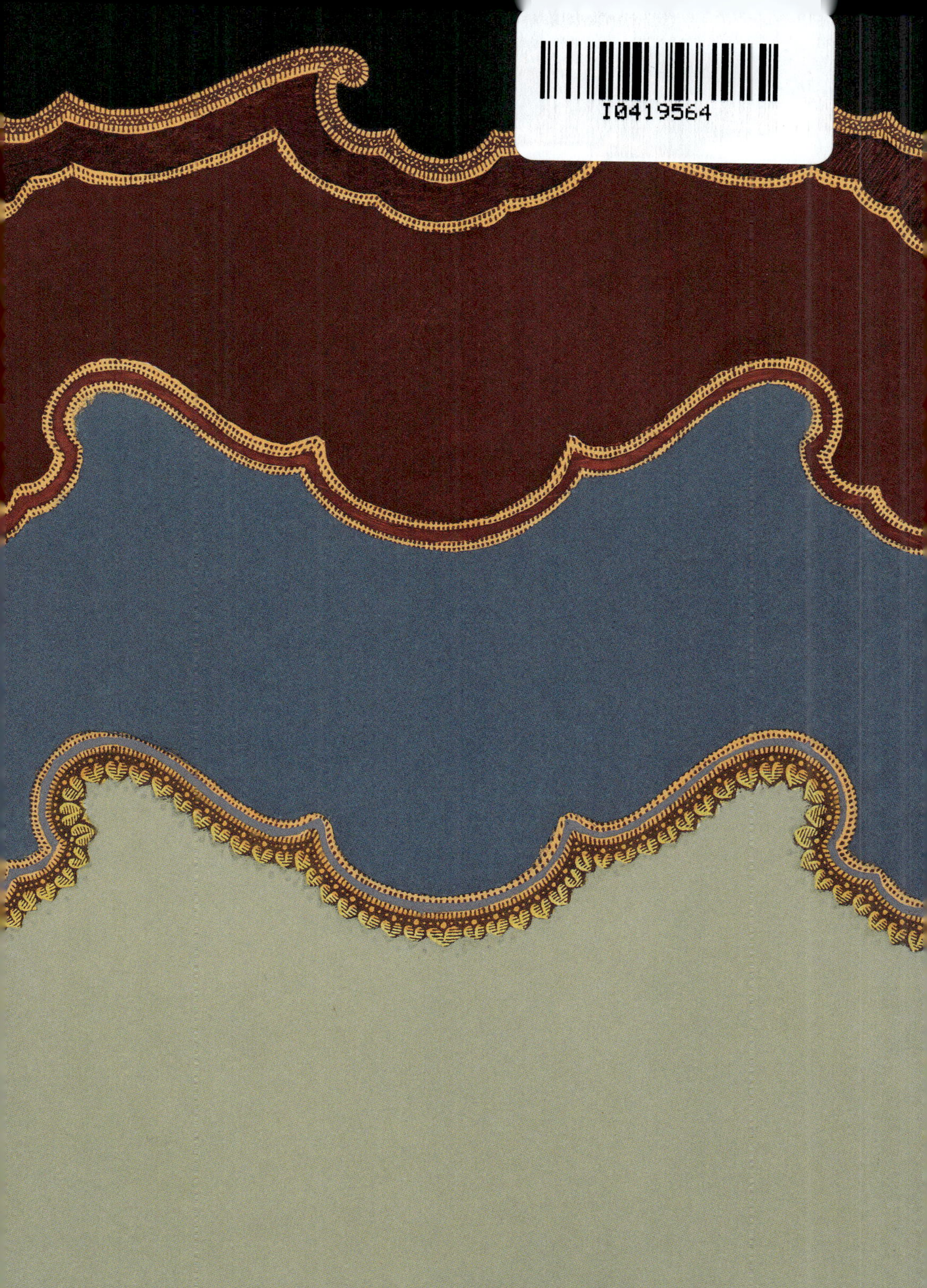
I0419564

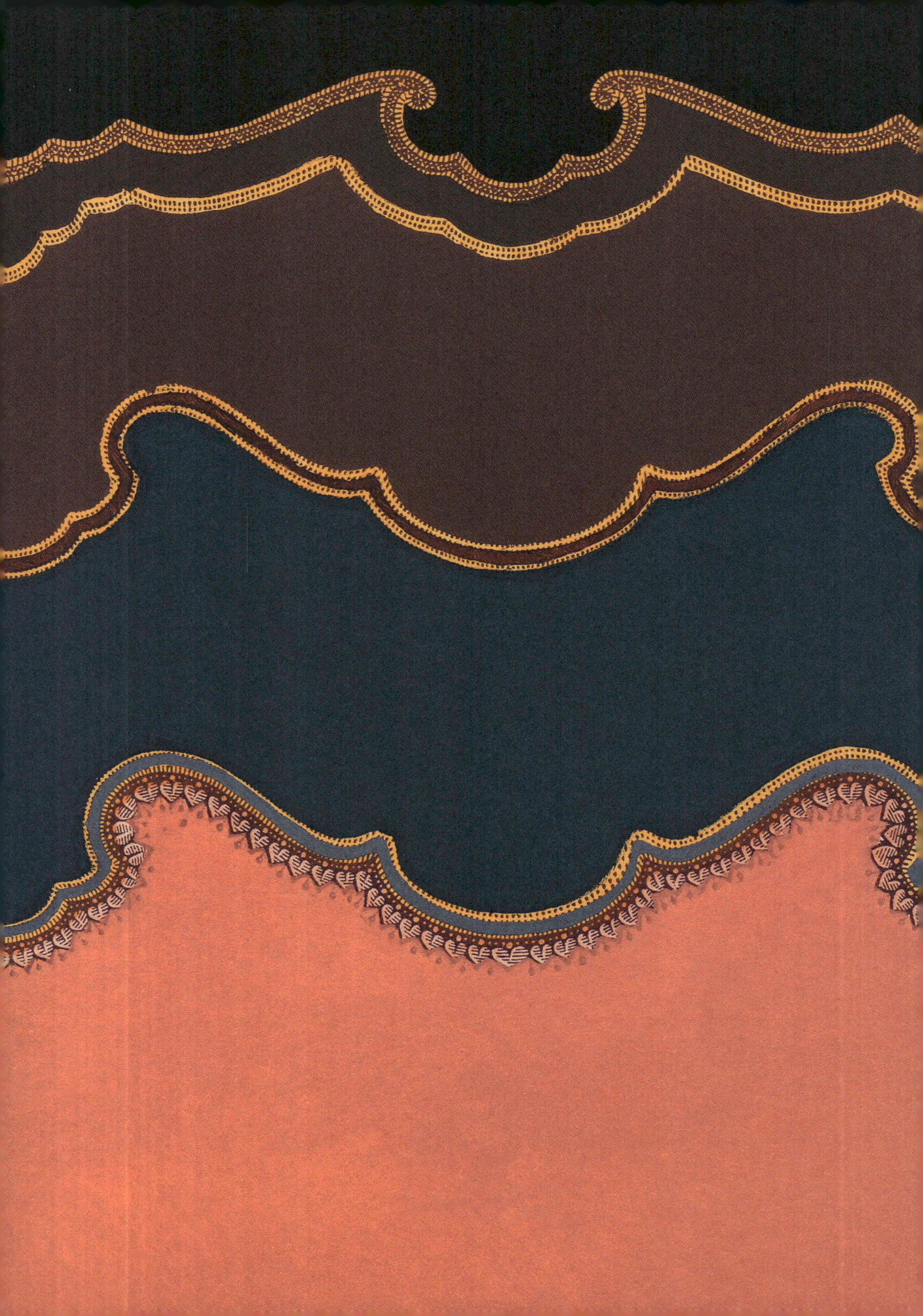

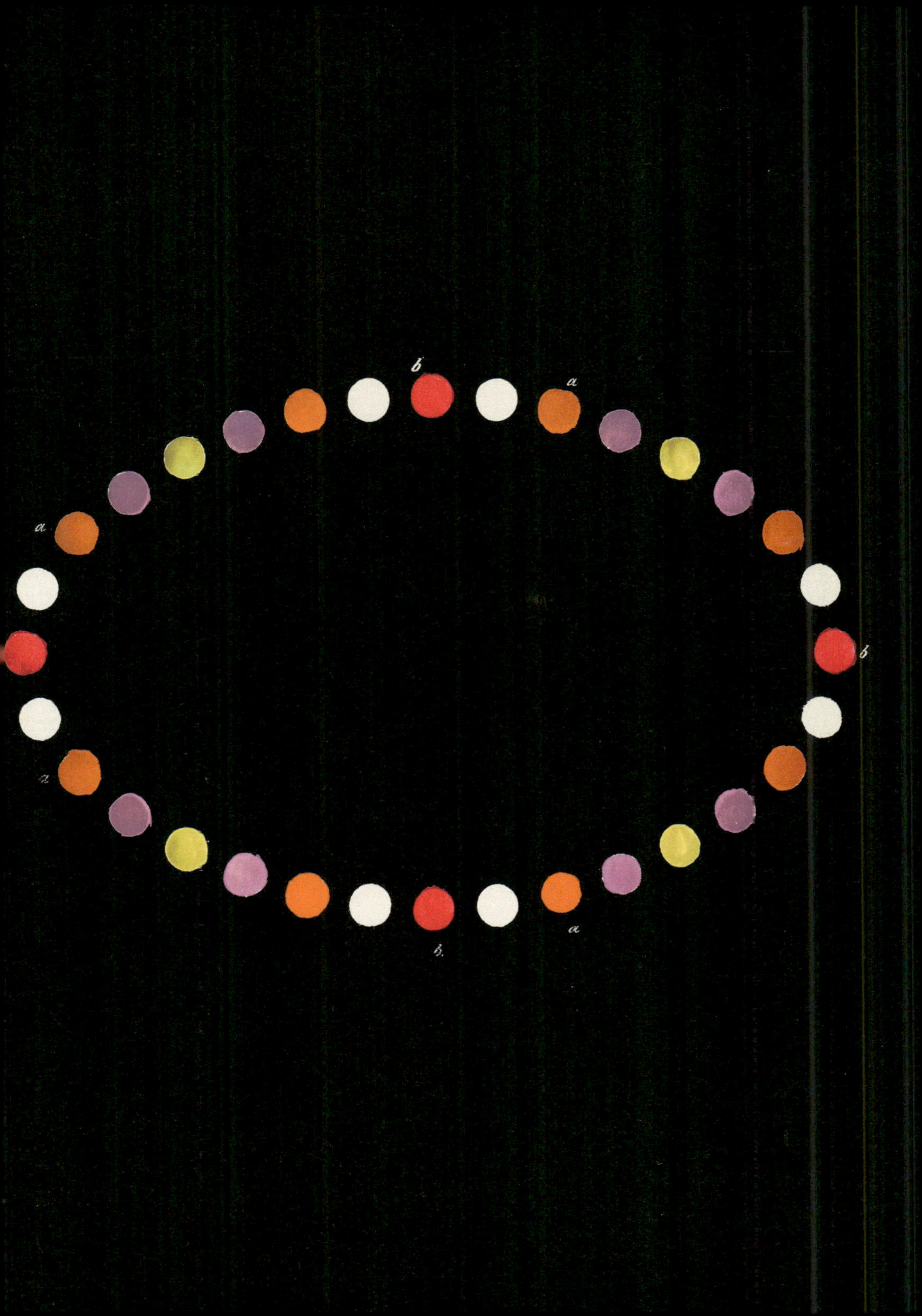
b
a
a
b
a
a
b.

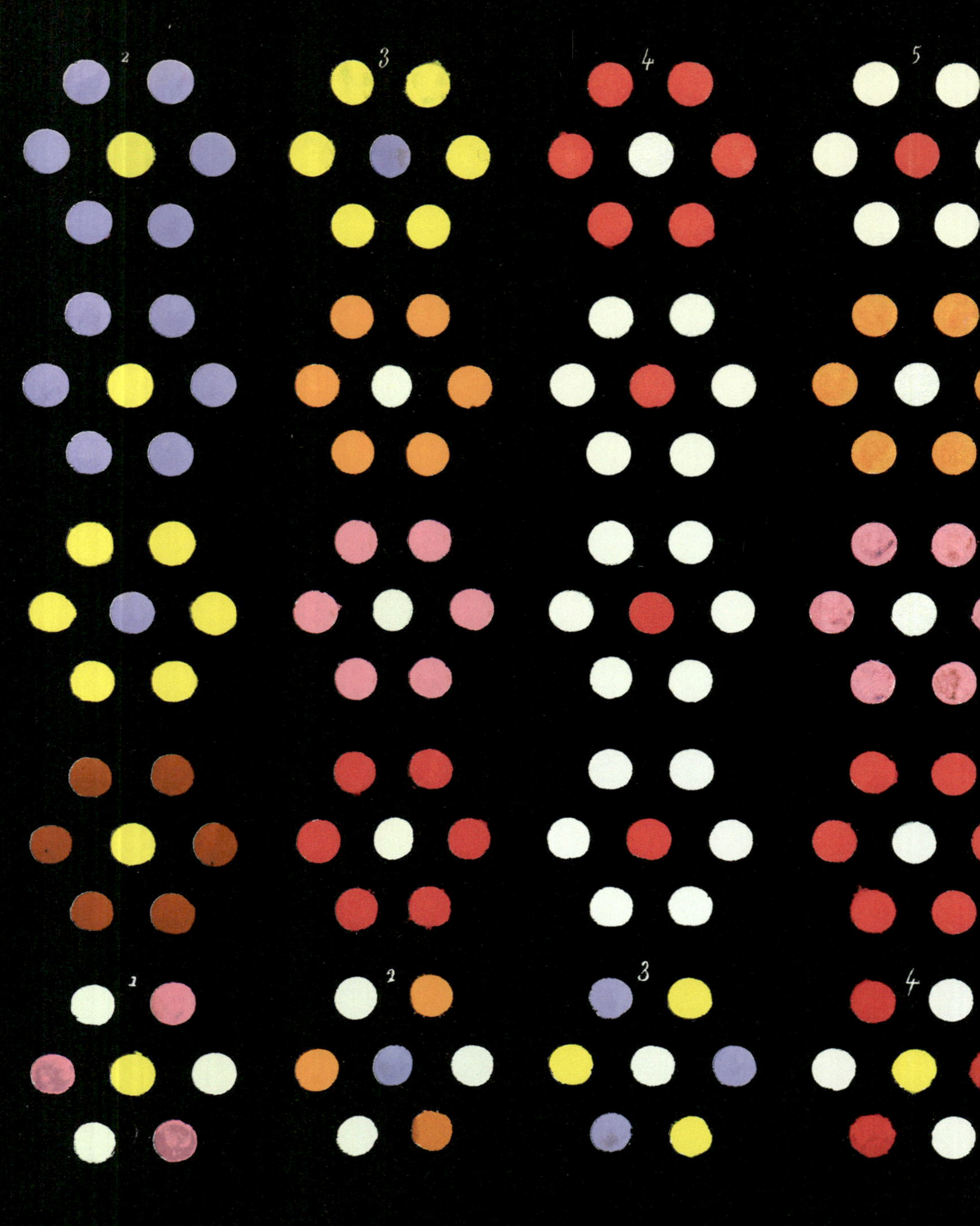
2
3
4
5
1
2
3
4

*Alexandra Loske*

# THE BOOK OF COLOUR CONCEPTS

TASCHEN

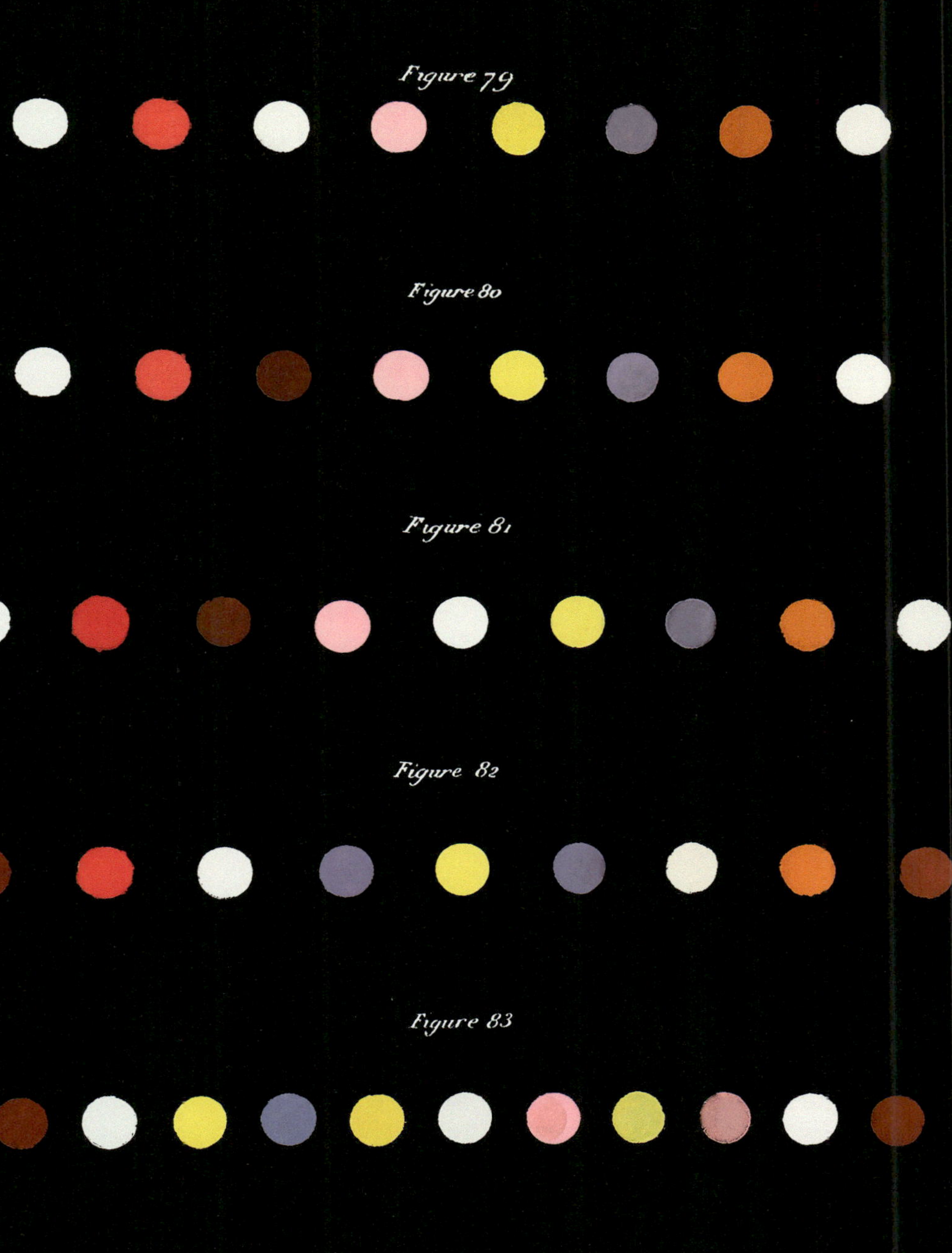
Figure 79
Figure 80
Figure 81
Figure 82
Figure 83

## Viridis species

Viridum aeris commune et hispaniense Creisocolla lazur ex reliquiis Malachitarum molitum, succus ex bacc. Merulae ex floribus Iridis succus [illegible] &c. Eorum explorata tantum habeo Viridum aeris commune Chrisocollam lazurium succum ex baccis merulae & ex floribus Iridis

## Caerulei species

Lazurium Smalta. Indicum. Flandrense quod Lagmoss agnominatur Isatidis Mirtillorum &c. Hoc ordine omitti possunt Isatidis & mirtillorum succi si cui compendium placeret.

## Receptissimorum colorum Vera exhibitio

Cerussa
Bleiweiss

Creta
Kreide

## Nitentium exhibitio

Argentum politum
Bruniert Silber

Aurum politum
Bruniert golde

Argentum madidum
Matt silber

Aurum madidum
Matt gold

Argentum molitum
Gemahlen silber

Aurum molitum
Gemahlen golde

Alexandra Loske

# COLOUR CONTROLLED AND SET FREE

## The Human History of Capturing Colour in Words and Images

Our world is full of colour. Most of us experience it in colour. The Earth is known as the 'Blue Planet' and optically we disappear into blue: when photographed in 1990 by the space probe *Voyager 1* from 6 billion kilometres away, we appeared, as the astronomer Carl Sagan described it a few years later, as "a pale blue dot", less than a pixel in size and hardly visible, but still of an identifiable colour. We turn into a spot of colour until we disappear from view. Colour, then, is one of the defining and unifying aspects of our lives, a universal and shared human experience, and it is not surprising that it has fascinated us from the beginning of history. The earliest manifestations of human creativity, in the form of carvings and markings on wood, bone and rock, show that we have always tried to make and use colour, chiefly to depict or copy what mattered to and what surrounded us. Although we only have fragmentary and faded visual and physical proof of this earliest human activity, it is possible that even at this early time colour was also used in a symbolic manner. The mineral pigments extracted from the earth by early humans were mixed with organic matter such as fat, grease or bodily fluids, and may well have acquired special or sacred meaning in the process, thus creating a first simple hierarchy of colours. We will never know exactly what our prehistoric ancestors thought about colour, but there is some evidence that certain colours were used in particular contexts.

We can trace an active intellectual engagement with colour throughout human history, from the simple concepts used in early art to the highly developed systems rooted in modern science, philosophy or the arts, categories which often overlap and make cross-references with each other. The aim of this book is to present an overview of human thinking and feeling about colour, the desire to create, arrange and systemise colour, to use and structure it, and to assign it complex meaning. Attempts at classifying and understanding colour have been numerous and have developed in a great variety of manifestations, from dualistic concepts of darkness and light to elaborate geometric patterns and systems that seek to give a specific shape to colour. With the development of language, writing and eventually print culture and sophisticated image reproduction methods, these concepts became more and more refined, complex, visually striking and also better recorded.

*Page 6*
Théodore Turquet de Mayerne
**Colour Circles from the De Mayerne Manuscript** (detail)
**Farbige Kreise aus dem De-Mayerne-Manuskript**
**Cercles chromatiques du manuscrit de Mayerne**
From: *Pictoria, sculptoria et quae subalternarum artium* (London, 1620–1646)
London, British Library

**Paintbox of the Vizier Amenemope**, *c.* 1427–1401 B.C.
**Malkasten des Wesirs Amenemope**
**Palette du vizir Amenemopet**
Boxwood with inscription inlaid in Egyptian blue; 2.2 x 21 x 3.6 cm (⅞ x 8¼ x 1⅜ in.)
Ohio, The Cleveland Museum of Art, Gift of the John Huntington Art and Polytechnic Trust

*Page 11*
Unknown Artist
**The Wilton Diptych**, *c.* 1395–1399
**Das Wilton-Diptychon**
**Diptyque de Wilton**
Tempera on panel, 37 x 53 cm (14⅝ x 20⅞ in.)
London, National Gallery, Bought with a special grant and contributions from Samuel Courtauld, Viscount Rothermere, C. T. Stoop and The Art Fund, 1929

This edition begins its visual journey through the history of colour concepts in the 17th century, the time of the earliest surviving illustrated manuscripts and printed sources that focus specifically on colour, and concludes in the mid-20th century, before the advent of the digital age. Just as much as each colour concept included here reflects the times in which it was created, so too does this book through the particular concepts that have been selected. There has been a sharp and growing interest in colour and colour history over the last few decades, and as the result of new research we are discovering new strands together with long-overlooked voices and examples of material culture (writers and educators, books, manuscripts, art and methods) that had either been forgotten or had never been considered as part of the colour canon.

No book on colour can provide an encyclopaedic record with a cultural, historical, geographical and thematic claim for completion. Some titles make deliberate omissions in order to focus on particular cultural or historic themes, others make choices that reflect the personal interests, tastes or expertise of the authors or editors. This book is, metaphorically speaking, a coat of many colours, and is as subjective in its selection as colour perception is deemed to be. The 41 works shown and discussed here are representative of the rich and varied history of colour concepts since the 17th century, and while we have selected many familiar examples of colour concepts that are firmly established in colour history, we hope to have succeeded in putting them in a wider cultural context and to have looked at them with fresh eyes. In addition to these 'classic' examples in their field we have made a particular effort to feature some lesser-known, or more obscure works that deserve to be considered for their aesthetic and theoretical appeal and importance. One further aim is to give more room to works on colour written, published and illustrated by women in the last two centuries. The historical and geographical range offered here is wide, with examples from Europe, the United States and parts of Asia, but we have also sought to be as inclusive as possible with regard to genre and style. A 20th-century educational colour primer can be as fascinating as Isaac Newton's (1643–1727) colour wheel from 1704 (p. 155), and they both play important roles in colour history.

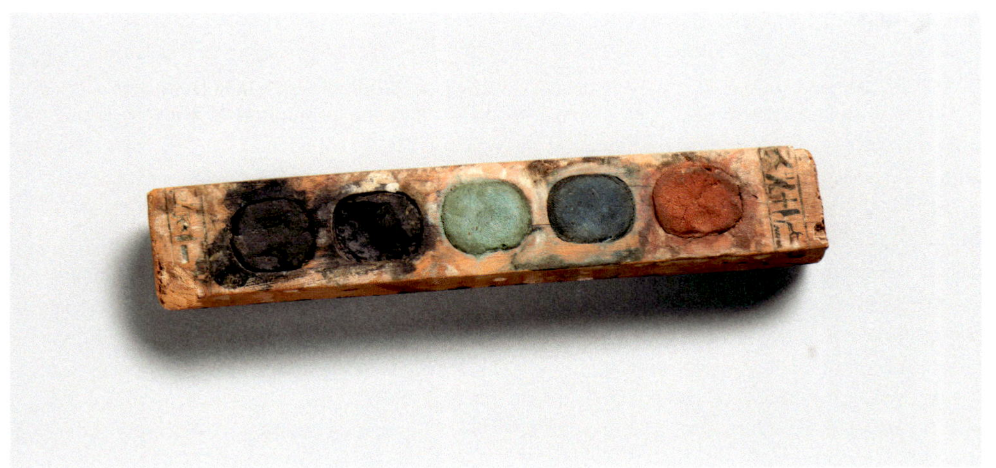

## Why Colour Concepts?

As an expansive and adaptable term, 'colour concept' is well suited to thinking about colour and trying to understand and systemise it. Yet rather than looking to find the perfect term it could perhaps be asked why the need is felt to systemise something that is so intangible, ever-changing, elusive and, to a certain degree, subjective. Until fairly recently, literature on colour didn't distinguish properly between material and immaterial colour, but once the difference was fully understood, it became clear that there are in fact many forms of colour that combine optical colour and the colours of solid materials. Colour easily slips away; it changes with the light, looks different at different times of the day, fades, darkens and can be unpredictable when combined, mixed or juxtaposed. Furthermore, it can be difficult to obtain, as pigment makers and historians can confirm, and it must have been frustrating for early humans to live in a world where the two dominant colours, the blue of the sky and the green of the plant world, were two of the most difficult to obtain. We may live in a world that is abundant with chlorophyll, but few plants make good green pigments. Colour is also infuriatingly fickle, unstable and often toxic, and was not always loved – for as the artist and writer David Batchelor has explained so beautifully in his essay *Chromophobia*, the loathing of colour is a significant part of western cultural history, rooted in "a fear of contamination and corruption by something that is unknown or appears unknowable [... manifesting] itself in the many and varied attempts to purge colour from culture, to devalue colour, to diminish its significance, to deny its complexity". Western attitudes to colour, or, more specifically, to highly saturated colours and polychromy Batchelor argued, were commonly associated with ideas of the foreign, oriental, primitive, feminine, vulgar, superficial or even pathological, in contrast to the Classical ideals of virginal white or colourless beauty. There is a long history in western culture of colour and darkness signifying dangerous or threatening 'otherness', and such a destabilising force needs either to be avoided or tamed. Creating colour systems or concepts is one way of taming colour, doing so intellectually at first, followed by measured use and application. If we impose an order on colour, even just theoretically, we have at least attempted to take control of something that is mutable and all-pervasive.

Fear, doubt and hatred of colour is of course only one side of the coin though. Our relationship with colour has always been multifaceted, and the last 50 or 60 years in particular – with the invention of colour film and photography, digital colour and the move to an almost fully coloured print culture – have not just made us more at ease with colour, but have resulted in an unprecedented accessibility to it. With hardly any exceptions, colour is now easily available and no longer exclusive, while there are likewise few limits to colour reproduction even if it is still the case that the quality varies.

## The Order of Colour: From Paintboxes to Palettes

Where textual sources for colour concepts are lacking, archaeology and material culture can give some insight into colour culture. At the very least, the colours used in art and decoration are an indicator of what pigments were available at certain times in history, and reveal details about techniques, painting materials, colour preferences and – when seen in their wider cultural context – perhaps the symbolic meanings of colours. One of the oldest surviving artists' palettes, a paintbox from the 18th Dynasty of Ancient Egypt that dates from *c.* 1427–1401 B.C. (p. 9), gives us a vivid and tactile understanding of which pigments were available to its owner, Amenemope, a vizier under Amenhotep II, but perhaps also which colours he preferred, and how he liked to arrange the cakes of red ochre, Egyptian blue, a mixed green and two charcoal blacks in his paintbox. Why did he choose to have two types of black? What did black mean to him, or in Ancient Egyptian culture in general? The arrangement of artists' materials may seem a long way removed from a complex three-dimensional colour model of the 20th century, but the underlying human desire is the same: to give an order to colour, whether for practical reasons, personal preference or even marketing purposes. Each painter's palette, in the case of the actual object with the remains of paint on it or as depicted in self-portraits, reveals a part of the artist's life and times, their practices and preferences. Even modern paintboxes that can be filled with manufactured watercolour cakes provide information about their users and owners: what size and quality of box could they afford, which colours did they pick, which ones get used the most, which ones are hardly ever used, and how are they arranged? As with the Ancient Egyptian example, a Reeves watercolour box from the early 20th century can also reveal much about what colours were available or were popular at the time. The Reeves paintbox shown here (p. 51) includes several colours that are named after Wilhelm Ostwald (1853–1932), an important German chemist and colour theorist.

## Picturing Colour Before the Modern Era

The main theme of this book concerns the visualisation of colour order and the ideas associated with these systems. While the concepts themselves can be traced back to the Classical world, the first illustrations of colours in the form of diagrams only appeared at the end of the 17th century. Until relatively recently, in material terms Classical culture had appeared to be largely colourless: the main colour association of Ancient Rome and Greece was whiteness, owing to the predominant images of white marble sculpture and buildings that have long lost their coloured surfaces. However, this general impression has been substantially modified by studies in the last few years into the polychrome nature of Greek and Roman sculpture and architecture.

Conceptually and linguistically, several traditions can be distinguished in the history of colour concepts. Empedocles (494–434 B.C.) is considered one of the first to have written on the subject, and from his surviving poetic fragments it is possible to discern a cosmological system based on the four elements of earth, fire, water and air from which he believed colours were derived. In the following century, Aristotle (384–322 B.C.) may have carried out simple optical experiments with coloured glass, and also examined colour vision and contrast. He proposed a polar system that ranged from divine white light, which made colours visible, through to darkness, represented by black. From white there evolved the hierarchical colours of yellow, green, blue and red, associated with earth, water, air and fire respectively. Aristotle's follower Theophrastus (372–287 B.C.) considered how we perceive or sense colours, and did so by referring to Democritus' (460–370 B.C.) view of the four basic colours, red, black, white and a greenish-yellow, which related to certain shapes, surface patterns and other sense-based attributes. For his part, the physician Hippocrates (460–375 B.C.) distinguished four colours that represented the main fluids or humours of the human body, which in turn were seen as the cause of certain character traits, namely white for phlegmatic, red for sanguine, yellow for choleric and black for melancholic.

Classical colour concepts and theoretical discussions of the subject have typically survived only in fragmented form, and with the additional inconvenience of the linguistic challenges they present. Colour is let down by language generally, since words cannot match the full complexity of colour or colour perception. Most languages only have a dozen or so basic colour terms, whereas the number of colours

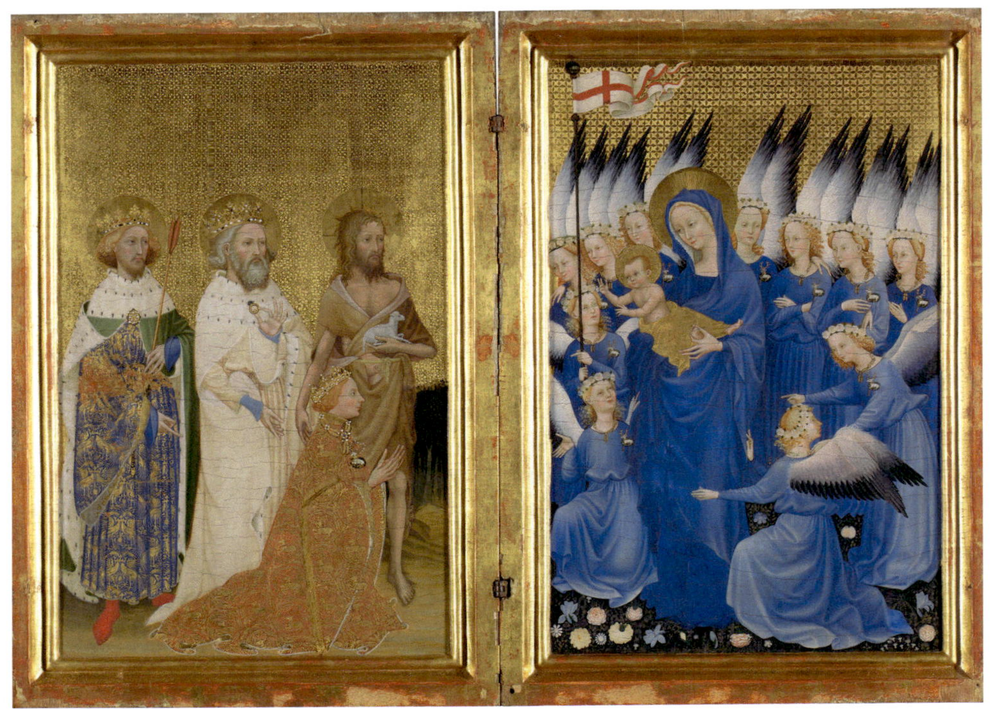

we can actually see is uncountable. This discrepancy becomes even more problematic when dealing with ancient languages, older texts or translations. There is also a lack of visual representations of colour concepts from the ancient world and earlier cultures, which makes it challenging to understand the earliest of these notions in any comprehensive manner. However, glimpses of the potent symbolic value of colours can be gleaned through certain archaeological finds, such as the theatrical masks found at Pompeii, both in the form of actual objects and as shown in fresco paintings, which were painted in colours expressing the four humours (p. 15). Despite the scarcity of specific literature on colour, we can nevertheless trace the development of several cultural concepts relating to it by way of the materiality of pigments and dyestuffs. As with the costly ultramarine pigment in medieval and Renaissance art (p. 11), the material value and rarity of certain colours in the ancient world led to them becoming associated with high-status figures and deities.

Throughout the Middle Ages, the basic Aristotelian framework of colour being situated between darkness and light (black and white) prevailed in the philosophical discourse on the subject, but there was also an increase in the number of more practical texts on colour. In the early 13th century, the Oxford University scholar and bishop of Lincoln Robert Grosseteste (*c.* 1175–1253) translated some of Aristotle's works and wrote his own treatise on colour in response, *De Colore*, in which he developed Aristotle's theories of colour being derived from light, while speculating on the amount of light that might be contained within individual colours. From around the time of the 15th century, colour gradually became more commercialised with the increase in global exchange and trade. Knowledge was now being captured in a more systematic way, as can be seen with the appearance of the first treatises on artistic techniques, painters' materials and artists' lives. Many of these texts are very technical and would not have reached a wide readership, especially in the pre–print age, but even so a number of written records have survived and these open a window on to the medieval world of artisanal colour, such as the somewhat earlier *De diversis artibus* (*On Diverse Arts*) by Theophilus Presbyter (fl. *c.* 1070–1125), which is essentially a book of colour recipes dating from the early 12th century. Many more artisanal writings followed in the 15th and 16th centuries, and while they are focused on technique and materiality, and do not provide philosophical discussions of colour concepts, they are nevertheless invaluable for the study of colour terminology and pigment history. Occasionally, we encounter an illustrated text that includes images of raw ingredients used to make pigments and paints, for example, the 15th- or 16th-century *Livre des simples médecines* (*The Book of Simple Medicines*, pp. 30, 33), which shows various organic and mineral substances such as squid ink, lapis lazuli and a mummy (for mummy brown) that were also believed to have therapeutic properties. The illustrations are straightforward and pictorial, but the objects are carefully arranged in the style of a collector's tray or a cabinet of curiosities.

Hippocrates' concept of the four humours that pervade the human body and spirit, and which could be represented by four colours, also continued to inform basic colour concepts throughout the Middle Ages and into the Renaissance. While images and artwork that deal specifically with colour theory and concepts are still unknown in this period, the first examples of colour being used to illustrate and enable order and classification in other contexts do begin to appear. For example, Ulrich Pinder's (d. 1519) uroscopic colour wheel from 1506 (p. 14) depicts 20 different shades of urine, which were used to diagnose

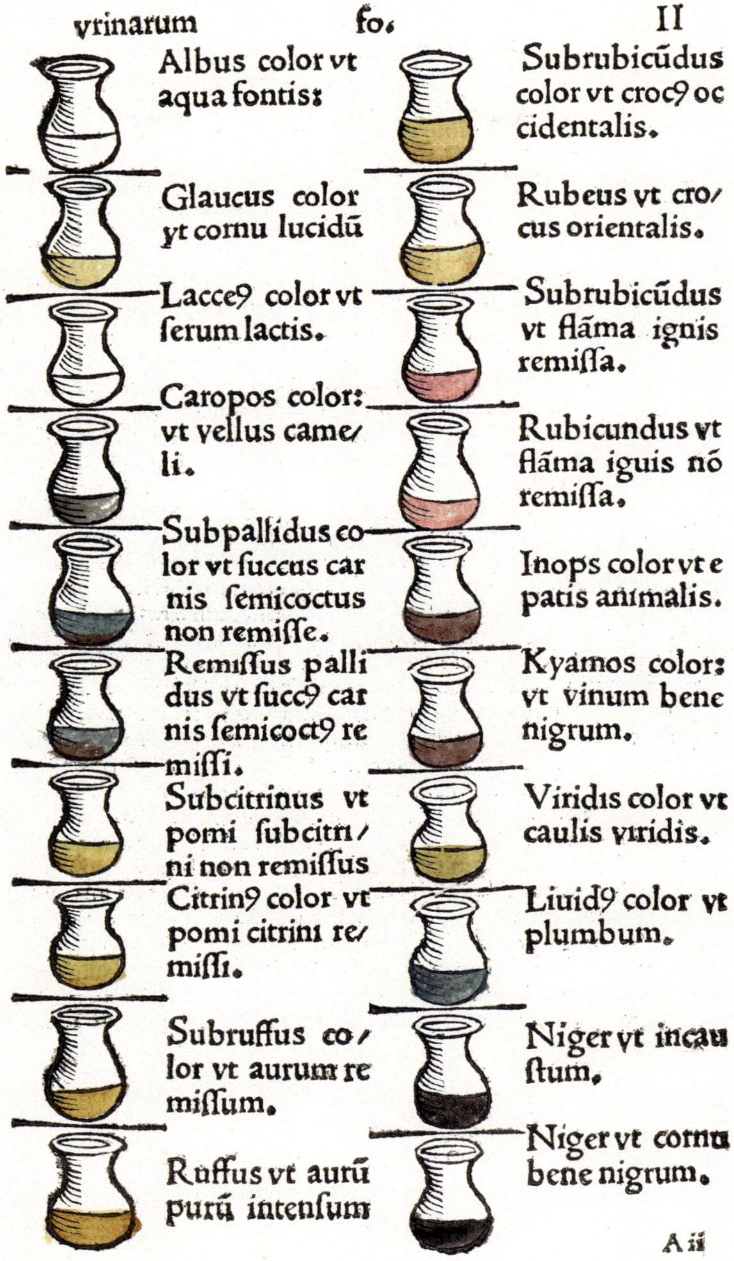

Albus color vt aqua fontis:

Glaucus color vt cornu lucidũ

Laccꝰ color vt ſerum lactis.

Caropos color: vt vellus cameli.

Subpallidus color vt ſuccus carnis ſemicoctus non remiſſe.

Remiſſus pallidus vt ſuccꝰ carnis ſemicoctꝰ remiſſi.

Subcitrinus vt pomi ſubcitrini non remiſſus

Citrinꝰ color vt pomi citrini remiſſi.

Subruffus color vt aurum remiſſum.

Ruffus vt aurũ purũ intenſum

Subrubicũdus color vt crocꝰ occidentalis.

Rubeus vt crocus orientalis.

Subrubicũdus vt flãma ignis remiſſa.

Rubicundus vt flãma iguis nõ remiſſa.

Inops color vt epatis animalis.

Kyamos color: vt vinum bene nigrum.

Viridis color vt caulis viridis.

Liuidꝰ color vt plumbum.

Niger vt incauſtum.

Niger vt cornu bene nigrum.

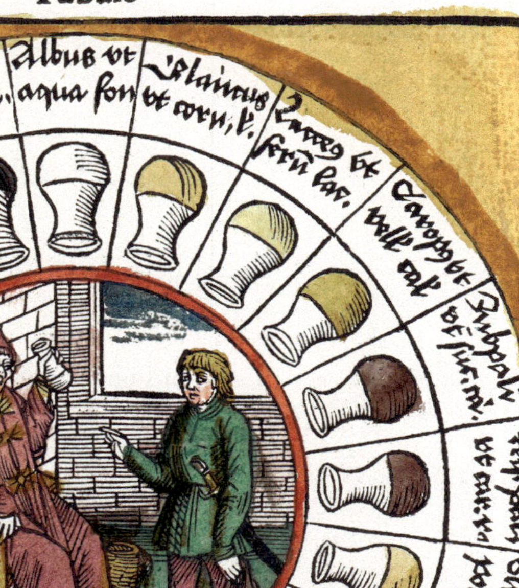
Tabule
Albus vt aqua fon

*Opposite and page 13*
Ulrich Pinder
**Urine Samples and Uroscopic Colour Wheel**
**Urinproben und Harnglasscheibe**
**Échantillons d'urine et Cercle chromatique uroscopique**
From: *Epiphanie medicorum. Speculum videndi urinas hominum* (Nuremberg, 1506)
Washington, D.C., Folger Shakespeare Library

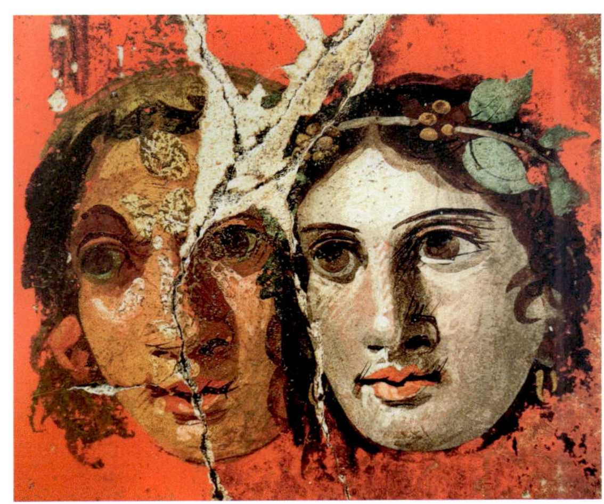

**Two Faces**
**Zwei Gesichter**
**Deux visages**
Fresco, 1st century A.D.
Pompeii, House of the Golden Bracelet

medical conditions. The pictorial urine flasks were hand-coloured, and this is an early example of a colour wheel based on nature's colours, not dissimilar to those included in Moses Harris's (1730–*c.* 1788) books on insects nearly three centuries later. In a similar manner, a wealth of encyclopaedic texts such as bestiaries, herbals, lapidaries and concordances may provide further direct or indirect information about the corresponding period's knowledge and use of colour.

The publication in 1435 of Leon Battista Alberti's (1404–1472) *De pictura* (*On Painting*) coincided with the rise of oil paint as a medium. On the subject of colour, which he considered an important and valuable element of painting, he proposed that all colours could be created by mixing together just four: red, green, blue and grey. He was a painter's writer, less concerned with coloured light than with physical colour, so the colour grey to which he gave such prominent status must be seen in the context of shading and creating three-dimensional effects in painting. Many texts written on the wider debate about the roles of drawing (*disegno*) and colour (*colore*) followed on from Alberti and his contemporaries, and there are also thoughts about colour from one of the greatest artists, Leonardo da Vinci (1452–1519), who in his various notebooks and collated writings mused on colour vision and perception, on the appearance of colour and the practical application of colour theory in painting. He proposed a colour concept, greatly influenced by Aristotle and Alberti, based on six "simple colours": red, yellow, green and blue, flanked by white and black. None of these medieval and early Renaissance texts include colour diagrams, so it is not possible to tell whether the proposed systems were envisaged as being linear or circular, two- or three-dimensional, but they are nevertheless fascinating precursors of modern colour theory.

## A New Chromatic Age: Colour from the 17th Century Onward

Although this book begins its journey through colour concepts in the later 17th century, when print culture had become well established, for various reasons many of the early examples of colour literature are still in manuscript form. The nascent spirit of the Enlightenment helped

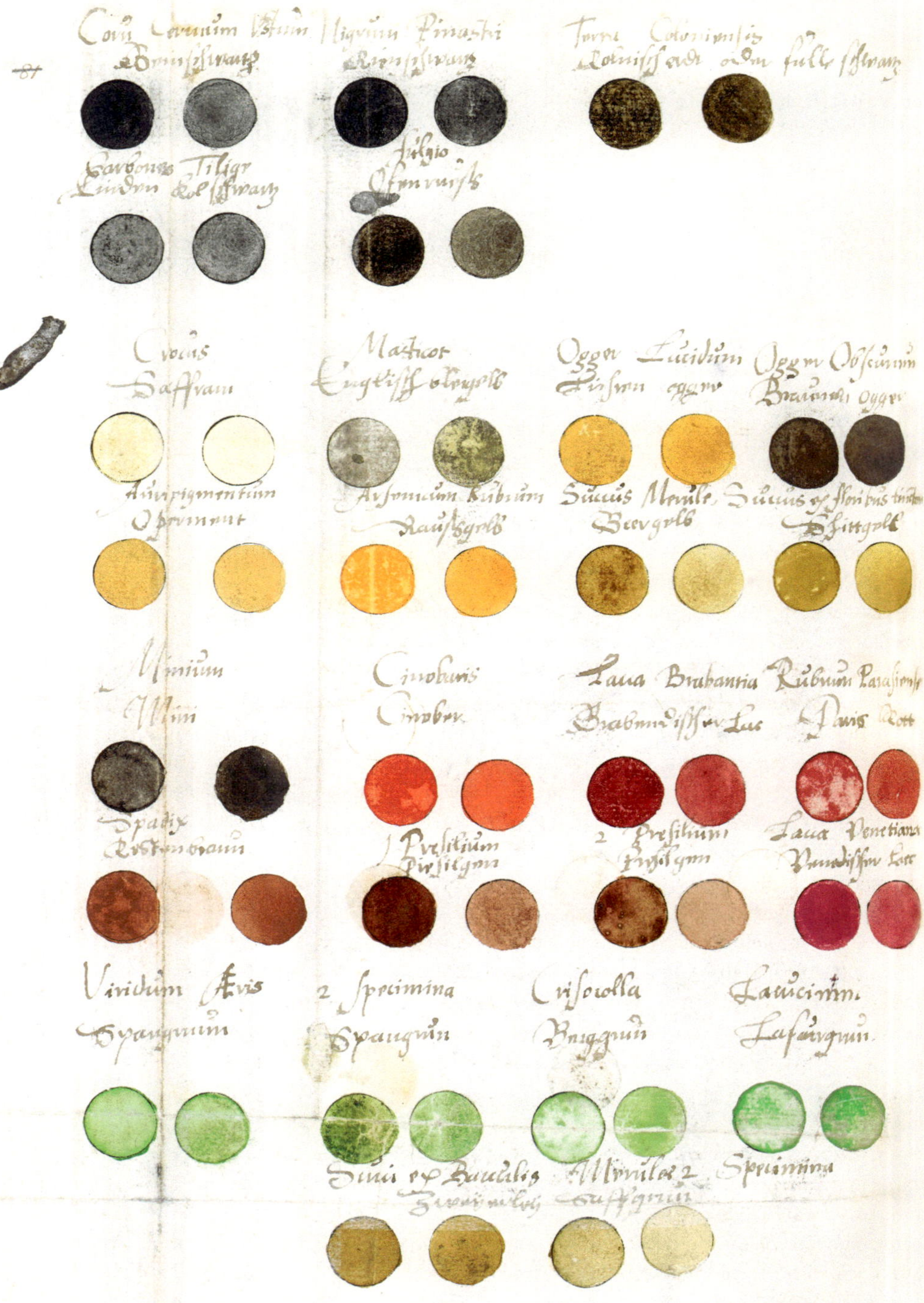
Crocus
Saffran
Masticot
Ogger Lucidum
Ogger Obscurum
Auripigmentum
Operment
Arsenicum Rubrum
Succus
Minium
Cinobaris
Cinober
Laca Brabantia
Rubrum Parasiense
Spadix
Presilium
2 Presilium
Laca Venetiana
Viridum Æris
Spangruen
2 Specimina
Spangruen
Crisocolla
2 Specimina

Théodore Turquet de Mayerne
**Arrangement of Colour Circles, Entitled 'True Presentation of the Most Common Colours'**
**Anordnung von farbigen Kreisen mit dem Titel „Wahre Aufstellung der Farben"**
**Agencement de cercles chromatiques, intitulé « Présentation des couleurs les plus courantes »**
From: *Pictoria, sculptoria et quae subalternarum artium* (London, 1620–1646)
London, British Library

*Page 18*
Louis Desplaces
**An Allegorical Monument to Isaac Newton and His Theories on Prisms**
**Allegorisches Denkmal für Isaac Newton und seine Prismentheorien**
**Monument allégorique en l'honneur de Isaac Newton et de ses théories sur les prismes**
From: *Tombeaux des princes, grands capitaines et autres hommes illustres* (Paris, 1741)
London, Wellcome Collection

promote the exchange of intellectual ideas across geographical and cultural boundaries, but while colour symbolism and meta-systems linked to religious beliefs, alchemy and folklore continued to exist, this was the age when colour became scientific and intellectualised. The general desire at this time to understand and classify the natural world included colour – as an optical phenomenon, a tool for depicting nature, and an expressive medium in the fine and decorative arts.

In a roughly (but not strictly) chronological order, each chapter of this book focuses on a specific theme or strand in the story of colour concepts. To be included, the featured books and manuscripts had to be concerned predominantly with colour in theory or practice, or else use colour in a coherent and inventive way, for instance as a tool to illustrate related concepts and ideas.

As noted, several works by women are featured, in order to address the historical gender imbalance in the field of colour literature, including educational books on colour and painting from the early 20th century, as, for example, the U.S. educator Bonnie Snow's (*c.* 1862–1925, pp. 22–23, 27) *The Theory and Practice of Color* (co-authored with Hugo B. Froehlich, 1918, pp. 352–361). One of the earliest examples of such a neglected source is Mary Gartside (*c.* 1755–1819, pp. 164–175), a British flower painter (p. 34 bottom) and teacher of watercolour painting, and the first woman known to have published a book on colour in English: *An Essay on Light and Shade, on Colours, and on Composition in General* (1805). For the second edition (1808) she changed the title to *An Essay on a New Theory of Colours*, thereby stressing the seriousness of her publication. Another example of a genre-bending publication by a woman from the wider circles of theosophists and spiritualists is *The New Science of Color* (1915) by the multinational and multicultural poet and actor Beatrice Irwin (1877–1956), who had a great interest in the potential of combining artificial coloured light with music. Now little known, her ideas on synaesthesia influenced several famous 20th-century artists, including Georgia O'Keeffe (1887–1986), who may well have indirectly made references to Irwin in some of her work. There are certain women in colour history who deserve to be in-

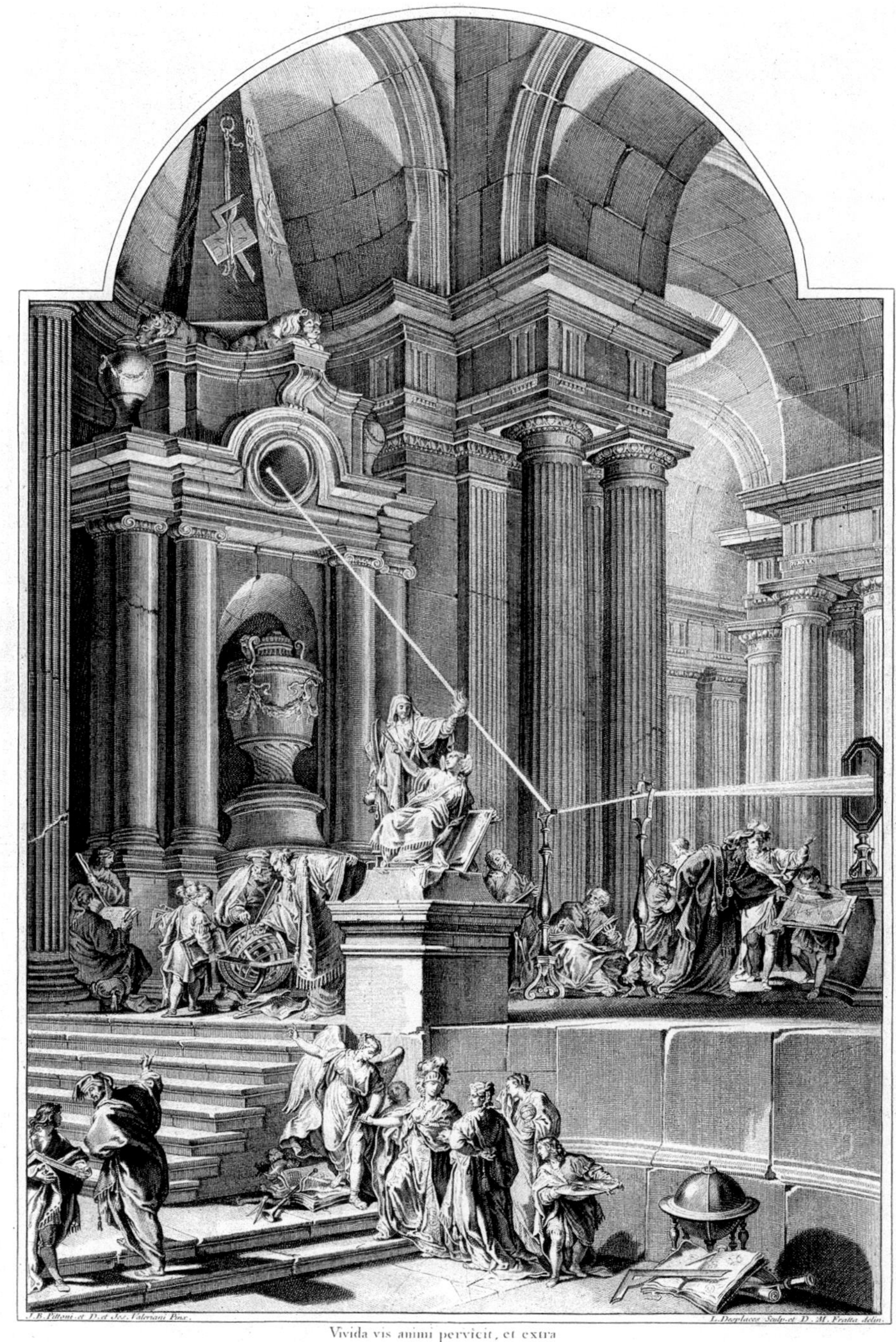


Vivida vis animi pervicit, et extra

cluded in the canon without having written a stand-alone theory of colour. Hilma af Klint (1862–1944) is one such, as is the British painter Winifred Nicholson (1893–1981), whose artistic output, in combination with her notes, letters and two short, published essays on colour, make her a great 20th-century colour theorist, despite never gathering her ideas and colour concepts into a concise format issued under one cover. Similar to Gartside, she appears to have developed an interest in colour theory through flower painting, and her earlier compositions were often set against illuminated landscapes or framed by windows, thus already demonstrating an interest in the interaction of light and colour (p. 34 top). This obvious interest in prismatic colour found a new lease of creativity when, in the mid-1970s when she was in her 80s, Nicholson was given two glass prisms. In the last few years of her life she created a fascinating series of so-called "prismatic paintings" in which she explored her experiments with prisms and light in visual form, often choosing a completely abstract style.

The first chapter of the present book, "Pyramids of Colour: Early Charts and Tables", offers a closer look at early illustrated books in western culture. The forerunner to these were a selection of charts produced previously by the alchemist and physician at the English court Théodore Turquet de Mayerne (1573–1655) that were included in the so-called "De Mayerne manuscript" (*Pictoria, sculptoria et quae subalternarum artium*), 1620–1646 (pp. 6, 16). This chart is relatively simple in its presentation of colours in the form of tables and neat circles. As such, it does not represent intellectual colour concepts, but should instead be seen in the wider context of painting handbooks, given that it provides much information on pigments and other artists' materials that were available at the time, and how they were mixed and classified. The chapter also shows how more complex charts and tables were created in the next century and subsequently found their way into print culture. The intellectualisation of colour concepts at this period is evident, as lists of colours become more elaborate and extensive and the first attempts at three-dimensional concepts are made. All such early charts, tables and diagrams were hand-coloured, despite the advances in colour printing, which means that each copy is an individual work of art. The practice of hand-colouring continued until well into the 19th century, and in some cases it wasn't replaced by mechanical colour reproduction until the 20th century.

In Chapter 2, "The Shape of Colour: Circles, Wheels and Globes", we examine how the simple visual concepts of colour order were developed further throughout the 18th and 19th centuries, which resulted in the emergence of a fascinating variety of geometric shapes and forms. Circles appear to have been the most prominent choice, leading to many variations of what we may now consider the classic colour wheel. Other shapes were used too though, while often a colour diagram will feature pictorial additions and embellishments, or a colour wheel will be accompanied by explanatory charts and tables, as, for example, in *The Natural System of Colours* (*c.* 1769–1776, pp. 118–123) by Moses Harris and the aforementioned works by Mary Gartside.

Aesthetically, 18th- and 19th-century colour diagrams are among the most impressive images in the history of colour literature, but despite their visual power they rarely exist without the written or printed word. Language, although no match for the visible colour spectrum, forms an important element in most of these diagrams, sometimes with intriguing and poetic results, as, for example, in the *Temperamentenrose* (1798/99) by Johann Wolfgang von Goethe (1749–1832) and Friedrich Schiller (1759–1805). One challenge commonly

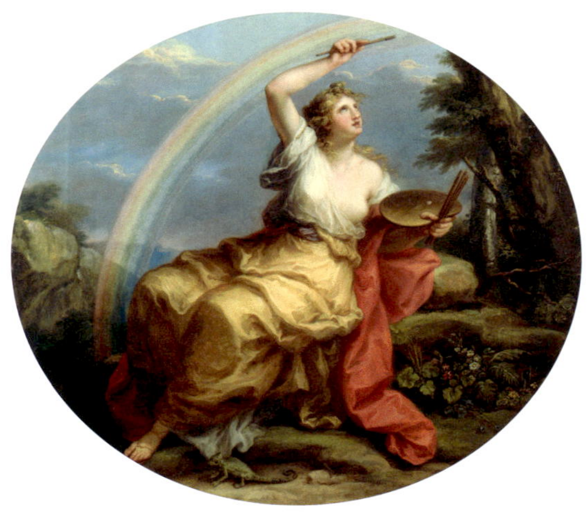

Angelica Kauffmann
**Colour**, 1778–1780
**Die Farbe / La Couleur**
Oil on canvas, 126 x 148.5 cm
(49 ½ x 58 ½ in.)
London, Royal Academy of Arts

John Everett Millais
**The Blind Girl**, 1856
**Das blinde Mädchen**
**La jeune Aveugle**
Oil on canvas, 81.2 x 52.3 cm
(32 x 20 ⅝ in.)
Birmingham Museums,
Presented by the Rt. Hon.
William Kendrick, 1892

faced by these diagrams was how to convey the three-dimensional aspect of colour order in a two-dimensional medium, and it is at this point that the first colour globes or balls make their appearance (see, for example, Philipp Otto Runge's (1777–1810) *Farben-Kugel* from 1810 (pp. 26, 124–125). Unfortunately, no three-dimensional models of colour globes survive from this time, but in 2016 the French-German artist Eva Bodinet constructed a model based on Runge's *Farben-Kugel* (p. 24), and in the past few years several commercial manufacturers have created ready-made 3D colour globes. Runge is also a poignant example of the increased sensibility and spirituality that was perceived in relation to colour during the Romantic era. Many artists, philosophers and writers of the later 18th and early 19th centuries adapted colour concepts to suit their individual belief systems and assigned them meanings that were highly symbolic. Between 1802 and 1810, Runge created a series of images showing the times of day, including *Der kleine Morgen* (*Little Morning*), which were representation of colour theory adapted to express his Christian beliefs (p. 29).

In Chapter 2 a widening range of colour studies also becomes apparent as the 19th century progresses, alongside the ways in which colour literature builds on and makes reference to earlier texts. Better documentation from this period reveals how some of these early works on colour influenced specific artists and teachers. In the 1820s, the artist J. M. W. Turner (1775–1851) taught the basics of colour theory as part of his role as Professor of Perspective at the Royal Academy of Arts in London. For this he created two lecture slides showing colour circles (pp. 38, 39), with the aim of explaining the difference between material and immaterial colours. These circles with their overlapping triangles of colour at the centre were very clearly influenced by Moses Harris's colour circles, which Turner had studied. Throughout his life, Turner had a keen interest in new pigments and colour theory, while he also owned and read many publications on colour and made the interaction between colour and light a key theme in his art (p. 41). Later in life, and just a few years after the first part of Goethe's main work on colour (*Zur Farbenlehre*, 1810–1812, pp. 184–191) had been published in English translation (*Goethe's Theory of Colours*, 1840), Turner painted two canvases in direct reference to the lessons in this text, and with a further possible nod to Harris (p. 65).

The following Chapter 3, "New Elucidations: The Rise of Colour Theory", elaborates further on some of the most important works on colour from the 19th century, and provides reasons for the sharp rise in the number of new theories and lengthy philosophical, scientific and practical treatises on colour. This chromatic revolution is intrinsically linked to the industrialisation of colour, specifically to new manufacturing, production and printing methods, but it has its origins in the early 18th century. An undisputed milestone in the history of colour concepts was written by Isaac Newton, and when *Opticks* was published in 1704 it was the fruit of many decades of research (pp. 154–163). The book included the first widely disseminated colour diagram, in the form of a wheel, which was based on Newton's experiments into splitting pure white light into spectral colours, using a prism. Newton's impact on scientific thinking throughout the 18th and into the 19th century was immeasurable, and his theories were adapted, admired, developed and criticised (p. 18). The fascination with the rainbow spectrum and with other findings of Newton's were, and still are frequently noted in the visual arts, as, for example, in Angelica Kauffmann's (1741–1807) painting *Colour* (p. 20), commissioned by the Royal Academy of Arts. Although an allegorical image, and thus not representing a colour concept *per se*, this painting illustrates an important point in colour history in that collectively the set that was commissioned from Kauffmann represented the significant "Elements of Art", namely Invention, Composition, Design and Colour. The female figure representing Colour dips her paintbrush into Newton's rainbow, pulling prismatic colour on to a physical palette, and in the process adapting optical colour theory to material colour while also relating it to the teaching practices at the newly founded Academy.

As the 19th century continued, Romantic concepts and attitudes, such as Runge's spiritual colour symbolism, gradually gave way to more technical and scientific studies, many of them linked to the manufacture of new pigments and dyestuffs. The quality of these new colours became a subject of study for the great British 'colourman' George Field (*c.* 1777–1854, pp. 200–207), who not only developed a colour theory of his own but also tested, produced and patented pigments. His colours were in demand with many 19th-century artists, including members of the Pre-Raphaelite Brotherhood and their followers, and their availability thus coincided with a renewed interest in medieval painting techniques and materials. The jewel-like brilliance and daring polychromy of paintings such as *Mariana* (1851, p. 55) by John Everett

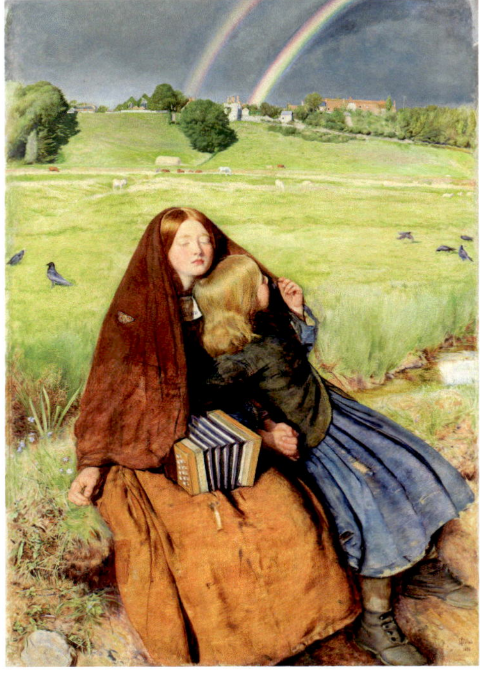

Bonnie Snow, Hugo B. Froehlich
**Instructions and Diagrams on the Painting of Windows**
**Anleitungen und Diagramme zum Malen von Fenstern**
**Instructions et graphiques pour la peinture des fenêtres**
From: *Text Books of Art Education*, vols. 1 (opposite) and 2 (below), New York, 1904
Sussex, collection of the author

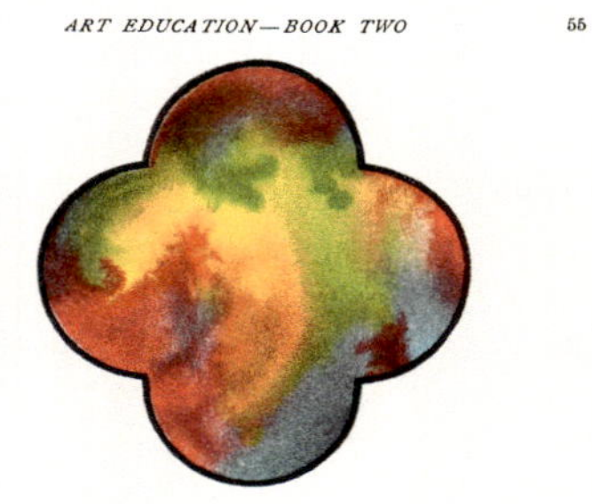

*ART EDUCATION—BOOK TWO* 55

What pleasure to paint a window like this, beautiful in shape, beautiful in color!

Draw a two-inch square. On this lay tablets—the inch square in the center, with semicircles about it. Draw around it. Draw around the semicircles.

Paint the shape with water. Drop in the fresh colors and let the water blend them.

Finish with the dark edge.

Millais (1829–1896) reflect this interest in good-quality pigments and a strong awareness of current colour concepts. It has even been suggested that Dante Gabriel Rossetti's (1828–1882) painting *Ecce Ancilla Domini! (The Annunciation*, 1849/50, p. 45) could have been inspired by Field's proposed colour symbolism. The intellectual attention given to colour literature and theory is widely evident among 19th-century western artists, and both Impressionism and Pointillism were directly influenced by Michel-Eugène Chevreul's (1786–1889) groundbreaking theory of simultaneous contrast in colours (from 1839 onward), which he developed while working for the Gobelins tapestry factory in Paris (pp. 216–227). The Post-Impressionist Vincent van Gogh (1853–1890) used the principles of colour contrast to astounding effect in his art, and it is significant that among his personal possessions was a red lacquer box containing several balls of coloured lengths of wool, twisted and combined in different variations just as if he had been creating colour harmonies in this way according to Chevreul's laws (p. 52). There is also a great awareness of colour contrast in the work of James McNeill Whistler (1834–1903), and while his direct engagement with colour literature is not recorded his interest in tonal harmony and colour symbolism is clear in the titles he gave to his paintings, such as "harmonies", "nocturnes" and "symphonies" of specific colours (pp. 58, 60).

*ART EDUCATION—BOOK ONE* 

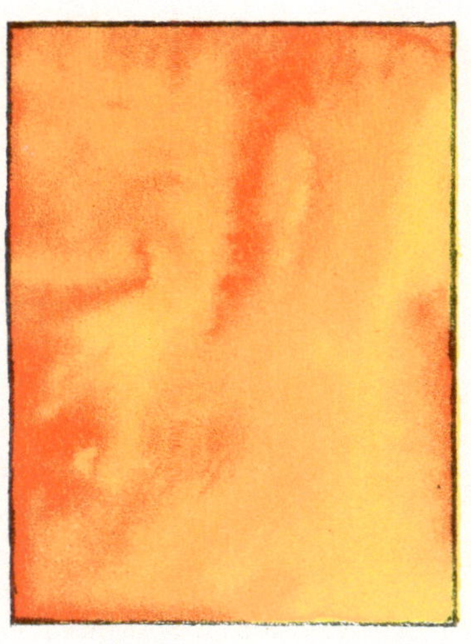

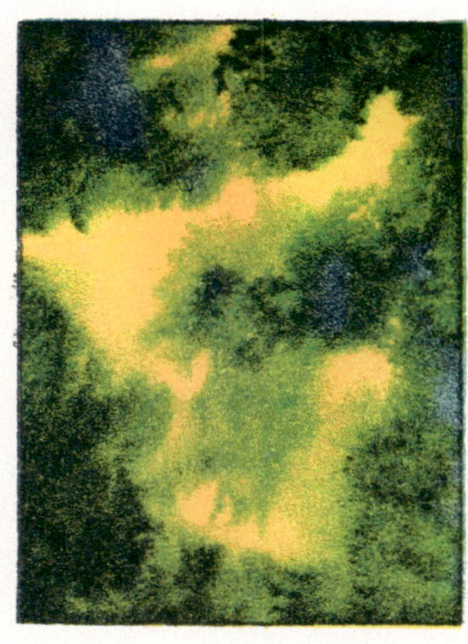

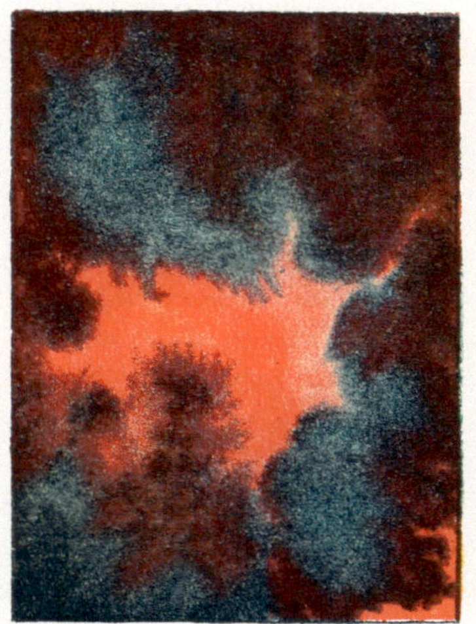

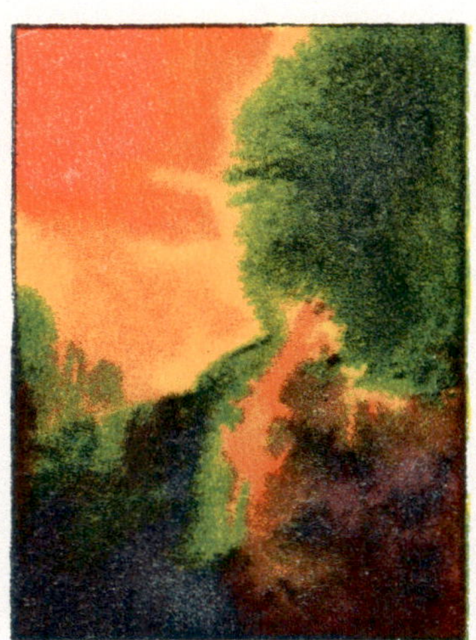

Eva Bodinet
**Colour Globe**, 2016
**Farbglobus**
**Sphère chromatique**
Sussex, collection of the author

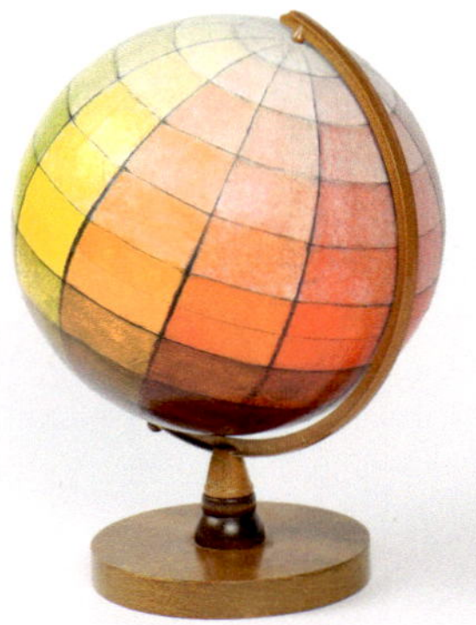

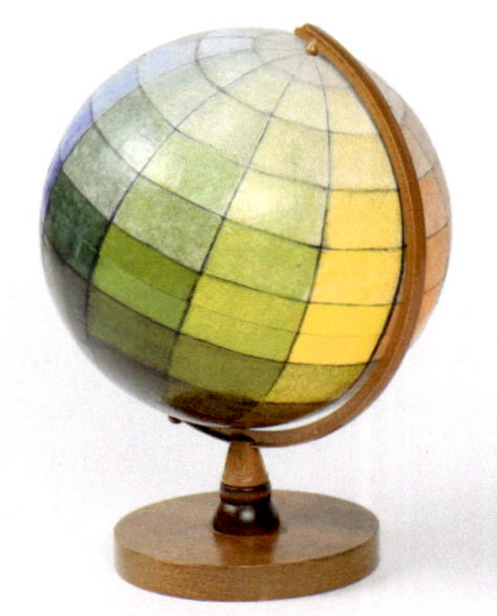

Chapters 4 and 5 deal with more technical and practical colour concepts. "Colours as Guiding Lights: Nomenclatures and Standards" is concerned with systematic lists of colours, often in relation to the natural world and taxonomical classification, which present fascinating attempts to create reliable nomenclatures and standards for use in art, manufacturing and the sciences. Some of these systems also aimed to provide a chronicle of historical colour, such as Elizabeth Burris-Meyer's (1899–1969) *Historical Color Guide* from 1938, which she later adapted for use in interior decoration, fashion and make-up (pp. 298–315). "Theory and Practice: The Teaching of Colour" focuses on the history of practical manuals of colour for painters and printers, from the early 19th to the early 20th century. The earlier colour manuals are still much indebted to the development of painting in watercolour, and many of them were intended for amateurs as painting materials became more affordable at the start of the 19th century. Painting was an acceptable pastime for women in the 18th and 19th centuries, and for that reason a good proportion of these manuals were aimed specifically at a female readership, although they were predominantly written by men. From the beginning of the 20th century, however, more women became active in writing educational and instructive colour manuals or primers, grasping their opportunities for writing, publishing and teaching in the field. Until now this has been a little-researched area of women's creative engagement, and because teaching manuals, especially those for younger children, were not considered serious texts they have typically not been well recorded and not many copies survive.

The early 20th century was marked as well by another surge in books about colour, many of them building on the works of the great colour theorists of the previous century but developing their concepts further, as is demonstrated in Chapter 6, "Colour Breaking Free: The Early 20th Century". Colour in this period cannot be properly evaluated without taking into account a range of scientific and artistic achievements, including the various advances in the understanding of colour vision and specifically the anatomy of the human eye, the electrification of the world and the resulting possibilities provided by artificial lighting, and the radical new use of colour as an expressive tool in the arts, for painting in particular. European avant-garde groups such as Der Blaue Reiter (The Blue Rider), the Fauvists and many of the Expressionists and early abstract artists actively engaged in colour theory. They embraced the symbolic and visual power of colour and depicted the world in subjective, non-realistic tones. For some, concepts of colour became the main subject of certain works, as seen, for example, in Franz Marc's (1880–1916) abstract painting *Kämpfende Formen* (*Fighting Forms*, p. 67) from 1914.

The highly coloured and increasingly mechanised first decades of the 20th century, when material colour could be bought ready-made and neatly packaged in almost every bright shade imaginable, were crying out for new attempts to give colour a definitive order. Some of the more influential results are discussed in Chapter 6, such as the complex work of Albert Henry Munsell (1858–1918) in America (pp. 380–389) and Wilhelm Ostwald in Europe. Both men created highly educational and adaptable systems that were based on a three-dimensional concept of colour, and indeed some of these three-dimensional models that were used in teaching have survived (see, for example, Ostwald's *Colour Solid* in the archives of Winsor & Newton). The early 20th century was also a period of improved research and publishing opportunities for women, which resulted in several notable examples of scientific studies by women on colour vision and psychology, colour in literature and poetry, historical colour theory and other aspects of colour history. Some of these books published between 1900 and the 1930s are among the most inventive and beautiful in colour history, as, for example, Emily Noyes Vanderpoel's (1842–1939) *Color Problems* (1902, pp. 364–379).

Chapter 7, "The Sound of Colour: Spiritualism, Occultism and Music", examines the synaesthetic associations between colour and music, and, by extension, movement, dance and spirituality. To some degree, the highly individual and often pseudo-scientific colour concepts published by the Theosophists, Anthroposophists and members of similar groups and movements around the start of the last century were a response to an increasingly mechanised world, but it is useful to review each of their colour concepts carefully and judge them not by their scientific accuracy but by their creative inventiveness and the social and historical circumstances that underpin them. You don't have to believe in colour auras, as illustrated and described by Annie Besant (1847–1933) and Charles Webster Leadbeater (1854–1934), but their attempt to give form and colour to thoughts and emotions is a fascinating comment on human nature at the time (pp. 412–439).

Analogies between colour and music have been a prominent theme in the history of colour concepts, and most of the texts mentioned in this chapter of the book discussed colour in relation to sound, music, poetry and dance, while many of them also combined mysticism with science, individual religious beliefs with colour theory, nature with spiritualism and historic texts on colour with current painting practice. This may well sound a bewildering and idiosyncratic mixture, and it often makes for difficult reading, but the visual representations of these concepts are captivating. The Australian artist Roy de Maistre (1894–1968) created many paintings on the subject, including a five-metre-long scroll that represented a "colour translation" of Haydn's *Trio in B Flat* (p. 76). The work of the Swedish mystic and anthroposophist Hilma af Klint was deeply rooted in occultism and colour symbolism, and in recent years she has been rediscovered and rightly praised for her visionary style. Although she never formulated a distinct col-

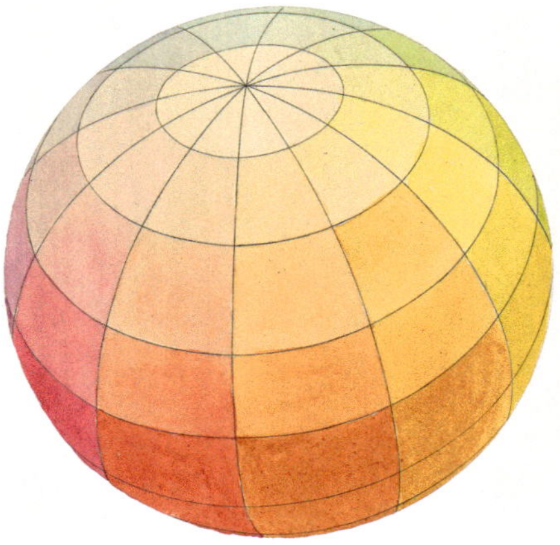

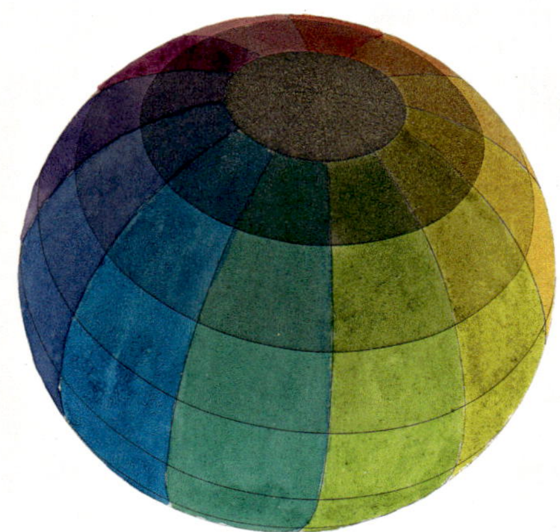

our theory, many of her large-scale paintings incorporate coloured circles, pyramids and images of optical colour, thereby creating a remarkably individual visual chromatic vocabulary in which realism was combined with abstraction (pp. 56, 68, 69).

This book cannot make any claim to being a global overview of historic colour concepts. It is, perhaps inevitably, predominantly western-centric in its selection of works, but Chapter 8 aims to redress this imbalance by looking east, beyond our more familiar western view, to provide a glimpse into Japanese colour concepts of the 19th and 20th centuries. It is not the author's intention to claim expertise in these regions' colour concepts, but rather to acknowledge their aesthetic appeal and to highlight how colour concepts from geographically distant parts of the world may relate to each other. Comparing something as abstract as colour is a potent example of what connects humans across the globe. One intriguing example of cross-cultural colour exchange can be noted in the afterlife of one of George Field's colour diagrams from the 1830s which recurs in a Japanese textbook for schoolchildren, *Gakko hitsuyo irozu mondo*, that was first published in 1876 (pp. 460–465).

The final chapter, "Interaction and Abstraction: Bauhaus and Beyond", considers colour in its most pure, reduced and elemental form as found in art, design, didactic literature and teaching in the early to mid-20th century. The road to abstraction was long and gradual, with contributions from various pioneers including Turner, Gartside, Whistler, af Klint and several artists from various European avant-garde groups, but the Bauhaus and its wider circle of influence became one of the leading representatives of modernism, progressiveness and, in stylistic terms, abstraction. Founded by the architect Walter Gropius (1883–1969) in Weimar in 1919, the short-lived school of art and design had its roots in German avant-garde and spiritualist groups, as well as the English Arts and Crafts movement. It was concerned with simplicity and functionality of design, based on giving artists a thorough training and on quality of craftsmanship. Members, teachers and students in the Bauhaus included Ludwig Mies van der Rohe, Paul Klee, Johannes Itten and Josef Albers, as well as

Philipp Otto Runge
**Colour Globe / Farben-Kugel**
**Sphère chromatique** (detail)
From: *Farben-Kugel; oder Construction des Verhältnisses aller Mischungen der Farben zu einander, und ihrer vollständigen Affinität* (Hamburg, 1810)
Hamburger Kunsthalle

Bonnie Snow
**Cover / Buchdeckel / Couverture**
From: *Text Books of Art Education*, vol. 1 (New York, 1904)
Sussex, collection of the author

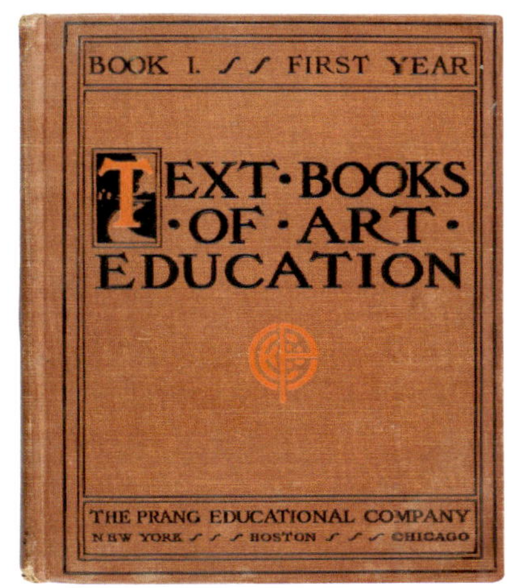


several women, whose roles in the Bauhaus story have only recently been fully acknowledged, such as Anni Albers, Marianne Brandt, Gertrud Arndt, Gertrud Grunow and Gunta Stölzl. In 1925 the Bauhaus moved to Dessau, where Gropius designed the iconic Bauhaus building (see p. 70), but in 1933, after a year's residency in Berlin, it was forced to close after having come under increasing pressure from the Nazis. Some of the members emigrated to England or the United States, where they were able to maintain ties with each other and continue their work. Although colour was only one element of the Bauhaus courses, it led to many related publications on colour, some of which are featured in this book's closing chapter, including a classic work on colour that was published nearly 30 years after the school's closure: Josef Albers's (1888–1976) *Interaction of Color* (1963, pp. 498–503). This and other, lesser-known works on colour by associated authors and artists are examples of a near-perfect synthesis of thinking about colour in terms of living and working with it, teaching it and applying it to art and design, while at the same time reflecting the modernist ideals of simplicity, geometry and abstraction. In art, the colour concepts and aesthetics of the Bauhaus are mirrored by the wider move towards abstraction in the 20th century, and the similarities in the use of colour with the extremely geometric work of modern masters such as Piet Mondrian (p. 74), Henri Matisse and Kazimir Malevich are obvious.

## The Timelessness of Colour Concepts

The abstract beauty of colour diagrams, of colour concepts made visual, gives them a timeless appeal. The simple, geometric shapes and forms created to form the framework of early colour charts and tables feel immediately accessible, because the same or similar forms still exist today in art, advertising and design, while colour circles, wheels, triangles, cubes and even more complex diagrams or organic forms are relatable across centuries. Colour theory and colour concepts continue to be a motif and source of inspiration for contemporary artists. Since 2009, the Icelandic-Danish artist Olafur Eliasson (b. 1967) has created a

Philipp Otto Runge
**Little Morning**, 1809/10
**Der kleine Morgen**
**Le Petit Matin**
Oil on canvas, 109 x 85.5 cm
(43 x 33 ½ in.)
Hamburger Kunsthalle

series of large colour wheels in which the various colours bled seamlessly into one another (p. 81), in similar fashion to one of Chevreul's colour wheels in his *Atlas* from 1861. A set of them, entitled *Turner colour experiments*, was displayed at Tate Britain in proximity to some of Turner's paintings. Just as Turner referenced Goethe and Harris in some of his work, so Eliasson referred back to colour theorists and artists before him, aiming to create his own new colour theory in art.

Human beings have always tried to tame and control colour, this ungraspable yet all-pervading element of our vision. Our attempts at capturing colour, by drawing circles, squares and lines around it, by squeezing it into lists or moulding it into three-dimensional shapes, are ultimately expressions of human thinking and creativity. The perfect colour concept may not yet have been formulated, but turning existing ideas about colour into words, images, diagrams and three-dimensional objects has resulted in a rich history of colour as visual art. Individual expertise, personal choices, new research discoveries and fresh thinking make every new book on colour history exciting, and the authors hope that the selection of colour concepts presented in these two volumes will provide some unexpected and inspiring views and stories that illuminate the history of colour further.

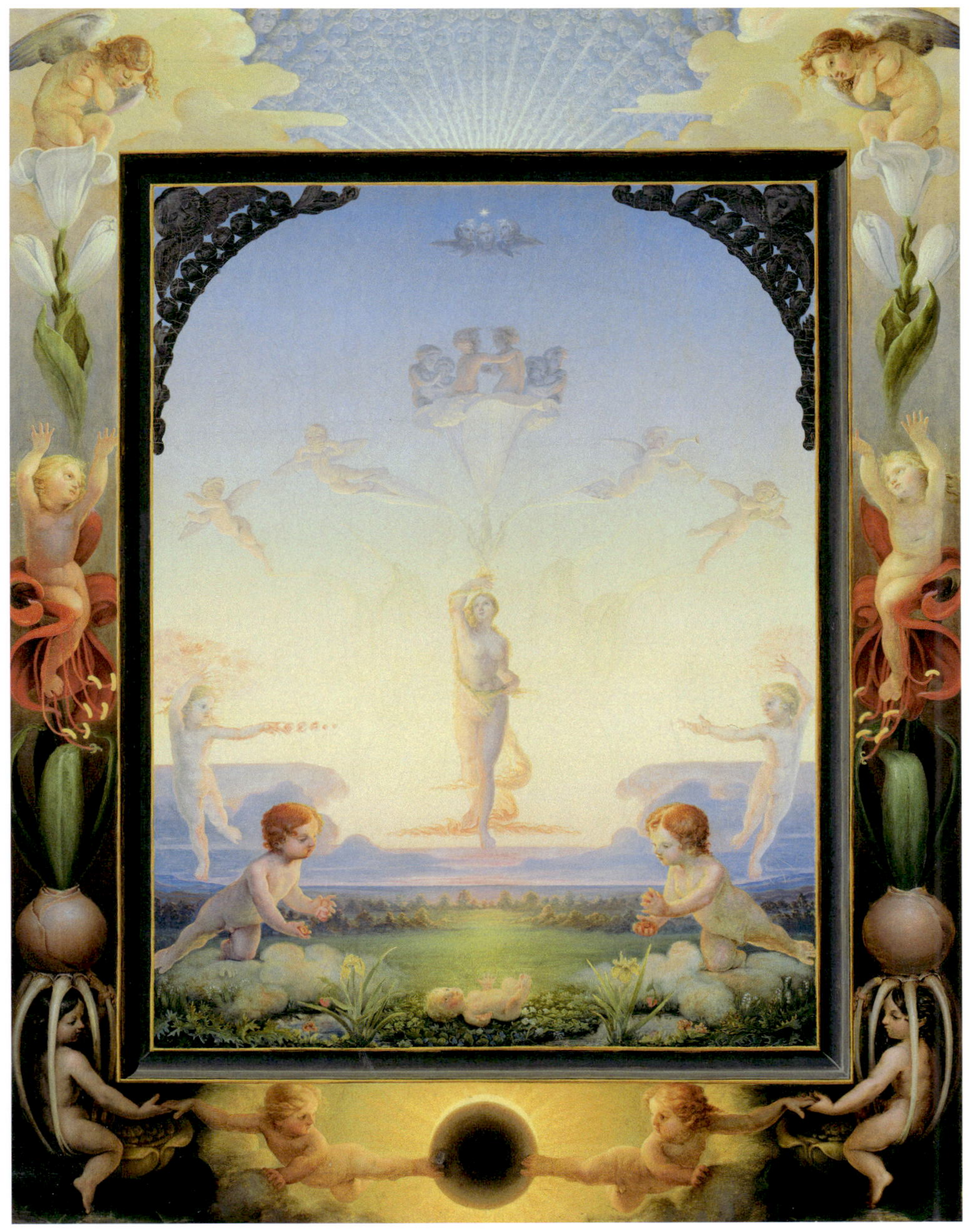

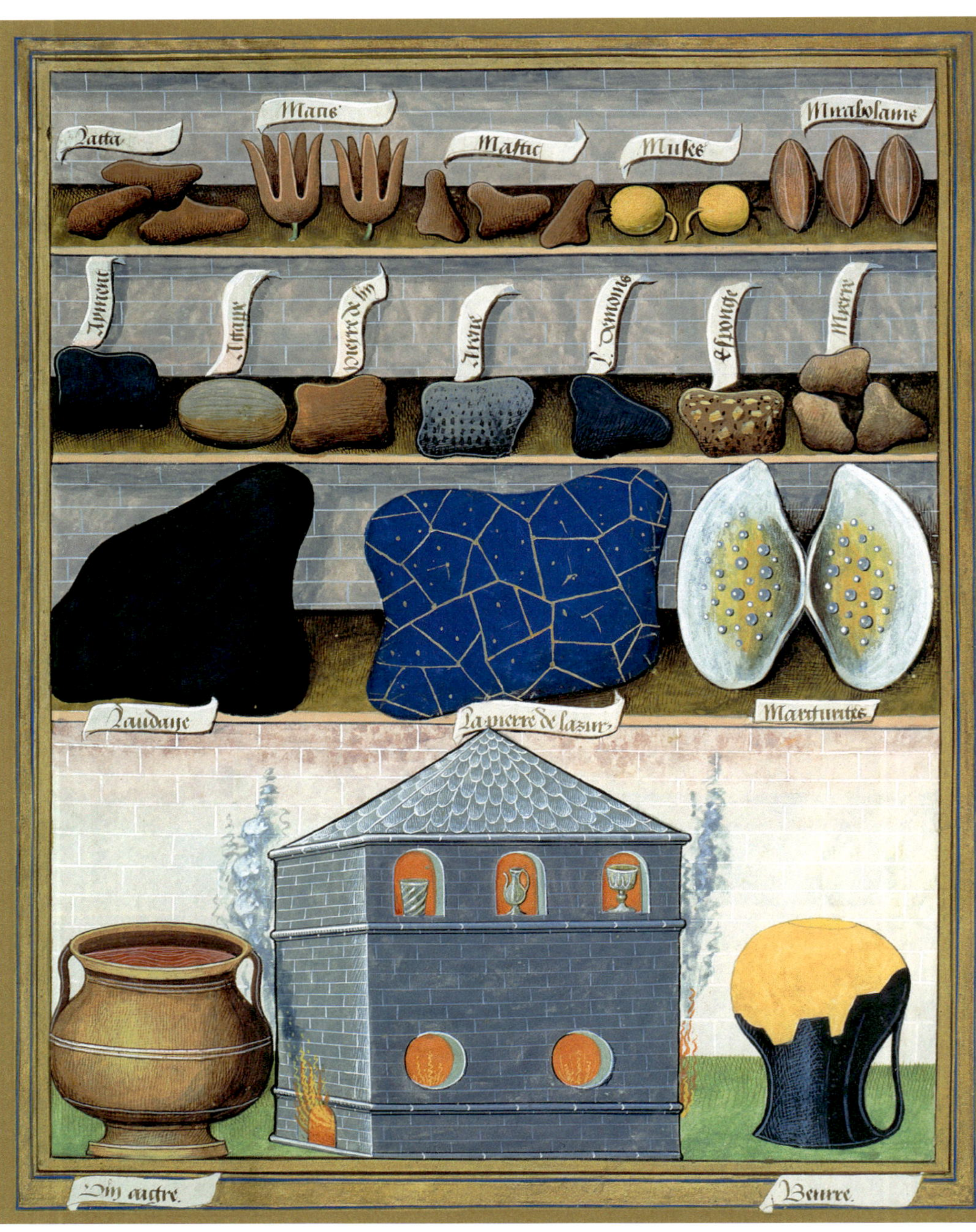
Macis
Mastic
Muscs
Mirabolans
Piment
Litarge
Esponge
Mirre
Laudane
La pierre de lazur
Margarites
Un aultre
Beurre

Alexandra Loske

# DIE KONTROLLE UND ENTFESSELUNG DER FARBEN

## Eine Geschichte des menschlichen Bestrebens, Farbe in Worten und Bildern zu erfassen

Unsere Welt ist voller Farbe. Die meisten erleben sie in Farbe. Die Erde ist als „Blauer Planet" bekannt, und optisch lösen wir uns in Blau auf: Als wir 1990 aus etwa sechs Milliarden Kilometern Entfernung von der Raumsonde *Voyager 1* fotografiert wurden, erschienen wir, wie der Astronom Carl Sagan es einige Jahre später formulierte, als „blassblauer Punkt": weniger als ein Pixel groß und kaum sichtbar, doch noch immer mit erkennbarer Färbung. Wir werden zum Farbfleck, bevor wir ganz aus dem Blickfeld verschwinden. Demnach ist Farbe einer der prägenden und verbindenden Aspekte unseres Lebens, eine wahrhaft universelle und von allen Menschen geteilte Erfahrung, und es überrascht nicht, dass sie uns schon immer fasziniert. Die frühesten Manifestationen menschlicher Kreativität in Form von Schnitzereien und Markierungen in und auf Holz, Knochen und Felsen zeigen, dass wir von jeher versucht haben, Farben herzustellen und zu verwenden, um vor allen Dingen abzubilden oder wiederzugeben, was uns beschäftigt und was uns umgibt. Wenngleich die Bilder und physischen Beweise dieser frühesten menschlichen Betätigung bruchstückhaft und verblasst sind, ist nicht auszuschließen, dass Farbe sogar in dieser Zeit auch als Symbol genutzt wurde. Die mineralischen Pigmente, die der frühe Mensch aus dem Boden gewann, wurden mit organischer Materie wie Fett, Schmalz oder Körperflüssigkeiten vermischt. Dabei könnten sie gut spezifische oder sakrale Bedeutungen angenommen haben, aus denen sich eine erste einfache Farbhierarchie entwickelte. Wir werden nie genau wissen, was unsere prähistorischen Vorfahren über Farbe dachten, doch gibt es Hinweise, dass bestimmte Farben in speziellen Zusammenhängen verwendet wurden.

Eine theoretische Auseinandersetzung mit Farbe lässt sich durch die gesamte Menschheitsgeschichte zurückverfolgen, von den einfachen Ausprägungen der frühen Kunst bis zu den hoch entwickelten Systemen, die in der modernen Wissenschaft, Philosophie oder Kunst verwurzelt sind – Kategorien, die sich häufig überschneiden und aufeinander beziehen. Seit jeher kreisen menschliche Gefühle und Gedanken um Farben und widmen sich dem Verlangen, Farben herzustellen, sie zu ordnen und zu systematisieren, sie zu nutzen und zu strukturieren und ihnen vielschichtige Bedeutungen

*Page 30 and opposite*
Robinet Testard
**Selected Minerals and Organic Matter**
**Anordnung von Mineralen und organischen Stoffen**
**Agencement de matières minérales et organiques**
From: Matthaeus Platearius, *Le Livre des simples médecines* (*c.* 1500)
St. Petersburg, Russian National Library

zuzuweisen. Die zahlreichen Bemühungen, sie zu klassifizieren und zu begreifen, schlugen sich in vielgestaltigen Erscheinungsformen nieder, von dualistischen Konzepten aus Dunkelheit und Licht bis zu ausgefeilten geometrischen Mustern und Systemen, die versuchen, Farbe mittels spezifischer Formen zu kategorisieren. Die Entwicklung der Sprache, der Schrift und schließlich des Druckwesens mit seinen ausgeklügelten Methoden der Bildreproduktion hat dazu geführt, dass diese Ideen immer anspruchsvoller, komplizierter, visuell verblüffender und zu guter Letzt auch besser dokumentiert wurden.

In diesem Buch beginnt die visuelle Reise durch die Geschichte der Farbtheorie zur Zeit der frühesten illustrierten Manuskripte und gedruckten Quellen aus dem 17. Jahrhundert, die sich speziell auf Farbe konzentrieren, und endet Mitte des 20. Jahrhunderts vor Anbruch des Digitalzeitalters. So wie jedes hier beschriebene Farbsystem ist auch das vorliegende Buch selbst mit seiner Auswahl an bestimmten Theorien ein Spiegel der Zeit, in der es verfasst wurde. Im Verlauf der letzten Jahrzehnte hat das Interesse an Farbe und Farbgeschichte deutlich zugenommen. Infolge aktueller Forschungen entdecken wir neue Stränge und lange Zeit übersehene Stimmen und Beispiele einer materiellen Kultur (Schriftsteller und Pädagogen, Bücher, Manuskripte, Kunst und Methoden), die entweder in Vergessenheit geraten waren oder bisher nie als Teil des Farbkanons galten.

Kein Buch über Farbe kann den Anspruch erheben, eine ebenso umfassende wie kulturell, historisch, geografisch und thematisch vollständige Dokumentation vorzulegen. Manche Titel nehmen bewusst Auslassungen vor, um den Fokus auf bestimmte kulturelle oder historische Themen zu lenken, andere treffen ihre Auswahl anhand der persönlichen Interessen, Vorlieben oder Fachkenntnisse der Autoren und Herausgeber. Dieses Buch ist, bildlich gesprochen, ein bunter Strauß und in seiner Auswahl so subjektiv wie die Farbwahrnehmung selbst. Die 41 hier gezeigten und besprochenen Werke stehen stellvertretend für die bewegte und abwechslungsreiche Geschichte der Farbtheorien seit dem 17. Jahrhundert. Während wir viele vertraute Beispiele für Farbsysteme ausgewählt haben, die in der Farbgeschichte fest verankert

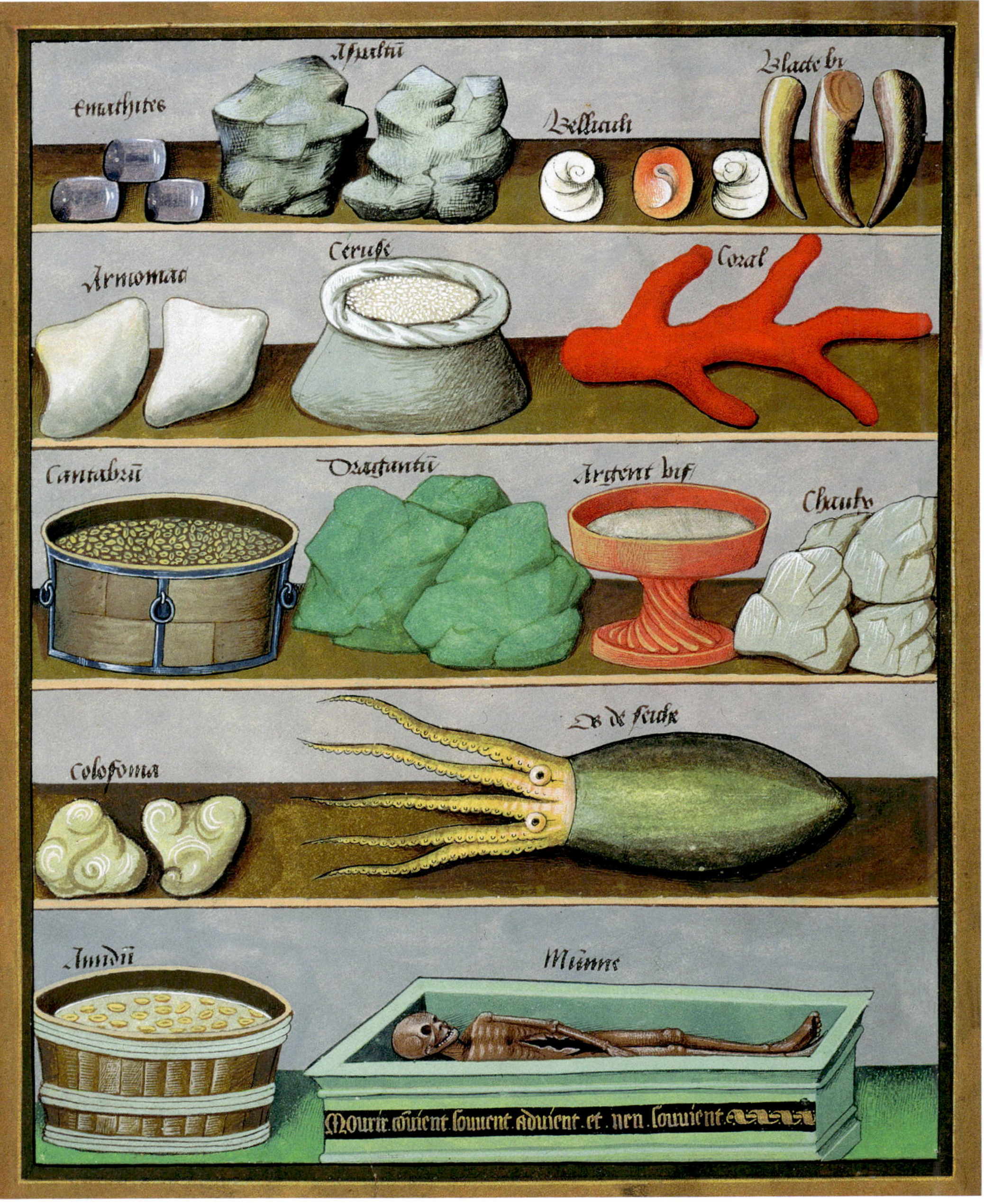
Ceruse
Coral

sind, konnten wir diese hoffentlich erfolgreich in einen größeren kulturellen Zusammenhang stellen und mit neuen Augen betrachten. Neben diesen „Klassikern“ ihres Fachs haben wir uns besonders darum bemüht, einige weniger bekannte oder ungewöhnlichere Werke zu präsentieren, die aufgrund ihrer ästhetischen und theoretischen Wirkung und Bedeutung Aufmerksamkeit verdienen. Darüber hinaus wollten wir mehr Raum Farbtraktaten geben, die in den letzten zweihundert Jahren von Frauen verfasst, publiziert und bebildert wurden. Die große historische und geografische Bandbreite dieses Buches reicht von Europa über die USA bis in asiatische Regionen, doch auch verschiedene Gattungen und Stile sollten so umfassend wie möglich abgedeckt werden. Eine lehrreiche Farbfibel aus dem 20. Jahrhundert kann genauso faszinierend sein wie Isaac Newtons (1643–1727) Farbkreis von 1704 (S. 155), und beide spielen in der Geschichte der Farben eine wichtige Rolle.

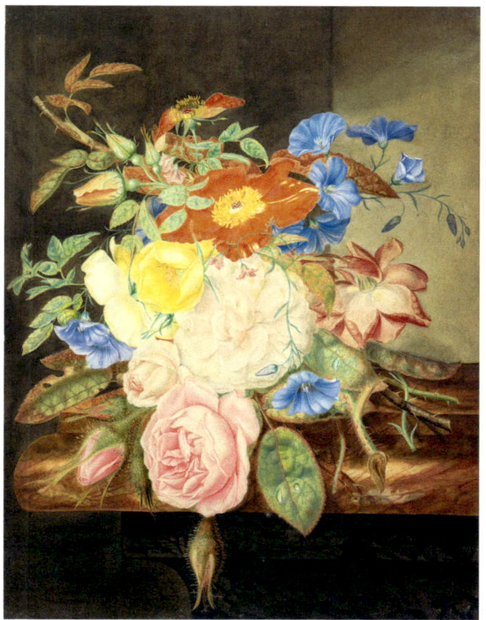

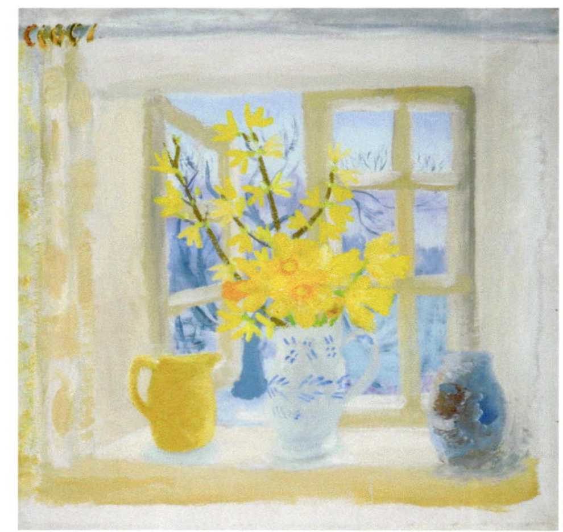

## Warum Farbtheorien?

Der weit gefasste und dehnbare Begriff „Farbtheorie“ lässt sich sehr gut auf das Nachdenken über Farben und den Versuch anwenden, sie zu verstehen und zu systematisieren. Doch anstatt nach dem perfekten Begriff zu suchen, könnte man vielleicht besser fragen, warum wir überhaupt das Bedürfnis verspüren, etwas so Ungreifbares, sich ständig Veränderndes, schwer Definierbares und in gewissem Maße Subjektives systematisch zu erfassen. Bis vor nicht allzu langer Zeit fand in der Farbliteratur keine saubere Trennung zwischen stofflicher und immaterieller Farbe statt. Doch nachdem man den Unterschied vollständig durchdrungen hatte, wurde klar, dass tatsächlich viele Formen von Farbe existieren, in denen sich immaterielle Farbe und die Farben von Feststoffen miteinander verbinden. Farben entgleiten uns leicht, sie verändern sich mit dem Licht, sehen je nach Tageszeit anders aus, verblassen, werden dunkler und können unkalkulierbar sein, wenn sie kombiniert, gemischt oder nebeneinandergesetzt werden. Darüber hinaus sind sie schwer nachzuahmen, wie Pigmenthersteller und Historiker bestätigen können. Für den frühen Men-

*Opposite top*
Winifred Nicholson
**Easter Monday**, *c.* 1950
**Ostermontag**
**Lundi de Pâques**
Oil on panel, 174 x 174 cm
(68 ½ x 68 ½ in.)
Carlisle, Tullie House
Museum and Art Gallery

*Opposite bottom*
Mary Gartside
**Mixed Flowers on a Slab, Including Roses, and Convolvulus**, *c.* 1785
**Gemischte Blumen auf einer Platte, darunter Rosen und Winden**
**Mélange de fleurs sur un bloc de pierre, avec roses et volubilis**
Watercolour and bodycolour on card, 36.1 x 27.7 cm (14 ¼ x 10 ⅞ in.)
Cambridge, Fitzwilliam Museum

schen muss es frustrierend gewesen sein, in einer Welt zu leben, deren vorherrschende Farben – das Blau des Himmels und das Grün der Pflanzenwelt – zugleich die beiden am schwierigsten herzustellenden waren. Wir mögen in einer Welt leben, die reich an Chlorophyll ist, doch nur wenige Pflanzen ergeben brauchbare grüne Pigmente. Farbe ist außerdem aufreizend launisch, instabil, oft giftig und wurde nicht immer geliebt – denn wie der Künstler und Schriftsteller David Batchelor in seinem Essay *Chromophobie* so wunderbar erklärt hat, ist die Abscheu vor der Farbe ein bedeutender Bestandteil der westlichen Kulturgeschichte und tief verwurzelt in einer „Angst vor Verunreinigung und Verderben durch etwas, das unbekannt ist und anscheinend auch unbekannt bleiben wird". Diese Angst oder Aversion „äußert sich in den zahlreichen unterschiedlichen Versuchen, Farbe aus der Kultur auszutreiben, zu entwerten, ihre Bedeutung zu schmälern, ihre Komplexität zu leugnen". Westliche Einstellungen zur Farbe oder, genauer gesagt, zu stark gesättigten Farben und zur Polychromie, so Batchelor, gingen im Gegensatz zu den klassischen Idealen von jungfräulichem Weiß oder farbloser Schönheit oft mit Vorstellungen einher, die das Fremde, Orientalische, Primitive, Weibliche, Vulgäre, Oberflächliche oder gar Pathologische einschließen. Die westliche Kultur blickte insofern auf eine lange Geschichte von Farbe und Dunkelheit als Sinnbilder für ein gefährliches oder bedrohliches „Anderes" zurück, und eine derart destabilisierende Kraft galt es entweder zu meiden oder zu bändigen. Farbsysteme oder Farbtheorien zu entwickeln, ist dabei eine Möglichkeit, Farbe zunächst gedanklich zu zähmen, um sie anschließend wohlüberlegt einzusetzen und aufzutragen. Wenn wir Farben eine Ordnung auferlegen, und sei es nur theoretisch, dann haben wir zumindest versucht, die Kontrolle über ein veränderliches und allgegenwärtiges Phänomen zu übernehmen.

Doch natürlich sind Furcht vor, Zweifel an und Hass auf Farbe nur eine Seite der Medaille. Unser Verhältnis zu Farbe war stets facettenreich. Vor allem die letzten fünfzig bis sechzig Jahre – in denen Erfindungen wie die Farbfotografie, der Farbfilm und das Farbfernsehen massentauglich wurden, digitale Farben aufkamen und das Druckwesen nahezu vollständig auf Farbe umstellte – haben nicht nur dazu geführt,

Johann Wolfgang von Goethe
**Chromatic Card Game; Two Picture Cards**
**Farbkartenspiel; zwei Bildkarten**
**Jeu de cartes chromatiques; deux cartes illustrées**
From: *Beyträge zur Optik* (Weimar, 1791)
Hand-coloured woodcuts, 5.8 x 10 cm (2 ¼ x 4 in.)
Klassik Stiftung Weimar

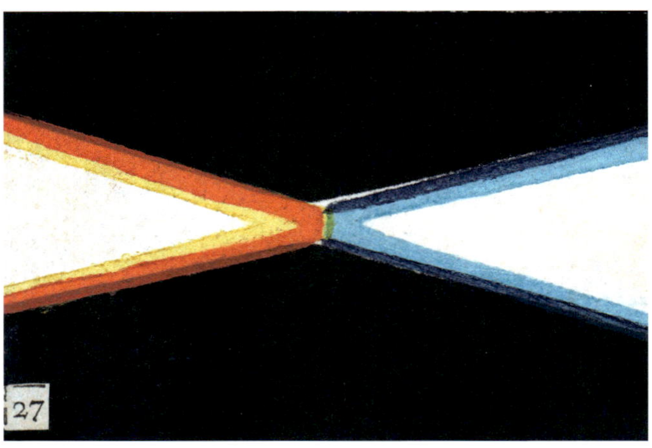


dass wir uns mit Farbe wohlfühlen, sondern haben uns diese auch so zugänglich gemacht wie niemals zuvor. Fast ausnahmslos ist Farbe heute ein bequem verfügbares Gut, das niemanden mehr ausschließt, und auch der Farbreproduktion sind trotz weiterhin auftretender Qualitätsschwankungen kaum noch Grenzen gesetzt.

## Die Ordnung der Farben: Vom Malkasten bis zur Palette

Wo Textquellen zur Farbtheorie fehlen, ermöglichen Archäologie und materielle Kultur Einblicke in die Farbkultur. Zumindest die in Kunst und Dekoration verwendeten Farben deuten darauf hin, welche Pigmente zu bestimmten Zeiten der Geschichte verfügbar waren, und geben detailliert Auskunft über Techniken, Malmittel, Farbvorlieben und – wenn man sie im größeren kulturellen Zusammenhang betrachtet – vielleicht auch über symbolische Farbbedeutungen. Eine der ältesten erhaltenen Künstlerpaletten, ein auf etwa 1427 bis 1401 vor unserer Zeitrechnung datierter Malkasten aus der 18. altägyptischen Dynastie (S. 9), vermittelt anschaulich und ganz unmittelbar, welche Pigmente ihrem Besitzer Amenemope, einem Wesir unter Amenhotep II., zur Verfügung standen, aber womöglich auch, welche Farben er bevorzugte und wie er die in Mulden gepressten Pigmente Roter Ocker, Ägyptisch Blau, Grün und zwei verschiedene Sorten Kohlenschwarz in seinem Kasten gern arrangierte. Wofür brauchte er zweimal Schwarz? Was bedeutete Schwarz für ihn oder die altägyptische Kultur insgesamt? Diese Anordnung von Künstlermaterialien scheint Lichtjahre entfernt von einem dreidimensionalen Farbmodell des 20. Jahrhunderts, doch das darunterliegende menschliche Bedürfnis ist dasselbe: den Farben eine Ordnung zu geben, ob aus praktischen Gründen, persönlicher Vorliebe oder gar zu Werbezwecken. Jede Malerpalette – als tatsächliches Objekt mit Farbresten darauf oder als Teil eines Selbstporträts – verrät etwas über Leben und Zeit des Künstlers, seine Malpraxis und seine Präferenzen. Selbst moderne Malkästen, die mit industriell gefertigten Wasserfarbtabletten bestückt werden können, geben Aufschluss über ihre Anwender und Besitzer: Welche Kastengröße und -qualität konnten sie sich leisten, welche Farben haben sie gewählt, welche wurden am meisten benutzt, welche so gut wie nie, und wie wurden die Farben angeordnet? Ähnlich wie das Beispiel aus dem alten Ägypten kann auch ein von Reeves in London hergestellter Aquarellmalkasten (S. 51) aus dem frühen 20. Jahrhundert viel darüber aussagen, welche Farben zur damaligen Zeit verfügbar oder populär waren. Das hier abgebildete Exemplar enthält mehrere Farben, deren Namensgeber der bedeutende deutsche Chemiker und Farbtheoretiker Wilhelm Ostwald (1853–1932) war.

## Abhandlungen über Farbe bis zur Frühen Neuzeit

Dieses Werk ist in erster Linie der Visualisierung von Farbordnungen und den damit verbundenen Ideen gewidmet. Während die Theorien selbst bis in die Antike zurückreichen, tauchten die frühesten Farbillustrationen in Form von Diagrammen erst Ende des 17. Jahrhunderts auf. Noch bis vor relativ kurzer Zeit erschien die antike Kultur unter Materialgesichtspunkten als überwiegend farblos. Aufgrund der vorherrschenden Bilder von weißen Skulpturen und Bauwerken, die ihre Farbe seit Langem eingebüßt hatten, wurden das alte Rom und die griechische Antike hauptsächlich mit der Farbe Weiß assoziiert. Dieser allgemeine Eindruck wurde jedoch von Studien aus den letzten Jahren widerlegt und durch ein polychromes Bild der griechischen und römischen Bildhauerei und Baukunst ersetzt.

In konzeptueller und sprachlicher Hinsicht lassen sich in der Geschichte der Farbtheorien mehrere Traditionen unterscheiden. Der griechische Philosoph Empedokles (494–434 v. Chr.) soll als einer der Ersten über das Thema geschrieben haben. Aus den erhaltenen Fragmenten seiner Dichtung ist ein kosmologisches System herauszulesen, das auf den vier Elementen Erde, Feuer, Wasser und Luft basiert, von denen er die Farben ableiten zu können glaubte. Im folgenden Jahrhundert könnte Aristoteles (384–322 v. Chr.) einfache optische Experimente mit farbigem Glas durchgeführt haben. Er untersuchte neben dem Farbensehen auch die Farbkontraste und schlug ein polares System vor – vom göttlichen weißen

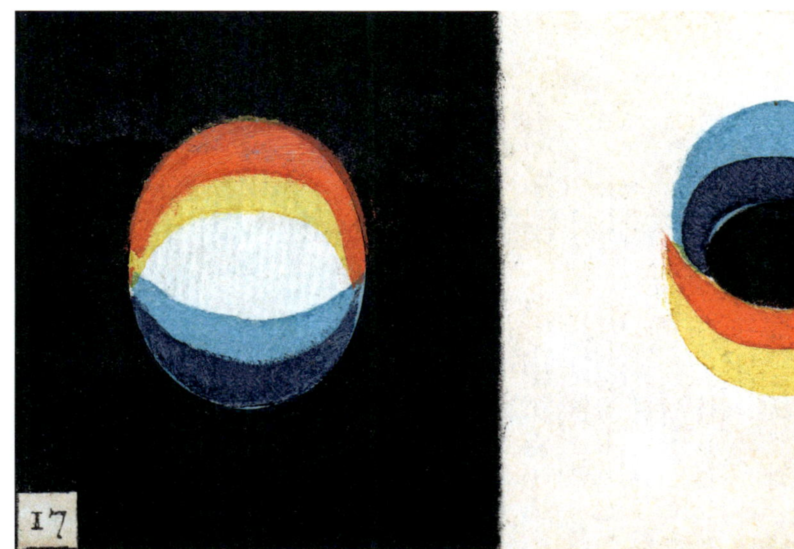


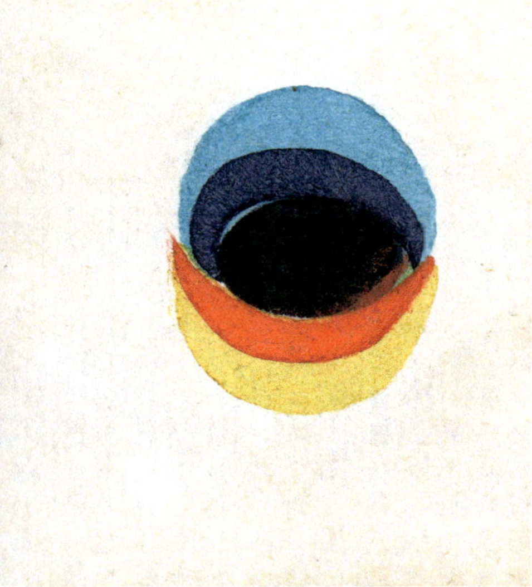

J. M. W. Turner
**Lecture Diagrams: Colour Circles No. 1 and 2**, *c.* 1824–1828
**Vorlesungsdiagramme: Farbkreise Nr. 1 und 2**
**Graphiques pédagogiques: cercles chromatiques nos 1 et 2**
Graphite and watercolour on paper;
No. 1: 55.6 x 76.2 cm (21⅞ x 30 in.),
No. 2: 55 x 75.8 cm (21⅝ x 29⅞ in.)
London, Tate Britain

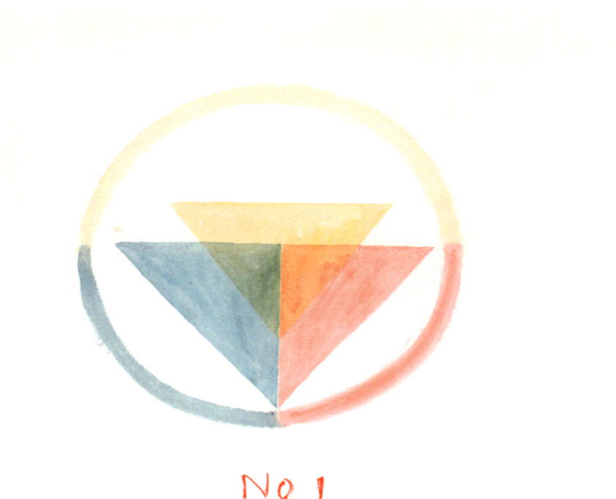


Licht, das Farbe sichtbar machte, bis zur Dunkelheit, die sich in Schwarz niederschlug. Aus Weiß entstand die Hierarchie der Farben Gelb, Grün, Blau und Rot, die in dieser Reihenfolge mit Erde, Wasser, Luft und Feuer assoziiert wurden. Der Aristoteles-Schüler Theophrast (372–287 v. Chr.) dachte darüber nach, wie wir Farben erkennen oder empfinden, und bezog sich dabei auf Demokrit (460–370 v. Chr.) und dessen Lehre von den vier Grundfarben Rot, Schwarz, Weiß und Grüngelb, die auf bestimmten Formen, Oberflächenmustern und anderen sinnesbezogenen Eigenschaften beruhten. Der griechische Arzt Hippokrates (460–375 v. Chr.) unterschied vier Farben, die die vier Grundsäfte oder Flüssigkeiten des menschlichen Körpers repräsentierten, von denen man ihrerseits annahm, dass sie für bestimmte Charakterzüge verantwortlich waren. So stand Weiß für phlegmatisch, Rot für sanguinisch, Gelb für cholerisch und Schwarz für melancholisch.

Klassische Farbsysteme und theoretische Erörterungen des Themas sind in der Regel nur bruchstückhaft erhalten und zudem mit großen sprachlichen Herausforderungen befrachtet. Sprache wird Farben grundsätzlich nicht gerecht, weil Worte außerstande sind, der vollen Komplexität von Farbe oder Farbwahrnehmung zu entsprechen. Die meisten Sprachen verfügen über etwa ein Dutzend grundlegende Farbbezeichnungen, während die Vielfalt der Farben, die wir tatsächlich sehen, unendlich ist. Diese Diskrepanz wird noch problematischer, wenn es um alte Sprachen, ältere Texte oder Übersetzungen geht. Der zusätzliche Mangel an visuellen Darstellungen von Farbsystemen aus der Antike und vorangegangenen Kulturen erschwert ein auch nur annähernd umfassendes Verständnis von den ältesten dieser Vorstellungen. Gleichwohl vermitteln bestimmte archäologische Funde flüchtige Eindrücke vom Symbolwert der Farben. Die in Pompeji ausgegrabenen Theatermasken etwa, sowohl in Objektform als auch auf Fresken, waren in Farben bemalt, die stellvertretend für die vier Temperamente standen (S. 15). Obwohl nur vereinzelt spezielle Farbliteratur überliefert ist, können wir anhand der materiellen Natur von Pigmenten und Farbstoffen die Entwicklung von Farbtheorien in verschiedenen Kulturen nachverfolgen. Ähnlich wie beim teuren Ultramarinpigment in der Kunst des Mittelalters und der

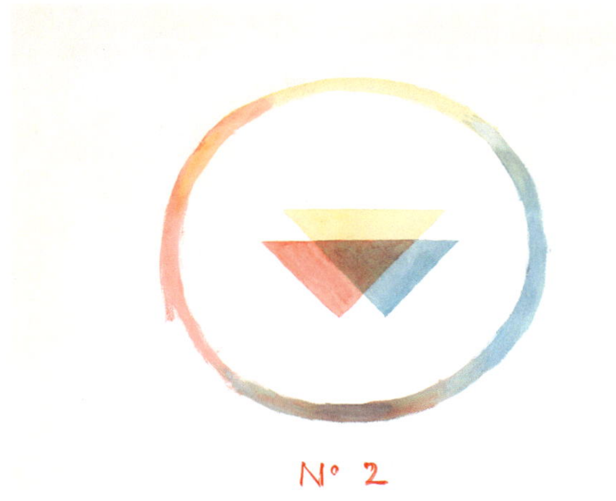


*Page 41*
J. M. W. Turner
**The Scarlet Sunset**, *c.* 1830–1840
**Der scharlachrote Sonnenuntergang**
**Coucher de soleil écarlate**
Watercolour and gouache on paper, 13.4 x 18.9 cm (5 ¼ x 7 ½ in.)
London, Tate Britain

Renaissance (S. 11) führten der Materialwert und die Seltenheit bestimmter Farben in der Antike dazu, dass sie mit hochrangigen Figuren und Gottheiten assoziiert wurden.

Während im philosophischen Farbdiskurs des Mittelalters das aristotelische Grundschema einer Farbenreihe zwischen Dunkelheit und Licht (Schwarz und Weiß) vorherrschte, nahm auch die Zahl der eher praktisch orientierten Texte zu. Im frühen 13. Jahrhundert übersetzte Robert Grosseteste (um 1175–1253), Gelehrter an der Universität Oxford und Bischof von Lincoln, einige aristotelische Schriften und verfasste als Antwort darauf seine eigene Abhandlung über Farbe. In *De Colore* entwickelte er Aristoteles' Theorie der Farbe als Ableitung des Lichts weiter und stellte Mutmaßungen über die Lichtmenge an, die in einzelnen Farben enthalten sein könnte. Etwa ab dem 15. Jahrhundert, getrieben vom wachsenden weltweiten Austausch und Handel, wurde Farbe zunehmend zum Wirtschaftsgut. Wie sich mit Erscheinen der ersten Abhandlungen zu künstlerischen Praktiken, Malmaterialien und Künstlerbiografien zeigte, wurde Wissen jetzt systematischer erfasst. Viele dieser Texte waren sehr technisch und erreichten keine große Leserschaft, erst recht nicht vor Anbruch des Druckzeitalters. Und doch haben sich allerlei schriftliche Aufzeichnungen erhalten, die ein Fenster zur mittelalterlichen Welt der handwerklich hergestellten Farben öffnen, etwa das bereits deutlich früher erschienene *De diversis artibus* („Über verschiedene Künste") von Theophilus Presbyter (tätig um 1070–1125), bei dem es sich im Kern um eine Sammlung von Farbrezepten aus dem frühen 12. Jahrhundert handelt (eine deutsche Gesamtausgabe erschien 1999 unter dem Titel *Theophilus Presbyter und das mittelalterliche Kunsthandwerk*). Viele weitere kunstpraktisch ausgerichtete Schriften folgten im 15. und 16. Jahrhundert, und obwohl sie sich auf Techniken und Materialien konzentrierten und keine philosophischen Auseinandersetzungen mit Farbtheorien liefern, sind sie für Studien zur Farbterminologie und Pigmentgeschichte von unschätzbarem Wert. Gelegentlich begegnen wir einem illustrierten Text mit Abbildungen von Rohzutaten für Pigmente und Malfarben. Das im 15. oder 16. Jahrhundert erschienene *Livre des simples médecines* beispielsweise (S. 30, 33) zeigt verschiedene organische und mineralische Substanzen wie Sepiatinte, Lapislazuli und eine Mumie (für Mumienbraun), denen man auch heilende Wirkungen zuschrieb. Die Illustrationen sind bildhaft und schlicht, die einzelnen Objekte jedoch sorgfältig angeordnet wie in einem Setzkasten oder Kuriositätenkabinett.

Die hippokratische Lehre von den vier Säften, die den menschlichen Körper und Geist durchdringen und von vier Farben symbolisiert werden, beeinflusste ebenfalls bis ins Mittelalter und die Frührenaissance die Entwicklung einfacher Farbsysteme. Während Bilder und Kunstwerke, die sich speziell mit Farbtheorien und -systemen beschäftigen, in dieser Periode noch unbekannt sind, beginnen erste Beispiele für die Verwendung von Farbe aufzutauchen, um mit ihrer Hilfe Ordnung und Systematik zu ermöglichen und abzubilden. Die 1506 von Ulrich Pinder (gest. 1519) vorgelegte Harnglasscheibe (S. 14) zum Beispiel zeigt zwanzig verschiedene Urinfarben, die herangezogen wurden, um Erkrankungen zu diagnostizieren. Mit ihren handkolorierten Abbildungen der einzelnen Harngläser stellt diese Urinschautafel ein frühes Beispiel für einen auf den Farben der Natur basierenden Farbkreis dar, der den fast dreihundert Jahre später veröffentlichten Farbkreisen in den Insektenbüchern eines Moses Harris (1730–um 1788) nicht unähnlich war. Auf vergleichbare Weise liefern zahlreiche enzyklopädische Textsammlungen wie Bestiarien, Kräuterbücher, Lapidarien und Konkordanzen direkt oder indirekt weitere Aufschlüsse zum Wissensstand und Farbeinsatz ihrer jeweiligen Zeit.

Die Veröffentlichung der von Leon Battista Alberti (1404–1472) verfassten bedeutenden kunsttheoretischen Abhandlung *Über die Malkunst*, die 1435 unter dem Titel *De pictura* erschien, fiel zusammen mit dem Aufstieg der Ölfarbe als Malmittel. Was die Farbe betraf, die er als wichtiges und wertvolles Element der Malerei ansah, ging Alberti davon aus, dass sich alle Farben herstellen ließen, indem man ganze vier von ihnen mischte: Rot, Grün, Blau und Grau. Als Kunsttheoretiker war er weniger mit farbigem Licht als mit physischer Farbe beschäftigt, sodass man die von ihm so herausragend positionierte Farbe Grau im Kontext von Schattierungen und dreidimensionalen Effekten in der Malerei betrachten muss. Viele Texte, die sich mit der ausführlichen Debatte über die Rollen von Zeichnung (*disegno*) und Farbe (*colore*) befassten, ergaben sich aus den Schriften Albertis und seiner Zeitgenossen. Auch Leonardo da Vinci (1452–1519), einer der größten Künstler der Geschichte, dachte über Farbensehen und Farbwahrnehmung, die Erscheinung von Farben und die praktische Anwendung von Farbtheorien in der Malerei nach, wie den Aufzeichnungen in seinen diversen Notizbüchern und gesammelten Schriften zu entnehmen ist. Seine stark von Aristoteles und Alberti beeinflusste Farbenordnung basierte auf sechs „Grundfarben“: Rot, Gelb, Grün und Blau, flankiert von Weiß und Schwarz. Da keiner dieser Texte aus dem Mittelalter und der Frührenaissance Farbdiagramme enthält, lässt sich nicht bestimmen, ob die vorgebrachten Systeme linear oder kreisförmig, zwei- oder dreidimensional gedacht waren, doch auch ohne dieses Wissen stellen sie faszinierende Vorläufer der modernen Farbenlehre dar.

## Das Zeitalter der Polychromie: Farbe ab dem 17. Jahrhundert

Obwohl die Reise dieses Werkes durch die Farbsysteme erst beginnt, als das Druckwesen im späteren 17. Jahrhundert bereits fest etabliert war, liegen zahlreiche frühe Beispiele der Farbliteratur aus unterschiedlichen Gründen nur in Manuskriptform vor. Der aufkeimende Geist der Aufklärung förderte den Austausch geistigen Gedankenguts über geografische und kulturelle Grenzen hinweg. Doch während Farbsymboliken und Metasysteme, die an religiöse Überzeugungen, Alchemie und Folklore geknüpft waren, in dieser Zeit fortbestanden, wurde die Farbe zum Gegenstand von Theorie und Wissenschaft. Das allgemeine Verlangen, die Natur zu verstehen und einzuteilen, schloss die Farbe mit ein – als optisches Phänomen, als Instrument der Naturdarstellung und als Ausdrucksmedium in Kunst und Kunsthandwerk.

In annähernd (aber nicht streng) chronologischer Reihenfolge konzentriert sich jedes Kapitel dieses Werkes auf einen bestimmten Gegenstand oder Strang in der Geschichte der Farbsysteme. Die hier vorgestellten Bücher oder Manuskripte beschäftigen sich vornehmlich mit Farbe in Theorie und Praxis oder befassen sich auf schlüssige und originelle Weise mit Farbe, etwa um auf sie bezogene Vorstellungen und Ideen zu veranschaulichen.

Um die historische Ungleichheit der Geschlechter in den Darstellungen über Farbliteratur zu korrigieren, werden in der vorliegenden Arbeit einige Werke aus Frauenhand präsentiert, darunter Farb- und Mallehrbücher aus dem frühen 20. Jahrhundert wie das 1918 von der US-amerikanischen Pädagogin Bonnie Snow (um 1862–1925, S. 22–23, 27) gemeinsam mit Hugo B. Froehlich publizierte *The Theory and Practice of Color* (S. 352–361). Als eines der frühesten Beispiele für eine kaum beachtete Autorin ist Mary Gartside (um 1755–1819, S. 164–175) zu nennen. Die britische Blumenmalerin (S. 34 unten) und Lehrerin für Aquarellmalerei veröffentlichte 1805 mit *An Essay on Light and Shade, on Colours, and on Composition in General* („Ein Aufsatz über Licht und Schatten, über Farben und über Komposition im Allgemeinen") als erste bisher bekannte Frau ein englischsprachiges Buch über Farbe. Für die zweite Fassung von 1808 änderte sie den Titel in *An Essay on a New Theory of Colours* („Ein Aufsatz über eine neue Farbenlehre") und hob damit die Ernsthaftigkeit

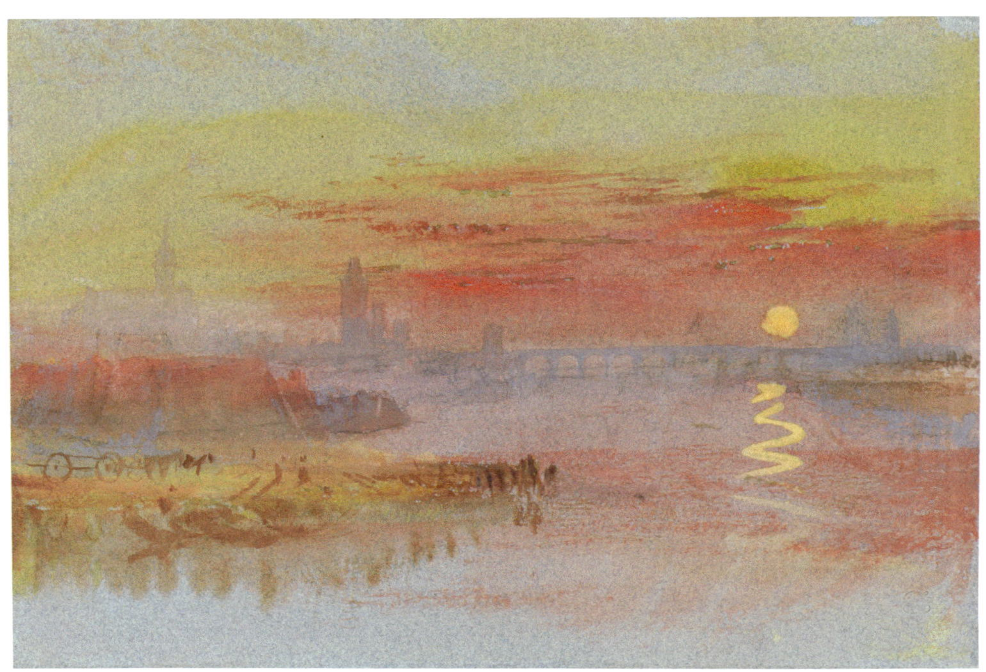

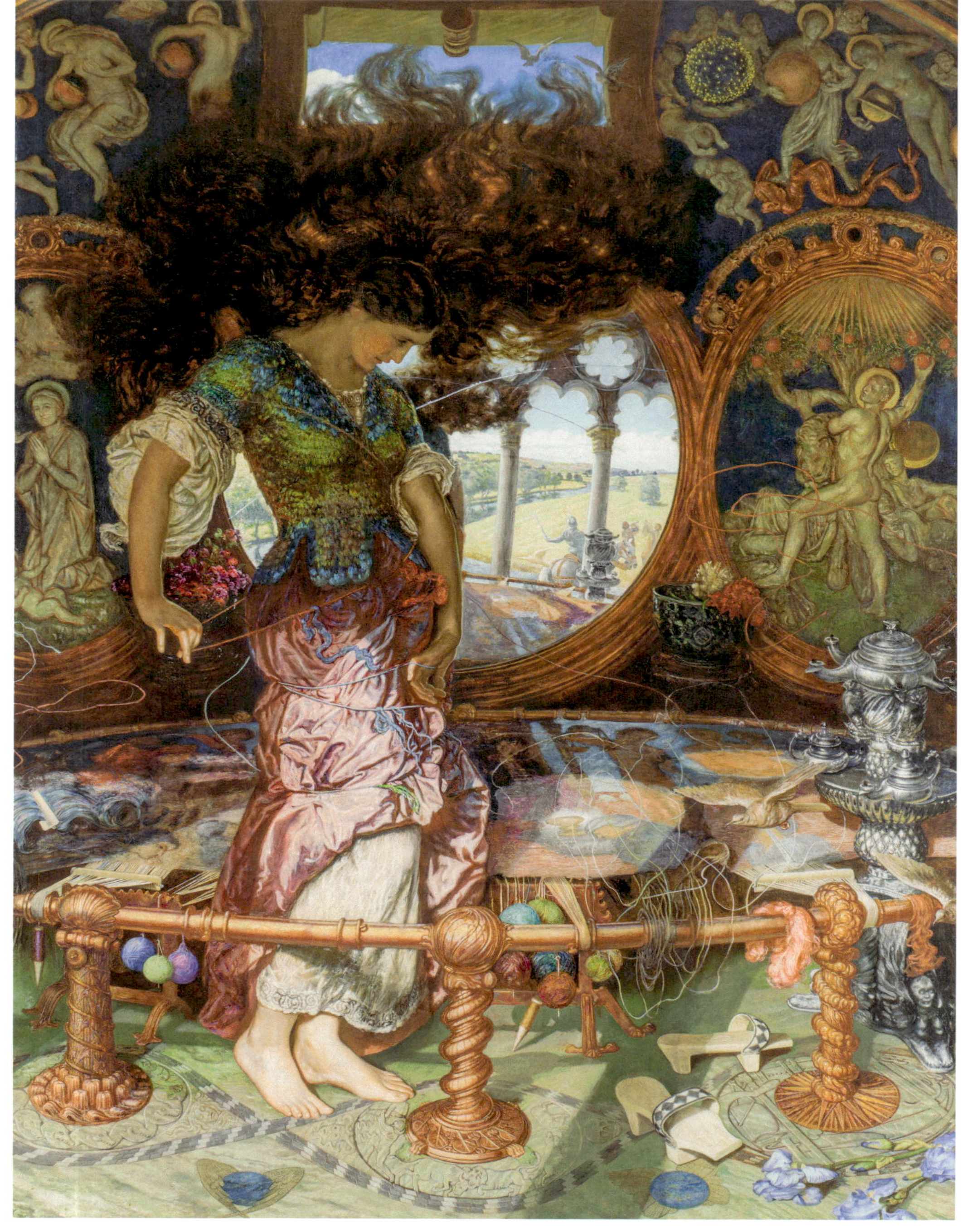

William Holman Hunt
**The Lady of Shalott**, *c.* 1888–1905
**Die Dame von Shalott**
**La Dame de Shalott**
Oil on canvas, 188.3 x 146.4 cm
(74 ⅛ x 57 ⅝ in.)
Hartford, Connecticut Wadsworth
Atheneum Museum of Art,
The Ella Gallup Sumner and Mary
Catlin Sumner Collection Fund

ihrer Publikation hervor. Ein weiteres Beispiel für eine gattungssprengende Publikation einer Frau aus dem erweiterten Kreis der Theosophen und Spiritisten ist *The New Science of Color* („Die neue Farbwissenschaft“, 1915) von Beatrice Irwin (1877–1956). Die global und kulturübergreifend tätige Lyrikerin und Schauspielerin interessierte sich sehr für das Potenzial der Verknüpfung von farbigem Kunstlicht und Musik. Mit ihren heute kaum noch bekannten synästhetischen Vorstellungen beeinflusste sie verschiedene Kunstschaffende des 20. Jahrhunderts, darunter auch Georgia O'Keeffe (1887–1986), in deren Arbeiten zuweilen ein indirekter Bezug auf Irwin anklingt. Bestimmte Frauen der Farbgeschichte verdienen in den Kanon aufgenommen zu werden, ohne eine eigenständige Farbenlehre formuliert oder verfasst zu haben. Hilma af Klint (1862–1944) gehört ebenso dazu wie die britische Malerin Winifred Nicholson (1893–1981). Nicholsons künstlerische Leistungen, ergänzt um ihre Notizen, Briefe und zwei kurze Aufsätze über Farbe, machen sie zu einer wichtigen Instanz der Farbtheorie im 20. Jahrhundert, obwohl sie ihre Ideen und Farbvorstellungen nie präzise zwischen zwei Buchdeckeln zusammengetragen hat. Ähnlich wie Mary Gartside scheint sie ihr Interesse an der Farbtheorie über die Blumenmalerei entwickelt zu haben. Schon in ihren frühen, oft vor beleuchteten Landschaften angesiedelten oder von Fenstern umrahmten Blumenkompositionen bewies sie ein Interesse am Zusammenspiel von Licht und Farbe (S. 34 oben). Dieses offensichtliche Interesse an prismatischen Farben erfuhr neuen kreativen Auftrieb, als die damals schon über achtzigjährige Künstlerin Mitte der 1970er-Jahre zwei Glasprismen geschenkt bekam. In ihren letzten Lebensjahren schuf Nicholson eine faszinierende Serie von „prismatischen Gemälden“, in denen sie ihre Experimente mit Prismen und Licht visuell ausforschte und dafür häufig einen ganz und gar abstrakten Malstil wählte.

Das erste Kapitel des vorliegenden Buches trägt den Titel „Farbpyramiden: Frühe Tafeln und Tabellen“ und nimmt frühe illustrierte Bücher der westlichen Kultur genauer in den Blick. Deren Vorläufer sind eine Auswahl von Tafeln, die zuvor der Alchemist und Arzt am englischen Hof, Théodore Turquet de Mayerne (1573–1655), erstellt und in das sogenannte

Dante Gabriel Rossetti
**Ecce Ancilla Domini!**
**The Annunciation**, 1849/50
**Die Verkündigung**
**L'Annonciation**
Oil on canvas, 72.4 x 41.9 cm
(28 ½ x 16 ½ in.)
London, Tate Britain

*Pages 47–49*
Attributed to George Barnard
**Colour Samples and Notes from a Sketchbook**, mid-19th century
**Farbmuster und Anmerkungen aus einem Skizzenbuch**
**Échantillons de couleurs et Extraits d'un carnet de croquis**
Sussex, collection of the author

De-Mayerne-Manuskript (*Pictoria sculptoria et quae subalternarum artium*, 1620–1646) aufgenommen hatte (S. 6, 16). Dieses ist vergleichsweise schlicht in seiner Präsentation der Farben in Form von Tabellen und sorgfältig gesetzten Kreisen. Insofern stellt es kein elaboriertes Farbsystem dar, sondern ist vielmehr im größeren Zusammenhang von Malhandbüchern zu betrachten – auch vor dem Hintergrund, dass es zahlreiche Informationen über damals verfügbare Pigmente und andere Künstlermaterialien enthält und Auskunft darüber gibt, wie diese gemischt und klassifiziert wurden. Das Kapitel führt außerdem vor Augen, wie im Jahrhundert darauf komplexere Tafeln und Tabellen erstellt wurden, die anschließend ihren Weg in die Druckerpresse fanden. In dieser Periode wurden die Farbsysteme zunehmend ausgearbeitet und differenziert. Farblisten werden aufwendiger und umfangreicher, Versuche einer Farbordnung erstmals dreidimensional. Da diese frühen Tafeln, Tabellen und Diagramme trotz der Fortschritte im Farbdruck ausnahmslos von Hand koloriert wurden, ist jede Ausfertigung ein individuelles Kunstwerk. Die Praxis der Handkolorierung setzte sich bis weit ins 19. Jahrhundert fort und wurde bisweilen erst im 20. Jahrhundert durch mechanische Farbreproduktionsverfahren ersetzt.

In Kapitel 2, „Farbanordnung: Kreise, Räder und Kugeln", untersuchen wir, wie die einfachen visuellen Konzepte der Farbordnung im 18. und 19. Jahrhundert zu einer faszinierenden Vielfalt geometrischer Formen und Strukturen weiterentwickelt wurden. Wenngleich auch andere Formen zum Einsatz kamen, führten Kreise als die wohl meistgewählte Form zu etlichen Variationen des aus heutiger Sicht klassischen Farbkreises. Oft weisen Farbdiagramme ergänzende Illustrationen und Ausschmückungen auf, oder ein Farbkreis wird von erläuternden Tafeln und Tabellen begleitet, wie zum Beispiel in *The Natural System of Colours* („Das natürliche System der Farben", um 1769–1776, S. 118–123) von Moses Harris und in den oben erwähnten Werken von Mary Gartside.

Ästhetisch zählen die Farbdiagramme des 18. und 19. Jahrhunderts zu den eindrucksvollsten Darstellungen in der Geschichte der Farbliteratur. Doch trotz ihrer visuellen Kraft kommen sie selten ohne das geschriebene oder gedruckte Wort aus. Obwohl die Sprache dem sichtbaren Farbspektrum hoffnungslos unterlegen ist, bildet sie in den meisten dieser Diagramme einen wichtigen Baustein mit zuweilen verblüffenden und poetischen Resultaten, so etwa in der von Johann Wolfgang von Goethe (1749–1832) und Friedrich Schiller (1759–1805) entwickelten *Temperamentenrose* (1798/99). Eine Hürde, die alle Diagramme gemeinhin zu bewältigen hatten, war die Wiedergabe des dreidimensionalen Aspekts der Farbordnung in einem zweidimensionalen Medium. An diesem Punkt treten die ersten Farbgloben oder Farbkugeln in Erscheinung, etwa die 1810 von Philipp Otto Runge (1777–1810) erdachte *Farben-Kugel* (S. 26, 124–125). Bedauerlicherweise haben sich keine räumlichen Modelle der damaligen Farbgloben erhalten. 2016 jedoch konstruierte die französisch-deutsche Künstlerin Eva Bodinet ein auf Runges *Farben-Kugel* basierendes Modell (S. 24), und in den letzten Jahren brachten mehrere kommerzielle Hersteller fertige Farbgloben auf den Markt. Runges Beispiel steht auch stellvertretend für die gesteigerte Empfindsamkeit und Spiritualität im Verhältnis zur Farbe, wie sie in der Romantik anzutreffen ist. Zahlreiche Künstler, Philosophen und Schriftsteller des späten 18. und frühen 19. Jahrhunderts passten Farbtheorien an ihre persönlichen Glaubenssätze an und wiesen ihnen hochgradig symbolische Bedeutungen zu. Zwischen 1802 und 1810 schuf Runge eine Serie von Tageszeitenbildern wie *Der kleine Morgen*, die als anschaulich gemachte Farbenlehre seine christlichen Überzeugungen ausdrücken sollten (S. 29).

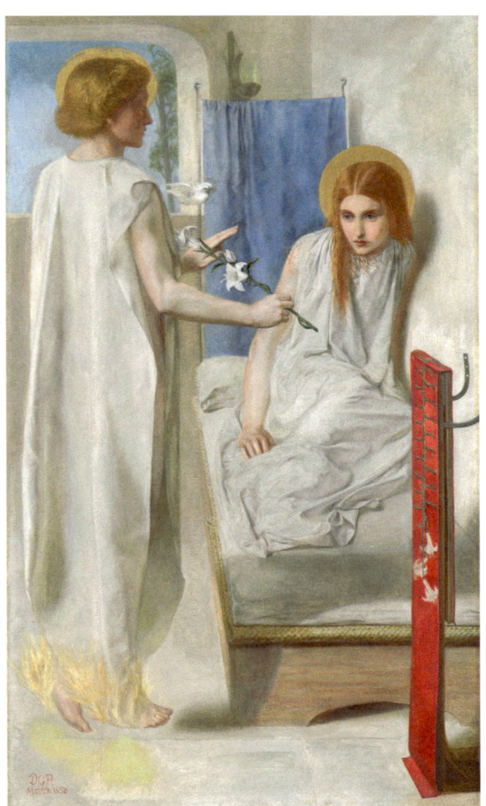

Kapitel 2 zeigt auch, wie im Verlauf des 19. Jahrhunderts die Bandbreite der Farbstudien immer größer wird, während die Farbliteratur auf früheren Texten aufbaut und sich auf sie bezieht. In den 1820er-Jahren zum Beispiel lehrte der Künstler Joseph Mallord William Turner (1775–1851) in seiner Funktion als Professor für Perspektive an der Royal Academy of Arts in London die Grundlagen der Farbtheorie. Um den Unterschied zwischen stofflichen und immateriellen Farben zu erläutern, fertigte er zwei große Vorlesungsdiagramme mit Farbkreisen an (S. 38, 39). Mit ihren überlappenden Farbdreiecken im Zentrum waren sie eindeutig von den Farbkreisen des Entomologen Moses Harris beeinflusst, die Turner studiert hatte. Zeitlebens interessierte sich Turner intensiv für neue Pigmente und Farbtheorien, las und besaß zahlreiche Publikationen über Farbe und machte das Zusammenspiel von Farbe und Licht zum zentralen Thema seiner Kunst (S. 41). In späteren Jahren – und nur kurz nachdem der erste Teil von *Zur Farbenlehre* (1810–1812, S. 184–191), Goethes Hauptwerk über Farbe, in einer englischen Übersetzung (*Goethe's*

*Theory of Colours*, 1840) erschienen war – schuf Turner zwei Gemälde, die sich unmittelbar auf die darin formulierten Aussagen bezogen und möglicherweise erneut auch auf Harris anspielten (S. 65).

Das folgende Kapitel 3, „Neue Erklärungen: Der Aufstieg der Farbtheorie", geht ausführlich auf einige der wichtigsten Farbtraktate des 19. Jahrhunderts ein und erläutert die Gründe für die drastische Zunahme an neuen Theorien und umfangreichen philosophischen, wissenschaftlichen und praktischen Abhandlungen über Farbe. Diese Farbrevolution ist untrennbar mit der Industrialisierung der Farbe verbunden, insbesondere mit neuen Fertigungs-, Produktions- und Druckverfahren, hat ihren Ursprung jedoch im frühen 18. Jahrhundert. Ein unumstrittener Meilenstein in der Geschichte der Farbsysteme wurde von Isaac Newton verfasst, der 1704 mit den *Opticks* die Früchte seiner jahrzehntelangen Farbforschungen veröffentlichte (S. 154–163). Das Buch enthielt – in Form eines Farbkreises – das erste an eine breite Leserschaft gerichtete Farbdiagramm. Es beruhte auf Newtons Versuchen, das weiße Licht mithilfe eines Prismas in Spektralfarben zu zerlegen. Wie wir heute wissen, war Newtons Einfluss auf die Wissenschaft des 18. und 19. Jahrhunderts unermesslich. Seine Theorien wurden adaptiert, bewundert, weiterentwickelt und kritisiert (S. 18). Die Faszination, die von den Regenbogenfarben und anderen Entdeckungen Newtons ausging, zeigt sich in der bildenden Kunst, etwa in dem allegorischen Gemälde *Colour* (S. 20), das Angelika Kauffmann (1741–1807) schuf. Obwohl es als Allegorie angelegt ist und damit an sich kein Farbsystem darstellt, veranschaulicht das Werk einen bedeutenden Aspekt der Farbgeschichte, denn zusammen repräsentieren diese vier Gemälde die maßgeblichen „Elemente der Kunst": Erfindung, Komposition, Zeichnung und Farbe. Letztere wurde damit endlich auf eine Ebene mit den drei übrigen Kategorien gehoben. In *Colour* taucht die Farbe in Gestalt einer weiblichen Figur ihren Pinsel in Newtons Regenbogen und zieht die prismatischen Farben auf eine physische Palette herunter. Auf diese Weise überträgt sie die Spektralfarbentheorie auf die stofflichen Farben, bringt sie jedoch gleichzeitig mit den Unterrichtspraktiken an der neu gegründeten Akademie in Verbindung.

Im fortschreitenden 19. Jahrhundert machten romantische Ideen und Einstellungen wie Runges Farbsymbolik allmählich Studien mit einer eher technischen und wissenschaftlichen Ausrichtung Platz, von denen viele in Zusammenhang mit der Herstellung neuer Pigmente und Farbstoffe standen. Die Qualität der neuen Farben wurde zum Forschungsfeld des bedeutenden britischen „Farbenmannes" George Field (um 1777–1854, S. 200–207), der nicht nur eine eigene Farbenlehre entwickelte, sondern auch Pigmente erprobte, herstellte und patentieren ließ. Seine Farben waren bei zahlreichen Künstlern des 19. Jahrhunderts gefragt, darunter auch bei Mitgliedern der Präraffaeliten und ihren Anhängern, und ihre Verfügbarkeit fiel zusammen mit einem wiedererwachten Interesse an mittelalterlichen Malmethoden und -materialien. Die juwelengleiche Leuchtkraft und gewagte Vielfarbigkeit von Gemälden wie *Mariana* (1851, S. 55) von John Everett Millais (1829–1896) spiegelten dieses Interesse an hochwertigen Pigmenten wider und verrieten ein ausgeprägtes Bewusstsein für die damals aktuellen Farbsysteme. Man vermutete sogar, dass das Gemälde *Ecce Ancilla Domini!* (*The Annunciation*, 1849/50, S. 45) von Dante Gabriel Rossetti (1828–1882) unmittelbar von der Symbolik der Farben nach George Field inspiriert war. Die Aufmerksamkeit, die man der Farbliteratur und -theorie entgegenbrachte, lässt sich in zahlreichen Werken westlicher Künstler des 19. Jahrhunderts erkennen. Sowohl der Impressionismus als auch

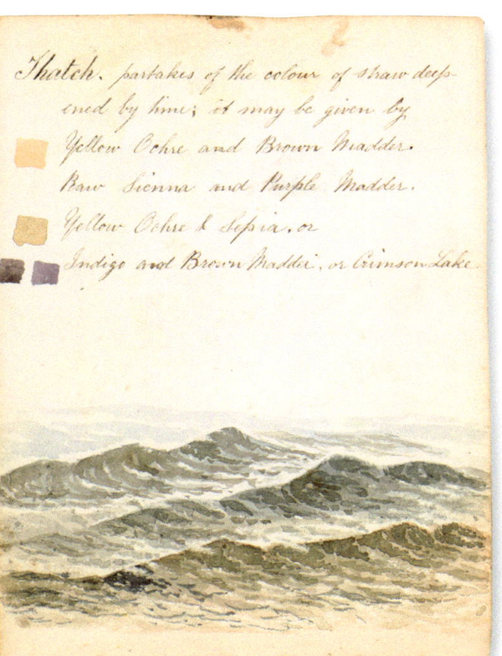

Thatch. partakes of the colour of straw deepened by time; it may be given by
Yellow Ochre and Brown Madder.
Raw Sienna and Purple Madder.
Yellow Ochre & Sepia, or
Indigo and Brown Madder, or Crimson Lake

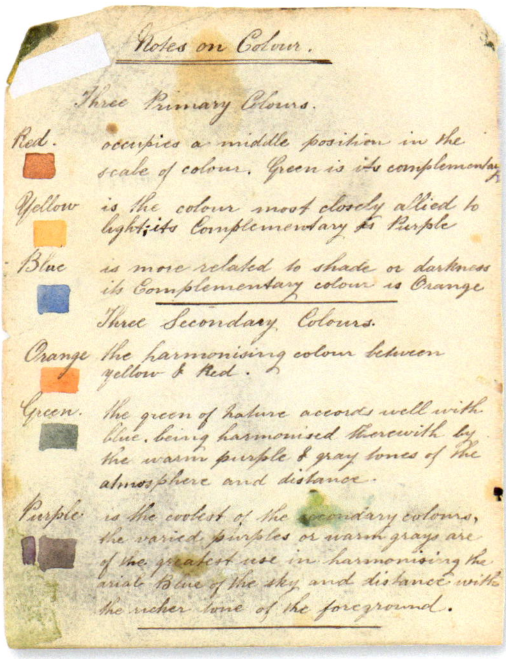

Notes on Colour.

Three Primary Colours.

Red. occupies a middle position in the scale of colour. Green is its complementary

Yellow is the colour most closely allied to light; its Complementary is Purple

Blue is more related to shade or darkness its Complementary colour is Orange

Three Secondary Colours.

Orange the harmonising colour between yellow & Red.

Green. the green of nature accords well with blue, being harmonised therewith by the warm purple & gray tones of the atmosphere and distance.

Purple is the coolest of the secondary colours, the varied purples or warm grays are of the greatest use in harmonising the aerial Blue of the sky and distance with the richer tone of the foreground.

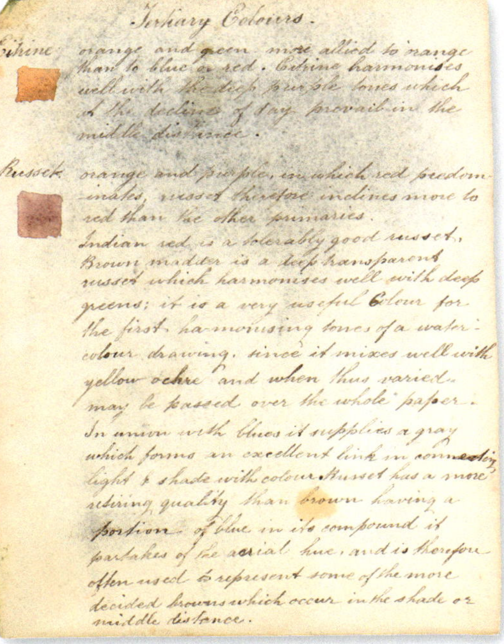

Tertiary Colours.

Citrine orange and green more allied to orange than to blue or red. Citrine harmonises well with the deep purple tones which at the decline of day prevail in the middle distance.

Russet orange and purple, in which red predominates, russet therefore inclines more to red than the other primaries.
Indian red is a tolerably good russet. Brown madder is a deep transparent russet which harmonises well with deep greens; it is a very useful Colour for the first harmonising tones of a water-colour drawing. since it mixes well with yellow ochre and when thus varied may be passed over the whole paper. In union with blues it supplies a gray which forms an excellent link in connecting light & shade with colour. Russet has a more retiring quality than brown having a portion of blue in its compound it partakes of the aerial hue, and is therefore often used to represent some of the more decided browns which occur in the shade or middle distance.

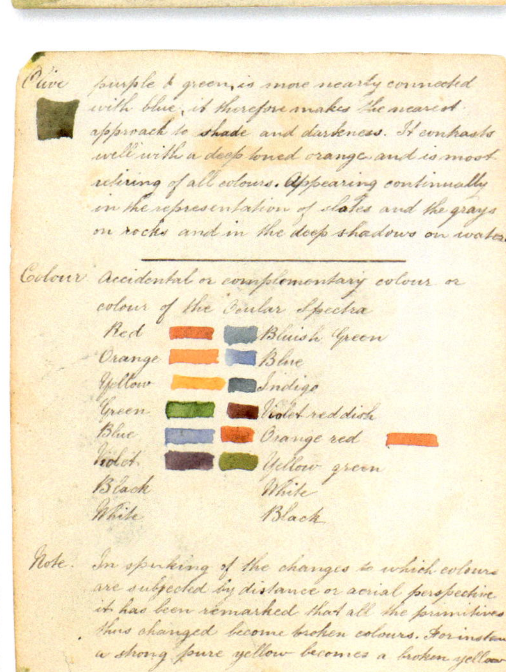

Olive purple & green, is more nearly connected with blue, it therefore makes the nearest approach to shade and darkness. It contrasts well with a deep toned orange and is most retiring of all colours. Appearing continually in the representation of slates and the grays on rocks and in the deep shadows on water.

Colour Accidental or complementary colour or colour of the Ocular Spectra

| Colour | |
|---|---|
| Red | Bluish Green |
| Orange | Blue |
| Yellow | Indigo |
| Green | Violet reddish |
| Blue | Orange red |
| Violet | Yellow green |
| Black | White |
| White | Black |

Note. In speaking of the changes to which colours are subjected by distance or aerial perspective it has been remarked that all the primitives thus changed become broken colours. For instance a strong pure yellow becomes a broken yellow

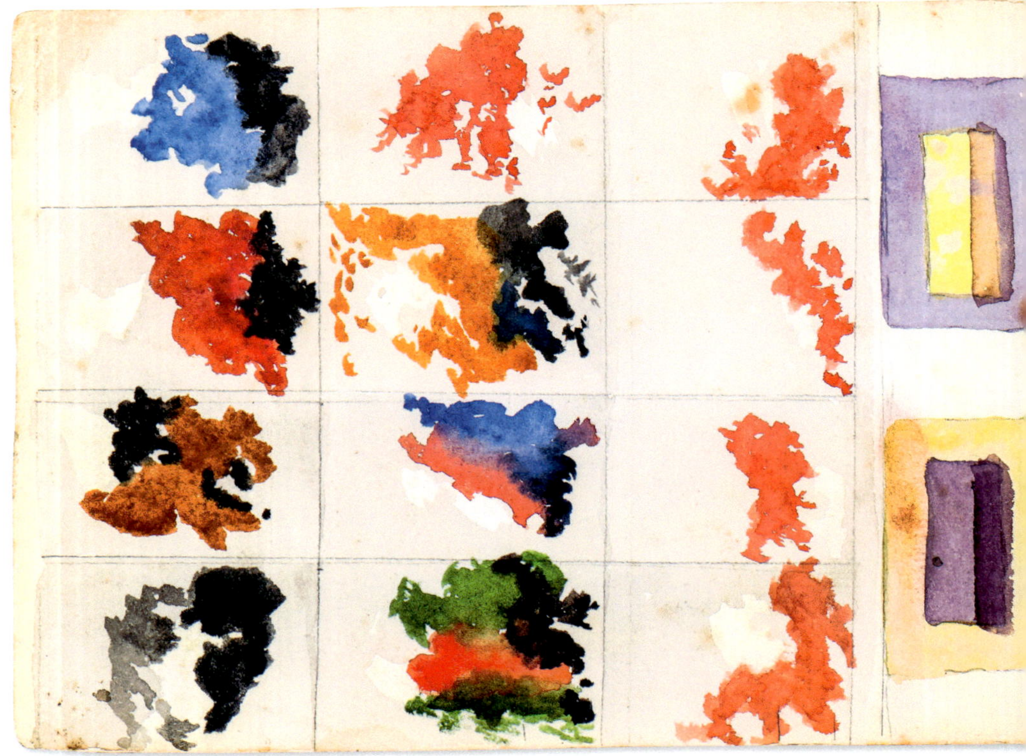

der Pointillismus wurden (ab 1839) direkt von der bahnbrechenden Theorie der simultanen Farbkontraste beeinflusst, die Michel-Eugène Chevreul (1786–1889) während seiner Tätigkeit für die staatliche Gobelinmanufaktur in Paris entwickelt hatte (S. 216–227). Der Post-Impressionist Vincent van Gogh (1853–1890) machte sich die Prinzipien des Farbkontrasts in seiner Malerei mit erstaunlicher Wirkung zunutze. Es ist bezeichnend, dass sich in seinem persönlichen Nachlass ein rotes Lackkästchen mit mehreren Knäueln aus bunten Wollfäden befand, die auf unterschiedliche Weisen aufgewickelt und kombiniert waren, so als hätte van Gogh auf diese Art harmonische Farbkombinationen nach den Gesetzen Chevreuls geschaffen (S. 52). Auch das Werk von James Abbott McNeill Whistler (1834–1903) strahlt ein großes Bewusstsein für Farbkontraste aus. Wenngleich seine unmittelbare Beschäftigung mit Farbliteratur nicht dokumentiert ist, äußert sich Whistlers Interesse an Farbharmonien und symbolischer Farbverwendung in den Titelbegriffen seiner Gemälde, die er – anstelle beschreibender Bezeichnungen – als „Harmonien", „Nachtstücke" oder „Symphonien" in bestimmten Farben bezeichnete (S. 58, 60).

In den Kapiteln 4 und 5 geht es um eher technisch und praktisch ausgerichtete Farbsysteme. „Farben als Orientierung: Nomenklaturen und Standards" beschäftigt sich mit systematischen Farblisten, die oft in Bezug zur Natur und zur taxonomischen Klassifikation stehen und faszinierende Versuche darstellen, verlässliche

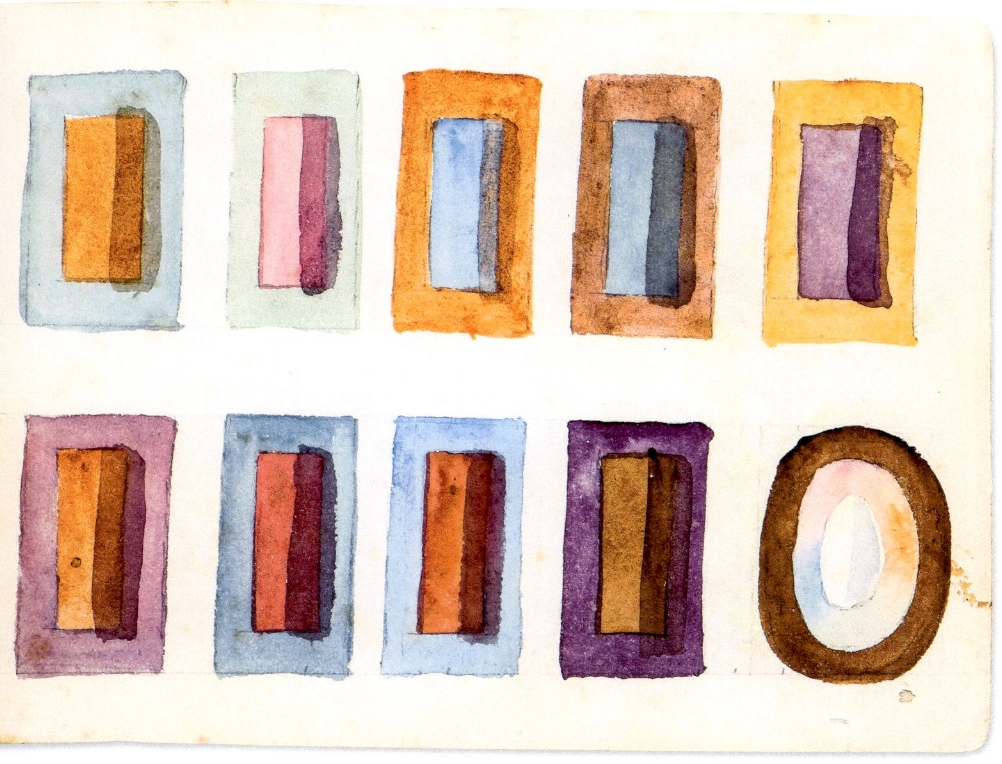

Terminologien und Standards zur Anwendung in Kunst, Industrie und Wissenschaft zu etablieren. Einige dieser Systeme zielten auch darauf ab, eine Chronik historischer Farben mitzuliefern, so etwa der 1938 erschienene *Historical Color Guide* von Elizabeth Burris-Meyer (1899–1969), den die Autorin später zum Leitfaden für Innenausstattung, Mode und Schönheitspflege umarbeitete (S. 298–315). Kapitel 5, „Theorie und Praxis: Unterweisungen in Farbe" konzentriert sich auf die Geschichte der praktischen Farbhandbücher für Maler und Drucker von Anfang des 19. bis Anfang des 20. Jahrhunderts. Die älteren Handbücher sind noch stark der Entwicklung der Aquarellmalerei verpflichtet und waren angesichts der zu Beginn des 19. Jahrhunderts erschwinglicher werdenden Malmaterialien überwiegend für Amateure bestimmt. Im 18. und 19. Jahrhundert war das Malen ein anerkannter Zeitvertreib für Frauen. Darum richtete sich ein Großteil der Handbücher, obwohl mehrheitlich von Männern abgefasst, speziell an eine weibliche Leserschaft. Seit Beginn des 20. Jahrhunderts ergriffen jedoch immer mehr Frauen die Gelegenheit, über dieses Thema zu schreiben, zu veröffentlichen und zu unterrichten, und verfassten ihrerseits Farblehrbücher und Farbfibeln. Bis heute ist dieses Feld der kreativen Beschäftigung von Frauen kaum erforscht, und weil Lehrbücher, insbesondere für jüngere Kinder, als Textgattung vernachlässigt wurden, sind sie in der Regel unzureichend dokumentiert und nur in wenigen Fällen erhalten.

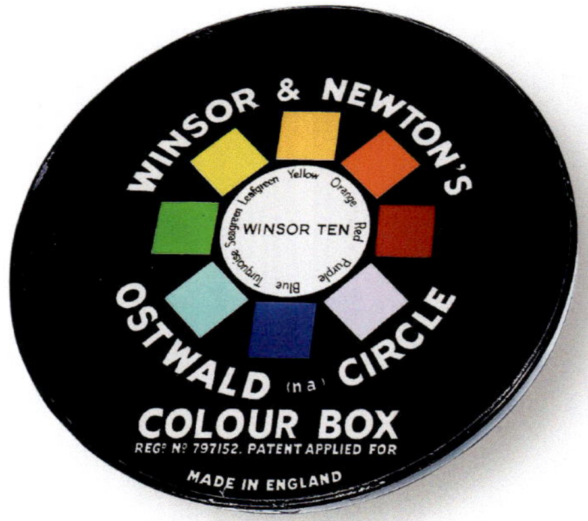


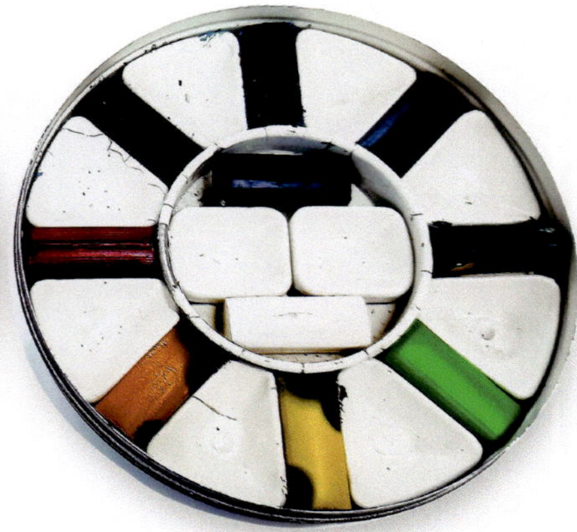

Neben den Handbüchern kam im frühen 20. Jahrhundert eine weitere Flut von Büchern über Farbe auf den Markt. Wie in Kapitel 6, „Farbe sprengt ihre Ketten: Das frühe 20. Jahrhundert“, dargelegt wird, knüpften viele von ihnen an die Werke der großen Farbtheoretiker des vorangegangenen Jahrhunderts an, entwickelten deren Konzepte jedoch weiter. Farbe lässt sich in dieser Periode nicht adäquat einschätzen, ohne eine Reihe von wissenschaftlichen und künstlerischen Errungenschaften zu berücksichtigen. Dazu zählen die Fortschritte in der Erforschung des Farbensehens und speziell der Anatomie des menschlichen Auges, die Elektrifizierung der Welt, die daraus resultierenden Möglichkeiten der künstlichen Beleuchtung und der radikal neue Einsatz von Farbe als Mittel des Ausdrucks in der Kunst, besonders in der Malerei. Vertreter avantgardistischer Gruppen und Strömungen in Europa – wie Der Blaue Reiter, die Fauvisten, viele Expressionisten und frühe abstrakte Künstler – befassten sich mit Farbtheorien. Sie machten sich die symbolische und visuelle Kraft der Farbe zu eigen und bildeten die Welt in subjektiven, nicht realistischen Tönen ab. Für manche unter ihnen wurden Farbauffassungen zum Hauptmotiv bestimmter Werke, zu sehen etwa in dem 1914 von Franz Marc (1880–1916) geschaffenen abstrakten Gemälde *Kämpfende Formen* (S. 67).

Die überaus bunten, von einer zunehmenden Mechanisierung geprägten ersten Dekaden des 20. Jahrhunderts, in denen man stoffliche Farben gebrauchsfertig und sauber verpackt in fast allen erdenklichen und leuchtenden Schattierungen kaufen konnte, schrien förmlich nach neuen Versuchen, den Farben eine ultimative Ordnung zu geben. Einige der einflussreicheren Arbeiten, etwa von Albert Henry Munsell (1858–1918) in den USA (S. 380–389) und Wilhelm Ostwald in Europa, werden in Kapitel 6 behandelt. Beide Männer entwickelten höchst lehrreiche und anpassungsfähige Systeme, die auf einer dreidimensionalen Farbtheorie beruhten; tatsächlich haben einige der räumlichen Modelle, die sie für ihre Unterrichtszwecke nutzten, die Zeiten überdauert (siehe zum Beispiel Ostwalds *Farbkörper* in den Archiven von Winsor & Newton). Dass sich im frühen 20. Jahrhundert auch die Forschungs- und Veröffentlichungsmöglichkeiten für Frauen verbesserten, führte zu bemerkenswerten wissen-

**Colour Box Depicting Wilhelm Ostwald's Colour Circle**
**Farbkasten mit Wilhelm Ostwalds Farbkreis**
**Boîte de couleurs reprenant le cercle chromatique d'Ostwald**
London, Slade School of Fine Art, Winsor and Newton Archive

**Reeves Watercolour Paintbox,** early 20th century
**Aquarellmalkasten von Reeves**
**Boîte d'aquarelle Reeves**
Sussex, collection of the author

schaftlichen Studien von Frauen zu Themen wie Farbensehen und Psychologie, Farbe in Literatur und Dichtung, historische Farbtheorie und zu weiteren Aspekten der Farbgeschichte. Einige dieser zwischen 1900 und den 1930er-Jahren erschienenen Bücher, wie die *Color Problems* („Farbproblematiken", 1902, S. 364–379) von Emily Noyes Vanderpoel (1842–1939), zählen zu den ideenreichsten und schönsten Publikationen in der Geschichte der Farben.

Kapitel 7, „Der Klang der Farbe: Spiritismus, Okkultismus und Musik", untersucht die synästhetischen Verbindungen zwischen Farbe und Musik und bezieht dabei Bewegung, Tanz und Spiritualität mit ein. In gewissem Maße waren die von Theosophen, Anthroposophen und Mitgliedern ähnlicher Gruppen und Bewegungen um die Wende zum letzten Jahrhundert publizierten, hochgradig individuellen und oft pseudowissenschaftlichen Farbtheorien eine Reaktion auf eine zunehmend mechanisierte Welt. Dennoch ist es ratsam und hilfreich, jede dieser Theorien gewissenhaft zu begutachten und sie nicht nach ihrer wissenschaftlichen Exaktheit, sondern nach ihrer kreativen Innovationskraft und den ihr zugrunde liegenden gesellschaftlichen und historischen Umständen zu beurteilen. Man muss nicht an die farbigen Auren glauben, die von Annie Besant (1847–1933) und Charles Webster Leadbeater (1854–1934) illustriert und beschrieben wurden, doch ihr Versuch, Gedanken und Gefühlen Form und Farbe zu geben, kommentiert auf faszinierende Weise kulturelle Einflüsse der Zeit (S. 412–439).

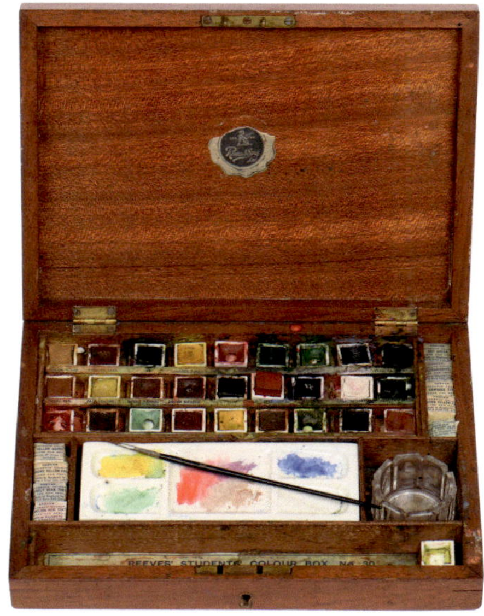

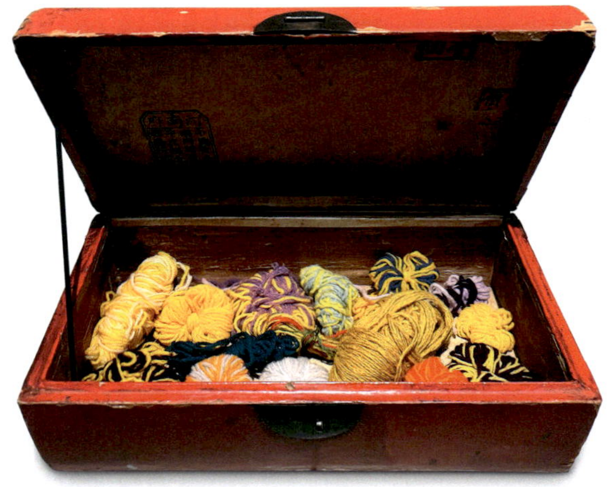

**Red Lacquer Box with Lengths of Coloured Wool Belonging to Vincent van Gogh**
**Rotes Lackkästchen mit farbigen Wollknäueln aus dem Besitz von Vincent van Gogh**
**Boîte de laque rouge de pelotes de laine ayant appartenu à Vincent van Gogh**
Amsterdam, Van Gogh Museum

Analogien zwischen Farbe und Musik bilden in der Geschichte der Farbsysteme ein herausragendes Thema. Die Mehrzahl der in diesem Kapitel vorgestellten Texte behandelt Farbe im Zusammenhang mit Klang, Musik, Poesie und Tanz, viele von ihnen kombinieren zudem Mystik mit Wissenschaft, individuelle religiöse Überzeugungen mit Farbtheorie, Natur mit Spiritualität und historische Texte über Farbe mit modernen Malpraktiken. Was sich nach einer verwirrenden und eigentümlichen Mischung anhören mag und oft schwierig zu lesen ist, besticht in der bildlichen Wiedergabe der einzelnen Konzepte aufs Äußerste. Der australische Künstler Roy de Maistre (1894–1968) schuf zahlreiche Gemälde zum Thema, unter anderem eine fünf Meter lange Bildrolle mit einer „Farbübersetzung" des *Trios in B-Dur* von Joseph Haydn (S. 76). Das Werk der schwedischen Mystikerin und Anthroposophin Hilma af Klint, die erst in den letzten Jahren wiederentdeckt und für ihren visionären Stil zu Recht gerühmt wurde, war tief im Okkultismus und in der Farbsymbolik verwurzelt. Obwohl sie nie eine eigene Farbenlehre formulierte, enthalten viele ihrer großformatigen Gemälde farbige Kreise, Pyramiden und Darstellungen immaterieller Farbe. In dem von ihr geschaffenen, bemerkenswert individuellen Farbvokabular verbanden sich Realismus und Abstraktion (S. 56, 68, 69).

Das vorliegende Buch kann keinerlei Anspruch erheben, einen umfassenden Überblick über die Geschichte der Farbtheorie zu liefern. In seiner Werkauswahl ist es vorwiegend – und vielleicht unausweichlich – auf die westliche Hemisphäre fixiert. Diesem Ungleichgewicht soll jedoch entgegengewirkt werden, indem Kapitel 8 nach Osten blickt, über unsere vertraute westliche Sichtweise hinaus, und einen Eindruck von den japanischen Farbsystemen des 19. und 20. Jahrhunderts vermittelt. Dabei geht es weniger um eine wissenschaftliche Untersuchung von Farbkonzepten dieser Regionen, als vielmehr um die Würdigung von deren ästhetischen Reiz. Zudem soll nachvollziehbar werden, dass zwischen Farbtheorien aus geografisch weit auseinanderliegenden Teilen der Erde Zusammenhänge bestehen können. Etwas so Abstraktes wie Farbe zu vergleichen, führt uns überzeugend vor Augen, was Menschen weltweit verbindet. Ein faszinierendes Beispiel für den interkulturellen Farbaustausch bildet das Nachleben eines Farbdiagramms von George Field aus den 1830er-Jahren, das in dem erstmals 1876 erschienenen japanischen Schulbuch *Gakko hitsuyo irozu mondo* (S. 460–465) wieder auftaucht.

Das letzte Kapitel, „Interaktion und Abstraktion: Vom Bauhaus in die Gegenwart", behandelt Farbe in ihrer reinsten, reduziertesten und elementarsten Form, wie man sie von Anfang bis Mitte des 20. Jahrhunderts in Kunst, Design, Lehrbüchern und Unterricht fand. Den langen, allmählichen Weg zur Abstraktion bereiteten neben Pionieren wie Turner, Gartside, Whistler oder af Klint auch Avantgardisten aus verschiedenen europäischen Künstlergruppen. Doch vor allem das Bauhaus mit seinem erweiterten Einflussbereich entwickelte sich zum führenden Vertreter von Modernismus, Fortschrittlichkeit und, stilistisch gesprochen, Abstraktion. 1919 von dem Architekten Walter Gropius (1883–1969) in Weimar gegründet, hatte die kurzlebige Schule für Kunst, Architektur und Design ihre Wurzeln in avantgardistischen und spirituellen Gruppen in Deutschland und in der englischen Arts-and-Crafts-Bewegung. Einfaches und funktionales Design, beruhend auf einer gründlichen künstlerischen Ausbildung und solidem Handwerk, bildete den Kern des Lehrbetriebs. Zu den Mitgliedern, Lehrern und Schülern am Bauhaus gehörten Ludwig Mies van der Rohe, Paul Klee, Johannes Itten und Josef Albers, aber auch mehrere Frauen, deren Rollen in der Geschichte des Bauhauses erst vor Kurzem umfassend gewürdigt wurden, darunter Anni Albers, Marianne Brandt, Gertrud Arndt, Gertrud Grunow und Gunta Stölzl. 1925 zog das Bauhaus nach Dessau um, wo Gropius das zur Ikone gewordene Bauhausgebäude entwarf (vgl. S. 70), doch schon 1933, nach der Vertreibung aus Dessau und lediglich einem Jahr mit Sitz in Berlin, musste das Bauhaus unter dem wachsenden Druck der Nationalsozialisten endgültig schließen. Einige seiner Mitglieder emigrierten nach England oder in die USA, wo sie Verbindung zueinander halten und ihre Arbeit fortsetzen konnten. Obwohl Farbe nur ein Bestandteil der Bauhausklassen war, entstanden zahlreiche einschlägige Publikationen über Farbe, von denen einige im Schlusskapitel dieses Buches vorgestellt werden. Darunter ist ein Klassiker der Farbliteratur, der knapp dreißig Jahre nach der Schließung der Schule veröffentlicht wurde: *Interaction of Color* (1963, S. 498–503) von Josef Albers (1888–1976), das 1970 unter gleichem Titel in einer deutschen Übersetzung erschien. Diese und andere, weniger bekannte Farbabhandlungen von gleichgesinnten Autoren sind Beispiele für eine nahezu vollkommene Synthese des Nachdenkens über Farbe – über das Leben und Arbeiten mit ihr, über den Farbunterricht und über die Anwendung von Farbe in Kunst und Design –, während sie gleichzeitig die modernen Ideale von Einfachheit, Geometrie und Abstraktion reflektieren. In der Kunst des 20. Jahrhunderts spiegeln sich die Farbtheorie und -ästhetik des Bauhauses nicht nur in der verbreiteten Annäherung an die Abstraktion wider; auch die Ähnlichkeiten im Farbgebrauch mit den extrem minimalistischen und geometrischen Werken von Meistern der Moderne wie Piet Mondrian (S. 74), Henri Matisse und Kasimir Malewitsch sind unübersehbar.

## Die Zeitlosigkeit von Farbtheorien

Die abstrakte Schönheit von Farbdiagrammen, von sichtbar gemachten Farbtheorien, verleiht ihnen einen zeitlosen Reiz. Die einfachen geometrischen Formen und Figuren, die geschaffen wurden, um frühen Farbtafeln und -tabellen ein Gerüst zu geben, erscheinen unmittelbar zugänglich, weil die gleichen oder ähnliche Formen in Kunst, Werbung und Design bis heute existieren. Farbkreise, Farbräder, Farbdreiecke, Farbwürfel und komplexere Farbdiagramme

John Everett Millais
**Mariana**, 1851
Oil on mahogany,
59.7 x 49.5 cm (23 ½ x 19 ½ in.)
London, Tate Britain

oder organische Formen bleiben über Jahrhunderte hinweg nachvollziehbar. Für zeitgenössische Künstler sind Farbtheorien und Farbsysteme Motiv und Inspirationsquelle zugleich. Seit 2009 hat der isländisch-dänische Künstler Ólafur Elíasson (geb. 1967) eine Reihe von großen Farbkreisen erschaffen, in denen die Farben, ähnlich wie in einem der Farbkreise aus dem 1861 erschienenen *Atlas* von Michel-Eugène Chevreul, nahtlos ineinander übergehen (S. 81). Eine Auswahl daraus mit dem Titel *Turner colour experiments* wurde in der Tate Britain in Nachbarschaft zu einigen Turner-Gemälden gezeigt. So wie sich Turner in manchen Werken auf Goethe und Harris bezog, so rekurrierte Elíasson in dem Bestreben, eine eigene Farbenlehre zu entwickeln, auf Farbtheoretiker und Künstler vor ihm.

Schon immer hat der Mensch versucht, Farbe, dieses ungreifbare, aber alles durchdringende Element unseres Sehens, zu bändigen und zu beherrschen. Unsere Versuche aber, Farbe einzufangen, indem wir Kreise, Quadrate und Linien um sie ziehen, indem wir sie in Listen zwängen oder in räumliche Formen pressen, sind letztlich Ausdruck des menschlichen Denkens und der menschlichen Kreativität. Die perfekte Farbtheorie mag noch nicht formuliert sein, doch vorhandene Ideen über Farbe in Worte, Bilder, Diagramme und dreidimensionale Objekte zu verwandeln, hat zu einer langen Geschichte der Farbe als Mittel und Inhalt der bildenden Kunst geführt. Individuelle Sachkenntnis, persönliche Vorlieben, aktuelle Forschungsergebnisse und neue Denkansätze machen jedes neue Buch über Farbgeschichte zum Abenteuer. Die Autorinnen hoffen, dass die in diesen beiden Bänden präsentierte Auswahl von Farbsystemen unerwartete und inspirierende Einblicke und Episoden bereithält, die ein neues Licht auf die Farbgeschichte werfen.

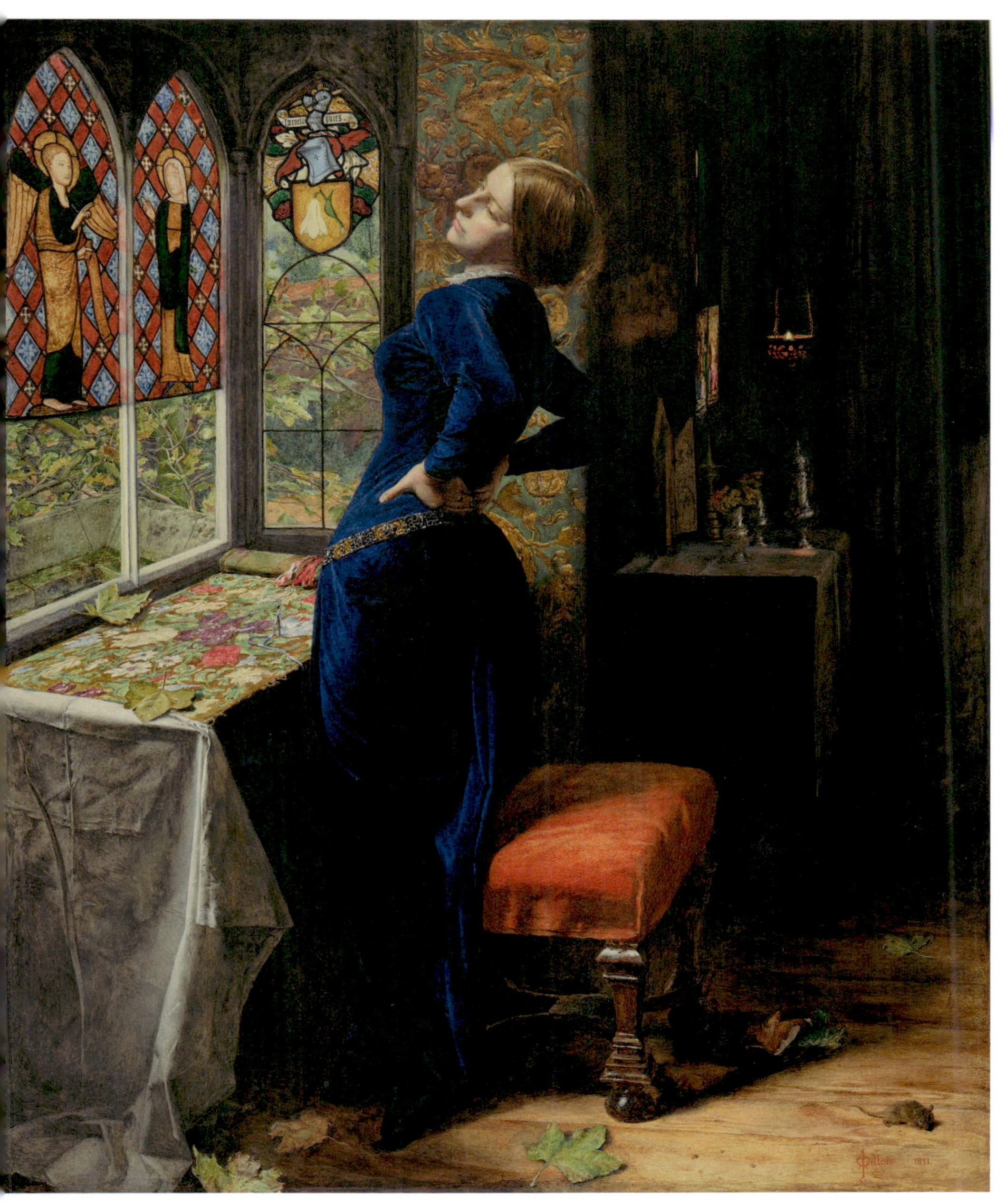

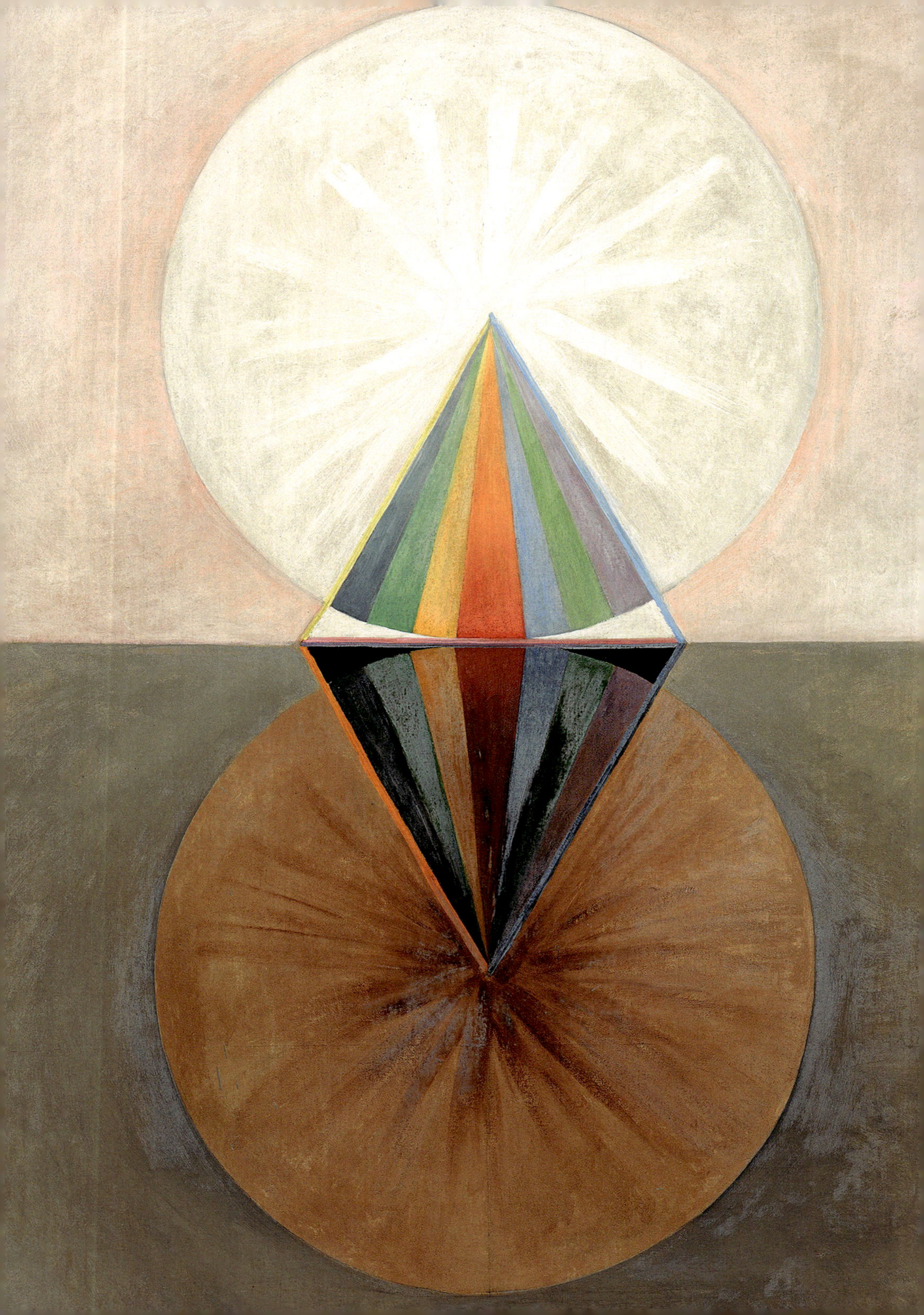

Alexandra Loske

# LA COULEUR MAÎTRISÉE ET LIBÉRÉE

## Comment l'être humain s'empare de la couleur par le mot et l'image

Notre monde regorge de couleurs. La plupart d'entre nous le vivent en couleurs. Nous disons de notre Terre qu'elle est la « planète bleue » et, d'un point de vue optique, nous nous noyons dans le bleu. Lorsqu'en 1990, la sonde spatiale *Voyager 1* nous a photographiés depuis une distance de six milliards de kilomètres, nous avions l'apparence, comme l'a décrit l'astronome Carl Sagan quelques années plus tard, d'un « point bleu pâle », mesurant moins d'un pixel et à peine visible, mais d'une teinte identifiable néanmoins. Nous sommes cette tache de couleur avant de disparaître. Ainsi la couleur est-elle l'un des aspects qui définissent et unifient notre existence et une caractéristique véritablement universelle que partagent tous les êtres humains. Il n'est donc pas surprenant qu'elle nous fascine depuis la nuit des temps. Les premières manifestations de la créativité humaine, sous la forme de gravures et de dessins sur bois, os ou roche, montrent que nous avons toujours cherché à fabriquer la couleur et à l'employer, avant tout pour représenter ou imiter ce qui a de l'importance à nos yeux et ce qui nous entoure. Bien que les traces physiques et visuelles de ces premières créations humaines soient fragmentaires et altérées, il est possible que, même aux temps primitifs, la couleur ait aussi été utilisée de manière symbolique. Les pigments minéraux extraits de la terre par les premiers humains étaient mélangés à des substances organiques, comme les graisses végétale et animale ou les humeurs du corps, et, ce faisant, pourraient bien avoir acquis une signification particulière ou sacrée, d'où serait née une hiérarchie chromatique simple. Si nous ne saurons jamais avec précision ce que nos ancêtres préhistoriques pensaient de la couleur, nous avons des preuves que certaines teintes étaient employées dans des contextes particuliers.

Il est possible de retracer, au fil de l'histoire humaine, l'intérêt intellectuel que nous nourrissons concrètement pour la couleur, depuis les conceptions rudimentaires des premières formes d'art jusqu'aux systèmes sophistiqués fondés sur la science moderne, la philosophie ou les arts, autant de catégories qui se recoupent et se répondent fréquemment. Cet ouvrage a pour objet de proposer un panorama de la réflexion et du ressenti de l'être humain à l'égard de la couleur, de son désir de créer, d'organiser et de systématiser la couleur, de l'employer et

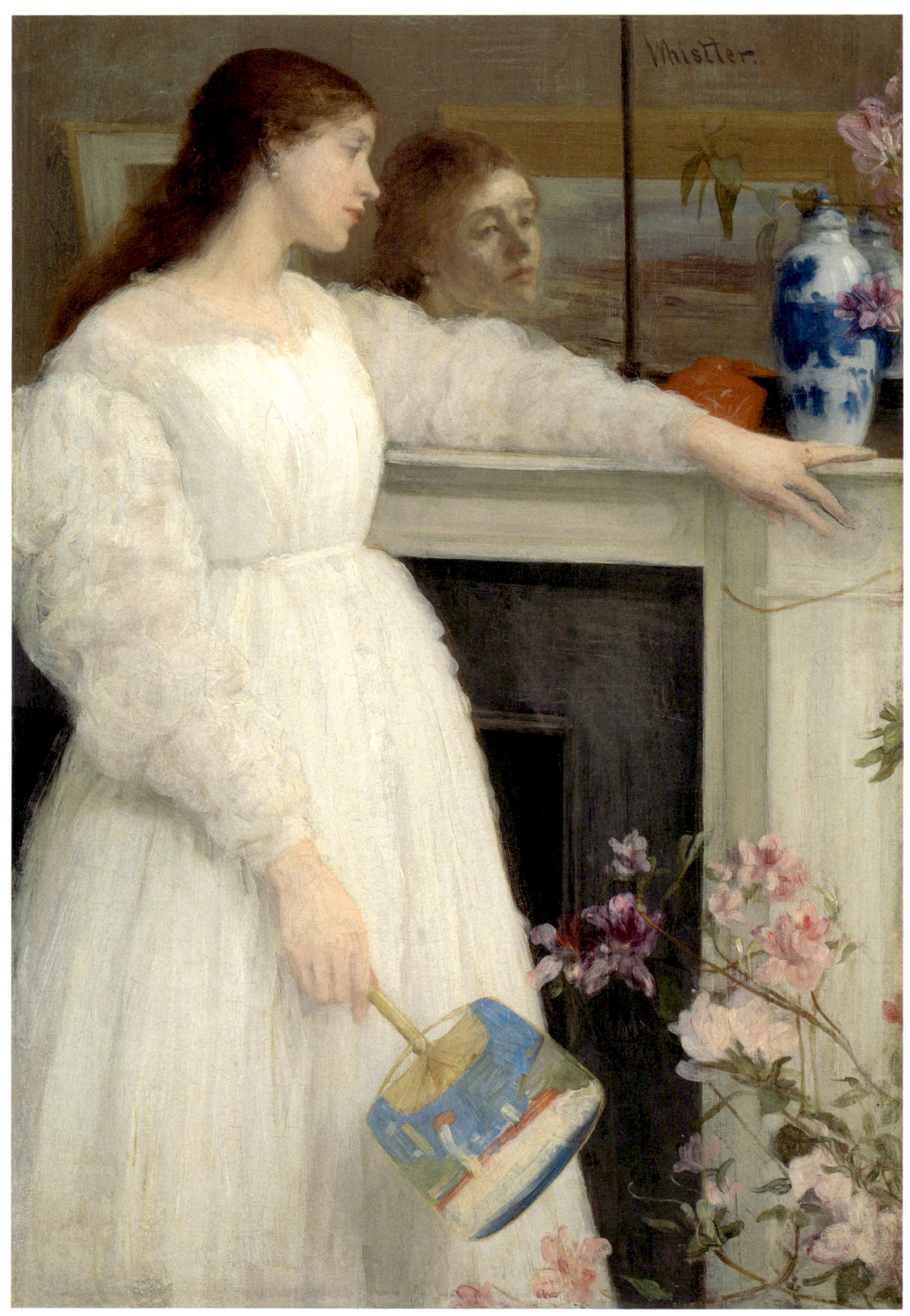
Whistler.

*Page 56*
Hilma af Klint
**The Swan (The SUW Series, Group IX: Part I, No. 12)**, 1914/15
**Der Schwan / Le Cygne**
Oil on canvas, 151.5 x 151 cm
(59 5/8 x 59 1/2 in.)
Stockholm, The Hilma af Klint Foundation

James McNeill Whistler
**Symphony in White, No. 2: The Little White Girl**, 1864
**Symphonie in Weiß, Nr. 2: Das kleine weiße Mädchen**
**Symphonie en blanc n° 2: la jeune fille en blanc**
Oil on canvas, 76.5 x 51.1 cm
(30 1/8 x 20 1/8 in.)
London, Tate Britain

de la structurer, de lui attribuer un sens complexe. Les innombrables tentatives de classification et de compréhension de la couleur ont suscité toutes sortes de manifestations, depuis les conceptions dualistes de l'obscurité et de la lumière jusqu'aux motifs et systèmes géométriques élaborés qui visent à donner une forme spécifique à la couleur. Avec le développement du langage, de l'écriture, puis de l'imprimerie et des méthodes sophistiquées de reproduction des images, ces conceptions ont gagné en raffinement et en complexité, pris des formes visuelles saisissantes, et sont aussi mieux conservées.

Notre voyage visuel à travers l'histoire des conceptions de la couleur commence au XVIIe siècle, époque dont datent les documents les plus anciens consacrés spécifiquement à la couleur – manuscrits illustrés et sources imprimées –, et s'achève au milieu du XXe siècle, avant l'avènement de l'ère numérique. Chacune des conceptions se fait l'écho du temps de sa création tout comme le présent ouvrage, à travers celles que nous avons retenues. Depuis une vingtaine d'années, la couleur et son histoire suscitent un intérêt marqué et grandissant. Grâce à de nouvelles recherches, nous découvrons des tendances, des voix et des exemples jusque-là négligés de la culture matérielle (écrivains, pédagogues, ouvrages, manuscrits, œuvres d'art, méthodes), oubliés ou jamais incorporés aux canons de la couleur.

Aucun ouvrage consacré à la couleur ne saurait offrir une vue d'ensemble encyclopédique ni prétendre à l'exhaustivité sur les plans culturel, historique, géographique et thématique. Certaines publications laissent délibérément des aspects de côté afin de mettre en lumière tel ou tel thème culturel ou historique, d'autres reflètent les intérêts, goûts ou savoirs de leur auteur ou directeur d'ouvrage. Métaphoriquement bigarré, le présent ouvrage présente, par ses choix, la même subjectivité que celle qu'on attribue à la perception des couleurs. Les 41 œuvres présentées et analysées ici sont représentatives de l'histoire riche et variée des conceptions de la couleur depuis le XVIIe siècle. Si nous avons choisi de nombreux exemples connus et bien établis dans l'histoire de la couleur, nous espérons être parvenues à les situer dans un contexte culturel plus vaste, en les abordant avec un œil neuf. Outre ces exemples considérés comme « caractéristiques » de leur domaine, nous nous sommes

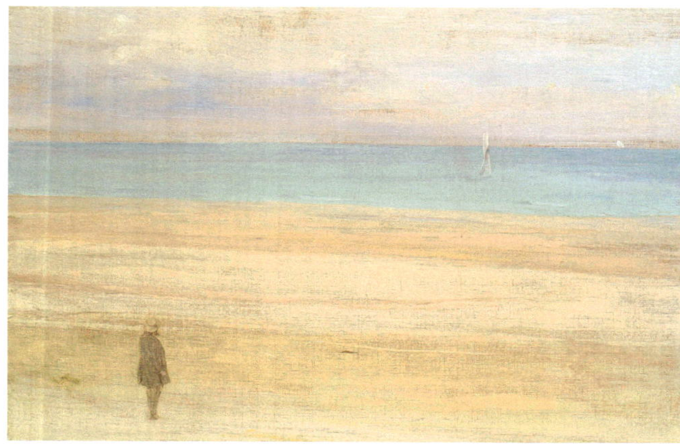

James McNeill Whistler
**Harmony in Blue and Silver: Trouville**, 1865
**Harmonie in Blau und Silber: Trouville**
**Harmonie en bleu et argent : Trouville**
Oil on canvas, 51 x 76.7 cm
(20 ⅛ x 30¼ in.)
Boston, Isabella Stewart Gardner Museum

efforcées de répertorier des œuvres méconnues ou ignorées, qui méritent d'être prises en compte pour leur intérêt et leur importance esthétiques et théoriques. Nous avons également cherché à mettre en lumière des œuvres écrites, publiées et illustrées par des femmes au cours des deux siècles passés. Notre spectre historique et géographique est vaste et nos exemples proviennent d'Europe, des États-Unis et de certaines régions d'Asie. Mais nous avons aussi voulu inclure autant de genres et de styles que possible. Un manuel élémentaire du XX^e siècle peut être aussi passionnant que le cercle chromatique élaboré par Isaac Newton (1643–1727) en 1704 (p. 155), chacun d'eux jouant un rôle essentiel dans l'histoire de la couleur.

## Des conceptions de la couleur, pour quoi faire ?

L'expression « conception de la couleur », malléable et appliquée à beaucoup d'aspects, convient bien à la réflexion sur ce sujet et aux tentatives de compréhension et de systématisation des couleurs. Pourtant, au lieu de chercher la meilleure appellation, on pourrait se demander pourquoi l'on éprouve le besoin de systématiser quelque chose d'aussi intangible, changeant, insaisissable et, dans une certaine mesure, subjectif. Jusqu'à une période relativement récente, les écrits consacrés à la couleur ne distinguaient pas clairement la couleur matérielle de la couleur immatérielle. Et dès lors que cette différence a été bien comprise, il est apparu qu'il existe en réalité de nombreuses formes chromatiques associant la couleur immatérielle aux teintes des matériaux solides. La couleur nous échappe facilement. Elle change en fonction de la lumière, prend une teinte différente selon le moment de la journée, pâlit, s'assombrit et peut se révéler imprévisible lorsqu'elle est combinée, mélangée ou juxtaposée. Qui plus est, elle peut être difficile à obtenir, comme peuvent le confirmer les fabricants de pigments et les historiens. Les premiers humains ont même dû être contrariés par le fait d'habiter un environnement où les deux couleurs dominantes, le bleu du ciel et le vert de la végétation, sont parmi les plus difficiles à fabriquer. Nous avons beau vivre dans un monde où la chlorophylle abonde, peu de végétaux permettent de réaliser de bons pigments verts. Sans compter que l'inconstante, l'instabilité et la toxicité fréquente de la couleur peuvent être exaspérantes. Et l'on n'a pas toujours aimé la couleur. Comme l'analyse brillamment l'artiste et écrivain David Batchelor dans *Chromophobia*, l'histoire de la culture occidentale se caractérise particulièrement par sa haine de la couleur, ancrée dans « la peur de la contamination et de la corruption par quelque chose qui est inconnu et semble inconnaissable [... et qui] se manifeste par les tentatives nombreuses et variées de débarrasser la culture de la couleur, de dévaluer celle-ci, de dénigrer son importance, de nier sa complexité ». Les attitudes de l'Occident à l'égard de la couleur ou, plus particulièrement, des couleurs très saturées et de la polychromie s'accompagnent généralement, selon Batchelor, de connotations en rapport avec l'étranger, l'oriental, le primitif, le féminin, le vulgaire, le superficiel, voire le pathologique, à l'opposé des notions classiques de blanc virginal ou de beauté incolore. La culture occidentale voit depuis fort longtemps la couleur et la noirceur comme les signifiants d'une altérité dangereuse ou menaçante, force déstabilisante qu'il s'agit d'éviter ou de dompter. La création de systèmes ou de conceptions chromatiques est une manière d'apprivoiser la couleur, intellectuellement d'abord, puis grâce à une utilisation et à une application mesurées. En imposant un ordre à la couleur, fût-ce de façon théorique, au moins tentons-nous de maîtriser une chose impermanente, mais omniprésente.

La peur, la défiance et la haine de la couleur ne sont, bien sûr, qu'un aspect des choses. Notre rapport à la couleur a toujours été multiforme. Les cinquante ou soixante dernières années, en particulier – dans le sillage de l'invention de la photographie et du cinéma en couleurs, de la couleur numérique, et la généralisation de l'impression en couleurs – nous ont accoutumés à la couleur comme jamais auparavant. À de très rares exceptions près, la couleur est désormais facilement accessible et n'est plus l'apanage de quelques-uns. La reproduction en couleurs connaît peu de limites, même si la qualité varie encore.

## L'ordre chromatique : de la boîte de couleurs à la palette

Là où les sources textuelles peuvent manquer, l'archéologie et la culture matérielle offrent une manière de comprendre les attitudes culturelles vis-à-vis de la couleur. À tout le moins, les teintes employées en peinture et en ornementation sont des indices qui nous renseignent sur les pigments disponibles à certaines époques et révèlent des détails relatifs aux techniques, aux matériaux picturaux, aux préférences chromatiques et éventuellement, d'un point de vue culturel plus large, aux significations symboliques assignées aux couleurs. L'une des plus anciennes palettes d'artiste qui soient parvenues jusqu'à nous – une palette de la 18<sup>e</sup> dynastie égyptienne, datant de vers 1427–1401 avant J.-C. (p. 9) – nous donne une idée tangible et tactile des pigments dont disposait son propriétaire, Amenemopet, vizir d'Amenhotep II. Elle nous renseigne aussi peut-être sur ses goûts en matière de couleur et sur sa manière de disposer dans sa palette les godets d'ocre rouge, de bleu égyptien et de vert mélangé, ainsi que deux sortes de noir. Pourquoi avait-il deux noirs différents ? Quelle était la signification du noir pour lui ou dans la culture de l'Égypte ancienne ? L'ordonnancement des matériaux de peinture peut sembler bien éloigné de la complexité d'un modèle chromatique tridimensionnel du XX<sup>e</sup> siècle. Pourtant, le désir sous-jacent est le même : attribuer à la couleur un ordre que ce soit pour des raisons pratiques ou des goûts individuels, voire à des fins commerciales. La palette d'un peintre, qu'il s'agisse de l'objet proprement dit et des restes de peinture qu'il porte ou tel qu'il est représenté dans les autoportraits, dévoile une partie de l'existence de l'artiste, de

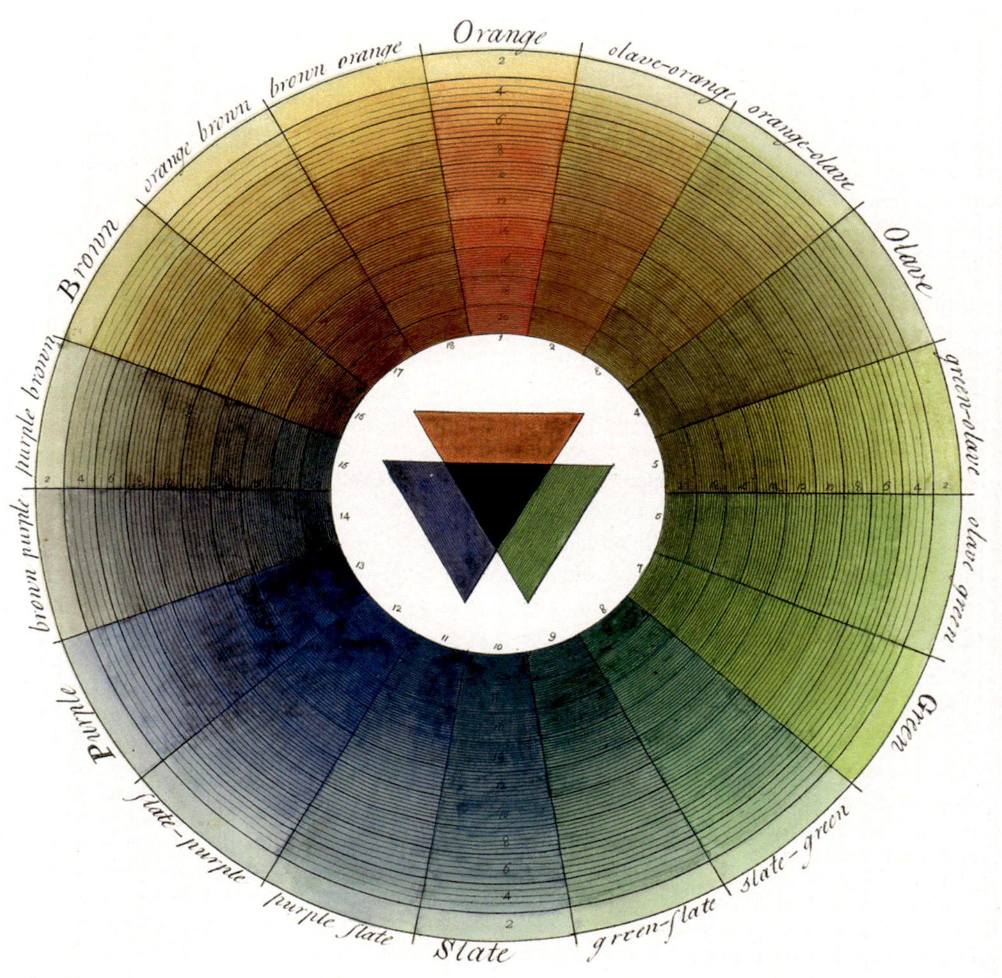
Orange
olave-orange
orange-olave
Olave
green-olave
olave green
Green
slate-green
green-slate
Slate
purple slate
slate-purple
Purple
brown purple
purple brown
Brown
orange brown
brown orange

Moses Harris
**Colour Circle, Prismatic**
**Farbkreis, prismatisch**
**Cercle chromatique, couleurs prismatiques**
From: *The Natural System of Colours* (London, *c.* 1769–1776)
Winterthur, Stadtbibliothek, Farbsammlung Werner Spillmann

*Page 65*
J. M. W. Turner
**Light and Colour (Goethe's Theory) – The Morning after the Deluge – Moses Writing the Book of Genesis**, *c.* 1843
**Licht und Farbe (Goethes Lehre) – der Morgen nach der Sintflut – Moses beim Schreiben der Genesis**
**Lumière et couleur (la théorie de Goethe) – le lendemain du déluge – Moïse écrivant le livre de la Genèse**
Oil on canvas, 78.7 x 78.7 cm (31 x 31 in.)
London, Tate Britain

ses pratiques et de ses préférences. Les boîtes de couleurs modernes, que l'on peut remplir de tablettes d'aquarelle industrielle, renseignent également aussi sur leurs utilisateurs et possesseurs : quelle taille et quelle qualité de boîte l'artiste avait-il ou elle les moyens de se procurer, quelles teintes a-t-il ou elle employées, quelles sont celles qui ont été le plus ou le moins utilisées, comment étaient-elles disposées ? De même que l'exemple de l'Égypte ancienne, une boîte d'aquarelle Reeves (p. 51) du début du XXe siècle peut en dire beaucoup sur la disponibilité des couleurs et leur popularité à cette époque. La boîte Reeves illustrée ici comprend plusieurs couleurs baptisées du nom de Wilhelm Ostwald (1853–1932), grand chimiste et théoricien de la couleur allemand.

## La représentation de la couleur avant l'époque moderne

Cet ouvrage a pour objet principal les systèmes de représentation visuelle de l'ordre chromatique et les idées qui les sous-tendent. Si les conceptions proprement dites remontent à l'époque classique, les premières illustrations de couleurs sous la forme de graphiques n'apparaissent qu'à la fin du XVIIe siècle. Jusqu'à une période relativement récente, la culture classique nous a semblé essentiellement incolore sur le plan matériel : le blanc est la teinte primordiale associée à la Rome et à la Grèce antiques, en raison des sculptures et des édifices de marbre blanc qui ont depuis longtemps perdu leurs surfaces colorées. Cependant, cette impression générale est bouleversée depuis quelques années par des études consacrées à la nature polychrome de la sculpture et des architectures grecque et romaine.

Sur les plans conceptuel et linguistique, on distingue plusieurs traditions dans l'histoire des conceptions de la couleur. Empédocle (494–434 av. J.-C.) serait l'un des premiers à avoir écrit sur le sujet. Les fragments de ses poèmes qui sont parvenus jusqu'à nous permettent de discerner une cosmologie fondée sur les quatre éléments – terre, feu, eau et air –, dont Empédocle pensait que les couleurs étaient dérivées. Au siècle suivant, Aristote (384–322 av. J.-C.) aurait réalisé des expériences optiques simples avec du verre coloré afin d'étudier la vision en couleurs et le contraste. Il propose un système polaire dont le spectre va de la lumière blanche divine, qui rend les couleurs visibles, à l'obscurité, figurée par le noir. À partir du blanc naît la hiérarchie des teintes jaune, verte, bleue et rouge, associées respectivement à la terre, à l'eau, à l'air et au feu. Élève d'Aristote, Théophraste (372–287 av. J.-C.) s'intéresse à la manière dont nous percevons ou ressentons les couleurs et se réfère à la conception des quatre couleurs – rouge, noir, blanc et jaune verdâtre – de Démocrite (460–370 av. J.-C.), associées à certaines formes et surfaces, ainsi qu'à d'autres aspects liés à nos sens. De son côté, le médecin Hippocrate (460–375 av. J.-C.) distingue quatre couleurs représentant les principaux fluides ou humeurs du corps humain, vues comme la cause de certains traits de caractère : blanc pour les flegmatiques, rouge pour les sanguins, jaune pour les colériques et noir pour les mélancoliques.

Les conceptions de la couleur et les discussions théoriques de l'époque classique n'existent plus que sous des formes fragmentées et comportent, en outre, l'inconvénient de présenter des difficultés linguistiques. La couleur est généralement mal servie par le langage car les mots sont impuissants à rendre toute la complexité des couleurs et de leur perception. La plupart des langues ne possèdent qu'une douzaine de termes pour qualifier les couleurs, alors que celles que nous sommes capables de voir sont innombrables. Cet écart est encore plus problématique en ce qui concerne les langues mortes, les textes anciens et leurs traductions. Nous manquons aussi de représentations visuelles des conceptions chromatiques du monde antique et des cultures premières, ce qui ne facilite pas la compréhension exhaustive des notions les plus anciennes. Néanmoins, il est possible d'avoir un aperçu de la puissante valeur symbolique des couleurs grâce à certaines découvertes archéologiques, comme les masques de théâtre trouvés à Pompéi, sous la forme d'objets ou d'images visibles sur les fresques, peints dans des teintes exprimant les quatre humeurs (p. 15). En dépit de la rareté des sources écrites consacrées à la couleur, nous pouvons retracer le développement de plusieurs conceptions culturelles en la matière grâce à la matérialité des pigments et des colorants. Comme dans le cas du pigment bleu outremer de la peinture médiévale et de la Renaissance (p. 11), la valeur matérielle et la rareté de certaines teintes ont conduit le monde antique à les associer à des figures de premier plan et à des divinités.

Si, tout au long du Moyen Âge, le système aristotélicien qui encadre la couleur entre l'obscurité et la lumière (le noir et le blanc) prévaut dans le discours philosophique sur le sujet, les manuels pratiques consacrés à la couleur se font aussi de plus en plus nombreux. Au début du XIIIe siècle, Robert Grosseteste (vers 1175–1253), érudit de l'université d'Oxford et évêque de Lincoln, en Angleterre, traduit certains ouvrages d'Aristote et, pour y répondre, rédige son propre traité des couleurs, *De colore*. Il y expose les théories chromatiques du philosophe grec et s'interroge sur la quantité de lumière que chaque couleur est susceptible de contenir. Vers le XVe siècle, la couleur devient peu à peu une marchandise, avec l'essor des échanges commerciaux. Les connaissances sont organisées de manière de plus en plus systématique et des premiers traités portant sur les techniques picturales, les matériaux des peintres et la vie des artistes voient le jour. Souvent très techniques, ils ont touché peu de lecteurs, en particulier avant le développement de l'imprimerie. Les manuscrits parvenus jusqu'à nous nous éclairent sur la fabrication artisanale des couleurs à l'époque médiévale. C'est notamment le cas d'un ouvrage du début du XIIe siècle, *De diversis artibus* (*Traité des divers arts*), dans lequel Théophile le moine (actif vers 1070–1125) propose principalement des recettes de couleurs. Bien d'autres ouvrages pratiques suivront au cours des XVe et XVIe siècles. Mettant

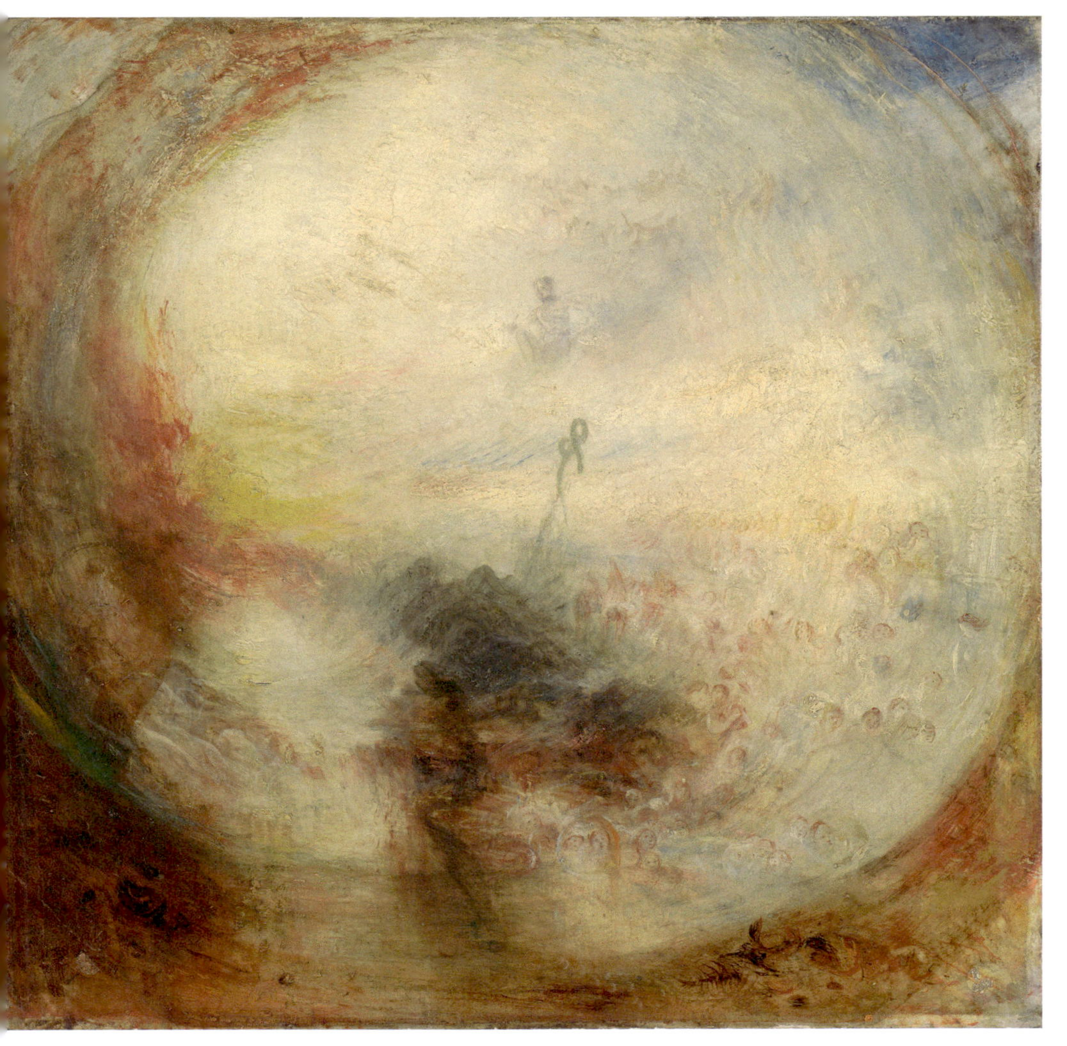

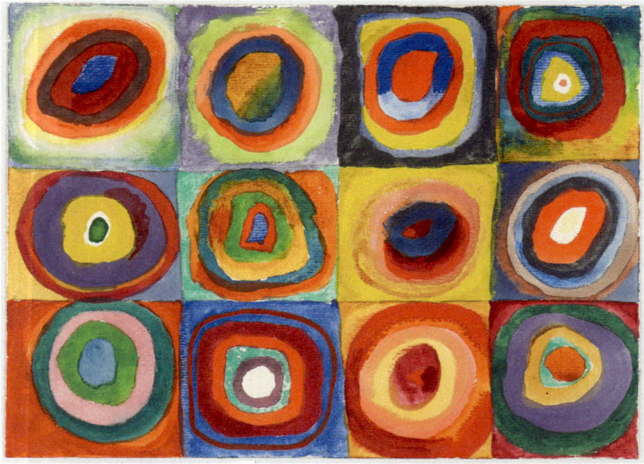

Wassily Kandinsky
**Color Study. Squares with Concentric Circles**, 1913
**Farbstudie. Quadrate mit konzentrischen Ringen**
**Étude de couleurs. Carrés et cercles concentriques**
Watercolour, gouache and crayon on paper, 23.8 x 31.4 cm (9⅜ x 12⅜ in.)
Munich, Lenbachhaus

Franz Marc
**Fighting Forms**, 1914
**Kämpfende Formen**
**Formes combattantes**
Oil on canvas, 91 x 131.5 cm (35⅞ x 51¾ in.)
Munich, Pinakothek der Moderne

l'accent sur les techniques et les matériaux, ils n'offrent aucune discussion philosophique des conceptions de la couleur, mais sont des sources précieuses pour l'étude de la terminologie chromatique et de l'histoire des pigments. On tombe parfois sur un texte comprenant des illustrations de matières premières employées pour fabriquer pigments et peintures. C'est, par exemple, *Le Livre des simples médecines* (p. 30, 33) – encre de calmar, lapis-lazuli et momie (pour le brun de momie) – dont on estimait aussi qu'elles possédaient des propriétés thérapeutiques. Il s'agit d'illustrations simples, mais les objets sont soigneusement disposés comme sur un plateau de collectionneur ou dans un cabinet de curiosités.

Les quatre humeurs qui, selon Hippocrate, sont omniprésentes dans le corps et l'esprit humain et peuvent être figurées par quatre couleurs, continuent de nourrir les conceptions chromatiques rudimentaires du Moyen Âge à la Renaissance. Si, au cours de cette époque, l'on ne connaît aucune image ou œuvre d'art traitant spécifiquement des théories et conceptions de la couleur, apparaissent néanmoins les premiers exemples d'utilisation des couleurs pour en illustrer et faciliter l'ordonnancement et la classification. Ainsi, le cercle chromatique uroscopique réalisé en 1506 (p. 14) par Ulrich Pinder (mort en 1519) représente vingt nuances d'urine, utilisées pour les diagnostics médicaux. Coloriées à la main, ces images de flacons d'urine offrent un des premiers exemples de cercle chromatique fondé sur les couleurs naturelles, assez semblable à ceux que l'on trouvera près de trois siècles plus tard dans les livres consacrés aux insectes de l'entomologiste anglais Moses Harris (1730–vers 1788). Dans la même veine, une foule d'écrits encyclopédiques tels que bestiaires, herbiers, lapidaires et index, comportent chacun des renseignements directs ou indirects sur les connaissances et l'usage des couleurs de leur époque.

En 1435, la publication de *De pictura* (*De la peinture*) par Leon Battista Alberti (1404–1472), coïncide avec l'avènement de la peinture à l'huile. Estimant que la couleur est un élément important et précieux de la peinture, Alberti avance que le mélange de quatre couleurs seulement – rouge, vert, bleu et gris – peut donner naissance à toutes les teintes.

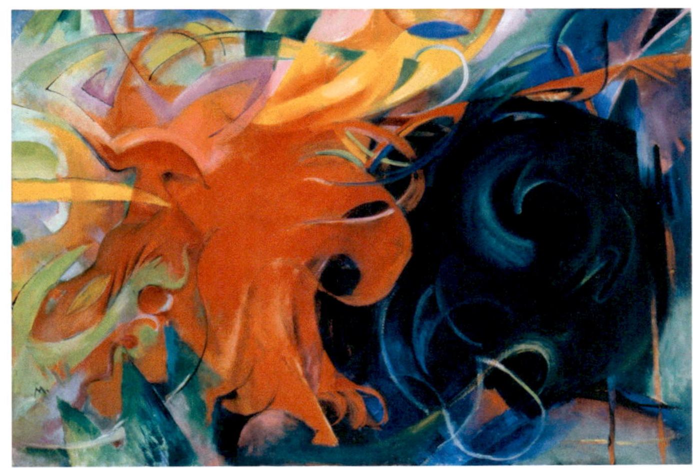

S'intéressant moins à la lumière colorée qu'à la couleur physique, il écrit à l'attention des peintres, de sorte que le gris, auquel il accorde une place de choix, doit être considéré sous l'angle des ombres et de l'effet de volume en peinture. De nombreux ouvrages portant sur le débat plus vaste des rôles respectifs du dessin (*disegno*) et de la couleur (*colore*) suivent les conceptions d'Alberti et de ses contemporains. L'un des plus grands artistes, Léonard de Vinci (1452–1519), nous a livré ses pensées sur le sujet dans divers carnets et recueils consacrés à la vision et à la perception des couleurs, à leur apparence et à l'application pratique de la théorie chromatique à la peinture. Il propose une conception simple, fortement influencée par Aristote et Alberti et fondée sur six « couleurs simples » : rouge, jaune, vert et bleu qu'encadrent le blanc et le noir. Aucun de ces textes datant du Moyen Âge et du début de la Renaissance n'étant illustré, il est impossible de savoir si les systèmes proposés étaient envisagés sous une forme linéaire ou circulaire, ou encore en deux ou trois dimensions. Néanmoins, ce sont des précurseurs fascinants de la théorie moderne des couleurs.

## Une nouvelle ère chromatique : la couleur depuis le XVII^e siècle

À la fin du XVII^e siècle, alors que l'imprimerie est déjà bien établie, pour diverses raisons, une grande partie des premiers écrits de l'époque sur la couleur sont des manuscrits. L'esprit naissant des Lumières favorise alors l'échange d'idées par-delà les frontières géographiques et culturelles. Si les symbolismes et métasystèmes chromatiques associés aux croyances religieuses, à l'alchimie et aux traditions populaires sont encore tenaces, la couleur commence à prendre une dimension scientifique et intellectualisée. On souhaite comprendre et catégoriser le monde naturel, y compris la couleur, considérée comme un phénomène optique, un instrument de description de la nature et un moyen d'expression dans les beaux-arts et les arts décoratifs.

Respectant un ordre relativement chronologique, chaque chapitre de cet ouvrage s'intéresse à un thème ou un aspect spécifique de l'histoire des concepts chromatiques. Les livres et manuscrits mentionnés ont été sélectionnés selon les critères suivants : avoir pour sujet principal la couleur sur le plan théorique ou pratique, ou

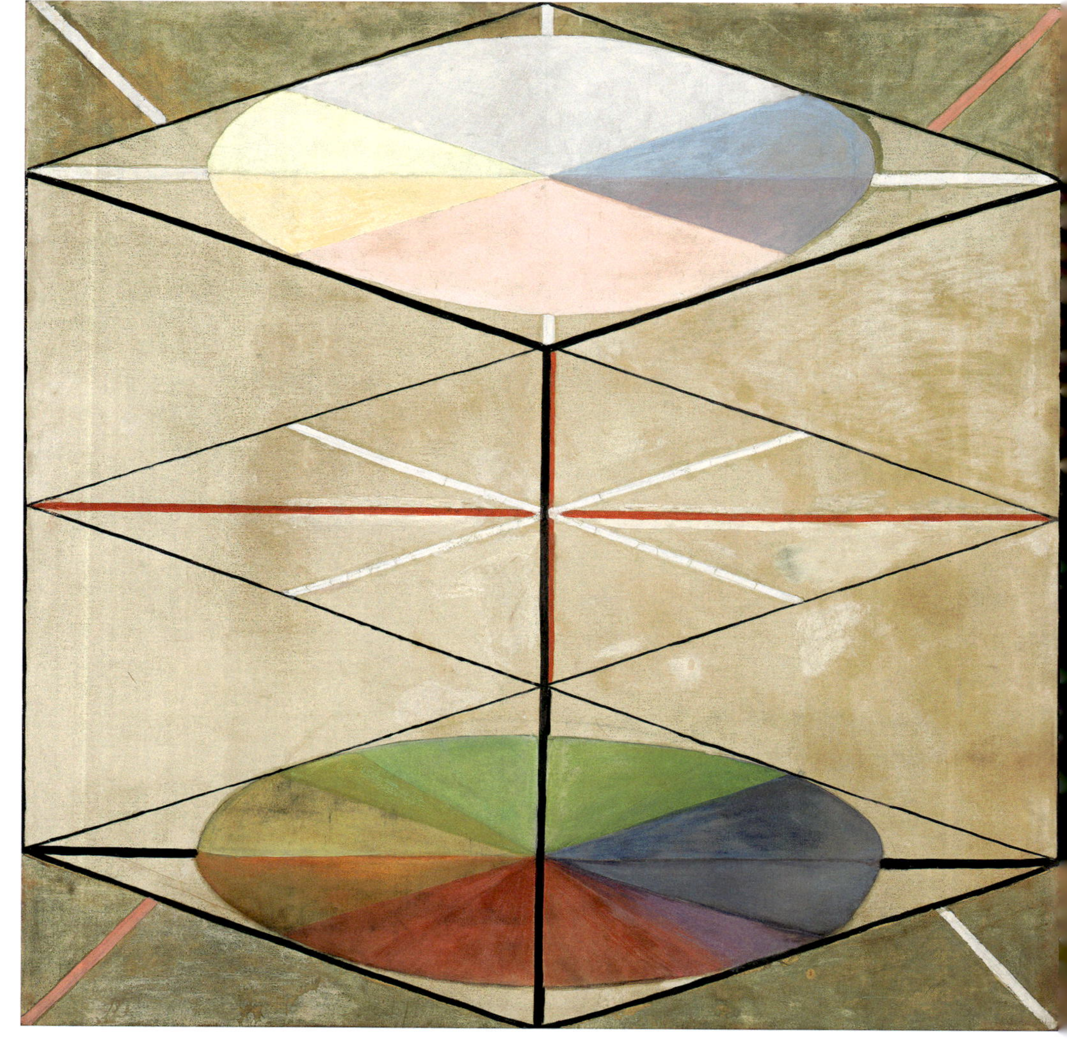

Hilma af Klint
**The Swan (The SUW Series, Group IX: Part I, No. 23)**, 1914/15
**Der Schwan / Le Cygne**
Oil on canvas, 152.5 x 150 cm (60 x 59 in.)
Stockholm, The Hilma af Klint Foundation

Hilma af Klint
**The Swan (The SUW Series, Group IX: Part I, No. 17)**, 1915
**Der Schwan / Le Cygne**
Oil on canvas, 150.5 x 151 cm (59 ¼ x 59 ½ in.)
Stockholm, The Hilma af Klint Foundation

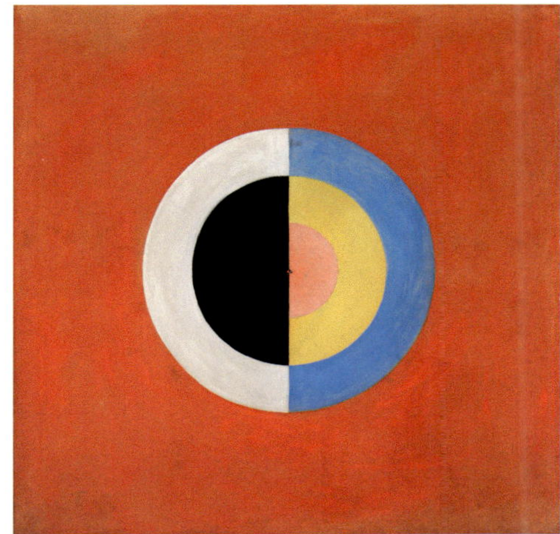

employer la couleur de manière cohérente et inventive comme, par exemple, pour l'illustration de concepts et d'idées relatifs à la couleur.

Nous présentons plusieurs œuvres dues à des femmes, ceci pour remédier au déséquilibre historique entre les hommes et les femmes ayant produit des écrits sur la couleur. Il s'agit notamment de livres éducatifs consacrés à la couleur en peinture au début du XX^e siècle, comme, par exemple, *The Theory and Practice of Color* (« La Théorie et pratique de la couleur », 1918, p. 352–361), de la pédagogue américaine Bonnie Snow (vers 1862–1925 ; coécrit avec Hugo B. Froehlich, p. 22–23, 27). Citons aussi Mary Gartside (vers 1755–1819, p. 164–175), peintre de fleurs britannique qui enseigna l'aquarelle et dont l'œuvre est négligée (p. 34 en bas). Elle est la première femme à avoir fait paraître un ouvrage consacré à la couleur en anglais : *An Essay on Light and Shade, on Colours, and on Composition in General* (« Essai sur la lumière et l'ombre, sur les couleurs, et sur la composition en général », 1805). Pour l'édition suivante (1808), elle donna un nouveau titre à son ouvrage, *An Essay on a New Theory of Colours* (« Essai sur une nouvelle théorie des couleurs »), afin de souligner le sérieux de sa publication. Des femmes ont également signé des ouvrages sortant des sentiers battus, de par leur appartenance à des cercles théosophes et spirites, comme *The New Science of Color* (« La nouvelle science de la couleur », 1915) de Beatrice Irwin (1877–1956), poétesse et actrice appartenant à plusieurs cultures, qui s'est beaucoup intéressée au potentiel que recèle l'association de la lumière artificielle colorée et de la musique. Aujourd'hui méconnues, ses réflexions sur la synesthésie ont influencé plusieurs artistes célèbres du XX^e siècle, comme Georgia O'Keeffe (1887–1986), dont certaines des œuvres pourraient bien faire allusion aux idées d'Irwin. Certaines femmes sont dignes de figurer au panthéon de l'histoire de la couleur sans pour autant avoir écrit une théorie à part entière sur le sujet. Hilma af Klint (1862–1944) en fait partie, de même que Winifred Nicholson (1893–1981). Par ses œuvres, ses notes, ses lettres et deux courts textes publiés à propos de la couleur, Nicholson est peut-être l'une des plus grandes théoriciennes du XXI^e siècle en ce domaine, bien qu'elle n'ait jamais réuni ses idées et conceptions en un seul volume concis. À l'instar de Gartside, c'est en peignant des fleurs qu'elle semble s'être inté-

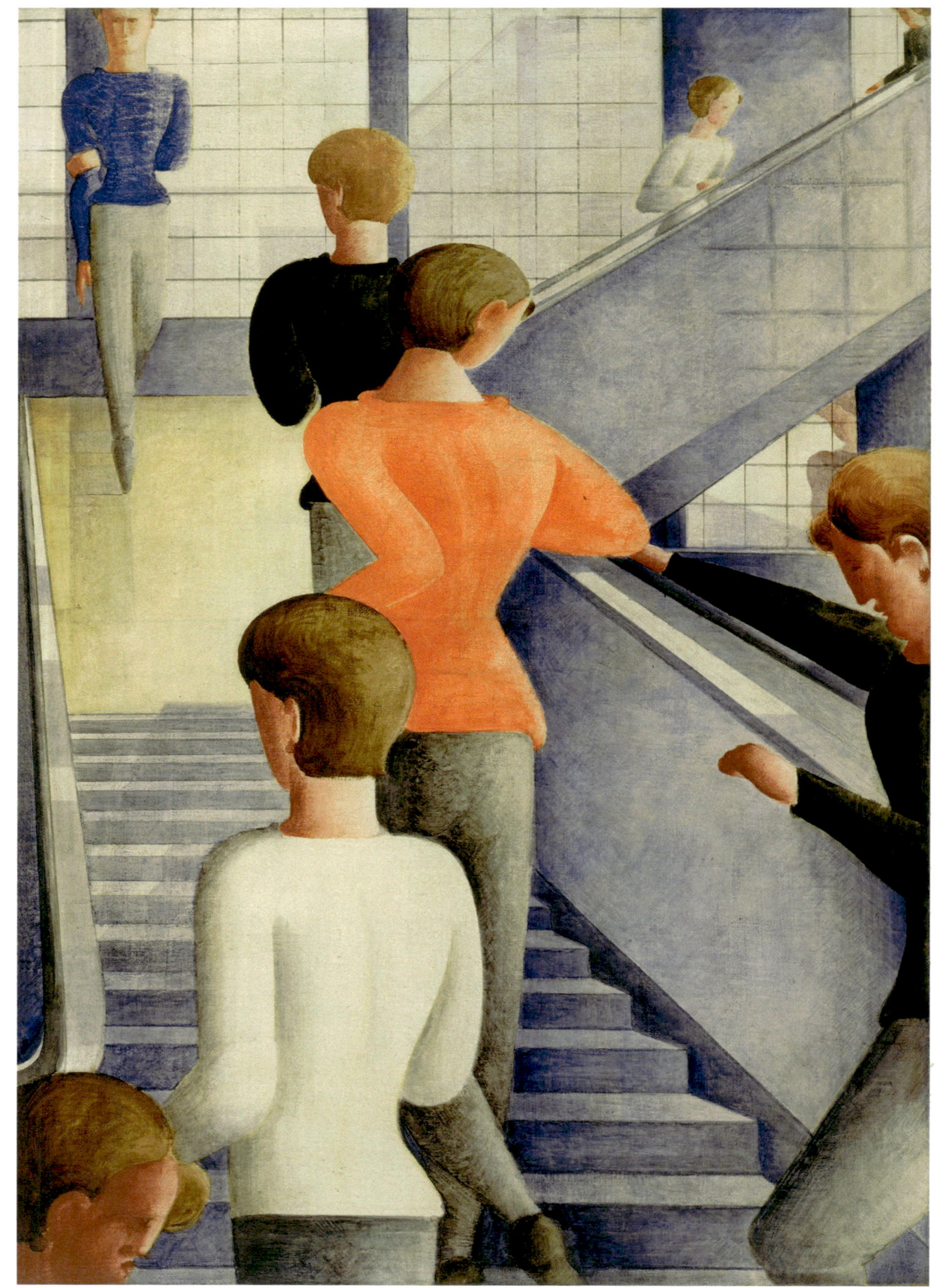

ressée à la théorie chromatique. Ses premières compositions ont souvent pour décor des paysages très éclairés ou encadrés par des fenêtres, indice précoce de son goût pour l'interaction de la lumière et de la couleur (p. 34 en haut). Cet intérêt manifeste pour les couleurs prismatiques trouve un nouveau débouché artistique lorsque, au milieu des années 1970, Nicholson, alors octogénaire, reçoit en cadeau deux prismes de verre. Au cours des dernières années de sa vie, elle réalise une série fascinante de « peintures prismatiques », où elle donne une forme visuelle aux expériences qu'elle a effectuées avec les prismes et la lumière, en recourant souvent à un style totalement abstrait.

Le premier chapitre, « Pyramides de la couleur : premiers graphiques et tableaux », s'intéresse aux premiers livres illustrés occidentaux. Les précurseurs de ces derniers sont une sélection de tableaux réalisés auparavant par Théodore Turquet de Mayerne (1573–1655), alchimiste et médecin à la cour d'Angleterre, lesquels figurent dans le « manuscrit de Mayerne » (*Pictoria, sculptoria et quae subalternarum artium*, 1620–1646, p. 6–16). Dans ce cas, les couleurs sont présentées de façon relativement simple, sous forme de tableaux et de cercles bien tracés. S'il ne s'agit pas d'une représentation de conceptions chromatiques nées de l'intellect, il faut la situer dans le contexte plus large des manuels de peinture, car ils offrent une mine de renseignements sur les pigments et d'autres matériaux dont les peintres disposaient à l'époque et sur la manière dont ceux-ci les mélangeaient et les organisaient. Ce chapitre montre également comment des graphiques et tableaux plus complexes sont créés au siècle suivant et diffusés via des ouvrages et autres documents imprimés. À cette époque, l'intellectualisation des concepts chromatiques est flagrante : les répertoires de couleurs sont de plus en plus élaborés et détaillés et l'on réalise les premières tentatives de conceptions tridimensionnelles. En dépit des progrès de l'imprimerie en couleurs, tous ces graphiques et tableaux sont coloriés à la main. Par conséquent, chaque exemplaire constitue une œuvre d'art à part entière. L'application des couleurs à la main est une pratique qui se poursuit au XIXe siècle et, dans certains cas, elle ne sera remplacée par la reproduction polychrome mécanique qu'au XXe siècle.

Le chapitre 2, « La forme de la couleur : cercles, disques et sphères », étudie comment les conceptions visuelles simples de la couleur sont approfondies au cours des XVIIIe et XIXe siècles et donnent naissance à une passionnante diversité de formes géométriques. Le cercle est, semble-t-il, privilégié et constitue l'origine de nombreuses variantes de ce qui est devenu le cercle chromatique classique. On fait aussi appel à d'autres formes ; souvent, un graphique de couleurs comporte des ajouts et des enrichissements picturaux, ou bien un cercle chromatique s'accompagne de diagrammes et tableaux explicatifs comme, par exemple, dans *The Natural System of Colours* (« Le système naturel des couleurs », vers 1769–1776, p. 118–123) de Moses Harris, ainsi que dans les œuvres de Mary Gartside.

Sur le plan esthétique, les graphiques chromatiques des XVIIIe et XIXe siècles font partie des plus belles images de la littérature consacrée à la couleur. Cependant, malgré leur puissance visuelle, elles s'accompagnent généralement de textes manuscrits ou imprimés. Bien qu'elle peine à exprimer tout le spectre des couleurs visibles, la langue joue un rôle important dans la plupart de ces graphiques, parfois avec des résultats enchanteurs et poétiques, notamment dans *Die Temperamentenrose* (« La rose des tempéraments », 1798/99) de Johann Wolfgang von Goethe (1749–1832) et Friedrich Schiller (1759–1805), par exemple. L'une des difficultés courantes consiste à figurer en deux dimensions l'aspect tridimensionnel de la couleur. C'est à ce stade qu'apparaissent les premières sphères chromatiques comme, par exemple, la *Farben-*

*Kugel* (1810, p. 26, 124–125) de Philipp Otto Runge (1777–1810). Malheureusement, aucun modèle de sphère chromatique de l'époque n'est parvenu jusqu'à nous. Toutefois, en 2016, l'artiste franco-allemande Eva Bodinet a créé une maquette inspirée de la *Farben-Kugel* (p. 24) et, ces dernières années, plusieurs fabricants ont réalisé pour le commerce des sphères chromatiques en 3D prêtes à l'emploi. Runge offre un exemple touchant de la sensibilité et de la spiritualité accrues des romantiques dans leur perception de la couleur. Bien des artistes, des philosophes et des écrivains de la fin du XVIIIe siècle et du début du XIXe ont adapté certaines conceptions chromatiques à leurs croyances personnelles en leur attribuant des significations hautement symboliques. De 1802 à 1810, Runge crée une suite d'images qui figurent les moments de la journée, notamment *Der kleine Morgen* (« *Le Petit Matin* », p. 29), et représentent une adaptation de la théorie des couleurs à l'expression de ses convictions chrétiennes.

Le chapitre 2 évoque l'expansion des études chromatiques au cours du XIXe siècle, parallèlement aux écrits sur la couleur s'appuyant sur les textes antérieurs. Nous nous intéressons notamment au peintre Joseph Mallord William Turner (1775–1851) qui, dans les années 1820, enseigne les fondamentaux de la théorie des couleurs, dans ses fonctions de professeur de perspective à la Royal Academy of Arts de Londres. Pour ce faire, il réalise deux grands dessins représentant des cercles chromatiques (p. 38, 39), afin d'expliquer ce qui distingue les couleurs matérielles des couleurs immatérielles. Ces cercles, qui entourent des triangles de couleur superposés, doivent beaucoup à ceux de Moses Harris, que Turner a étudiés. Tout au long de sa vie, le peintre anglais ne cessera de réfléchir à la création de nouveaux pigments et à la théorie chromatique. Il possède et lit de nombreux ouvrages sur le sujet et fait de l'interaction de la couleur et de la lumière l'un des thèmes majeurs de son œuvre (p. 41). Par la suite et quelques années après la parution de la première partie du principal ouvrage de Goethe sur le sujet *Zur Farbenlehre* (*Traité des couleurs*, 1810–1812, p. 184–191) dans une traduction en anglais (*Goethe's Theory of Colours*, 1840), Turner peint deux toiles qui font directement référence aux leçons de Goethe et, peut-être aussi, allusion à Harris (p. 65).

Le chapitre 3, « Nouveaux éclaircissements : les progrès de la théorie des couleurs », aborde de manière plus approfondie certaines des plus grandes œuvres du XIXe siècle portant sur la couleur et offre des explications quant à la brusque augmentation des théories nouvelles et des longs traités philosophiques, scientifiques et pratiques sur le sujet. Si cette révolution chromatique est intimement liée à l'industrialisation de la couleur, en particulier aux nouvelles méthodes de fabrication, de réalisation et d'impression, ses racines se situent au début du XVIIIe siècle. L'un des ouvrages ayant incontestablement fait date dans l'histoire des conceptions chromatiques est dû à Isaac Newton. En 1704, celui-ci fait paraître *Opticks*, fruit de décennies de recherches sur la couleur (p. 154–163). On y trouve, sous la forme d'un disque, le premier graphique des couleurs ayant été diffusé à grande échelle : il s'inspire des expériences du scientifique anglais sur la fragmentation de la lumière blanche en spectres de couleurs à l'aide d'un prisme. Comme on le sait aujourd'hui, l'influence de Newton sur la pensée scientifique des XVIIIe et XIXe siècles est inestimable et ses théories ont été adaptées, admirées, prolongées et critiquées (p. 18). La fascination exercée par le spectre de l'arc-en-ciel et par d'autres découvertes de Newton a été, et est encore, souvent présente dans les arts visuels. En témoigne, par exemple, *Colour* (p. 20), peinture allégorique d'Angelica Kauffmann (1741–1807) commandée par la Royal Academy of Arts. Allégorie et non figuration d'une conception chromatique en tant que telle, cette œuvre illustre un moment impor-

*Page 70*
Oskar Schlemmer
**Bauhaus Stairway**, 1932
**Bauhaustreppe**
**L'Escalier du Bauhaus**
Oil on canvas, 162.3 x 114.3 cm
(64 x 45 in.)
New York, Museum of Modern Art, Gift of Philip Johnson

Hilde Boos-Hamburger
**Cover and Colour Samples**
**Buchumschlag und Farbmuster**
**Couverture et Échantillons de couleurs**
From: *Die Schöpferische Kraft der Farbe* (Basel, 1942)
Sussex, collection of the author

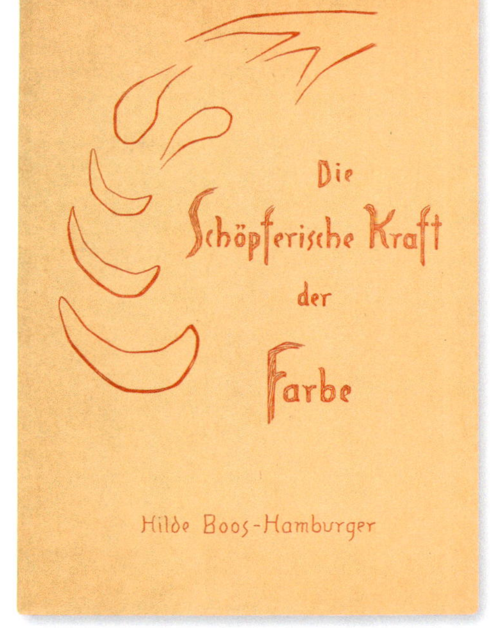


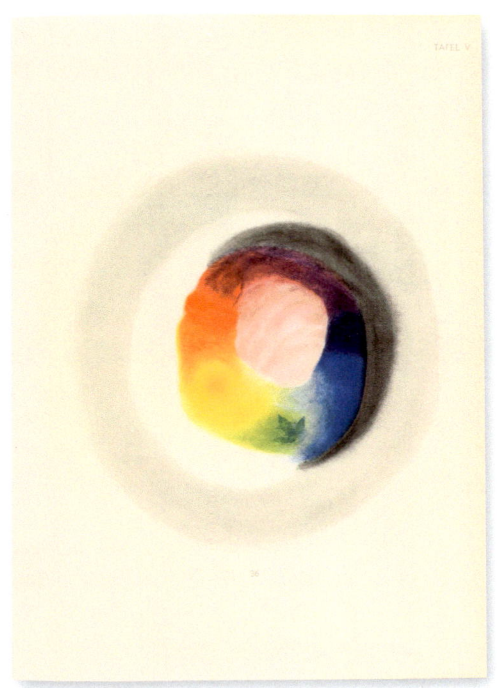

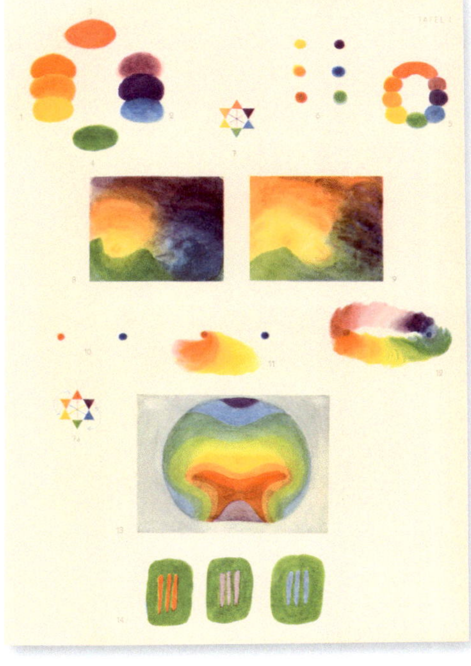

Piet Mondrian
**Composition with Red, Yellow and Blue**, *c.* 1937–1942
**Komposition mit Rot, Gelb und Blau**
**Composition en rouge, jaune et bleu**
Oil on canvas, 72.5 x 69 cm (25 ⅝ x 27 ¼ in.)
London, Tate Modern

Wassily Kandinsky
**Yellow-Red-Blue**, 1925
**Gelb-Rot-Blau**
**Jaune-rouge-bleu**
Oil on canvas, 127 x 200 cm (50 x 78 ¾ in.)
Paris, Centre Georges Pompidou

*Page 76*
Roy de Maistre
**Colour Music (enclosed roll),** *c.* 1934
**Farbenmusik (beidseitig aufgerollt)**
**Musique chromatique (rouleau)**
Gouache on piano roll, 31 x 1,606 cm (12 ¼ x 632 ¼ in.)
New South Wales Art Gallery, Gift of Sir John Rothenstein in memory of the artist, 1969

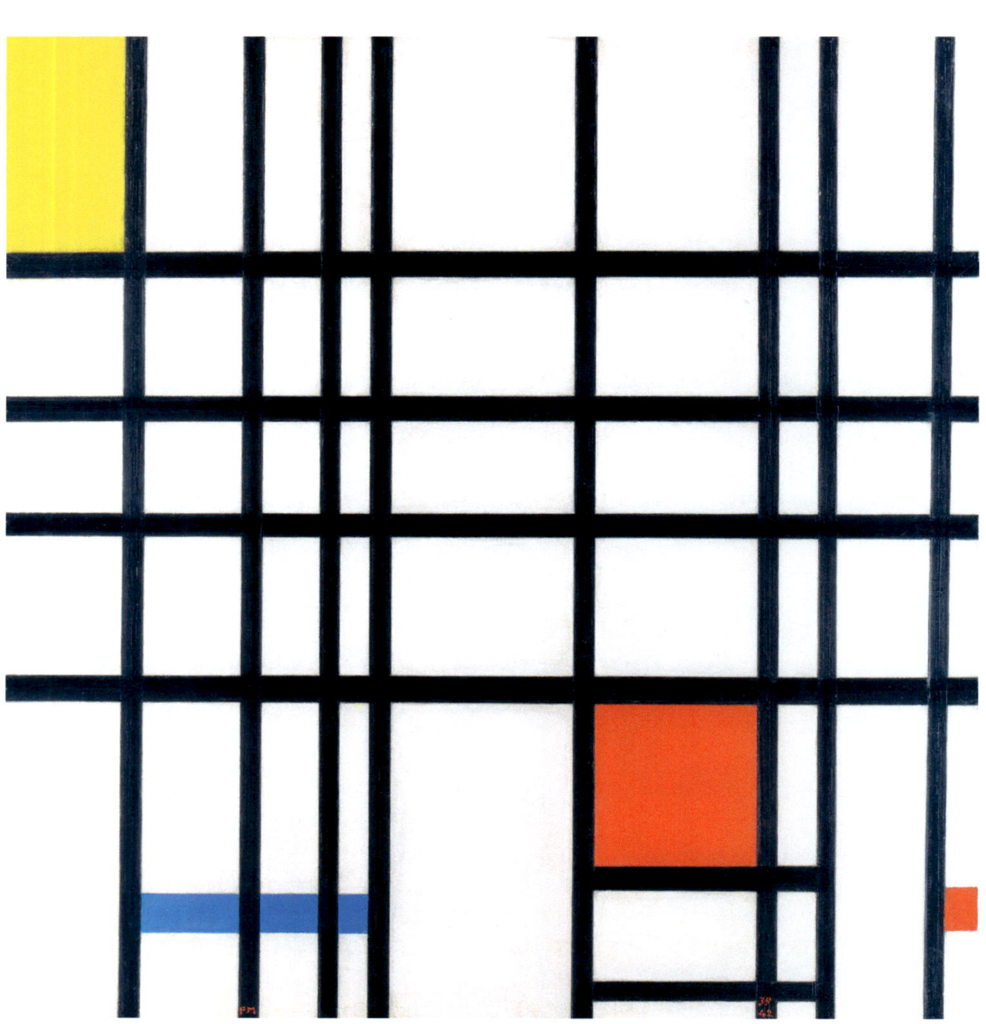

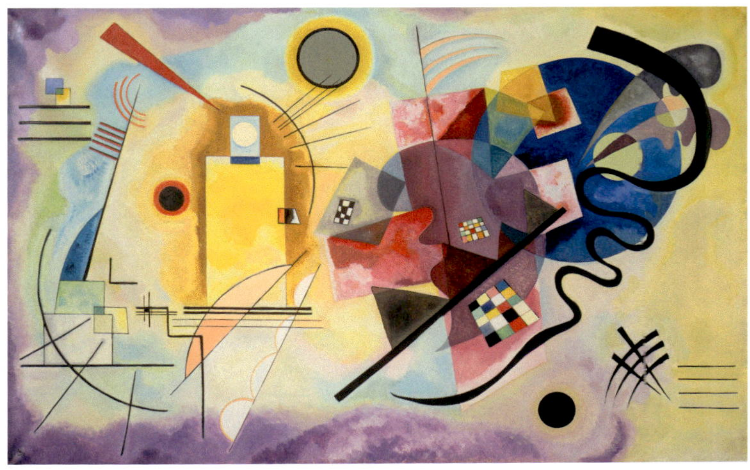

tant de l'histoire de la peinture car l'ensemble commandé à Kauffmann représente les grands « Éléments de l'art » – l'invention, la composition, la conception et la couleur – et place la couleur sur un pied d'égalité avec les trois autres catégories. La femme qui incarne la couleur trempe son pinceau dans l'arc-en-ciel de Newton et en extrait la couleur prismatique pour la poser sur une palette bien concrète. Ce faisant, elle adapte la théorie des couleurs immatérielles à la couleur matérielle, tout en l'associant à l'enseignement pratiqué à la Royal Academy of Arts qui vient d'être fondée.

Au fil du XIX^e siècle, les conceptions et attitudes romantiques, comme le symbolisme chromatique spirituel de Runge, cèdent peu à peu le pas à des études plus techniques et scientifiques, dont beaucoup sont liées à la fabrication de pigments et de colorants nouveaux. La qualité de ces nouvelles teintes est l'objet d'une étude de George Field (vers 1777–1854, p. 200–207), grand coloriste britannique qui a élaboré sa propre théorie des couleurs, mais aussi expérimenté, fabriqué et fait breveter des pigments. Ses couleurs sont très demandées par de nombreux peintres de ce siècle, notamment par les membres de la Confrérie préraphaélite et leurs disciples. La disponibilité de ces teintes coïncide avec un regain d'intérêt pour les techniques et les matériaux de la peinture médiévale. Des peintures comme *Mariana* (1851, p. 55) de John Everett Millais (1829–1896), remarquable par un éclat rappelant celui des bijoux et une polychromie audacieuse, illustrent cet intérêt pour les pigments de bonne qualité et une conscience aiguë des théories sur la couleur alors en vogue. D'aucuns avancent même qu'une œuvre de Dante Gabriel Rossetti (1828–1882), *Ecce Ancilla Domini! (The Annunciation*, 1849/50, p. 45), aurait été directement inspirée par le symbolisme des couleurs proposé par George Field. L'intérêt intellectuel accordé aux écrits et aux théories consacrés à la couleur est flagrant chez les peintres occidentaux du XIX^e siècle. L'impressionnisme et le pointillisme sont sous l'influence de la théorie pionnière du contraste simultané des couleurs qu'a élaborée Michel-Eugène Chevreul (1786–1889) à partir de 1839, lorsqu'il travaillait à la Manufacture des Gobelins, à Paris (p. 216–237). Le postimpressionniste Vincent van Gogh (1853–1890) applique les principes de Chevreul

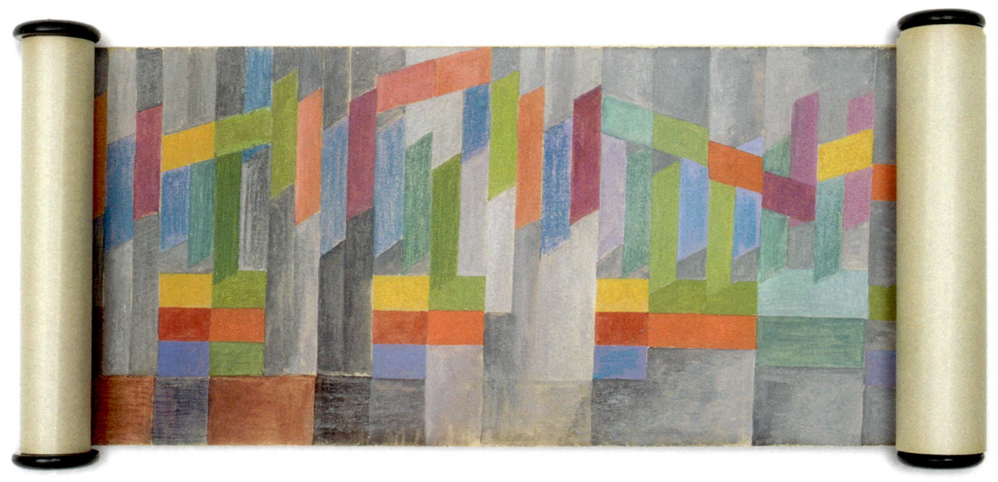

dans ses œuvres d'une manière stupéfiante. Il est révélateur que, parmi les biens personnels de l'artiste, se trouve une boîte de laque rouge contenant plusieurs pelotes de laine de couleur, emmêlées et associées selon différentes variations, comme s'il avait ainsi créé des harmonies chromatiques suivant les lois de Chevreul (p. 52). L'œuvre de James McNeill Whistler (1834–1903) exprime également une grande conscience du contraste des couleurs. Si nous ne disposons d'aucune trace de son intérêt pour les ouvrages consacrés à la couleur, son goût de l'harmonie tonale et du symbolisme chromatique est évident dans les titres qu'il a donnés à ses peintures, où figurent des termes comme « harmonies », « nocturnes » et « symphonies » de couleurs particulières (p. 58, 60), au détriment de toute description narrative.

Les chapitres 4 et 5 s'intéressent plus en détail aux conceptions techniques et pratiques de la couleur. « La couleur éclairante : nomenclatures et normes » traite des répertoires de couleurs, souvent en rapport avec le monde naturel et les classifications taxinomiques, qui présentent des tentatives séduisantes de création de nomenclatures et de normes fiables, utilisables dans les arts, la fabrication et les sciences. Certains répertoires visent aussi à faire l'histoire de la couleur, comme l'*Historical Color Guide* (« Guide historique de la couleur », 1938) d'Elizabeth Burris-Meyer (1899–1969), que celle-ci a ensuite adapté pour être utilisé dans la décoration intérieure, la mode et le maquillage (p. 298–315). Le chapitre 5 retrace l'histoire des manuels pratiques destinés aux peintres et aux imprimeurs, du début du XIX^e^ siècle au début du XX^e^. Les premiers manuels décrivant les couleurs doivent encore beaucoup à l'évolution de la peinture à l'aquarelle et nombre d'entre eux s'adressent aux amateurs car les fournitures artistiques sont de plus en plus abordables au début du XIX^e^ siècle. La peinture étant devenue un passe-temps féminin convenable aux XVIII^e^ et XIX^e^ siècles, une grande partie de ces manuels est destinée tout particulièrement aux femmes, bien que leurs auteurs soient majoritairement des hommes. Mais à partir du début du XX^e^ siècle, de plus en plus de femmes se consacrent à la rédaction de manuels pédagogiques et s'emparent des possibilités qui s'offrent à elles d'écrire, de publier et d'enseigner sur ce thème. Jusqu'à maintenant, ce domaine de la création féminine a été très peu étudié. Peu pris au sérieux, ces ouvrages pédagogiques, notamment ceux qui s'adressent aux jeunes enfants, ont été mal répertoriés et il n'en subsiste que peu d'exemplaires.

Le début du XX^e^ siècle est marqué par une nouvelle vague de livres consacrés à la couleur, dont beaucoup s'appuient sur les ouvrages des grands théoriciens du siècle précédent et en développent les conceptions. Tel est le sujet du chapitre 6, « La libération de la couleur au début du XX^e^ siècle ». On ne saurait analyser les concepts chromatiques de cette époque sans tenir compte de toutes sortes de réalisations scientifiques et artistiques, qui comprennent notamment les progrès effectués dans la compréhension de la vision en couleurs et, tout particulièrement, l'anatomie de l'œil humain, l'électrification et les possibilités qu'offrent l'éclairage électrique, ainsi que l'emploi radicalement nouveau de la couleur comme moyen d'expression artistique, notamment en peinture. Des collectifs européens d'avant-garde comme Der Blaue Reiter (Le Cavalier bleu) et le fauvisme s'intéressent activement à la théorie de la couleur, de même que de nombreux expressionnistes et les premiers peintres abstraits. Ils s'approprient le pouvoir symbolique et visuel de la couleur et représentent le monde qui nous entoure dans des tonalités subjectives et dépourvues de réalisme. Certains artistes font même des conceptions chromatiques le thème de leurs œuvres, comme, par exemple, Franz Marc (1880–1916) avec une peinture abstraite intitulée *Kämpfende Formen* (*Combat de formes*, p. 67) datant de 1914.

Au cours des premières décennies du XX^e^ siècle, très colorées et de plus en plus mécanisées, la couleur matérielle s'achète désormais sous une forme prête à l'emploi et dans de belles boîtes qui contiennent presque toutes les teintes vives qu'on puisse imaginer. Cette période incite fortement à tenter derechef d'établir un ordre chromatique une fois pour toutes. Les productions les plus marquantes dans ce domaine sont évoquées au chapitre 6 comme, par exemple, les œuvres d'Albert Henry Munsell (1858–1918) aux États-Unis (p. 380–389) et de Wilhelm Ostwald en Europe. Ces deux hommes sont les auteurs de systèmes très pédagogiques et adaptables, fondés sur une conception tridimensionnelle de la couleur. Certaines de leurs maquettes en volume, employées dans leurs enseignements, sont même parvenues jusqu'à nous (voir, par exemple, le « Corps coloré » d'Ostwald, conservé dans les archives de Winsor & Newton). Au début du XX^e^ siècle, les femmes bénéficient de nouvelles possibilités de recherche et de publication donnant lieu à plusieurs études scientifiques remarquables, que celles-ci réalisent sur la vision et la psychologie des couleurs, la couleur en littérature et en poésie, l'histoire des théories des couleurs, ainsi que d'autres aspects historiques. Publiés entre 1900 et 1930, certains de ces ouvrages figurent parmi les plus beaux et les plus inventifs de l'histoire de la couleur, comme, par exemple, *Color Problems* (« Problèmes de couleurs », 1902, p. 364–379) d'Emily Noyes Vanderpoel (1842–1939).

Le chapitre 7, « Le son de la couleur : spiritisme, occultisme et musique », étudie les associations synesthésiques de la couleur et de la musique et, par extension, avec le mouvement, la danse et la spiritualité. Dans une certaine mesure, les conceptions très personnelles et pseudoscientifiques des théosophes, anthroposophes et membres de groupes et mouvements de nature semblable au début du XX^e^ siècle sont suscitées par une réaction à un monde de plus en plus mécanisé. Toutefois, il faut rendre compte avec soin de chacune de ces conceptions chromatiques et ne pas les évaluer à l'aune d'une précision scientifique, mais selon leur inventivité artistique et les circonstances sociales et historiques qui les sous-tendent. Il n'est pas nécessaire de croire en l'existence

Yves Klein
**Blue Sponge Relief: RE 19, 1958**
**Blaues Schwammrelief**
**Relief éponge bleu**
Pigment in synthetic resin on sponge, pebbles and board, 200 x 165 cm (78¾ x 65 in.)
Cologne, Museum Ludwig

*Page 81*
Olafur Eliasson
**Colour experiment no. 57, 58,** 2014
**Farbexperiment**
**Expérience chromatique**
Oil on canvas, ϕ 190 cm (74¾ in.)

*Pages 82–83*
**Shopfront of Myland's Paints, Stockwell Road, London,** 1906
**Schaufenster von Myland, Stockwell Road, London**
**Devanture du magasin Myland, Stockwell Road, Londres**
Photograph

d'auras colorées, telles que les illustrent et décrivent Annie Besant (1847–1933) et Charles Webster Leadbeater (1854–1934). Pourtant, les tentatives de ces auteurs pour donner forme et couleur aux pensées et aux émotions constituent des points de vue fascinants sur la nature humaine (p. 412–439).

L'histoire des concepts chromatiques est dominée par les analogies entre couleur et musique. La plupart des écrits cités dans ce chapitre étudient les rapports des couleurs avec les sons, la musique, la poésie et la danse. Un grand nombre associe également mysticisme et science, convictions religieuses personnelles et théorie chromatique, nature et spiritisme, textes historiques sur la couleur et pratiques picturales de leur époque. On peut voir en cette énumération un mélange singulier et déconcertant. Ces ouvrages sont souvent difficiles à lire, mais les représentations visuelles de ces conceptions sont attrayantes. Le peintre australien Roy de Maistre (1894–1968) est l'auteur de nombreuses peintures sur ce thème, notamment un rouleau de cinq mètres de long représentant une « traduction en couleurs » du *Trio en si bémol majeur* de Haydn (p. 76). L'œuvre d'Hilma af Klint, mystique et anthroposophe suédoise, s'enracine dans l'occultisme et le symbolisme chromatique. On assiste depuis ces dernières années à une redécouverte de son œuvre, dont le style visionnaire est salué, à juste titre. Bien qu'elle n'ait jamais rédigé de théorie chromatique de son cru, nombre de ses peintures de grandes dimensions se composent de cercles et pyramides chromatiques et d'images de la couleur immatérielle. En résulte un langage visuel et chromatique remarquablement personnel, où cohabitent réalisme et abstraction (p. 56, 68, 69).

Le présent ouvrage ne prétend pas être exhaustif. Si les sources retenues sont principalement occidentales, chose quasi inévitable, le chapitre 8 vise à rétablir l'équilibre en dépassant les points de vue usuels en Occident et en s'intéressant aux conceptions orientales. Il donne un aperçu des approches japonaises de la couleur en vigueur durant les XIXᵉ et XXᵉ siècles. Loin de nous ériger en spécialistes des conceptions de la couleur de ces régions du monde, nous en reconnaissons néanmoins l'attrait esthétique et souhaitons montrer comment des concepts chromatiques géographiquement éloignés peuvent entrer en dialogue. Comparer quelque

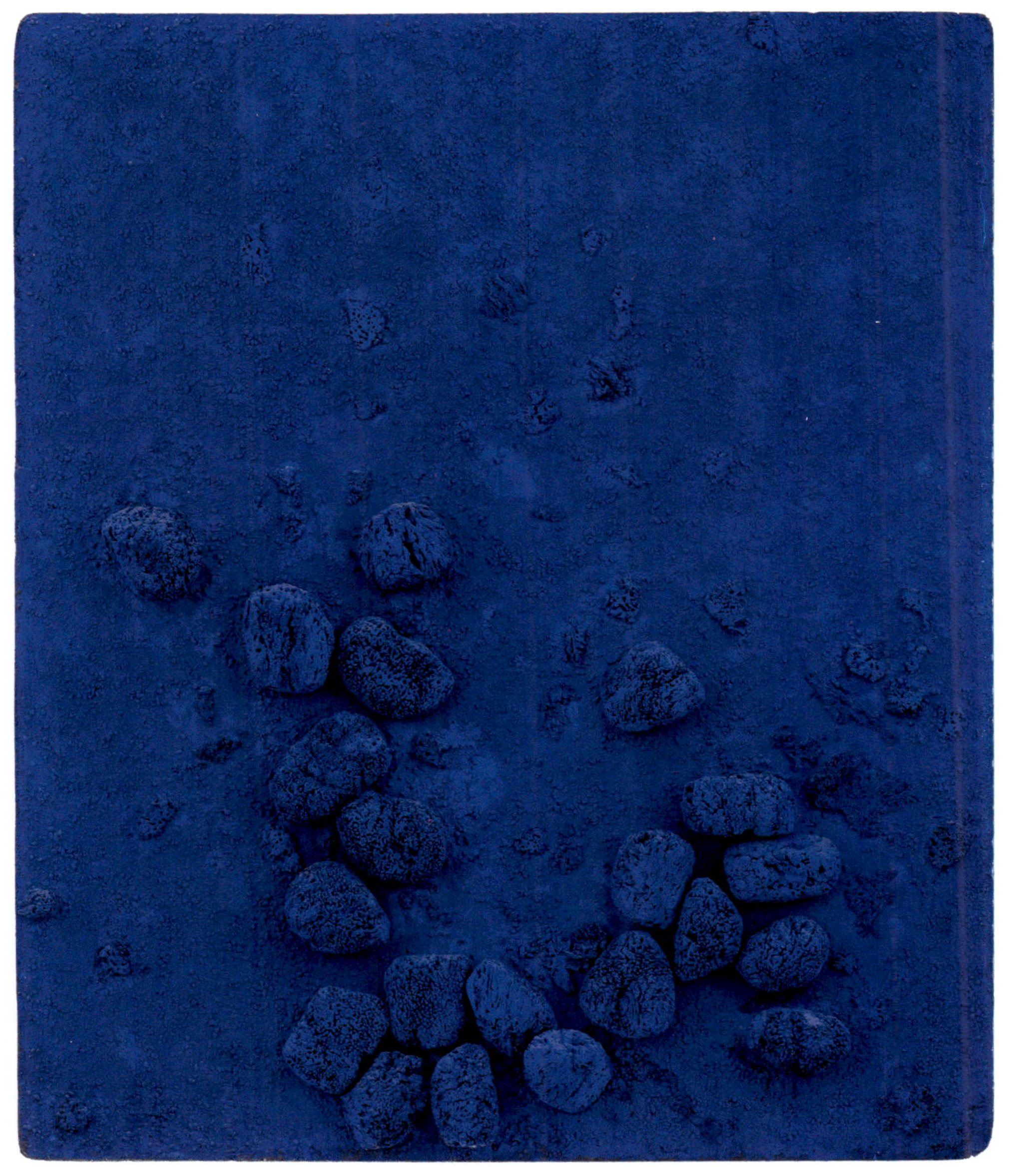

chose d'aussi abstrait que la couleur révèle avec beaucoup de force ce qui relie les êtres humains de par le monde. Un exemple captivant des échanges interculturels sur la couleur nous est donné par la pérennité des graphiques chromatiques créés par George Field dans les années 1830, qui réapparaissent dans un manuel scolaire japonais, *Gakko hitsuyo irozu mondo*, paru pour la première fois en 1876 (p. 460–465).

Le dernier chapitre, « Interaction et abstraction : le Bauhaus et après », évoque la couleur sous sa forme la plus pure, la plus réduite et la plus élémentaire dans la peinture, le design, les ouvrages didactiques et l'enseignement de la première moitié du XX^e siècle. Le cheminement vers l'abstraction est long et jalonné d'étapes nourries des contributions de divers pionniers, comme Turner, Gartside, Whistler, af Klint et d'autres artistes membres de différentes avant-gardes européennes. Mais c'est le Bauhaus qui, avec ses cercles d'influence, devient l'un des phares du modernisme, du progressisme et, d'un point de vue stylistique, de l'abstraction. Fondée en 1919 à Weimar par l'architecte Walter Gropius (1883–1969), cette éphémère école d'art et de design trouve ses origines dans l'avant-garde allemande et les cercles spiritistes, ainsi que dans le mouvement anglais Arts and Crafts. Elle met l'accent sur la simplicité et la fonctionnalité et s'attache à offrir aux artistes une formation complète en soulignant la qualité de la facture. Parmi les membres, enseignants et étudiants du Bauhaus, on compte notamment Ludwig Mies van der Rohe, Paul Klee, Johannes Itten et Josef Albers, ainsi que plusieurs femmes, comme Anni Albers, Marianne Brandt, Gertrud Arndt, Gertrud Grunow et Gunta Stölzl, dont le rôle que celles-ci ont joué dans l'histoire de l'école n'est véritablement reconnu que depuis peu. En 1925, le Bauhaus est transféré à Dessau, où Gropius a conçu le fameux bâtiment qui l'accueille (voir p. 70). En 1933, au terme d'une année à Berlin, où l'école a de nouveau déménagé, celle-ci est contrainte à la fermeture sous la pression croissante des nazis. Certains de ses membres émigrent en Angleterre ou aux États-Unis, où ils parviennent à maintenir leurs relations et à poursuivre leur travail. Si la couleur n'est qu'un élément parmi d'autres des cours dispensés au Bauhaus, elle suscite de nombreuses publications, dont un ouvrage qui fait référence sur le sujet, paru près de trente ans après la fermeture de l'école : *Interaction of Color* (*L'Interaction des couleurs*, 1963, p. 498–503) de Josef Albers (1888–1976). Cette œuvre, ainsi que des publications moins célèbres dues à des écrivains et artistes associés au Bauhaus, témoignent d'une synthèse quasi parfaite de la pensée sur la couleur, prenant en compte la vie et le travail parmi les couleurs, l'enseignement de la couleur et son application à la peinture et au design, sans négliger la réflexion portant sur les idéaux modernistes de simplicité, de géométrie et d'abstraction. En peinture, les conceptions chromatiques et l'esthétique du Bauhaus se retrouvent dans l'évolution plus large vers l'abstraction qui a lieu au XX^e siècle. Les œuvres extrêmement minimalistes et géométriques de maîtres de la peinture moderne comme Piet Mondrian (p. 74), Henri Matisse et Kazimir Malévitch présentent des similitudes manifestes dans leur usage de la couleur.

## Intemporalité des conceptions chromatiques

Par leur beauté abstraite et la manière visuelle dont les conceptions chromatiques sont rendues, les représentations de la couleur exercent une fascination intemporelle. Les formes simples et géométriques créées pour façonner l'aspect des premiers graphiques et tableaux chromatiques nous parlent immédiatement, car des formes identiques ou similaires peuplent la peinture, la publicité et le design d'aujourd'hui. De même,

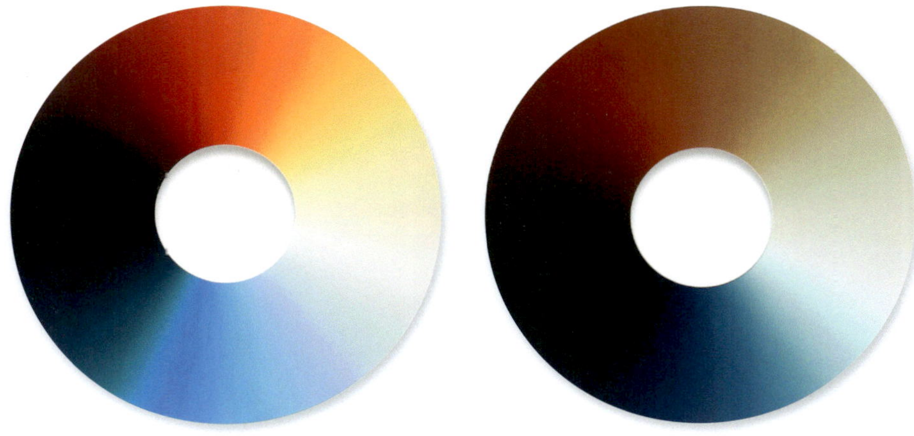

les cercles, disques, triangles et cubes, ainsi que les graphiques ou formes organiques encore plus complexes, entretiennent un dialogue à travers les siècles. Les théories et conceptions des couleurs demeurent un thème et une source d'inspiration chez les artistes contemporains. Depuis 2009, l'artiste islando-danois Olafur Eliasson (né en 1967) a réalisé une série de grands disques chromatiques, dans lesquels les couleurs se fondent imperceptiblement les unes dans les autres (p. 81), à la manière des disques de Chevreul dans son *Atlas* de 1861. Une sélection des disques d'Eliasson a été exposée à la Tate Britain, à Londres, sous le titre *Turner colour experiments* (« Expériences chromatiques de Turner »), en regard de peintures de Turner. De même que, dans certaines de ses œuvres, Turner fait allusion à Goethe et à Harris, Eliasson évoque les théoriciens de la couleur et les peintres qui l'ont précédé, mais cherche également à proposer une théorie des couleurs dans l'art de son cru.

De tout temps, l'être humain a tenté d'apprivoiser et de maîtriser la couleur, cet aspect insaisissable mais omniprésent de notre vision, même si nos efforts pour circonscrire la couleur à des cercles, des carrés et des traits, pour la faire entrer de force dans des listes ou lui faire prendre des formes en trois dimensions, ne sont en fin de compte que des expressions de la pensée et de la créativité humaines. Peut-être reste-t-il à formuler la conception chromatique parfaite. Néanmoins, la transformation d'idées sur la couleur en mots, images, diagrammes et volumes a produit une riche histoire de la couleur, véritable art visuel à part entière. Les savoirs individuels, les choix personnels, les découvertes et le renouvellement de la pensée font que chaque nouvel ouvrage sur le sujet est une réalisation stimulante. Nous espérons que notre sélection de conceptions et théories de la couleur offrira une variété inattendue d'opinions et de récits, ainsi que des sources d'inspiration, et qu'elle éclairera l'histoire de la couleur d'une lumière nouvelle.

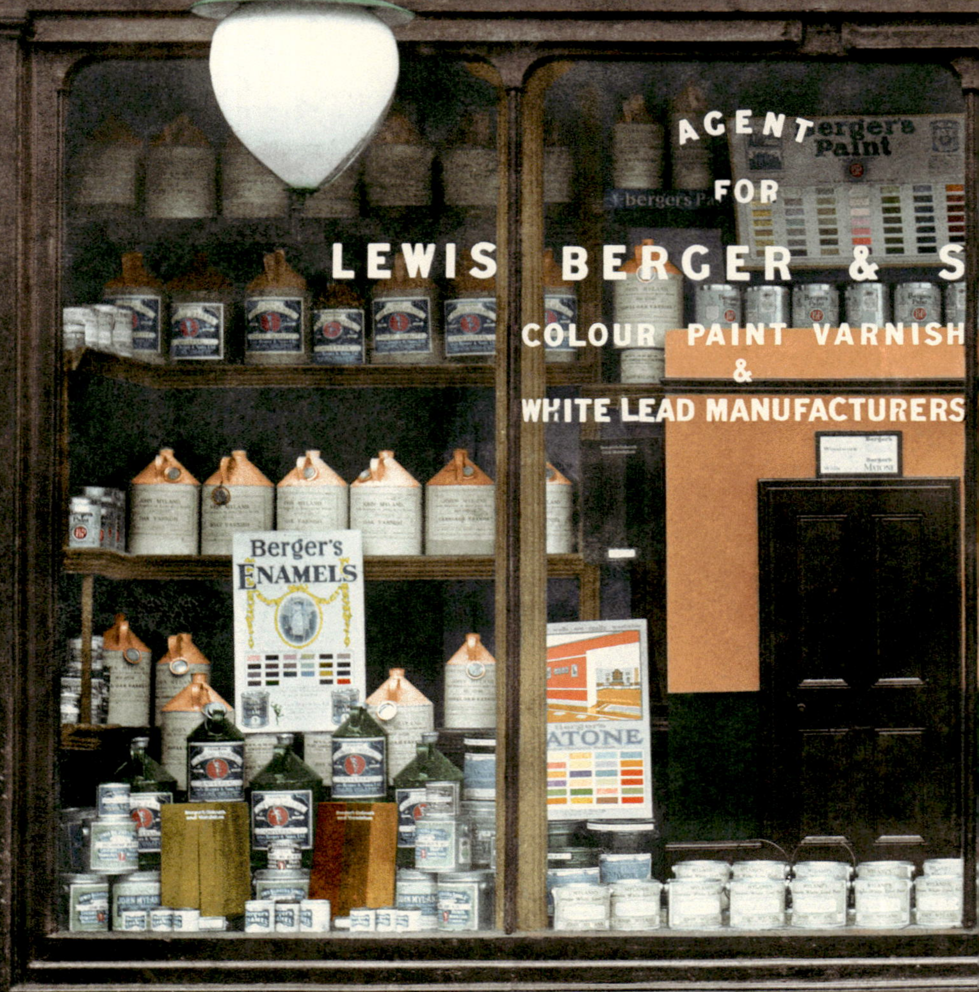
OILS, COLORS
128 JOHN
Berger's Paint
AGENT FOR
LEWIS BERGER & S
COLOUR PAINT VARNISH
&
WHITE LEAD MANUFACTURERS
Berger's ENAMELS
ATONE

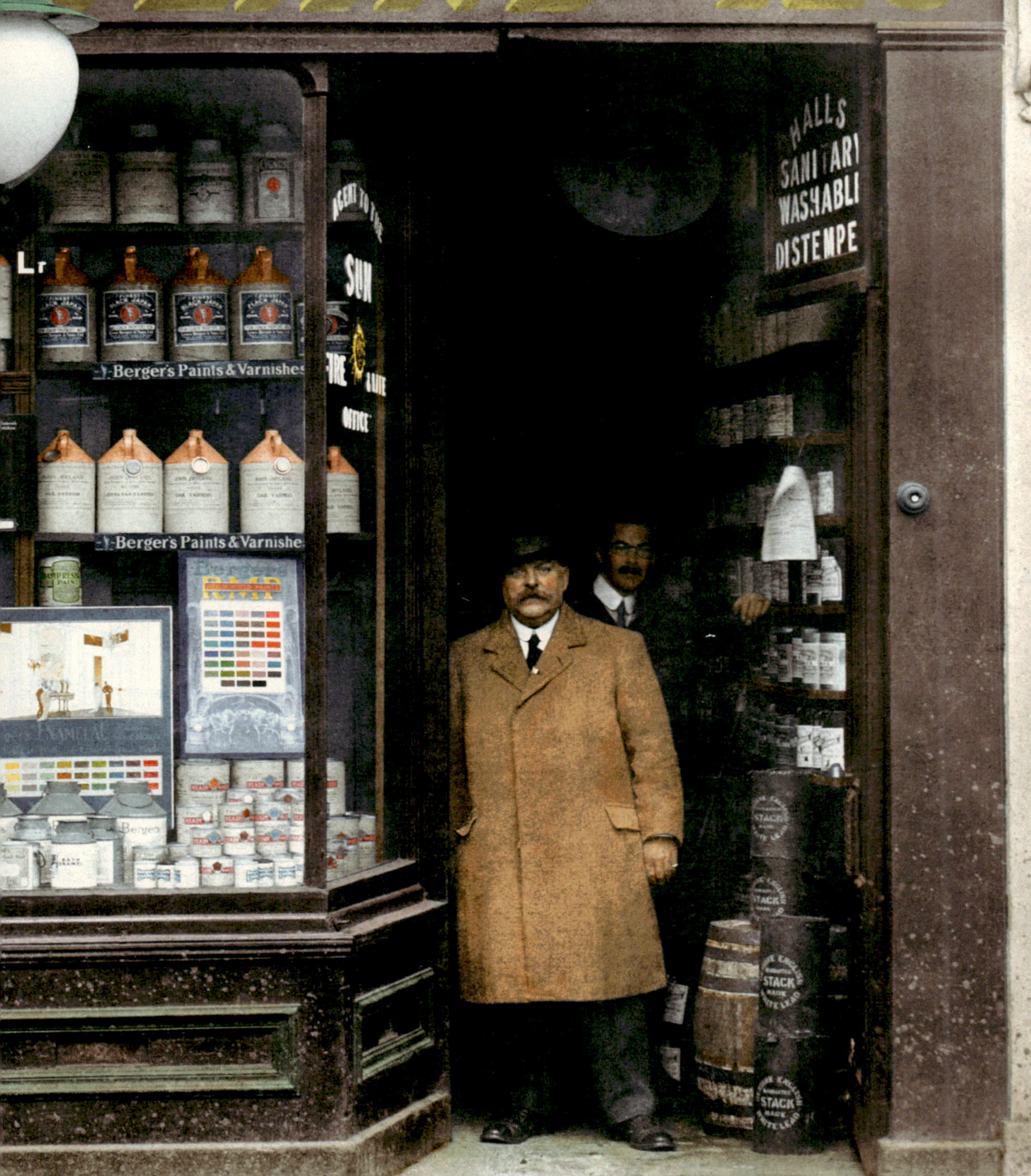

LEAD &c
YLAND 128
Berger's Paints & Varnishe
Berger's Paints & Varnishe
AGENT TO THE
SUN
FIRE & LIFE
OFFICE
HALLS
SANITARY
WASHABL
DISTEMPE
STACK
STACK
STACK
STACK

# Regiſter.

N°: Bij fol: 25:

N°: Bij fol: 26:

N°: Bij fol: 27:

N°: Bij fol: 28:

N°: Bij fol: 29

N°: Bij fol: 30:

N°: Bij fol: 31:

N°: Bij fol: 32:

N°: Bij fol: 33:

N°: Bij fol: 34:

N°: Bij fol: 35:

N°: Bij fol: 36:

## Chapter 1

# *Pyramids of Colour:* EARLY CHARTS AND TABLES

## 1692–1794

### A. Boogert (forename and dates unknown)

# KLAER LIGHTENDE SPIEGEL DER VERFKONST

## A Clearly Lit Mirror of Painting

*19 pages, 16 x 9.5 cm / 6 ¼ x 3 ¾ in., Delft, 1692*
*Aix-en-Provence, Bibliothèque Méjanes*

This is one of the most beautiful early books about colour in existence, yet it is shrouded in mystery, and was, as far as is known, never actually published. It survives as a manuscript originally written in Delft in 1692, comprising nearly 900 pages of elegant longhand text in Dutch, illustrated on almost every page with colour samples in watercolour and gouache. The otherwise unidentified author, A. Boogert, added that name to the title-page and to the end of the introduction. The relatively small bound manuscript has been in the collection of the Bibliothèque Méjanes for many years but was brought to wider attention in 2014 by the book historian Erik Kwakkel via social media. Since coming to light, the manuscript has been a source of widespread fascination and the subject of much academic research, although very little has been published about it so far. Comparisons have been drawn with colour guides produced by paint-makers from around the same time, and it is certainly tempting to think of it as a 17th-century colour catalogue for designers, or a list of paints available in Delft in the 1690s, but the real story behind the manuscript and its purpose might well be more complex. It is a striking object, largely because of its brilliant and well-preserved colour samples, which were painted directly on to the paper, but also because of the notably modern-looking, abstract simplicity of their design. The samples are all presented in clearly defined squares or rectangles that collectively occupy most of the illustrated pages, beginning with a section of 42 pages showing one colour on each page in three stages of dilution, followed by 323 plates showing colours mixed in five ratios, resulting in a total of 1,615 samples. A detailed "register" of colours completes the manuscript.

Boogert presented this work throughout in the manner of a finished printed book, repeating the title *Klaer Lightende Spiegel der*

1

2

3

1

2

3

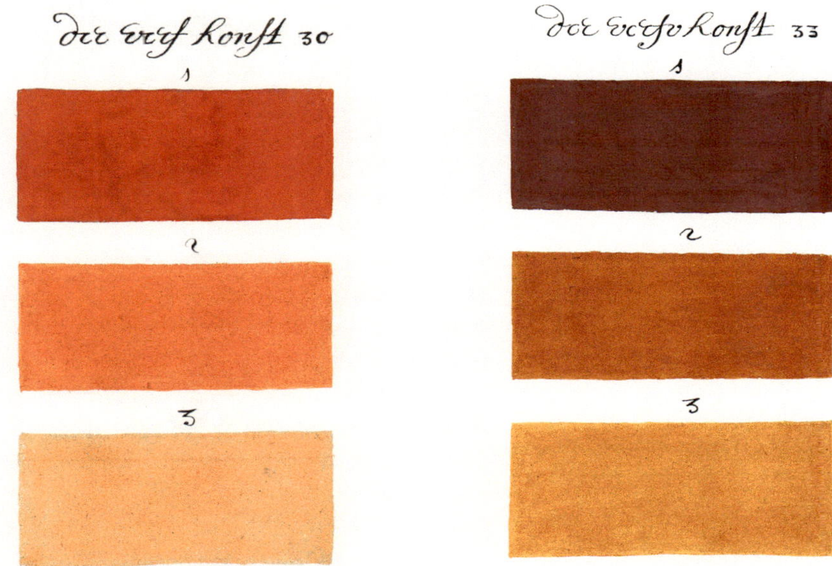


*Verfkonst* (literally, 'A clearly lit / illuminated mirror of painting', but it could be read as 'An enlightened reflection on painting') at the top of each illustrated double-page, which suggests the author had every intention for it to be published. It is hard to imagine how the plates could have been reproduced in print format at this early date, and that was perhaps part of the reason why it was never properly issued. It is nevertheless clear that Boogert intended it to be a comprehensive and practical painting compendium that would be helpful in colouring engravings and drawing from nature, while the text also included advice on how to prepare paints. This may explain the prominent image of a butterfly depicted on the title-page, a symbol of the complexities of colour in the natural world, and also the iconography of the frontispiece, which shows an artist (or engraver) copying a large portrait painting, behind whom an assistant is preparing pigment by grinding it with a muller while another person is waiting to transfer the colour to a palette. Boogert's book was perhaps too complex in its design for late 17th-century print culture, but it certainly strikes a chord with the 21st-century world of digital and social media.

## Klar leuchtender Spiegel der Malkunst

Dieses Buch zählt zu den schönsten noch existierenden Frühwerken über Farbe. Doch es ist von Geheimnissen umwittert und wurde, soweit man weiß, niemals wirklich veröffentlicht. Erhalten ist das Originalmanuskript, das 1692 in Delft verfasst wurde, fast neunhundert Seiten in eleganter niederländischer Schreibschrift umfasst und auf fast jeder Seite mit Farbmustern in Wasserfarbe und Gouache bebildert ist. Der ansonsten unbekannte Autor setzte den Namen A. Boogert auf die Titelseite und ans Ende der Einleitung. Das vergleichsweise kleine, gebundene Manuskript befand sich über viele Jahr in der Bibliothèque Méjanes, bevor der Buchhistoriker Erik Kwakkel es 2014 über die sozialen Medien einer breiten Öffentlichkeit zugänglich machte. Seit es auf diese Weise bekannt wurde, fasziniert das Manuskript Wissenschaftler, Buchliebhaber, Designer und Farbhistoriker gleichermaßen und wurde zum Gegenstand zahlreicher wissenschaftlicher Untersuchungen, wenngleich bislang nur sehr wenig darüber publiziert wurde. Man hat es mit Handbüchern von Farbenherstellern aus etwa derselben Zeit verglichen, doch so verlockend es auch sein mag, dieses Buch als Farbenkatalog für Gestalter aus dem 17. Jahrhundert oder als Liste der in den 1690er-Jahren in Delft verfügbaren Farben zu betrachten, könnte die wahre Geschichte hinter dem Manuskript und seiner Zielsetzung weitaus vielschichtiger sein. Vor allem wegen seiner leuchtenden und gut erhaltenen Farbmuster, die direkt auf das Papier gemalt wurden, aber auch wegen der gestalterisch bemerkenswert modern wirkenden, abstrakten Einfachheit dieser Farbflächen ist es ein faszinierendes Objekt. Die Muster werden ausnahmslos in gleichmäßig angeordneten Quadraten oder Rechtecken präsentiert, die zusammen den größten Teil der illustrierten Seiten einnehmen. Sie beginnen mit einem 42-seitigen Abschnitt, der auf jeder Seite eine Farbe in drei Verdünnungszuständen zeigt. Auf ihn folgen 323 Tafeln mit Farben in fünf Mischungsverhältnissen und insgesamt 1.615 Mustern. Ein ausführliches „Register" der Farben rundet das Manuskript ab.

Boogert präsentierte das Werk durchgehend in der Art eines fertig gedruckten Buches und wiederholte den Titel *Klaer Lightende Spiegel der Verfkonst* (wörtlich „Klar leuchtender/illuminierter Spiegel der Malkunst", aber auch zu lesen als „Eine aufgeklärte Betrachtung über das Malen") am Kopf jeder illustrierten Doppelseite, was auf seine feste Veröffentlichungsabsicht hindeutet. Es ist schwer vorstellbar, wie die Tafeln zu diesem frühen Zeitpunkt im Druckformat hätten reproduziert werden sollen, und womöglich war das einer der Gründe, warum das Buch nie als solches erschien. Dennoch steht außer Frage, dass es von Boogert als umfassendes und praktisches Malhandbuch konzipiert war, das bei der Kolorierung von Stichen und beim Zeichnen nach der Natur hilfreich sein sollte, während der Text auch Ratschläge für die Herstellung von Farben enthält. Das mag die prominente Abbildung eines Schmetterlings auf der Titelseite erklären, eines Symbols für die Vielfalt der Farben in der Natur, und auch die Ikonografie des Frontispizes, das einen Künstler (oder Kupferstecher) beim Kopieren eines großen Porträtgemäldes zeigt, hinter dem ein Assistent mit einem Mahlstein Pigmente zubereitet, während eine weitere Person bereitsteht, um die Farbe auf eine Palette zu übertragen. Boogerts Buch war in seiner Gestaltung vielleicht zu komplex für das Druckwesen des späten 17. Jahrhunderts, doch es trifft mit Sicherheit den Nerv der digitalen und sozialen Medienwelt des 21. Jahrhunderts.

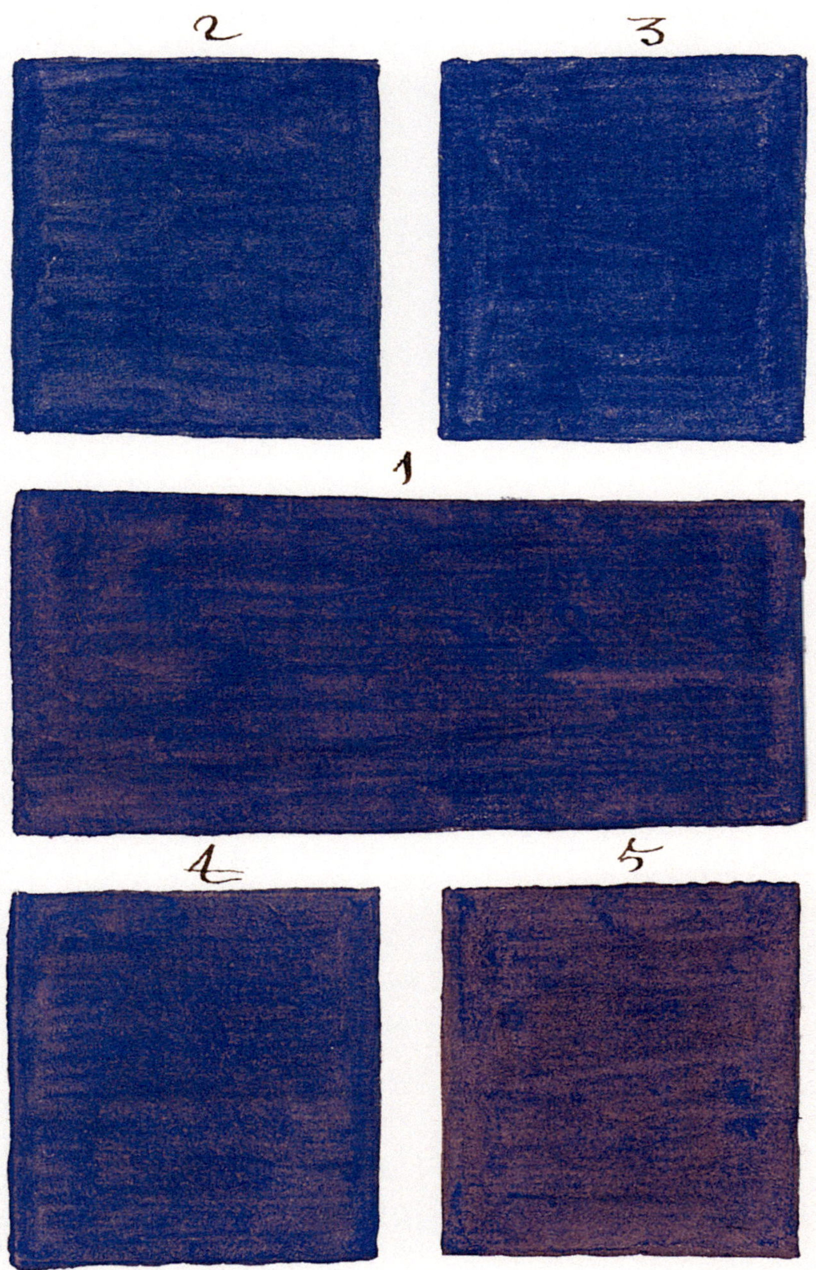
2
3
1
4
5

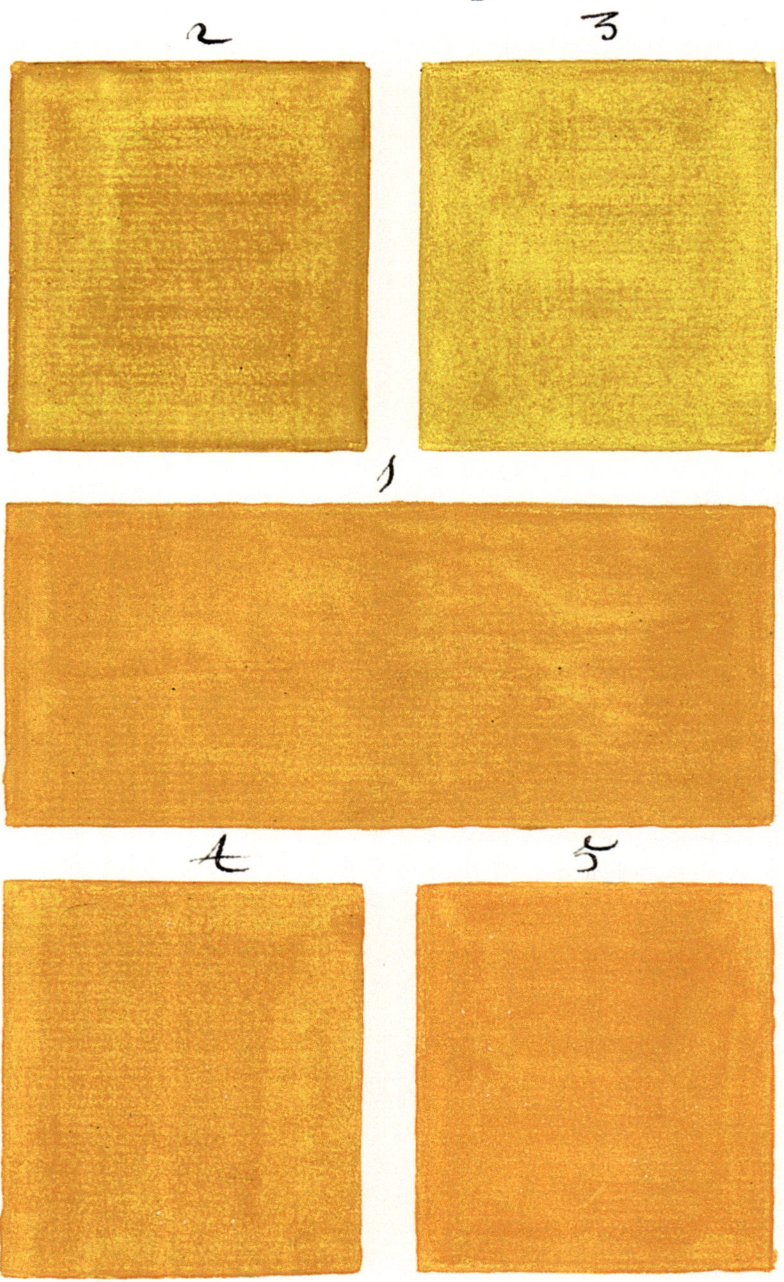
2
3
1
4
5

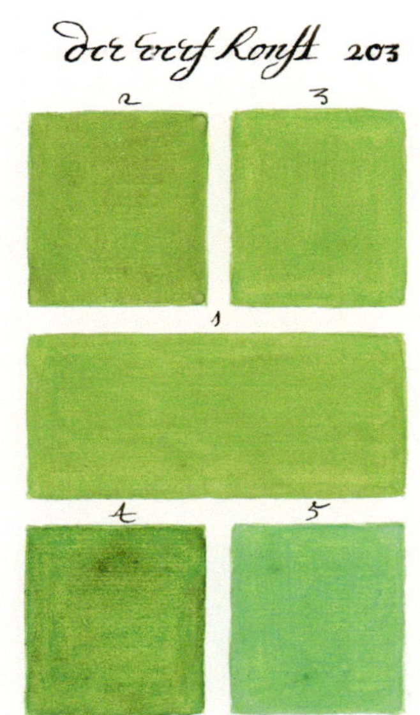


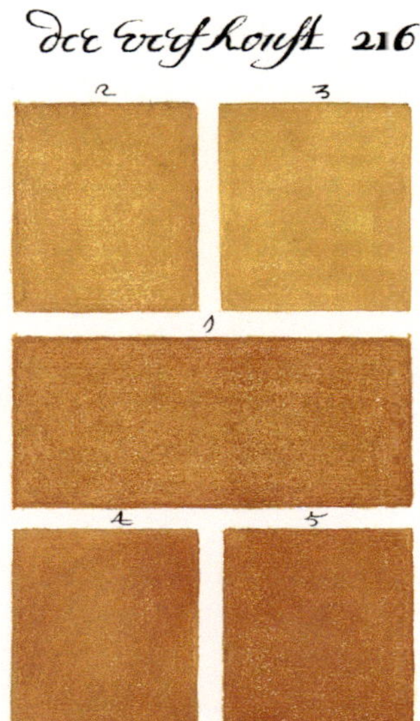


## Miroir bien éclairé de la peinture

Il s'agit là d'un des plus beaux ouvrages primitifs sur la couleur ayant survécu. Pourtant, il constitue une énigme car, en l'état actuel des connaissances, il n'a jamais été publié. Il n'en existe qu'un manuscrit rédigé à Delft en 1692, comprenant près de 900 pages avec un texte en néerlandais à l'écriture élégante, presque chaque page étant illustrée d'échantillons de couleurs à l'aquarelle et à la gouache. Le nom de l'auteur, A. Boogert, dont on ne sait rien d'autre, figure sur la page de titre et à la fin de l'introduction. Ce manuscrit relié aux dimensions relativement réduites est conservé à la bibliothèque Méjanes d'Aix-en-Provence depuis de nombreuses années. Mais ce n'est qu'en 2014 que l'historien du livre Erik Kwakkel l'a mis en lumière sur les réseaux sociaux. Depuis lors, l'ouvrage fascine les spécialistes, les bibliophiles, les graphistes et les historiens de la couleur et fait l'objet de nombreuses recherches universitaires, bien que fort peu d'études aient été publiées jusqu'ici à son sujet. Ce manuscrit a été comparé à des guides chromatiques réalisés par des fabricants de peintures de la même époque. Il est certes tentant d'y voir un catalogue de couleurs destiné aux illustrateurs du XVIIe siècle, ou une liste des peintures disponibles à Delft dans les années 1690. Pourtant, son histoire et sa destination véritables pourraient bien être plus complexes. C'est un objet hors du commun, principalement en raison de ces échantillons de couleurs vives fort bien conservés, peints à même le papier, mais aussi pour la simplicité abstraite et remarquablement moderne de sa mise en page. Ces échantillons sont tous présentés sous forme de carrés ou de

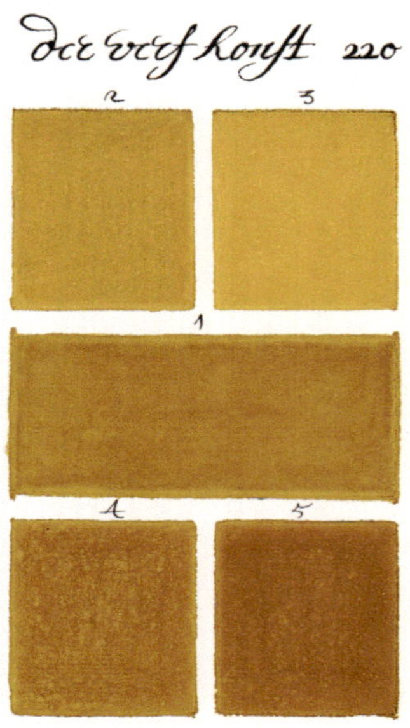


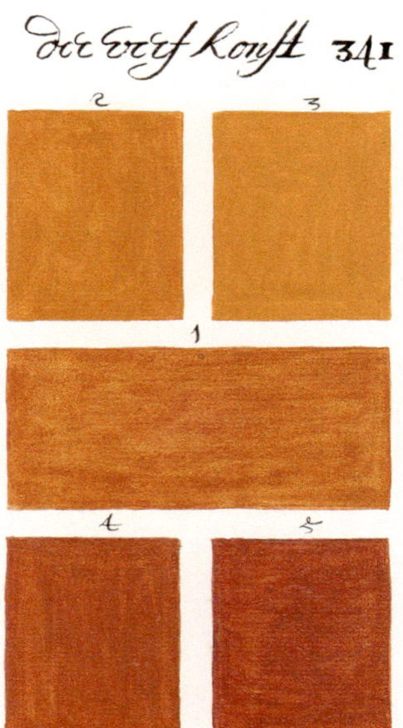


rectangles bien délimités qui remplissent la plupart des pages illustrées : la première section de 42 pages, à raison d'une teinte par page selon trois états de dilution, est suivie de 323 planches de couleurs avec cinq nuances, pour un total de 1 615 échantillons. Un « registre » de couleurs complète le manuscrit.

Boogert présente cette œuvre à la manière d'un livre achevé et imprimé, dont il répète le titre *Klaer Lightende Spiegel der Verfkonst* (littéralement, « Miroir bien éclairé de la peinture », ou encore « Réflexion éclairée sur la peinture ») en haut de chaque double page illustrée, signe que son auteur avait bien l'intention de le voir publié. Il est difficile d'imaginer comment les planches auraient pu être reproduites par impression à cette époque, raison possible pour laquelle l'ouvrage n'a jamais paru. Néanmoins, il est évident que Boogert souhaitait en faire un précis complet et pratique sur la peinture, qui soit utile pour colorier des gravures et des dessins effectués d'après nature et qui s'accompagne d'un texte comportant des conseils sur la manière de préparer les peintures. Ceci expliquerait la présence sur la page de titre d'une grande image de papillon, symbole des complexités chromatiques du monde naturel, ainsi que l'iconographie du frontispice : on y voit un peintre (ou un graveur) occupé à copier un grand portrait, derrière lequel un assistant prépare un pigment en le concassant avec un pilon, tandis qu'un autre personnage attend de transférer la couleur sur une palette. Peut-être la conception de l'ouvrage de Boogert était-elle trop complexe pour les techniques d'impression du XVIIe siècle. Elle semble plus en phase avec le monde numérique et les réseaux sociaux du XXIe siècle.

der verf Konst 

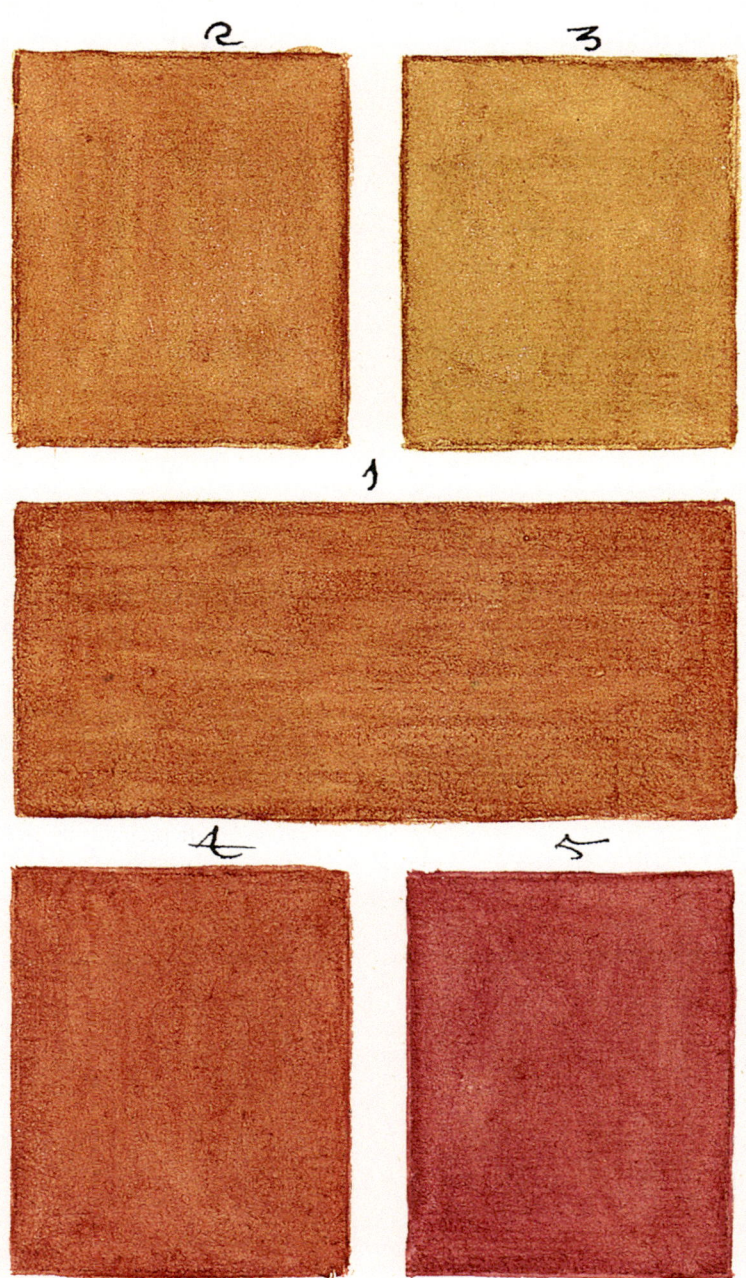

# Regisster.

N1: Bij fol: 25:

N1: Bij fol: 26:

N1: Bij fol 27:

N1: Bij fol: 28:

N1: Bij fol: 29

N1: Bij fol: 30:

N1 Bij fol: 31:

N1: Bij fol: 32:

N1: Bij fol: 33:

N1: Bij fol: 34:

N1: Bij fol: 35:

N1: Bij fol: 36:

# Register.

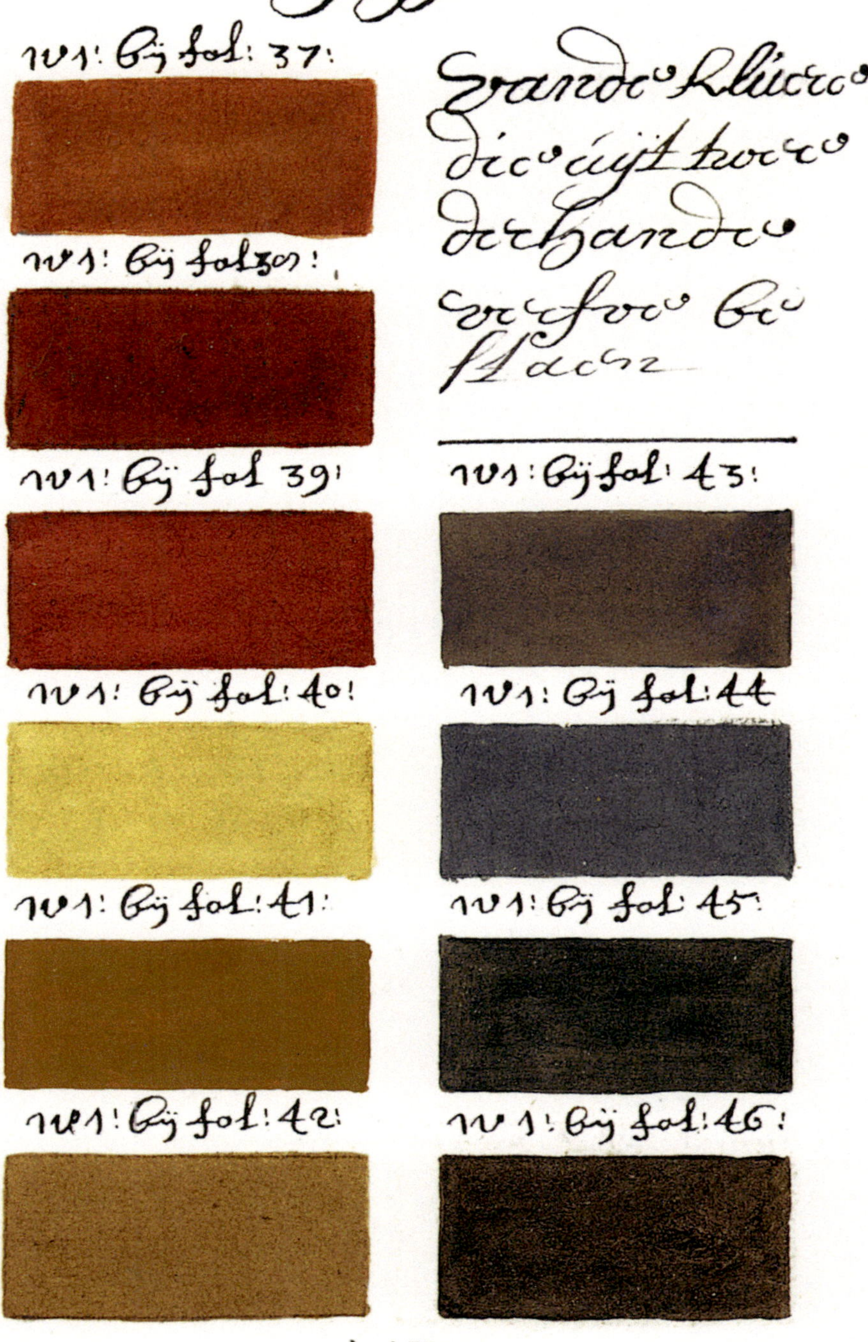


A:1:X:

# Regisster.

N1: Bij fol: 141:

N1: Bij fol: 142:

N1: Bij fol: 143:

N1: Bij fol: 144:

N1: Bij fol: 145:

N1: Bij fol: 146:

N1: Bij fol: 147:

N1: Bij fol: 148:

N1: Bij fol: 149:

waer de kleure
die door lack
moet worde
getempert

N1: Bij fol: 150:

N1: Bij fol: 151:

# Regisster.

N1: Bij fol: 311:

N1: Bij fol: 316:

N1: Bij fol: 312:

N1: Bij fol: 317:

N1: Bij fol: 313:

N1: Bij fol: 318

Vande kleuren die door sap groen worden getempert

N1: Bij fol: 319:

N1: Bij fol: 314

N1: Bij fol: 320

N1: Bij fol: 315

N1: Bij fol: 321:

# Registter.

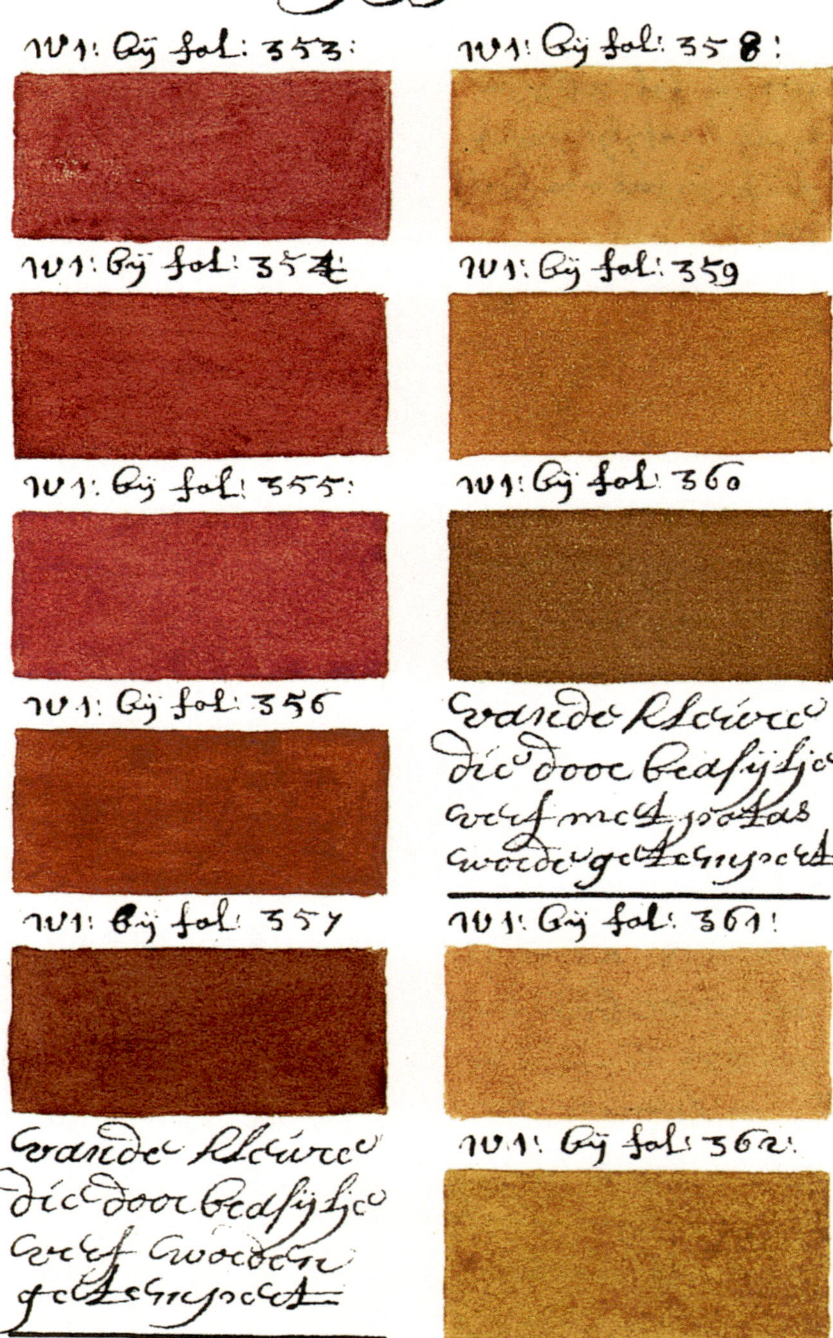

N 1: Bij fol: 353:

N 1: Bij fol: 354

N 1: Bij fol: 355:

N 1: Bij fol: 356

N 1: Bij fol: 357

van de kleure
die door bedsijde
verf worden
getenyseert

N 1: Bij fol: 358:

N 1: Bij fol: 359

N 1: Bij fol: 360

van de kleure
die door bedsijde
verf met potas
worde getenyseert

N 1: Bij fol: 361!

N 1: Bij fol: 362:

# Regisster.

N1: bij fol: 289:

van de kleuren
die door saffe
raen worde
getempert

N1: bij fol: 290

N1: bij fol: 291:

N1: bij fol: 292:

N1: bij fol: 293

N1: bij fol: 294:

N1: bij fol: 295:

N1: bij fol: 296:

N1: bij fol: 297:

N1: bij fol: 298:

N1: bij fol: 299:

## Johann Ferdinand von Schönfeld (1750–1821)

# WIENER FARBENKABINET

## oder vollständiges Musterbuch aller Natur-, Grund- und Zusammensetzungsfarben

### A Viennese Cabinet of Colours

*10 plates, 24.1 x 21 cm / 9 ½ x 8 ¼ in., Vienna, Prague, 1794*
*Washington, D.C., Smithsonian Libraries*

To appreciate the scope of this extraordinary book about colour it is instructive to look further at its long and detailed full title: "a complete book of samples of all natural, basic and combined colours, how these have been perceived since painting was invented through until the present day, containing 5,000 painted samples after nature, and with a name assigned to each (...) followed by a detailed description of all colour secrets, for dyeing silk (etc. ...) for use by all naturalists, parents and teachers, painters, dyers, printers, manufacturers, artists and craftspeople, and any other persons who deal with colour". This ambitious range of purpose and content of what is essentially a colour manual was perhaps only matched by Michel-Eugène Chevreul's publications nearly half a century later (pp. 216–237).

This is a large-format, two-volume work with more than 430 pages of text, and yet the identity of the author remains unknown, and von Schönfeld was in fact the publisher. From the introduction it seems possible that the text was put together as a collaborative effort by members of the Viennese Academy of Fine Arts, and perhaps their associates. The text itself is divided into 14 sections, beginning with essays on the colours black, blue, yellow, red, green, brown and white, relating to the colours themselves and as used by painters, printers, dyers and various other people working with crafts. There are further sections on watercolours and inks, miniature painting, painting materials and techniques, as well as recipes for lacquers and other finishes, followed by an extensive index ("Real-Register").

A simple table for mixing colours appears on page 264 of volume 1, similar to the later *Farb-Tabelle* by Johann Heinrich Meynier, but the tables that make the *Farbenkabinet* so very special are attached at the end of volume 2, where there are dozens of plates each with etched grids of 48 boxes, on to which narrow hand-painted colour strips have been pasted, following the colour range discussed previously. The exact number of plates that were intended

# Sechste Stammtafel. Blauschwärzliche und blaue Farben.

| Nr. 241. Tiefstahlblau. | Nr. 257. Schöndunkelblau. | Nr. 273. Himmelblau. |
|---|---|---|
| Nr. 242. Finsterstahlblau. | Nr. 258. Starklasurblau. | Nr. 274. Lebhaftblau. |
| Nr. 243. Dunkelstahlblau. | Nr. 259. Kräftiglasurblau. | Nr. 275. Himmelschön. |
| Nr. 244. Starkstahlblau. | Nr. 260. Gemeinlasurblau. | Nr. 276. Saphirblau. |
| Nr. 245. Kräftigstahlblau. | Nr. 261. Ganzlasurblau. | Nr. 277. Lieblichblau. |
| Nr. 246. Vollstahlblau. | Nr. 262. Mittellasurblau. | Nr. 278. Sanftblau. |
| Nr. 247. Ganzstahlblau. | Nr. 263. Kornblumenblau. | Nr. 279. Feinblau. |
| Nr. 248. Gemeinstahlblau. | Nr. 264. Helllasurblau. | Nr. 280. Lichtblau. |
| Nr. 249. Mittelstahlblau. | Nr. 265. Lichtlasurblau. | Nr. 281. Hellblau. |
| Nr. 250. Stahlblau. | Nr. 266. Mattlasurblau. | Nr. 282. Blaßblau. |
| Nr. 251. Hellstahlblau. | Nr. 267. Schwachlasurblau. | Nr. 283. Zartblau. |
| Nr. 252. Lichtstahlblau. | Nr. 268. Blaßlasurblau. | Nr. 284. Bleichblau. |
| Nr. 253. Mattstahlblau. | Nr. 269. Bleichlasurblau. | Nr. 285. Wasserfarbe. |
| Nr. 254. Blaßstahlblau. | Nr. 270. Hochlasurblau. | Nr. 286. Diamantfarbe. |
| Nr. 255. Bleichstahlblau. | Nr. 271. Weißlichlasurblau. | Nr. 287. Blaulichweiß. |
| Nr. 256. Weißlichstahlblau. | Nr. 272. Höchsteslasurblau. | Nr. 288. Weißblau. |

Wiener

# Farbenkabinet;

oder

## vollständiges Musterbuch

aller

### Natur- Grund- und Zusammensetzungsfarben,

wie solche
seit Erfindung der Malerei bis auf gegenwärtige Zeiten
gesehen worden,
mit

**fünftausend nach der Natur gemalten Abbildungen,**

und der Bestimmung des Namens einer jeden Farbe,
dann

**einer ausführlichen Beschreibung aller Farbengeheimnisse, in**

Seide- Baum- und Schafwolle, Lein- Leder- Rauch- und Pelzwaaren, Papier,
Holz und Bein, u. s. w., schön und dauerhaft zu färben.

Herausgegeben
zum
Gebrauche aller Naturforscher, Eltern und Erzieher, Maler, Färber, Drucker,
Fabrikanten, Künstler und Handwerker, und überhaupt aller Menschen,
die sich mit Farben beschäftigen.

Wien und Prag,
im Verlage der v. Schönfeldschen Handlung, 1794.

to be included cannot be stated for certain as only a handful of copies of the *Farbenkabinet* survive in public libraries worldwide, and none seem complete. Based on the figure of 5,000 colour samples given on the book's title-pages, this would correspond to 105 plates; the Smithsonian Libraries copy, a selection of plates from which are shown here, contains 54 plates, making a total of 2,592 colour samples. Leafing through these pages with their thousands of strips of colour painted and pasted in more than 200 years ago is a bewildering optical experience, not dissimilar in its way to looking at modern abstract paintings by Bridget Riley (b. 1931) or Frank Stella (1936–2024). The *Farbenkabinet* is a book of superlatives, and solid proof that by the end of the 18th century colour had become properly respected as an important element of the arts, design, manufacture and education.

# Zehnte Stammtafel. Blaurothe Farben.

| | | |
|---|---|---|
| Nr. 433. Hyacinthenblau. | Nr. 449. Dunkellila. | Nr. 465. Dunkelpfirsichblüthroth. |
| Nr. 434. Gemeinhyacinthenblau. | Nr. 450. Starklila. | Nr. 466. Starkpfirsichblüthroth. |
| Nr. 435. Mittelhyacinthenblau. | Nr. 451. Kräftiglila. | Nr. 467. Kräftigpfirsichblüthroth. |
| Nr. 436. Ganzhyacinthenblau. | Nr. 452. Vollila. | Nr. 468. Vollpfirsichblüthroth. |
| Nr. 437. Hellhyacinthenblau. | Nr. 453. Ganzlila. | Nr. 469. Ganzpfirsichblüthroth. |
| Nr. 438. Lichthyacinthenblau. | Nr. 454. Gemeinlila. | Nr. 470. Gemeinpfirsichblüthroth. |
| Nr. 439. Schwachhyacinthenblau. | Nr. 455. Mittellila. | Nr. 471. Mittelpfirsichblüthroth. |
| Nr. 440. Cichorienblau. | Nr. 456. Lila. | Nr. 472. Pfirsichblüthroth. |
| Nr. 441. Hellcichorienblau. | Nr. 457. Helllila. | Nr. 473. Hellpfirsichblüthroth. |
| Nr. 442. Lichtcichorienblau. | Nr. 458. Lichtlila. | Nr. 474. Lichtpfirsichblüthroth. |
| Nr. 443. Blaßcichorienblau. | Nr. 459. Blaßlila. | Nr. 475. Blaßpfirsichblüthroth. |
| Nr. 444. Bleichcichorienblau. | Nr. 460. Bleichlila. | Nr. 476. Bleichpfirsichblüthroth. |
| Nr. 445. Mattcichorienblau. | Nr. 461. Schwachlila. | Nr. 477. Schwachpfirsichblüthroth. |
| Nr. 446. Schwachcichorienblau. | Nr. 462. Mattlila. | Nr. 478. Mattpfirsichblüthroth. |
| Nr. 447. Hochcichorienblau. | Nr. 463. Hochlila. | Nr. 479. Hochpfirsichblüthroth. |
| Nr. 448. Höchstescichorienblau. | Nr. 464. Höchsteslila. | Nr. 480. Höchstespfirsichblüthroth. |

## Wiener Farbenkabinet

Um die Reichweite dieses außergewöhnlichen Buches über Farbe würdigen zu können, hilft ein Blick auf seinen detailreichen Titel: „Musterbuch aller Natur-, Grund- und Zusammensetzungsfarben, wie solche seit Erfindung der Malerei bis auf gegenwärtige Zeiten gesehen worden, mit fünftausend nach der Natur gemalten Abbildungen, und der Bestimmung des Namens einer jeden Farbe, dann einer ausführlichen Beschreibung aller Farbengeheimnisse, in Seide [...] u. s. w. [...] zu färben. Herausgegeben zum Gebrauche aller Naturforscher, Eltern und Erzieher, Maler, Färber, Drucker, Fabrikanten, Künstler und Handwerker, und überhaupt aller Menschen, die sich mit Farben beschäftigen." An diese ambitionierte Fülle von Absichten und Inhalten eines eigentlichen Farbhandbuchs kamen vermutlich nur Michel-Eugène Chevreuls Publikationen knapp fünfzig Jahre später heran (S. 216–237).

Der Verfasser dieses großformatigen zweibändigen Werks mit mehr als 430 Textseiten ist unbekannt. Schönfeld war de facto der Herausgeber. Der Einleitung nach scheint es möglich, dass der Text von Migliedern der Wiener vereinigten Akademie der bildenden Künste und deren Mitarbeitern zusammengestellt wurde. Er ist in 14 Abschnitte unterteilt und beginnt mit Abhandlungen über die Farben Schwarz, Blau, Gelb, Rot, Grün, Braun und Weiß, in denen die Farben an sich und ihre Verwendung durch Maler, Drucker, Färber und andere Künstler und Handwerker erörtert werden. Weitere Abschnitte sind den Wasserfarben und Tuschen, der Miniaturmalerei, Malmaterialien und -techniken sowie Rezepten für Lacke und andere Firnisse gewidmet, gefolgt von einem ausführlichen „Real-Register".

Eine Tafel zur Farbenmischung, die der späteren *Farb-Tabelle* von Johann Heinrich Meynier ähnelt, erscheint in Band 1 auf Seite 264. Die Tafeln aber, die das *Farbenkabinet* so besonders machen, sind am Ende des zweiten Bandes angehängt, wo schmale, handbemalte Farbstreifen, die dem Farbspektrum folgen, auf Dutzende gestochene Raster mit jeweils 48 Kästchen aufgeklebt wurden. Die genaue Anzahl der ursprünglich geplanten Farbtafeln ist nicht sicher zu bestimmen, da die nur wenigen, in öffentlichen Bibliotheken erhaltenen Exemplare des *Farbenkabinets* alle unvollständig sind. Legt man die fünftausend im Titel genannten Farbmuster zugrunde, dann müsste es 105 Tafeln geben. Das Exemplar der Smithsonian Libraries, aus dem hier einige Tafeln gezeigt werden, enthält 54 Tafeln mit insgesamt 2.592 Mustern. Diese Seiten mit ihren abertausend vor mehr als zweihundert Jahren bemalten und eingeklebten Farbstreifen durchzublättern, ist ein verblüffendes optisches Erlebnis und der Betrachtung moderner abstrakter Gemälde von Bridget Riley (geb. 1931) oder Frank Stella (1936–2024) nicht unähnlich. Das *Farbenkabinet* ist ein Beweis dafür, dass Farbe im ausgehenden 18. Jahrhundert als wichtiges Element in Kunst, Gestaltung, Industrie und Bildung hoch geschätzt wurde.

# Einundzwanzigste Stammtafel. Schwach rothe Farben.

| | | |
|---|---|---|
| Nr. 961. Dunkelkupferroth. | Nr. 977. Dunkelschönziegelroth. | Nr. 993. Dunkelbolus. |
| Nr. 962. Starkkupferroth. | Nr. 978. Starkschönziegelroth. | Nr. 994. Starkbolus. |
| Nr. 963. Kräftigkupferroth. | Nr. 979. Kräftigschönziegelroth. | Nr. 995. Kräftigbolus. |
| Nr. 964. Vollkupferroth. | Nr. 980. Vollschönziegelroth. | Nr. 996. Vollbolus. |
| Nr. 965. Ganzkupferroth. | Nr. 981. Ganzschönziegelroth. | Nr. 997. Ganzbolus. |
| Nr. 966. Gemeinkupferroth. | Nr. 982. Gemeinschönziegelroth. | Nr. 998. Gemeinerbolus. |
| Nr. 967. Mittelkupferroth. | Nr. 983. Mittelschönziegelroth. | Nr. 999. Mittelbolus. |
| Nr. 968. Kupferroth. | Nr. 984. Schönziegelroth. | Nr. 1000. Bolus. |
| Nr. 969. Hellkupferroth. | Nr. 985. Hellschönziegelroth. | Nr. 1001. Hellbolus. |
| Nr. 970. Lichtkupferroth. | Nr. 986. Lichtschönziegelroth. | Nr. 1002. Lichterbolus. |
| Nr. 971. Schwachkupferroth. | Nr. 987. Schwachschönziegelroth. | Nr. 1003. Schwachbolus. |
| Nr. 972. Mattkupferroth. | Nr. 988. Mattziegelschönroth. | Nr. 1004. Matterbolus. |
| Nr. 973. Blaßkupferroth. | Nr. 989. Blaßschönziegelroth | Nr. 1005. Blaßerbolus. |
| Nr. 974. Bleichkupferroth. | Nr. 990. Bleichschönziegelroth. | Nr. 1006. Bleicherbolus. |
| Nr. 975. Hochkupferroth. | Nr. 991. Hochschönziegelroth. | Nr. 1007. Hochbolus. |
| Nr. 976. Höchsteskupferroth. | Nr. 992. Höchstesschönziegelroth. | Nr. 1008. Höchstesbolus. |

# Siebenunddreißigste Stammtafel. Gelbgrünliche Farben.

| | | |
|---|---|---|
| Nr. 1729. Tieffrühlingsgrün. | Nr. 1745. Dunkelgranatengrün. | Nr. 1761. Dunkelgrünlichgelb. |
| Nr. 1730. Dunkelfrühlingsgrün. | Nr. 1746. Starkgranatengrün. | Nr. 1762. Starkgrünlichgelb. |
| Nr. 1731. Starkfrühlingsgrün. | Nr. 1747. Kräftiggranatengrün. | Nr. 1763. Kräftiggrunlichgelb. |
| Nr. 1732. Kräftigfrühlingsgrün. | Nr. 1748. Vollgranatengrün. | Nr. 1764. Vollgrünlichgelb. |
| Nr. 1733. Vollfrühlingsgrün. | Nr. 1749. Ganzgranatengrün. | Nr. 1765. Ganzgrünlichgelb. |
| Nr. 1734. Ganzfrühliugsgrün. | Nr. 1750. Gemeingranatengrün. | Nr. 1766. Gemeingrünlichgelb. |
| Nr. 1735. Gemeinfrühlingsgrün. | Nr. 1751. Mittelgranatengrün. | Nr. 1767. Mittelgrünlichgelb. |
| Nr. 1736. Mittelfrühlingsgrün. | Nr. 1752. Granatengrün. | Nr. 1768. Grünlichgelb. |
| Nr. 1737. Frühlingsgrün. | Nr. 1753. Hellgranatengrün. | Nr. 1769. Hellgrünlichgelb. |
| Nr. 1738. Hellfrühlingsgrün. | Nr. 1754. Lichtgranatengrün. | Nr. 1770. Lichtgrünlichgelb. |
| Nr. 1739. Lichtfrühlingsgrün. | Nr. 1755. Schwachgranatengrün. | Nr. 1771. Schwachgrünlichgelb. |
| Nr. 1740. Schwachfrühlingsgrün. | Nr. 1756. Mattgranatengrün. | Nr. 1772. Mattgrünlichgelb. |
| Nr. 1741. Mattfrühlingsgrün | Nr. 1757. Blaßgranatengrün. | Nr. 1773. Blaßgrünlichgelb. |
| Nr. 1742. Blaßfrühlingsgrün. | Nr. 1758. Bleichgranatengrün. | Nr. 1774. Bleichgrünlichgelb. |
| Nr. 1743. Bleichfrühlingsgrün. | Nr. 1759. Hochgranatengrün. | Nr. 1775. Hochgrünlichgelb. |
| Nr. 1744. Hochfrühlingsgrün. | Nr. 1760. Höchstesgranateugrün. | Nr. 1776. Höchstesgrünlichgelb. |

## Cabinet des couleurs viennois

Pour bien saisir l'envergure de ce livre extraordinaire, il est utile de prêter attention à son titre : « Cabinet de couleurs viennois, ou Ouvrage complet d'échantillons de toutes les couleurs naturelles, fondamentales et combinées, comment celles-ci sont perçues depuis l'invention de la peinture jusqu'à nos jours, avec 5 000 échantillons peints d'après nature, chacun portant une désignation [...] suivis d'une description détaillée de tous les secrets de la couleur, pour la teinture de la soie [etc. ...] à l'usage de tous les naturalistes, parents et professeurs, peintres, teinturiers, imprimeurs, fabricants, peintres et artisans et toute personne faisant usage de la couleur. » L'ambition des objectifs et du contenu de ce qui est essentiellement un manuel des couleurs n'a peut-être trouvé d'équivalent qu'avec les publications de Chevreul, près d'un demi-siècle plus tard (p. 216–237).

Il s'agit d'un ouvrage de grand format, en deux volumes, avec plus de 430 pages de texte, mais dont l'auteur demeure inconnu. L'introduction laisse penser que le texte est dû à un collectif de membres de l'École des beaux-arts de Vienne et, peut-être, de confrères. Divisé en 14 sections, le texte s'ouvre par des essais dédiés aux couleurs noir, bleu, jaune, rouge, vert, brun et blanc, portant sur la nature de ces couleurs et leur emploi par les peintres, les imprimeurs, les teinturiers et autres artisans. Suivent des sections traitant des aquarelles et des encres, de la miniature, des techniques et matériaux picturaux, des recettes de laques et autres matériaux de finition, ainsi qu'un index exhaustif.

La page 264 du volume 1 figure un simple tableau pour le mélange des couleurs, semblable à la *Farb-Tabelle* que concevra plus tard Johann Heinrich Meynier. Mais ce sont les tableaux en fin du volume 2 qui font du *Farbenkabinet* un ouvrage si singulier. Il s'agit de dizaines de planches illustrées à l'eau-forte, comprenant chacune une grille de 48 cases, sur lesquelles de fines bandes de couleurs peintes à la main ont été collées, selon la gamme chromatique évoquée plus haut. Il est impossible de mentionner le nombre exact de planches qui devaient composer l'ouvrage car il ne reste que très peu d'exemplaires du *Farbenkabinet*, conservés dans des bibliothèques publiques du monde entier, mais dont aucun ne semble complet. Le chiffre de 5000 échantillons figurant sur les pages de titre laisse penser qu'il devait y avoir 105 planches. L'exemplaire des Bibliothèques de la Smithsonian Institution, dont proviennent les planches reproduites ici, en comporte 54, pour un total de 2 592 échantillons. Contempler ces pages et leurs milliers de bandes de papier est une expérience optique stupéfiante, qui n'est pas sans rappeler l'effet produit par les peintures abstraites de Bridget Riley (née en 1931) ou de Frank Stella (1936–2024). Le *Farbenkabinet* est la preuve tangible qu'à la fin du XVIII^e^ siècle, la couleur s'est désormais acquis le respect qui lui est dû comme élément essentiel des arts, du dessin, de la fabrication et de l'éducation.

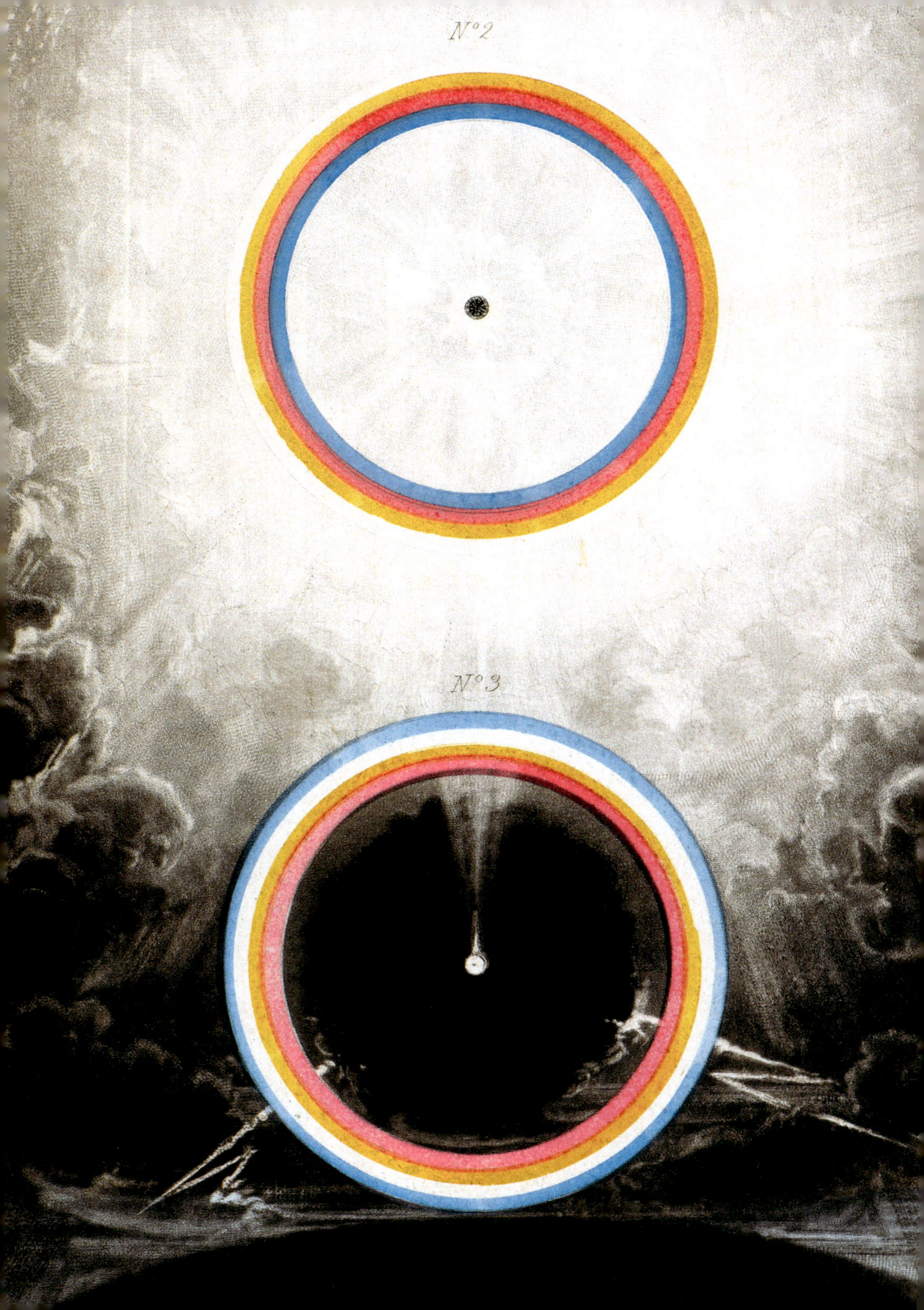
N° 2
N° 3

Chapter 2

# *The Shape of Colour:* CIRCLES, WHEELS AND GLOBES

1708–1896

## Attributed to Claude Boutet (dates unknown)

# TRAITÉ DE LA PEINTURE EN MIGNATURE

### A Treatise on Painting in Miniature

*2 plates, 15.5 x 8.6 cm / 6 ⅛ x 3 ⅜ in., The Hague, 1708*
*Winterthur, Stadtbibliothek, Farbsammlung Werner Spillmann*

The pair of diagrams shown here are perhaps the first colour wheels actually to appear in colour in western print culture. They were published just four years after Isaac Newton's uncoloured wheel and were likely influenced by that form on the basis of their circular design, although they are also something of a mystery. They appear in some copies of a substantial practical handbook on colour, *Traité de la peinture en mignature*, which included when it was published in 1708 a small section on painting in pastel, "Traité de la peinture au pastel". The main part of the text was first published in around 1673 and is often attributed to the French painter Claude Boutet, but this is not certain, and furthermore it may not have been Boutet who created these plates, which appear only in some of the later editions. Aside from such questions of authorship, the book contains detailed recipes and advice on how to prepare pigments and use colours when painting portraits, landscapes, flowers and other subjects. In that respect it doesn't differ greatly from other 17th- and 18th-century artists' manuals, but the carefully designed and hand-coloured engravings depicting the colour wheels are very special. Their presence in a handbook for artists, and the added figurative scenes beneath the wheels showing allegorical putti as portrait painters, makes clear that their purpose is to illustrate material colour, in contrast to Newton's colour wheel which was concerned in the main with the optical spectrum. A pair of colour wheels would usually represent an attempt to visualise secondary or tertiary colour mixtures, effectively creating another layer of colour, but in this case there is no recognisable arrangement of primaries and secondaries based on the pure, unmixed colours of red, yellow and blue. The circle on the left contains seven colours, named as violet, blue, green, yellow, orange, fire red and crimson, while the circle on the right extends this scheme to a 12-colour arrangement, adding golden yellow, red, purple, sea green and yellow-green. These additional five colours are not all mixtures of the colours found in the first wheel, and indeed they include a simple red, one of the pure "primitives" mentioned in the accompanying text. The hand-colouring in the few surviving examples of this book varies considerably, which in turn adds further mystery to this pair of charming early colour wheels for painters.

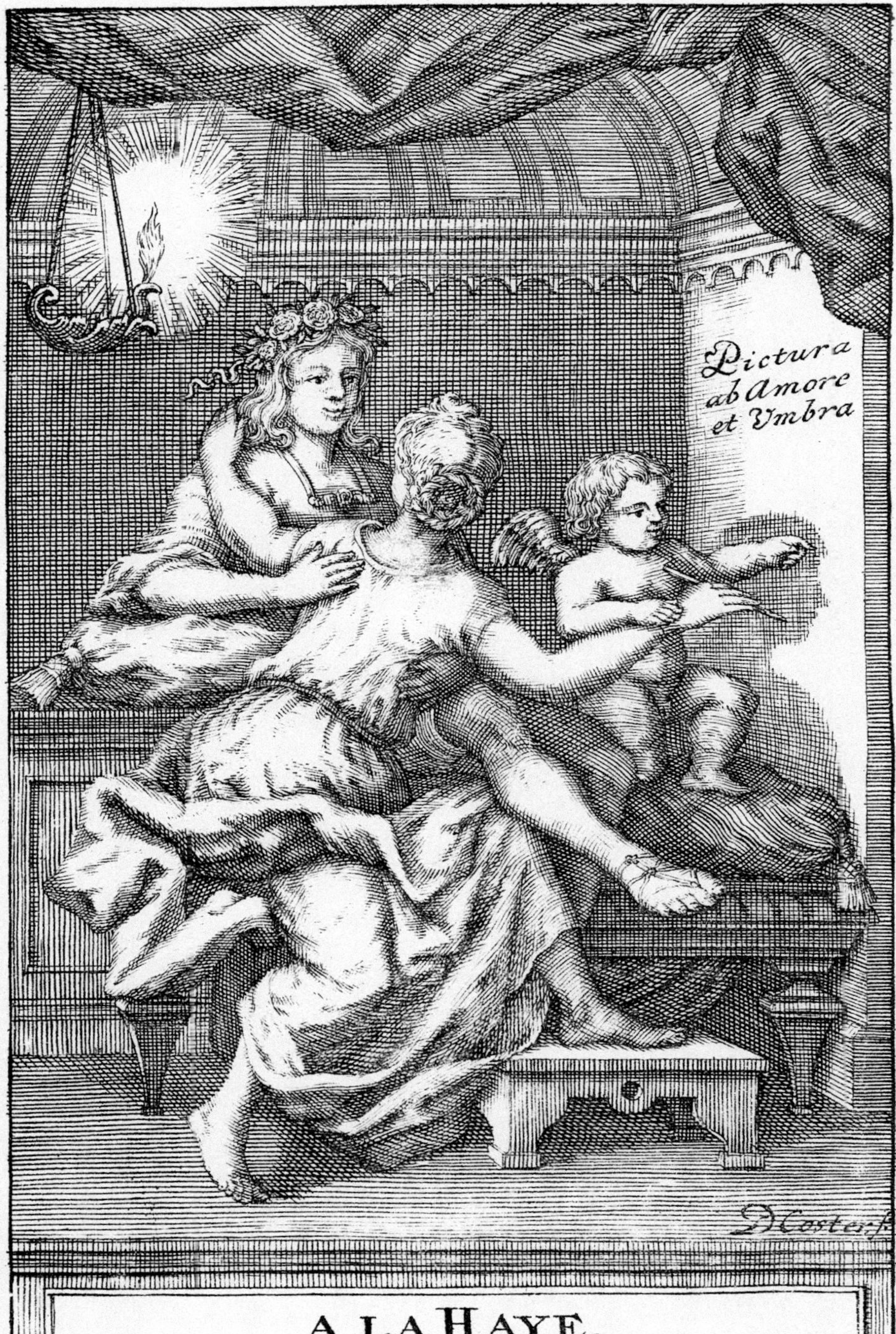
Pictura
ab Amore
et Vmbra
D. Coster f.
A LA HAYE,
Chez LOUIS & HENRY VAN DOLE.

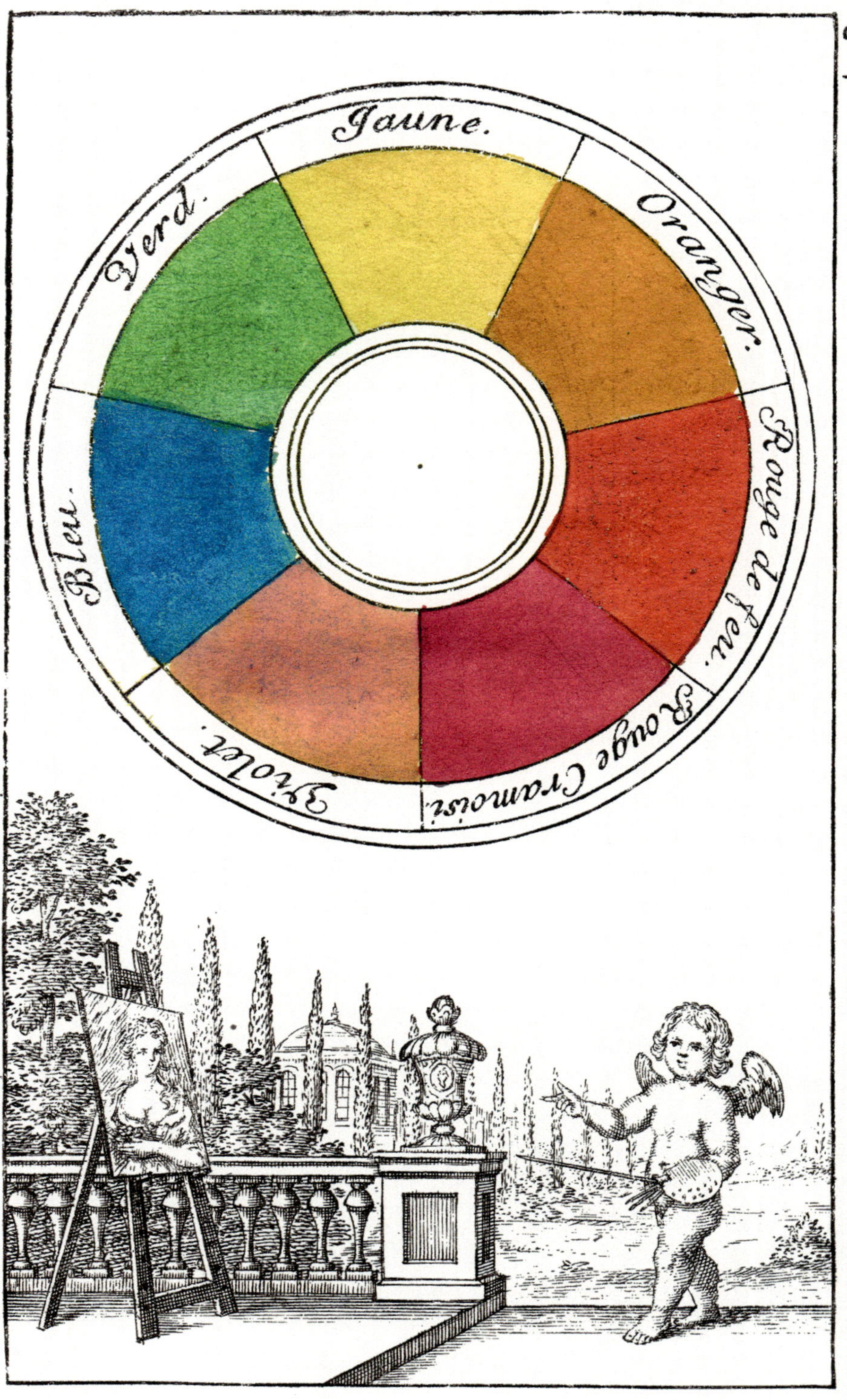
Jaune.
Oranger.
Rouge de feu.
Rouge Cramoisi
Violet.
Bleu.
Verd.

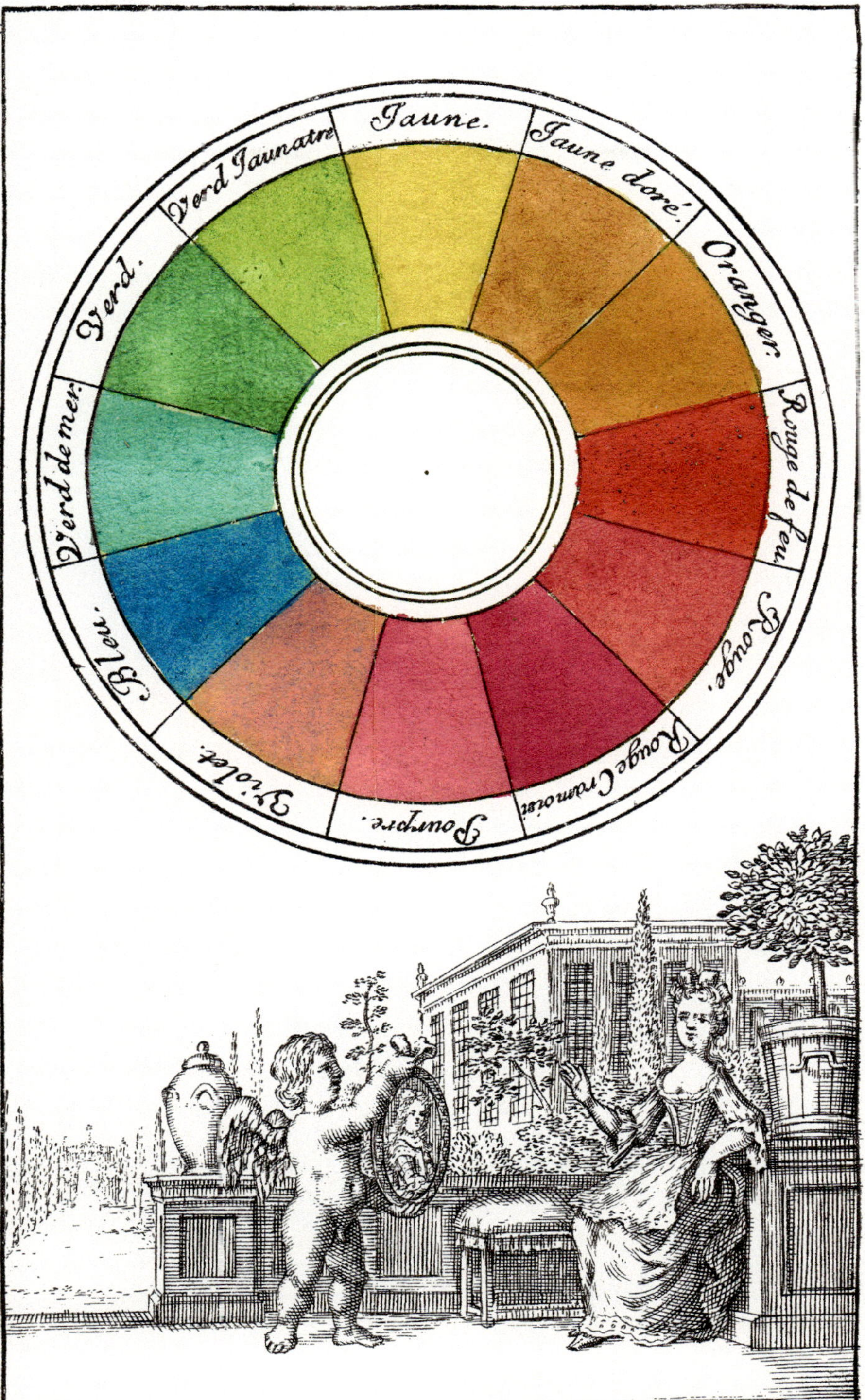

Jaune.
Jaune doré.
Oranger.
Rouge de feu.
Rouge.
Rouge Cramoisi
Pourpre.
Violet.
Bleu.
Verd de mer.
Verd.
Verd Jaunatre

## Die Kunst der Miniaturmalerei

Bei dem hier gezeigten Diagrammpaar handelt es sich um die womöglich ersten Farbkreise, die in einer westlichen Publikation tatsächlich in Farbe erschienen. Sie kamen nur vier Jahre nach Isaac Newtons nicht koloriertem Farbkreis heraus, wurden in ihrer Kreisform vermutlich von diesem beeinflusst – und geben doch auch Rätsel auf. Abgedruckt waren sie in einigen Exemplaren des praktischen Farbhandbuchs *Traité de la peinture en mignature*, das bei seiner Veröffentlichung 1708 mit „Traité de la peinture au pastel" auch einen kurzen Abschnitt über Pastellmalerei enthielt. Der Hauptteil des Textes wurde erstmals um 1673 veröffentlicht und wird häufig, wenn auch nicht mit letzter Sicherheit, dem französischen Maler Claude Boutet zugeschrieben. Auch die Tafeln, die nur in einigen späteren Auflagen vorkommen, stammen möglicherweise nicht von ihm. Abgesehen von solchen Urheberschaftsfragen sind die im Buch enthaltenen detaillierten Rezepte interessant, ebenso die Erläuterungen, wie Pigmente zuzubereiten und Farben einzusetzen sind, um Porträts, Landschaften, Blumen und andere Motive zu malen. In dieser Hinsicht unterscheidet es sich nicht sehr von anderen Künstlerhandbüchern des 17. und 18. Jahrhunderts, wären da nicht die in Kupfer gestochenen, ungewöhnlichen Abbildungen der beiden sorgfältig gestalteten und handkolorierten Farbkreise. Diese Darstellung in einem Handbuch für Künstler und die darunter eingefügten Figurenszenen, in denen allegorische Putti als Porträtmaler auftreten, machen deutlich, dass die Kreise, anders als Newtons Farbkreis, bei dem das prismatische Spektrum im Vordergrund stand, stoffliche Farben verbildlichen sollten. Ein Bild von zwei Farbkreisen stellte üblicherweise den Versuch dar, sekundäre oder tertiäre Farbmischungen abzubilden und dadurch eine weitere Farbebene zu erzeugen, doch in diesem Fall ist keine Anordnung von Primär- und Sekundärfarben auf Basis der reinen, unvermischten Farben Rot, Gelb und Blau erkennbar. Der linke Kreis enthält sieben Farben, die mit Violett, Blau, Grün, Gelb, Orange, Feuerrot und Karminrot bezeichnet sind, der rechte erweitert dieses Schema unter Hinzunahme von Goldgelb, Rot, Purpur, Meergrün und Gelbgrün auf zwölf Farben. Nicht alle fünf zusätzlichen Töne wurden aus den Farben des ersten Kreises gemischt, sogar ein einfaches Rot ist dabei, eine der im Begleittext erwähnten reinen „Urfarben". Dass die Handkoloration in den wenigen noch erhaltenen Exemplaren des Buches erheblich variiert, lässt dieses Paar früher Farbkreise für Maler noch rätselhafter erscheinen.

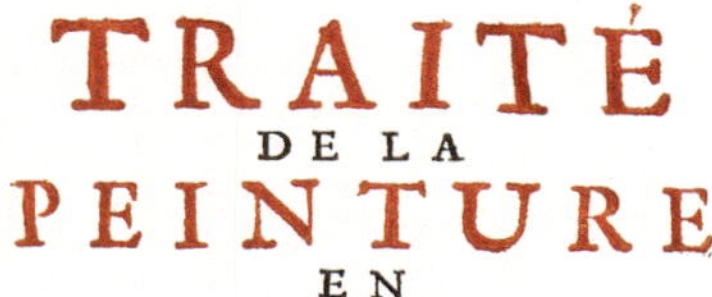

TRAITÉ
DE LA
PEINTURE
EN
MIGNATURE.

Pour apprendre aisément à Peindre sans Maître.

*Ouvrage corrigé & augmenté sur le plan de l'ancien de diverses Instructions Préliminaires sur la Peinture en général, & de Préceptes sur le Dessein pour en faciliter l'Etude & la Pratique.*

AUQUEL ON A AJOÛTÉ

Un petit Traité de la Peinture au Pastel, avec la Méthode de composer les Pastels.

*La Manière de Laver proprement toutes sortes de Plans.*

Le Secret de faire les plus belles Couleurs, l'Or Bruny, l'Or en Coquille, & le Vernis de la Chine.

*Avec une Explication par ordre Alphabétique de tous les Termes propres au Dessein & à la Peinture.*

A LA HAYE,
Chez Loüis & Henry van Dole, Marchands Libraires, dans le Pooten.

M. D. CCVIII.

## Traité de la peinture en mignature

Les deux graphiques montrés ici sont peut-être les premiers cercles chromatiques à avoir paru en couleurs dans l'histoire de l'édition occidentale. Publiés à peine quatre ans après le disque sans couleurs d'Isaac Newton, ils sont probablement influencés par cette forme, qui fonde leur conception circulaire, même s'ils conservent aussi un certain mystère. Ils apparaissent dans certains exemplaires d'un copieux manuel pratique sur la couleur, le *Traité de la peinture en mignature*, qui comprenait, à sa publication en 1708, un petit *Traité de la peinture au pastel*. La majeure partie du texte est d'abord publiée vers 1673 et souvent attribuée au peintre français Claude Boutet, mais sans certitude. De plus, Boutet ne semble pas avoir été le créateur de ces gravures, qui n'apparaissent que dans certains tirages plus tardifs. Mis à part cette question de paternité, l'ouvrage contient des recettes et conseils détaillés pour la préparation des pigments et l'utilisation des couleurs pour peindre des portraits, des paysages, des fleurs ou d autres sujets. De ce point de vue, il ressemble beaucoup à d'autres traités artistiques des XVII^e et XVIII^e siècles, mais les délicates gravures coloriées à la main pour représenter les cercles chromatiques y sont particulièrement remarquables. Leur présence dans un manuel à l'usage des artistes, et les scènes figuratives sous les cercles, où des *putti* allégoriques se font portraitistes, mettent en évidence que le propos est bien ici d'illustrer la couleur matérielle, par contraste avec le cercle chromatique de Newton, qui représente globalement le spectre visible. Les cercles chromatiques allant par deux constituent habituellement une tentative de visualisation des mélanges de couleurs secondaires et tertiaires, créant de fait une autre couche colorée ; or dans ce cas-ci, nul assemblage visible de couleurs primaires et secondaires basées sur les couleurs pures et non mélangées rouge, jaune et bleu. Le cercle de gauche contient sept couleurs (« violet, bleu, verd [*sic*], jaune, orange, rouge de feu, rouge cramoisi »), tandis que le cercle de droite enrichit la représentation jusqu'à disposer 12 teintes, en ajoutant « jaune doré, rouge, pourpre, verd [*sic*] de mer et verd-jaunatre ». Ces cinq couleurs supplémentaires ne sont pas du tout présentées comme des mélanges des couleurs appartenant au premier cercle. Elles comprennent d'ailleurs un rouge simple, l'une des couleurs « primitives » mentionnées dans le texte d'accompagnement. La coloration manuelle varie énormément d'un exemplaire à l'autre, parmi ceux qui nous sont parvenus, ce qui ajoute une touche de mystère à ces deux charmants cercles chromatiques destinés aux peintres.

## Moses Harris (1730–*c.* 1788)

# THE NATURAL SYSTEM OF COLOURS

*3 plates, 35.3 x 25.5 cm | 13 ⅞ x 10 in., London, c. 1769–1776*
*Winterthur, Stadtbibliothek, Farbsammlung Werner Spillmann*

Moses Harris was an English entomologist who wrote and illustrated this short early book with a colour system designed for painters and illustrators, while acknowledging the influence of Isaac Newton. As the continuation of his title explains, his system was intended to show the "*Regular and Beautiful Order and Arrangement, Arising from the Three Premitives* [sic], *Red, Blue, and Yellow*". No date is given in the first edition, but it was probably published between 1769 and 1776. It was dedicated to the President of the Royal Academy of Arts in London, Sir Joshua Reynolds (1723–1792), and was the first in a series of important works on colour that originated from the circle of people associated with the Royal Academy in the decades after it was founded in 1768, a fact that underlines the changing attitudes to colour at this time in art and art education.

The weighting of text (just eight pages, including the dedication) to images (two plates showing magnificent colour wheels together with charts in some copies showing examples of colour mixtures) and the aspirational design of Harris's illustrations are a clear indication of the importance he assigned to the accurate depiction of colours in the natural world. The two wheels are copperplate engravings, comprising respectively 18 sectors of "prismatic" and "compound" colour mixtures divided and numbered according to 20 degrees of intensity, with ten degrees delineated in the images. Each wheel carries a total of 360 colours. The book's subtitle however states only 660 different colours in total, as the mixtures green, orange and purple are shown in both circles. In the center of each circle are overlapping triangles of the "primitive" colours red, yellow and blue, and the "mediates" orange, green and purple, each having a black centre representing the subtractive colour mixture. A brief accompanying list of the primaries and secondaries provides equivalents of these colours from the worlds of pigments and flora.

A second, posthumous edition was published in 1811, with newly cut plates. Harris's work was widely discussed, taught and reproduced by a number of artists, teachers and scholars in the early 19th century, including Turner, Thomas Phillips and William Benjamin Sarsfield Taylor (1781–1850). In 1963 the American writer Faber Birren produced a facsimile edition of this extraordinary book and called it "perhaps the rarest known book in the literature of color". Of the orginal editions (this one and the 1811 reprint) fewer than 10 copies are currrently recorded in libraries worldwide.

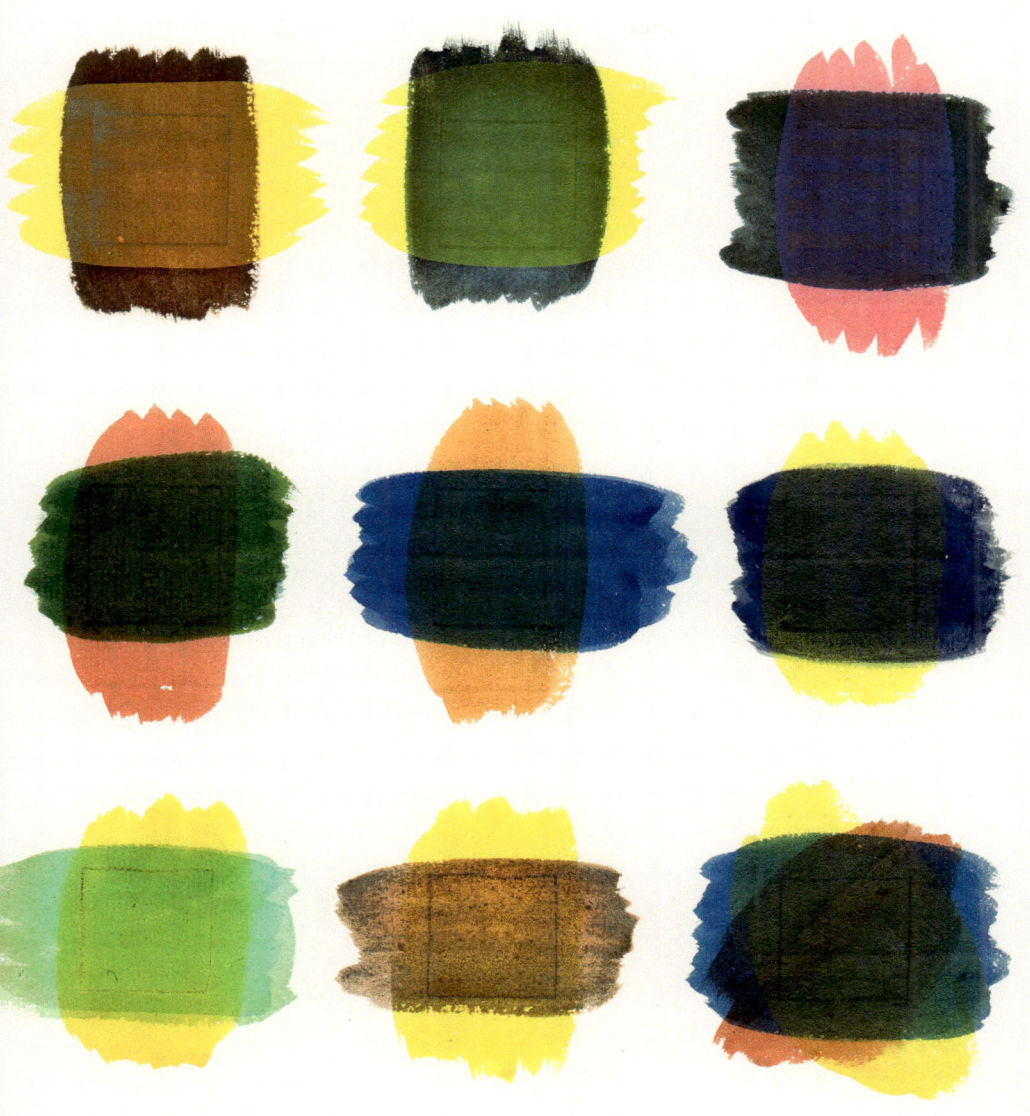

PRISMATIC

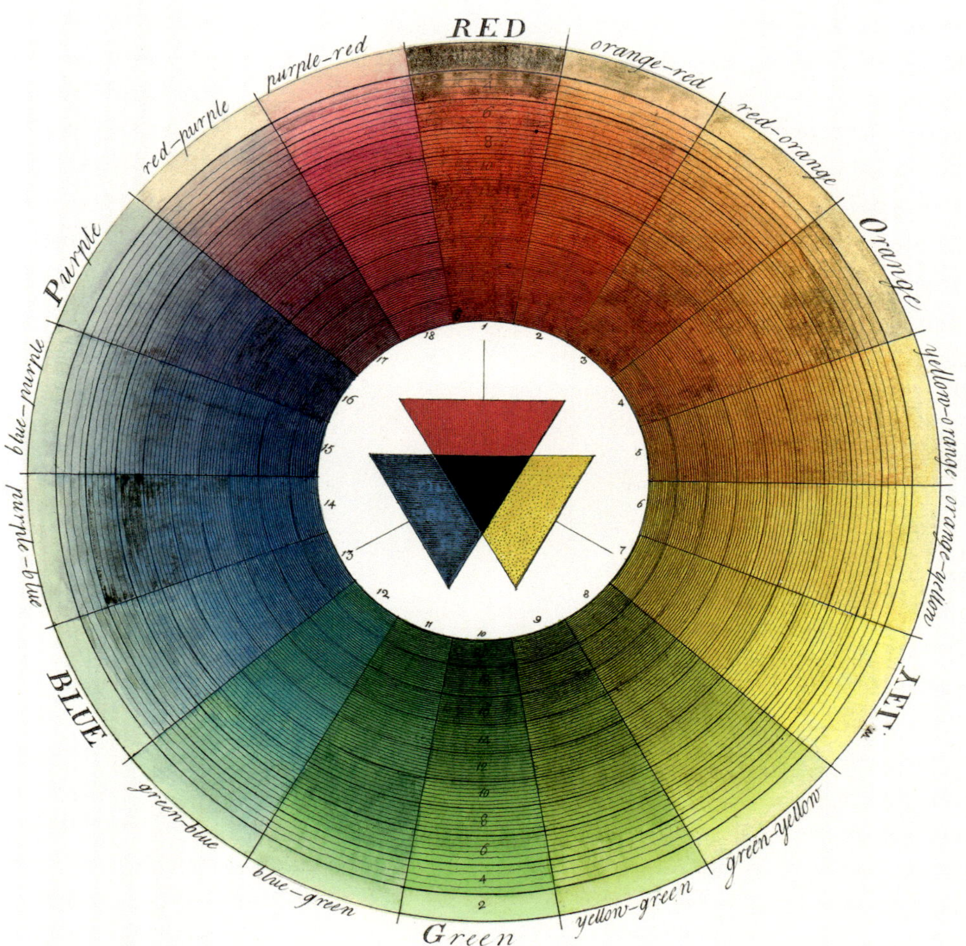


Mos. Harris inv.t et

## Das natürliche System der Farben

Schon früh verfasste der englische Entomologe Moses Harris dieses kurze Büchlein und bebilderte es mit einem Farbsystem, das sich an Maler und Illustratoren richtete, wobei er den Einfluss Isaac Newtons durchaus eingestand. Wie die Fortsetzung des Titels seiner Abhandlung erklärt, sollte sein System die „regelmäßige und schöne Ordnung und Gliederung" zeigen, „die aus den drei Urfarben Rot, Blau und Gelb erwächst". Die erste Auflage ist nicht datiert, erschien jedoch vermutlich zwischen 1769 und 1776. Sie war Sir Joshua Reynolds (1723–1792) gewidmet, dem Präsidenten der Royal Academy of Arts in London, und bildete den Auftakt zu einer Reihe von bedeutenden Farbtraktaten aus dem Umkreis der Akademie in den Jahrzehnten nach ihrer Gründung 1768. Dies unterstreicht den Wandel in den Einstellungen zur Farbe, der sich damals im Bereich der Kunst und Kunsterziehung vollzog.

Die Gewichtung von Text (nur acht Seiten einschließlich Widmung) und Bildern (zwei Tafeln mit prächtigen Farbkreisen, in einigen Exemplaren ergänzt um Tabellen mit Beispielen für Farbmischungen) und die anspruchsvolle Gestaltung der Illustrationen sind ein deutlicher Hinweis auf die Bedeutung, die Harris der exakten Wiedergabe von natürlichen Farben zuschrieb. Die in Kupfer gestochenen Farbkreise bestehen aus jeweils 18 Sektoren mit „prismatischen" und „gemischten" Farben, unterteilt und nummeriert in zwanzig Intensitätsgrade, die sich in den Abbildungen auf zehn Stufen verteilen. Jeder Kreis enthält insgesamt 360 Farben. Im Untertitel des Buches ist jedoch nur von 660 verschiedenen Farben die Rede, da die Mischfarben Grün, Orange und Violett in beiden Kreisen vertreten sind. Das Zentrum der Kreise bilden sich überlappende Dreiecke aus den „Urfarben" Rot, Gelb und Blau und den „Zwischenfarben" Orange, Grün und Violett. Das schwarze Dreieck in der Mitte steht in beiden Fällen stellvertretend für die subtraktive Farbmischung. Eine kurze Begleitliste der Primär- und Sekundärfarben im Text steuert Entsprechungen aus der Pigment- und Pflanzenwelt bei.

1811 erschien postum eine zweite Auflage des Buches mit neu gestochenen Kupfertafeln. Harris' Werk wurde im frühen 19. Jahrhundert von zahlreichen Künstlern, Pädagogen und Wissenschaftlern wie William Turner, Thomas Phillips oder William Benjamin Sarsfield Taylor (1781–1850) umfassend diskutiert, in der Lehre verwendet und reproduziert. 1963 gab der amerikanische Schriftsteller Faber Birren eine Faksimile-Ausgabe dieses außergewöhnlichen Buches heraus und bezeichnete es als „das vielleicht seltenste bekannte Buch in der Literatur über Farben". Von der Originalausgabe (und dem Nachdruck von 1811) sind derzeit weniger als 10 Exemplare in Bibliotheken weltweit verzeichnet.

## Le système naturel des couleurs

Moses Harris est un entomologiste anglais, auteur et illustrateur de ce bref ouvrage, l'un des tout premiers à proposer un système chromatique destiné aux peintres et illustrateurs, tout en reconnaissant l'influence d'Isaac Newton. Comme l'explique la suite du titre, son système a pour objectif de montrer « L'ordre et la disposition réguliers et beaux découlant des trois premitives [*sic*], rouge, bleu et jaune ». Aucune date ne figure dans la première édition, mais elle a probablement été publiée entre 1769 et 1776. Dédicacé au président de la Royal Academy of Arts à Londres, Sir Joshua Reynolds (1723–1792), l'ouvrage est le premier d'une série de titres importants consacrés à la couleur, tous signés par des personnes associées à la Royal Academy dans les décennies qui suivent sa fondation en 1768, indice du changement d'attitude vis-à-vis de la couleur à cette époque, en peinture comme dans l'enseignement artistique.

La proportion du texte (huit pages tout juste, dédicace comprise) par rapport aux images (deux gravures figurant deux splendides cercles chromatiques, accompagnés, dans certains exemplaires, de tableaux donnant des exemples de mélanges de couleurs) et l'ambitieuse qualité des illustrations d'Harris indiquent clairement l'importance qu'il attribue à une représentation précise des couleurs du monde naturel. Les deux cercles, gravés au burin sur cuivre, présentent les couleurs « prismatiques » et les couleurs « composées ». Chacun est constitué de 18 segments, divisés en 20 degrés d'intensité numérotés, et présente donc 360 couleurs. Le sous-titre du livre n'évoque quant à lui que 660 couleurs différentes au total, puisque les mélanges violet, orange et vert apparaissent dans les deux cercles. Au centre du premier cercle sont superposés trois triangles des couleurs « primitives » rouge, jaune et bleu ; au centre du second, trois triangles des couleurs « médiates » violet, orange et vert. Dans les deux cas, le centre noir représente le mélange soustractif des couleurs. Une brève liste des couleurs primaires et secondaires en indique les équivalents dans l'univers des pigments et de la flore.

Une seconde édition, posthume, paraît en 1811 avec de nouvelles gravures. Les travaux d'Harris ont été largement discutés, enseignés et reproduits par de nombreux artistes, professeurs et élèves au début du XIXe siècle, dont Turner, Thomas Phillips ou encore William Benjamin Sarsfield Taylor (1781–1850). En 1963, l'écrivain états-unien Faber Birren a réalisé une édition en fac-similé de cet ouvrage extraordinaire, dont il disait que c'était « peut-être l'ouvrage le plus rare dans l'histoire des livres consacrés à la couleur ». Aujourd'hui, il ne reste des éditions originales (qu'il s'agisse de cette édition ou de la réimpression de 1811) que moins de 10 exemplaires recensés dans des bibliothèques de par le monde.

THE NATURAL

SYSTEM of COLOURS,

Wherein is diſplayed the regular and beautiful Order and Arrangement,

Ariſing from the Three Premitives, *Red*, *Blue*, and *Yellow*,

The manner in which each Colour is formed, and its Compoſition,

The dependance they have on each other, and by their

HARMONIOUS CONNECTIONS

Are produced the Teints, or Colours, of every Object in the Creation,

And thoſe Teints, tho' ſo numerous as 660, are all compriſed in Thirty Three Terms, only

By MOSES HARRIS,

AUTHOR of the AURELIAN, &c. &c.

Printed at LAIDLER's Office, Princes-ſtreet, Liceſter-Fields.

# COMPOUND

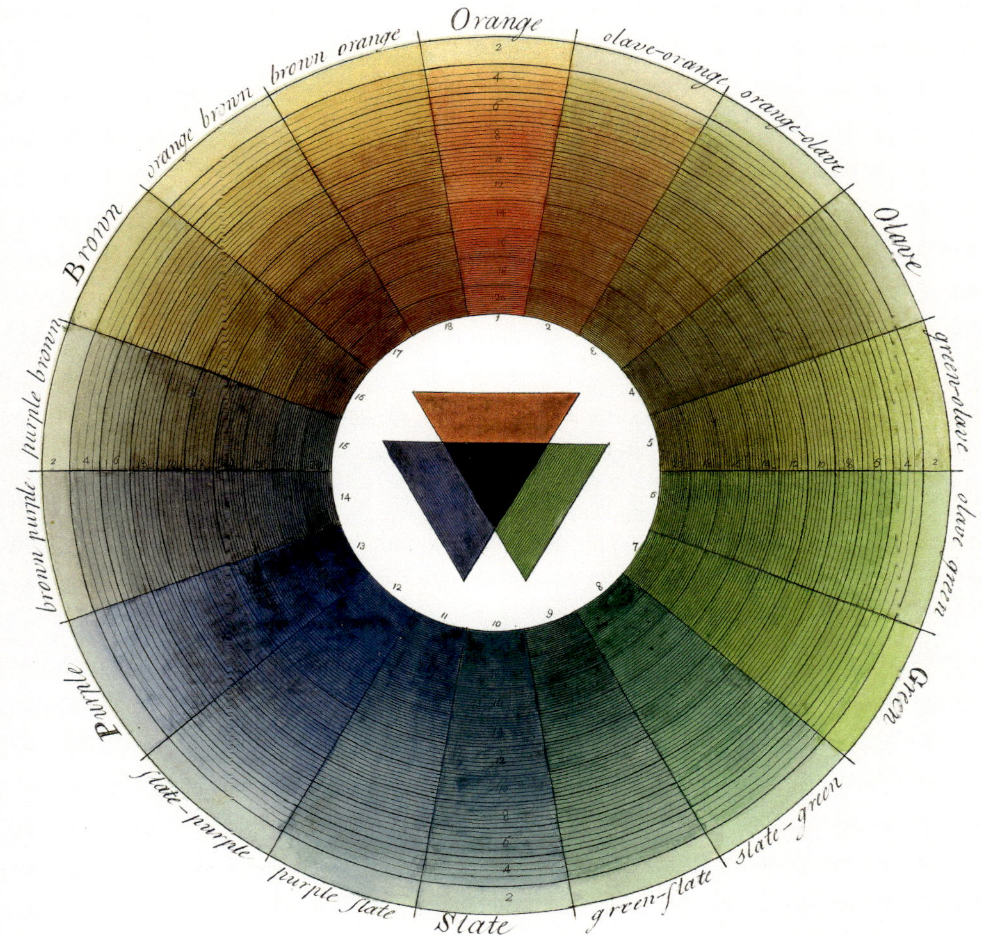


Moses Harris inv^t et sc^t

## Philipp Otto Runge (1777–1810)

# FARBEN-KUGEL

## oder Construction des Verhältnisses aller Mischungen der Farben zu einander, und ihrer vollständigen Affinität

### Colour Globe

*1 plate, 21.6 x 18.7 cm | 8 ½ x 7 ⅜ in., Hamburg, 1810*
*Hamburger Kunsthalle*

It is to the German Romantic painter Philipp Otto Runge that credit is due for the first visually convincing three-dimensional concept of colour. The multi-dimensionality of colour order had of course been considered earlier, as in 1611 when the Finnish-Swedish astronomer Aron Sigfrid Forsius (1550–1624) presented a colour diagram that seems to have been intended to represent a three-dimensional shape, while a similar notion is evident in the pyramidal forms devised by Tobias Mayer, but when Runge gave his diagram the form of a sphere and presented it in the style of a terrestrial globe his model gained a more familiar, and seemingly tactile quality. The development of this spherical form, which was still limited to the two-dimensional format of a flat print, occupied much of Runge's time in the last few years of his life. His research was informed from 1806 onwards by lengthy written exchanges on colour with Goethe, who was sent a copy of the manuscript of *Farben-Kugel* prior to its publication. By coincidence, Runge's *Farben-Kugel* and the first part of Goethe's *Zur Farbenlehre* were both published in 1810, within a few months of each other, and Goethe praised the brilliance of Runge's concept in personal letters and in the later historical part of *Zur Farbenlehre*. It was, however, to be Runge's last work as he died from tuberculosis the same year.

Runge's hand-coloured etching shows the colour globe in four views, with one perspective view aligned so that the white region at the top (equivalent to the North Pole on a terrestrial globe) marks the pure white culmination of the greyscale that runs vertically through the globe, while a second perspective view shows the opposite black region (equivalent to the South Pole) that represents the darkening of the greyscale. A cross-section through the poles depicts the complementaries red and green on opposite sides of the globe as a series of concentric rings, while another cross-section represented as a 12-part colour wheel slices through the equator, around which run the pure colours, without any addition of white or black. While in practical terms this was far from being a perfect three-dimensional colour model, it worked well conceptually because it made it easy to perceive the range of colour mixtures, shades and tints within the form of the globe. The perspective views meanwhile add a sense of movement and dynamism to the model. Runge also added coloured plates in this work showing examples of colour harmonies and contrasts in the form of simple squares.

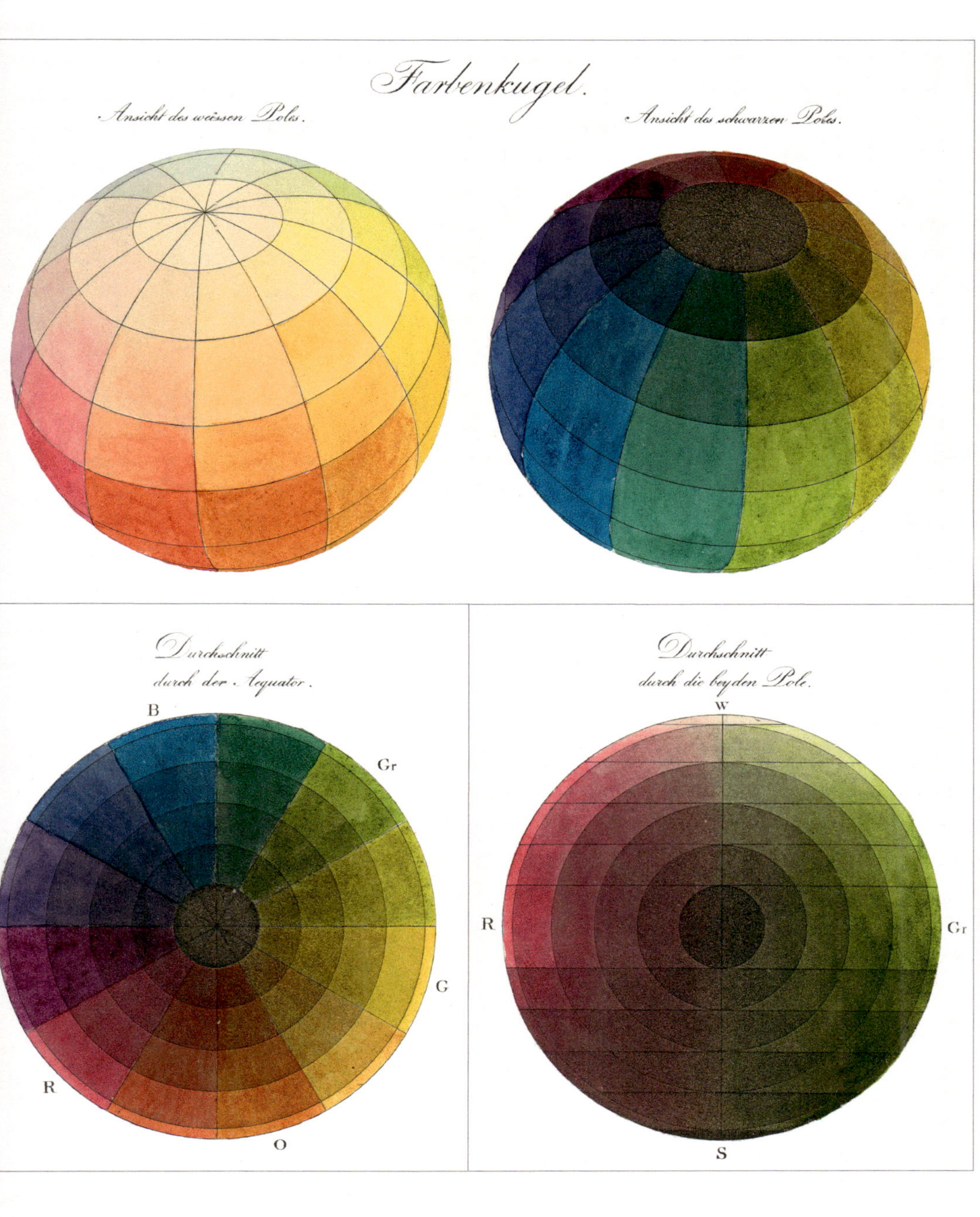
Farbenkugel.
Ansicht des weissen Poles.
Ansicht des schwarzen Poles.
Durchschnitt
durch der Aequator.
B
Gr
G
O
R
Durchschnitt
durch die beyden Pole.
W
R
Gr
S

## Farben-Kugel

Dem deutschen Maler der Romantik Philipp Otto Runge ist das erste visuell überzeugende dreidimensionale Farbsystem zu verdanken. Die Mehrdimensionalität der Farbenordnung wurde natürlich bereits früher erwogen, etwa als 1611 der finnisch-schwedische Astronom Aron Sigfrid Forsius (1550–1624) ein Farbdiagramm vorlegte, das allem Anschein nach eine dreidimensionale Form darstellen sollte. Eine ähnliche Vorstellung spricht aus den von Tobias Mayer entworfenen pyramidalen Figuren. Doch als Runge seinem Diagramm die Form einer Kugel gab und diese im Stil eines Erdballs präsentierte, erlangte sein Modell eine vertrautere und scheinbar haptische Qualität. Die Entwicklung dieser Kugelform, die jedoch auf das zweidimensionale Format der Druckseite beschränkt war, nahm Runge in den letzten Jahren seines Lebens stark in Anspruch. Seine Forschung war seit 1806 vom Austausch längerer Briefe über Farbe zwischen ihm und Goethe geprägt, dem er eine Kopie des Manuskripts von *Farben-Kugel* schickte, bevor das Buch erschien. Durch Zufall lagen zwischen der Veröffentlichung von Runges *Farben-Kugel* und dem ersten Teil von Goethes *Zur Farbenlehre* im Jahr 1810 nur wenige Monate. Goethe lobte die Brillanz der Runge'schen Theorie in persönlichen Briefen und später im historischen Teil von *Zur Farbenlehre*. Sie sollte Runges letztes Werk sein, denn noch im selben Jahr starb der Künstler an Tuberkulose.

Runges handkolorierte Radierung zeigt seine Farben-Kugel in vier Ansichten, von denen eine perspektivische Aufsicht so ausgerichtet ist, dass die weiße Region oben (dem Nordpol eines Erdglobus entsprechend) den reinweißen Endpunkt der Grauskala markiert, die senkrecht durch die Kugel verläuft. Eine zweite Perspektive zeigt die gegenüberliegende (dem Südpol entsprechende) schwarze Region, die den dunkler werdenden Teil der Grauskala repräsentiert. Ein Schnitt durch die Pole bildet die Komplementärfarben Rot und Grün auf entgegengesetzten Seiten der Kugel in konzentrischen Ringen ab, während ein weiterer Schnitt in Form eines zwölfteiligen Farbkreises durch den Äquator verläuft. Seinen äußeren Ring bilden die reinen Farben, denen weder Weiß noch Schwarz beigemischt wurde. War die Kugel in praktischer Hinsicht auch bei Weitem kein perfektes dreidimensionales Farbmodell, so funktionierte sie doch als Konzept, weil sie es einem erleichterte, sich das Spektrum der Farbmischungen, Töne und Schattierungen in der Kugelform vorzustellen. Die perspektivischen Ansichten des Modells erzeugen derweil einen Eindruck von Bewegung und Dynamik. Darüber hinaus fügte Runge seinem Buch auch Farbtafeln mit Beispielen für Farbharmonien und -kontraste in Form einfacher Quadrate hinzu.

FARBEN-KUGEL

oder

Construction des Verhältnisses aller Mischungen der Farben zu einander, und ihrer vollständigen Affinität,

mit angehängtem

Versuch einer Ableitung der Harmonie in den Zusammenstellungen der Farben.

Von

Philipp Otto Runge, Mahler.

Nebst einer Abhandlung

über die Bedeutung der Farben in der Natur,

von Hrn. Prof. Henrik Steffens in Halle.

Mit einem Kupfer, und einer beygelegten Farbentafel.

Hamburg,

bey Friedrich Perthes.

1810.

## Sphère chromatique

C'est au peintre romantique allemand Philipp Otto Runge que l'on doit la première représentation convaincante d'une conception chromatique en trois dimensions. La multidimensionnalité de l'ordre chromatique avait bien sûr été envisagée avant : dès 1611, l'astronome finno-suédois Aron Sigfrid Forsius (1550–1624) a proposé un graphique de couleurs qui semble avoir été conçu pour représenter une forme tridimensionnelle, tandis que cette même notion est évidente dans les formes pyramidales imaginées par Tobias Mayer. Mais lorsque Runge dessine une forme sphérique à la façon d'un globe terrestre, sa représentation prend une tournure familière et devient presque possible à toucher. L'élaboration de cette forme sphérique, qui était à l'époque limitée par l'impression en deux dimensions, a beaucoup occupé Runge dans les dernières années de sa vie. Ses recherches se nourrissent, à partir de 1806, par son abondante correspondance avec Goethe, à qui il fait parvenir un exemplaire manuscrit de sa *Farben-Kugel* avant publication. Le hasard fera que le livre de Runge et la première partie du *Zur Farbenlehre* de Goethe paraissent tous les deux en 1810, à quelques mois d'intervalle. Goethe fera l'éloge de la remarquable conception de Runge dans des lettres personnelles et, ultérieurement, dans la partie historique de son *Zur Farbenlehre*. Runge publie là son dernier ouvrage, et meurt de la tuberculose la même année.

Coloriée à la main, la gravure à l'eau-forte de Runge présente une sphère chromatique sous quatre angles. L'une des vues en perspective est orientée de manière que la zone blanche au sommet (l'équivalent du pôle Nord d'un globe terrestre) indique le point culminant, d'un blanc pur, de l'échelle des gris qui traverse verticalement le centre de la sphère. Une deuxième perspective montre la zone opposée (l'équivalent du pôle Sud), noire, qui représente l'obscurcissement de l'échelle des gris. En bas à droite, une coupe longitudinale par les pôles montre le rouge et le vert, complémentaires et diamétralement opposés, et déclinés sur une série d'anneaux concentriques ; en bas à gauche, une coupe transversale au niveau de l'équateur représente un disque chromatique en 12 parties, où sont figurées les couleurs pures, sans aucune adjonction de blanc ou de noir. Bien qu'en termes pratiques cette modélisation chromatique tridimensionnelle soit loin d'être parfaite, elle fonctionne bien sur le plan conceptuel car elle rend facilement perceptibles, au sein d'une même sphère, les gammes de mélanges de couleurs, les nuances et les teintes. L'inclinaison des axes des sphères, quant à elle, insuffle du mouvement et du dynamisme à la représentation. Runge a également intégré des planches coloriées à son ouvrage, montrant des exemples d'harmonies et de contrastes chromatiques sous la forme de simples carrés.

## Wilhelm von Bezold (1837–1907)

# DIE FARBENLEHRE IM HINBLICK AUF KUNST UND KUNSTGEWERBE

### Colour Theory in Relation to Art and Art Industry

*3 plates, 22.1 x 13.7 cm | 8 ¾ x 5 ⅜ in., Braunschweig, 1874*
*Munich, Bayerische Staatsbibliothek*

Wilhelm von Bezold was a physics professor at the Royal Bavarian Polytechnic School in Munich, whose range of interests included technology, science, architecture and the decorative arts. He is perhaps best known for his work with Ernst Wilhelm von Brücke (1819–1892) during which they discovered the 'Bezold–Brücke effect', the perceptual change in the hue of a colour relative to the intensity of light.

Bezold's substantial work on colour theory presented here reflects the developments in colour and optical science in the later 19th century, in particular the research of James Clerk Maxwell (1831–1879) and Hermann von Helmholtz (1821–1894) who had both recently made significant contributions in the study of trichromatic vision. The chromolithographic plates in Bezold's *Die Farbenlehre* are of a superior quality, as may be seen with plate I which shows the spectrum of sunlight accompanied by the respective spectra of yellow (gamboge) and (Prussian) blue followed by mixtures of the two, as observed through a prism and against a black ground. This explains the black background colour of the plates, which also offsets the colours to dramatic effect. Plate II features a pair of saturated colour wheels, also placed on a black background. In an age before colour photography (Maxwell was working on it at the time, but the world was still many decades away from it being widely available), these plates must have looked quite spectacular. Bezold noted in the book that he himself considered the colour plates to be a success, but at the same time he remarked on the challenges and limitations of colour printing. His colour wheels relate to an innovative three-dimensional colour concept in the form of a cone, based on 10 colours with a greyscale running through its centre, and culminating in black at the top of the cone. A translation of Bezold's book was published just two years later in Boston, with the title *The Theory of Color in Its Relation to Art and Art-Industry*, while a new and revised edition of the original work appeared in Germany in 1921, a testament to the high regard in which Bezold's work on colour was still held at that date.

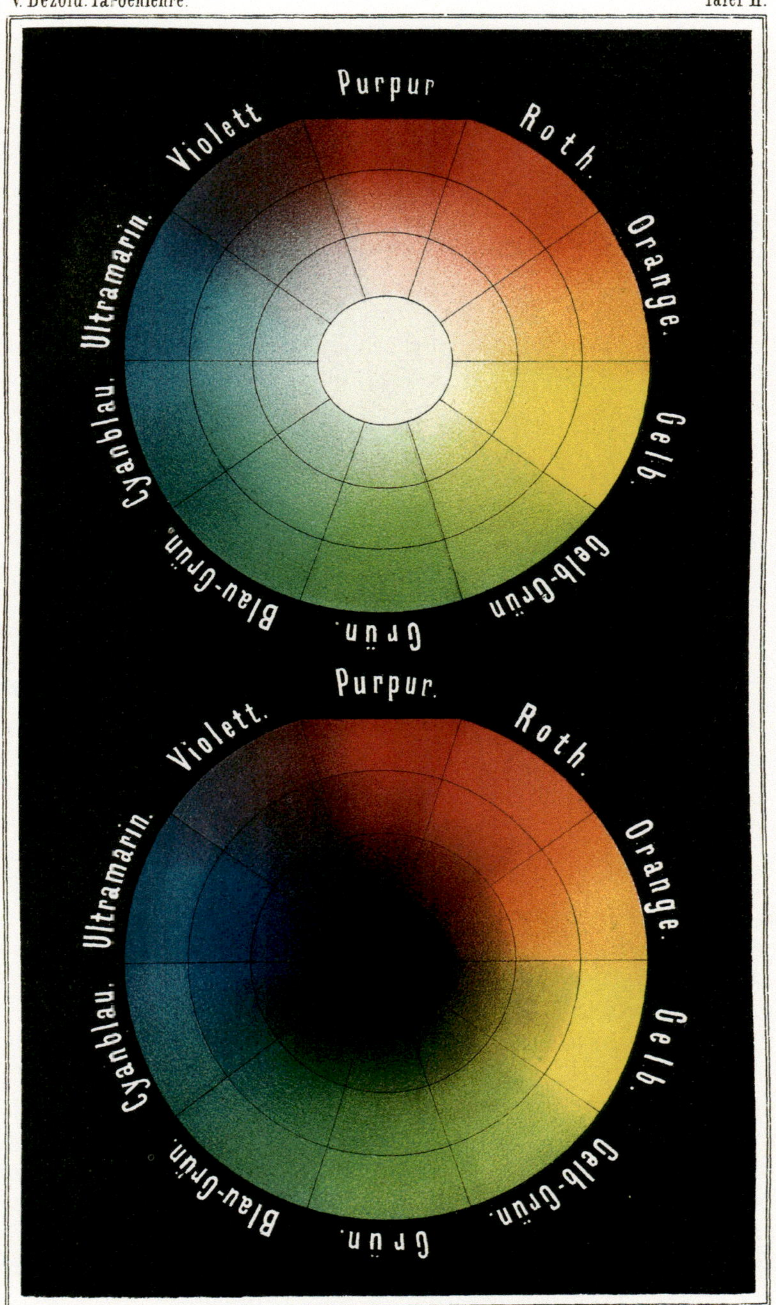


Chromolith. v. A. Schütze, Berlin. Braunschweig, Verlag von G. Westermann.

DIE FARBENLEHRE

IM HINBLICK AUF

KUNST UND KUNSTGEWERBE

VON

DR. WILH. v. BEZOLD,

ORD. PROFESSOR DER PHYSIK AM KÖNIGLICHEN POLYTECHNICUM IN MÜNCHEN.

MIT 63 FIGUREN UND 9 TAFELN.

BRAUNSCHWEIG,
DRUCK UND VERLAG VON GEORGE WESTERMANN.
1874.

## Die Farbenlehre im Hinblick auf Kunst und Kunstgewerbe

Wilhelm von Bezold war Physikprofessor an der Polytechnischen Schule München und interessierte sich neben Technik und Wissenschaft auch für Architektur und Kunstgewerbe. Bekannt ist er wohl vor allem für seine Zusammenarbeit mit Ernst Wilhelm von Brücke (1819–1892). Gemeinsam entdeckten die beiden Wissenschaftler den nach ihnen benannten Bezold-Brücke-Effekt, die Veränderung eines empfundenen Farbtons in Abhängigkeit von der Intensität des Lichts.

Bezolds hier vorgestelltes bedeutendes Werk zur Farbtheorie spiegelt die Entwicklungen von Farbwissenschaft und Optik im ausgehenden 19. Jahrhundert wider, insbesondere die Arbeiten von James Clerk Maxwell (1831–1879) und Hermann von Helmholtz (1821–1894), die beide kurz zuvor wesentliche Beiträge zur Erforschung des Dreifarbensehens geleistet hatten. Die hohe Qualität der farblithografischen Tafeln in *Die Farbenlehre* zeigt sich gleich in Tafel I, auf der das Sonnenspektrum und die entsprechenden Spektren der Farben Gummigutt (Gelb) und Preußischblau zu sehen sind, gefolgt von Mischungen der beiden Farben, jeweils betrachtet durch ein Prisma vor schwarzem Hintergrund. Dies erklärt die schwarze Hintergrundfarbe der Tafeln und setzt zugleich die Buntfarben auf dramatische Weise dagegen ab. Tafel II zeigt ein Paar gesättigte Farbkreise, ebenfalls auf schwarzem Grund. In der Zeit vor der Farbfotografie (sie wurde etwa zeitgleich von Maxwell entwickelt, doch die Welt war noch Jahrzehnte von ihrer allgemeinen Verfügbarkeit entfernt) müssen diese Farbtafeln spektakulär gewirkt haben. Im Buch merkte Bezold an, dass er selbst sie für einen Erfolg hielt, äußerte sich jedoch auch über die Herausforderungen und Grenzen des Farbdrucks. Seine Farbkreise beziehen sich auf ein innovatives dreidimensionales Farbsystem in Kegelform, basierend auf zehn Farben und einer Grauachse im Zentrum, die an der Kegelspitze in Schwarz gipfelt. Während nur zwei Jahre später in Boston eine englische Übersetzung des Buches mit dem Titel *The Theory of Color in Its Relation to Art and Art-Industry* herauskam, zeugt die 1921 in Deutschland erschienene überarbeitete Auflage des Originalwerks davon, wie angesehen Bezolds Farbtheorie damals immer noch war.

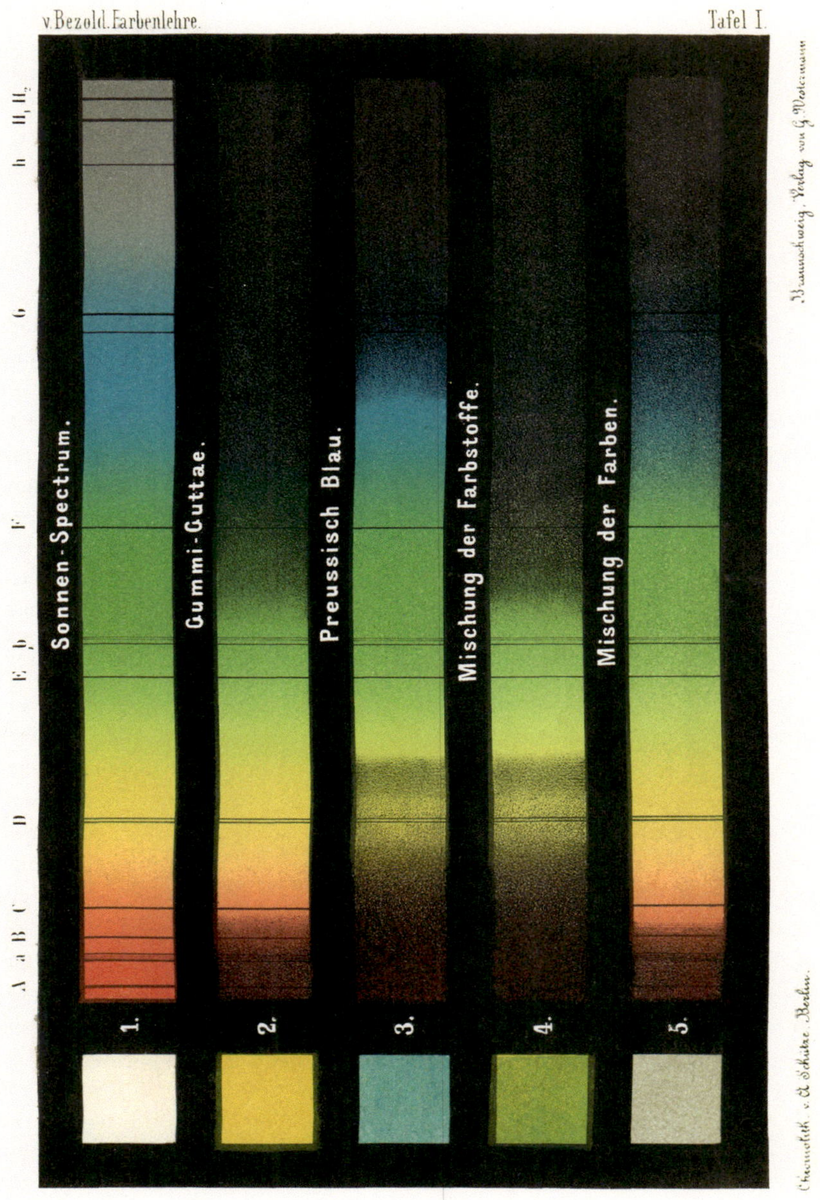
v. Bezold. Farbenlehre.
Tafel I.
Sonnen-Spectrum.
Gummi-Guttae.
Preussisch Blau.
Mischung der Farbstoffe.
Mischung der Farben.
1.
2.
3.
4.
5.
Braunschweig, Verlag von G. Westermann
Chromolith. v. A. Schütze. Berlin.

## La théorie de la couleur en relation avec l'art et les métiers de l'art

Wilhelm von Bezold est professeur de physique à l'École polytechnique royale de Bavière, à Munich, qui forme tout à la fois à la technologie, à l'architecture, aux sciences et aux arts décoratifs. C'est sans doute pour ses travaux avec Ernst Wilhelm von Brücke (1819–1892) qu'il est le plus connu : ils ont ensemble découvert ce qui sera appelé l'effet Bezold-Brücke, qui désigne le changement de perception des nuances d'une couleur selon l'intensité de la lumière.

Ce qui est présenté ici du travail approfondi de Bezold sur la théorie des couleurs reflète les avancées scientifiques en matière chromatique et optique de la fin du XIXe siècle. Deux autres éminents chercheurs, James Clerk Maxwell et Hermann von Helmholtz (1821–1894), viennent à l'époque d'apporter leurs importantes contributions dans l'étude de la vision trichromatique. Les planches chromolithographiques de *Die Farbenlehre* sont de qualité supérieure, comme on peut l'observer sur la planche I : le spectre de la lumière du soleil y est accompagné des spectres respectifs du jaune (gomme-gutte) et du bleu (de Prusse) qui sont suivis du mélange des deux, tels qu'observés à travers un prisme et sur un fond noir. Ainsi s'explique le noir employé pour le fond, qui renforce l'effet spectaculaire des couleurs des planches. La planche II présente deux cercles de couleurs saturées, également placés sur un fond noir. Ces planches devaient être très impressionnantes à voir en ces temps antérieurs à la photographie en couleurs (Maxwell était déjà en train d'en développer la technique, mais elle ne se répandrait largement dans le monde que bien des décennies plus tard). Bezold note dans son ouvrage qu'il est satisfait des planches en couleurs, mais il souligne dans le même temps les limites et le défi que représente l'impression en couleurs. Ses cercles découlent d'un concept chromatique tridimensionnel novateur : une forme conique comprenant 10 couleurs, avec une échelle de gris structurant le centre, et qui culmine au sommet du cône avec le noir. Une traduction en anglais du livre de Bezold est publiée à peine deux ans plus tard à Boston, sous le titre *The Theory of Color in Its Relation to Art and Art-Industry*. Une nouvelle édition revue et corrigée de l'ouvrage original paraît en Allemagne en 1921, ce qui témoigne de la haute considération dans laquelle le travail de Bezold est tenu à l'époque.

v. Bezold, Farbenlehre.

Tafel III.

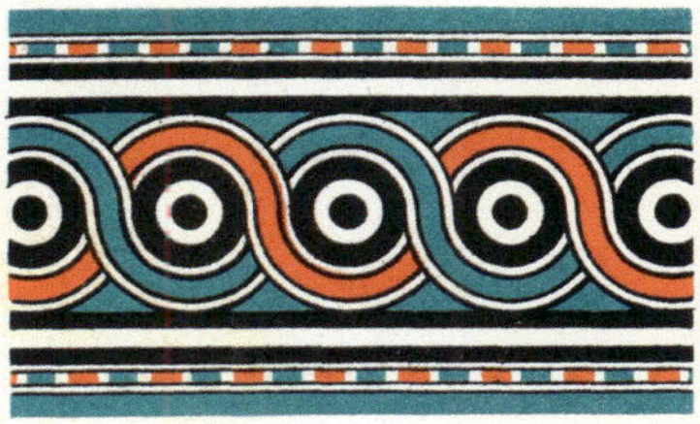

Fig. 1.

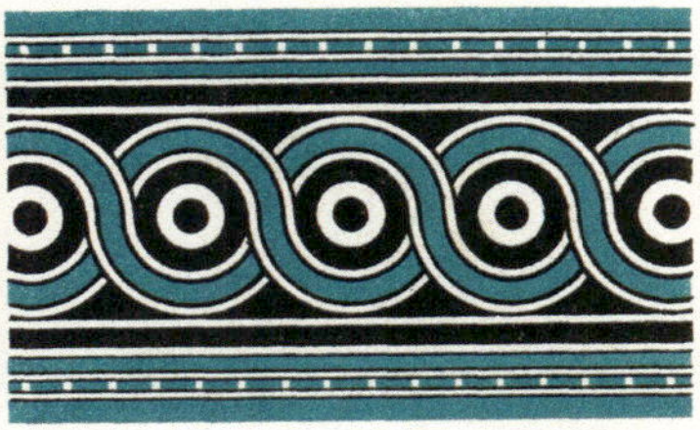

Fig. 2.

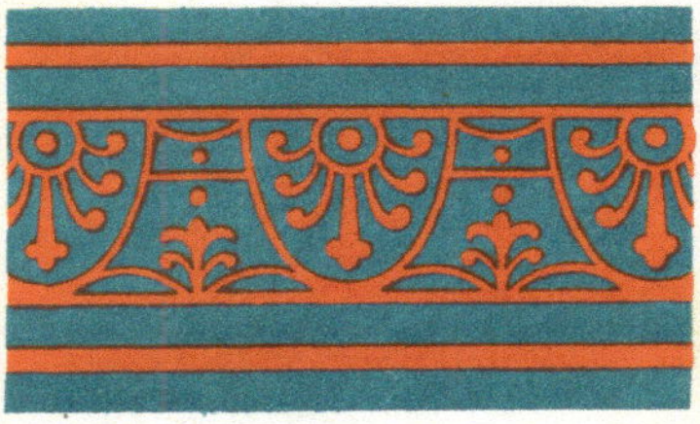

Fig. 3.

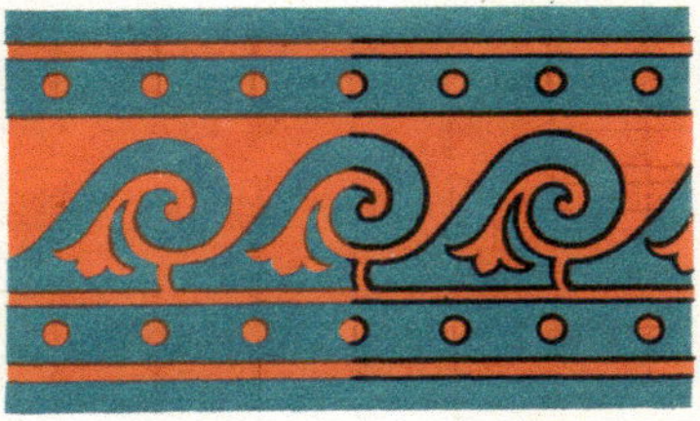

Fig. 4.

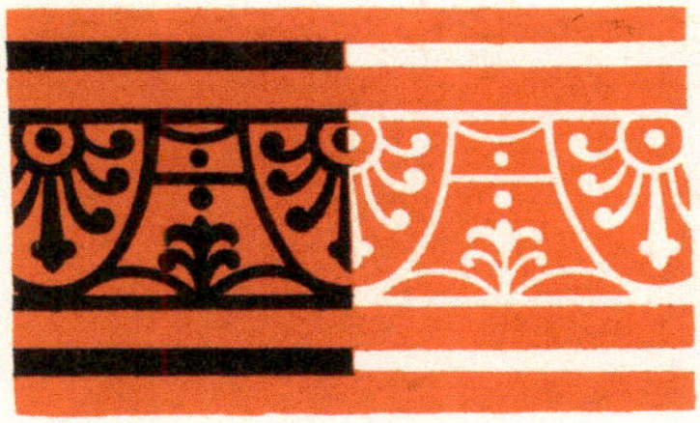

Fig. 5.

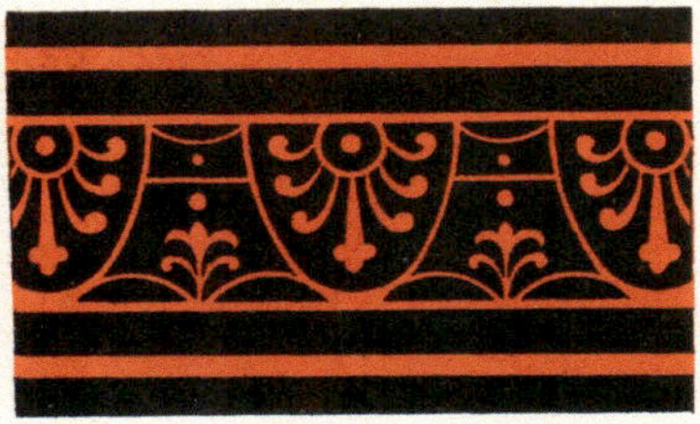

Fig. 6.

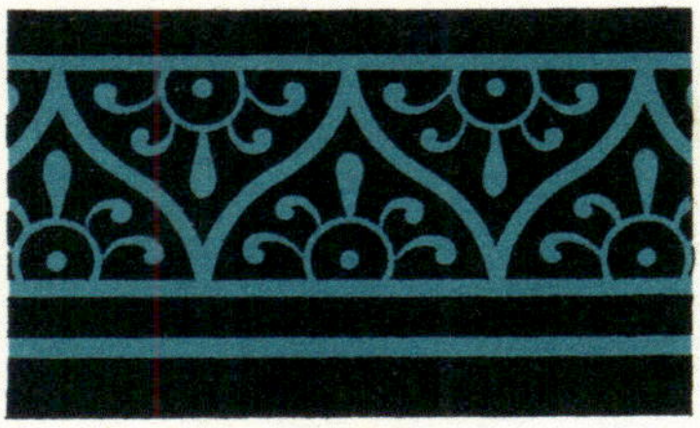

Fig. 7.

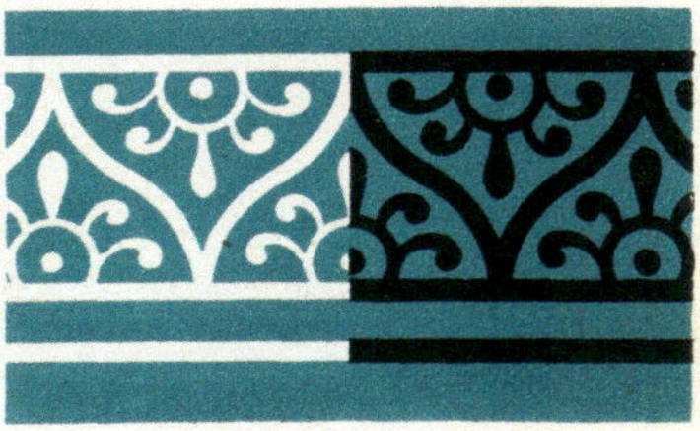

Fig. 8.

Chromolith. v. A. Schütze Berlin.

Braunschweig, Verlag von G. Westermann.

## Edwin D. Babbitt (1828–1905)

# THE PRINCIPLES OF LIGHT AND COLOR

*4 plates, 24.2 x 16.5 cm | 9 ½ x 6 ½ in., New York, 1878*
*London, Royal College of Art, Colour Reference Library*

Edwin Dwight Babbitt was a New York–born teacher and stationery maker, who decided to pursue a radical career change in mid-life. Seemingly without any formal training he became a self-declared physician and mystic healer, being listed in a directory from the 1870s as a "magnetist and author of a health guide". In 1878 he published this lengthy work on the healing qualities of colour and light, which marked him as one of the pioneers of the alternative medicine method of chromotherapy. Now largely discredited as pseudoscience, the purported healing powers of colour (always in connection with light) had been investigated and discussed since earlier historical times, and found a receptive audience in the late 19th century, an age characterised by quackery and various misconceptions in the world of medicine. Babbitt was strongly criticised by several figures during his later career, but the fascination with the "elaborate and elegant (book by) this bold speculator", as one critic put it, was evident, not least when it was translated into a number of other languages.

The 200,000 words of Babbitt's text were embellished with 204 photoengravings and four coloured plates prepared by the New York printer John Fahnestock, who received a special acknowledgement from the author for creating illustrations "which for beauty I have not seen surpassed on either side of the ocean". One of the plates features a 14-part colour wheel in the shape of a stylised flower-head that identifies the qualities of the different colours in categories marked around the circumference. In keeping with Babbitt's belief in the therapeutic effect of individual colours he chose a pale sky-blue paper, since he considered it to be handsome and "soothing to the nerves of the eye".

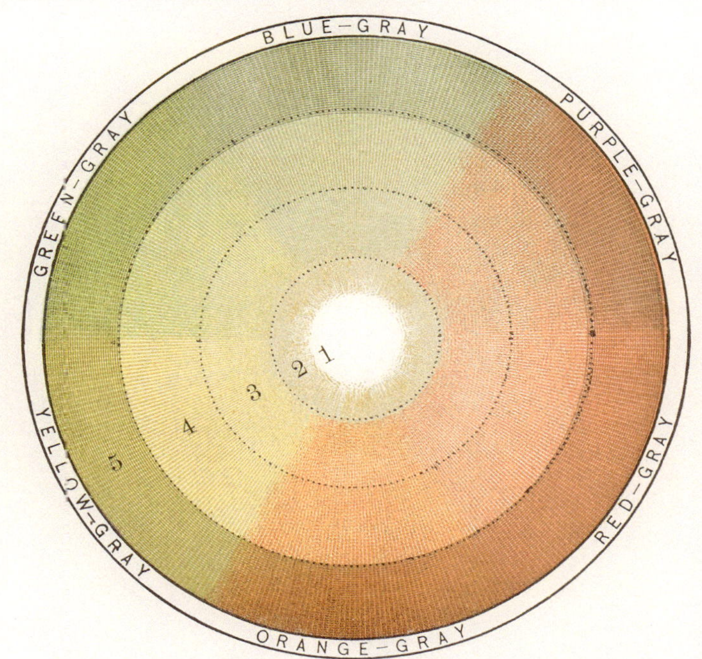


VARIOUS SHADES OF GRAY ARRANGED IN ANALOGICAL HARMONY.

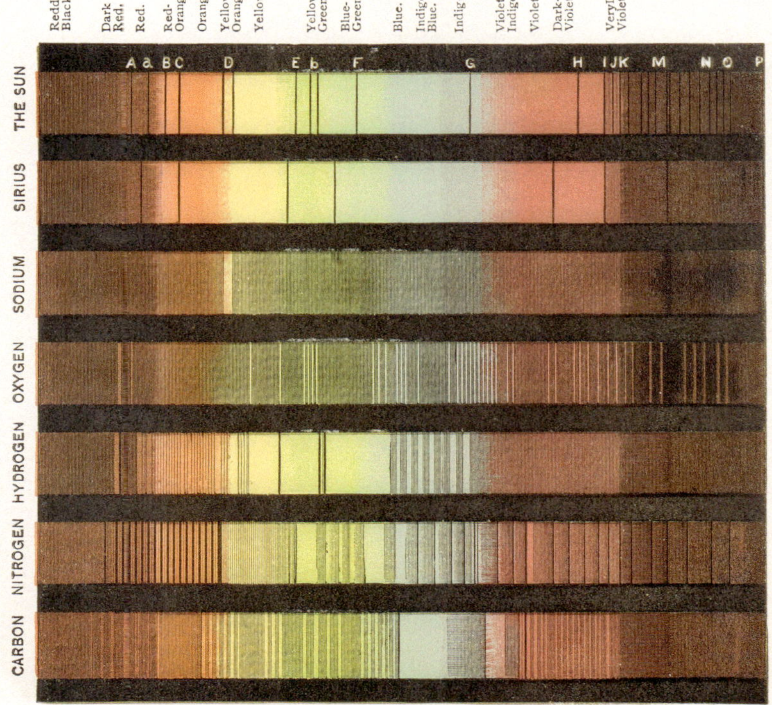


SPECTRA OF THE SUN, SIRIUS, AND SEVERAL ELEMENTS.

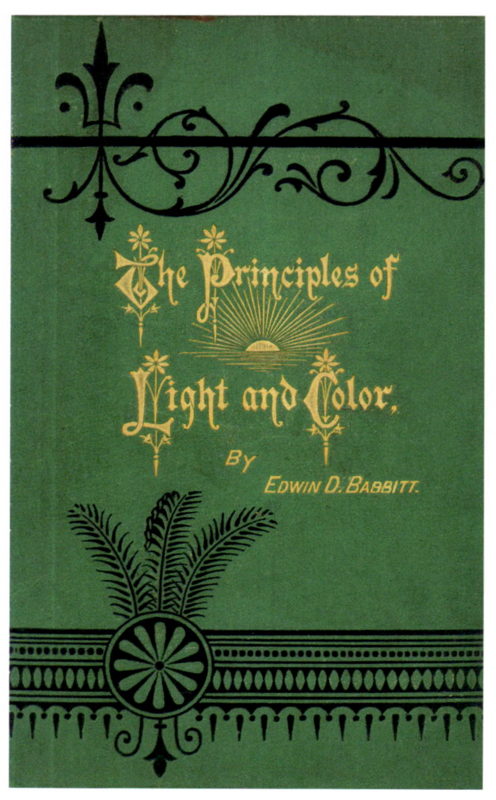


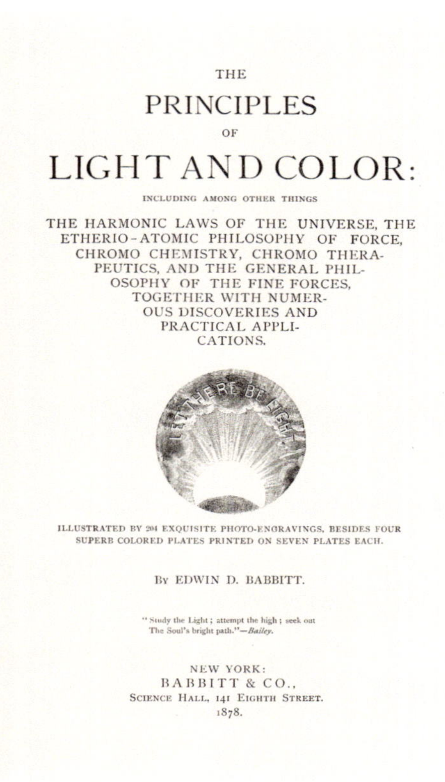

THE
PRINCIPLES
OF
LIGHT AND COLOR:
INCLUDING AMONG OTHER THINGS
THE HARMONIC LAWS OF THE UNIVERSE, THE ETHERIO-ATOMIC PHILOSOPHY OF FORCE, CHROMO CHEMISTRY, CHROMO THERAPEUTICS, AND THE GENERAL PHILOSOPHY OF THE FINE FORCES, TOGETHER WITH NUMEROUS DISCOVERIES AND PRACTICAL APPLICATIONS.



ILLUSTRATED BY 204 EXQUISITE PHOTO-ENGRAVINGS, BESIDES FOUR SUPERB COLORED PLATES PRINTED ON SEVEN PLATES EACH.

By EDWIN D. BABBITT.

"Study the Light; attempt the high; seek out
The Soul's bright path."—*Bailey.*

NEW YORK:
BABBITT & CO.,
SCIENCE HALL, 141 EIGHTH STREET.
1878.

Among the objects he devised to assist with colour therapy were Chromolenses, double convex lenses made of different coloured glass that were hollow and could be filled with water, which would then focus the colour into a ray and transfer its healing powers to the individual; and the Chromolume, a panel of stained-glass with 16 sections of coloured panes that could be placed in sunlight so that the patient could bathe in the healing, coloured light. Babbitt was also a businessman, and his book included ordering information and price lists for these and other items. For all its contested content, as, for example, Babbitt's diagram of the imagined shape of an atom or his claim that coloured light could be an alternative for anaesthetics, the book is a fascinating snapshot of early ideas about colour psychology, psychotherapy and the effects of colour on mood, especially in architectural spaces.

# BABBITT'S PRINCIPLES OF LIGHT AND COLOR.—PLATE II

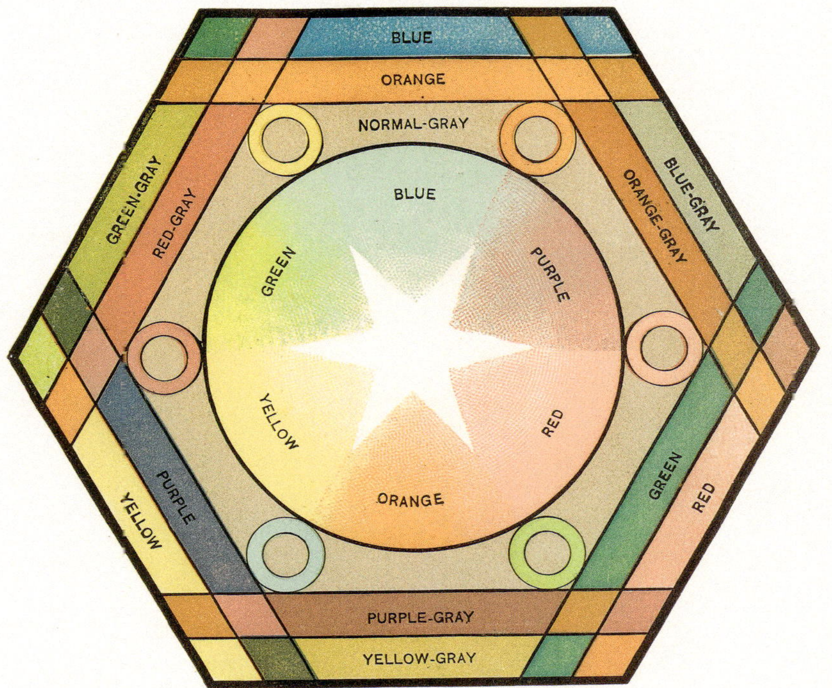


## CHROMATIC HARMONY OF GRADATION AND CONTRAST.

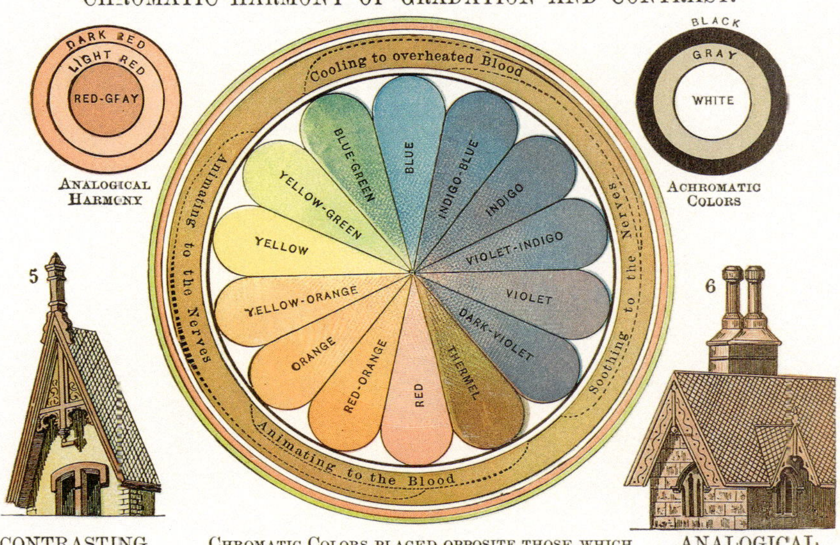


CONTRASTING HARMONY

CHROMATIC COLORS PLACED OPPOSITE THOSE WHICH FORM A CHEMICAL AFFINITY WITH THEM

ANALOGICAL HARMONY

In the above elaborate combination of colors the artist has found it impossible to get every feature accurate, although he has many beautiful and pure tints. The grays on both plates I. and II. are not sufficiently subdued, the chromatic colors standing out too brilliantly, the red, for instance, in the house, fig. 6, being too strong, etc. For description of plates see pp. 63, 65, 66, 69, 71, etc. The spectra are described on p. 217.

# BABBITT'S PRINCIPLES OF LIGHT AND COLOR.--PLATE III.

NORTH.

BLUE-GREEN. BLUE. INDIGO VIOLET RED.

YELLOW-GREEN.

GRAY WITH SLIGHT BLUE TINGE.

WEST.

YELLOW.

EAST.

ORANGE.

RED-GRAY.

RED.

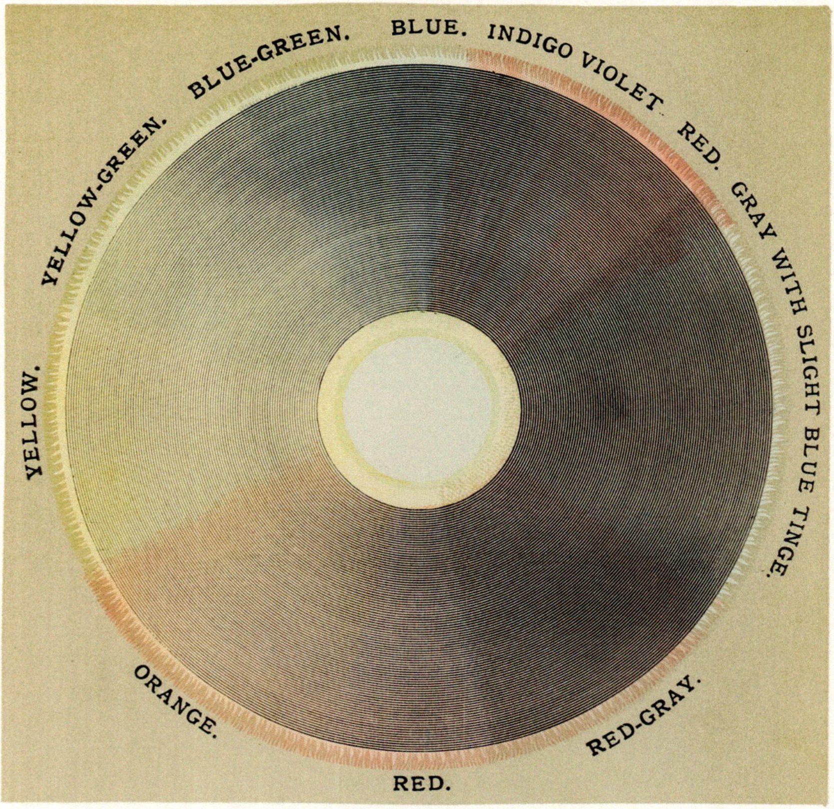

SOUTH.

## TERRESTRIAL DYNAMICS.—RADIATION OF ODIC LIGHTS AND COLORS.

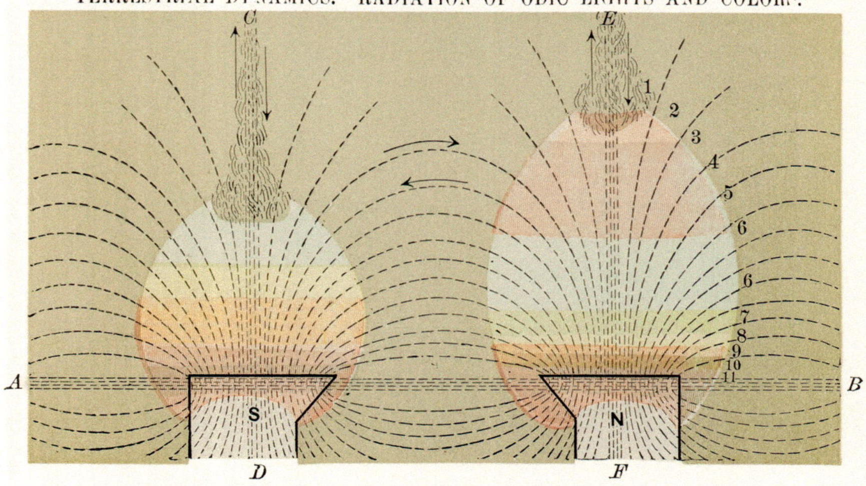


## ODIC FLAMES FROM THE POLES OF A HORSE-SHOE MAGNET.

The colors are not put on very accurately nor blended properly in these magnets, but the reader can consult page 434, with which and these colors he may be able to gain a fair conception of the radiations.

## Die Grundsätze von Licht und Farbe

In der Mitte seines Lebens beschloss der in New York geborene Lehrer und Schreibwarenhersteller Edwin Dwight Babbitt, sich beruflich radikal zu verändern, und erklärte sich, anscheinend ohne jede formale Ausbildung, zum Arzt und mystischen Heiler. In einem Verzeichnis aus den 1870er-Jahren wird er als „Magnetist und Autor eines Gesundheitsratgebers" geführt. 1878 veröffentlichte Babbitt dieses seitenstarke Werk über die heilenden Eigenschaften von Farbe und Licht, das ihn in der alternativen Medizin zum Pionier der Farbtherapie machte. Die angeblichen Heilkräfte von Farbe (stets im Zusammenhang mit Licht), die heute weithin als pseudowissenschaftlich angezweifelt werden, waren in der Geschichte schon seit Langem erforscht und diskutiert worden. Im späten 19. Jahrhundert, einer Zeit der Quacksalberei und allerlei falscher Vorstellungen in der Welt der Medizin, fanden sie ein aufnahmebereites Publikum. Babbitt wurde im weiteren Verlauf seiner Karriere von mehreren Seiten scharf kritisiert, doch die Begeisterung für das „ausführliche und elegante [Buch] dieses kühnen Spekulanten", wie ein Kritiker es ausdrückte, war offensichtlich – nicht zuletzt, als es in zahlreiche andere Sprachen übersetzt wurde.

Die zweihunderttausend Worte des Buchtextes waren mit 204 Fotogravüren und vier Farbtafeln ausgeschmückt. Letztere hatte der New Yorker Drucker John Fahnestock produziert, der von Babbitt mit einem besonderen Dank bedacht wurde; er habe Abbildungen geschaffen, „die ich an Schönheit auf beiden Seiten des Ozeans niemals übertroffen sah". Eine Tafel zeigt einen 14-teiligen Farbkreis in Form einer stilisierten Blüte, auf deren äußerem Ring die Eigenschaften der unterschiedlichen Farben vermerkt sind. Seinem Glauben an die therapeutische Wirkung einzelner Farben entsprechend, wählte Babbitt ein blasshimmelblaues Papier, das aus seiner Sicht attraktiv und „beruhigend für die Nerven des Auges" war. Als Hilfsmittel für die Farbtherapie entwickelte er unter anderem die „Chromo-Lenses" (Farblinse), eine bikonvexe hohle Linse aus farbigem Glas, die sich mit Wasser füllen ließ, um die Farbe zu einem Strahl zu bündeln und ihre Heilkräfte auf den Anwender zu übertragen. Eine weitere Erfindung von ihm war das „Chromolume" (Farblicht), eine Art Buntglasfenster im Holzrahmen mit 16 verschiedenen Farbzonen, das ins Sonnenlicht gestellt werden konnte, um die Patienten im heilenden Farblicht baden zu lassen. Da Babbitt auch Geschäftsmann war, enthielt sein Buch Bestellangaben und Preislisten zu diesen und anderen Artikeln. Trotz aller umstrittenen Inhalte, etwa Babbitts Diagramm vom vermeintlichen Aussehen eines Atoms oder seiner Behauptung, farbiges Licht könnte eine Alternative zu Betäubungsmitteln darstellen, ist das Buch eine faszinierende Momentaufnahme früher Vorstellungen von Farbpsychologie, Farbpsychotherapie und der Wirkung von Farben auf die menschliche Stimmung, insbesondere im architektonischen Raum.

## Les principes de la lumière et de la couleur

Edwin Dwight Babbitt, enseignant natif de New York et papetier, prend un tournant radical au milieu de sa vie. Apparemment sans la moindre formation, il s'autoproclame médecin et guérisseur mystique, et figure dans l'annuaire, à partir des années 1870, en tant que « magnétiseur et auteur d'un guide pour la santé ». En 1878, il fait paraître ce long ouvrage sur les propriétés curatives de la couleur et de la lumière, qui le place parmi les pionniers de la méthode de soin alternative appelée chromothérapie, depuis qualifiée de pseudoscience et donc discréditée. Les prétendus pouvoirs guérisseurs de la couleur (toujours en relation avec la lumière), qui faisaient déjà de très longue date l'objet de maints recherches et débats, trouvent un fort écho auprès du public de la fin du XIXe siècle, une époque qui voit croître le charlatanisme et nombre d'idées farfelues dans le domaine médical. Babbitt est sévèrement critiqué par plusieurs figures importantes à la fin de sa carrière, mais l'ouvrage « élaboré et élégant [de] cet impudent spéculateur », selon les mots d'un contempteur, opère une évidente fascination, y compris lorsqu'il est traduit dans de nombreuses langues.

Le texte de Babbitt, fort de 200 000 mots, est orné de 204 photogravures et quatre planches en couleurs, préparées par l'imprimeur new-yorkais John Fahnestock. Pour l'occasion, l'auteur remercie tout particulièrement celui-ci pour la création des illustrations « dont [il] n'a rien vu de comparable en beauté d'un côté comme de l'autre de l'océan ». L'une des planches représente un cercle chromatique en 14 parties, sous forme de fleur stylisée, et identifie les qualités des différentes couleurs par des catégories inscrites sur tout le pourtour. Croyant fermement à l'effet thérapeutique de chaque couleur prise individuellement, Babbitt a choisi un papier bleu ciel clair, qu'il tient pour beau et « apaisant pour les nerfs des yeux ». Il est également le concepteur de plusieurs objets employés pour pratiquer la thérapie par la couleur : ses « Chromo-lenses » (lunettes chromatiques) sont des lunettes à doubles verres convexes, taillés dans du verre coloré et creux, et que l'on remplit d'eau. Ainsi, la couleur se focalise en un rayon qui transmet son pouvoir guérisseur à la personne. Son « Chromolume » est un vitrail composé de 16 sections de verre coloré et que l'on place face aux rayons du soleil, de façon que la personne soit baignée par la lumière colorée et curative. Babbitt est par ailleurs un homme d'affaires : son volume inclut les renseignements permettant de passer commande et la liste des tarifs pour tous les objets et articles. L'ouvrage comprend encore d'autres éléments fortement contestés, comme le schéma imaginé par Babbitt pour représenter la forme d'un atome, ou encore l'affirmation selon laquelle la lumière colorée serait une alternative possible aux anesthésiques. Cependant, il constitue un aperçu fascinant des premières idées en matière de psychologie des couleurs, de psychothérapie par les couleurs et d'effets de la couleur sur l'humeur, notamment dans la conception des espaces architecturaux.

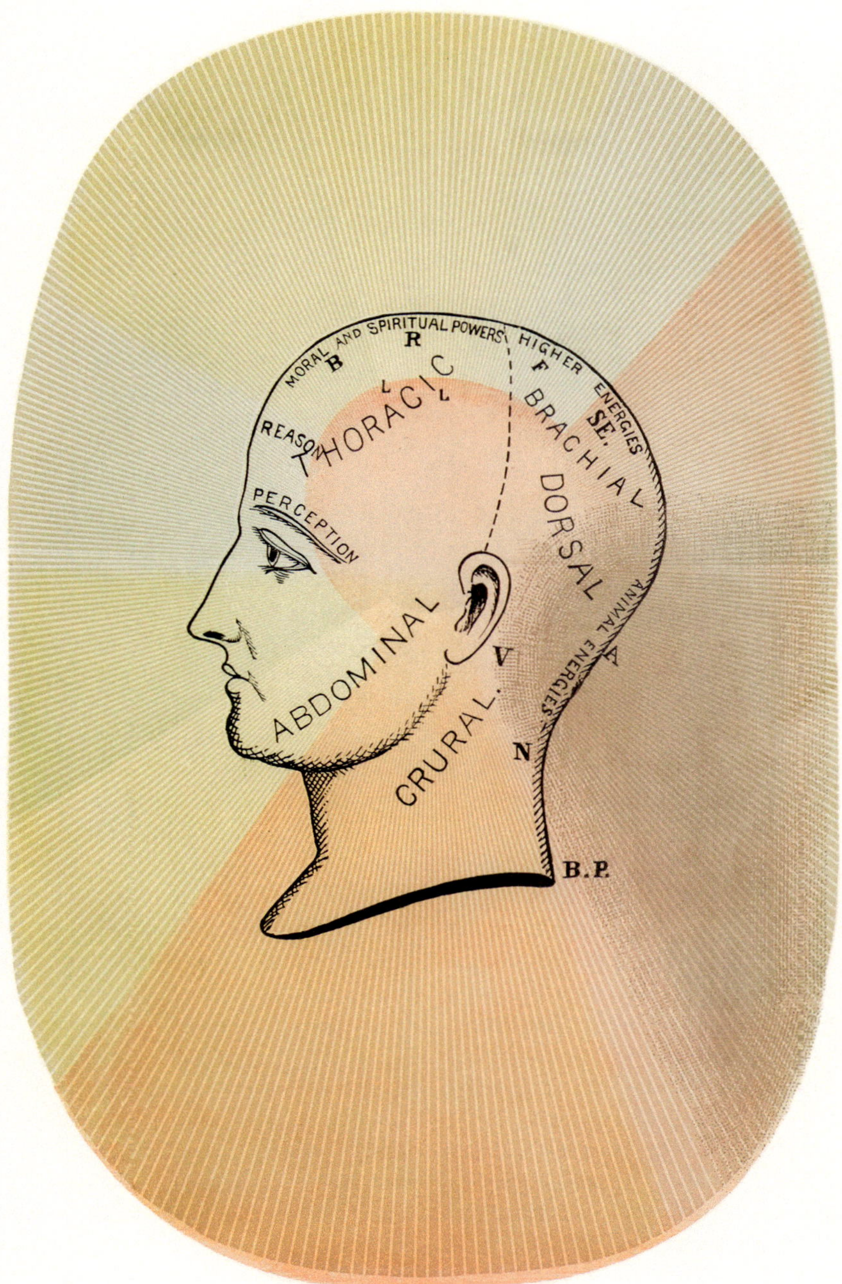


## PSYCHIC LIGHTS AND COLORS.

On the lower face of the above the artist has placed the green and yellow too low. The yellow should come over the mouth, then a slight orange merging into a red at the chin, which continues all the way to the occiput, at which last point it assumes a more muddy cast.

## Robert Steinheil (1863–1944)

# LA REPRODUCTION DES COULEURS

## par la superposition des trois couleurs simples

### The Reproduction of Colours

*19 plates, 36 x 29 cm | 14 1⁄8 x 11 3⁄8 in., Paris, 1896*
*Los Angeles, Getty Research Institute*

Robert Steinheil's book is a masterpiece of late 19th-century decorative book design and illustration, and as such it is also self-referential, for this work is a celebration of the technical possibilities offered by halftone colour printing in the 1890s. The full title, *La Reproduction des Couleurs par la superposition des trois couleurs simples*, makes clear that the book's purpose is to demonstrate how to reproduce colour by overlaying the "simple" chromatic primaries yellow, red and blue. The cover is typical of aesthetic *fin-de-siècle* style, with its elaborate title graphics on the front board coloured in prismatic shading. The title-page gives a further taste of the quality of the illustrations that follow, with its decorative luminous semicircle of 660 individual tints, illustrating the principles of simultaneous colour contrasts.

The book was printed by the historic French firm Berger-Levrault et Cie, and comprises 43 pages of letterpress main text, including a glossary of colour terms, a taxonomy of colour (with reference to Chevreul, Lacouture and others as influences) together with alphabetical and numerical tables of all the "nuances" of colour shown in the illustrations. The text is followed by an "Atlas" of 150 colour plates, printed on three types of paper in different batches of the copies, showing the series of colour combinations. These mostly take the form of colour wheels with sectors divided into 10 gradations that illustrate the printing process and provide exact proportions for each nuance or shade, identified by three numbers. There are 16 plates showing colour overlays in numbered 10 x 10 grid systems, while the final colour plate is an assemblage of several overlays in different shapes and patterns, including the semicircular image from the title-page repeated at the centre. In total, the plates show almost 15,000 individual colours. This is a highly ambitious book about colour printing, produced at the highest level of expertise, and is a magnificent testament to the technological achievements of the industrial age. The print run must have been small, as it is now one of the rarest of historical books on colour.

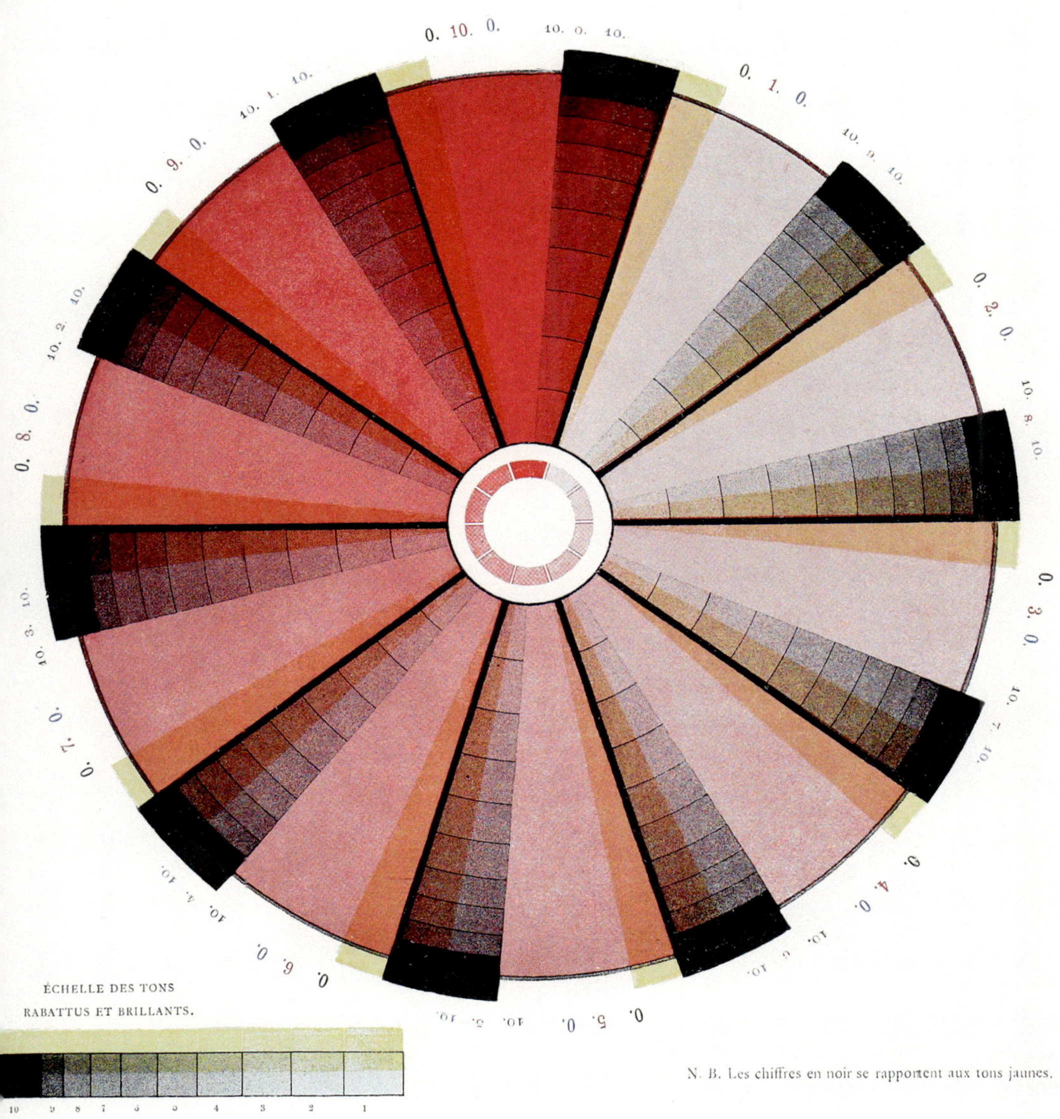


N. B. Les chiffres en noir se rapportent aux tons jaunes.

LE ROUGE.

Ses tons lavés et leurs gammes.

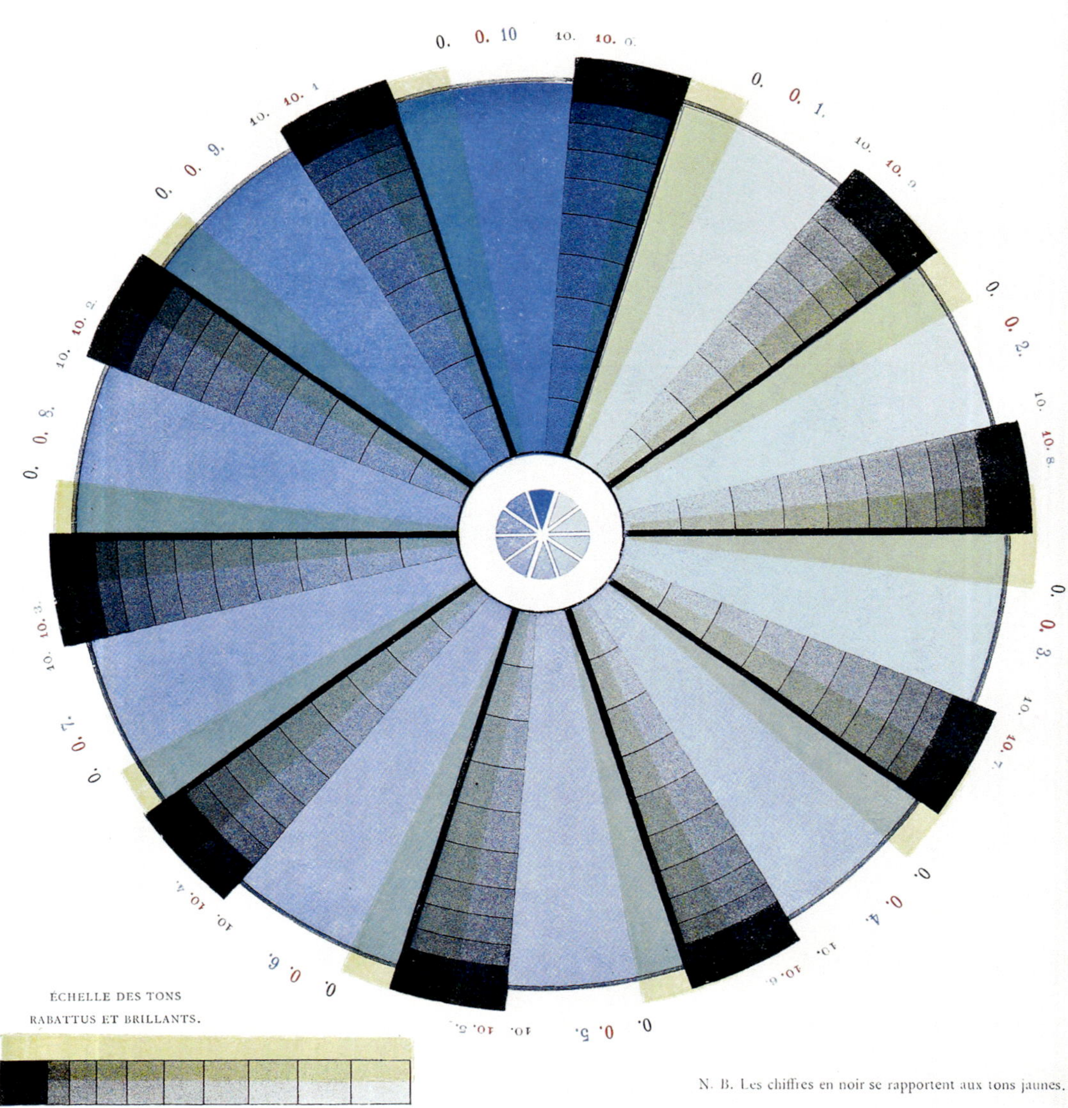


N. B. Les chiffres en noir se rapportent aux tons jaunes.

LE BLEU.

Ses tons lavés et leurs gammes.

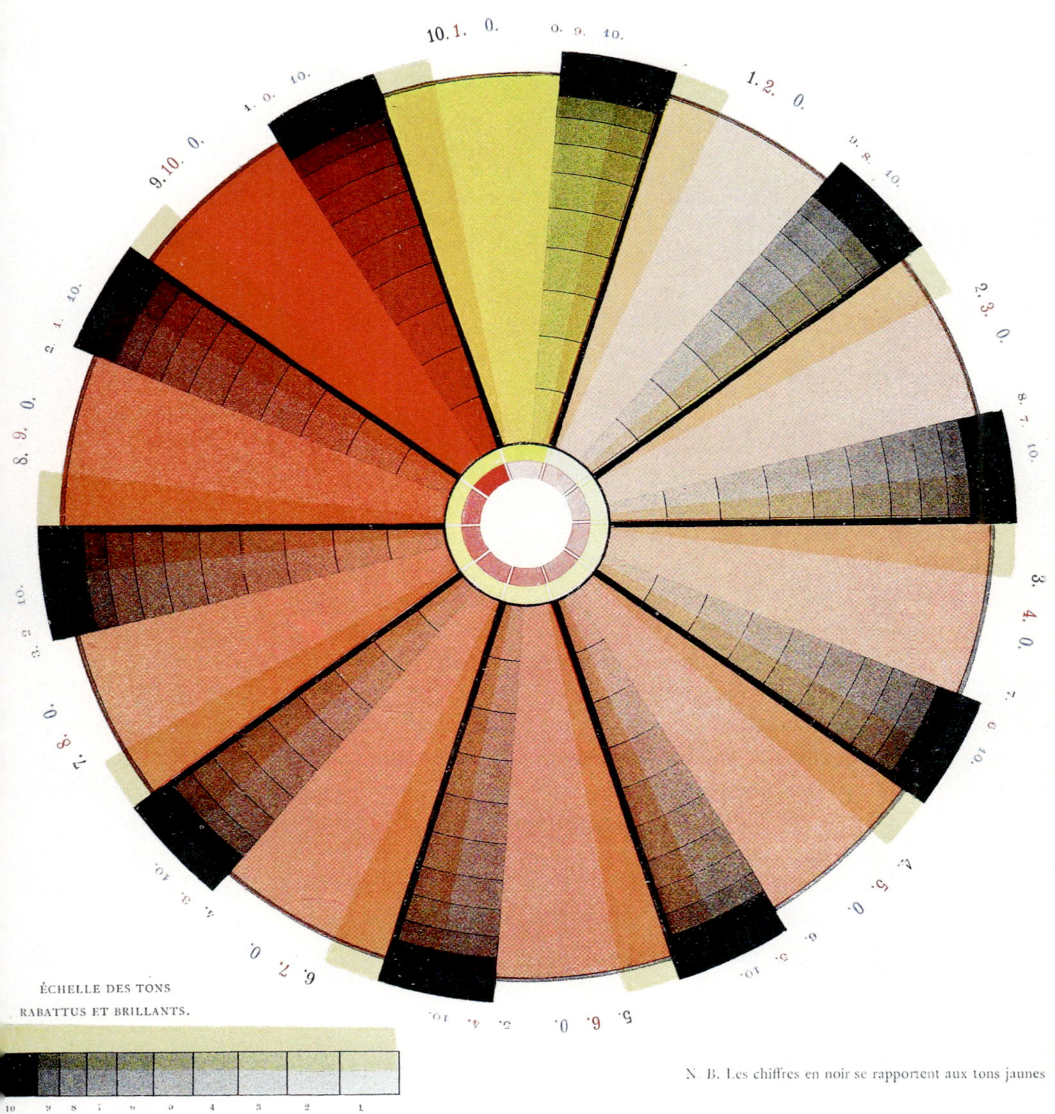


N. B. Les chiffres en noir se rapportent aux tons jaunes

LES NUANCES 10.1.0. et 9.10.0.

Leurs tons lavés et leurs gammes.

## Die Reproduktion von Farben

Robert Steinheils Buch ist ein Meisterwerk der dekorativen Buchgestaltung und -illustration des späten 19. Jahrhunderts und als solches auch selbstreferenziell, da es die technischen Möglichkeiten des Farbrasterdrucks in den 1890er-Jahren zelebrierte. Der vollständige Titel, *La Reproduction des Couleurs par la superposition des trois couleurs simples*, macht deutlich, dass das Buch demonstrieren sollte, wie Farbe reproduziert wird, indem man die „einfachen" Primärfarben Gelb, Rot und Blau übereinanderlegt. Der Bucheinband mit seiner kunstvollen, in prismatischer Abstufung gedruckten Titelgrafik auf dem Vorderdeckel ist typisch für die Ästhetik des Fin de Siècle. Die Titelseite liefert einen weiteren Vorgeschmack auf die folgenden Abbildungen. Ihr schmückender, leuchtkräftiger Halbkreis aus 660 einzelnen Farbtönen veranschaulicht die Grundsätze der simultanen Farbkontraste.

Das von dem alteingesessenen französischen Unternehmen Berger-Levrault et Cie gedruckte Werk enthält 43 Buchdruckseiten Haupttext, darunter ein Glossar der Farbbegriffe und eine Farbtaxonomie (mit Hinweisen auf Einflüsse von Chevreul, Lacouture und anderen) nebst alphabetischen und numerischen Tabellen aller in den Abbildungen vorkommenden farblichen „Nuancen". Auf den Text folgt ein „Atlas" von 150 Farbtafeln, der je nach Charge des Buches auf drei verschiedenen Papiertypen gedruckt wurde und die Serie der Farbkombinationen zeigt. Diese nehmen größtenteils die Form von Farbkreisen an, deren in zehn Abstufungen unterteilte Sektoren das Druckverfahren abbilden und für jede Nuance oder Schattierung genaue, durch drei Zahlen bestimmte Mischverhältnisse angeben. Auf 16 Tafeln sind Farbüberlagerungen in nummerierten Rastern aus jeweils zehn mal zehn Feldern zu sehen, während die letzte Farbtafel aus einer Ansammlung mehrerer Überlagerungen in verschiedenen Formen und Mustern besteht, darunter als Wiederholung im Zentrum die halbkreisförmige Abbildung von der Titelseite. Insgesamt zeigen die Tafeln fast fünfzehntausend Einzelfarben. Das äußerst ambitionierte, mit einem Höchstmaß an Fachwissen produzierte Buch über den Farbdruck zeugt auf prachtvolle Weise von den technologischen Errungenschaften des Industriezeitalters. Seine Auflage muss klein gewesen sein, denn es zählt heute zu den seltensten historischen Büchern über Farbe.

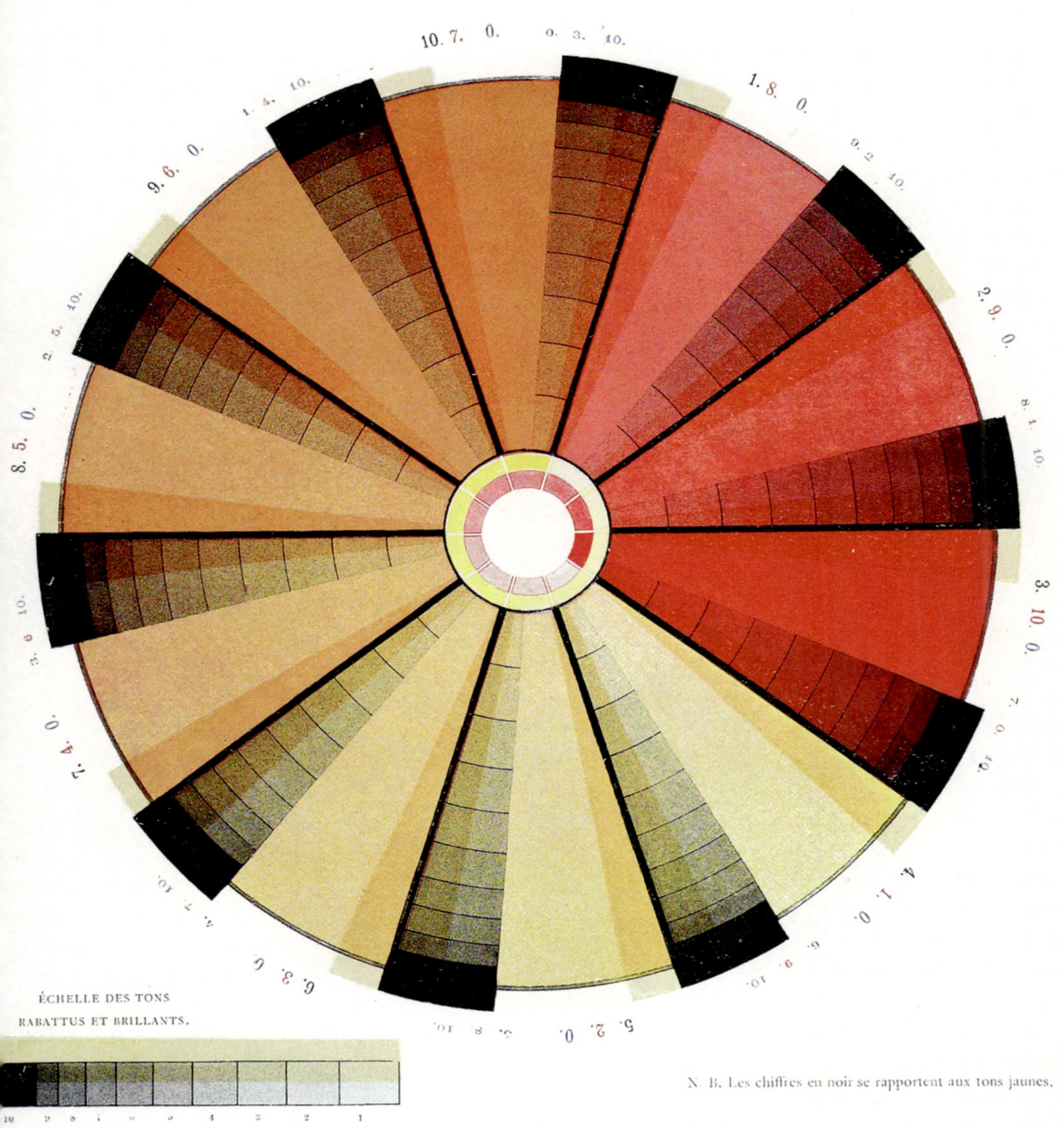


N. B. Les chiffres en noir se rapportent aux tons jaunes.

## LES NUANCES 10.7.0. et 3.10.0.

Leurs tons lavés et leurs gammes.

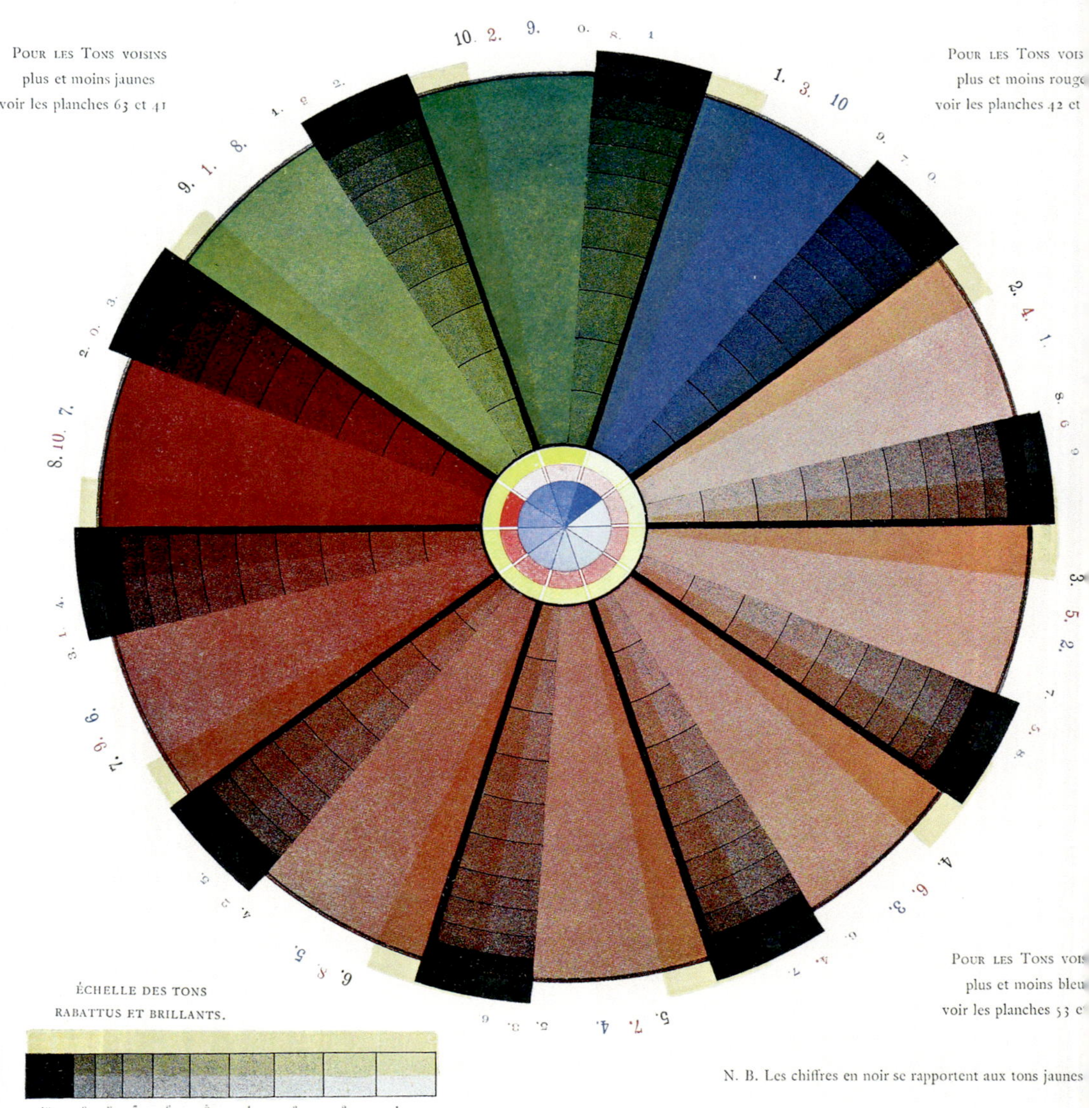


LES NUANCES 10.2.9, 8.10.7 et 1.3.10.

Leurs tons lavés et leurs gammes.

## La Reproduction des Couleurs

Le livre de Robert Steinheil est un chef-d'œuvre consacré au dessin et à l'illustration éditoriale de la fin du XIXe siècle. À ce titre, on peut dire qu'il est autoréférentiel, dans la mesure où il célèbre les possibilités techniques offertes par l'impression en couleurs demi-teintes des années 1890. Le titre complet, *La Reproduction des Couleurs par la superposition des trois couleurs simples*, pose clairement que le propos du livre est de démontrer comment reproduire des couleurs en superposant celles appelées « simples », autrement dit les couleurs primaires, jaune, rouge et bleu. La couverture est typique du style esthétique fin-de-siècle, avec son lettrage recherché aux nuances prismatiques. La page de titre donne un avant-goût de la qualité des illustrations qui suivent : elle figure un lumineux demi-cercle décoratif de 660 teintes différentes, qui représente les principes des contrastes simultanés des couleurs.

Imprimé par la très ancienne maison française Berger-Levrault et Cie, le livre contient 43 pages de texte typographié, dont un glossaire chromatique, une taxonomie de la couleur (qui reconnaît l'influence de Chevreul, Lacouture et d'autres), ainsi que des tables alphabétique et numérique de toutes les nuances de couleurs utilisées dans les illustrations. Le texte est suivi d'un « Atlas » de 150 planches en couleurs qui figurent les séries de combinaisons chromatiques et sont imprimées sur trois types de papier différents selon les lots d'exemplaires. La plupart des planches se présentent sous la forme de cercles chromatiques dont les portions sont divisées en 10 gradations, qui illustrent le processus d'impression et indiquent les proportions exactes pour chaque nuance, identifiée par trois numéros. Il y a par ailleurs 16 planches qui montrent les superpositions de couleurs par un système de grilles numérotées 10 x 10, la dernière étant un assemblage de plusieurs superpositions de formes et motifs différents, dont la figure en demi-cercle de la page de titre, reproduite ici au centre. Au total, les planches rassemblent près de 15 000 couleurs différentes. Un ouvrage extrêmement ambitieux sur l'impression en couleurs, produit avec un très haut niveau de savoir-faire, qui reste un magnifique témoignage des réussites technologiques de l'ère industrielle. En raison d'un tirage probablement réduit, l'ouvrage est devenu l'un des livres historiques sur la couleur les plus rares.

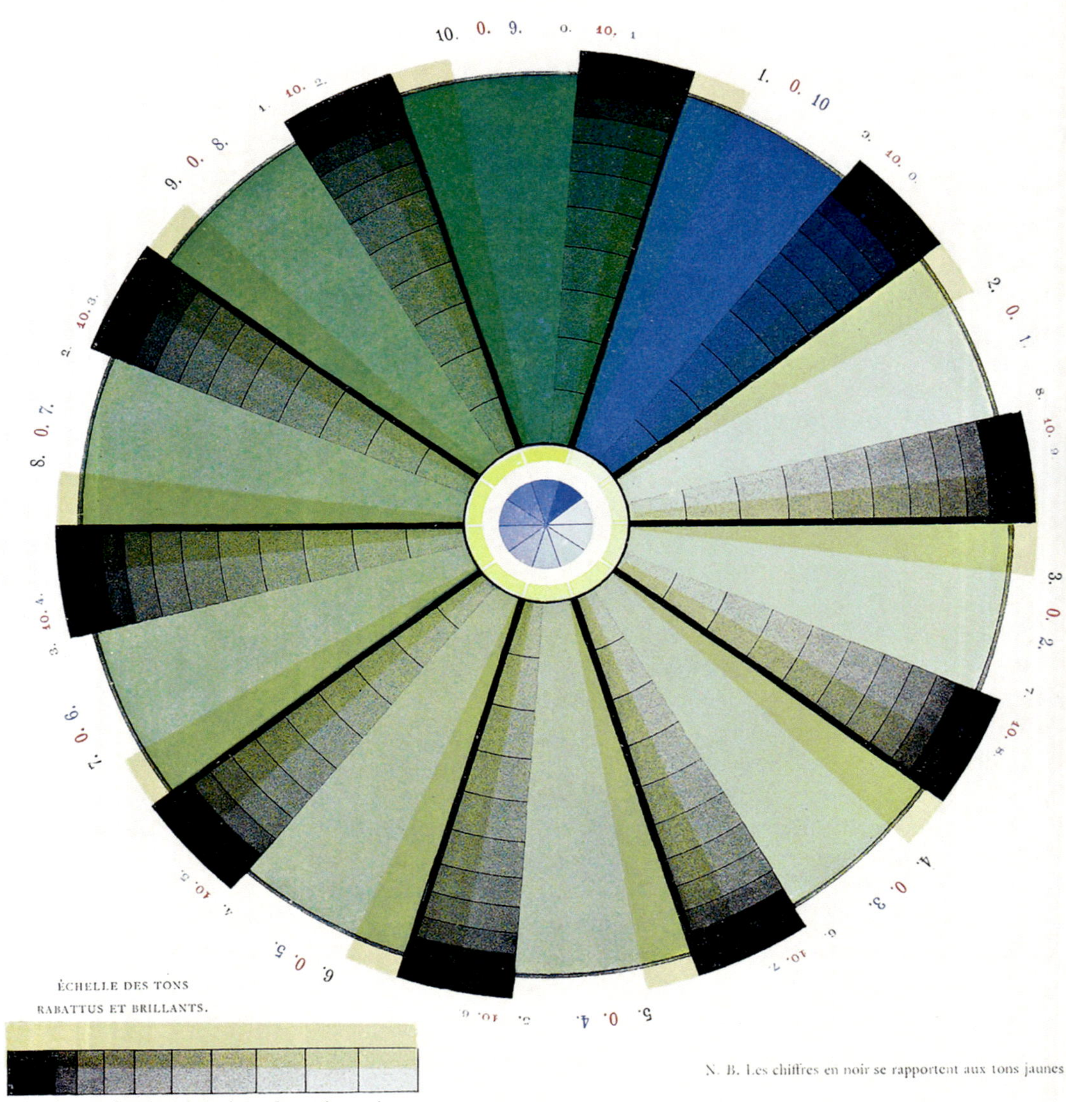


LES NUANCES 10.0.9. et 1.0.10.

Leurs tons lavés et leurs gammes.

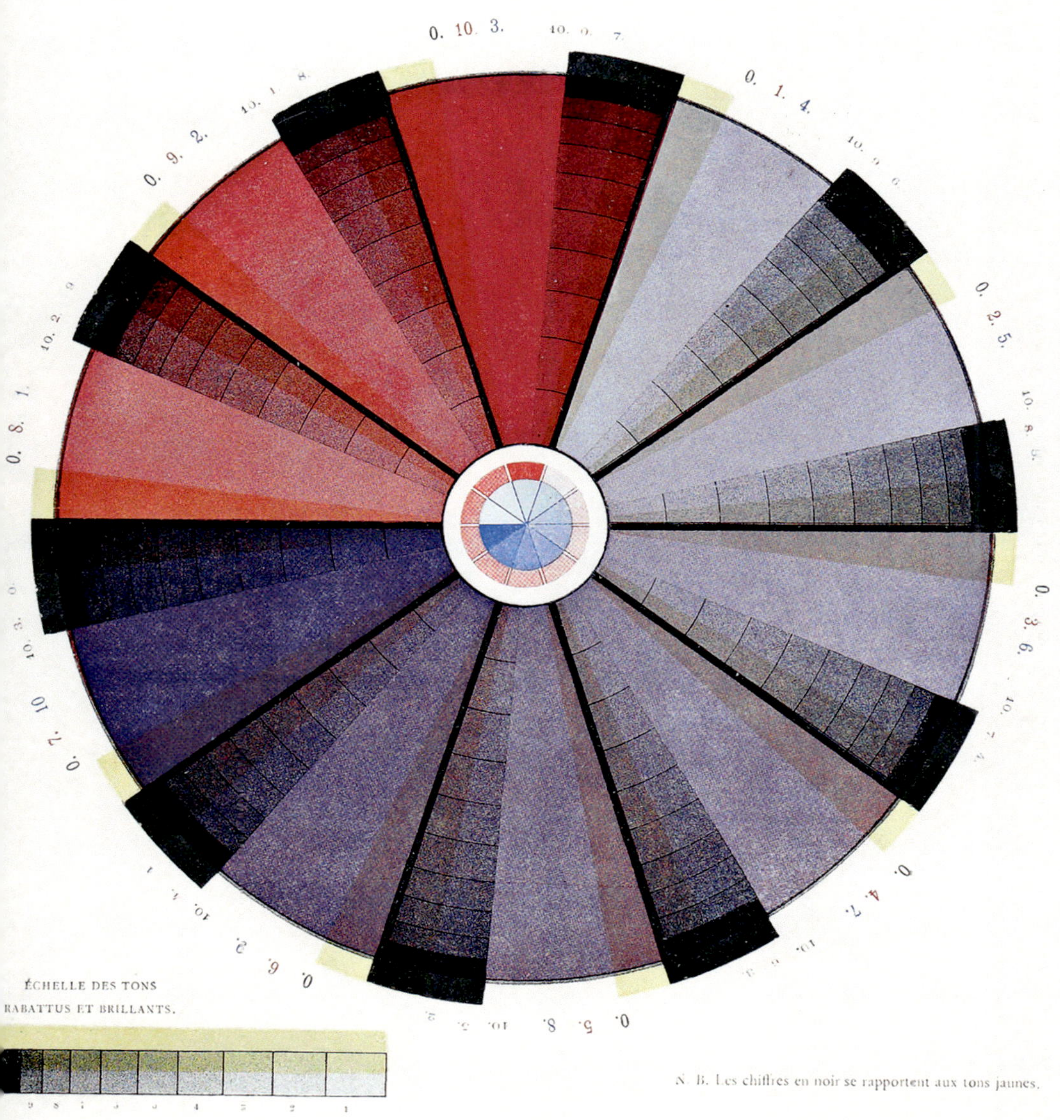


N. B. Les chiffres en noir se rapportent aux tons jaunes.

LES NUANCES 0.10.3. et 0.7.10.

Leurs tons lavés et leurs gammes.

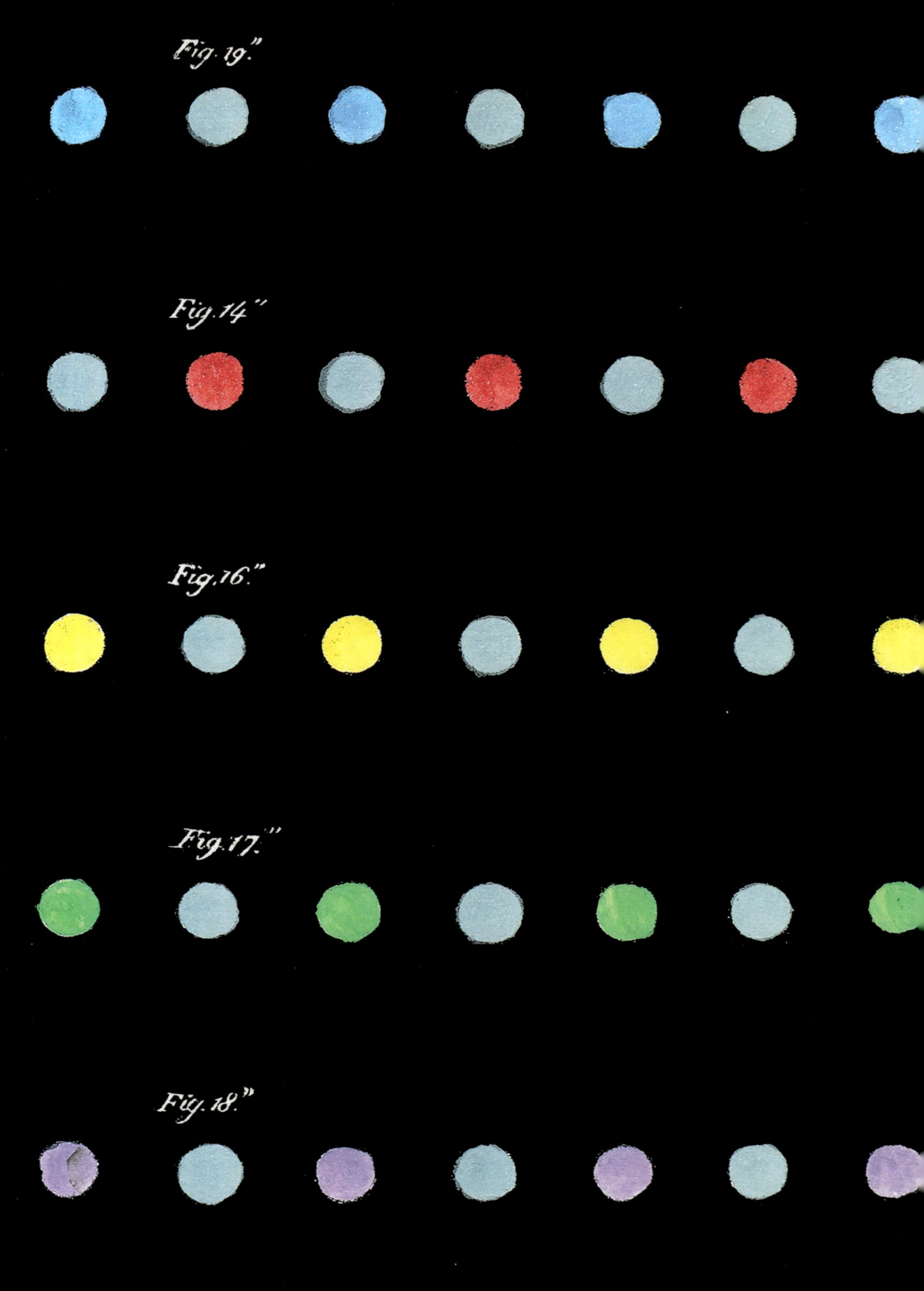
Fig. 19."
Fig. 14."
Fig. 16."
Fig. 17."
Fig. 18."

## Chapter 3

# *New Elucidations:* THE RISE OF COLOUR THEORY

## 1704–1864

## Isaac Newton (1643–1727)

# OPTICKS

## or, A Treatise of the Reflexions, Refractions, Inflexions and Colours of Light

*13 plates, 25 x 21 cm | 9 7/8 x 8 1/4 in., London, 1704*
*Washington, D.C., Library of Congress*

Newton's *Opticks* of 1704 is regularly named as one of the milestones in colour history. It made an immediate impact on the arts and sciences in the 18th century, although it is worth noting that Newton had been occupied with the subject of colour for decades before this book was published, and that he was himself part of a long line of other figures who worked with colour concepts and research. He was certainly not the first to have carried out optical studies, but in terms of scale and thoroughness his work stands out by some distance from that of both his contemporaries and his predecessors. Newton's status and reputation, together with advances in the print culture of his day, also helped to disseminate and popularise his work, with this book being translated into several languages soon after the first edition in English. It was discussed, developed and adapted from a number of critical perspectives by several other writers in the 18th and 19th centuries, and even today there is hardly a text, programme or talk on colour that does not mention Newton. That first small prism he bought in the 1660s when still a young man has thrown a very long ray of colour across the centuries, and his colour circle is one of the most important and recognisable diagrams in the history of science.

Newton began experimenting with prisms at Woolsthorpe Manor, his home in Lincolnshire, in 1666. He first presented the results of his "crucial experiment" of splitting pure sunlight into the prismatic colour spectrum in the *Philosophical Transactions of the Royal Society* in London in 1671. With this experiment he proved that the colours of the spectrum visible to the human eye cannot be split further into more colours, and in fact form white light again when redirected through a second prism, thus laying out the principles of additive, or immaterial, colour mixture. At first, Newton noted five identifiable colours but later settled on seven, which he understood to be analogous to musical scales, namely red, orange, yellow, green, blue, indigo and violet. Despite the linear appearance of colour order in his experiments he envisioned a circular shape to represent it from an early stage, eventually creating the (uncoloured) colour wheel that was printed in *Opticks*. There are hundreds of engravings in *Opticks*, illustrating the many stages and aspects of Newton's decades of research, but the surprisingly small colour wheel, with its uneven proportional divisions, is the most potent and influential of his diagrams. Within a few years it was adapted by other researchers, in an attempt to meet the needs of artists working with material colour.

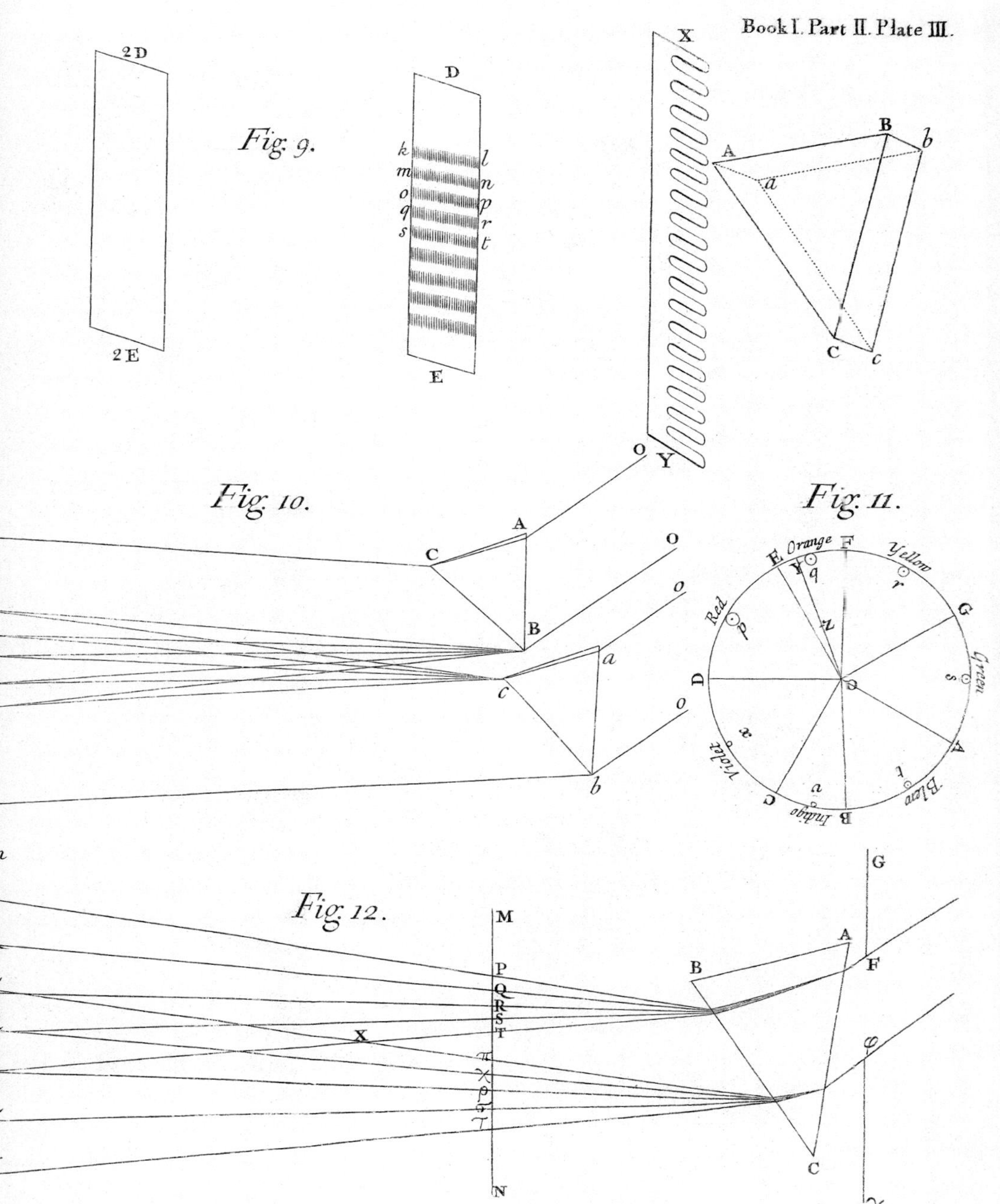
Fig. 9.
2D
2E
D
E
k
l
m
n
o
p
q
r
s
t
X
Y
O
A
B
b
a
C
c
Fig. 10.
Fig. 11.
Orange
Yellow
Red
Green
Blue
Indigo
Violet
Fig. 12.
M
P
Q
R
S
T
N
G
F
X

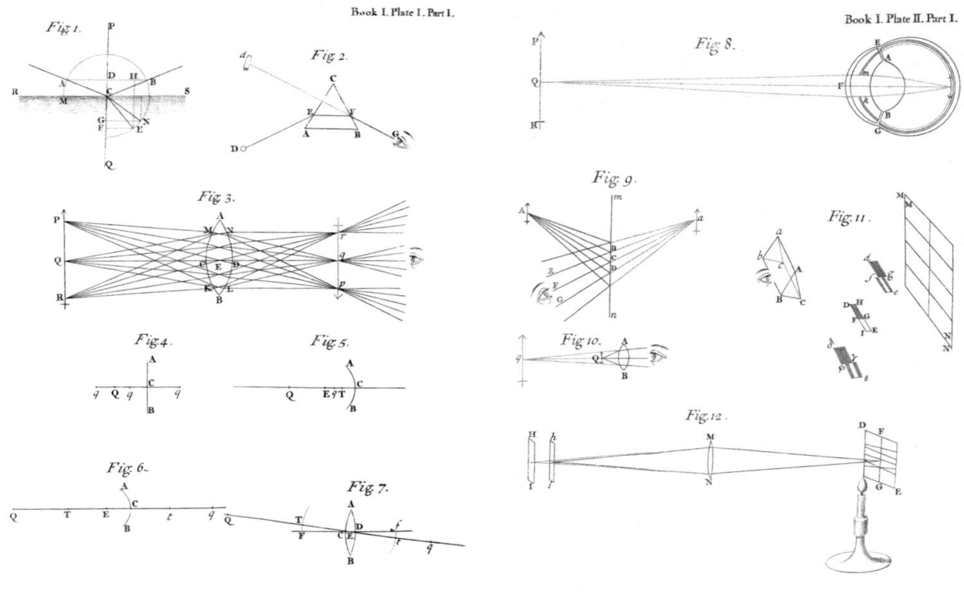


## Optik: oder Abhandlung über Spiegelungen, Brechungen, Beugungen und Farben des Lichts

Newtons *Opticks* aus dem Jahr 1704 wird regelmäßig als Meilenstein der Farbgeschichte bezeichnet. Das Buch hatte unmittelbare Auswirkungen auf die Kunst und Wissenschaft des 18. Jahrhunderts. Nicht zu vergessen ist jedoch, dass sich Newton bereits Jahrzehnte vor dessen Veröffentlichung mit dem Thema Farbe befasst hatte und selbst zu einer Vielzahl von Personen gehörte, die sich mit Farbsystemen und Farbforschung beschäftigten. Er war mit Sicherheit nicht der Erste, der optische Studien durchführte, doch im Hinblick auf Umfang und Gründlichkeit hebt sich seine Arbeit deutlich von der seiner Zeitgenossen und Vorgänger ab. Newtons Stellung und Reputation, aber auch die Fortschritte im Druckwesen seiner Zeit, halfen sein Werk zu verbreiten und bekannt zu machen. Kurz nach Erscheinen der englischen Erstauflage wurde das Buch in mehrere Sprachen übersetzt. Im 18. und 19. Jahrhundert wurde es von anderen Autoren aus unterschiedlichen Perspektiven besprochen, weiterentwickelt und angepasst, und selbst heutzutage gibt es kaum einen Text, ein Programm oder eine Diskussion über Farbe, in denen Newton nicht erwähnt wird. Das erste kleine Prisma, das er in den 1660er-Jahren als junger Mann erwarb, hat einen sehr langen Farbstrahl durch die Jahrhunderte geworfen, und sein Farbkreis zählt zu den wohl wichtigsten Diagrammen der Wissenschaftsgeschichte mit besonderem Wiedererkennungswert.

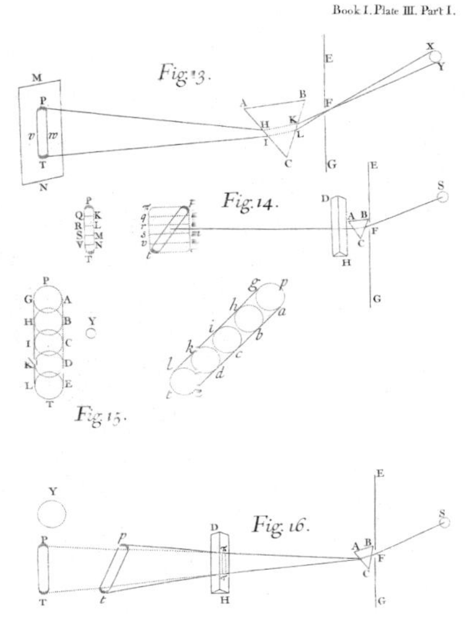


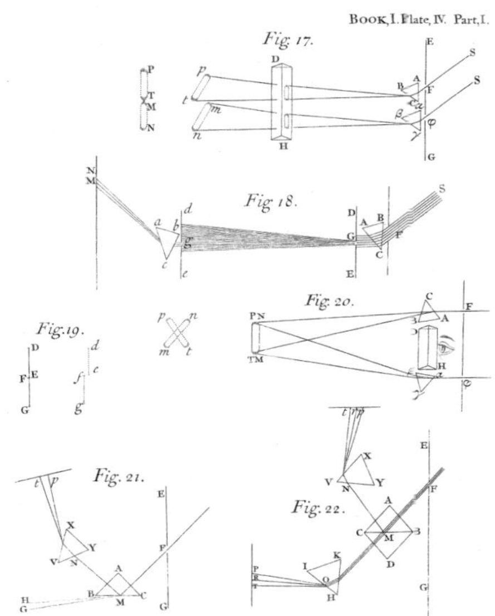


Newton begann 1666 in seinem Elternhaus Woolsthorpe Manor in der englischen Grafschaft Lincolnshire mit Prismen zu experimentieren. In den *Philosophical Transactions of the Royal Society* veröffentlichte er 1671 erstmals die Ergebnisse seines „entscheidenden Versuchs“, das Sonnenlicht in die Farben des prismatischen Spektrums aufzuspalten. Mit diesem Versuch bewies er, dass sich die für das menschliche Auge sichtbaren Spektralfarben nicht in weitere Farben aufspalten lassen und bei Umlenkung durch ein zweites Prisma tatsächlich wieder weißes Licht ergeben. Damit hatte er die Grundsätze der additiven oder immateriellen Farbmischung dargelegt. Anfangs notierte Newton fünf identifizierbare Farben, entschied sich dann aber für sieben, die er mit den sieben Stufen der Tonleiter gleichsetzte: Rot, Orange, Gelb, Grün, Blau, Indigo und Violett. Trotz der linearen Ordnung der Farben in seinen Experimenten malte er sich für ihre Darstellung schon früh eine Kreisform aus und schuf schließlich den in *Opticks* abgedruckten (nicht kolorierten) Farbkreis. In Hunderten von Stichen veranschaulicht das Buch die vielen Stadien und Aspekte der jahrzehntelangen Forschungen Newtons, doch der überraschend kleine Farbkreis mit seinen verschieden großen Unterteilungen ist das wirkungsvollste und einflussreichste seiner Diagramme. In dem Versuch, die Bedürfnisse von Künstlern zu erfüllen, die mit stofflichen Farben arbeiteten, wurde der Kreis innerhalb weniger Jahre von anderen Forschern übernommen und weiterentwickelt.

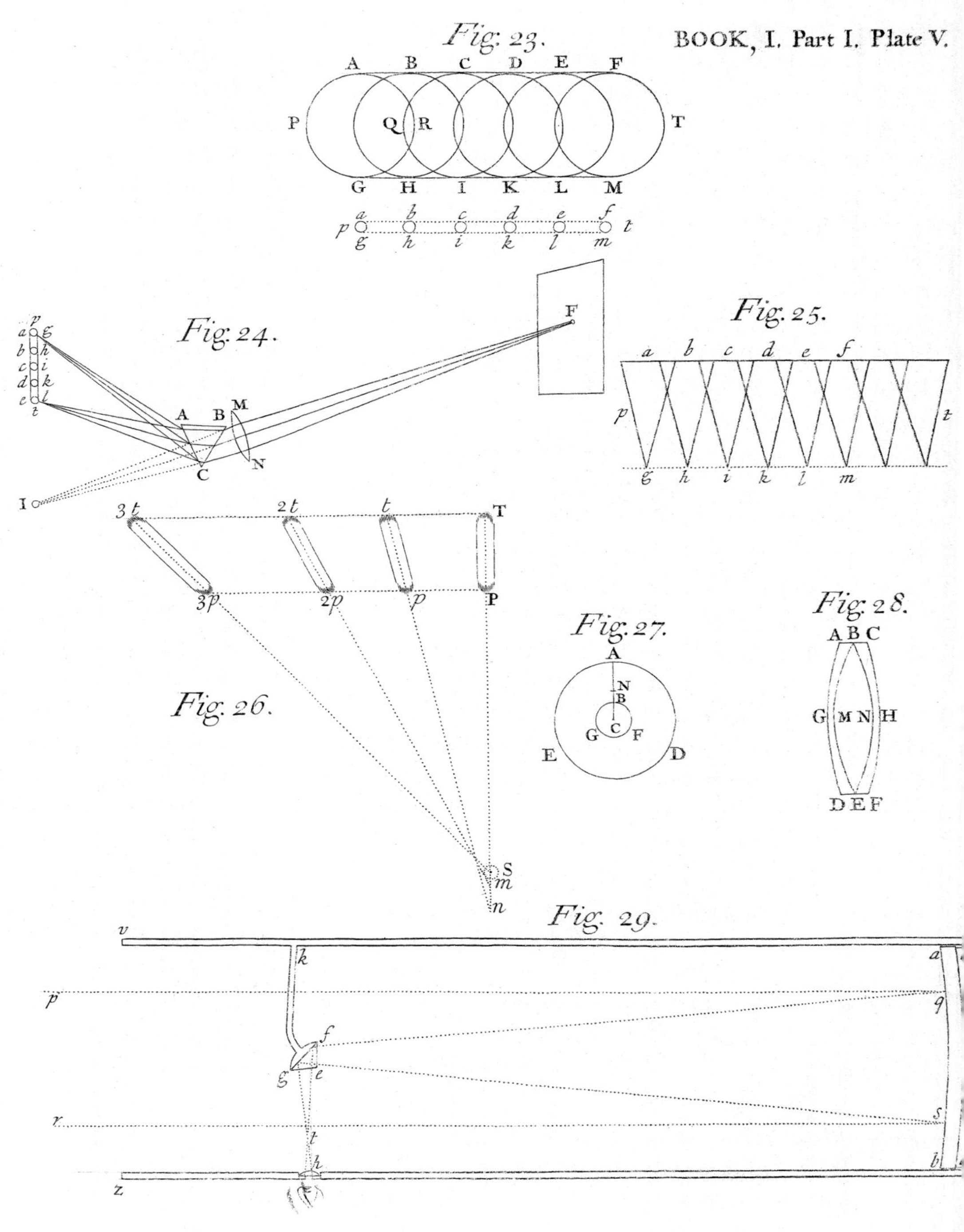
Fig: 23.
Fig: 24.
Fig: 25.
Fig: 26.
Fig: 27.
Fig: 28.
Fig: 29.

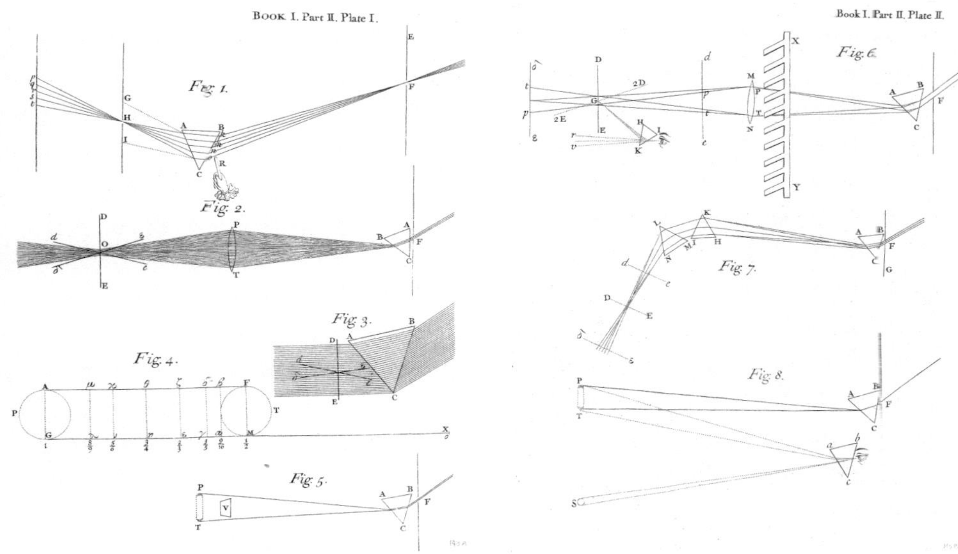


## Traité d'optique sur les réflexions, réfractions, inflexions et couleurs de la lumière

Couramment considéré comme l'un des ouvrages majeurs de l'histoire de la couleur, l'*Opticks* de Newton a paru en 1704 et a imprimé sa marque sur les arts et les sciences du XVIIIe siècle. Quand paraît son traité, Newton s'intéresse au sujet depuis plusieurs décennies déjà. Il s'inscrit dans une longue lignée d'auteurs ayant étudié la couleur et les manières de la concevoir. S'il n'est pas le premier à avoir réalisé des recherches en optique, il se distingue grandement de ses prédécesseurs comme de ses contemporains par l'ampleur et la profondeur de ses travaux. Le statut et la notoriété de Newton, ainsi que les progrès de l'imprimerie, lui permettent de diffuser auprès d'un vaste public cet ouvrage qui, peu après sa première édition en anglais, sera traduit dans plusieurs langues. Son traité est analysé, enrichi et adapté grâce aux divers points de vue critiques de plusieurs auteurs des XVIIIe et XIXe siècles. Aujourd'hui encore, rares sont les textes, programmes de recherche ou conférences sur la couleur qui ne citent pas Newton. Le petit prisme qu'il achète au cours de sa jeunesse dans les années 1660 diffusera à travers les siècles un immense rayon de couleur. Son cercle chromatique est l'un des graphiques les plus marquants et reconnaissables de l'histoire des sciences.

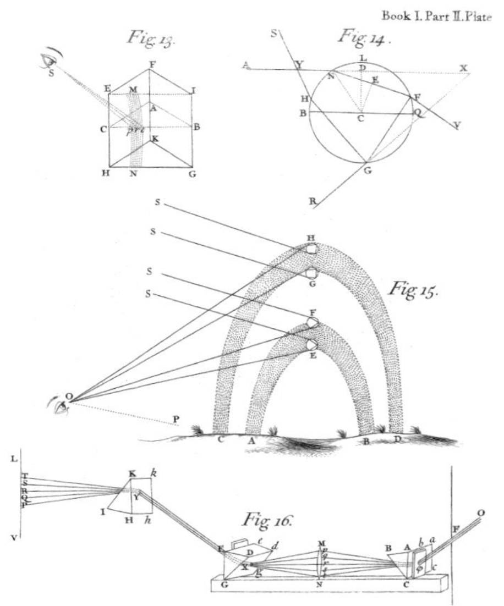


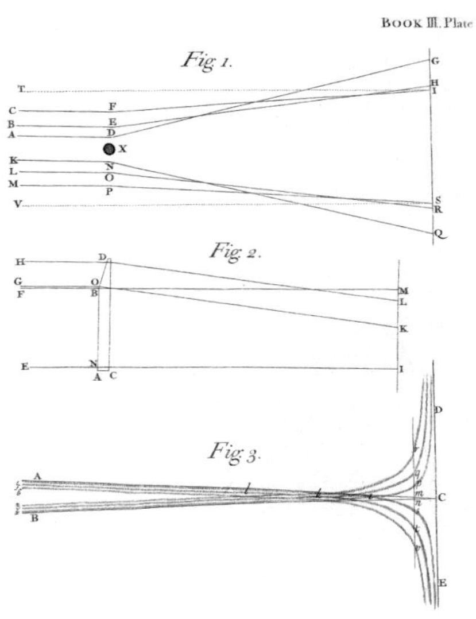


C'est en 1666 que Newton réalise ses premières expérimentations avec des prismes dans son manoir de Woolsthorpe, dans le Lincolnshire. Il présente les résultats de son « expérience capitale » – la division de la lumière solaire pure en un spectre de couleurs prismatiques – dans les *Philosophical Transactions of the Royal Society*, à Londres en 1671. Cette manipulation lui permet de démontrer que les couleurs du spectre visible par l'œil humain se limitent à un nombre donné de teintes et qu'elles se recomposent sous la forme de lumière blanche lorsqu'on les dirige vers un second prisme. Il établit ainsi les principes du mélange additif, ou immatériel, des couleurs. Newton identifie d'abord cinq couleurs, puis sept, qu'il estime analogues à des gammes musicales : rouge, orange, jaune, vert, bleu, indigo et violet. Malgré l'aspect linéaire de l'ordre chromatique de ses expériences, il conçoit très tôt l'idée d'une forme circulaire pour représenter celui-ci et créera le cercle chromatique (mais incolore) qui figure dans *Opticks*. Ce traité contient des centaines de gravures illustrant les nombreux aspects et étapes des longues recherches de Newton. Pourtant, c'est un petit cercle chromatique, étonnamment modeste avec ses divisions inégalement proportionnées, qui constitue son graphique le plus frappant et dont l'influence sera gigantesque. En quelques années, il est remanié par plusieurs chercheurs qui tentent de le mettre au service des peintres travaillant avec la couleur matérielle.

# Quadr. Tab. I.

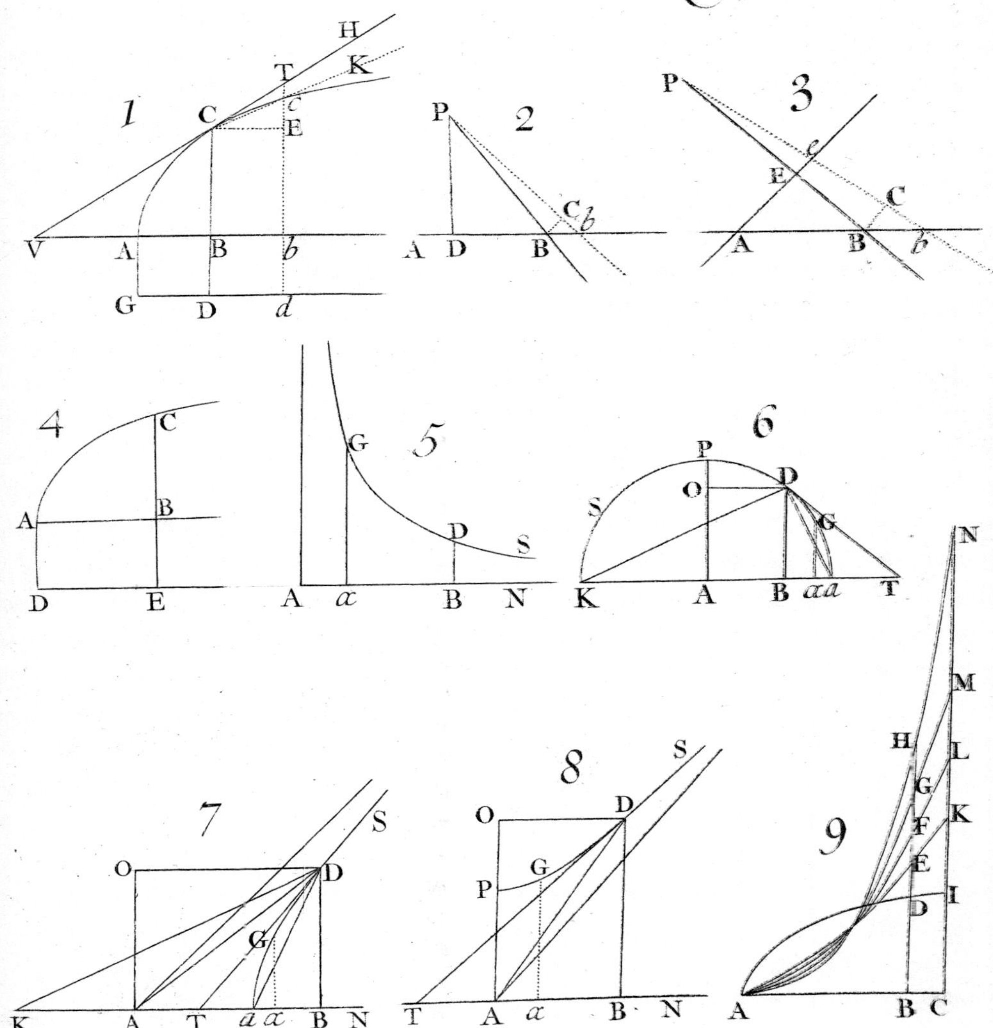
1
H
T
K
C
c
E
V
A
B
b
G
D
d
2
P
C
b
A
D
B
3
P
e
E
C
A
B
b
4
C
A
B
D
E
5
G
D
S
A
α
B
N
6
P
D
O
S
G
K
A
B
aa
T
7
O
D
S
G
K
A
T
a α
B
N
8
S
O
D
G
P
T
A
α
B
N
9
N
M
H
L
G
F
K
E
D
I
A
B
C

*Fig. 5.*

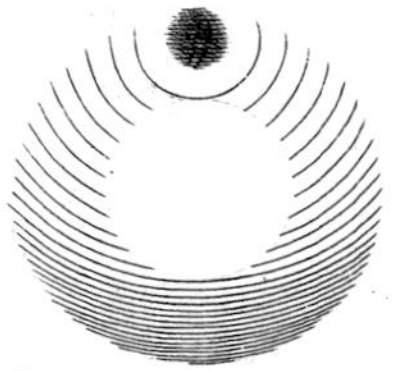

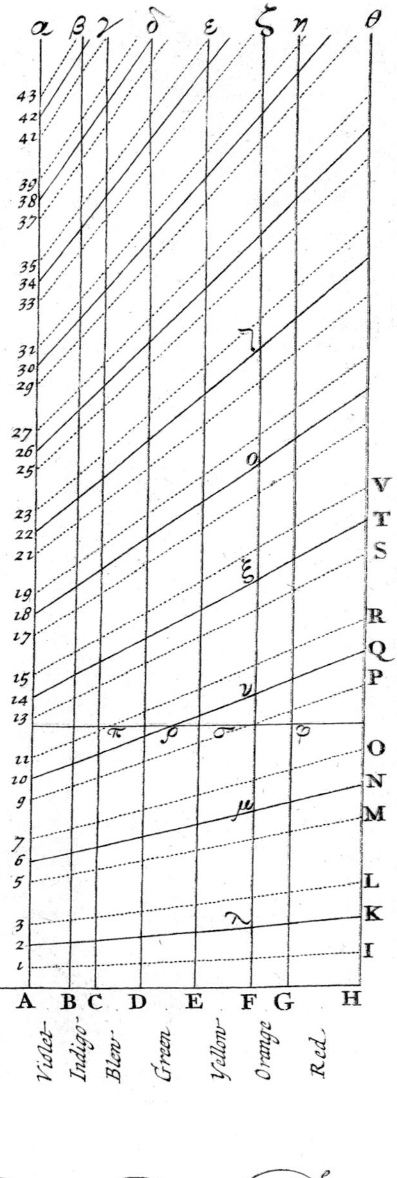

*Fig. 6.*

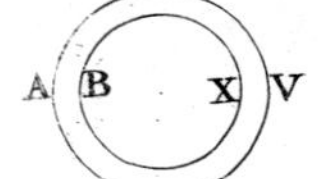

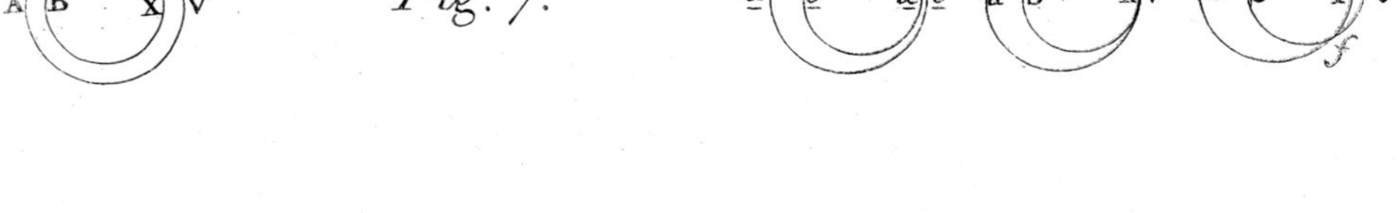

*Fig. 7.*

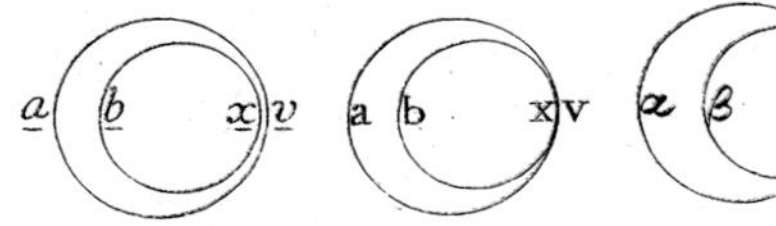

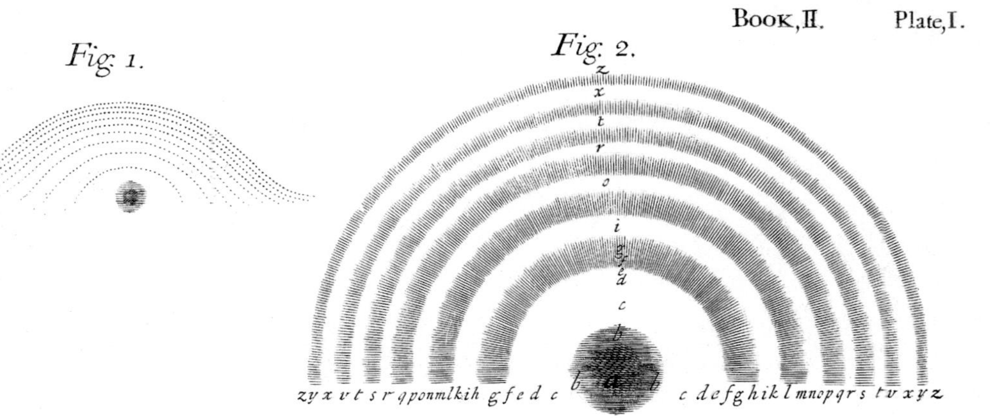
Fig: 1.
Fig: 2.
z x t r o i g f e d c b
z y x v t s r q p o n m l k i h g f e d c b a b c d e f g h i k l m n o p q r s t v x y z

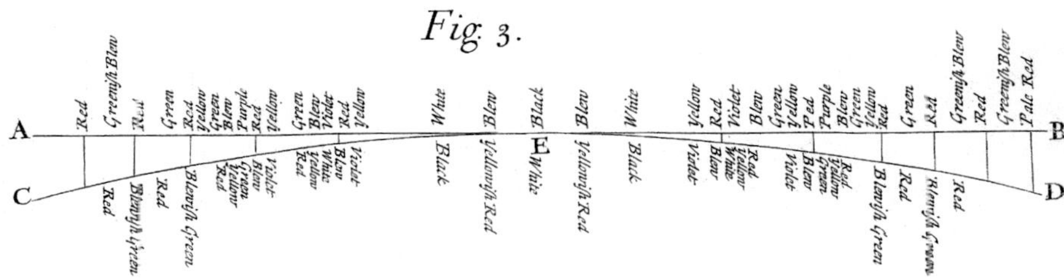
Fig: 3.
A
B
C
D
E
White
Blew
Black
Blew
White
Black
Yellowish Red
White
Yellowish Red
Black

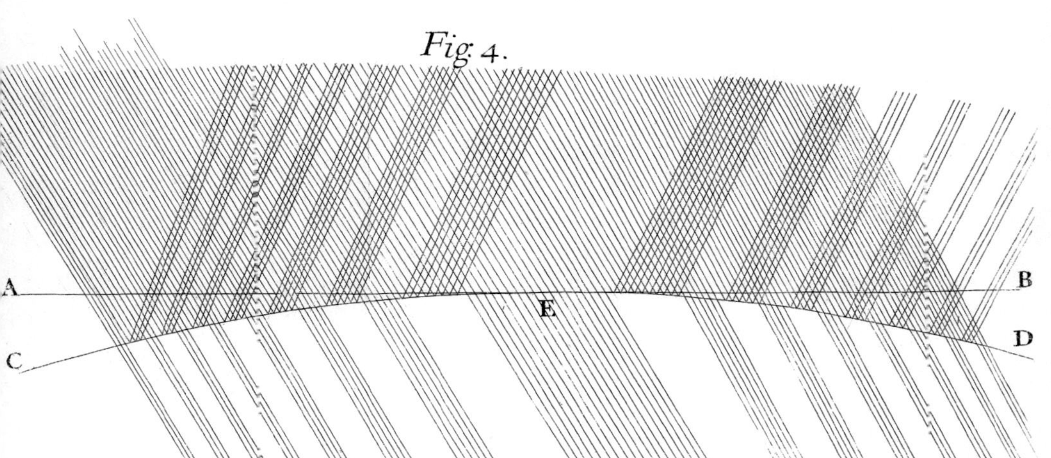
Fig: 4.
A
B
C
D
E

## Mary Gartside (*c.* 1755–1819)

# AN ESSAY ON LIGHT AND SHADE, ON COLOURS, AND ON COMPOSITION IN GENERAL

*10 plates, 3 illustrated pages, 29 x 22.5 cm | 11 ⅜ x 8 ⅞ in., London, 1805*
*Sussex, collection of the author*

The English flower painter Mary Gartside was very likely the first woman to have published illustrated books on colour. Women were not excluded from colour history, and had played a part as allegorical figures, colourists, assistants, illuminators, translators, teachers and in other roles, but rarely had they been able to participate as authors or theorists. One early exception is Catherine Perrot (1620–169?), who taught art at the French court and published a treatise on painting miniatures in 1686. In some ways, Gartside's road to publishing books on colour was similar, since she too worked as a painting teacher, which was an acceptable occupation for a woman at the time and also justified writing about it. Very little is known about her life, but she secured the patronage of Lady Sophia Grey of Dunham Massey, in Cheshire, and managed to carve out a lifelong career in art which included publishing a pamphlet and three books on colour between around 1804 and 1808. Although she could not enrol at the Royal Academy as a student, she exhibited some of her botanical drawings there in 1781 and at other venues in London until 1808, thereby establishing a personal network of artists, teachers, botanists and colour researchers, while always carefully operating within what was socially acceptable for an unmarried woman in Georgian England. But there is more to the story of Mary Gartside.

Her books, of which *An Essay on Light and Shade* was the first, were overtly conceived as watercolour painting manuals for young women, but beyond that Gartside succeeded in placing herself within a tradition of colour theorists, adding the words "new theory" to the title of her second book. Her work mentioned other researchers, among them Isaac Newton and Moses Harris, making it clear that she

# Yellow · 2.

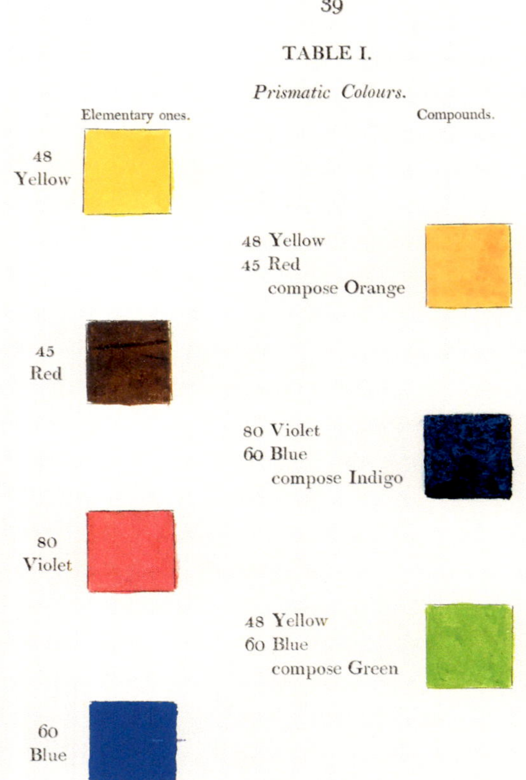


had a sound knowledge of colour discourse, and it is possible that she knew James Sowerby (pp. 176–183) in person.

*An Essay on Light and Shade* is illustrated with two pictorial plates (soft-ground etchings), two coloured tables, a further coloured engraving showing a colour circle described as a "ball" and eight plates of colour "blots". It is these last eight plates that have given Gartside a special place in colour history. While essentially examples of her colour theory applied to composition and the harmonious arrangement of colours (white, yellow, orange, green, scarlet, blue, violet and crimson), they are not coloured

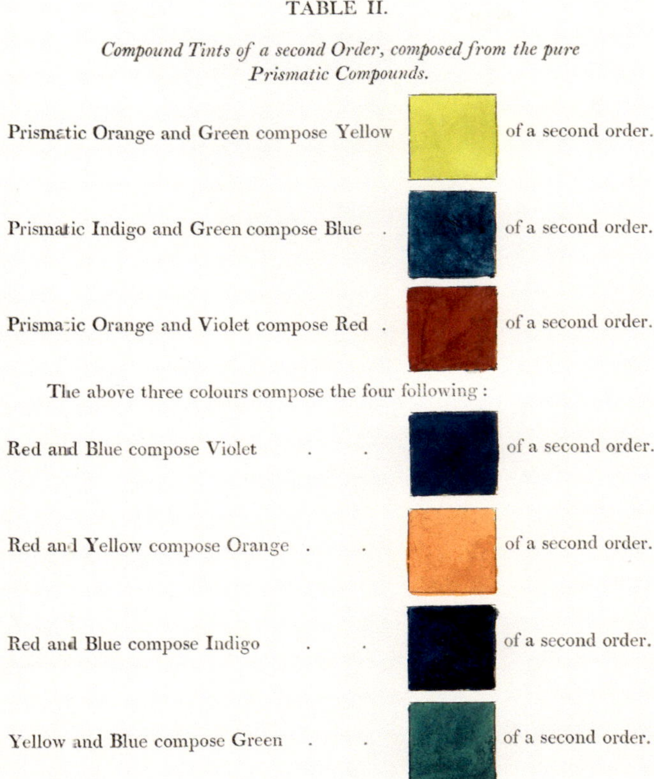

41

TABLE II.

*Compound Tints of a second Order, composed from the pure Prismatic Compounds.*

| | |
|---|---|
| Prismatic Orange and Green compose Yellow | of a second order. |
| Prismatic Indigo and Green compose Blue . | of a second order. |
| Prismatic Orange and Violet compose Red . | of a second order. |

The above three colours compose the four following :

| | |
|---|---|
| Red and Blue compose Violet . . | of a second order. |
| Red and Yellow compose Orange . . | of a second order. |
| Red and Blue compose Indigo . . | of a second order. |
| Yellow and Blue compose Green . . | of a second order. |

engravings but freely painted masses of colour that vaguely resemble flowers seen through wet glass, and because they were hand-painted the images are different in each copy of the book. The concept was very clearly Gartside's own, but she could not have painted all the blots herself for the entire print run, and it is likely that she used some of her students to help out. Gartside's colour blots were inventive, radical, ambitious and suffused with an abstract beauty that has only recently begun to be recognised and appreciated.

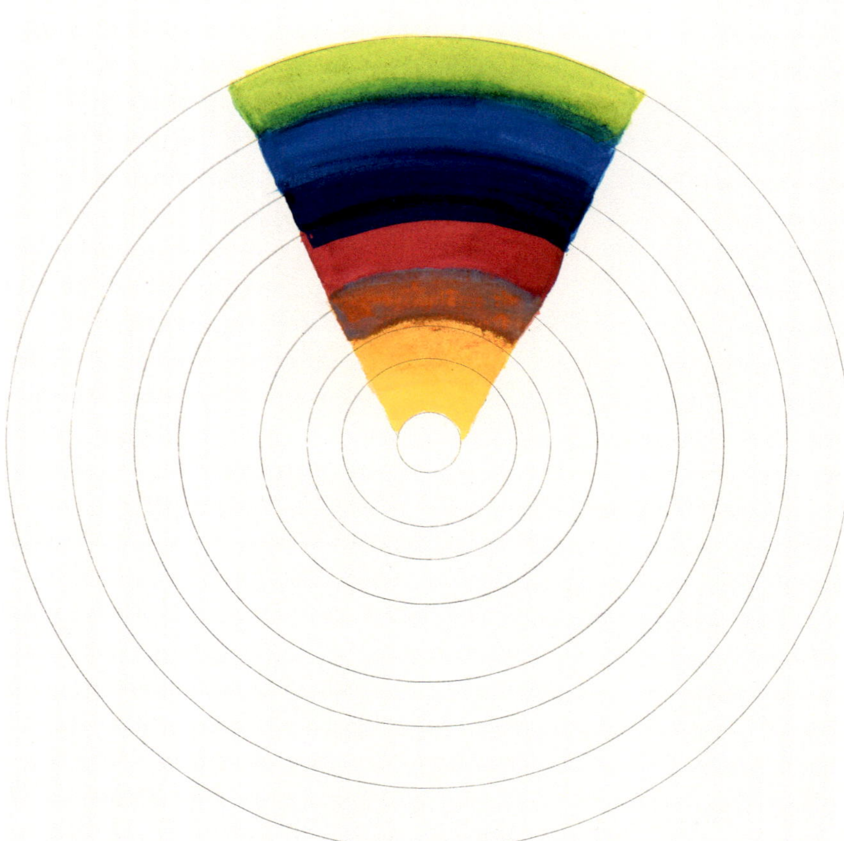

*It has already been said that it is not meant to arrange the colours in circles in a Picture: for besides the absurdity of that, the proper quantity of each could not be observed as may be seen here, if each circle was filled with its own colour. Therefore nothing more must be looked for in this than the proper situation for each colour in respect to the others, which is shewn by the small portion that is coloured, and if the effect of Light & Shade on a Ball and concave object is considered, it may be known directly what degree of brilliancy or shade should be given to each colour in every different part of it. This Idea will be of use if kept in mind when Painting Objects from nature.*

Published as the Act directs, Nov$^{r}$ 1. 1804, by T. Gardiner, Princes Street, Cavendish Square

## Ein Aufsatz über Licht und Schatten, über Farben und über Komposition im Allgemeinen

Die englische Blumenmalerin Mary Gartside war die höchstwahrscheinlich erste Frau, die ein illustriertes Buch über Farbe veröffentlichte. Auch Frauen haben in der Geschichte der Farbtheorie eine Rolle gespielt, zum Beispiel als allegorische Figuren, Koloristinnen, Helferinnen, Illuminatorinnen, Übersetzerinnen oder Lehrerinnen, doch selten waren sie in der Lage gewesen, einen Beitrag als Autorinnen oder Theoretikerinnen zu leisten. Eine frühe Ausnahme bildete Catherine Perrot (1620–169?), die am französischen Hof Kunst unterrichtete und 1686 eine Abhandlung über Miniaturmalerei herausgab. In mancherlei Hinsicht verlief Gartsides Weg zur Veröffentlichung von Farbenbüchern ähnlich, denn auch sie unterrichtete Malerei, was als Beschäftigung für Frauen damals akzeptiert wurde und auch rechtfertigte, dass sie darüber schrieben. Über Gartsides Leben ist sehr wenig bekannt. Man weiß, dass sie sich die Unterstützung von Lady Sophia Grey aus Dunham Massey in der Grafschaft Cheshire erwarb und es ihr gelang, ein Leben lang im Bereich der Kunst zu arbeiten und um 1804 bis 1808 eine Broschüre und drei Bücher über Farbe zu publizieren. Obwohl sie sich nicht als Studentin an der Royal Academy of Arts einschreiben konnte, stellte Gartside dort 1781 und an anderen Orten in London bis 1808 ihre botanischen Zeichnungen aus und baute sich auf diese Weise ein persönliches Netzwerk aus Künstlerinnen und Künstlern, Lehrern, Botanikern und Farbforschern auf. Gleichzeitig achtete sie sorgsam darauf, nur in einem Rahmen zu agieren, der für eine unverheiratete Frau im georgianischen England gesellschaftlich anerkannt war. Doch das ist nicht die ganze Geschichte von Mary Gartside.

Ihre Bücher, von denen *An Essay on Light and Shade* das erste war, waren offenkundig als Aquarellmalhandbücher für junge Frauen angelegt. Darüber hinaus jedoch stellte sich Gartside erfolgreich in eine Tradition von Farbtheoretikern, indem sie dem Titel ihres zweiten Buches die Worte „neue Farbenlehre" hinzufügte. In ihrem Werk erwähnte sie andere Forscher, darunter Isaac Newton und Moses Harris, und machte deutlich, dass sie sich im Farbdiskurs auskannte. Persönlich bekannt war sie möglicherweise mit James Sowerby (S. 176–183).

*An Essay on Light and Shade* ist mit zwei malerischen Tafeln (Weichgrundätzungen), zwei farbigen Tabellen, einem weiteren kolorierten Stich eines als „Ball" bezeichneten Farbkreises und acht Tafeln mit farbigen „Flecken" bebildert. Diese letzten acht Tafeln brachten Gartside eine Sonderstellung in der Geschichte der Farben ein. Im Wesentlichen handelt es sich dabei um Beispiele für ihre Farbtheorie, angewandt auf den Bildaufbau und die harmonische Anordnung von Farben (Weiß, Gelb, Orange, Grün, Scharlachrot, Blau, Violett und Karminrot). Doch anstelle von kolorierten Stichen sind frei aufgetragene Farben zu sehen, die entfernt an Blüten hinter nassen Glasscheiben erinnern, und weil sie von Hand gemalt wurden, unterscheiden sich die Bilder von Buch zu Buch. Das Konzept stammte zweifellos von Gartside selbst. Da sie jedoch unmöglich alle Flecken der gesamten Auflage eigenhändig gemalt haben kann, ließ sie sich wahrscheinlich von ihren Schülerinnen helfen. Gartsides Farbflecken waren originell, radikal, ambitioniert und sind zudem von einer abstrakten Schönheit, die erst seit Kurzem Anerkennung und Würdigung erfahren hat.

## Essai sur la lumière et l'ombre, sur les couleurs et sur la composition en général

Peintre de fleurs, l'Anglaise Mary Gartside est très probablement la première femme à avoir publié des ouvrages illustrés ayant pour thème la couleur. Si les femmes ont joué un rôle dans l'histoire de la couleur, en y contribuant notamment comme figures allégoriques, coloristes, assistantes, enlumineuses, traductrices, pédagogues, rares sont celles qui ont pu accéder au statut d'autrices ou de théoriciennes. L'une des toutes premières exceptions est Catherine Perrot (1620–169?), qui enseigna la peinture à la cour de France et publia un traité sur l'art de la miniature en 1686. À certains égards, Gartside suit une voie semblable avant de faire paraître des livres traitant de la couleur, puisqu'elle enseigne aussi la peinture, activité acceptable pour une femme de son époque et prétexte à publier. On sait fort peu de choses de sa biographie, si ce n'est qu'elle a obtenu le patronage de Lady Sophia Grey de Dunham Massey, dans le Cheshire, et parviendra à mener une carrière artistique tout au long de sa vie. Elle est l'autrice d'un opuscule et de trois ouvrages consacrés à la couleur, parus entre 1804 et 1808. Bien qu'elle ne puisse s'inscrire à la Royal Academy, elle y expose une partie de ses dessins botaniques en 1781 et dans d'autres salons londoniens jusqu'en 1808. Elle se crée ainsi un réseau de peintres, enseignants, botanistes et chercheurs sur la couleur, en veillant constamment à rester dans les limites de ce que la société anglaise permet à une femme célibataire à l'époque georgienne. Mais l'histoire de Mary Gartside ne s'arrête pas là.

Ses ouvrages, dont le premier est cet « Essai sur la lumière et l'ombre », prennent la forme délibérée de manuels d'aquarelle destinés aux jeunes femmes. Mais leur autrice parvient à s'inscrire dans une lignée de théoriciens de la couleur en ajoutant au titre de la nouvelle édition les mots « nouvelle théorie ». Elle y cite d'autres chercheurs, comme Isaac Newton et Moses Harris et montre, par là même, qu'elle a une connaissance solide du discours sur la couleur. Il est même possible qu'elle ait rencontré James Sowerby (p. 176–183).

*An Essay on Light and Shade* est illustré de deux planches descriptives (eaux-fortes au vernis mou), de deux tableaux de couleurs, d'une autre gravure en couleurs représentant un cercle chromatique qualifié de « boule » et de huit planches de « taches » de couleurs. C'est grâce à ces dernières planches que Gartside occupe une place particulière dans l'histoire de la couleur. Il s'agit avant tout d'exemples de sa théorie chromatique appliquée à la composition et à l'organisation harmonieuse des teintes (blanc, jaune, orange, vert, écarlate, bleu, violet et cramoisi). Ce ne sont pas des gravures colorées, mais des taches de couleurs qui ressemblent un peu à des fleurs vues à travers du verre humide. Peintes à la main, ces images diffèrent d'un exemplaire à l'autre de l'ouvrage. Si Gartside est bien l'autrice de cette conception, il est impossible qu'elle ait peint elle-même les taches de tous les exemplaires du tirage et elle a probablement bénéficié de l'aide de ses disciples. Tout à la fois inventives, radicales et ambitieuses, ses taches de couleurs se caractérisent par une beauté abstraite qui n'est reconnue et appréciée que depuis peu.

White. 1.

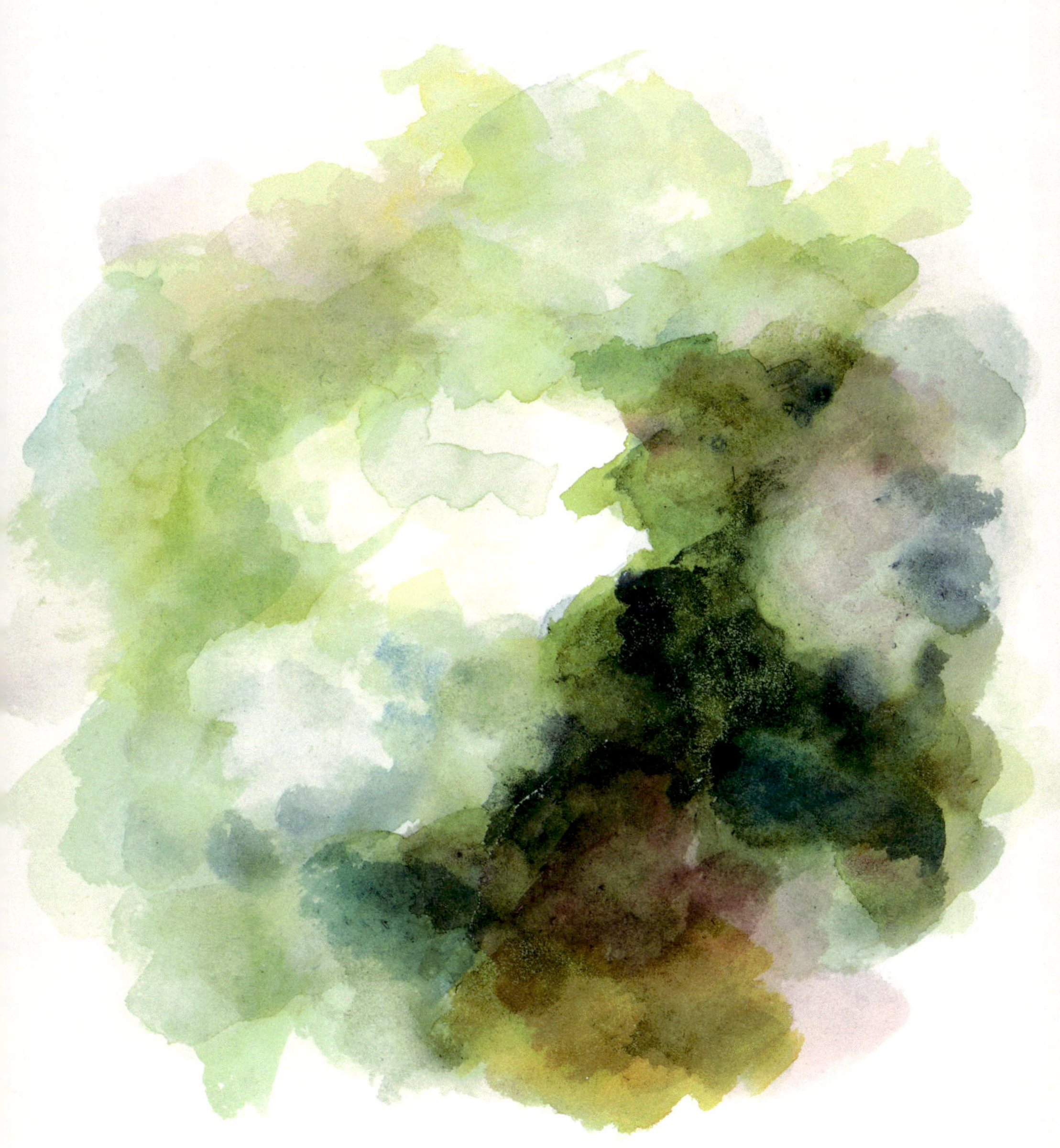

*Scarlet. 5.*

Blue. 6.

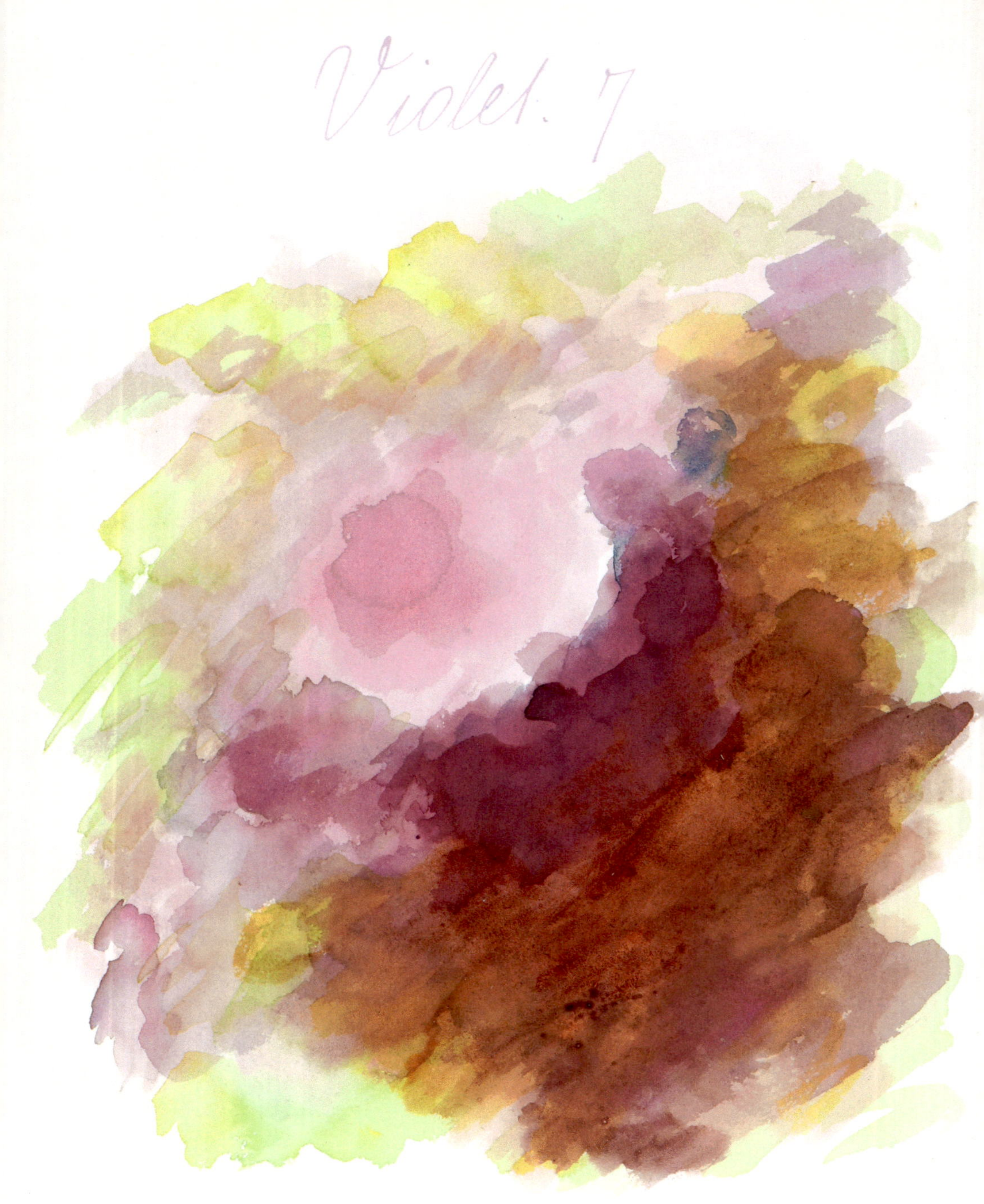
Violet. 7

Crimson.

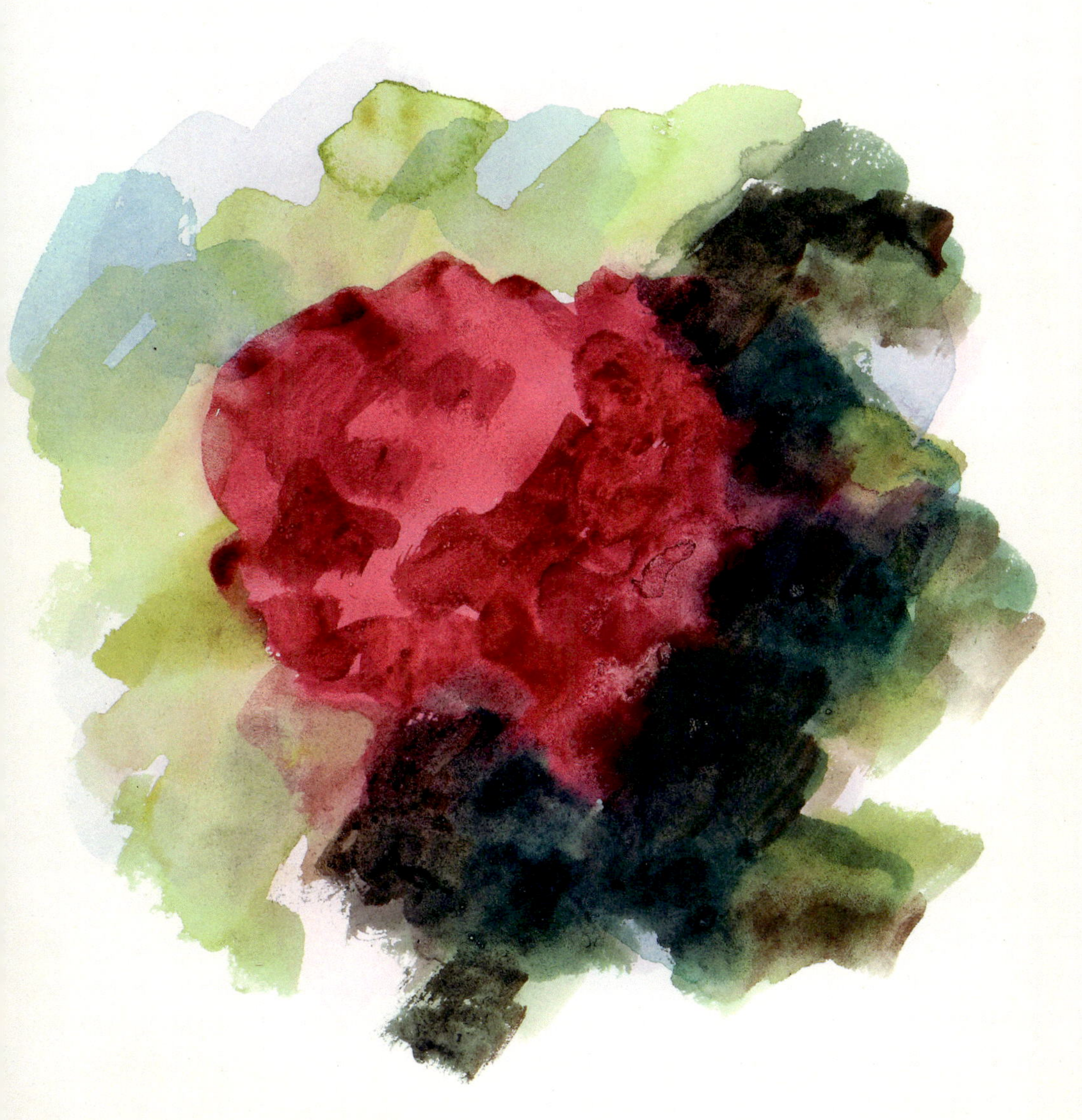

## James Sowerby (1757–1822)

# A NEW ELUCIDATION OF COLOURS, ORIGINAL PRISMATIC, AND MATERIAL

## Showing Their Concordance in Three Primitives, Yellow, Red, and Blue

*7 plates, 31 x 25.5 cm / 12 ¼ x 10 in., London, 1809*
*London, Wellcome Collection*

The naturalist James Sowerby published this book at an exciting time for anyone interested in this field. A few years earlier, the polymath Thomas Young (1773–1829) had presented his theory of trichromatic colour vision, while Runge and Goethe were both busy at this time working on their colour concepts and imminent publications. It is probable that Sowerby would have heard that Mary Gartside's wondrously illustrated book on colour and flower painting had gone into a second edition in 1808 (now titled *An Essay on a New Theory of Colours*), and to this wealth of major new works on colour he added his own, *A New Elucidation of Colours*, which he dedicated to Newton, whose *Opticks* had been published just over 100 years earlier. A "new" approach then, an attempt to redirect the emphasis to light and shade and the differences between colours, but an approach that still paid homage to Newton's achievements. Sowerby also attempted to remove confusion and explain the difference between additive (immaterial) and subtractive (material) colour mixtures, while as a naturalist and prolific illustrator he shared with Moses Harris a concern with the subtleties of colour in the natural world, concentrating in particular on the painters' primaries red, yellow and blue and choosing as their "most perfect" pigment equivalents carmine, gamboge and Prussian blue. Sowerby was the inventor of a Chromatometer, a type of prism to measure the amount of dark and light in colours and which was presented and described in *A New Elucidation*. The device was meant to be used with the plates in the book that show bands of colour or black (Goethe had done something similar in 1791; see pp. 36, 37). Sowerby's main colour diagram, the "Chromatic Scale" (Table 5), is an elegant variation on a colour wheel, overlaid with a three-banded triangle in which the primaries in their purest form are located on the outer bands in the middle portions between the vertices, with the tints becoming brighter towards the centre. The three additional diamonds added to the bottom of the triangle contain further mixtures, in a similar way to Harris's second colour wheel, resulting in a total of 63 colours, plus the white central triangle. It is a beautifully executed diagram, using layers of transparent watercolour paint, albeit one that remained firmly two-dimensional.

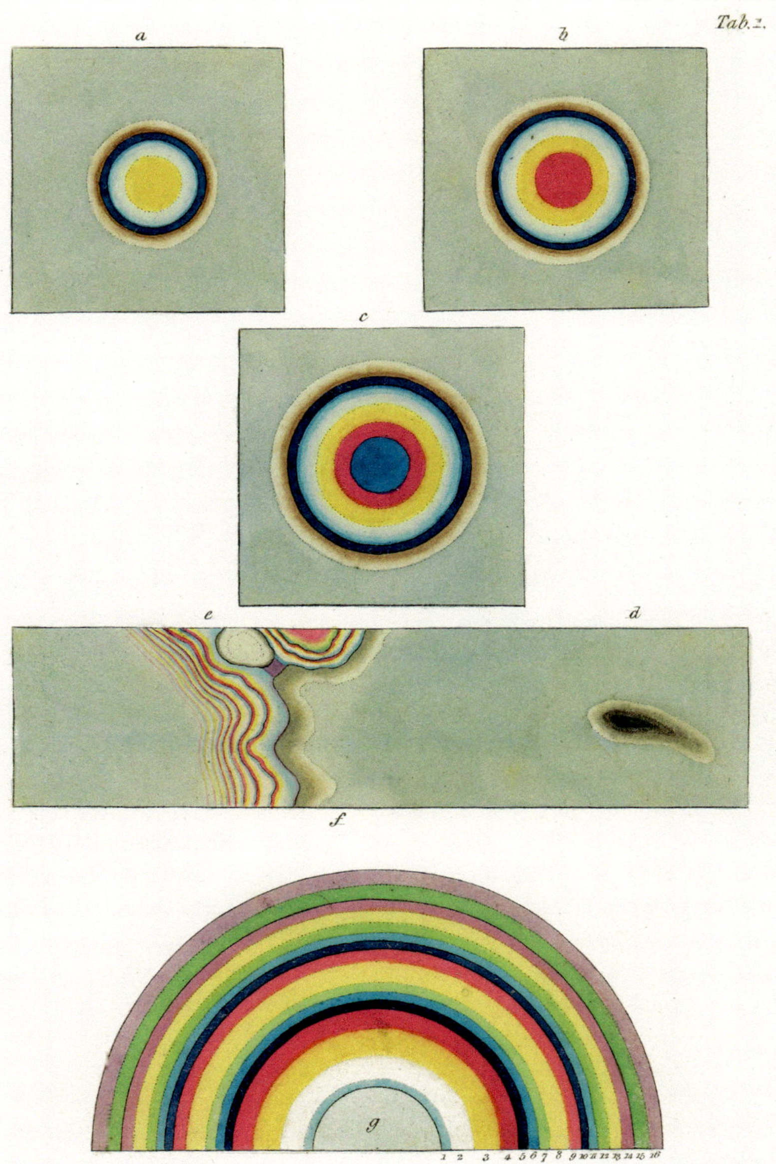


Oct. 1. 1807. Publish'd by Jas. Sowerby London.

## Neue Erläuterung der Farben, original prismatisch und stofflich; mit einer Demonstration ihrer Übereinstimmung in den drei Grundfarben Gelb, Rot und Blau

Der Naturforscher James Sowerby veröffentlichte dieses Buch in einer für alle Farbinteressierten aufregenden Zeit. Wenige Jahre zuvor hatte der Universalgelehrte Thomas Young (1773–1829) seine Theorie des Dreifarbensehens vorgelegt, während Runge und Goethe mit der Arbeit an ihren Farbsystemen und bevorstehenden Publikationen beschäftigt waren. Sowerby dürfte auch davon gehört haben, dass Mary Gartsides wundersam illustriertes Buch über Farbe und Blumenmalerei 1808 in zweiter Auflage erschienen war (jetzt mit dem Titel *An Essay on a New Theory of Colours*). Zu dieser Fülle bedeutender neuer Werke über Farbe steuerte er mit *A New Elucidation of Colours* sein eigenes Buch bei und widmete es Newton, dessen *Opticks* gut hundert Jahre zuvor erschienen war. Ein „neuer" Ansatz also, ein Versuch, die Betonung auf Licht und Schatten und auf die Unterschiede zwischen den Farben umzulenken, der jedoch gleichwohl den Errungenschaften Newtons verpflichtet war. Sowerby versuchte auch, die Verwirrung zu beseitigen und den Unterschied zwischen additiven (immateriellen) und subtraktiven (stofflichen) Farbmischungen zu erklären, während er als Naturforscher und produktiver Illustrator mit Moses Harris ein Interesse für die farblichen Feinheiten in der Natur teilte. Dabei konzentrierte er sich mit Rot, Gelb und Blau speziell auf die Primärfarben der Malerei und wählte als ihre „perfektesten" Pigmententsprechungen Karmin, Gummigutt und Preußischblau. Sowerby war der Erfinder des „Chromatometers", einer Vorrichtung, die ein Prisma und einen schwarzen Keil auf Papier umfasste und von ihm mit einem Barometer zum Messen von Farben verglichen wurde. Es bildete einen wichtigen Teil von *A New Elucidation* und war mit den Tafeln im Buch zu verwenden, die farbige oder schwarze Streifen zeigten (Goethe hatte 1791 etwas Ähnliches vorgelegt; siehe S. 36–37).

Sowerbys Hauptfarbdiagramm ist die „Chromatische Skala" (Tafel 5), eine elegante Variante eines Farbkreises mit einem dreistreifigen Dreieck darin, auf dem die Primärfarben in ihrer reinsten Form in den mittleren Abschnitten der drei äußeren Streifen platziert sind. Zur Mitte hin werden die Farbtöne heller. Die drei zusätzlichen Rauten an der unteren Spitze des Dreiecks enthalten ähnlich wie Harris' zweiter Farbkreis weitere Farbmischungen, sodass sich neben dem zentralen weißen Dreieck insgesamt 63 Farbtöne ergeben. Für das schön ausgeführte, aber streng zweidimensionale Diagramm wurden transparente Wasserfarben schichtweise übereinander aufgetragen.

Tab. 3.

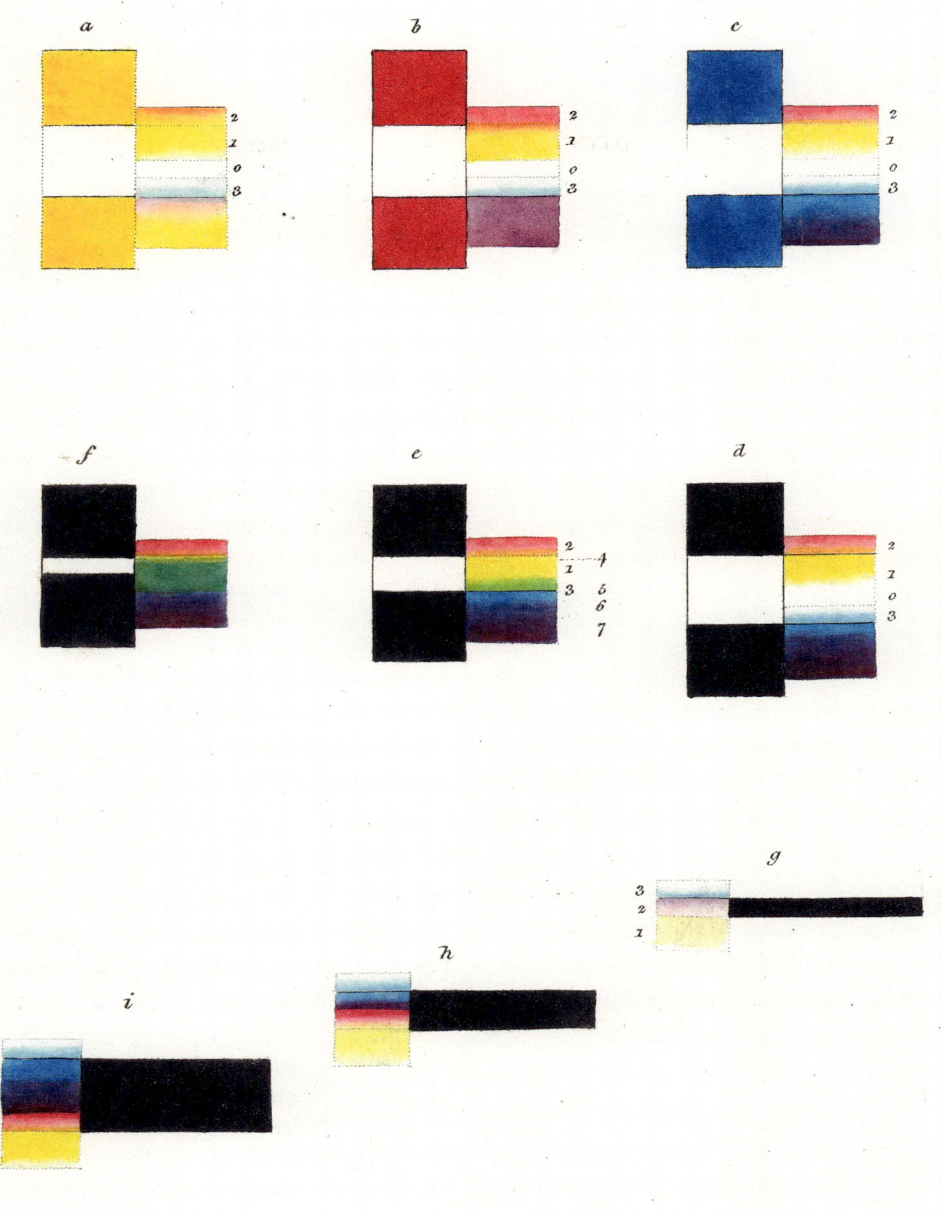


Nov. 1. 1807. Publish'd by Jas. Sowerby London.

## Nouvelle élucidation des couleurs, prismatiques et matérielles, et montrant leur correspondance avec les trois couleurs primaires, jaune, rouge et bleu

Naturaliste anglais, James Sowerby publie cet ouvrage à un moment passionnant pour quiconque s'intéresse au sujet. Quelques années plus tôt, l'érudit Thomas Young (1773–1829) a présenté sa théorie de la vision trichromatique, tandis que Runge et Goethe travaillaient à leurs conceptions respectives et à leurs publications imminentes. Il est probable que Sowerby ait entendu parler de la parution de la seconde édition du livre merveilleusement illustré que Mary Gartside consacre à la couleur et à la peinture de fleurs, paru en 1808 sous le titre *An Essay on a New Theory of Colours* (« Essai sur une nouvelle théorie des couleurs »). À cet ensemble d'œuvres nouvelles et importantes, Sowerby ajoute sa propre contribution – « Nouvelle élucidation des couleurs » – qu'il dédie à Newton, dont l'*Opticks* a paru plus d'un siècle plus tôt. Il s'agit donc d'une approche « nouvelle », d'une tentative de revenir à l'examen de la lumière et de l'ombre et des différences entre les couleurs, qui rend néanmoins hommage aux avancées de Newton. Sowerby cherche également à clarifier les choses et à expliquer la différence entre mélanges de couleurs additif (immatériel) et soustractif (matériel). Naturaliste et illustrateur prolifique, il partage aussi l'attention que porte Moses Harris aux subtilités des couleurs du monde naturel, s'intéresse en particulier aux couleurs primaires des peintres – rouge, jaune et bleu – et choisit comme équivalents « les plus parfaits » le carmin, la gomme-gutte et le bleu de Prusse. Sowerby est aussi l'inventeur d'un « chromatomètre », dispositif composé d'un prisme et d'un coin noir, destiné à la mesure des couleurs et qu'il compare à un « baromètre » chromatique, auquel est consacrée une partie importante de son ouvrage. Cet appareil devait être utilisé avec les planches du livre montrant des bandes de couleurs ou de noir (Goethe avait réalisé un dispositif identique en 1791; voir p. 36, 37).

L'« échelle chromatique » (Table 5), le principal graphique de couleurs de Sowerby, est une variante élégante du cercle chromatique, auquel se superpose un triangle à trois bandes, où les couleurs primaires les plus pures se situent dans les bandes périphériques des portions centrales, entre les sommets du triangle, et s'éclaircissent vers le centre. Les trois losanges ajoutés au bas du triangle contiennent d'autres mélanges de couleurs, à la manière du cercle des couleurs secondaires de Harris, et rassemblent en tout 63 teintes, en plus du triangle blanc situé au centre. Ce graphique magnifiquement réalisé superpose des couches d'aquarelle translucide, mais conserve un aspect résolument bidimensionnel.

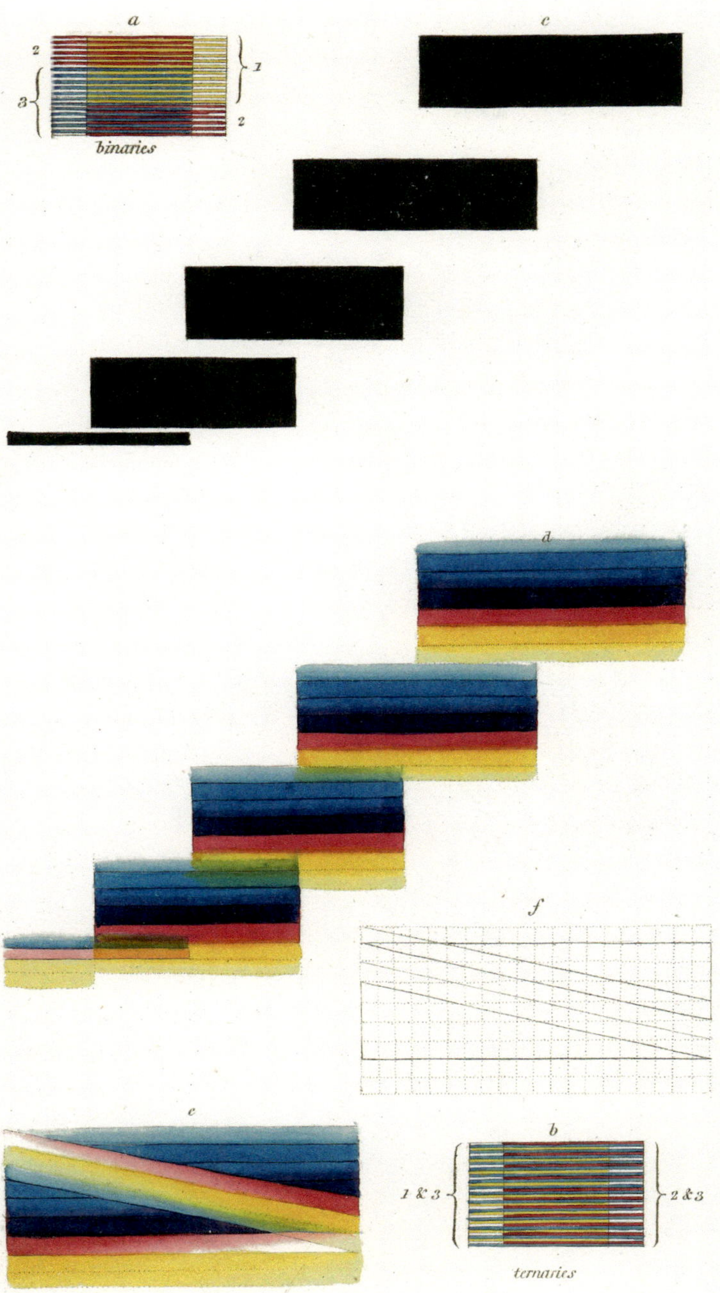
a
2
1
3
2
binaries
c
d
f
e
b
1 & 3
2 & 3
ternaries

# Chromatic Scale.

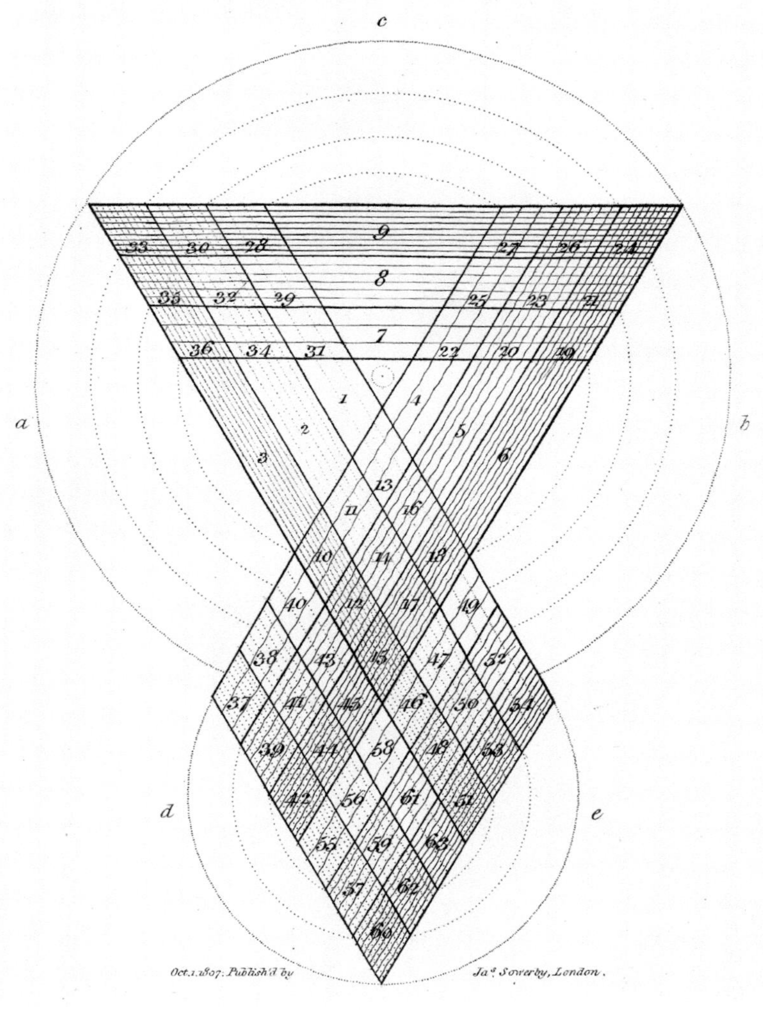

*Tab.*

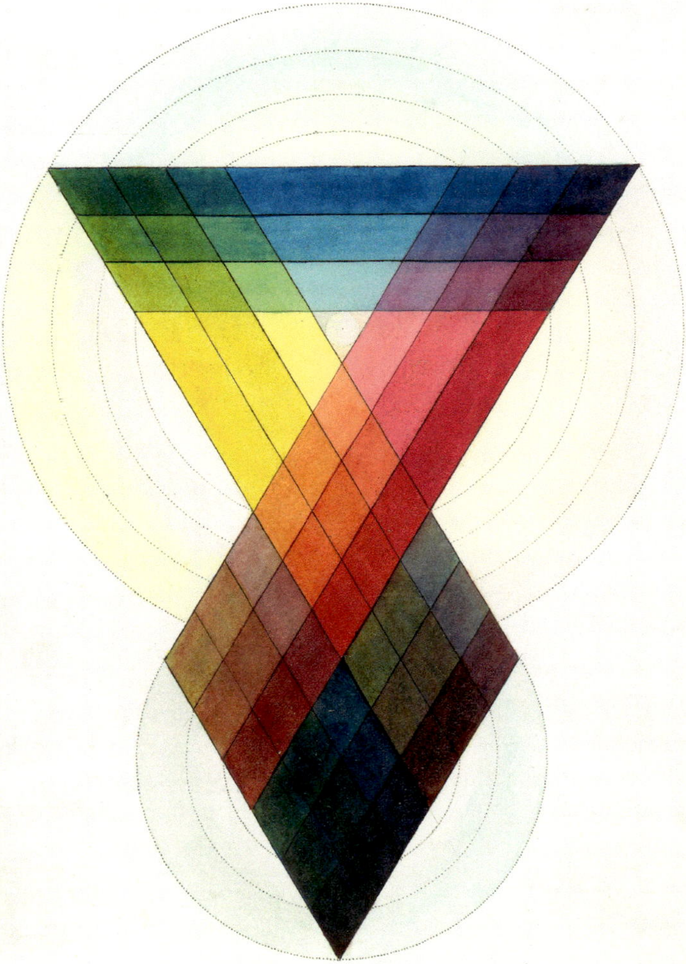

*Oct 2 1807, Publish'd by Ja.s Sowerby London.*

## Johann Wolfgang von Goethe

# ZUR FARBENLEHRE

## On Colour Theory

*16 plates, 23 x 19.3 cm | 9 x 7⅝ in., Vienna, 1810–1812*
*Berlin, Universitätsbibliothek der Humboldt-Universität*

It is hard to overestimate the significance of Goethe's *Zur Farbenlehre*, which was the result of more than 20 years of research. It was first published in Tübingen in 1810 in three volumes, as two volumes of text and one volume, an "Atlas", of 17 engraved plates, 12 of them hand-coloured. Goethe himself, in characteristically boastful style, considered that he was "the only person who knows the truth in the difficult science of colours", and was immensely proud of this work.

Two decades earlier he had published a short treatise on colour, *Beyträge zur Optik*, which was in part a critical attack on Newton's *Opticks* and in which Goethe proposed a dualistic colour system based on the polarity of darkness and light, represented by the "pure" colours blue and yellow from which all other colours can be produced, including the "impure" red. Goethe argued further that black and white are not colours, but representations of total darkness and the brightest light. Readers were encouraged to recreate certain experiments with a prism, using a set of printed coloured playing-cards that accompanied the book (pp. 36, 37). Over the following 20 years Goethe extended and developed his theory, often as a result of discussions with other artists and writers, and this culminated in *Zur Farbenlehre*, one of the most comprehensive texts on colour written since Newton's great work. However, where Newton had sought to be as objective and rational as possible, Goethe's approach reflected the different times in which he lived, and indeed in the Romantic Age subjective experience and emotions associated with colour were often considered more important than hard scientific facts and experimental predictability. As such Goethe paved the way for new attitudes in relation to colour, for example in psychology, while his legacy was and remains considerable, far beyond the limits of the German-speaking world. The first English edition of the main "didactic" part of his *Farbenlehre* was translated by Charles Lock Eastlake and published in London in 1840 as *Goethe's Theory of Colours*, but the manuscript may have been in circulation in the British art world from as early as 1820, since it would seem to have directly inspired Turner (p. 65) and several other artists.

I

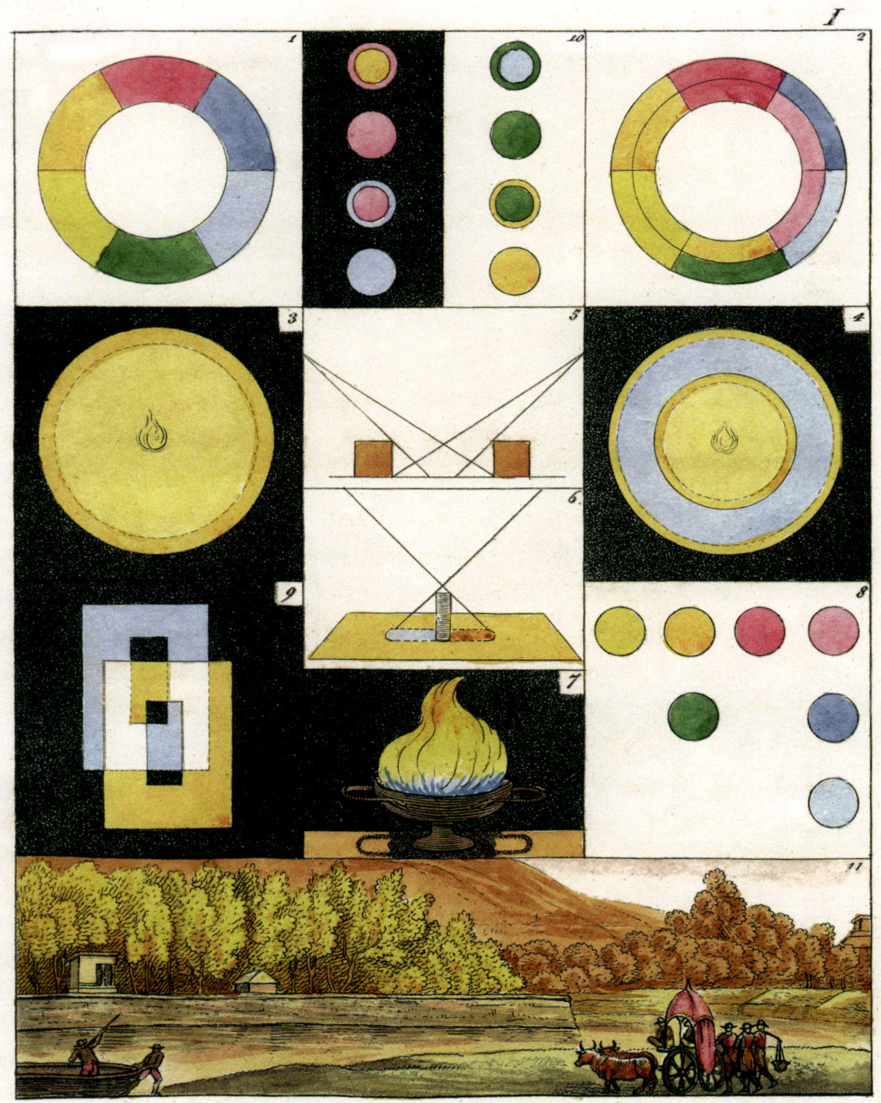

II.

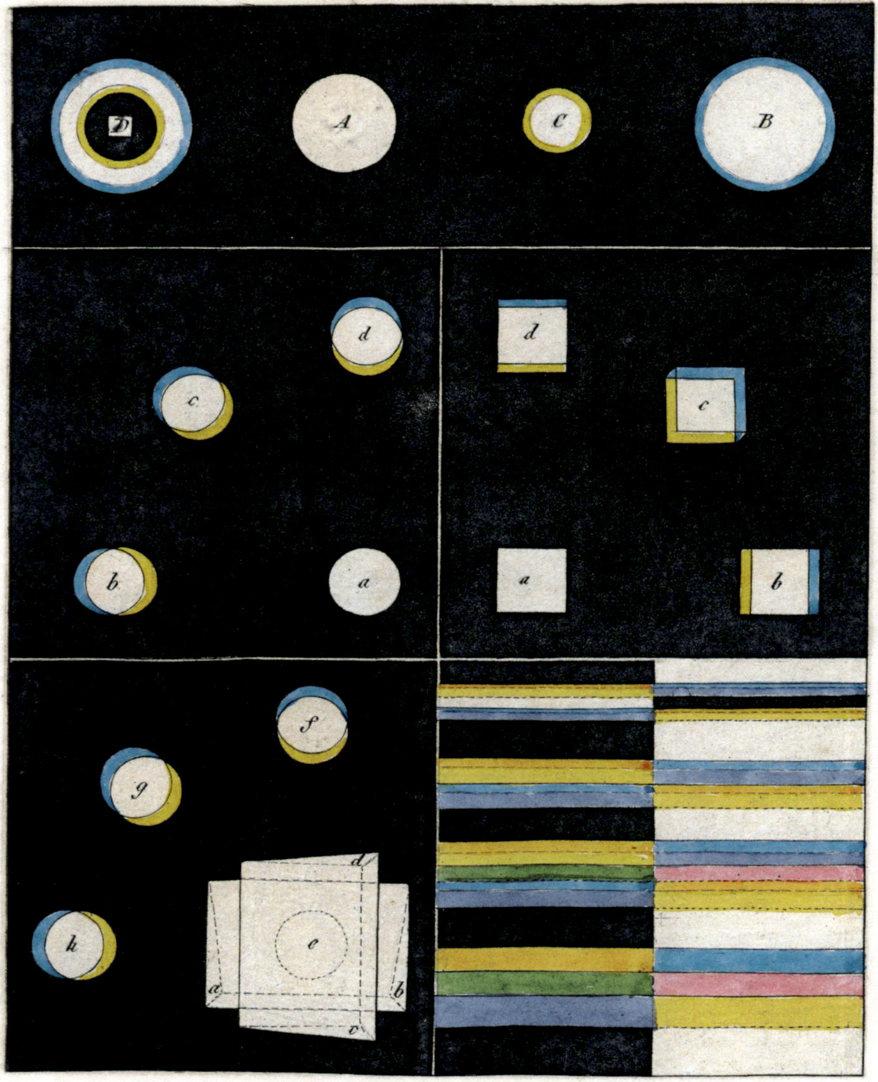

## Zur Farbenlehre

Die Bedeutung des von Goethe verfassten Werks *Zur Farbenlehre*, dem mehr als zwanzig Jahre Forschungsarbeit vorausgingen, ist nicht hoch genug einzuschätzen. Es erschien 1810 in Tübingen in zwei Textbänden und einem „Atlas“ aus 17 Kupfertafeln, von denen zwölf handkoloriert waren. Goethe selbst befand, er sei „in der schwierigen Wissenschaft der Farbenlehre der Einzige [...], der das Rechte weiß“, und war enorm stolz auf sein Werk.

Zwei Jahrzehnte zuvor hatte er mit *Beyträge zur Optik* (1791/92) eine kurze zweiteilige Abhandlung über Farbe veröffentlicht, die in Teilen kritisch mit Newtons *Opticks* ins Gericht ging und in der Goethe ein dualistisches Farbsystem vorschlug, das auf der Polarität von Dunkelheit und Licht beruhte. Diese wurden von den „reinen“ Farben Blau und Gelb repräsentiert, aus denen sich alle anderen Farben herstellen ließen, auch das „nie ganz reine“ Rot. Goethe argumentierte weiter, dass Schwarz und Weiß keine Farben seien, sondern Repräsentanten der völligen Finsternis und des hellsten Lichts. Die Leserschaft wurde ermuntert, bestimmte Experimente mit einem Prisma nachzuvollziehen und hierfür die gedruckten und kolorierten Spielkarten zu verwenden, die dem ersten Teil der *Beyträge* beilagen (S. 36, 37). In den folgenden zwanzig Jahren baute Goethe diese Theorie aus und entwickelte sie weiter, oft aufgrund von Diskussionen mit anderen Künstlern und Schriftstellern. Am Ende dieser Entwicklung stand *Zur Farbenlehre*, eine der umfänglichsten Schriften über Farbe seit Newtons bedeutendem Werk. Doch während Newton so objektiv und rational wie möglich hatte sein wollen, spiegelte Goethes Ansatz die anderen Zeiten wider, in denen er lebte – und tatsächlich wurden subjektives Erleben und mit Farbe in Verbindung gebrachte Gefühle in der Romantik oft für wichtiger gehalten als harte wissenschaftliche Fakten und experimentelle Berechenbarkeit. Insofern bereitete Goethe den Weg für neue Betrachtungsweisen von Farbe, etwa in der Psychologie, und sein Vermächtnis weit über die Grenzen des deutschsprachigen Raums hinaus ist bis heute beträchtlich. Die erste englischsprachige Ausgabe des „didaktischen“ Hauptteils von *Zur Farbenlehre* wurde von Charles Lock Eastlake übersetzt und kam 1840 unter dem Titel *Goethe's Theory of Colours* in London heraus. Das Manuskript könnte in der britischen Kunstwelt jedoch schon seit 1820 in Umlauf gewesen sein, da es Turner und mehrere andere Künstler unmittelbar beeinflusst zu haben scheint (S. 65)

## Traité des couleurs

L'importance du *Zur Farbenlehre* de Goethe, résultat de plus de deux décennies de recherches, est inestimable. Paru pour la première fois en 1810 à Tübingen, il se compose de trois volumes, deux tomes de texte et un « Atlas » de 17 planches gravées, dont 12 coloriées à la main. Extrêmement fier de son œuvre, Goethe se proclame « seule personne connaissant la vérité dans la science difficile des couleurs ».

Vingt ans auparavant, il avait publié un petit traité en deux parties sur le même sujet, *Beyträge zur Optik* (1791–1792), qui se voulait une critique sévère de l'*Opticks* de Newton, dans laquelle il proposait en outre un système chromatique duel, fondé sur l'opposition entre obscurité et lumière, laquelle était représentée par les couleurs « pures » bleu et jaune, d'où peuvent naître toutes les autres couleurs, y compris le rouge « impur ». Goethe allait plus loin en affirmant que le noir et le blanc ne sont pas des couleurs mais des représentations de l'obscurité totale et de la lumière la plus vive. Il encourageait ses lecteurs à refaire certaines de ses expériences à l'aide d'un prisme et d'un jeu de cartes à jouer imprimées en couleurs, qui accompagne la première partie de *Beyträge zur Optik* (p. 36, 37). C'est souvent à la suite de discussions avec d'autres artistes et écrivains que Goethe approfondira sa théorie et aboutira au *Zur Farbenlehre*, l'un des textes les plus détaillés sur le sujet depuis la grande œuvre de Newton. Tandis que le scientifique anglais visait avant tout l'objectivité et la rationalité, Goethe est le produit de son temps. À l'époque romantique, l'expérience subjective et les émotions en rapport avec les couleurs sont fréquemment considérées comme plus importantes que les faits scientifiques tangibles et le caractère prévisible de l'expérimentation. Ainsi Goethe a-t-il ouvert la voie à de nouvelles manières d'appréhender la couleur, en psychologie par exemple. Son héritage demeure considérable et dépasse largement les frontières du monde germanophone. Due à Charles Lock Eastlake, la première édition traduite en anglais de la partie principale, « didactique », du *Zur Farbenlehre* a paru à Londres en 1840 sous le titre *Goethe's Theory of Colours*. Toutefois, le manuscrit de cette édition pourrait avoir circulé parmi les peintres britanniques dès 1820, car il semble avoir directement inspiré Turner et d'autres artistes (p. 65).

IV

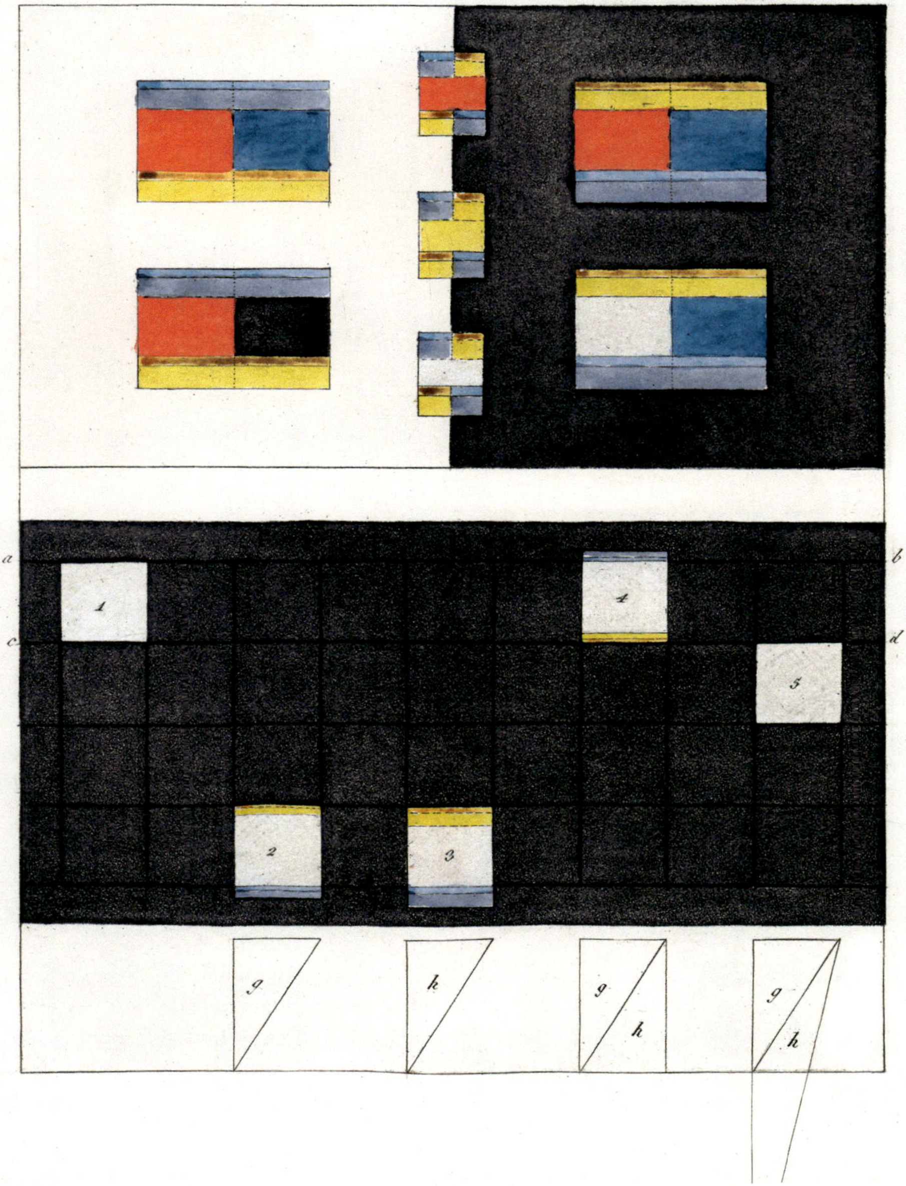

XIII.

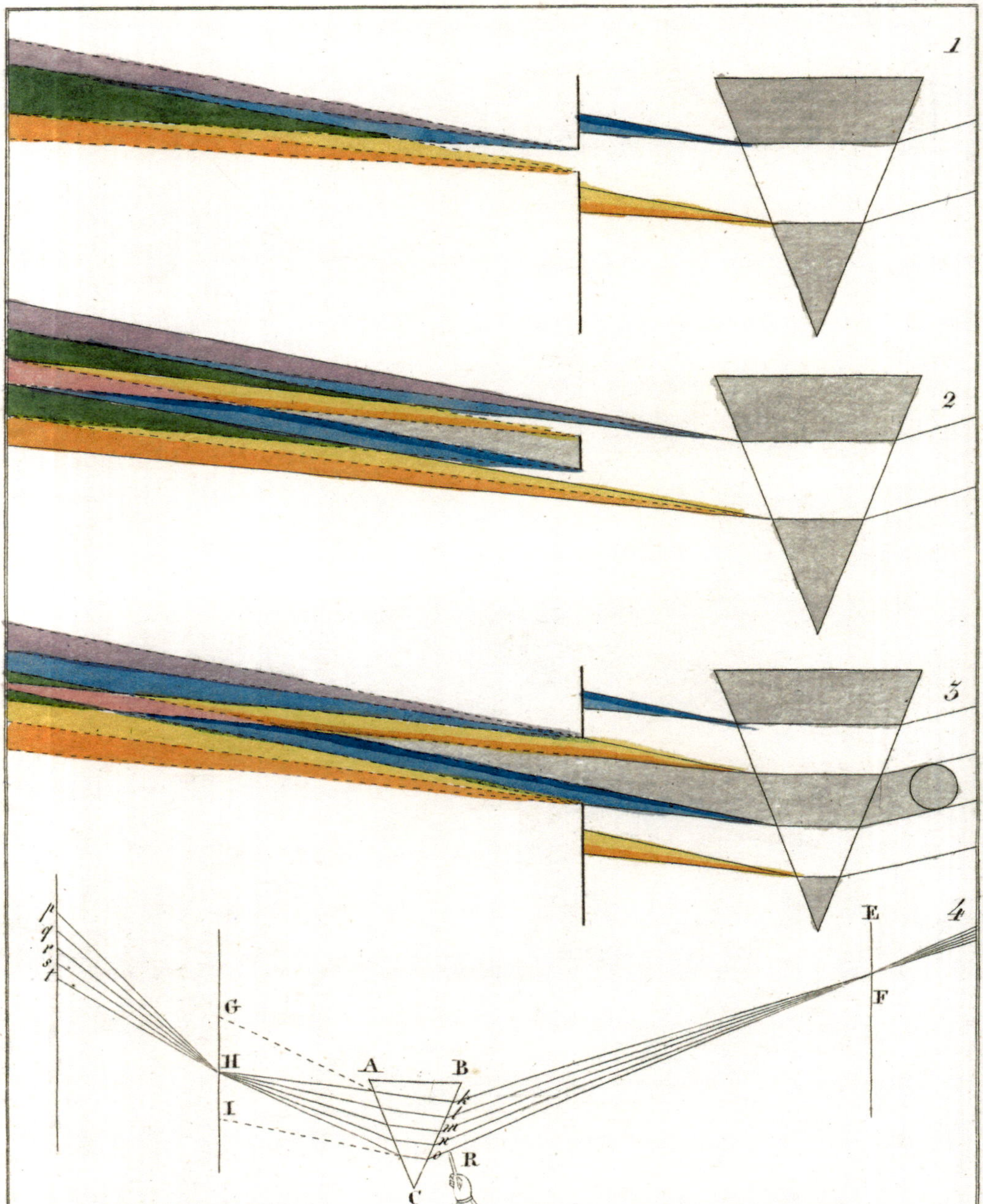

1

2

3

4

p q r s t

G H I

A B C

k l m n o R

E F

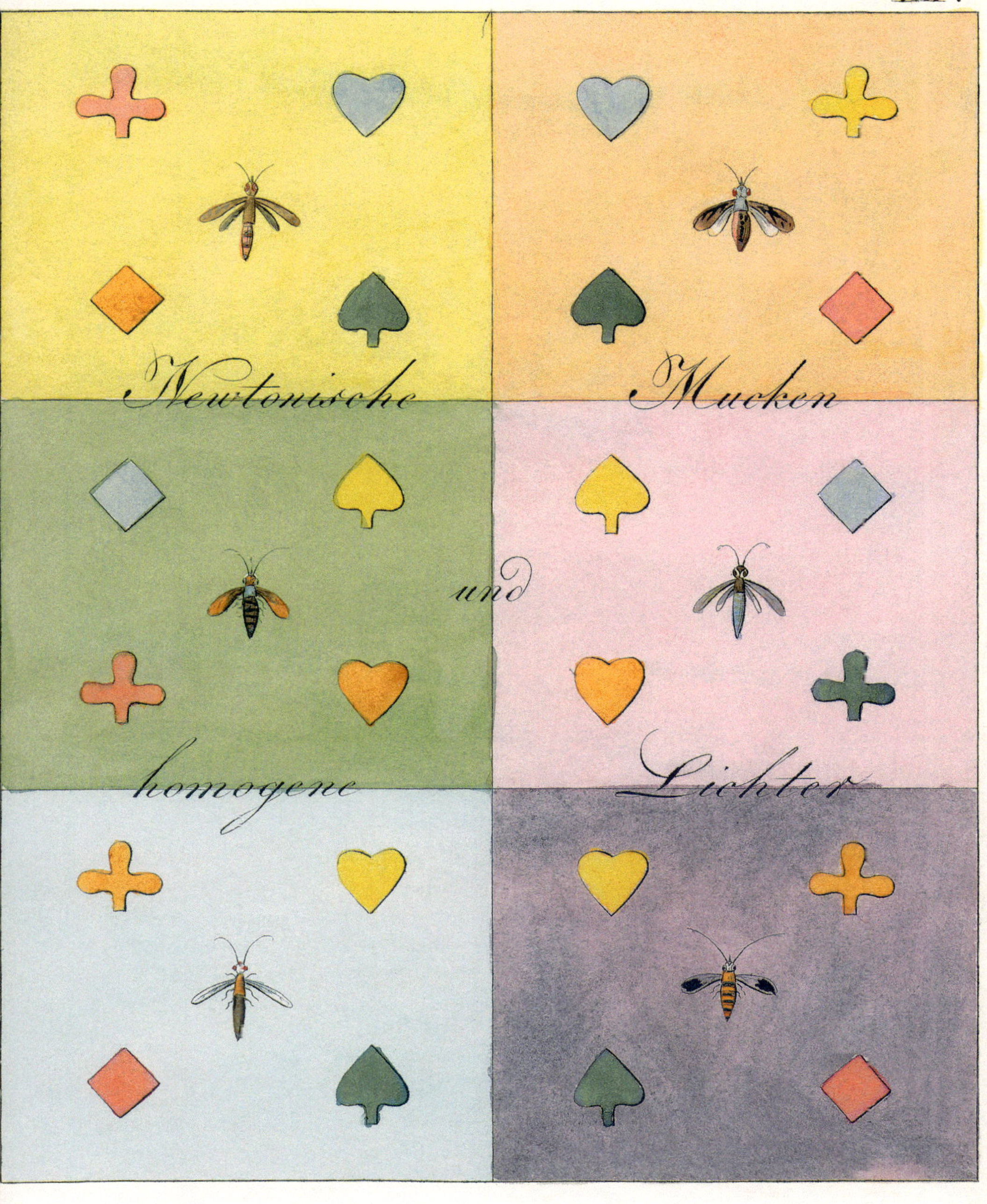
Newtonische Mucken
und
homogene Lichter

## Matthias Klotz (1748–1821)

# GRÜNDLICHE FARBENLEHRE

## A Comprehensive Doctrine on Colour

*7 plates, 41.5 x 33.5 cm | 16 ⅜ x 13 ¼ in., Munich, 1816*
*Munich, Bayerische Staatsbibliothek*

Matthias Klotz's *Gründliche Farbenlehre* was many years in the making and contains some of the most beautiful illustrations of all 19th-century books on colour, and yet this work is not very well known. The author, a portrait painter from Strasbourg, obtained a position as a scenic artist for theatre and stage sets at the Bavarian court in the 1770s, and this work would doubtless have given him a heightened sense of the interaction between colour, perspective and light. In the decades before his *Gründliche Farbenlehre* was published, Klotz wrote several pamphlets and booklets, some of them running to dozens of pages, announcing the comprehensive colour theory he was in the process of developing. He also approached Goethe about a possible collaboration but was met with silence (although Goethe did make some notes about Klotz in his diaries).

Klotz's intention was to provide a broad scientific and artistic overview of colour theory, and structured his treatise in two sections. The first part introduced *Chromatische Farbenlehre* (Chromatic colour theory) and dealt with material colour and the painter's three primaries, yellow, blue and red (he called the latter *purpur*, or purple), and their relations to black and white, or darkness and light; the second part was entitled *Prismatik* (Prismatics) and elaborated on various optical experiments similar to those Goethe had undertaken. When the book was eventually published it was met with both praise and criticism, as with the reviewer in 1817 who commented on the author's age at the time, thereby implying that his theory was old-fashioned while also deploring his lack of scientific expertise – but still writing gushingly about the book's illustrations. The seven plates, originally designed as fold-outs, are very early examples of the 'painterly' method of lithographic printing, including what is possibly the first depiction of a greyscale. Four of the plates were meant to be coloured, including the sophisticated 24-part colour wheel, which represented a three-dimensional colour solid, but when the book was published buyers had a choice between coloured and uncoloured copies (for those who might want to colour the plates in themselves). Of the 500 copies printed 45 were coloured by Klotz himself, and while his attempt to produce a work that would be equal to Goethe's was ultimately futile, the result was certainly beautiful.

# Dreiquelliger Ursprung aller Färbigkeit, durch Natur und Kunst in prismatischer Richtigkeit und Energie

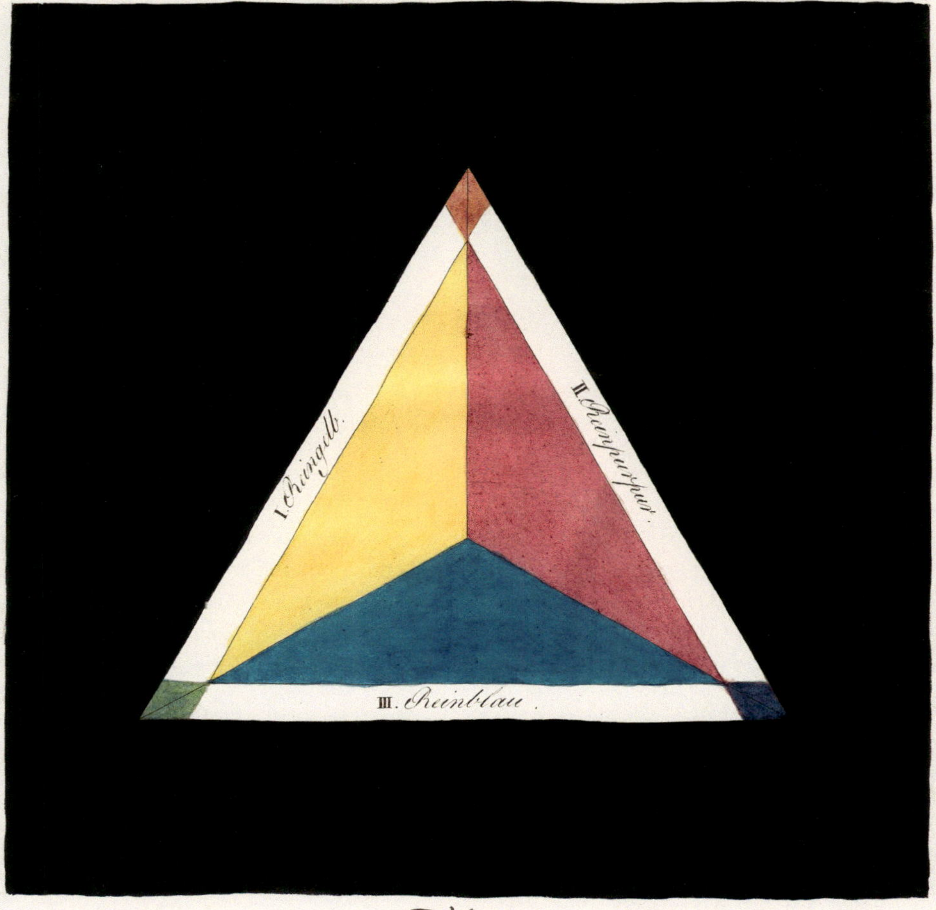


Tab. I.

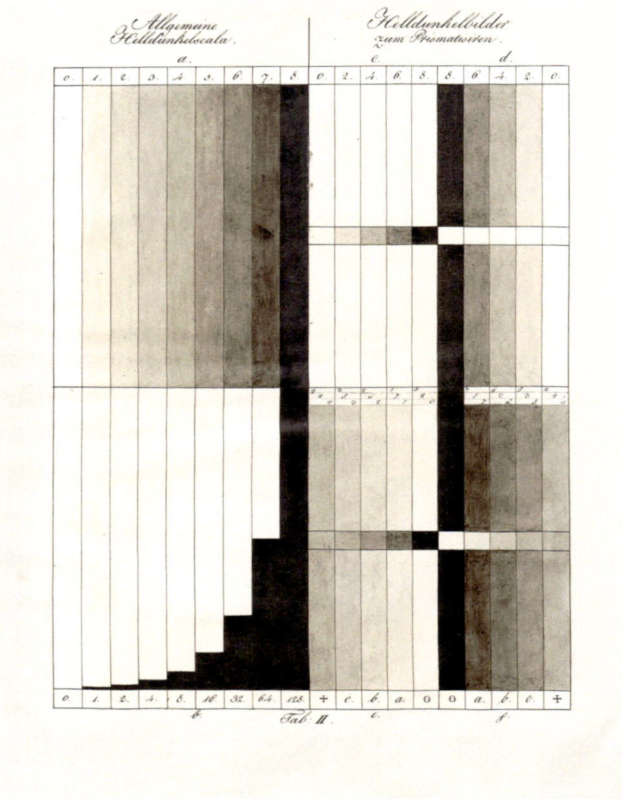


## Gründliche Farbenlehre

Die Entstehung der *Gründlichen Farbenlehre* von Matthias Klotz zog sich über viele Jahre hin. Obwohl das Buch unter allen Farbenbüchern des 19. Jahrhunderts einige der schönsten Illustrationen enthält, ist es nicht sehr bekannt. Der Autor, ein Porträtmaler aus Straßburg, kam in den 1770er-Jahren als Kulissenmaler für Bühnenbilder an den bayrischen Hof. Diese Arbeit verschaffte ihm ohne Zweifel ein gesteigertes Gespür für das Zusammenspiel von Farbe, Perspektive und Licht. In den Jahrzehnten vor Erscheinen seiner *Gründlichen Farbenlehre* verfasste Klotz mehrere Aufsätze und teils mehrere Dutzend Seiten lange Broschüren, in denen er die umfassende Farbtheorie ankündigte, die gerade von ihm entwickelt wurde. Wegen einer möglichen Zusammenarbeit wandte er sich auch an Goethe, stieß dort jedoch auf Schweigen (auch wenn sich in Goethes Tagebüchern einige Notizen über Klotz finden).

Klotz' Ziel war ein breit angelegter wissenschaftlicher und künstlerischer Überblick über die Farbtheorie, den er in zwei Abschnitte gliederte. Der erste Teil stellte die „Chromatische Farbenlehre" vor und befasste sich mit stofflicher Farbe, mit Gelb, Blau und Rot (Letzteres wurde Purpur genannt) als den drei Urfarben der Malerei und mit deren Beziehungen zu

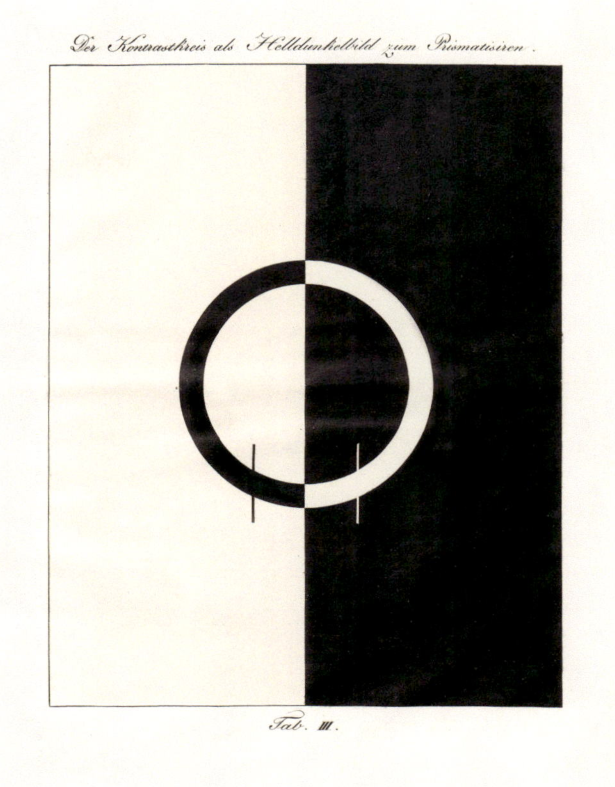


Schwarz und Weiß oder Dunkelheit und Licht. Der zweite Teil trug die Überschrift „Prismatik" und ging ausführlich auf verschiedene optische Experimente ein, wie sie in ähnlicher Weise auch Goethe durchgeführt hatte. Als das Buch schließlich veröffentlicht wurde, schlugen ihm Lob und Kritik entgegen. So kommentierte ein Kritiker 1817 das damalige Alter des Autors, um anzudeuten, dass seine Theorie altmodisch war, und bemängelte Klotz' fehlende wissenschaftliche Kompetenz, äußerte sich hingegen überschwänglich zu den Illustrationen des Buches. Die sieben ursprünglich zum Ausklappen konzipierten Tafeln bilden sehr frühe Beispiele für die „malerische" Methode der Lithografie einschließlich der vielleicht ersten Abbildung einer Grauskala. Vier Tafeln sollten farbig sein, darunter der ausgeklügelte 24-teilige Farbkreis, der stellvertretend für einen dreidimensionalen Farbkörper stand. Doch als das Buch veröffentlicht wurde, hatten Käuferinnen und Käufer die Wahl zwischen Ausfertigungen in Farbe und in Schwarz-Weiß (für jene, die ihre Tafeln vielleicht selbst ausmalen wollten). Von den fünfhundert Exemplaren wurden 45 von Klotz selbst koloriert. Während sein Versuch, ein Werk auf Augenhöhe mit Goethes *Zur Farbenlehre* zu produzieren, am Ende vergeblich war, besteht an der Schönheit seines Werks sicherlich kein Zweifel.

## Principes fondamentaux de la couleur

Il a fallu de nombreuses années à Matthias Klotz pour rédiger *Gründliche Farbenlehre* (« Principes fondamentaux de la couleur »), dont les illustrations sont parmi les plus belles de tous les ouvrages du XIX^e siècle sur le sujet. Pourtant, cette œuvre reste méconnue. Portraitiste strasbourgeois, Klotz est engagé comme peintre de théâtre et de décors à la cour de Bavière au cours des années 1770. Cette fonction l'a assurément doté d'une connaissance fine de l'interaction des couleurs, de la perspective et de la lumière. Au fil des décennies qui précèdent la parution de cet ouvrage, il rédige plusieurs opuscules et brochures qui comptent parfois plusieurs dizaines de pages et sont autant d'étapes annonçant sa grande théorie des couleurs. Il sollicite également Goethe pour envisager une collaboration, mais sa demande reste sans réponse (bien que Goethe mentionne Klotz dans ses journaux).

Dans son traité en deux parties, Klotz propose un vaste panorama scientifique et artistique des théories des couleurs. La première partie, « Chromatische Farbenlehre » (« Théorie chromatique »), traite de la couleur matérielle et des trois couleurs primaires du peintre, jaune, bleu et rouge (désignant cette dernière par le substantif *Purpur*, pourpre), dans leurs rapports avec le noir et le blanc, ou l'obscurité et la lumière. Intitulée « Prismatik », la deuxième partie entre dans les détails de diverses expériences optiques, semblables à celles que Goethe a réalisées. Lors de sa parution, l'ouvrage reçoit autant d'éloges que de critiques : l'auteur d'un compte rendu de 1817 souligne l'âge de l'auteur, sous-entend ainsi que sa théorie est démodée et déplore l'absence de savoir-faire scientifique, mais commente les illustrations du livre sur un ton dithyrambique. Initialement conçues pour être dépliées, les sept planches figurent parmi les tout premiers exemples de la méthode « picturale » d'impression lithographique et pourraient constituer la première description d'une échelle des gris. Quatre des planches auraient dû être en couleurs, notamment le cercle chromatique divisé en 24 sections qui représente un solide en trois dimensions. Mais le livre paraît en deux versions, avec ou sans couleurs (pour les lecteurs qui souhaiteraient colorier eux-mêmes les planches). Sur les 500 exemplaires imprimés, 45 sont coloriés à la main par Klotz en personne. Si sa tentative de réaliser une œuvre qui soit l'égale de celle de Goethe s'avère vaine, le résultat n'en est pas moins superbe.

# Buntfarbsystem in prismatisch-theoretischer Ordnung.

| | Nomenklatur | Gelb | Purpur | Blau | | | Dunkel | Hell | | | Gelb | Purpur | Blau | Nomenklatur | |
|---|---|---|---|---|---|---|---|---|---|---|---|---|---|---|---|
| | Weis | I | II | III | | | im hellen Felde | im dunkeln Felde | | | I | II | III | Schwarz: dunkle Unfarbe. | |
| | Helle Unfarbe | — | — | — | | | | | | + | 4 | 4 | 4 | | |
| Schwache gelb | noch heller | 1 | — | — | C°°° | 48 | | | 48 | Dc | 3 | 4 | 4 | noch mehr | Gebrochenviolet |
| | heller | 2 | — | — | C°° | 2 | | | 2 | Db | 2 | 4 | 4 | gebrochener | |
| | hell | 3 | — | — | C° | 4 | | | 4 | Da | 1 | 4 | 4 | gebrochen | |
| | Reingelb | 4 | — | — | C | 6 | | | 6 | D | — | 4 | 4 | Richtigviolet | |
| Rothgelb | 1 tes | 4 | 1 | — | E | 12 | | | 12 | F | — | 3 | 4 | 3 tes | Violblau |
| | 2 tes | 4 | 2 | — | G | 1 2 | | | 1 2 | H | — | 2 | 4 | 2 tes | |
| | 3 tes | 4 | 3 | — | J | 1 | | | 1 | K | — | 1 | 4 | 1 tes | |
| | Richtigroth | 4 | 4 | — | L | | | | | M | — | — | 4 | Reinblau | |
| Rothpurpur | 3 tes | 3 | 4 | — | N | 4 1 | | | 4 1 | O | 1 | — | 4 | 1 tes | Grünblau |
| | 2 tes | 2 | 4 | — | P | 2 | | | 2 | Q | 2 | — | 4 | 2 tes | |
| | 1 tes | 1 | 4 | — | R | 1 | | | 1 | S | 3 | — | 4 | 3 tes | |
| | Reinpurpur | — | 4 | — | T | 12 | | | 12 | V | 4 | — | 4 | Richtiggrün | |
| Violpurpur | 1 tes | — | 4 | 1 | W | 1 | | | 1 | X | 4 | — | 3 | 3 tes | Grüngelb |
| | 2 tes | — | 4 | 2 | Y | 2 | | | 2 | Z | 4 | — | 2 | 2 tes | |
| | 3 tes | — | 4 | 3 | B | 1 4 | | | 1 4 | A | 4 | — | 1 | 1 tes | |
| | Richtigviolet | — | 4 | 4 | D | 1 | | | 1 | C | 4 | — | — | Reingelb | |
| Violblau | 3 tes | — | 3 | 4 | F | 2 | | | 2 | E | 4 | 1 | — | 1 tes | Rothgelb |
| | 2 tes | — | 2 | 4 | H | 1 | | | 1 | G | 4 | 2 | — | 2 tes | |
| | 1 tes | — | 1 | 4 | K | 12 | | | 12 | J | 4 | 3 | — | 3 tes | |
| | Reinblau. | — | — | 4 | M | | | | | L | 4 | 4 | — | Richtigroth | |
| Schwache Blau | hell | — | — | 3 | M° | 6 | | | 6 | La | 4 | 4 | 1 | gebrochen | Gebrochenroth. |
| | heller | — | — | 2 | M°° | 4 2 | | | 4 2 | Lb | 4 | 4 | 2 | gebrochener | |
| | noch heller | — | — | 1 | M°°° | 48 | | | 48 | Lc. | 4 | 4 | 3 | noch mehr. | |
| | Helle Unfarbe. | — | — | — | O | | | | | + | 4 | 4 | 4 | | |

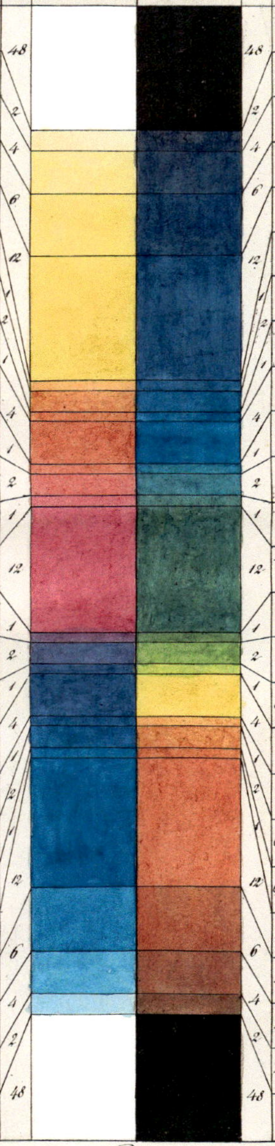

Tab: IV.

Entstehung der Mittelfarben aus den Urfarben

durch Ausdehnung aus dem innern Dunkel ins äußere Hell: | durch Ausdehnung aus dem äußern Dunkel ins innere Hell:

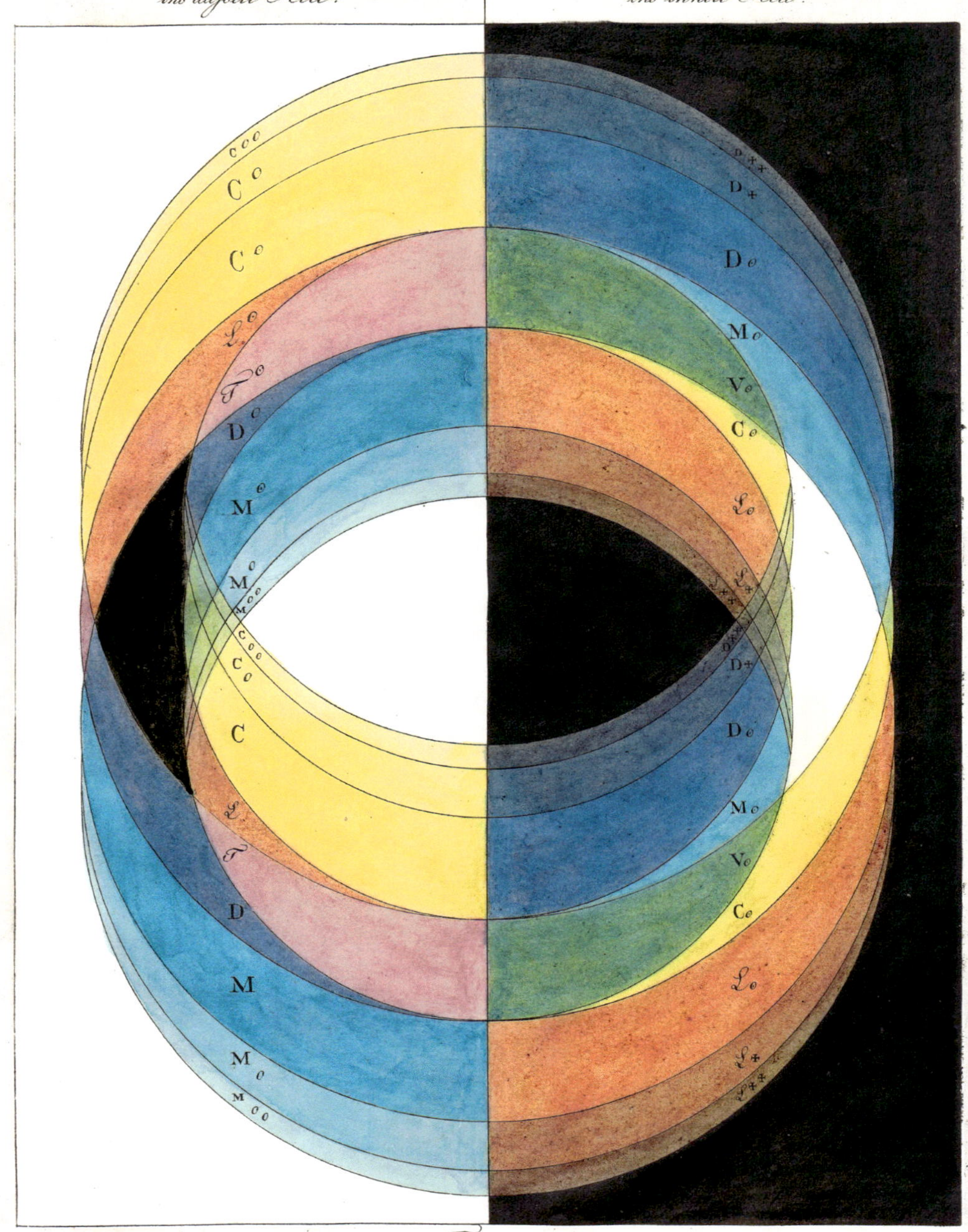


Tab. V.

Farbkanon für die Kunst, der nehmliche, wie für die Prismatik, nur anders geordnet.

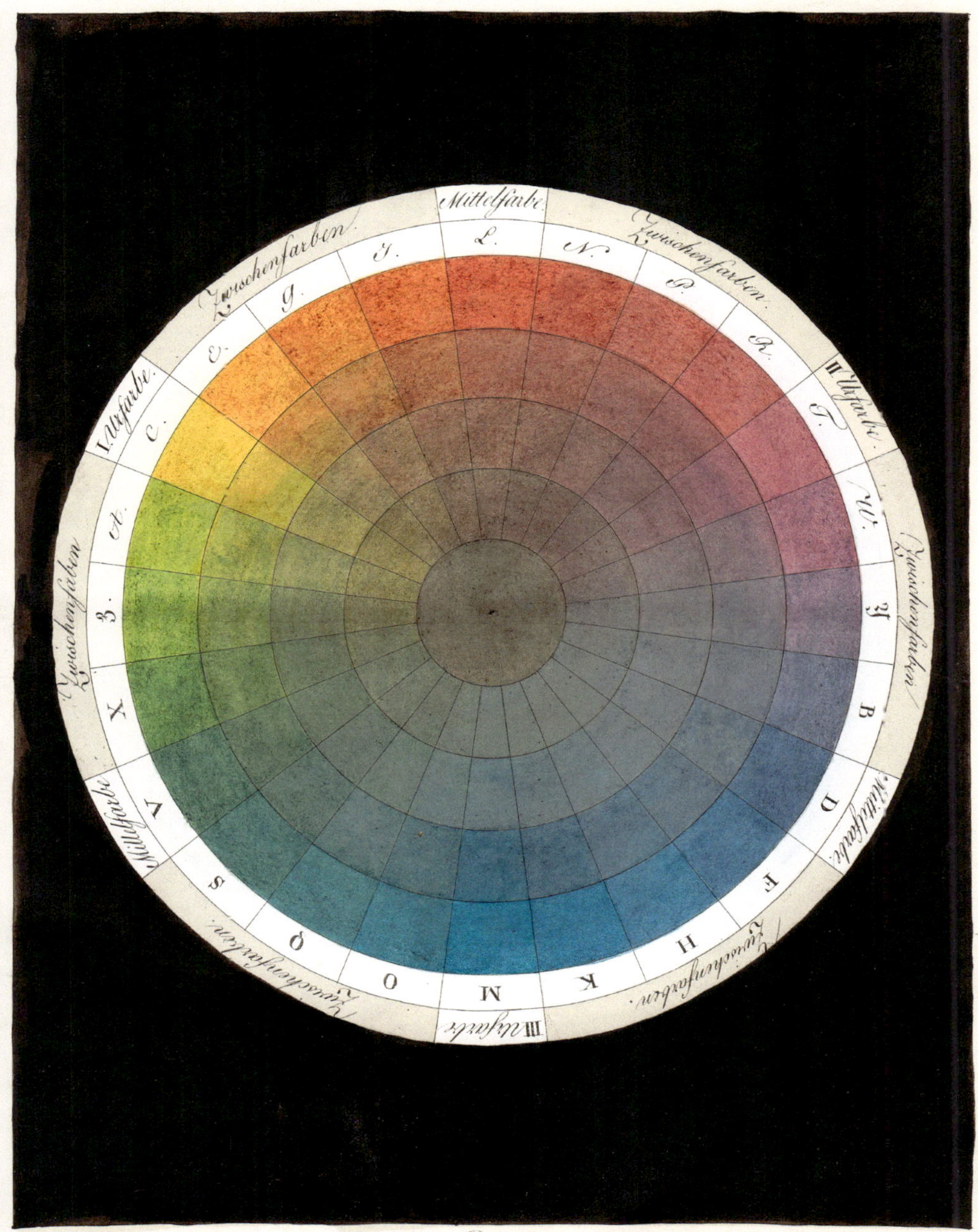


Tab. VI.

## George Field (*c.* 1777–1854)

# CHROMATICS

## or, An Essay on the Analogy and Harmony of Colours

*6 plates, 8 illustrated pages, 30.5 x 24.5 cm | 12 x 9 ⅝ in., London, 1817*
*Sussex, collection of the author*

The entrepreneurial chemist George Field was also a pigment and dye maker and a colour researcher, as well as being extremely well connected in art circles in Britain in the early part of the 19th century. During his relatively long and successful life he provided many artists with high-quality pigments and paints, and published many books, including several on colour, which combined chemistry with theory, religious beliefs with colour order, and music with colour harmonies. Field had been experimenting with the manufacture of colours since 1804 and invented a number of tools and machines for use in pressing, filtering and producing pigments and dyes. Over the years he operated pigment factories in Bristol, London and Syon Hill Park in Middlesex, and from 1808 he began supplying pigments to artists, artists' suppliers, printers and publishers, including William Winsor and Henry Newton who later founded the art material suppliers Winsor & Newton. Field was a practising Christian and made analogies between the three primary colours and the Christian concept of the Holy Trinity. For their earthly representations he selected a trio of pure and stable pigments, namely red madder, lemon yellow and ultramarine blue.

Field's first book on colour, *Chromatics, or, An Essay on the Analogy and Harmony of Colours*, was published in an edition of 250 copies. Ever keen to invent words, it seems, he explained that "*Chromatics* denotes the science of the relations of *light*, *shade*, and *colours*." Field recognised the importance of presenting colour concepts visually and took great care with the book's illustrations. The diagrams develop gradually, with the triangles that represent the trichromatic system serving as a guiding shape from which horizontal mixture charts, hexagons and eventually star shapes are derived, the stars being a variation on the familiar colour wheel. As with Newton and others, Field believed there was a strong connection between colour and music, an analogy he first discussed in *Chromatics* and which he visualised as an image of musical scales and their colour equivalents. This diagram, too, is based on a triangle. All the illustrations in *Chromatics* are hand-coloured, possibly done by Field himself or else under his close supervision. The intricate colour patterns of the sequence of five stars are especially impressive.

## EXAMPLE IX.

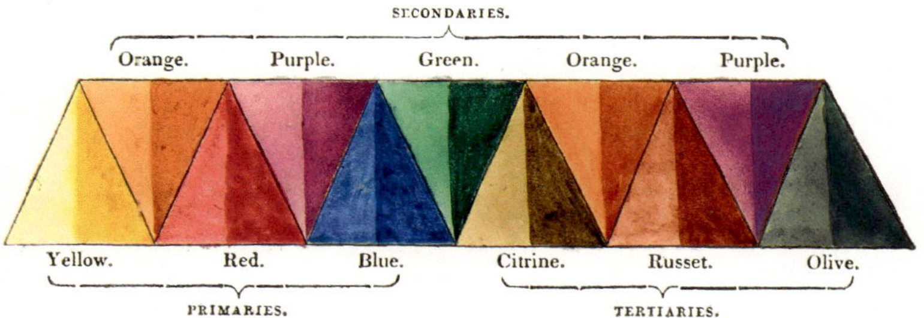


§ 20. Such are the *particular* distinctions, relations, and gradations of colours, as determined by the various predominance of their first principles through an orderly and infinite progress to the neutral grey; the position at which this predominance terminates, and the equilibrium of these first principles is re-established in unity according to a naturally perfect system.

§ 21. As the *neutralization or negation of colours* depends upon the reunion of the three primaries, (§ 8) it is evident that each of the *primary colours* is neutralized by that

# PARTICULAR RELATIONS

OF

# COLOURS.

§ 6. THE principles of light and shade, in their sensible state, have two extremes and a mean, denominated, inherently, WHITE, BLACK, and GREY; the intermedia or degrees of which are indefinite or infinite.

### EXAMPLE I.

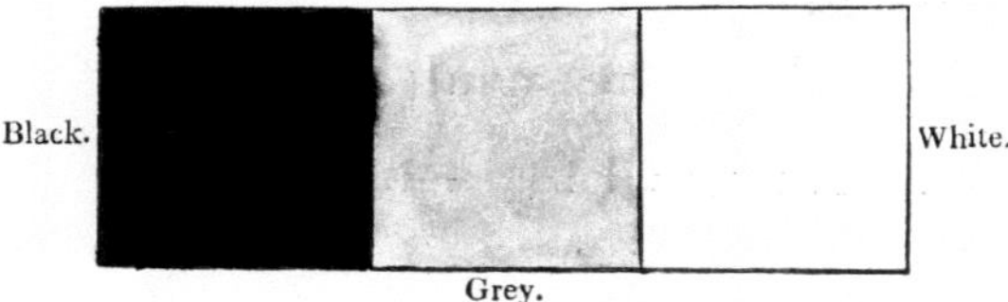

## Chromatik; oder Ein Versuch über die Analogie und Harmonie der Farben

Der geschäftstüchtige Chemiker George Field war auch Pigment- und Farbstoffhersteller und als aktiver Farbforscher in den Kreisen der britischen Kunstwelt des frühen 19. Jahrhunderts außerordentlich gut vernetzt. Im Verlauf seines recht langen und erfolgreichen Lebens versorgte er zahlreiche Künstler mit hochwertigen Pigmenten und Farben und veröffentlichte viele Bücher, darunter die Farbenbücher, die Chemie mit Theorie, religiöse Überzeugungen mit Farbordnungen und Musik mit Farbharmonien verknüpften. Seit 1804 hatte Field mit Verfahren zur Farberzeugung experimentiert und eine Reihe von Werkzeugen und Maschinen zum Pressen, Filtern und Herstellen von Pigmenten und Farbstoffen erfunden. Im Laufe der Jahre betrieb er Pigmentfabriken in Bristol, London und Syon Hill Park in der Grafschaft Middlesex. Von 1808 an lieferte er Pigmente an Künstler, Künstlerbedarfsläden, Druckereien und Verleger, darunter William Winsor und Henry Newton, die später Winsor & Newton gründeten, einen Fachhandel für Künstlermaterialien. Als praktizierender Christ stellte Field Analogien zwischen den drei Primärfarben und dem christlichen Konzept der heiligen Dreifaltigkeit her. Für ihre Darstellung wählte er mit Krapprot, Zitronengelb und Ultramarinblau drei reine und stabile Pigmente aus.

Fields erstes Buch über Farbe, *Chromatics, or, An Essay on the Analogy and Harmony of Colours*, erschien in einer Auflage von 250 Exemplaren. Als begeisterter Wortschöpfer, so scheint es, erklärte er: „*Chromatik* bezeichnet die Wissenschaft von den Beziehungen zwischen *Licht*, *Schatten* und *Farben*." Field erkannte, wie wichtig es war, Farbtheorien in Bildern darzulegen, und verwandte große Sorgfalt auf die Illustrationen des Buches. Die Diagramme entwickeln sich Schritt für Schritt, wobei die Dreiecke, die das trichromatische System darstellen, als Leitform dienen, aus der sich waagerechte Farbmischungsgrafiken, Sechsecke und schließlich Sterne ergeben, Letztere als Variationen des vertrauten Farbkreises. Wie Newton und andere Farbforscher glaubte Field fest an eine starke Beziehung zwischen Farbe und Musik, eine Analogie, die er zuerst in *Chromatics* erörterte und als Abbildung von Tonleitern und ihren farblichen Entsprechungen anschaulich machte. Auch dieses Diagramm basiert auf der Dreiecksform. Alle Illustrationen in *Chromatics* wurden, möglicherweise von Field selbst oder unter seiner strengen Aufsicht, von Hand koloriert. Die Abfolge der fünf Sterne mit ihren komplizierten Farbmustern ist besonders beeindruckend.

## La chromatique ou Essai sur l'analogie et l'harmonie des couleurs

Chimiste doué pour les affaires, George Field est également fabricant de pigments et de teintures et spécialiste des couleurs. En ce début du XIX<sup>e</sup> siècle, il est extrêmement bien introduit dans tous les cercles artistiques britanniques. Tout au long d'une vie relativement longue et bien remplie, il fournit de nombreux artistes en pigments et peintures de qualité et publie plusieurs ouvrages. Ceux consacrés à la couleur établissent des liens entre la chimie et la théorie, les croyances religieuses et l'ordre chromatique, ou encore la musique et les harmonies chromatiques. Field commence ses expérimentations en matière de fabrication de couleurs dès 1804 et met au point un certain nombre d'outils et de machines pour presser, filtrer et produire des pigments et des teintures. Au fil des années, il dirigera plusieurs fabriques de pigments à Bristol, Londres et Syon Hill Park dans le Middlesex. À partir de 1808, il fournit en pigments les peintres, les imprimeurs, les éditeurs et les marchands de couleurs, notamment William Winsor et Henry Newton qui fonderont la maison de matériel de beaux-arts Winsor & Newton. Chrétien pratiquant, Field établit des analogies entre les trois couleurs primaires et le concept de la Sainte Trinité. Il choisit, pour leur représentation matérielle, un trio de pigments purs et stables : garance, jaune citron et bleu outremer.

Premier opus que Field consacre à la couleur, *Chromatics, or, An Essay on the Analogy and Harmony of Colours* est tiré à 250 exemplaires. L'homme aime, semble-t-il, inventer de nouveaux mots : ainsi explique-t-il que « *la chromatique* désigne la science des relations entre la *lumière*, l'*ombre* et les *couleurs* ». Field comprend l'importance d'une représentation visuelle des concepts chromatiques et apporte le plus grand soin aux illustrations de son livre. Les graphiques se déclinent progressivement, et le système trichromatique représenté par des triangles sert de forme de référence d'où dérivent ensuite des tableaux de mélanges horizontaux, hexagonaux puis en forme d'étoile, ces derniers étant des variations du cercle chromatique classique. À l'instar de Newton et d'autres, Field croit aux rapports étroits entre la couleur et la musique et étudie cette analogie pour la première fois dans *Chromatics*. Il représente celle-ci par une gamme de notes accompagnées de leurs équivalents colorés et agencés en petits triangles. Toutes les illustrations de *Chromatics* sont peintes à la main, peut-être par Field lui-même ou sous sa supervision. Les motifs colorés complexes des cinq étoiles sont particulièrement remarquables.

## EXAMPLE XVI.

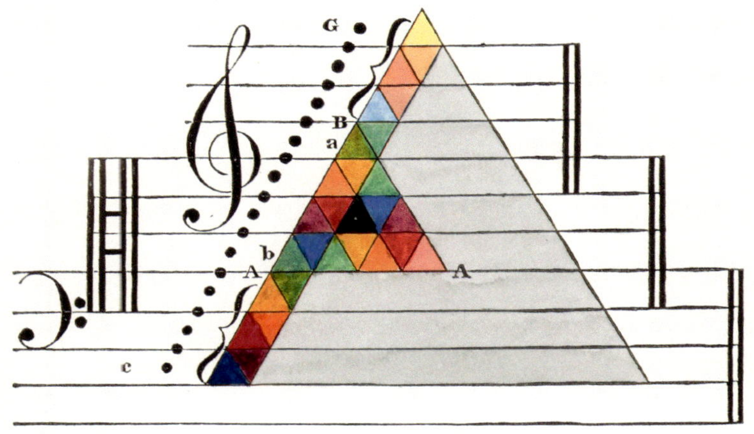


ANALOGOUS SCALE OF SOUNDS AND COLOURS.

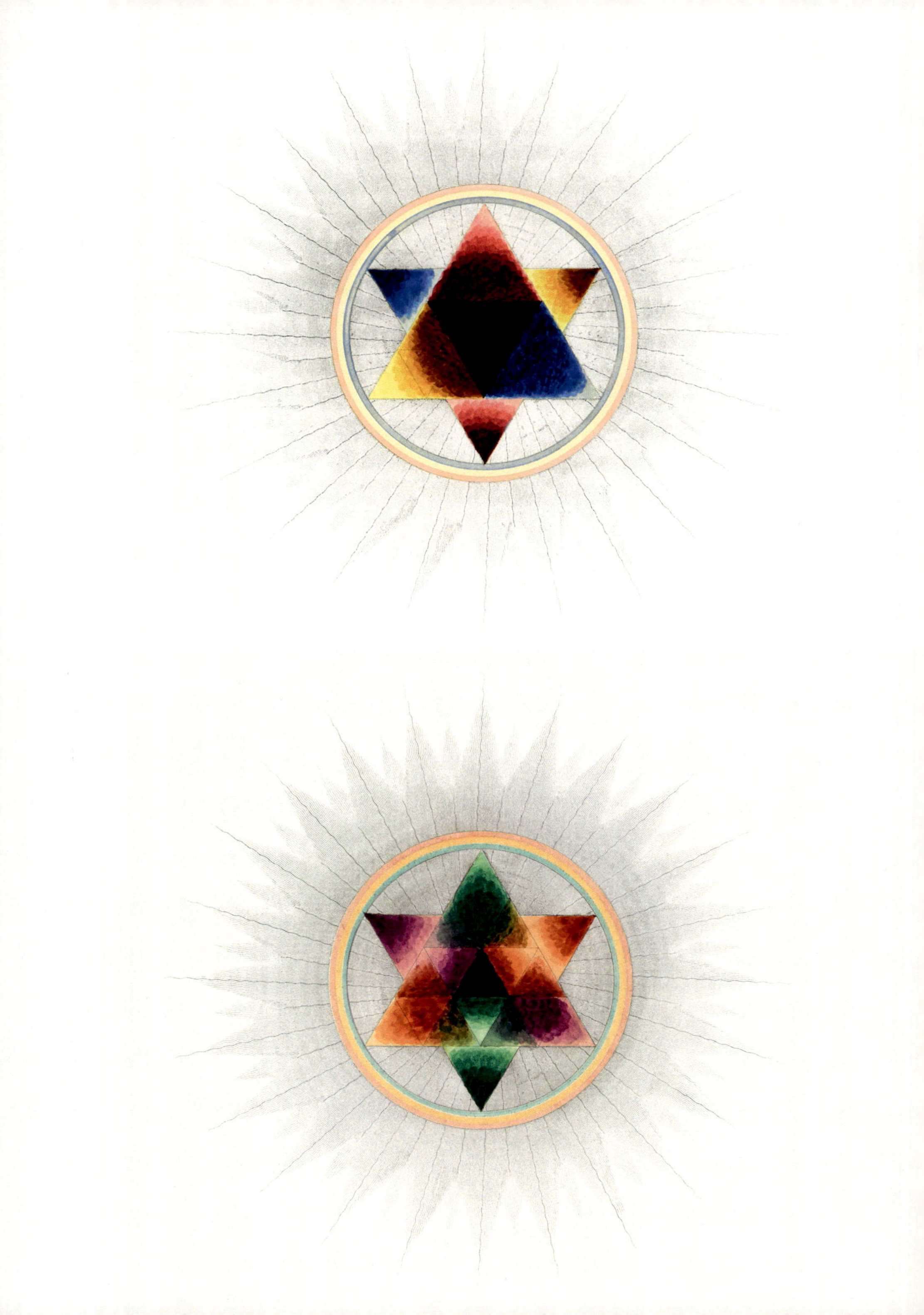

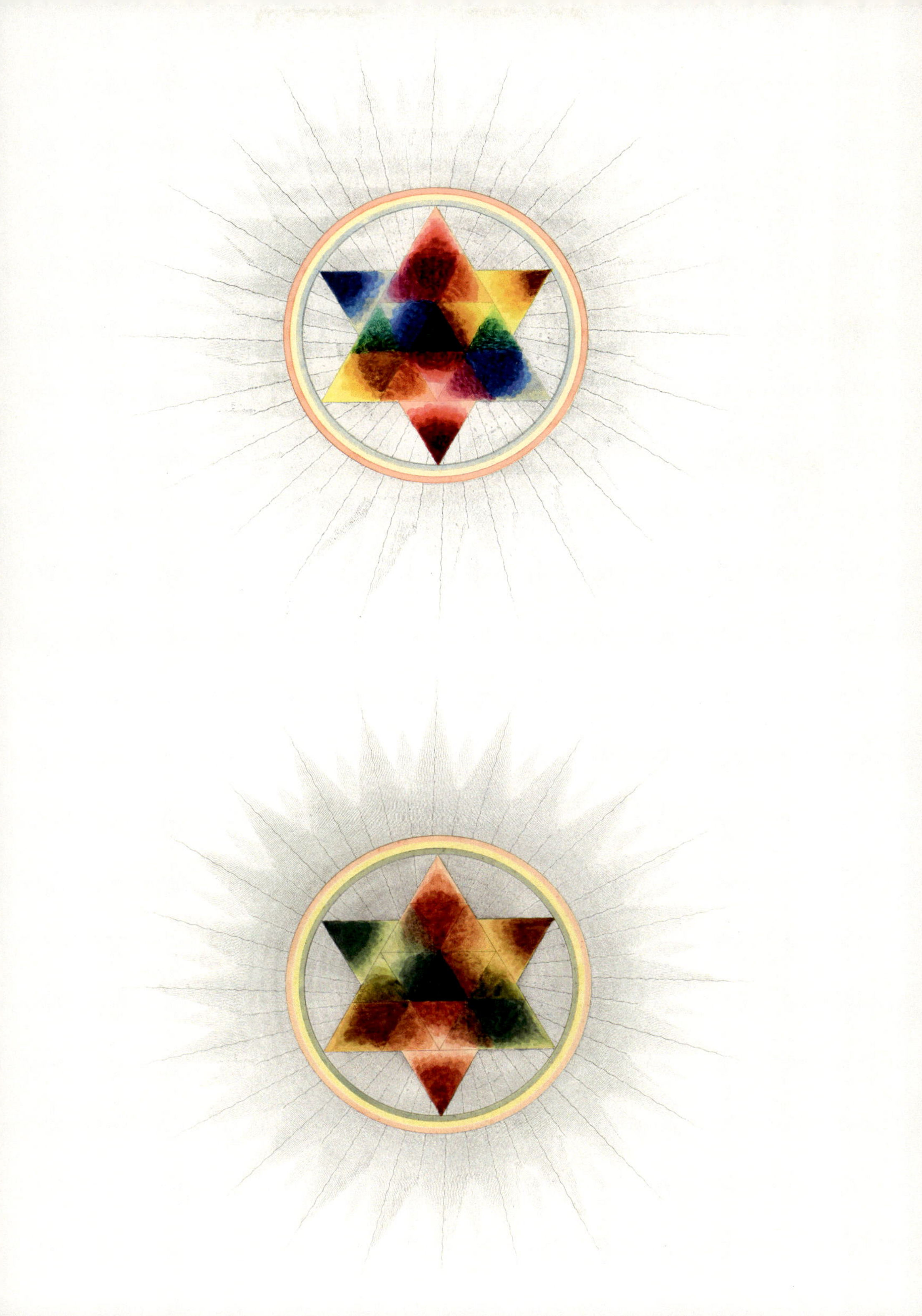

## Charles Hayter (1761–1835)

# A NEW PRACTICAL TREATISE ON THE THREE PRIMITIVE COLOURS

## Assumed as a Perfect System of Rudimental Information

*6 plates, 26.5 x 21 cm | 10 ⅜ x 8 ¼ in., London, 1826*
*London, Wellcome Collection*
*Los Angeles, Getty Research Institute (frontispiece)*

Charles Hayter was an art teacher to members of the British royal family, some of whom, especially the sisters of George IV, showed a great interest in botanical illustration and painting technique. Hayter published his treatise at a time when painting in watercolour was becoming an increasingly popular and affordable pastime, although, while it is certainly a practical handbook, he was also keen to present his work as a serious theoretical system. The last part of the subtitle informs the reader that this book offers "some practical rules for reflections; and Sir Isaac Newton's distribution of the colours in the rainbow". A book then that helped people paint, but which also provided the intellectual and historical background to colour theory.

By the 1820s painting manuals were being published in large numbers (see Chapter 5), with some of them cheerfully embracing mechanical colour-printing methods while others still relied on the hand-colouring of engravings. Hayter's confident claim that he had produced a "perfect system of rudimental information" should perhaps be interpreted as a marketing device, conveying the message that even though it was a book about the basics of painting, it was perfect in that respect. Hayter also wanted it to be affordable, and remarked that he would have liked to include more colour illustrations but was aware of the effect this would have had on the price. His strategy seems to have worked since *A New Practical Treatise* went into a second edition the same year, followed by five further editions through until 1845. The frontispiece shown here (p. 209) was originally uncoloured, but a later owner of the copy coloured it in by hand.

Visually and conceptually, the hand-coloured illustrations in Hayter's book are clearly influenced by those of Moses Harris, whose work he had encountered in 1813 and most of all in the best-known of Hayter's plates, "The Painters Compass" (p. 214), which shows three colour wheels, each with increasing levels of brightness in three stages, from the centre to the outer edge. Where Harris's wheels have a central triangle, Hayter used overlapping discs to represent material colour, while to the right of the wheels there are two vertical scales of warm (yellow, orange, red, purple and indigo) and cold (indigo, blue, green, yellow and pale yellow) colours, both bookended by black and white.

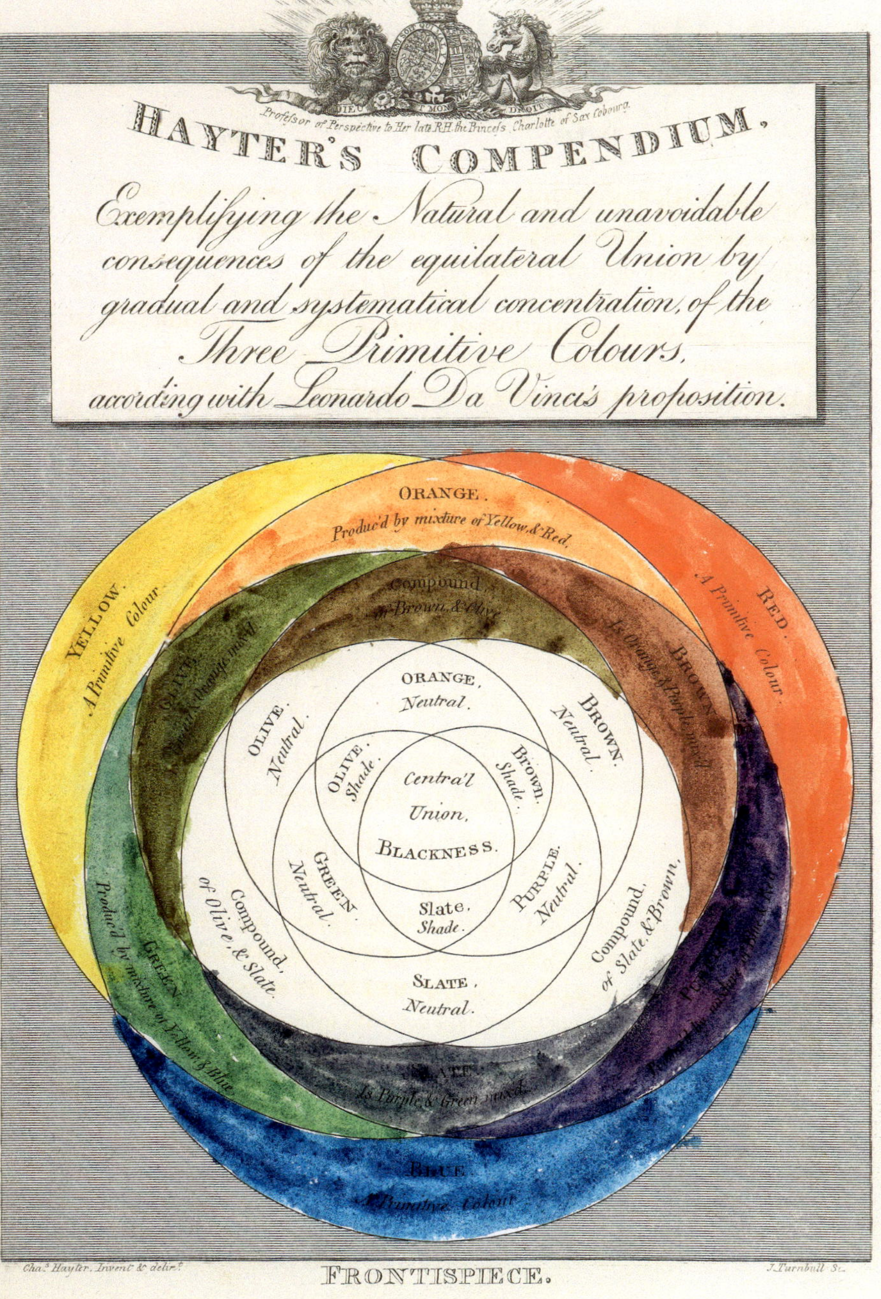


Chas. Hayter. Invent & delint. FRONTISPIECE. J. Turnbull Sc.

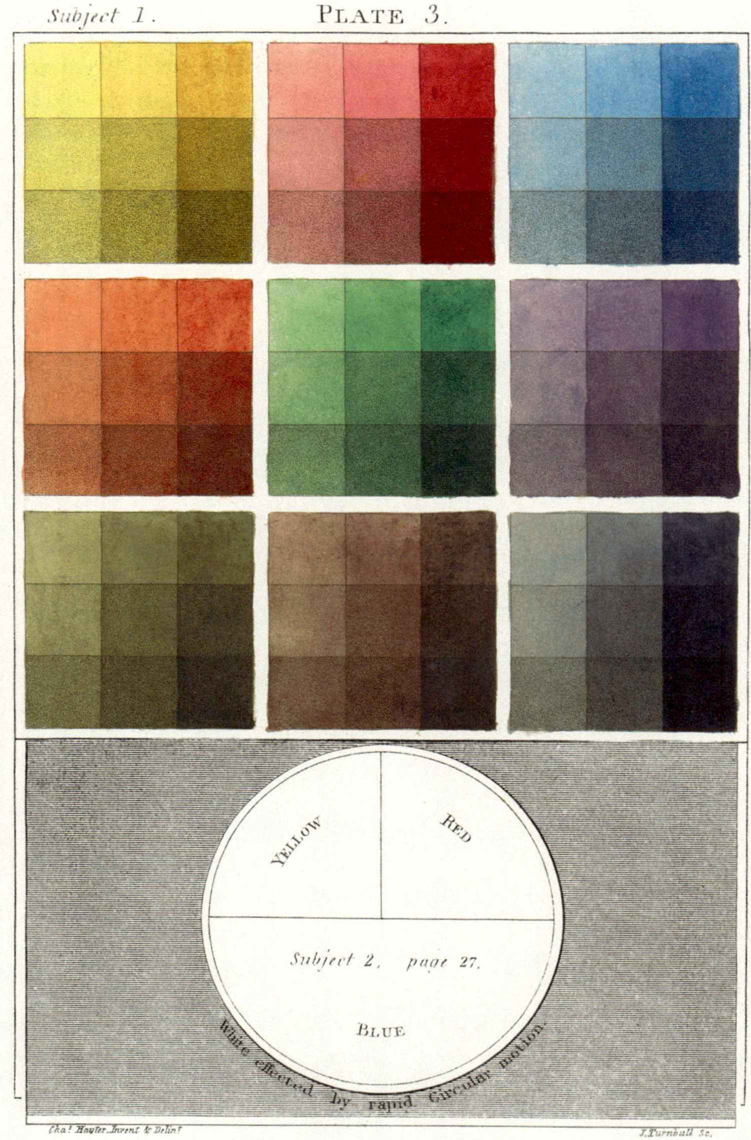
Subject 1.
PLATE 3.
YELLOW
RED
Subject 2, page 27.
BLUE
White effected by rapid Circular motion.
Chas. Hayter. Invent & Delint
J. Turnbull Sc.

## Neue praktische Abhandlung über die drei Urfarben

Charles Hayter war Kunstlehrer am britischen Königshaus, wo sich vor allem die Schwestern von George IV. sehr für botanische Illustrationen und Maltechniken interessierten. Er veröffentlichte seine Abhandlung zu einer Zeit, in der die Aquarellmalerei als Freizeitbeschäftigung immer beliebter und erschwinglicher wurde. Zwar hatte Hayter ein praktisches Handbuch geschrieben, doch wollte er sein Werk auch als ernsthaftes theoretisches System verstanden wissen. Der letzte Teil des Untertitels informiert die Leserschaft über „einige praktische Regeln für Spiegelungen; und Sir Isaac Newtons Verteilung der Farben im Regenbogen", die im Buch zu finden seien – einem Buch also, das Anleitungen zum Malen enthielt, aber auch den geistigen und historischen Hintergrund zur Farbtheorie mitlieferte.

In den 1820er-Jahren kamen Malhandbücher in großer Zahl auf den Markt. Einige griffen beherzt die mechanischen Farbdruckverfahren auf, andere setzten nach wie vor auf handkolorierte Kupferstiche. Hayters selbstbewusste Behauptung, er habe ein „perfektes System elementarer Informationen" geschaffen, sollte man vielleicht als Marketingtrick mit der Botschaft interpretieren, dass man es hier zwar mit einem Buch über das Einmaleins der Malerei zu tun habe, es als solches aber perfekt sei. Hayter wollte auch, dass das Buch bezahlbar blieb, und merkte an, er hätte gern mehr farbige Abbildungen eingefügt, sei sich aber der damit verbundenen Auswirkungen auf den Preis bewusst gewesen. Seine Strategie scheint aufgegangen zu sein, denn noch im selben Jahr erschien eine zweite Auflage von *A New Practical Treatise*, auf die bis 1845 fünf weitere folgten. Die hier gezeigte Frontispiz-Radierung (S. 209) war ursprünglich nicht koloriert, wurde aber von einem Besitzer des Exemplars mit der Hand koloriert.

Optisch und konzeptuell sind die handkolorierten Abbildungen in diesem Buch deutlich von denen eines Moses Harris beeinflusst, dessen Werk Hayter 1813 kennengelernt hatte. Dies gilt vor allem für die bekannteste seiner Tafeln, die den Titel „Der Malerkompass" (S. 214) trägt. Sie zeigt drei Farbkreise mit drei jeweils von innen nach außen angeordneten Helligkeitsstufen. Während bei Harris Dreiecke das Zentrum bilden, wählte Hayter für die stofflichen Grundfarben einander überlappende Scheiben. Rechts neben die Kreise setzte er, jeweils eingerahmt von Schwarz und Weiß, zwei senkrechte Skalen mit warmen (Gelb, Orange, Rot, Violett und Indigo) und kalten Farben (Indigo, Blau, Grün, Gelb und Hellgelb).

## Nouveau traité pratique sur les trois couleurs primaires

Certains membres de la famille royale britannique à qui Charles Hayter enseigne les arts, notamment les sœurs du roi George IV, s'intéressent particulièrement à l'illustration botanique et aux techniques picturales. Lorsque Hayter publie son traité, l'aquarelle est en train de devenir un passe-temps de plus en plus populaire et abordable. Pourtant, même si l'ouvrage est un manuel pratique, son auteur se propose également d'y présenter un système théorique sérieux. La dernière partie du sous-titre informe le lecteur que le livre offre des « règles pratiques permettant la réflexion ; et la distribution des couleurs dans l'arc-en-ciel telle qu'établie par sir Isaac Newton ». En somme, un ouvrage qui aide tout un chacun à peindre autant qu'il présente les bases intellectuelles et historiques de la théorie des couleurs.

Dans les années 1820, les manuels de peinture sont désormais monnaie courante (voir le chapitre 5). Certains adoptent allègrement les méthodes mécaniques d'impression polychrome, d'autres reposent toujours sur une mise en couleurs manuelle de gravures. Pour sa part, Hayter affirme avec assurance avoir mis au point un « système parfait d'informations rudimentaires », peut-être une formule publicitaire pour faire passer l'idée qu'il propose, certes, les bases de la peinture, mais sous une forme parfaite. Hayter souhaite aussi que son livre soit bon marché : il souligne qu'il aurait aimé y intégrer davantage d'illustrations en couleurs, mais qu'il est conscient de l'impact qu'elles auraient eu sur le prix. Sa stratégie semble avoir durablement fonctionné : son « Nouveau traité pratique sur les trois couleurs primaires » est réédité la même année, puis de nouveau à cinq reprises jusqu'en 1845. L'eau-forte illustrant le frontispice (p. 209) et présentée ici était initialement sans couleurs. C'est l'un des possesseurs de cet exemplaire qui l'a coloriée à la main.

En termes visuels et conceptuels, les illustrations coloriées à la main d'Hayter sont clairement influencées par celles de Moses Harris, dont il a découvert les travaux en 1813. C'est le cas notamment de sa célèbre « Boussole des peintres » (p. 214), constituée de trois cercles chromatiques présentant chacun trois degrés d'intensité, qui vont croissant depuis le centre vers l'extérieur. Là où Harris dessinait des triangles au centre, Hayter choisit de superposer des disques représentant les couleurs matérielles. À droite des cercles, deux échelles verticales présentent des gradations baptisées « effet chaud » (jaune, orange, rouge, violet et indigo) et « effet froid » (indigo, bleu, vert, jaune et jaune clair), encadrées à chaque extrémité par le noir et le blanc.

PLATE 1.

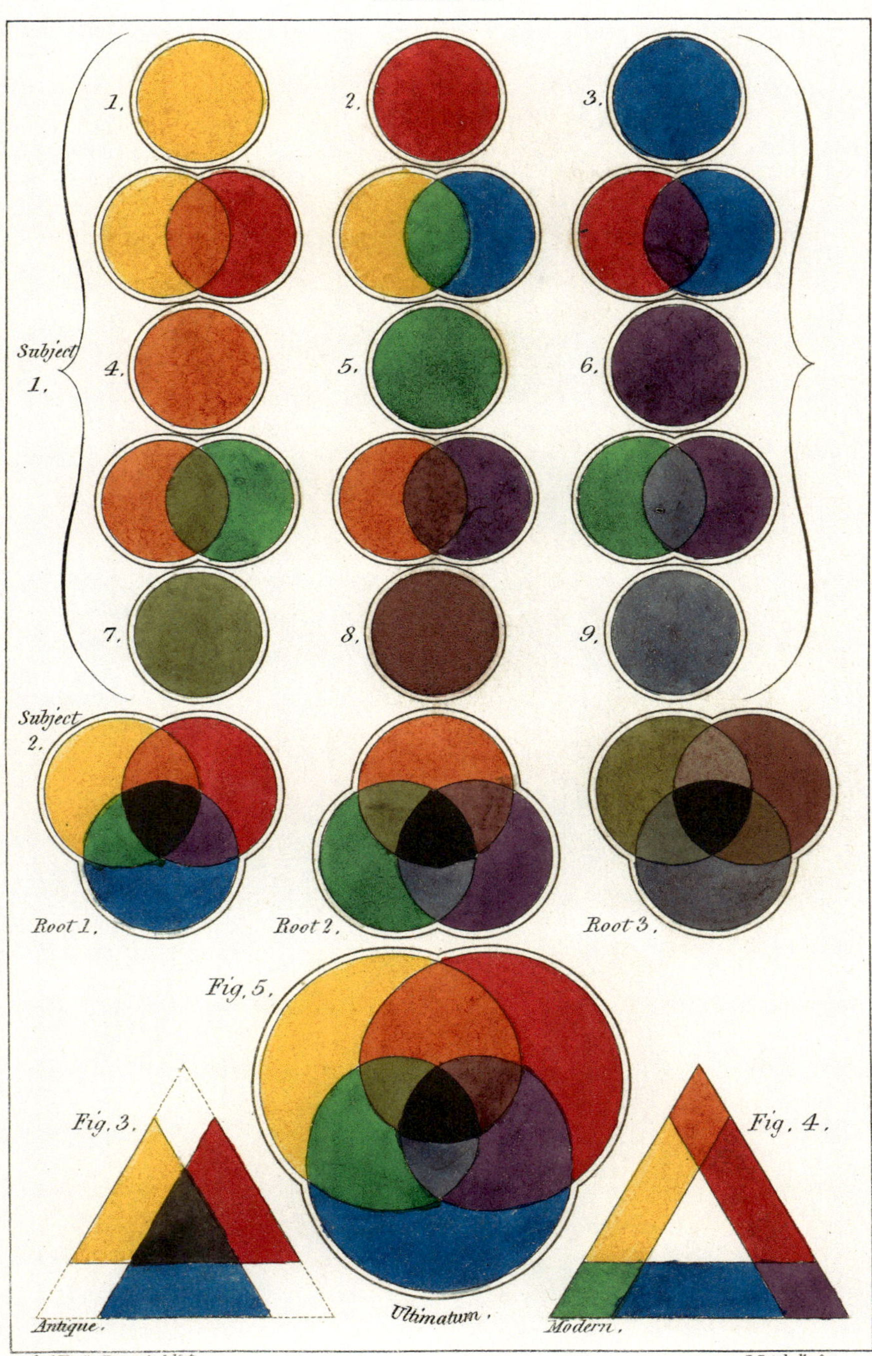


Cha.s Haytir Invent & delin.t J. Turnbull. Sc.

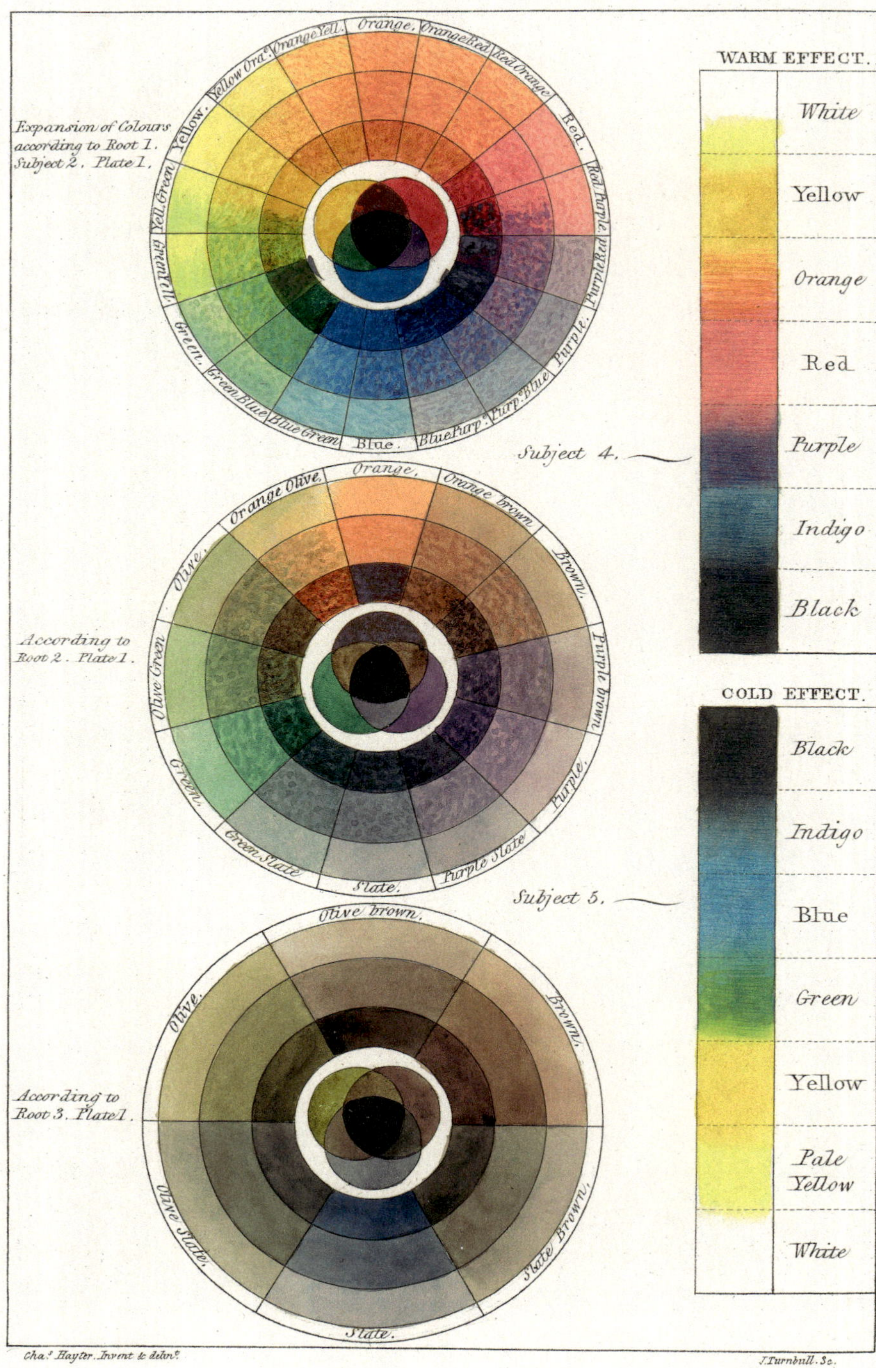
PL. 2.
THE PAINTERS COMPASS.
Expansion of Colours according to Root 1. Subject 2. Plate 1.
Orange.
Orange Red
Red Orange
Red.
Red Purple.
Purple Red.
Purple.
Purp. Blue
Blue Purp.
Blue.
Blue Green
Green Blue
Green.
Green Yell.
Yell. Green
Yellow.
Yellow Ora.
Orange Yell.
Subject 4.
According to Root 2. Plate 1.
Orange.
Orange brown
Brown.
Purple brown
Purple.
Purple Slate
Slate.
Green Slate
Green.
Olive Green
Olive.
Orange Olive.
Subject 5.
According to Root 3. Plate 1.
Olive brown.
Brown.
Slate Brown.
Slate.
Olive Slate.
Olive.
WARM EFFECT.
White
Yellow
Orange
Red
Purple
Indigo
Black
COLD EFFECT.
Black
Indigo
Blue
Green
Yellow
Pale Yellow
White
Chas. Hayter. Invent & delin.
J. Turnbull. Sc.

PLATE 4.

THE RAINBOW.

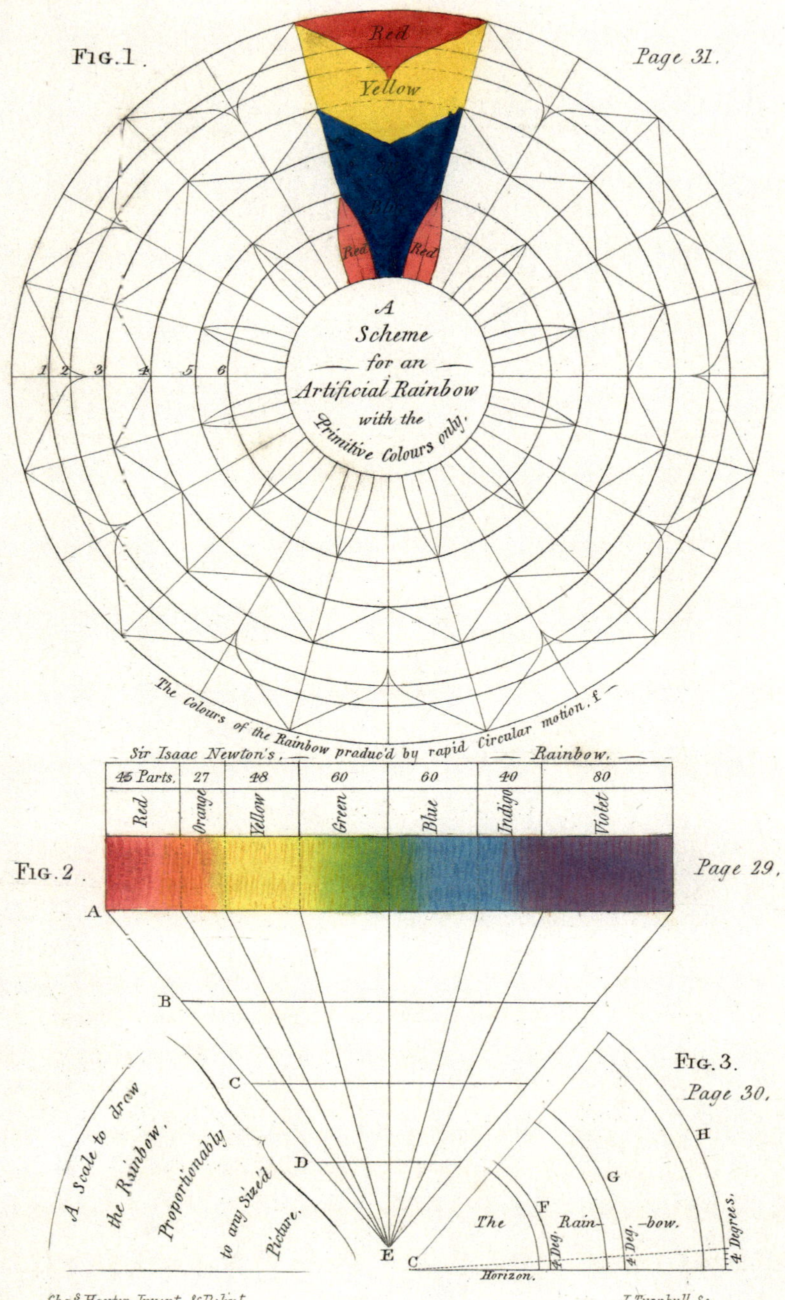


Chas. Hayter Invent & Delint. J. Turnbull, Sc.

## Michel-Eugène Chevreul (1786–1889)

# DE LA LOI DU CONTRASTE SIMULTANÉ DES COULEURS

**On the Principles of Simultaneous Contrast in Colours**

*33 plates, 27.4 x 24 cm | 10 ¾ x 9 ½ in., Paris, 1839*
*London, Royal College of Art, Colour Reference Library*

In the 19th century Michel-Eugène Chevreul was for France what Goethe was for Germany and George Field for England: the author who produced the most wide-ranging, substantial and influential work in the field of colour at this period. However, the three decades that separate Goethe's *Zur Farbenlehre* and Chevreul's *De la loi du contraste simultané des couleurs* reveal how quickly the world was changing during the early years of the 19th century.

When he was younger Chevreul had worked at the Muséum National d'Histoire Naturelle in Paris as an assistant to the chemist and pharmacist Nicolas-Louis Vauquelin, whom he succeeded as Professor of Chemistry at the museum. During his time as a consultant for the famous Gobelin tapestry factories in the 1820s, Chevreul began to formulate his laws of simultaneous colour contrast after having observed how the proximity of colours in woven fabrics affects how they are processed by the human eye. He poured his findings and years of related research into *De la loi du contraste simultané des couleurs*, which was first published in 1839 and within a year had been translated into German, with an English edition following in 1854. From the outset, the book was directed unapologetically at many different disciplines, though with a strong focus on manufacturing. This was the first peak of the industrial age, and Chevreul was well aware of the impact of new technology, such as steam power and electricity, on the arts. As such, his work differs significantly from Goethe's much more philosophical colour theory.

The book presented here, with its 735 pages of text, was accompanied by an experimental volume of around 40 lithographed plates, many of them coloured and some of them triple-folded. In order to demonstrate his notions of colour contrast, Chevreul placed hundreds of small, coloured dots against backgrounds of different colours, combining lithography and hand-colouring. He also introduced an uncoloured 72-part colour wheel, which he ingeniously turned into a three-dimensional object by attaching an overlay section along its radius. This represented the greyscale and could be lifted away from the surface of the diagram.

Figure 89

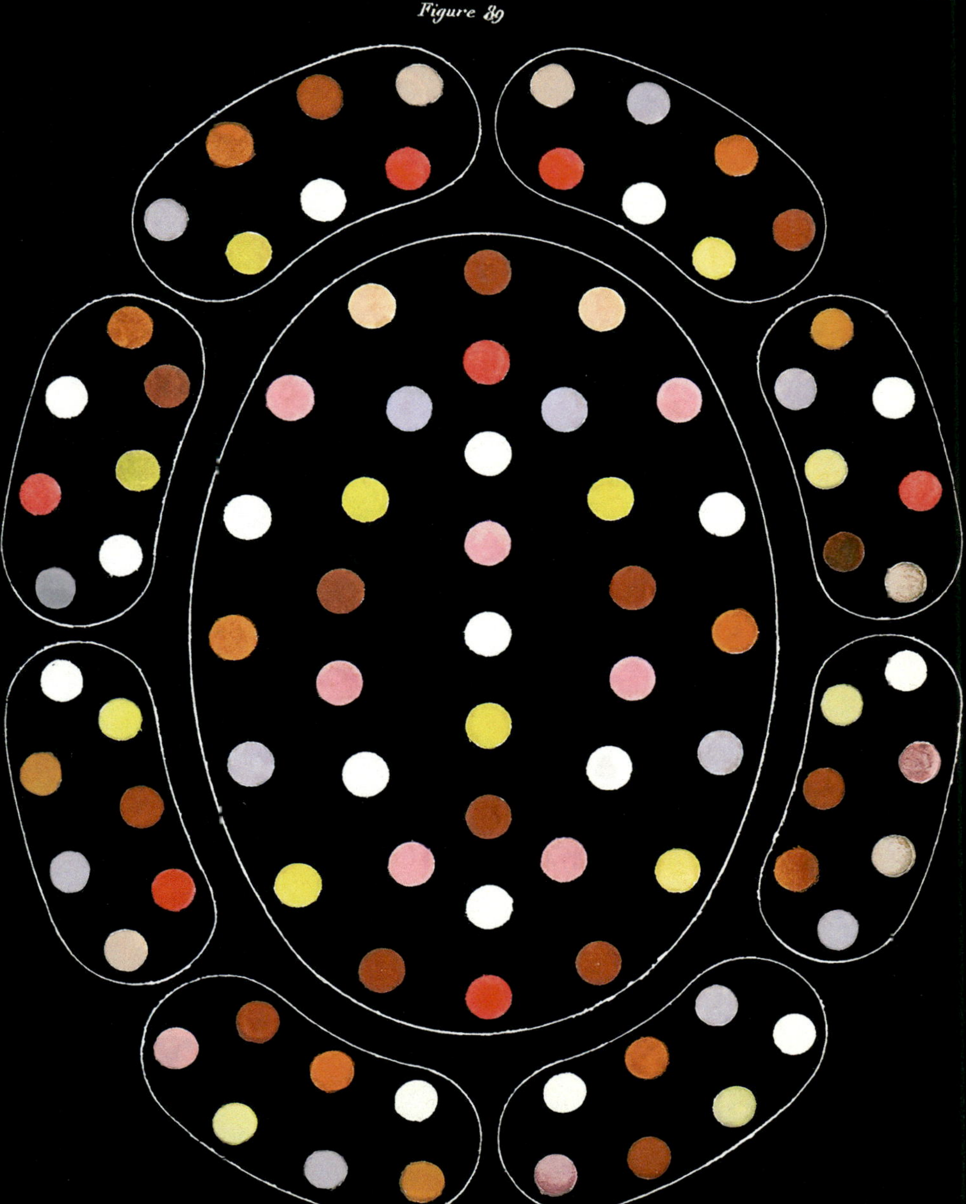

## Vom Prinzip des simultanen Farbkontrasts

Im 19. Jahrhundert war Michel-Eugène Chevreul für Frankreich, was Goethe für Deutschland und George Field für England war: der Autor, der in dieser Zeit die am breitesten gefächerten, gewichtigsten und einflussreichsten Arbeiten zur Farbforschung produzierte. Dennoch legen die drei Jahrzehnte, die zwischen Goethes *Zur Farbenlehre* und Chevreuls *De la loi du contraste simultané des couleurs* liegen, auf faszinierende Weise offen, wie schnell sich die Welt im ersten Drittel des 19. Jahrhunderts veränderte.

Als junger Mann hatte Chevreul im Muséum national d'Histoire naturelle in Paris als Assistent des Chemikers und Apothekers Nicolas-Louis Vauquelin gearbeitet, dem er dort als Professor für Chemie nachfolgte. Während seiner Zeit als Berater der berühmten staatlichen Gobelinmanufaktur in den 1820er-Jahren begann Chevreul seine Gesetze des simultanen Farbkontrasts zu formulieren, nachdem er beobachtet hatte, dass die Nähe von Farben in gewebten Stoffen Einfluss darauf hat, wie das Auge sie verarbeitet. Seine Befunde und jahrelangen Forschungen zu verwandten Phänomenen ließ er in *De la loi du contraste simultané des couleurs* einfließen, das 1839 erschien und binnen eines Jahres ins Deutsche übersetzt wurde. Eine englische Ausgabe folgte 1854. Von Anfang an richtete sich das Buch unmissverständlich an viele verschiedene Disziplinen, wenn auch mit besonderem Fokus auf die Warenherstellung. Das Industriezeitalter hatte seinen ersten Höhepunkt erreicht, und Chevreul war sich über die Auswirkungen, die neue Technologien wie die Dampfkraft oder die Elektrizität auf die Kunst hatten, ganz im Klaren. Insofern unterscheidet sich sein Werk erheblich von Goethes weitaus philosophischer angelegter Farbtheorie.

Das hier vorgestellte Buch mit seinen 735 Textseiten wurde von rund vierzig lithografischen Bildtafeln in einem experimentellen „Atlas“ begleitet, viele davon koloriert und einige dreimal gefaltet. Um seine Vorstellungen vom Farbkon-trast zu demonstrieren, setzte Chevreul in einer Kombination aus Lithografie und manueller Kolorierung Hunderte von kleinen farbigen Punkten auf verschieden eingefärbte Hintergründe. Darüber hinaus führte er einen 72-teiligen Farbkreis ein, den er auf geniale Weise in ein dreidimensionales Objekt verwandelte, indem er auf seinem Radius eine Grauskala in Form eines aufstellbaren Viertelkreises anbrachte.

Planche 2.

Fig 4

Fig. 5

Fig 6

Fig 7

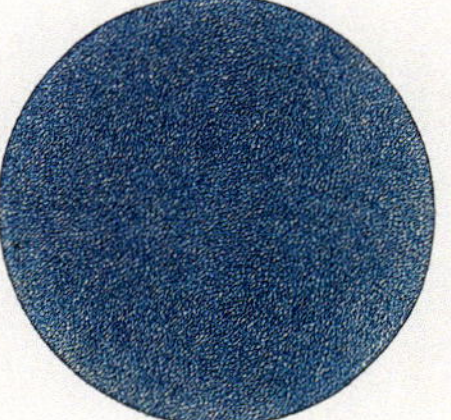

*H. Legrand sc.*

Fig. 8

Fig. 9

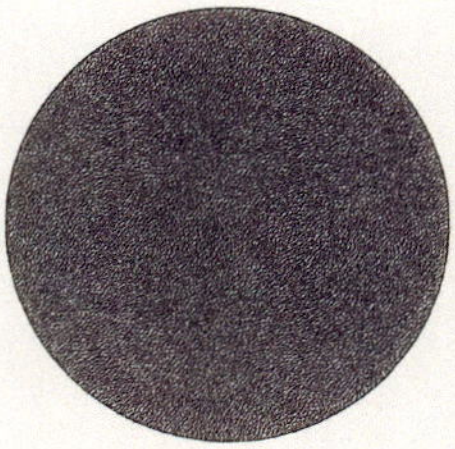

Fig. 10

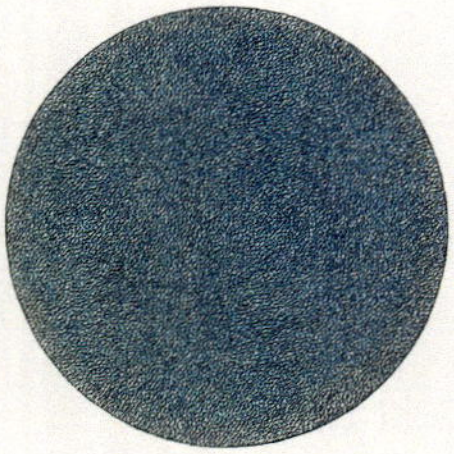

Fig. 11

Fig. 12.

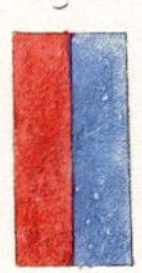


H. Legrand sc.

## De la loi du contraste simultané des couleurs

Au XIXe siècle, Michel-Eugène Chevreul est à la France ce que Goethe est à l'Allemagne et George Field à l'Angleterre : l'auteur le plus prolifique et le plus influent en matière de travaux sur la couleur. Mais l'écart qui sépare *Zur Farbenlehre* (*Traité des couleurs*) de Goethe et l'ouvrage de Chevreul, qui paraît trois décennies plus tard, est révélateur de la rapidité fascinante avec laquelle le monde change en ce début de siècle.

Dans sa jeunesse, Chevreul a travaillé au Muséum national d'histoire naturelle de Paris en tant qu'assistant du chimiste et pharmacien Nicolas-Louis Vauquelin, auquel il succèdera comme professeur de chimie dans l'institution. Dans les années 1820, il œuvre comme conseiller de la célèbre Manufacture des Gobelins. C'est en observant que l'œil humain traite différemment les couleurs rapprochées dans les tissages qu'il commence à formuler ses lois du contraste simultané des couleurs. Les recherches qu'il mène au fil des années seront la matière première de cet ouvrage publié en 1839, traduit en allemand dès l'année suivante, puis en anglais en 1854. Le livre, d'emblée destiné à différentes disciplines, privilégie cependant le domaine de la fabrication. En cette première heure de gloire de l'ère industrielle, Chevreul est tout à fait conscient de l'impact des technologies nouvelles, telles que la machine à vapeur ou l'électricité, sur la production artistique. En cela, son ouvrage se distingue grandement de la théorie de la couleur, beaucoup plus philosophique, de Goethe.

Dans le livre présenté ici, les 735 pages de texte sont assorties d'une partie expérimentale contenant une quarantaine de planches, dont beaucoup sont en couleurs et certaines en trois pans dépliables. Pour démontrer la notion de contraste des couleurs, Chevreul peint des centaines de petites pastilles sur des fonds de différentes couleurs, en combinant lithographie et coloriage manuel. Il propose également, pour représenter l'échelle des gris, un cercle chromatique sans couleurs de 72 sections, qui se mue en objet en trois dimensions par l'apposition d'un rabat le long de son rayon.

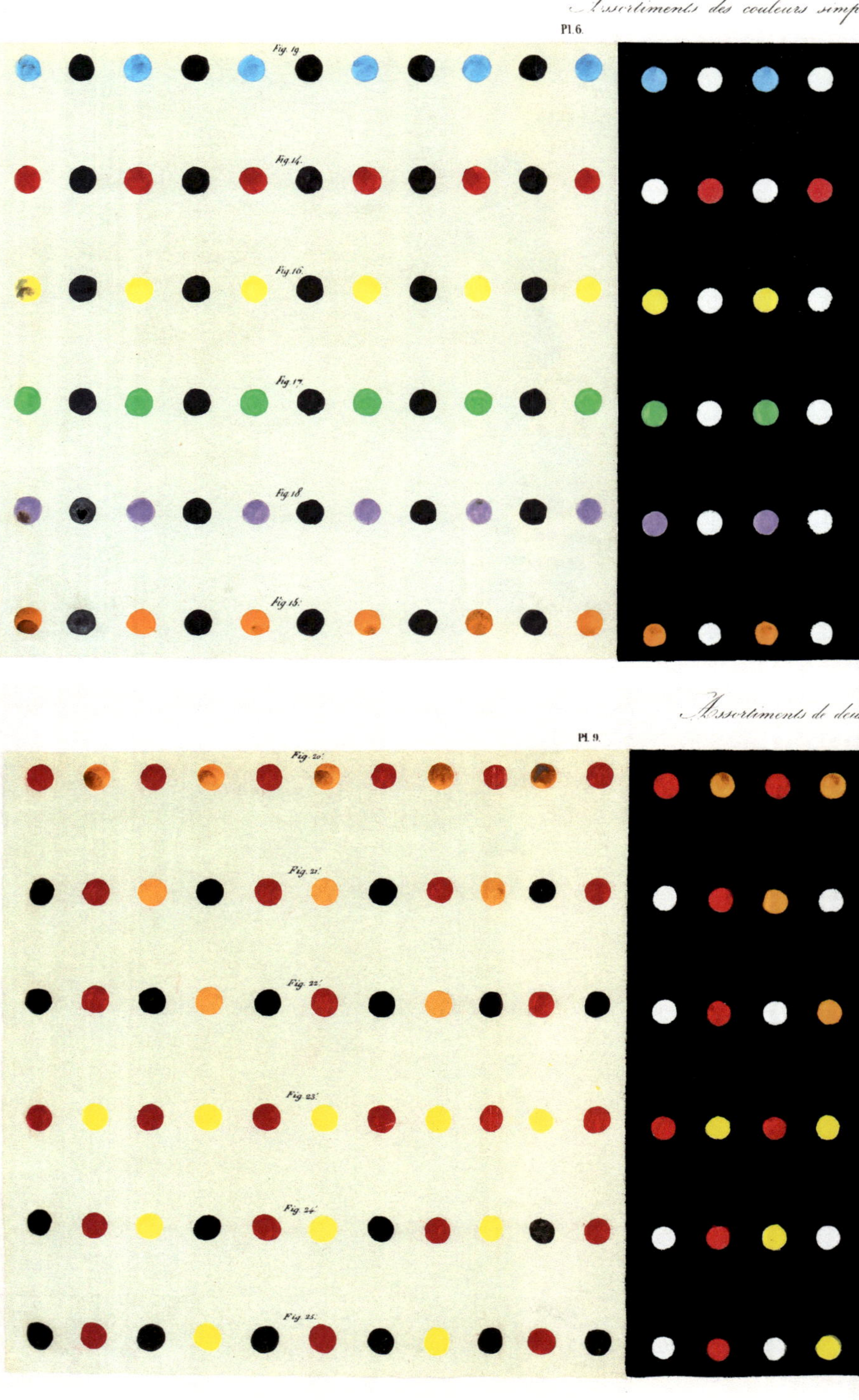
Assortiments des couleurs simples
Pl. 6.
Fig. 19.
Fig. 14.
Fig. 16.
Fig. 17.
Fig. 18.
Fig. 15.
Assortiments de deux
Pl. 9.
Fig. 20'.
Fig. 21'.
Fig. 22'.
Fig. 23'.
Fig. 24'.
Fig. 25'.

artistes avec le blanc, le noir et le gris.

Pl. 5.

Pl. 7.

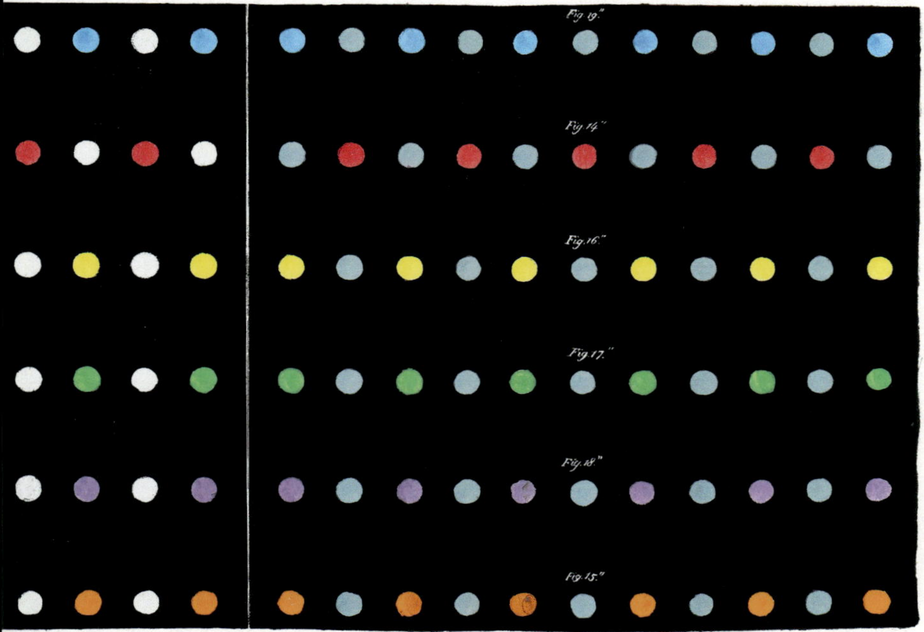

Fig. 13.

Fig. 14.

Fig. 16.

Fig. 17.

Fig. 18.

Fig. 15.

Lith. Kaeppelin, 17 Quai Voltaire, Paris.

avec le blanc, le noir et le gris.

Pl. 8.

Pl. 10.

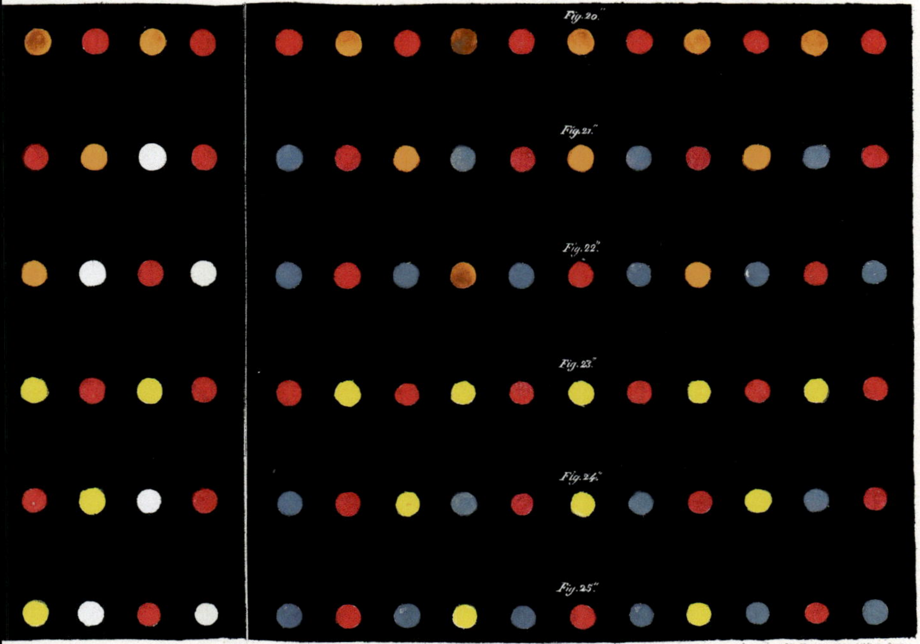

Fig. 20.

Fig. 21.

Fig. 22.

Fig. 23.

Fig. 24.

Fig. 25.

Lith. Kaeppelin, 17 Quai Voltaire, Paris.

PL. 34.

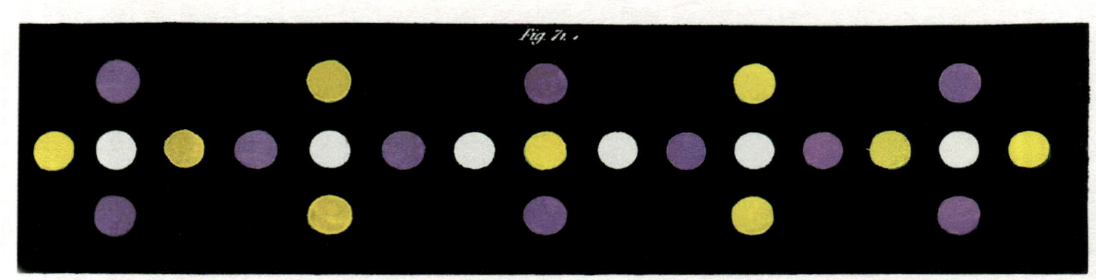


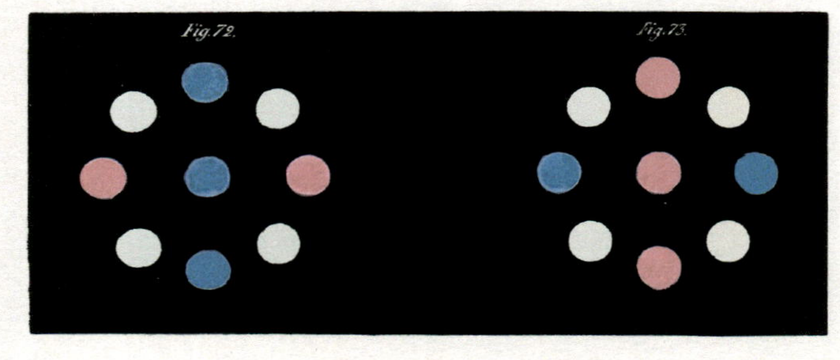

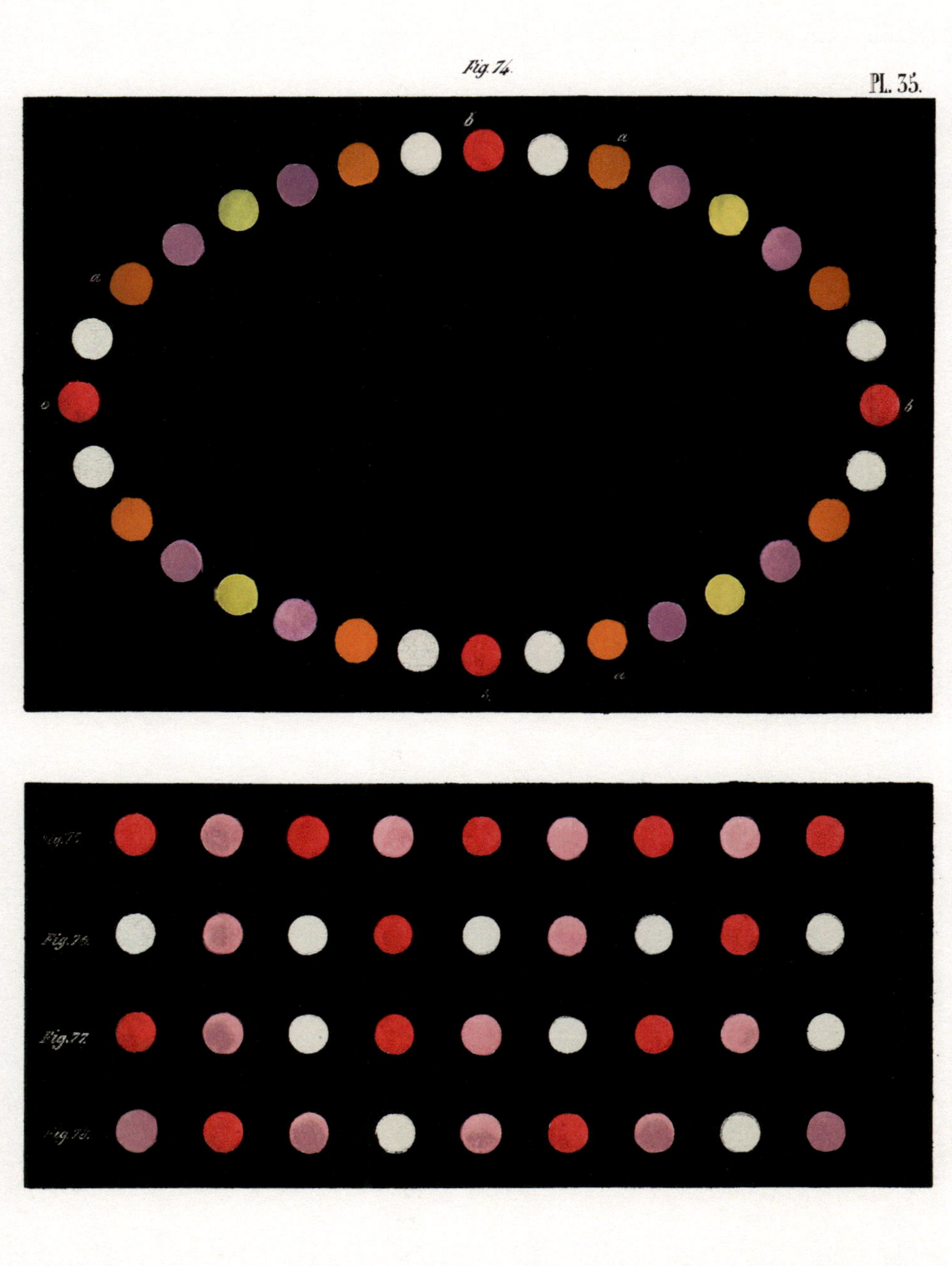
Fig. 74.
PL. 35.
b
a
a
b
b
a
b
Fig.77.

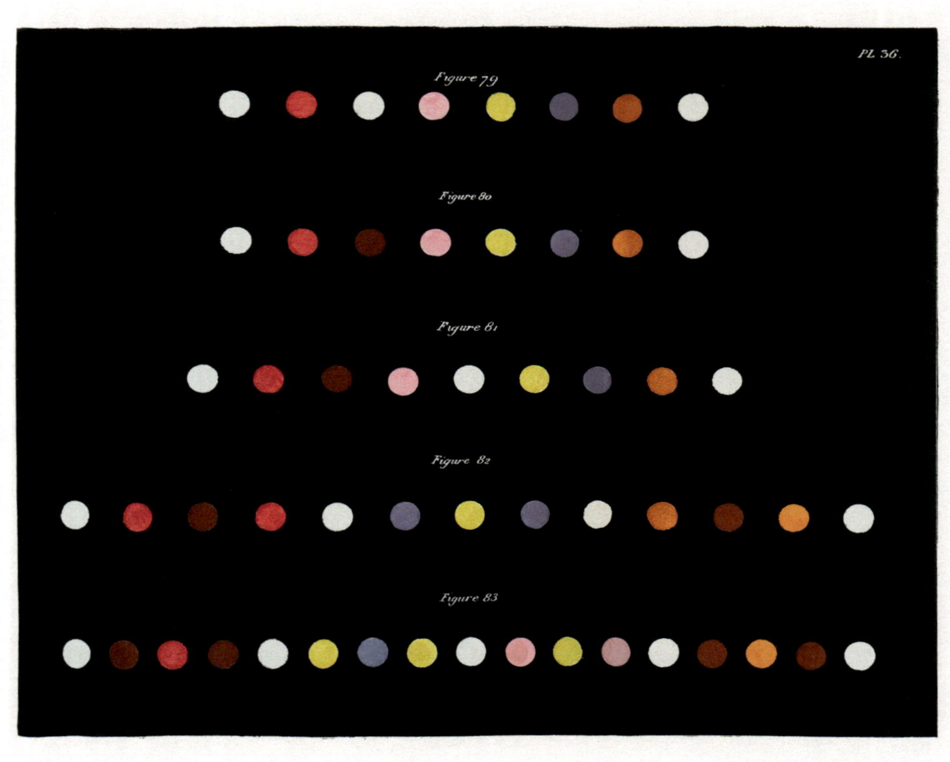
Pl. 36.
Figure 79
Figure 80
Figure 81
Figure 82
Figure 83

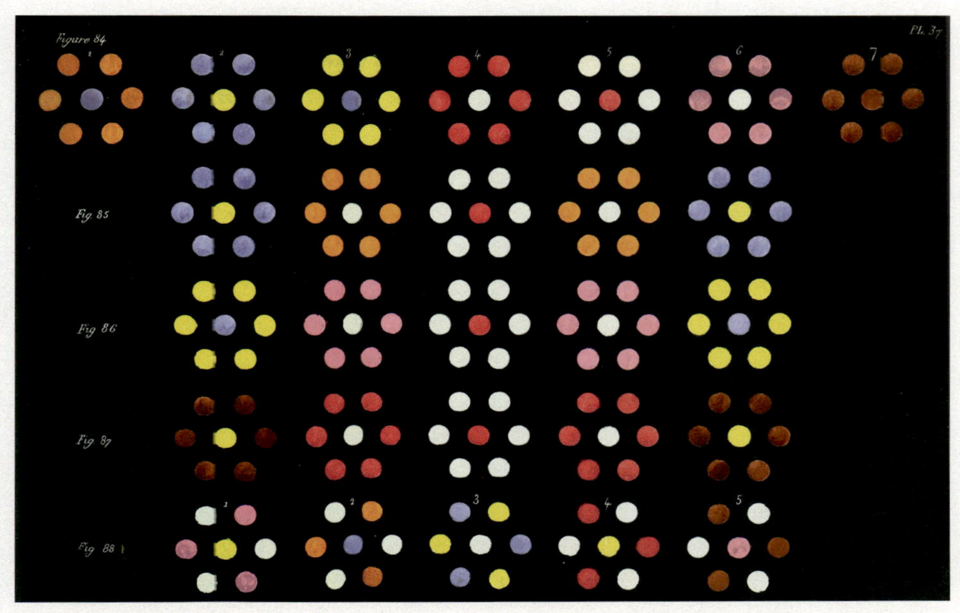
Figure 84
Pl. 37
Fig. 85
Fig. 86
Fig. 87
Fig. 88

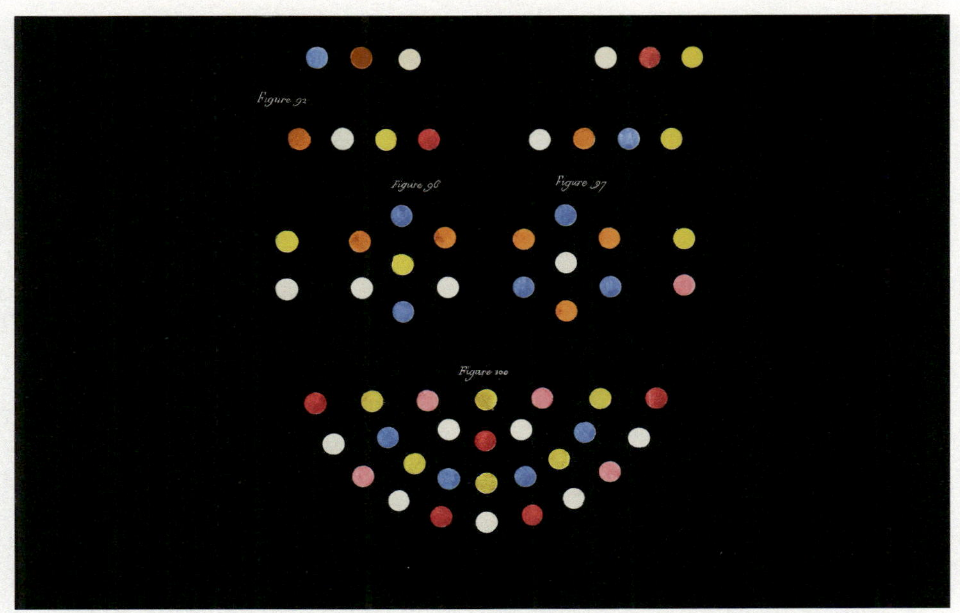
Figure 92
Figure 96
Figure 97
Figure 100

## Michel-Eugène Chevreul

# DES COULEURS

### et de leurs applications aux arts industriels à l'aide des cercles chromatiques

### On Colours, and Their Uses in the Industrial Arts as Considered with the Aid of Chromatic Circles

*13 plates, 37 x 29 cm | 14 ⅝ x 11 ⅜ in., Paris, 1864*
*New Haven, Yale University, Robert B. Haas Family Arts Library Special Collections, Faber Birren Collection of Books on Color*

The success of Chevreul's *De la loi du contraste simultané des couleurs* of 1839 resulted in the book being issued in several further editions, in which Chevreul constantly sought to improve the visual representations of his colour concepts. By the 1860s chromolithographic colour printing had been significantly refined, making possible the publication of a number of magnificently illustrated books that showcased an increasingly colourised world. This later work by Chevreul is one of those masterpieces.

In 1855 Chevreul had started working in conjunction with the engraver René-Henri Digeon, and together they produced a large set of colour circles, using a four-stage printing process, the stunning *Cercles chromatiques de M. E. Chevreul* (1855). This work had been based on the original uncoloured circle from 1839, and in 1861 the section of plates from *De la loi du contraste simultané des couleurs* was itself printed again, as *Exposé d'un moyen de définir et de nommer les couleurs* (A proposal for a method to be used for defining and naming colours), which was included in the 33rd volume of the *Mémoires de l'Académie des Sciences*. In 1864 it was further extended and published as a title on its own, as the edition shown here: *Des couleurs et de leurs applications aux arts industriels à l'aide des cercles chromatiques*.

A long fold-out plate, "Couleurs d'un Spectre Solaire" (Colours of a solar spectrum), displays the full linear prismatic spectrum of visible colours against a dark background and was intended as a standard for the different hues to be found in the accompanying circles. Other plates show columns of colours in subtle gradations, formed by additions of white and black (for example, "Gamme chromatique bleu", p. 230).

Digeon and Chevreul's group of 12 full-page colour circles is unrivalled in 19th-century print culture with regard to their technical and conceptual brilliance. The first circle shows the pure prismatic colours at a stage of maximum saturation. This is repeated in the second circle, but with a division into 72 sections, which is then used in all the subsequent circles. The remaining 10 circles show the development from this state of maximum brightness to almost complete darkness, with the increasing addition of black. The last few circles show astonishingly subtle shades of grey and black, with just a hint of colour in each of them.

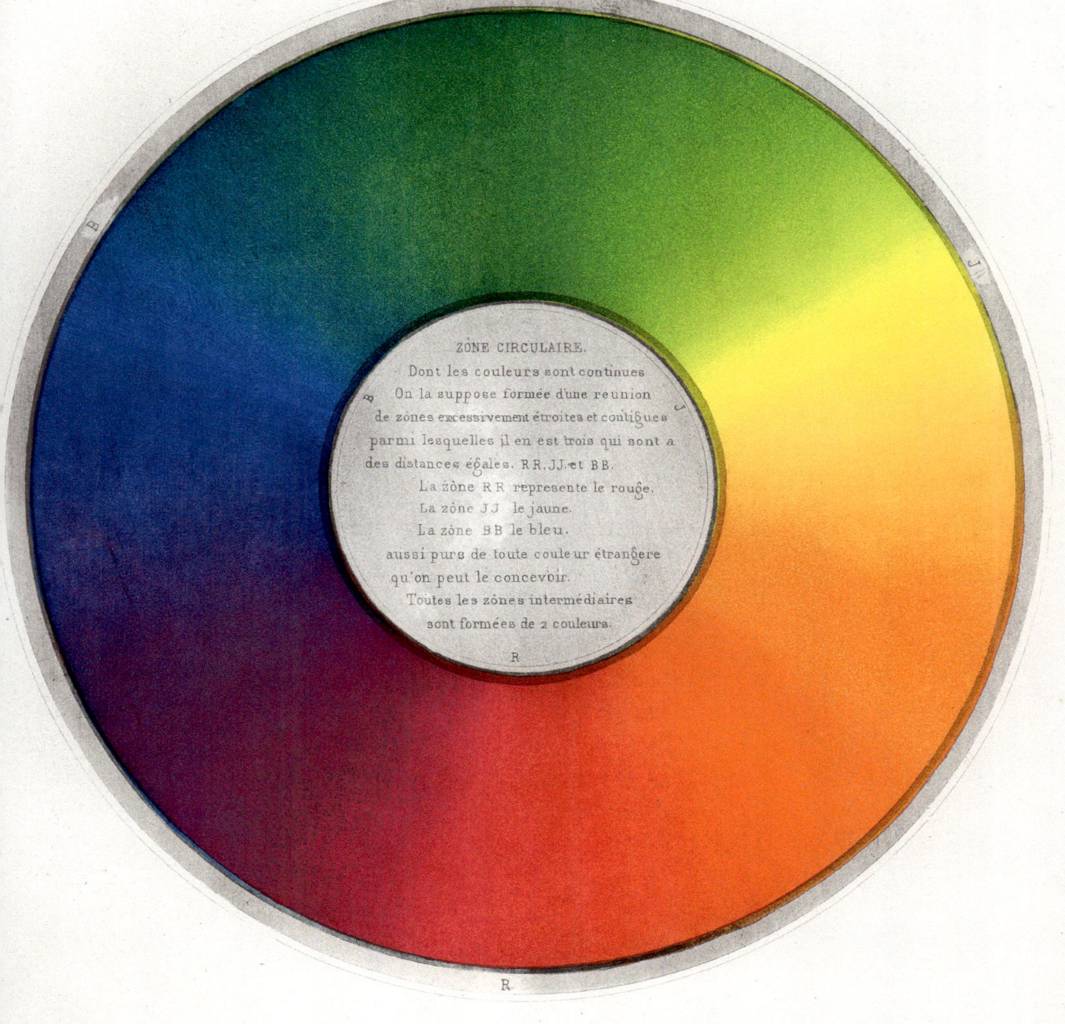
ZÔNE CIRCULAIRE.
Dont les couleurs sont continues
On la suppose formée d'une reunion
de zônes excessivement étroites et contigues
parmi lesquelles il en est trois qui sont a
des distances égales. RR, JJ et BB.
La zône RR represente le rouge,
La zône JJ le jaune.
La zône BB le bleu.
aussi purs de toute couleur étrangere
qu'on peut le concevoir.
Toutes les zônes intermédiaires
sont formées de 2 couleurs.
B
J
R
B
J
R

Digeon sc. Publié par J.B. BAILLIÈRE et FILS, à Paris. Lamoureux Imp

# MANIÈRE

Dont Mr Chevreul conçoit qu'une couleur qui est indéfinie en allant du blanc au noir, est distinguée en parties définies qu'il appelle tons.

*Il désigne les tons d'une même couleur par le mot :*

GAMME DE CETTE COULEUR.

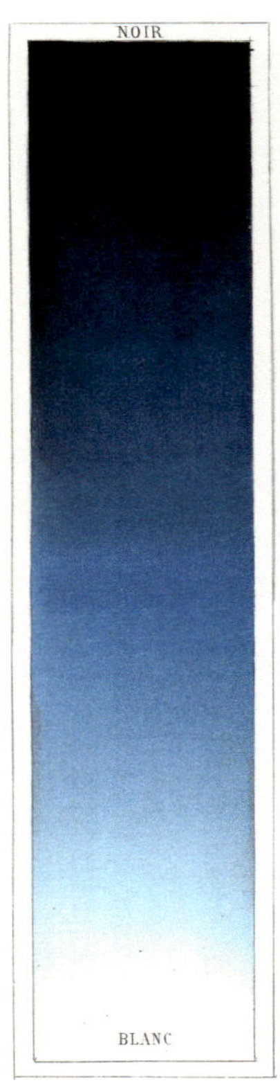


Fig. 1.

Exemple de la graduation d'une couleur.

On va du blanc au noir.

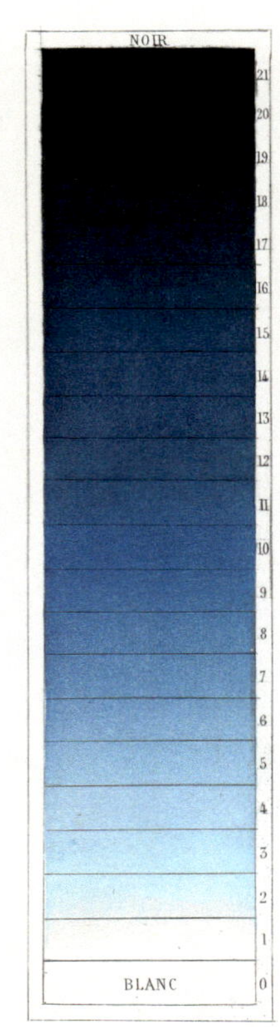


Fig. 2.

C'est la figure 1 divisée en 22 parties superficielles égales

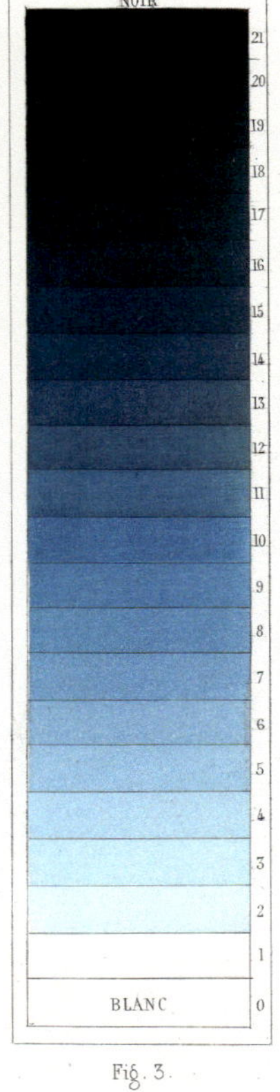


Fig. 3.

C'est la figure 2 avec la différence que la couleur qui est graduée d'une manière continue dans la figure 2 sur chaque partie superficielle en allant du blanc au noir, est repartie d'une manière uniforme sur chaque partie superficielle ; dès lors la couleur est discontinue dans l'ensemble des parties superficielles.

C'est ainsi que la fig. 3 représente ce que Mr Chevreul appelle la gamme des tons bleus au nombre de vingt.

On peut dire que le blanc est zéro et que le noir est le ton 21

Digeon sc.

Lamoureux

Publié par J.B. BAILLIÈRE et FILS, à Paris.

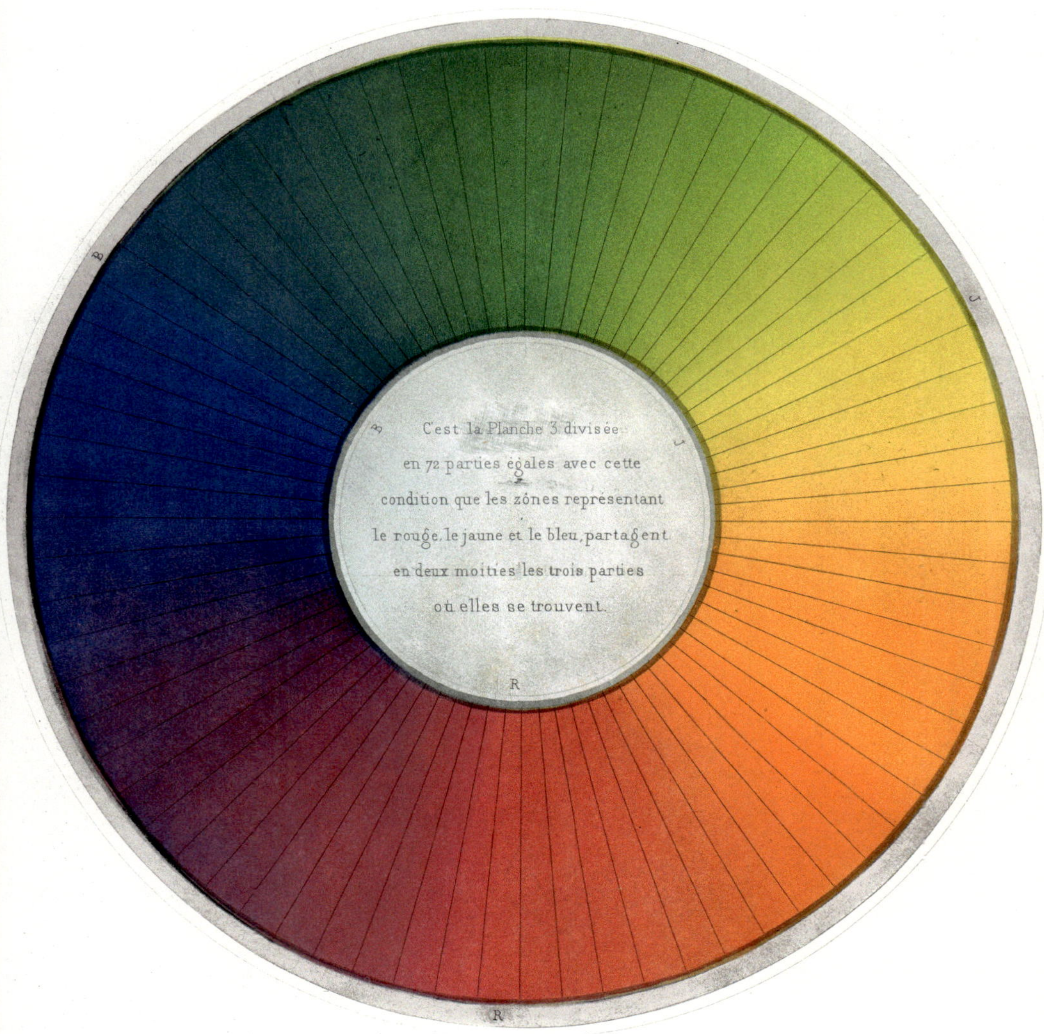


Si on se représente chaque partie de la zône Pl. 4. uniformément teinte de la *Couleur nuancée* dont elle est couverte, on aura *72 Couleurs types* suffisamment distinctes pour qu'on puisse y rapporter les couleurs franches, comme on rapporte les tons d'une même couleur à la figure 3. de la Planche 2.

*Observation*: La conséquence du mélange uniforme de la couleur est toute simple pour toutes les parties qui ne renferment que deux couleurs: mais les parties divisées par RR. JJ. BB. renfermant trois couleurs, doivent être l'objet d'une remarque particulière. Elles comprennent en effet chacune trois couleurs, par exemple, la moitié de la partie représentant le rouge qui est du coté du jaune contient du jaune, comme la moitié qui regarde le bleu contient du bleu. Dès lors, par le mélange, la partie rouge doit être mêlée de jaune et de bleu, à la vérité en très petite quantité, mais ce mélange ne change pas la qualité du rouge autrement qu'en l'ombrant un peu, par la raison que des couleurs matérielles complémentaires donnent du Noir par leur mélanges.

Si l'on se représentait la zône circulaire colorée par la transmission ou la réflexion des rayons colorés du prisme, le rouge, au lieu d'être ombré, serait éclairci parce que les lumières colorées complémentaires reproduisent du blanc par leur mélange.

Publié par J. B. BAILLIERE et FILS, à Paris

Lamoureux lith.

CHEVREUL

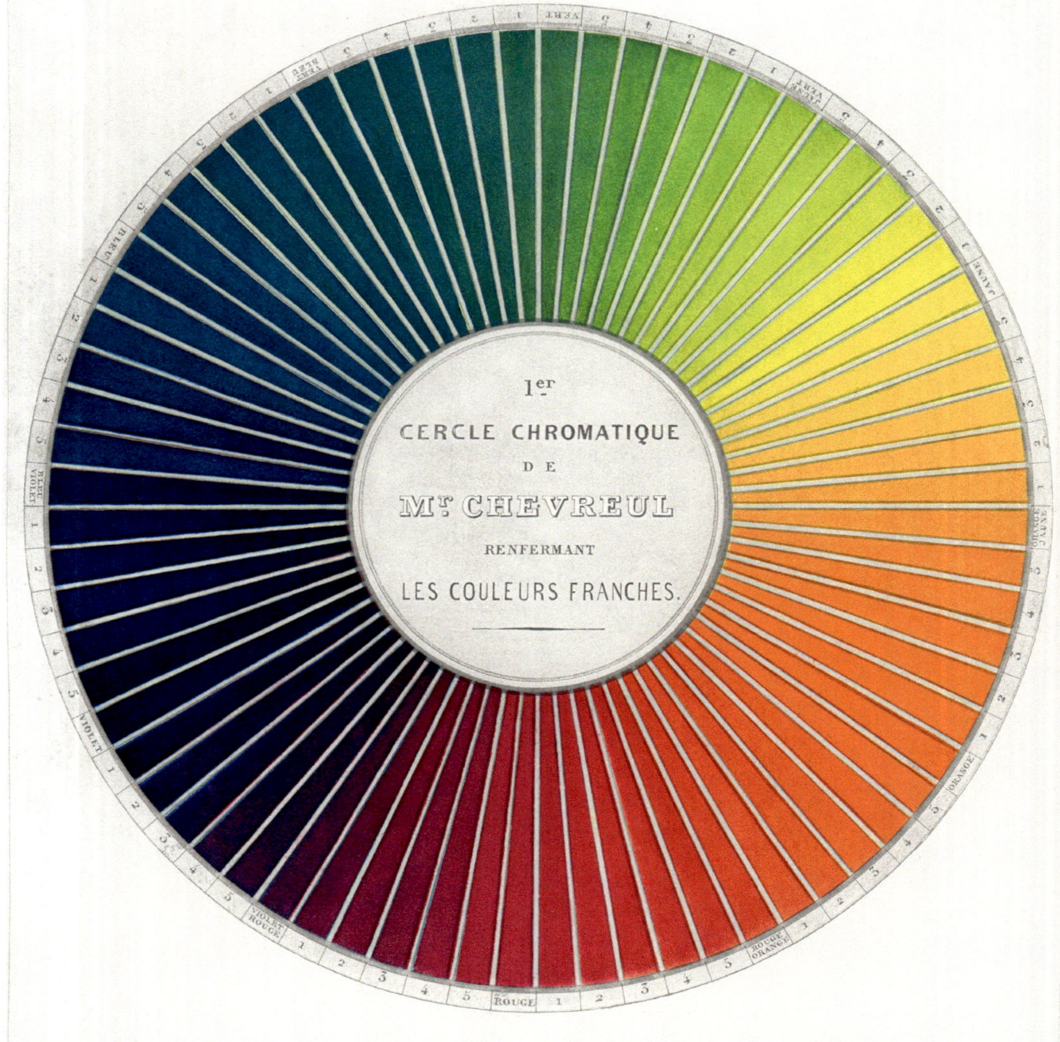


Pigeon sc. Publié par J.B. BAILLIÈRE et FILS, à Paris. Lamoureux Imp.

## Über Farben und ihre Anwendungen in Industrie und Gewerbe mithilfe von Farbkreisen

Der Erfolg von Chevreuls *De la loi du contraste simultané des couleurs* (1839) bescherte dem Buch mehrere Neuauflagen, in denen der Autor laufend versuchte, die bildlichen Darstellungen seiner Farbsysteme zu verbessern. In den 1860er-Jahren hatte sich die Farblithografie erheblich weiterentwickelt und machte die Herausgabe prachtvoll illustrierter Bücher möglich, die eine zunehmend eingefärbte Welt darboten. Dieser spätere Band aus Chevreuls Hand ist eines jener Meisterwerke.

Chevreul hatte 1855 eine Zusammenarbeit mit dem Kupferstecher René-Henri Digeon begonnen. Gemeinsam schufen sie mithilfe eines vierstufigen Druckverfahrens die überwältigenden *Cercles chromatiques de M. E. Chevreul* (1855), eine umfangreiche Serie von Farbkreisen, die auf dem ursprünglichen, nicht kolorierten Kreis von 1839 beruhte. 1861 wurde der Farbatlas aus *De la loi du contraste simultané des couleurs* nachgedruckt und als *Exposé d'un moyen de définir et de nommer les couleurs* („Vorschlag für eine Methode der Bestimmung und Benennung von Farben") als Teil des 33. Bandes der *Mémoires de l'Académie des Sciences* veröffentlicht. Hier gezeigt werden Tafeln aus der erweiterten Fassung, die 1864 unter dem Titel *Des couleurs et de leurs applications aux arts industriels à l'aide des cercles chromatiques* („Über Farben und ihre Anwendungen in Industrie und Gewerbe mithilfe von Farbkreisen") als eigenständiges Werk erschien.

Eine lange Ausklapptafel mit dem Titel „Couleurs d'un spectre solaire" (Farben eines Sonnenspektrums) zeigt das komplette prismatische Spektrum der sichtbaren Farben in linearer Form vor einem dunklen Hintergrund und sollte als Maßstab für die verschiedenen Farbtöne in den folgenden Farbkreisen dienen. Auf weiteren Tafeln sind Farbsäulen in feinen Abstufungen zu sehen, die durch Hinzugabe von Weiß oder Schwarz entstehen (zum Beispiel die „Gamme chromatique bleu" oder „Blaue Farbskala", S. 230).

Die Gruppe der zwölf ganzseitigen Farbkreise von Digeon und Chevreul ist in ihrer technischen und konzeptuellen Brillanz im Druckwesen des 19. Jahrhunderts einmalig. Der erste Kreis zeigt die reinen prismatischen Farben im Zustand maximaler Sättigung. Im zweiten Kreis wiederholt sich das Bild, nun jedoch mit einer Unterteilung in 72 Abschnitte, die in allen folgenden Kreisen beibehalten wird. Die restlichen zehn Kreise zeigen die Entwicklung von diesem Zustand maximaler Leuchtkraft bis hin zu fast völliger Dunkelheit durch ansteigendes Zusetzen von Schwarz. Die letzten Kreise bestechen mit erstaunlich feinen, nur einen Hauch Buntfarbe enthaltenden Schattierungen von Grau und Schwarz.

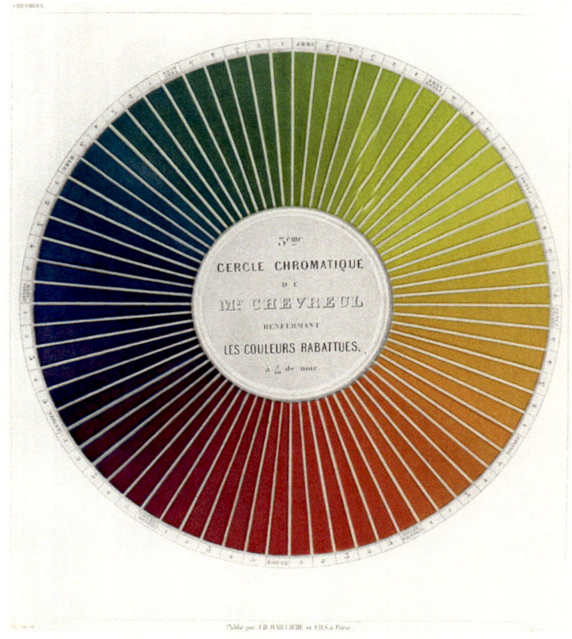


## Des couleurs et de leurs applications aux arts industriels à l'aide des cercles chromatiques

Le succès rencontré par *De la loi du contraste simultané des couleurs* en 1839 permet à Chevreul d'améliorer progressivement les représentations visuelles de ses conceptions chromatiques dans plusieurs rééditions. L'impression par chromolithographie s'est considérablement améliorée et, dans les années 1860, de nombreux ouvrages superbement illustrés voient le jour. Dans le monde de plus en plus coloré qui se déploie, le nouvel ouvrage de Chevreul fait figure de chef-d'œuvre.

En 1855, Chevreul entame une collaboration avec le graveur René-Henri Digeon. Ensemble, ils produisent toute une panoplie de cercles chromatiques en utilisant un processus d'impression en quatre étapes : ce sont les éblouissants *Cercles chromatiques de M. E. Chevreul* (1855), issus du cercle sans couleurs de 1839. En 1861, les planches figurant dans *De la loi du contraste simultané des couleurs* sont également réimprimées sous le titre *Exposé d'un moyen de définir et de nommer les couleurs*, qui sera inclus dans le 33e volume des *Mémoires de l'Académie des Sciences*. En 1864, cet opus est encore augmenté et doté d'un titre propre, comme sur l'édition présentée ici : *Des couleurs et de leurs applica-*

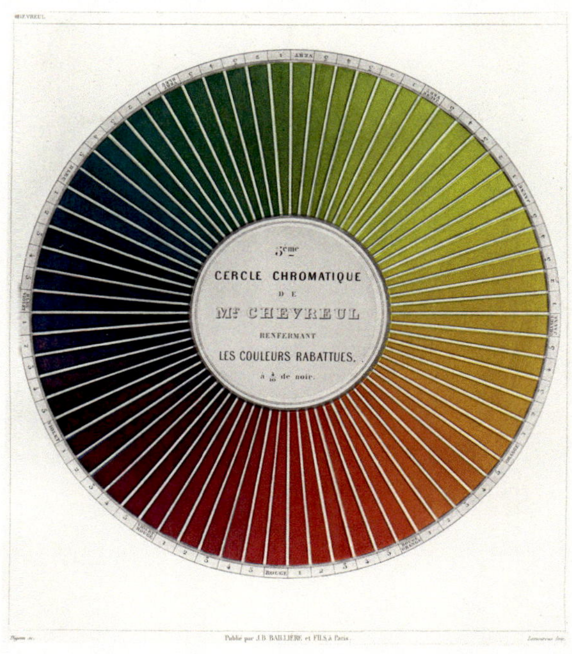


*tions aux arts industriels à l'aide des cercles chromatiques.*

Une longue planche dépliable intitulée « Couleurs d'un spectre solaire » montre la décomposition complète du spectre prismatique des couleurs visibles sur un fond sombre et sert de référence pour les différentes teintes que l'on trouve dans les cercles. D'autres planches montrent les couleurs disposées en colonnes dont les gradations subtiles sont obtenues par ajout de blanc et de noir (voir par exemple la gamme chromatique des bleus, p. 230).

Les 12 pleines pages de cercles chromatiques de Digeon et Chevreul restent un sommet absolu dans toute la production éditoriale du XIXe siècle, tant au plan technique que conceptuellement. Les couleurs prismatiques pures du premier cercle sont figurées dans leur saturation maximale. Cette présentation se répète dans le deuxième cercle, mais avec une division en 72 sections que l'on retrouve dans tous les cercles suivants. Les dix cercles restant montrent la déclinaison depuis le stade de luminosité maximale jusqu'à l'obscurité presque totale, au gré de l'ajout de noir. Les tout derniers cercles présentent les gris et les noirs au moyen d'infimes touches de couleur étonnamment subtiles.

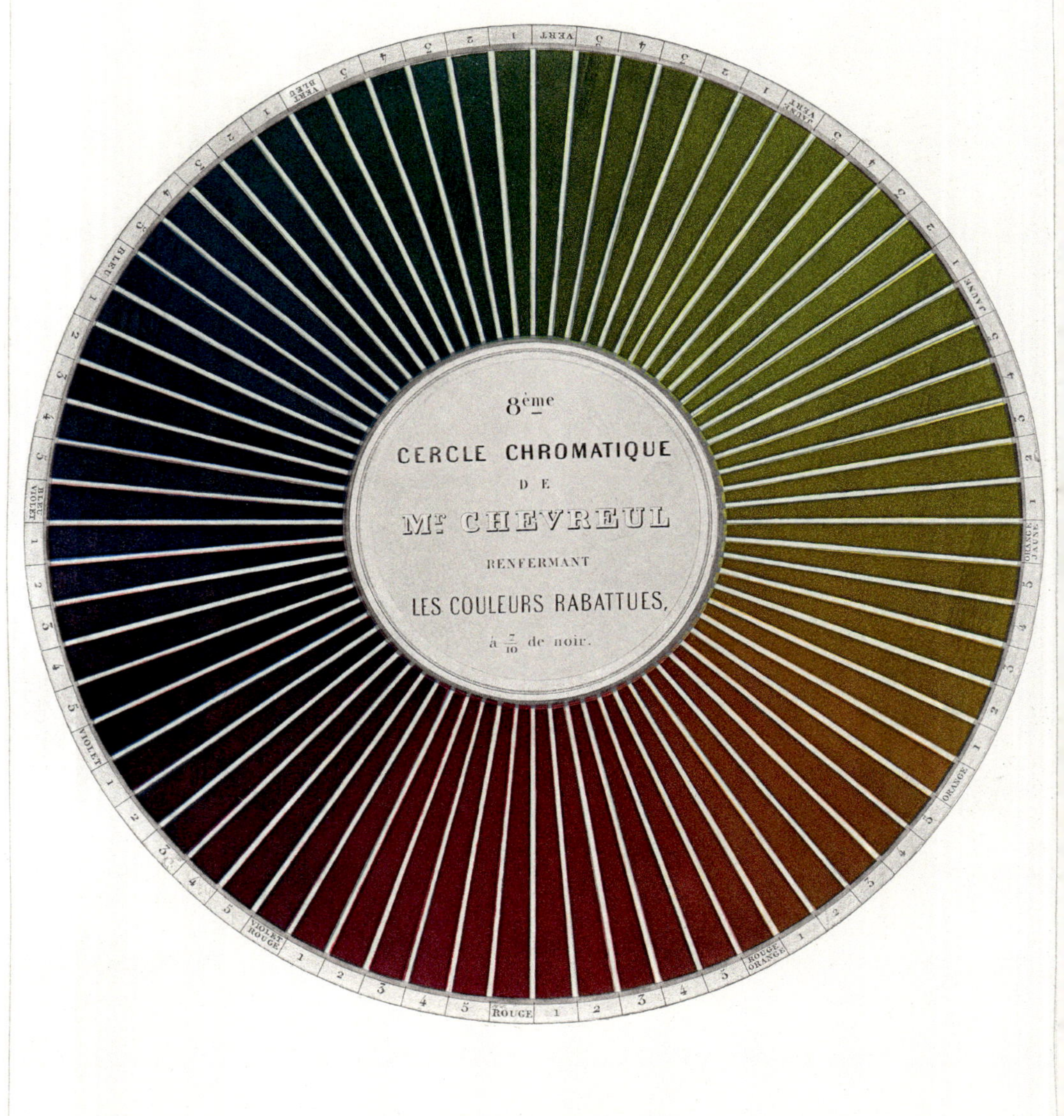


Digeon sc. Publié par J.B. BAILLIÈRE et FILS, à Paris. Lamoureux Imp.

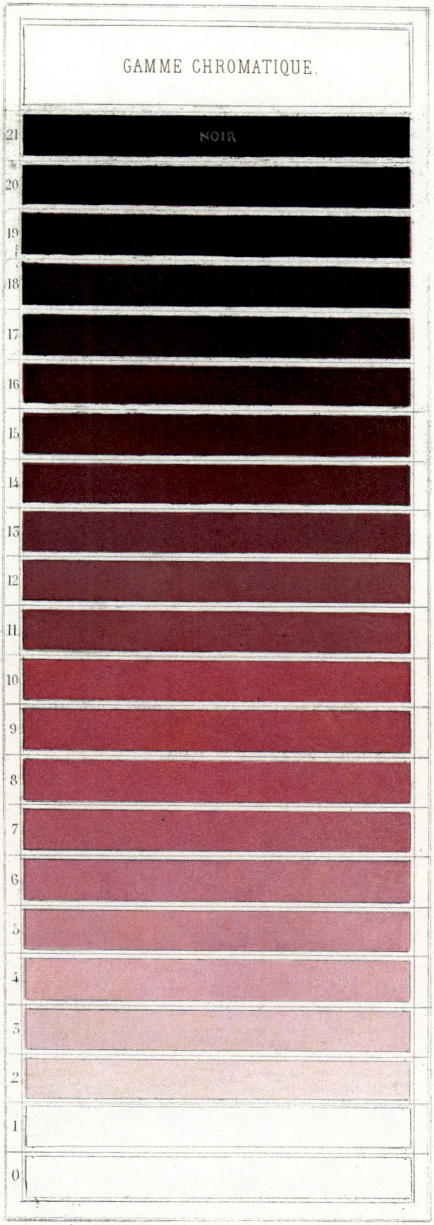

# GAMME CHROMATIQUE.

21 NOIR
20
19
18
17
16
15
14
13
12
11
10
9
8
7
6
5
4
3
2
1
0

*Digeon sc.* Publié par J.B. BAILLIÈRE et FILS, à Paris. Imp. [illegible]

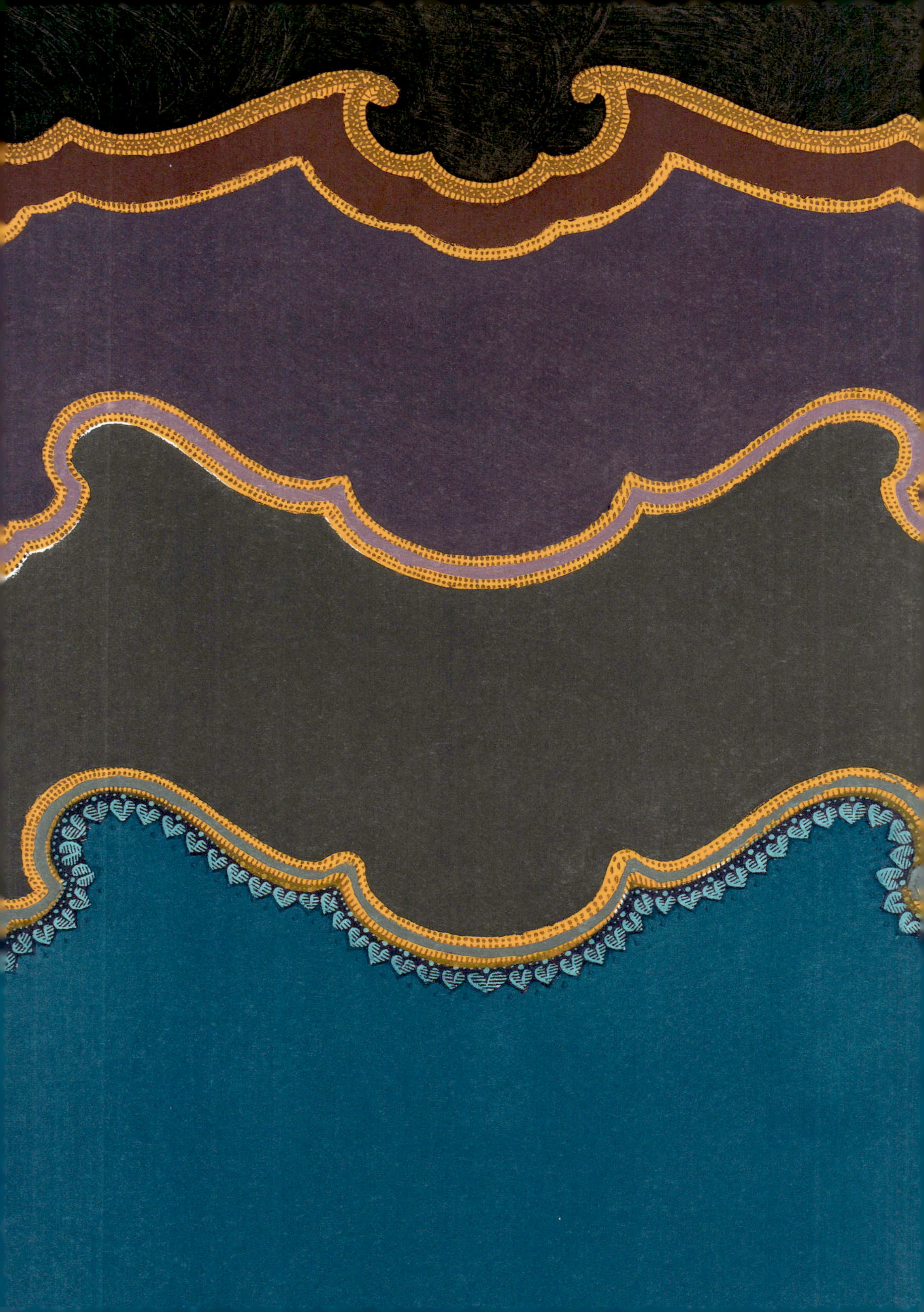

Chapter 4

# *Colours as Guiding Lights:* NOMENCLATURES AND STANDARDS

**1821–1950**

## Patrick Syme (1774–1845)

# WERNER'S NOMENCLATURE OF COLOURS

*13 illustrated pages, 24 x 15 cm / 9 ½ x 5 ⅞ in., Edinburgh, 1821*
*Fife, University of St Andrews Library, Department of Special Collections*

A book about colour that reveals much about how 18th-century thinking, knowledge, research and print culture influenced developments in the early 19th century, *Werner's Nomenclature of Colours* is a work that manages to connect different disciplines, languages and cultures, as well as countries and people. Its own history is complex and fascinating, and benefits from the (true) story that the young Charles Darwin kept a copy of it in his coat pocket on his voyage to South America and Australia aboard HMS *Beagle* in the 1830s. Its small size may have been one reason why he took it along during his search for new species, but it had more to offer than mere portability.

The titular Werner was the German geologist Abraham Gottlob Werner, who in 1774 published a book on rocks and minerals, *Von den äußerlichen Kennzeichen der Foßilien* (On the external characteristics of mineral remains), which included a section about colour, albeit with no illustrations. Werner grouped his list of 54 individual colours into eight families (white, grey, black, blue, green, yellow, red and brown) and this list soon became an internationally influential standard for colour classification. Werner's book was translated into Hungarian, French and English before Patrick Syme, a flower painter at the Wernerian and Caledonian Horticultural Societies in Edinburgh, published his own English translation in 1814, with a second edition appearing in 1821.

Syme added two further colour groups (purple and orange) and doubled the list of individual colours to 108, adding another two in the translation's second edition. His aim was to provide a colour reference work that would be useful for "the Arts and Sciences, Particularly Zoology, Botany, Chemistry, Mineralogy, and Morbid Anatomy", and especially so in fieldwork. His most important addition, however, to Werner's original work was a set of plates depicting all the individual colours, with small hand-painted squares for each one. They are presented as charts, and Syme also noted equivalents for most of the colours using sources from the animal (including humans and insects) vegetable and mineral kingdoms. Emphasis was placed on the appearance and recognisability of each colour, to aid taxonomical identification. Within that, some of the names given to the colours are conspicuously visceral, such as "Veinous" and "Arterial Blood Red", "Liver Brown" and "Skimmed Milk White", the latter being found in the "white of the human eyeballs".

## WHITES.

| Nº | Names. | Colours. | Animal. | Vegetable. | Mineral. |
|---|---|---|---|---|---|
| 1 | Snow White. | | Breast of the black headed Gull. | Snow-Drop. | Carara Marble and Calc Sinter. |
| 2 | Reddish White. | | Egg of Grey Linnet. | Back of the Christmas Rose. | Porcelain Earth. |
| 3 | Purplish White. | | Junction of the Neck and Back of the Kittiwake Gull. | White Geranium or Storks Bill. | Arragonite. |
| 4 | Yellowish White. | | Egret. | Hawthorn Blossom. | Chalk and Tripoli. |
| 5 | Orange coloured White. | | Breast of White or Screech Owl. | Large Wild Convolvulus. | French Porcelain Clay. |
| 6 | Greenish White. | | Vent Coverts of Golden crested Wren. | Polyanthus Narcissus. | Calc Sinter. |
| 7 | Skimmed milk White. | | White of the Human Eyeballs. | Back of the Petals of Blue Hepatica. | Common Opal. |
| 8 | Greyish White. | | Inside Quill-feathers of the Kittiwake. | White Hamburgh Grapes. | Granular Limestone. |

# BLUES

| No. | Names | Colours | ANIMAL | VEGETABLE | MINERAL |
|---|---|---|---|---|---|
| 24 | *Scotch Blue* | | *Throat of Blue Titmouse.* | *Stamina of Single Purple Anemone.* | *Blue Copper Ore.* |
| 25 | *Prussian Blue.* | | *Beauty Spot on Wing of Mallard Drake.* | *Stamina of Bluish Purple Anemone.* | *Blue Copper Ore* |
| 26 | *Indigo Blue* | | | | *Blue Copper Ore.* |
| 27 | *China Blue* | | *Rhynchites Nitens* | *Back Parts of Gentian Flower.* | *Blue Copper Ore from Chessy.* |
| 28 | *Azure Blue.* | | *Breast of Emerald crested Manakin* | *Grape Hyacinth. Gentian.* | *Blue Copper Ore.* |
| 29 | *Ultra marine Blue.* | | *Upper Side of the Wings of small blue Heath Butterfly.* | *Borrage.* | *Azure Stone or Lapis Lazuli.* |
| 30 | *Flax-flower Blue.* | | *Light Parts of the Margin of the Wings of Devil's Butterfly.* | *Flax flower.* | *Blue Copper Ore* |
| 31 | *Berlin Blue.* | | *Wing Feathers of Jay.* | *Hepatica.* | *Blue Sapphire.* |
| 32 | *Verditter Blue* | | | | *Lenticular Ore.* |
| 33 | *Greenish Blue* | | | *Great Fennel Flower.* | *Turquois. Flour Spar.* |
| 34 | *Greyish Blue.* | | *Back of blue Titmouse* | *Small Fennel Flower.* | *Iron Earth.* |

# PURPLES.

| No. | Names | Colours | Animal | Vegitable | Mineral |
|---|---|---|---|---|---|
| 35 | Bluish Lilac Purple. | | Male of the Lebellula Depressa. | Blue Lilac. | Lepidolite. |
| 36 | Bluish Purple. | | Papilio Argeolus. Azure Blue Butterfly. | Parts of White and Purple Crocus. | |
| 37 | Violet Purple. | | | Purple Aster | Amethyst. |
| 38 | Pansy Purple. | | Chrysomela Goettingensis. | Sweet-scented Violet. | Derbyshire Spar. |
| 39 | Campa-nula Purple. | | | Canterbury Bell. Campanula Persicifolia. | Fluor Spar. |
| 40 | Imperial Purple. | | | Deep Parts of Flower of Saffron Crocus. | Fluor Spar. |
| 41 | Auricula Purple. | | Egg of largest Blue-bottle. or Flesh Fly. | Largest Purple Auricula. | Fluor Spar. |
| 42 | Plum Purple. | | | Plum. | Fluor Spar. |
| 43 | Red Lilac Purple | | Light Spots of the upper Wings of Peacock Butterfly. | Red Lilac. Pale Purple Primrose. | Lepidolite. |
| 44 | Lavender Purple | | Light Parts of Spots on the under Wings of Peacock Butterfly. | Dried Lavender Flowers. | Porcelain Jasper. |
| 45 | Pale Blackish Purple. | | | | Porcelain Jasper. |

## Werners Nomenklatur der Farben

*Werner's Nomenclature of Colours* ist ein Farbenbuch, das viel über den Einfluss verrät, den die Vorstellungen und das Wissen, die Forschung und das Druckwesen des 18. Jahrhunderts auf die Entwicklungen des frühen 19. Jahrhunderts ausübten. Es gelingt dem Buch, verschiedene Disziplinen, Sprachen und Kulturen, aber auch Länder und Menschen miteinander zu verknüpfen. Seine Entstehung ist komplex und faszinierend. Dahinter verbirgt sich die (wahre) Geschichte, dass ein Exemplar des Buches in der Manteltasche des jungen Charles Darwin steckte, als dieser in den 1830er-Jahren an Bord der HMS *Beagle* auf Expeditionsreise nach Südamerika und Australien ging. Unter anderem das kleine Format mag ihn bewogen haben, das Buch auf der Suche nach neuen Arten bei sich zu tragen, doch tatsächlich hatte es weit mehr zu bieten, als nur leicht transportierbar zu sein.

Der titelgebende Werner war der deutsche Geologe Abraham Gottlob Werner, der 1774 ein Buch über Steine und Minerale herausgab. *Von den äußerlichen Kennzeichen der Foßilien* enthielt auch einen Abschnitt über Farbe, allerdings ohne Abbildungen. Werner stellte eine Liste von 54 Einzelfarben auf, die er in acht Farbfamilien (Weiß, Grau, Schwarz, Blau, Grün, Gelb, Rot und Braun) zusammenfasste. Binnen kurzer Zeit entwickelte sich die Liste zur international einflussreichen Norm für Farbeinteilungen. Werners Buch wurde ins Ungarische, Französische und Englische übersetzt, bevor Patrick Syme, ein Blumenmaler der Wernerian Society und der Caledonian Horticultural Society in Edinburgh, 1814 seine eigene englische Übersetzung veröffentlichte, die 1821 in zweiter Auflage erschien.

Syme fügte Werners Liste zwei weitere Farbgruppen (Purpur und Orange) hinzu, verdoppelte die Liste der Einzelfarben auf 108 und erweiterte sie für die zweite Auflage auf 110. Ihm schwebte ein Farbhandbuch vor, das für „die Kunst und Wissenschaft, insbesondere die Zoologie, Botanik, Chemie, Mineralogie und pathologische Anatomie" nützlich wäre, vor allem in der Feldforschung.

Seine wichtigste Beigabe zu Werners Werk waren jedoch die Tafeln, auf denen sämtliche Einzelfarben in kleinen handbemalten Quadraten abgebildet waren. Syme präsentierte sie in Tabellenform und notierte für die meisten Farben Entsprechungen aus dem Reich der Tiere (einschließlich Menschen und Insekten), der Pflanzen und der Minerale. Betont wurden Erscheinung und Erkennbarkeit einer Farbe, um taxonomische Bestimmungen zu erleichtern. Einige Farbbezeichnungen sind auffallend viszeral, etwa „Venen" und „Arterienblutrot", „Leberbraun" oder „Magermilchweiß", von denen Letzteres im „Weiß des menschlichen Augapfels" zu finden war.

## GREENS.

| No. | Names | Colours | ANIMAL | VEGETABLE | MINERAL |
|---|---|---|---|---|---|
| 54 | *Grass Green* | | *Scarabæus Nobilis.* | *General Appearance of Grass Fields. Sweet Sugar Pear* | *Uran Mica.* |
| 55 | *Duck Green* | | *Neck of Mallard* | *Upper Disk of Yew Leaves.* | *Ceylanite* |
| 56 | *Sap Green.* | | *Under Side of lower Wings of Orange tip Butterfly.* | *Upper Disk of Leaves of woody Night Shade.* | |
| 57 | *Pistachio Green.* | | *Neck of Eider Drake* | *Ripe Pound Pear. Hypnum like Saxifrage.* | *Crysolite.* |
| 58 | *Asparagus Green.* | | *Brimstone Butterfly.* | *Variegated Horse-Shoe Geranium.* | *Beryl.* |
| 59 | *Olive Green.* | | | *Foliage of Lignum vitæ.* | *Epidote Olvene Ore.* |
| 60 | *Oil Green.* | | *Animal and Shell of common Water Snail.* | *Nonpareil Apple from the Wall.* | *Beryl* |
| 61 | *Siskin Green.* | | *Siskin.* | *Ripe Coalmar Pear. Irish Pitcher Apple.* | *Uran Mica* |

# YELLOWS.

| No. | Names | Colours. | ANIMAL | VEGETABLE | MINERAL |
|---|---|---|---|---|---|
| 62 | Sulphur Yellow. | | Yellow Parts of large Dragon Fly. | Various Coloured Snap dragon. | Sulphur |
| 63 | Primrose Yellow. | | Pale Canary Bird. | Wild Primrose | Pale coloured Sulphur. |
| 64 | Wax Yellow. | | Larva of large Water Beetle. | Greenish Parts of Nonpareil Apple. | Semi Opal. |
| 65 | Lemon Yellow. | | Large Wasp or Hornet. | Shrubby Goldylocks. | Yellow Orpiment. |
| 66 | Gamboge Yellow. | | Wings of Goldfinch. Canary Bird. | Yellow Jasmine. | High coloured Sulphur. |
| 67 | Kings Yellow. | | Head of Golden Pheasant. | Yellow Tulip. Cinque foil. | |
| 68 | Saffron Yellow. | | Tail Coverts of Golden Pheasant. | Anthers of Saffron Crocus. | |

## Nomenclature des couleurs de Werner

Très révélatrice de la manière dont la pensée, les connaissances, les recherches et l'imprimerie du XVIII^e siècle ont influencé le début du siècle suivant, la « Nomenclature des couleurs de Werner » s'intéresse à la couleur en parvenant à couvrir toute une variété de disciplines, de langues, de cultures, de pays et de personnalités. Complexe et passionnante, l'histoire de cet ouvrage bénéficie en outre de l'affirmation (vraie) selon laquelle le jeune Charles Darwin en conservait un exemplaire dans la poche de son manteau, au cours du voyage qu'il effectua en Amérique du Sud et en Australie à bord du HMS *Beagle* dans les années 1830. C'est peut-être en raison de son petit format que le scientifique anglais l'emporta dans sa quête d'espèces nouvelles. Mais ce livre a bien d'autres atouts.

Le Werner du titre est le géologue allemand Abraham Gottlob Werner qui, en 1774, publia un ouvrage portant sur les roches et les minéraux, *Von den äußerlichen Kennzeichen der Foßilien* (*Traité des caractères extérieurs des fossiles*), dont une partie est consacrée à la couleur, bien qu'elle soit dépourvue d'illustrations. Werner classe 54 teintes en huit familles de couleurs (blanc, gris, noir, bleu, vert, jaune, rouge et brun), liste qui deviendra vite une référence internationale majeure pour les catégorisations chromatiques. L'ouvrage de Werner fut traduit en hongrois, français et anglais, avant que Patrick Syme, peintre de fleurs aux Sociétés horticoles werneriennes et calédoniennes à Édimbourg, ne publie sa propre traduction anglaise en 1814, suivie d'une seconde édition en 1821.

À la liste de Werner, Syme ajoute deux groupes (violet et orange) et double le nombre de teintes (108), la seconde édition en comptant deux supplémentaires. Il souhaite proposer un ouvrage de référence sur la couleur au profit « des arts et des sciences, en particulier de la zoologie, de la botanique, de la chimie, de la minéralogie et de l'anatomie morbide », et singulièrement pour le travail de terrain. Mais l'apport décisif de Syme à l'œuvre de Werner consiste en un ensemble de planches représentant toutes les teintes sous la forme de petits carrés peints, réunis dans des tableaux. Syme répertorie également des équivalents de la plupart des teintes, empruntées aux règnes animal (y compris l'être humain et les insectes), végétal et minéral. Il met l'accent sur les caractères extérieurs et reconnaissables de chaque couleur, afin d'effectuer une identification taxonomique. Au sein de cette classification, certaines appellations attribuées aux teintes sont notoirement anatomiques comme, par exemple, « rouge veineux », « rouge artériel », « brun foie » et « blanc du lait écrémé », teinte que l'on trouve dans le « blanc du globe oculaire humain ».

## RED.

| Nº | Names. | Colours. | Animal. | Vegetable. | Mineral. |
|---|---|---|---|---|---|
| 91 | *Carmine Red.* | | | *Raspberry, Cocks Comb, Carnation Pink.* | *Oriental Ruby.* |
| 92 | *Lake Red.* | | | *Red Tulip, Rose Officinalus.* | *Spinel.* |
| 93 | *Crimson Red.* | | | | *Precious Garnet.* |
| 94 | *Purplish Red.* | | *Outside of Quills of Terico.* | *Dark Crimson Officinal Garden Rose.* | *Precious Garnet.* |
| 95 | *Cochineal Red.* | | | *Under Disk of decayed Leaves of None-so-pretty.* | *Dark Cinnaber* |
| 96 | *Veinous Blood Red.* | | *Veinous Blood.* | *Musk Flower, or dark Purple Scabious.* | *Pyrope.* |
| 97 | *Brownish Purple Red.* | | | *Flower of deadly Nightshade.* | *Red Antimony Ore.* |
| 98 | *Chocolate Red.* | | *Breast of Bird of Paradise.* | *Brown Disk of common Marigold.* | |
| 99 | *Brownish Red.* | | *Mark on Throat of Red-throated Diver.* | | *Iron Flint.* |

# BROWNS.

| N.º | Names. | Colours. | ANIMAL. | VEGETABLE. | MINERAL. |
|---|---|---|---|---|---|
| 100 | *Deep Orange-coloured Brown.* | | *Head of Pochard. Wing coverts of Sheldrake.* | *Female Spike of Catstail Reed.* | |
| 101 | *Deep Reddish Brown.* | | *Breast of Pochard, and Neck of Teal Drake.* | *Dead Leaves of green Panic Grass.* | *Brown Blende.* |
| 102 | *Umber Brown.* | | *Moor Buzzard.* | *Disk of Rubeckia.* | |
| 103 | *Chesnut Brown.* | | *Neck and Breast of Red Grouse.* | *Chesnuts.* | *Egyptian Jasper.* |
| 104 | *Yellowish Brown.* | | *Light Brown Spots on Guinea-Pig, Breast of Hoopoe.* | | *Iron Flint, and common Jasper.* |
| 105 | *Wood Brown.* | | *Common Weasel. Light parts of Feathers on the Back of the Snipe.* | *Hazel Nuts.* | *Mountain Wood.* |
| 106 | *Liver Brown.* | | *Middle Parts of Feathers of Hen Pheasant, and Wing coverts of Grosbeak.* | | *Semi Opal.* |
| 107 | *Hair Brown.* | | *Head of Pintail Duck* | | *Wood Tin.* |
| 108 | *Broccoli Brown.* | | *Head of Black headed Gull.* | | *Zircon.* |
| 109 | *Clove Brown.* | | *Head and Neck of Male Kestril.* | *Stems of Black Currant Bush.* | *Axinite, Rock Cristal.* |
| 110 | *Blackish Brown.* | | *Stormy Petril. Wing Coverts of black Cock. Forehead of Foumart.* | | *Mineral Pitch.* |

## David Ramsay Hay (1798–1866)

# THE PRINCIPLES OF BEAUTY IN COLOURING SYSTEMATIZED

*12 plates, 20 x 14 cm | 7 ⅞ x 5 ½ in., Edinburgh & London, 1845*
*University of North Carolina at Chapel Hill, Louis Round Wilson Special Collections Library*

David Hay was a Scottish artist and interior decorator, and one of the first people to apply colour theory to interior design. In 1828, when he was setting up his own business in Edinburgh (the house-painting firm Nicholson and Hay), he published *The Laws of Harmonious Colouring Adapted to House Painting* in which he laid out his ideas on colour and aesthetics, with specific reference to the analogy between colour and music. It went into six expanded editions and marked the beginning of a long writing career, and by the time Hay published the first edition of *The Principles of Beauty in Colouring Systematized* he had received a royal warrant from Queen Victoria and other high-profile commissions.

Hay's books are fundamental works in the field of architectural colour because of the fact that they present a fully developed sense not only of the application of colour theory to interior design but also the importance of colour perception. Hay noted that while the beauty of colour generally depends on contrast, this does not mean that the arrangements with the greatest contrasts are necessarily the most desirable. The real skill, he argued, lies in combining primary, secondary and tertiary colours in such a way that they result in the most harmonious composition, or "melody". He was also acutely

# EXAMPLE I.

## THE PRIMARY AND SECONDARY COLOURS.

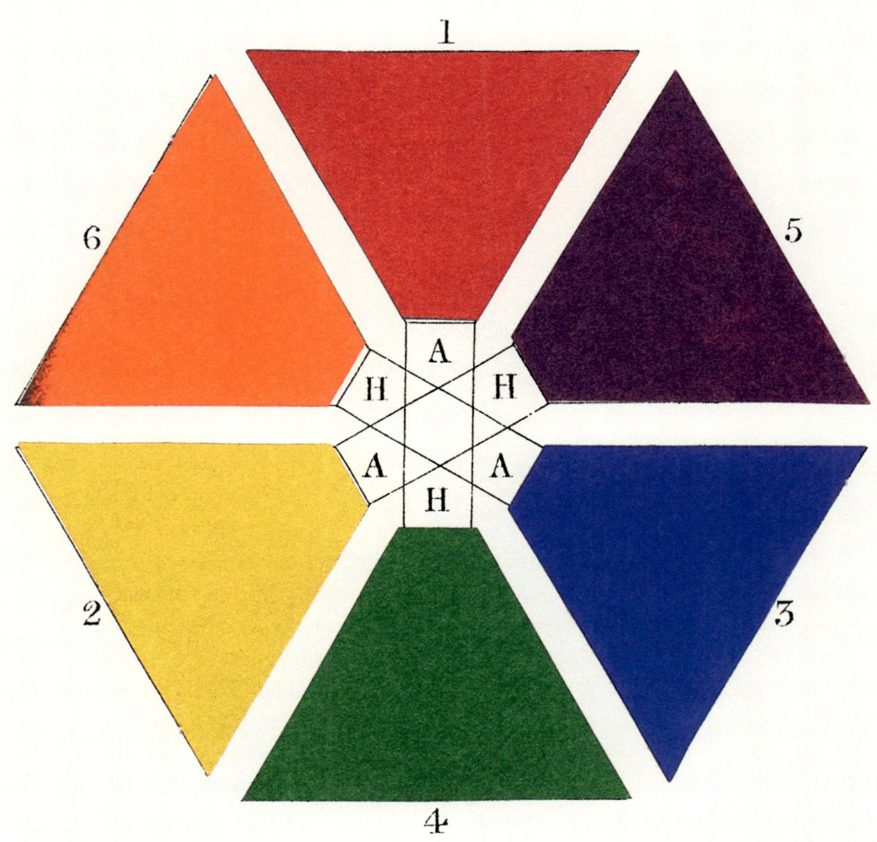


D.R. Hay Invt.

Lizars Sc.

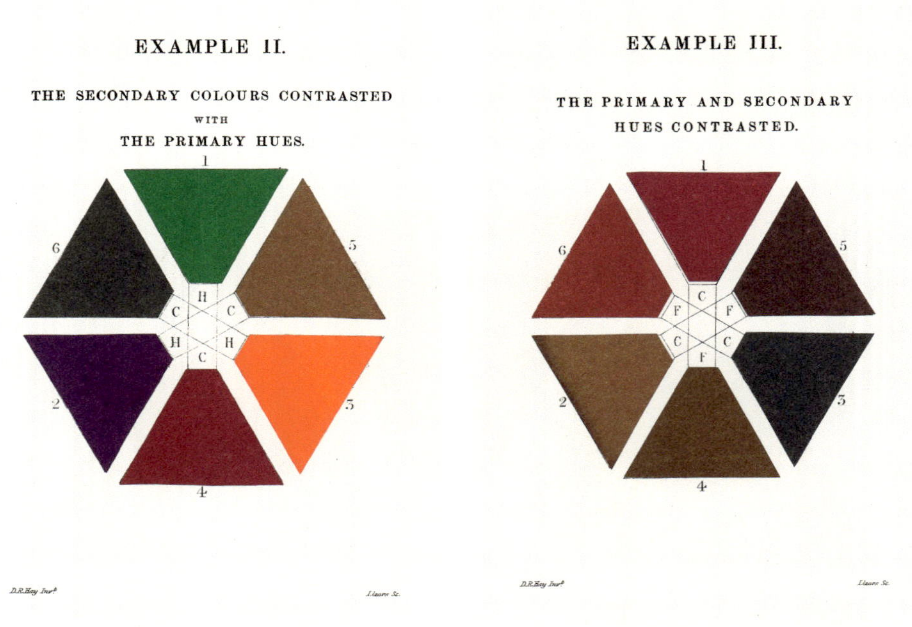


aware of the relationship between colour and light, not just in a Newtonian sense but in the way surfaces and spaces are illuminated, for example, how light extends into a room at different times of the day.

Illustrations formed a vital part of Hay's many publications on colour, and he also stressed the need for maximum clarity and simplicity, presenting his most important images as both labelled tables and engravings within the running text, and then again as coloured plates. With very few exceptions he used geometric shapes to illustrate his "laws" and "principles", rather than depicting images of architectural interiors or decorative objects. His *Principles of Beauty* contains 14 plates of diagrams showing combinations of primaries, secondaries and tertiaries, each taking the shape of a colour wheel created from six numbered trapezoid parts (that is triangles with one point cut off to allow for a letter and connecting lines to be added in the engraving), apart from one example (plate 8, p. 257) in which the colours are arranged in a column of triangles. As in Syme's *Werner's Nomenclature* (see pp. 240–249) the colour shapes were cut from hand-painted sheets of paper and pasted on to the plates, a method Hay continued to use for all his books on colour despite the fact that lithographic illustrations had become more usual by the 1830s.

# EXAMPLE IV.

## BINARY MODIFICATIONS
## OF
## THE SECONDARY COLOURS.

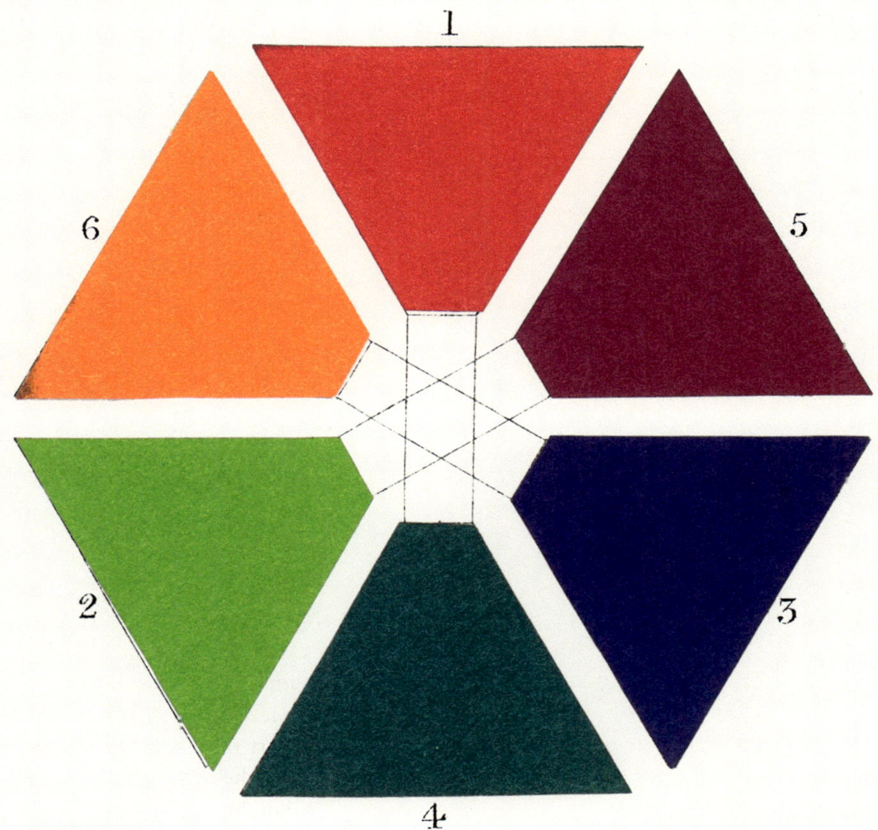


D.R.Hay Invt.

# EXAMPLE V.

## THE PRIMARY AND SECONDARY COLOURS TEMPERED.

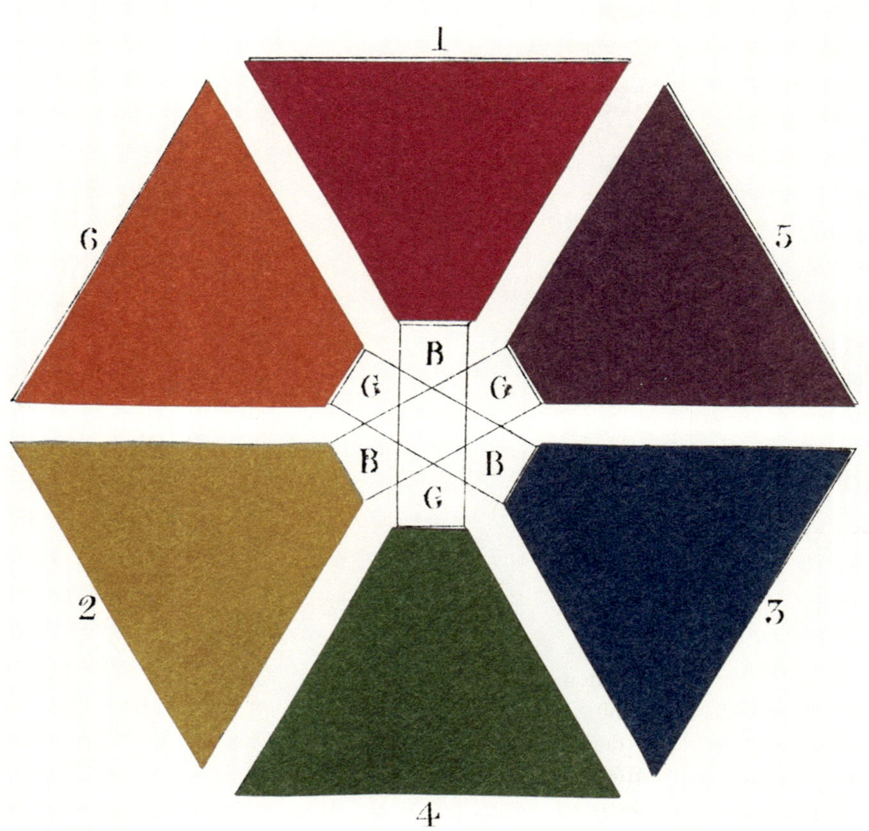


D.R.Hay Invt. Lizars Sc.

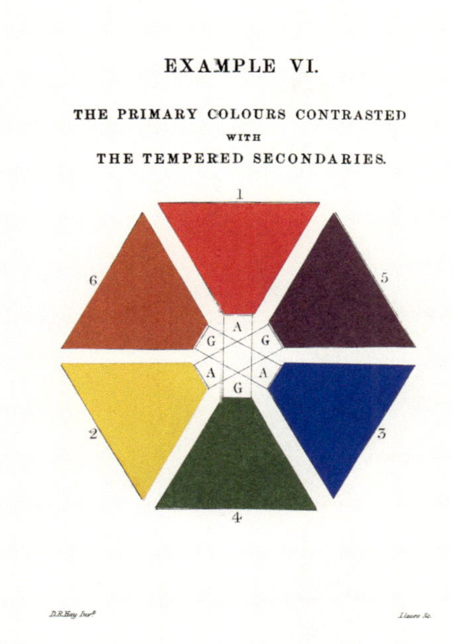


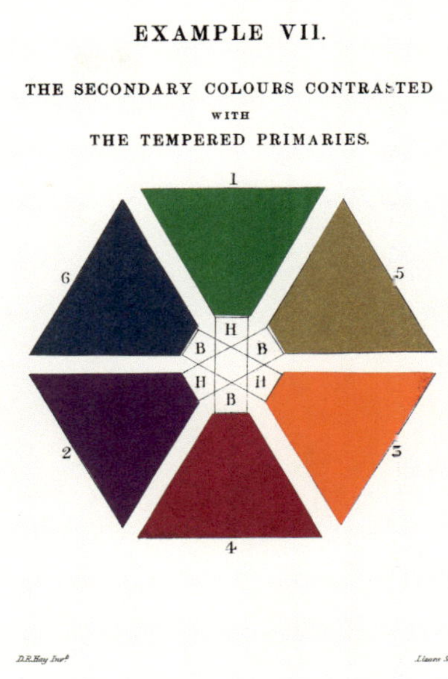


## Systematisierte Darstellung der Prinzipien der Schönheit in der Farbgebung

Der schottische Künstler und Innenarchitekt David Hay war einer der Ersten, der die Farbtheorie auf Fragen der Innenausstattung anwandte. Als er 1828 in Edinburgh sein eigenes Unternehmen gründete (den Malerbetrieb Nicholson und Hay), veröffentlichte er *The Laws of Harmonious Colouring Adapted to House Painting*. Darin erläuterte er seine Auffassungen von Farbe und Ästhetik und ging speziell auf die Analogie von Farbe und Musik ein. Das Buch erlebte sechs erweiterte Auflagen und markierte den Beginn einer langen Autorenkarriere. Als schließlich die erste Auflage von *The Principles of Beauty in Colouring Systematized* erschien, hatte Hay bereits für Königin Victoria und andere hochrangige Auftraggeber gearbeitet.

Hays Bücher sind Grundlagenwerke im Bereich der Architekturfarben, weil sie von einem ausgeprägten Sinn nicht nur für die Anwendung der Farbtheorie auf die Innenarchitektur, sondern auch für die Bedeutung der Farbwahrnehmung durchdrungen sind. Hay stellte fest, dass die Schönheit von Farben zwar grundsätzlich vom Kontrast abhänge, dies aber nicht heiße, dass die Arrangements mit den stärksten Kontrasten zwangsläufig auch die erstrebenswertesten seien. Die wahre Kunst bestehe vielmehr darin, Primär-, Sekundär- und Tertiärfarben so zu kombinieren, dass sie zur harmonischsten Komposition oder „Melodie“ führten. Auch

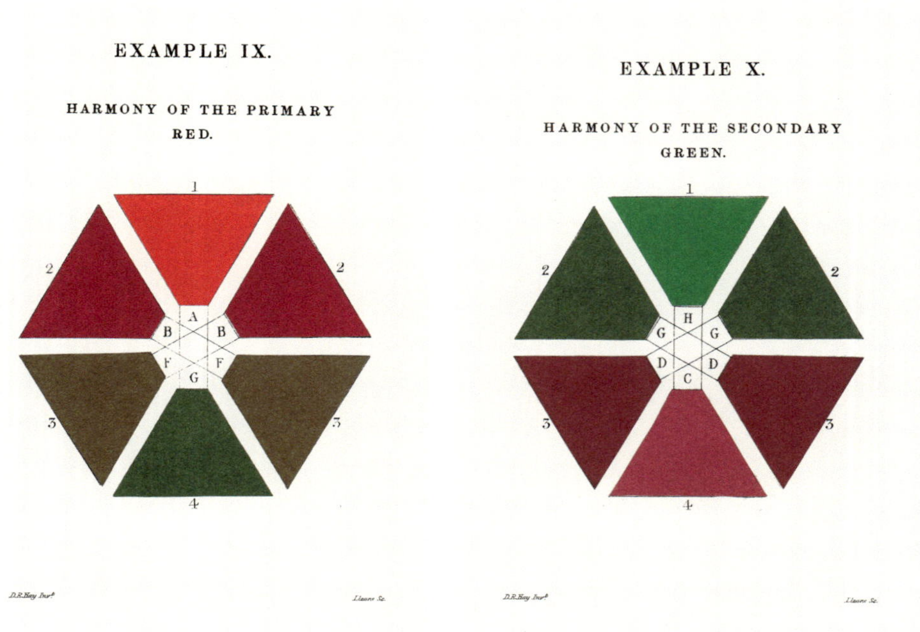


der Beziehung zwischen Farbe und Licht war sich Hay aufs Äußerste bewusst, nicht nur im Newton'schen Sinne, sondern zum Beispiel auch im Hinblick auf die Art und Weise, wie Oberflächen und Räume beleuchtet werden oder wie sich Licht zu verschiedenen Tageszeiten im Raum verteilt.

Illustrationen bildeten einen wesentlichen Bestandteil der vielen Publikationen Hays über Farbe. Dabei betonte er die Notwendigkeit von maximaler Klarheit und Einfachheit und präsentierte seine wichtigsten Abbildungen zunächst als beschriftete Tafeln und Stiche im Fließtext und ein zweites Mal in Form von Farbtafeln. Mit sehr wenigen Ausnahmen verwendete er zur Veranschaulichung seiner „Gesetze“ und „Prinzipien“ geometrische Formen, anstatt Bilder von Innenräumen oder Dekorationsgegenständen zu zeigen. *The Principles of Beauty* enthält 14 Diagrammtafeln mit Kombinationen von primären, sekundären und tertiären Farben, die sich zu Farbkreisen aus jeweils sechs nummerierten Trapezformen zusammenfinden (also Dreiecken, denen eine Spitze abgeschnitten wurde, um an ihrer Stelle einen Buchstaben und Verbindungslinien in die Platte zu stechen). Nur in einem Fall (Tafel 8, S. 257) sind die Farben zu einer Säule aus Dreiecken arrangiert. Wie in *Werner's Nomenclature* von Patrick Syme (S. 240–249) wurden die Farbformen aus handbemalten Papierbögen ausgeschnitten und auf die Tafeln geklebt. Hay blieb dieser Methode in allen seinen Büchern treu, obwohl lithografische Tafeln schon in den 1830er-Jahren gebräuchlicher geworden waren.

# EXAMPLE VIII.

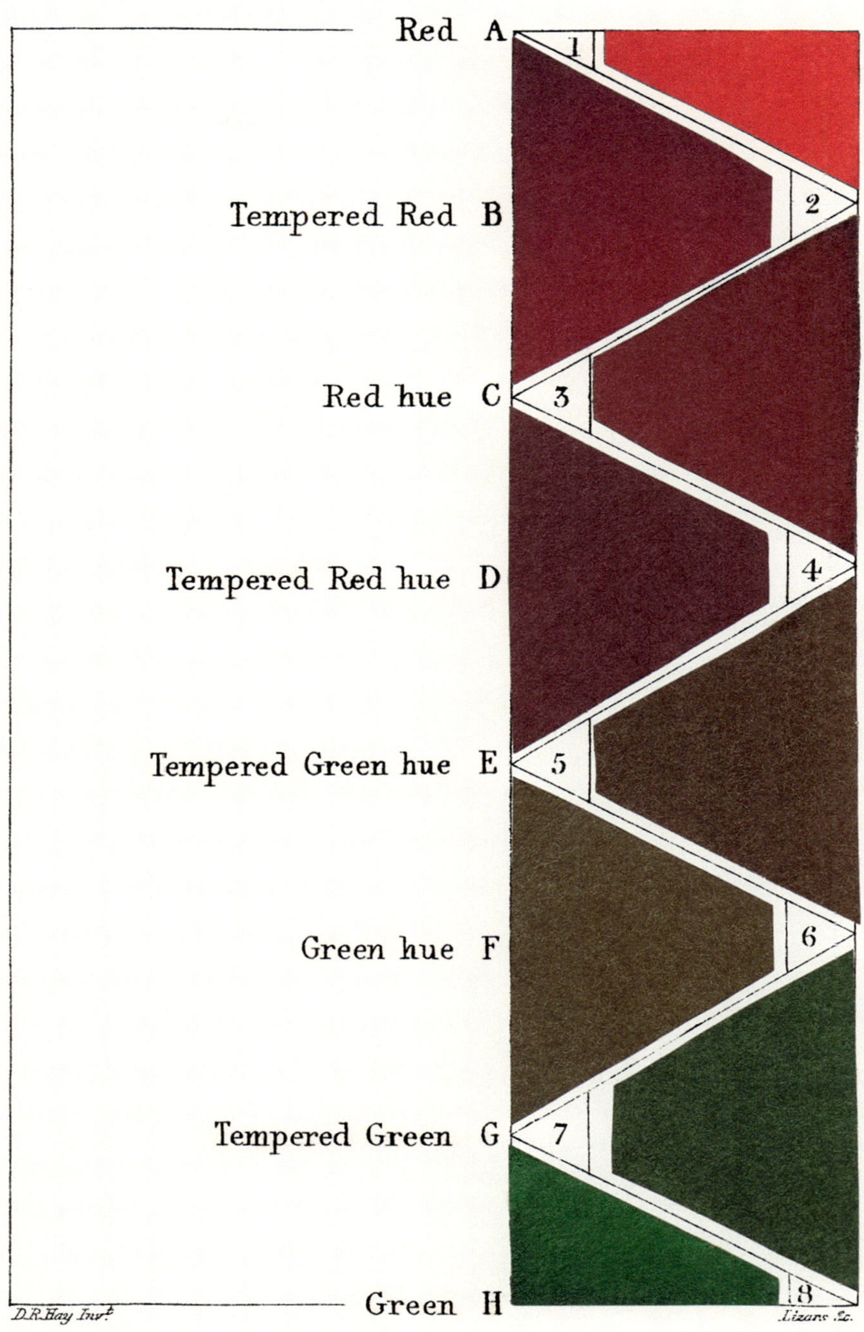

## Principes systématisés de la beauté appliqués à la coloration

Peintre et décorateur d'intérieur écossais, David Hay est l'un des premiers à appliquer une théorie des couleurs à l'architecture d'intérieur. En 1828, l'année où il crée à Édimbourg son entreprise de peinture d'intérieur (Nicholson & Hay), il publie *The Laws of Harmonious Colouring Adapted to House Painting* («Les lois de l'harmonie des couleurs adaptées à la peinture d'intérieur»), où il expose ses idées sur la couleur et l'esthétique, en faisant particulièrement allusion à l'analogie entre couleur et musique. L'ouvrage connaît six éditions augmentées et marque pour Hay le début d'une longue carrière d'auteur. Lorsqu'il fait paraître ses «Principes systématisés de la beauté appliqués à la coloration», il bénéficie déjà du statut de fournisseur officiel de la reine Victoria et a pour clients d'autres commanditaires prestigieux.

Si les œuvres de Hay sont fondamentales dans l'usage de la couleur en architecture, c'est parce qu'elles témoignent d'une maîtrise totale de l'application des théories chromatiques à la décoration d'intérieur, mais aussi de l'importance du rôle que joue la perception des couleurs. Soulignant que la beauté des couleurs est généralement tributaire du contraste, Hay précise toutefois qu'il n'est pas nécessairement souhaitable de disposer celles-ci dans le but d'obtenir les contrastes les plus frappants. À ses yeux, le véritable savoir-faire consiste à réussir la combinaison des couleurs primaires, secondaires et tertiaires de sorte qu'elles produisent la plus harmonieuse des compositions, qu'il qualifie de «mélodie». En outre, Hay possède une connaissance fine des rapports entre couleur et lumière, non seulement au sens newtonien, mais dans la manière dont les surfaces et les espaces sont éclairés: comment, par exemple, la lumière du jour se diffuse dans une pièce en fonction de l'heure.

L'illustration est un élément essentiel des nombreux ouvrages qu'a consacrés Hay à la couleur. Il insiste, en outre, sur la nécessité d'un propos absolument clair et simple et incorpore au corps du texte ses images les plus importantes sous forme de gravures et de tableaux légendés, suivis de nouvelles planches en couleurs. À de rares exceptions près, il préfère, pour illustrer ses «lois» et «principes», recourir à des figures géométriques plutôt qu'à des images d'intérieurs ou d'objets décoratifs. Ses *Principles of Beauty* contiennent 14 planches de graphiques représentant des combinaisons de couleurs primaires, secondaires et tertiaires. Chaque graphique a la forme d'un cercle chromatique composé de six trapèzes numérotés (c'est-à-dire des triangles dont un angle est tronqué afin de permettre l'ajout dans la gravure d'une lettre et de traits de liaison). La planche 8 (p. 257) y fait exception puisque les couleurs y sont disposées en une colonne de triangles. Comme dans *Werner's Nomenclature* de Syme (voir p. 240–249), les figures de couleurs sont découpées dans des morceaux de papier peints et collées sur les planches, méthode employée par Hay dans tous ses livres sur la couleur, alors que les lithographies étaient devenues monnaie courante dans les années 1830.

# EXAMPLE XI.

## HARMONY OF THE PRIMARY YELLOW.

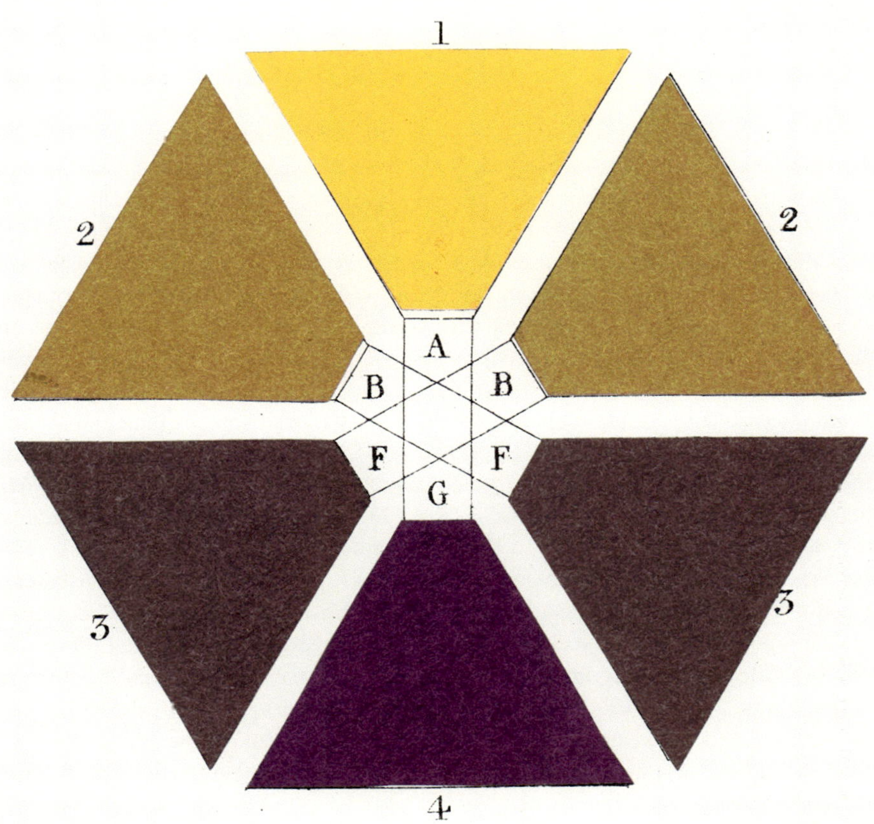


D.R.Hay Invt. Lizars Sc.

## David Ramsay Hay

# A NOMENCLATURE OF COLOURS

### Applicable to the Arts and Natural Sciences

*18 plates, 21 x 15 cm | 8 ¼ x 5 ⅞ in., Edinburgh & London, 1846*
*Fife, University of St Andrews Library, Department of Special Collections*

In the same way as many of his contemporaries, Hay promoted a trichromatic, subtractive system based on primary, secondary and tertiary colours. He was extremely well informed about developments and publications in this field and frequently acknowledged and praised theorists of his day and from the past, including Goethe (by way of Eastlake's translation), David Brewster and George Field. Hay's *Nomenclature of Colours* was clearly influenced by his countryman Patrick Syme's new edition of *Werner's Nomenclature* (1814 and 1821), even if he considered it "a very imperfect work".

*A Nomenclature* (first published in 1845) was Hay's most ambitious and assured work on colour, and was based on a mathematical system for the proportions of different colours and hues. The subtitle announced that his object was to create a reference work that would be "applicable to the Arts and Natural Sciences; to Manufactures, and other Purposes of General Utility", thereby making it similar in scope to Chevreul's *De la loi du contraste simultané des couleurs* from 1839 (pp. 216–227) which also stressed the applicability of colour theory to a wide range of disciplines.

With this work being a nomenclature, Hay devoted a significant portion of the book to the naming of colours. Consequently, he did not just provide a reliable mathematical formula for defining a particular colour, but also looked to clarify his approach. He populated his system with simple colour names, "not given arbitrarily, but according to the primary elements from which each colour, hue, tint, or shade is derived", eschewing known pigment names or fanciful descriptions. The purpose was to examine and describe how a colour, hue or shade appeared, looked and felt, rather than being concerned with exactly what substance it was made of. The design used in the book's 40 plates is an elegant augmentation of the triangular compositions Hay had employed in his earlier book, with each plate now showing two engraved pyramidal structures formed of three coloured equilateral triangles, with hand-painted samples once again pasted into the design. In total he presented 240 colours, in various proportions, combinations and with the addition of white and black, thereby creating an extraordinary record of the colours known in Britain during the 1840s. Hay continued to write and publish books on colour, beauty and design until 1856. His friend, the Scottish painter David Roberts (1796–1864), referred to him as "the first intellectual housepainter".

# Plate 1.

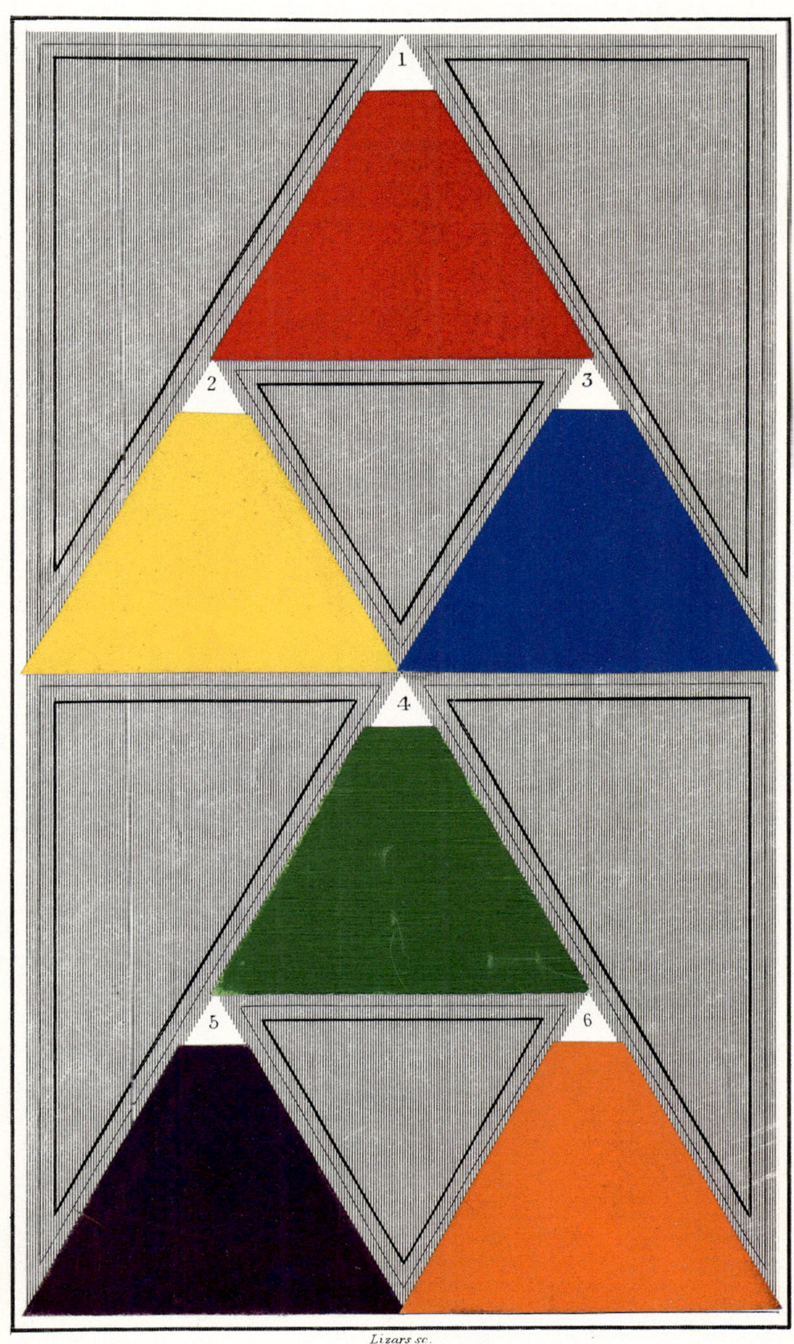


*Lizars sc.*

Plate 4.

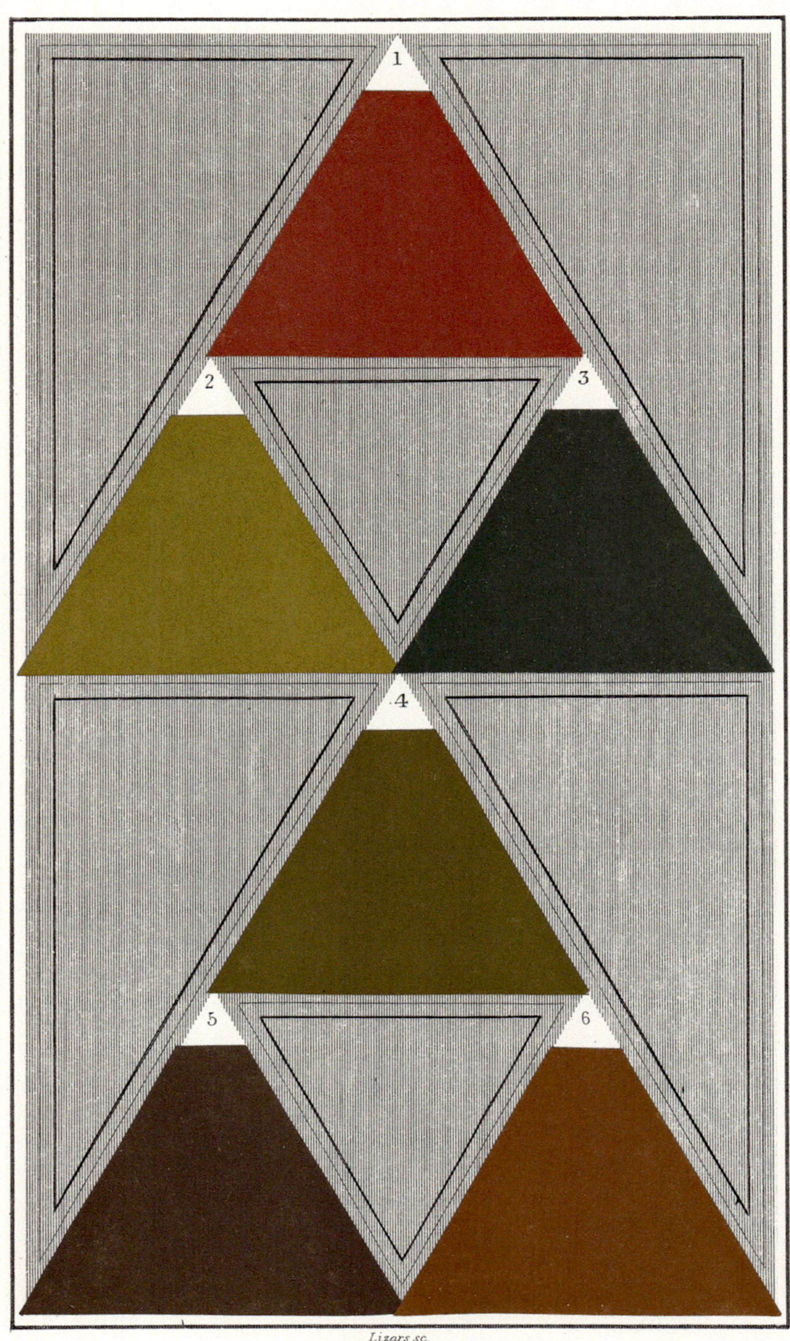


*Lizars sc.*

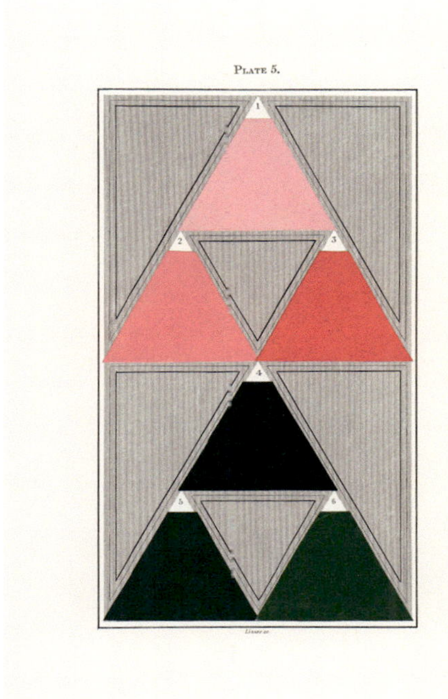


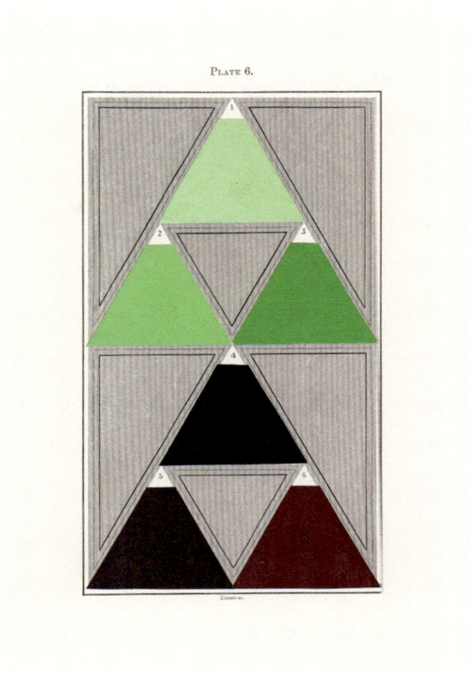


## Nomenklatur der Farben, anwendbar auf die Künste und Naturwissenschaften

Wie viele seiner Zeitgenossen propagierte Hay ein trichromatisches, subtraktives System auf der Grundlage von Primär-, Sekundär- und Tertiärfarben. Er war über die Entwicklungen und Publikationen in diesem Bereich außergewöhnlich gut informiert und lobte und würdigte oftmals andere Theoretiker der Vergangenheit oder Gegenwart, wie Goethe (anhand von Eastlakes Übersetzung), David Brewster oder George Field. Indes war sein *A Nomenclature of Colours* deswegen stark von Patrick Symes Neuauflage der *Werner's Nomenclature* (1814 und 1821) beeinflusst, obwohl Hay das Buch seines Landsmannes für „ein sehr unvollkommenes Werk“ hielt.

*A Nomenclature of Colours* (1845 erstmals veröffentlicht) war Hays ehrgeizigste und sicherste Arbeit über Farbe und beruhte auf einem mathematischen System für die Zusammensetzung verschiedener Farben und Schattierungen. Im Untertitel erklärte er, ein Nachschlagewerk angestrebt zu haben, das „auf die Künste und Naturwissenschaften anwendbar [sein würde]; auf Hersteller und andere Zwecke von allgemeinem Nutzen“. Damit stellte er das Buch in eine Reihe mit Chevreuls *De la loi du contraste simultané des couleurs* von 1839 (S. 216–227), das ebenfalls die Anwendbarkeit der Farbtheorie auf ein breites Spektrum von Fachgebieten hervorhob.

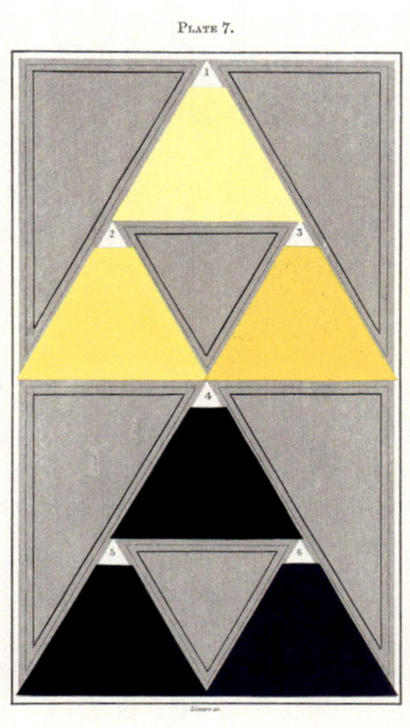


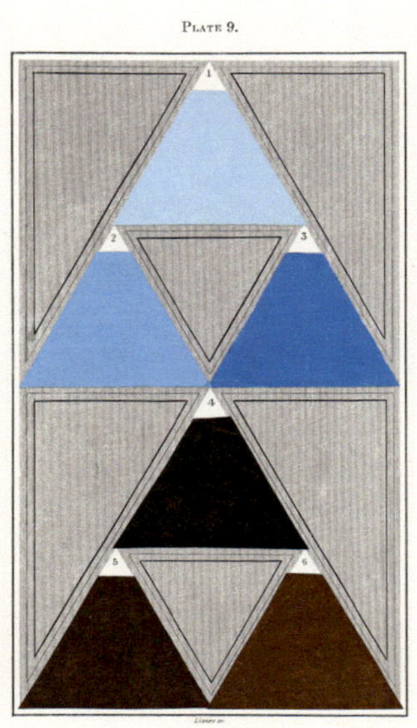


Da sein Buch eine Nomenklatur war, widmete Hay einen bedeutenden Teil des Werks der Benennung von Farben. So stellte er für die Bestimmung einer konkreten Farbe nicht nur eine verlässliche mathematische Formel bereit, sondern wollte mit seinem Ansatz auch mehr Klarheit schaffen. Hay stattete sein System mit einfachen Farbnamen aus, die „nicht willkürlich vergeben [werden], sondern nach den primären Bestandteilen, aus denen jede Farbe, Tönung, Nuance oder Schattierung herrührt". Dabei vermied er bekannte Pigmentnamen oder der Fantasie entsprungene Bezeichnungen. Sein Buch sollte analysieren und beschreiben, wie eine Farbe, Tönung oder Schattierung erschien, aussah und sich anfühlte, anstatt sich damit zu beschäftigen, aus welcher Substanz sie genau bestand. Das Layout der vierzig Bildtafeln stellt eine elegante Erweiterung der Dreieckskompositionen dar, die Hay für sein früheres Buch verwendet hatte. Jede Tafel zeigt jetzt zwei gestochene, aus jeweils drei gleichseitigen Dreiecken bestehende Pyramidenstrukturen, in die handbemalte Farbmuster eingeklebt wurden. Insgesamt präsentierte Hay 240 Farben in verschiedenen Mischungsverhältnissen und Kombinationen mit varriierenden Weiß- und Schwarzanteilen und schuf damit ein außergewöhnliches Verzeichnis der im Großbritannien der 1840er-Jahre bekannten Farben. Noch bis 1856 verfasste und veröffentlichte Hay Bücher über Farbe, Schönheit und Gestaltung. Ein Freund, der schottische Maler David Roberts (1796–1864), bezeichnete ihn als „den ersten intellektuellen Anstreicher".

PLATE 11.

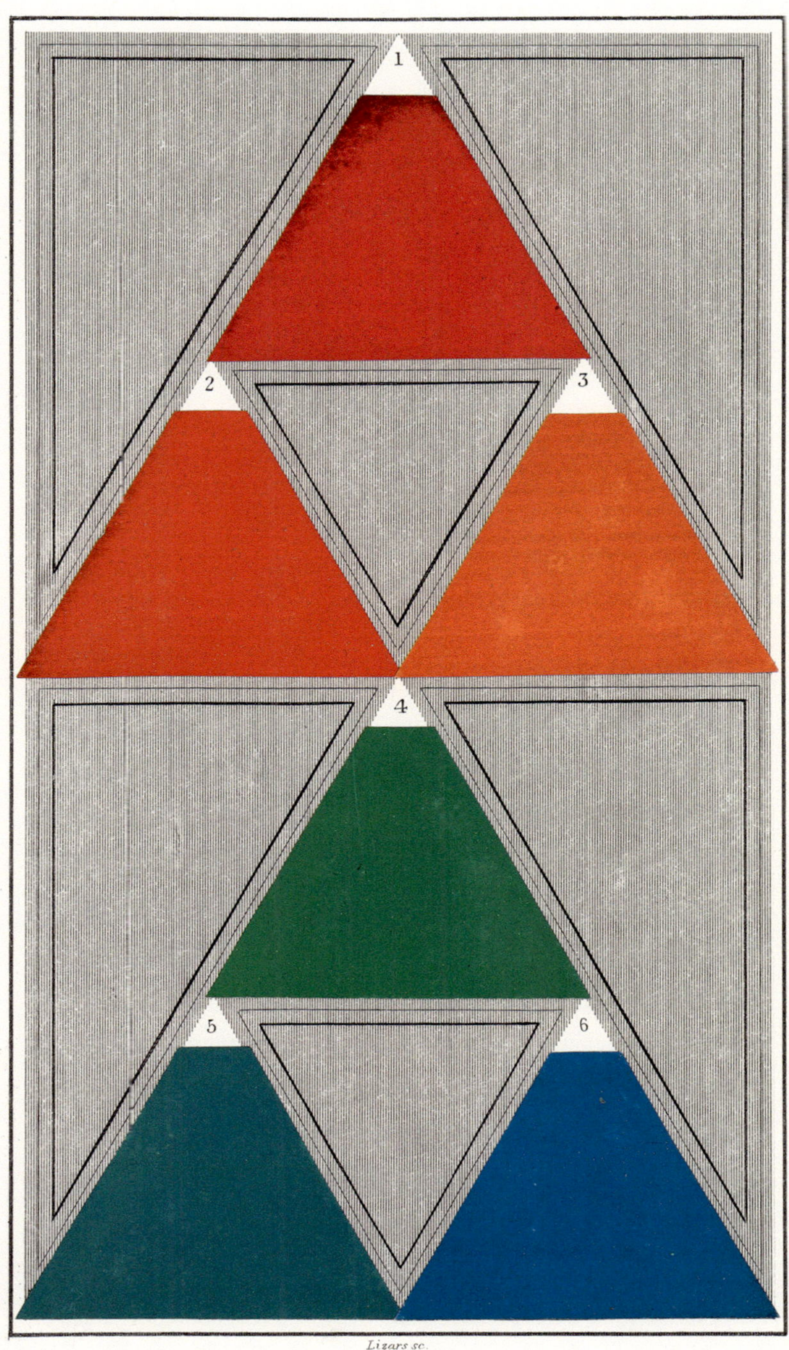


*Lizars sc.*

## Plate 12.

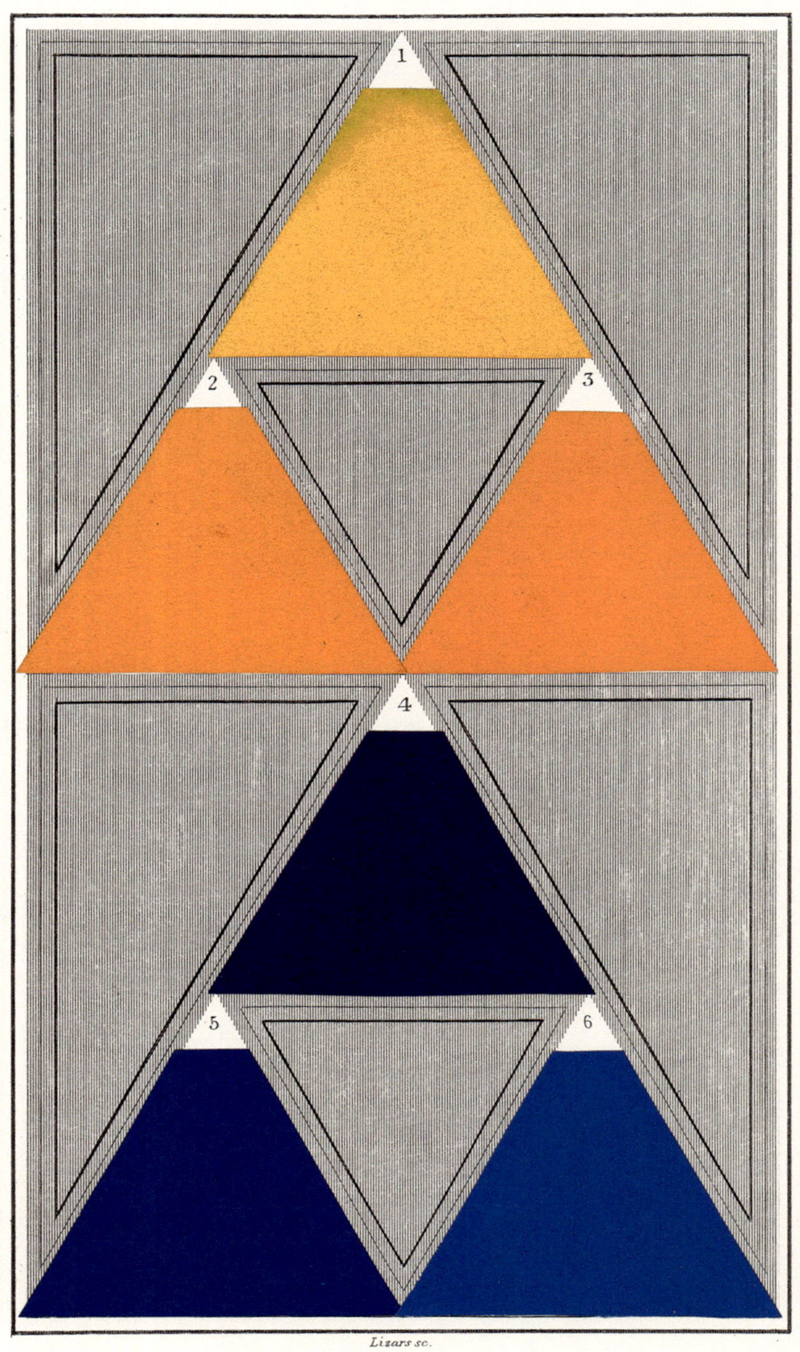


*Lizars sc.*

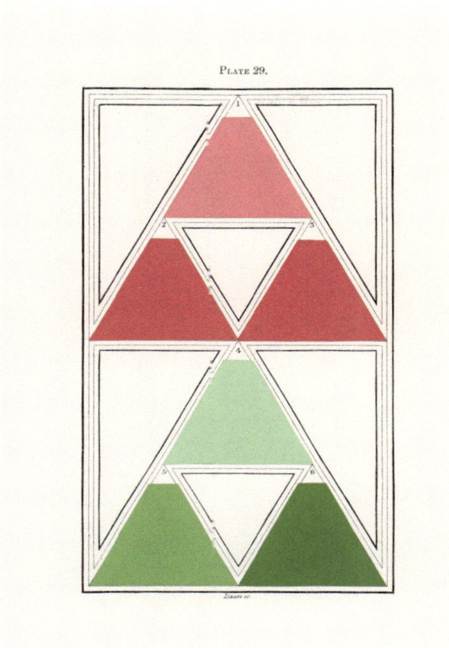


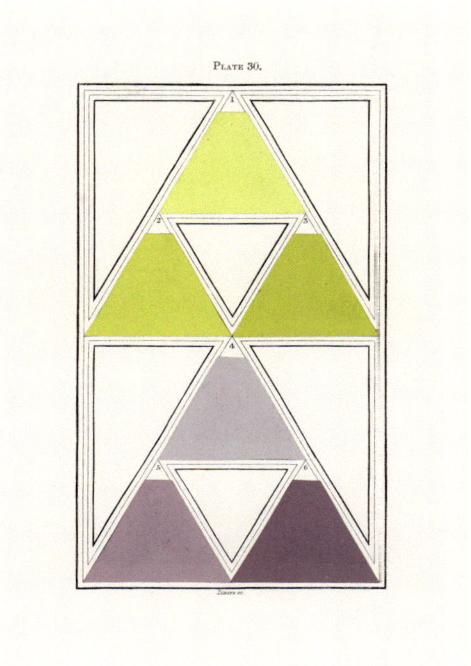


## Nomenclature des couleurs, applicable aux arts et aux sciences naturelles

À l'instar de bien d'autres de ses contemporains, Hay se prononce en faveur d'un système soustractif trichromatique, fondé sur les couleurs primaires, secondaires et tertiaires. Très au fait des recherches et publications en la matière, il reconnaît souvent sa dette à l'égard de théoriciens du passé et de son temps, dont il fait l'éloge, comme Goethe (via la traduction anglaise d'Eastlake), David Brewster et George Field. Sa « Nomenclature des couleurs » doit en effet beaucoup à la nouvelle édition de l'ouvrage de son compatriote Patrick Syme, *Werner's Nomenclature* (1814, puis 1821), qu'il considère pourtant comme « un ouvrage très imparfait ».

Œuvre la plus ambitieuse et la plus aboutie de David Hay, la *Nomenclature* (publié la première fois en 1845) est fondée sur un système mathématique de détermination des proportions entre les différents tons et couleurs. Selon son sous-titre, l'objectif est de proposer un ouvrage de référence « applicable aux arts et aux sciences naturelles ; aux manufactures et autres visées d'utilité générale ». Ce livre est donc d'une ambition semblable à celle de Chevreul avec *De la loi du contraste simultané des couleurs*, paru en 1839 (p. 216–227), lequel a aussi pour but d'appliquer la théorie des couleurs à toutes sortes de domaines.

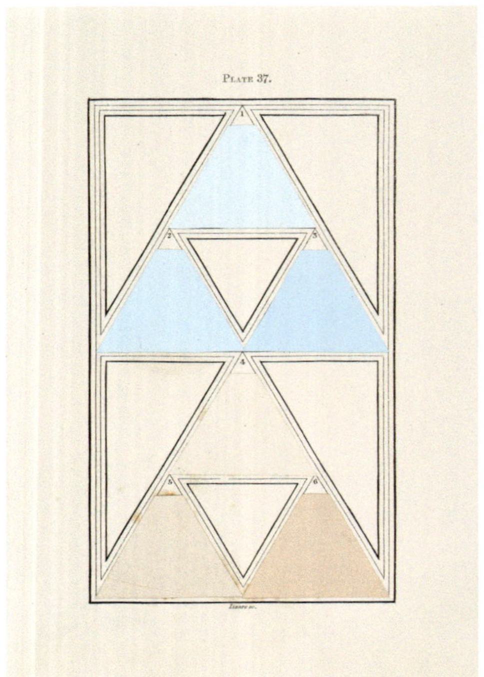


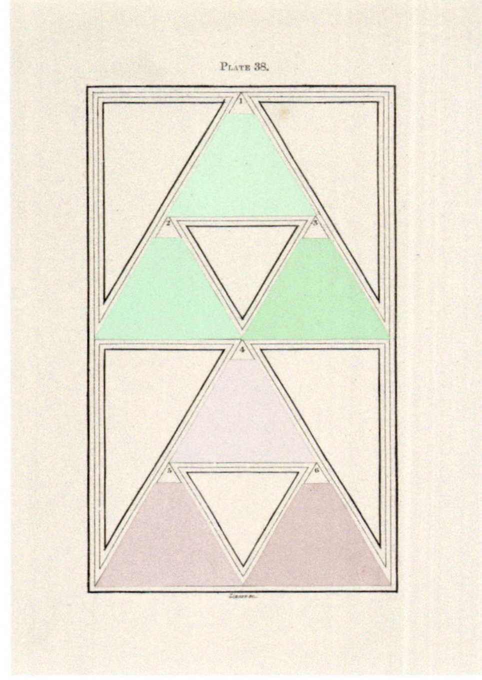


Puisqu'il s'agit d'une nomenclature, Hay consacre une partie importante de l'ouvrage à la désignation des couleurs. Par conséquent, il ne se contente pas de fournir une formule mathématique fiable pour définir telle ou telle teinte mais cherche à expliciter sa démarche. Il dote son système de noms de couleurs simples, « qui ne sont pas choisis de manière arbitraire, mais en fonction des éléments principaux dont sont issus chaque couleur, ton, teinte ou nuance », en écartant les appellations des pigments connus et les descriptions fantaisistes. Hay s'attache avant tout à étudier et décrire l'aspect d'une couleur, d'une teinte ou d'une nuance et à la sensation qu'elle suscite, plutôt qu'à définir avec précision ce qui la composent. Les 40 planches de l'ouvrage reprennent et augmentent avec élégance les compositions triangulaires que l'auteur a employées dans ses livres précédents. Chaque gravure présente désormais deux structures pyramidales formées par trois triangles équilatéraux, contenant des échantillons peints à la main et, là encore, collés. Hay donne ainsi à voir 240 couleurs en diverses proportions et combinaisons, auxquelles s'ajoutent le blanc et le noir. Cet ouvrage constitue un témoignage extraordinaire des couleurs que l'on connaissait en Grande-Bretagne dans les années 1840. Hay publiera d'autres ouvrages consacrés à la couleur, à la beauté et à la décoration jusqu'en 1856. Ami de Hay, le peintre écossais David Roberts (1796–1864) qualifiait celui-ci de « premier peintre d'intérieur intellectuel ».

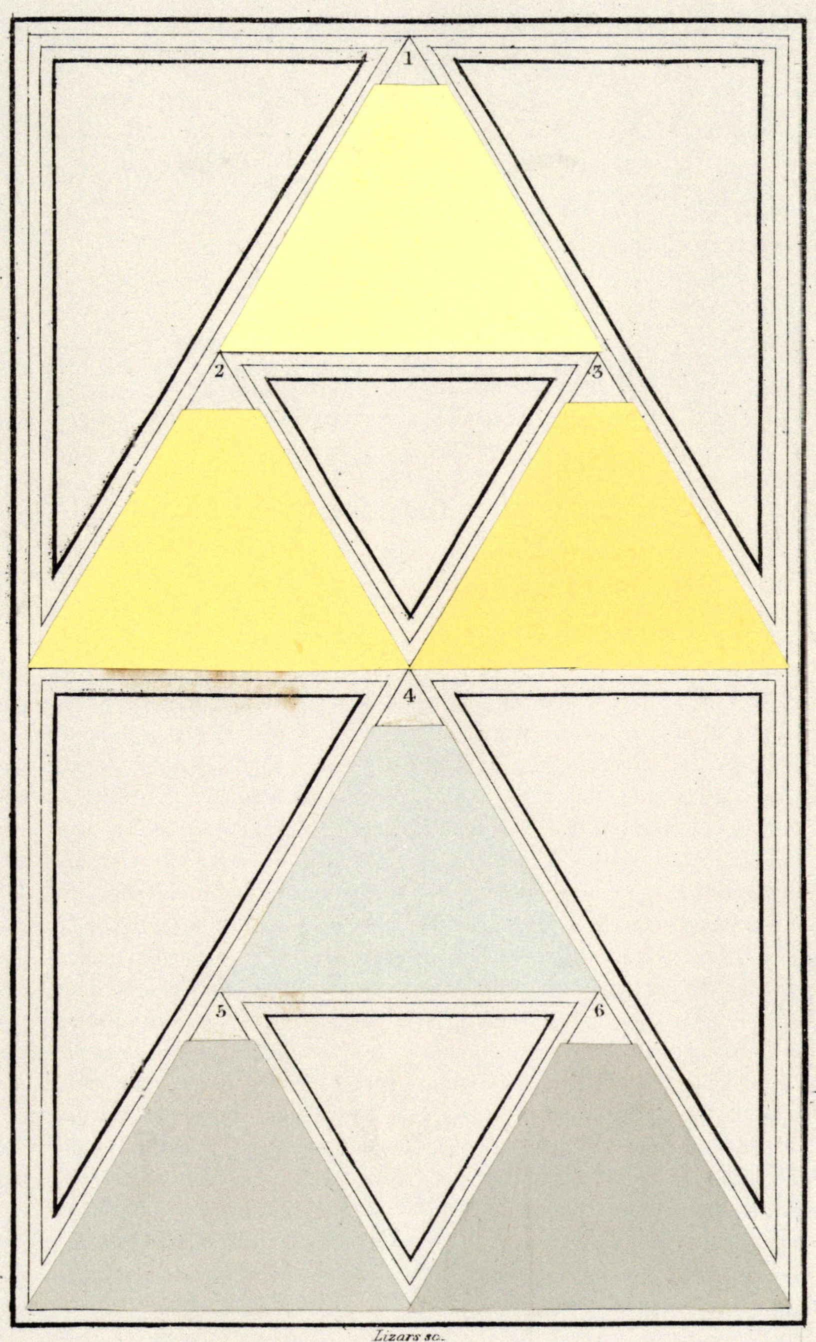


Lizars sc.

## Édouard Guichard (1815–1889)

# L'HARMONIE DES COULEURS / DIE HARMONIE DER FARBEN

### The Harmony of Colours

*29 plates, 34.3 x 26.7 cm | 13 ½ x 10 ½ in., Paris | Frankfurt am Main, 1880–1882*
*Washington, D.C., Smithsonian Libraries*

Édouard Guichard was a French designer, architect and decorator, yet considering the outstanding typographical and chromatic beauty of the book on colour harmony he produced it is surprising how seldom it is mentioned in recent literature on colour and design history. The original French work, *L'Harmonie des couleurs*, was published in several instalments in Paris between 1880 and 1882 by Ad. Goubaud et Fils. The authorised German edition, with a translation by Georg Krebs, must have been in preparation almost simultaneously and in fact surpasses the French edition with regard to the quality of both the paper and the illustrations. There are only a dozen pages of introductory text by Guichard, but the illustrations in the folio volume are accompanied by extensive descriptive captions. As with many later 19th-century writers on colour arrangement and the decorative arts, Guichard was heavily influenced by Chevreul, and perhaps directly inspired by the technical brilliance of the plates in Chevreul's *Atlas* volume from 1864 (pp. 228–237). The German title-page also announced what made Guichard's book so special, specifically the 1,300 examples it contained of harmonious colour combinations and arrangements for use in the art industry, interior decoration, fashion and make-up. These are presented in 166 colour plates, some on double-pages, depicting textile patterns, decorative objects against different background colours, strictly typographical arrangements, figurative and ornamental designs, and entirely abstract compositions, all of them illustrating colour harmony and contrast. No other book before had displayed such variety in depicting colour arrangements. The printing techniques show the full range of what could be achieved with colour reproduction in later 19th-century print culture, including plates in pochoir, a number of screen-printed plates illustrating advertising posters and chromolithographs of superior quality contributed by F. Appel. It is sometimes described as a pattern book, but is much more than that since it is unquestionably a book about colour and design, showcasing the best of what printers and printing technology were capable of producing at this date. Fewer than 10 copies of each edition, the French and the German, are recorded in the collections of libraries and museums worldwide, which strongly suggests they were published in only very small print runs.

Guichard, however, did not stop at this point, and in 1882 a continuation of his work was published in Paris by H. Cagnon, appearing as a three-volume, trilingual (French-English-German) set with the title *La Grammaire de la couleur / Grammar of Colour / Die Grammatik der Farben*, in an oblong format and this time with 765 coloured plates.

# HARMONIE DER FARBEN

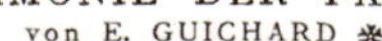

von E. GUICHARD ✻

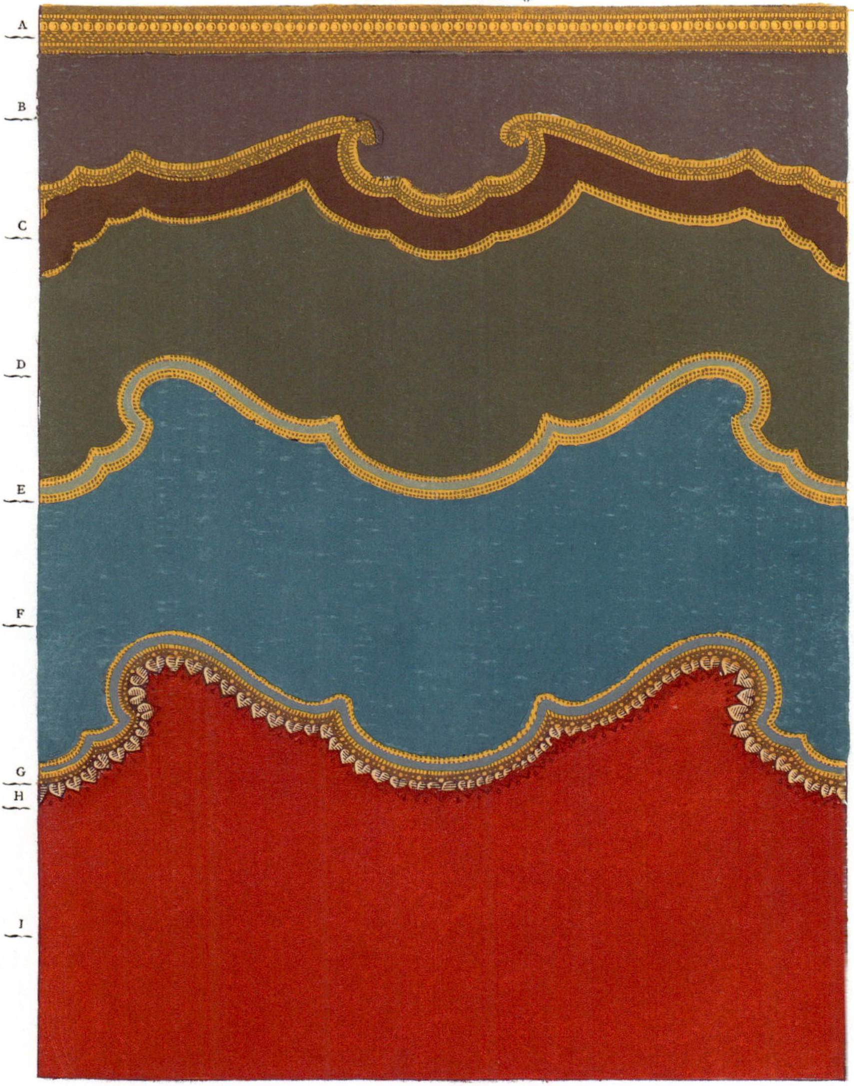

1

A

B

C

D

E

F

G

H

I

## TAPETEN

Wenn die Grundfarbe einer Tapete wie I ist, so kann der Fries wie F und die Borde wie A, G und H sein.

## VORHÄNGE und PORTIÈREN

Ist die Farbe der Tapete wie I, so kann die Grundfarbe der Vorhänge wie F sein, mit Bordüren wie I und Franzen oder Gimpe wie A, G und H. — Wählt man die Vorhänge von derselben Farbe wie die Tapete, so wird man gut thun, um Eintönigkeit zu vermeiden die Farbe F für die Gallerieüberhänge (lambrequins) der Fenster zu nehmen.

## THÜREN, LAMBRIS und KARNIESSE (GESIMSE, franz. CORNICHES)

Zu den Thüren und Lambris nimmt man die Farben B, C, D und E. — Der Theil des Karniesses, welcher den Plafond berührt, muss in etwas lichteren Farbentönen gehalten sein als die Thüren und Lambris; — man nehme dazu daher nur die Töne C, D, E, nämlich die Farbe C als Grundfarbe des Karniesses, die Farbe D für die Wölbung desselben und die Farbe E für das an den Plafond angrenzende Gesims. — Die Farbe A kann in bescheidenem Mass zu feinen Zwischenlinien benutzt werden; statt dessen kann man übrigens auch Gold nehmen oder diese Verzierung ganz weglassen.

## FRAUENKLEIDUNG

Die soeben angeführten Farbenzusammenstellungen werden auch bei der feinen Damentoilette ihre Wirkung nicht verfehlen.

*Alle Rechte vorbehalten.*

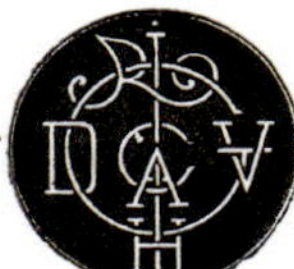

(Verlag von Wilh. Rommel in Frankfurt a. M.)

# HARMONIE DER FARBEN

von E. GUICHARD ✻

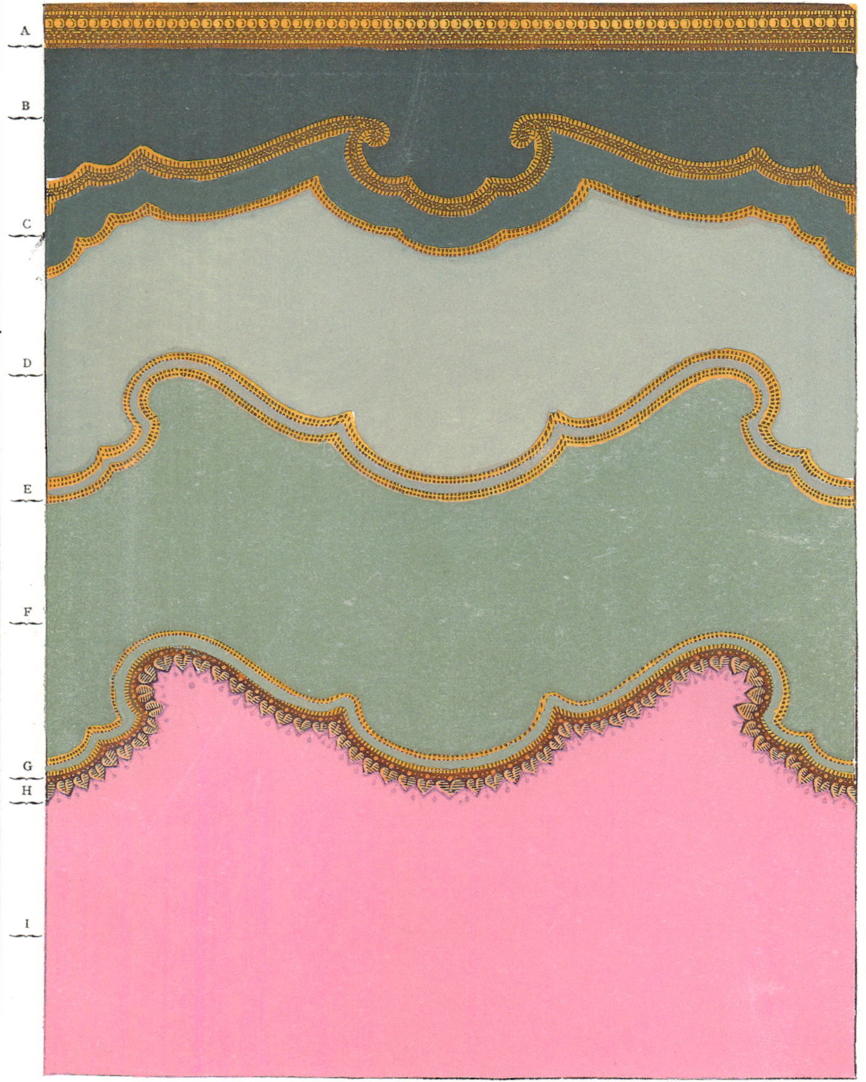


## TAPETEN

Wenn die Grundfarbe einer Tapete wie I ist, so kann der Fries wie F und die Borde wie A, O und H sein.

## VORHÄNGE und PORTIÈREN

Ist die Farbe der Tapete wie I, so kann die Grundfarbe der Vorhänge wie F sein, mit Bordüren wie I und Franzen oder Gimpen wie A, G und H. — Wählt man die Vorhänge von derselben Farbe wie die Tapete, so wird man gut thun, um Eintönigkeit zu vermeiden, die Farbe F für die Gallerieüberhänge (lambrequins) der Fenster zu nehmen.

## THÜREN, LAMBRIS und KARNIESSE (GESIMSE, franz. CORNICHES)

Zu den Thüren und Lambris nimmt man die Farben B, C, D und E. — Der Theil des Karniesses, welcher den Plafond berührt, muss in etwas lichteren Farbentönen gehalten sein als die Thüren und Lambris; — man nehme dazu daher nur die Töne C, D, E, nämlich die Farbe C als Grundfarbe des Karniesses, die Farbe D für die Wölbung desselben und die Farbe E für das an den Plafond angrenzende Gesims. — Die Farbe A kann in bescheidenem Mass zu feinen Zwischenlinien benutzt werden; statt dessen kann man übrigens auch Gold nehmen oder diese Verzierung ganz weglassen.

## FRAUENKLEIDUNG

Die soeben angeführten Farbenzusammenstellungen werden auch bei der feinen Damentoilette ihre Wirkung nicht verfehlen.

*Alle Rechte vorbehalten.*

(Verlag von Wilh. Rommel in Frankfurt a. M.)

## Die Harmonie der Farben

Édouard Guichard war ein französischer Gestalter, Architekt und Innenausstatter. Trotz der herausragenden drucktechnischen und farblichen Schönheit seines Buches über Farbharmonien wird der Titel in der jüngeren Literatur zur Farb- und Designgeschichte erstaunlich selten erwähnt. Die französische Originalausgabe, *L'Harmonie des couleurs*, erschien zwischen 1880 und 1882 in mehreren Lieferungen bei Ad. Goubaud et Fils in Paris. Die autorisierte deutsche Ausgabe, übersetzt von Georg Krebs, muss fast zeitgleich in Vorbereitung gewesen sein und übertrifft in Papier- und Abbildungsqualität sogar ihr französisches Pendant. Während die von Guichard verfasste Einleitung nur ein Dutzend Seiten lang ist, begleiten ausführliche Beschreibungen in den Legenden die Abbildungen des deutschen Foliobandes. Wie viele Autoren des späteren 19. Jahrhunderts, die über Farbkombinationen und dekorative Kunst schrieben, war Guichard stark von Chevreul beeinflusst und womöglich unmittelbar inspiriert von der technischen Brillanz der Tafeln in dessen Farbatlas aus dem Jahr 1864 (S. 228–237). Wie die deutsche Titelseite verriet, waren es die 1.300 Beispiele für harmonische Farbverbindungen zur Anwendung in Kunstindustrie, Raumausstattung, Mode und Kosmetik, die Guichards Buch so besonders machten und auf 166 teils doppelseitigen Farbtafeln präsentiert wurden. Darauf abgebildet sind Stoffmuster, Dekorationsobjekte vor verschiedenen Hintergrundfarben, streng auf Buchstaben und Schrift basierende Arrangements, figurative und ornamentale Muster sowie ganz und gar abstrakte Kompositionen, die allesamt der Veranschaulichung von Farbharmonien und Farbkontrasten dienen. Kein anderes Buch hatte jemals eine solche Vielfalt in der Darstellung von Farbarrangements geboten. Die Druckverfahren führen in voller Bandbreite vor Augen, was im Druckwesen des späten 19. Jahrhunderts in der Farbreproduktion möglich war. Tafeln in Schablonendruck wechseln sich ab mit Siebdrucktafeln für den Plakatdruck und Farblithografien von höchster Qualität aus der Druckerei F. Appel in Paris. Das mitunter als Musterbuch bezeichnete Werk ist viel mehr als das – es ist ohne Frage ein Buch über Farbe und Gestaltung, in dem das Beste vorgeführt wird, was Druckereien und Druckverfahren in dieser Zeit zu leisten vermochten. Dass in Bibliotheken und Museen weltweit jeweils nur weniger als zehn Exemplare der französischen und der deutschen Ausgabe verzeichnet sind, lässt stark darauf schließen, dass beide in nur sehr kleiner Auflage erschienen.

Für Guichard war damit noch nicht Schluss. Ebenfalls 1882 erschien bei H. Cagnon in Paris eine Fortsetzung seines Werks. Die dreibändige, im Querformat aufgelegte Publikation mit einem erläuternden Text in drei Sprachen und dem Titel *La Grammaire de la couleur / Grammar of Colour / Die Grammatik der Farben* umfasste diesmal 765 Farbtafeln.

## L'Harmonie des couleurs

Dessinateur, architecte et décorateur français, Édouard Guichard est l'auteur d'un ouvrage sur l'harmonie des couleurs d'une exceptionnelle beauté typographique et chromatique. Il est donc surprenant que ce livre soit rarement cité dans les ouvrages récents consacrés à l'histoire de la couleur et du dessin. *L'Harmonie des couleurs* a paru initialement en français en plusieurs tomes de 1880 à 1882, chez l'éditeur parisien Ad. Goubaud et Fils. L'édition allemande autorisée, dans une traduction de Georg Krebs, a probablement été réalisée presque en même temps que l'édition française et surpasse même celle-ci quant à la qualité du papier et des illustrations. Si l'introduction de Guichard ne comprend qu'une douzaine de pages, les images du volume in-folio allemand s'accompagnent de légendes extrêmement détaillées. De même que de nombreux auteurs d'ouvrages portant sur l'ordonnancement des couleurs dans les arts décoratifs à la fin du XIXe siècle, Guichard est très influencé par Chevreul, voire directement inspiré par l'excellence technique des planches de l'*Atlas* de ce dernier, paru en 1864 (p. 228–237). La page de titre de l'édition allemande annonce ce qui rend l'ouvrage de Guichard si singulier, à savoir les 1300 exemples de combinaisons et de dispositions harmonieuses des couleurs, appliquées aux métiers de l'art, à la décoration d'intérieur, à la mode et au maquillage. Présentés dans 166 planches en couleurs, parfois sur des doubles pages, ces exemples proposent des motifs textiles, des objets décoratifs sur différents fonds colorés, des arrangements strictement typographiques, des dessins figuratifs et ornementaux et des compositions abstraites, tous destinés à illustrer l'harmonie et le contraste des couleurs. Aucun ouvrage antérieur n'offre une telle variété dans la représentation des compositions chromatiques. Les techniques d'impression témoignent de toutes les possibilités offertes par la reproduction en couleurs à la fin du XIXe siècle : des planches au pochoir, plusieurs sérigraphies illustrant des affiches publicitaires, ainsi que des chromolithographies d'excellente qualité réalisées par F. Appel. Parfois qualifié d'album d'échantillons, l'ouvrage est bien plus que cela : il a incontestablement pour objet la couleur et la conception graphique et donne à voir ce que les imprimeurs et les techniques d'impression de l'époque pouvaient réaliser de mieux. Moins de dix exemplaires de chaque édition sont conservés dans les bibliothèques et les musées du monde entier, signe que le tirage a dû être très limité.

Guichard n'en est pas resté là. En 1882, la suite de cette œuvre paraît à Paris chez H. Cagnon, en trois volumes trilingues sous le titre *La Grammaire de la couleur / Grammar of Colour / Die Grammatik der Farben* et dans un format oblong, avec cette fois 765 planches en couleurs.

# HARMONIE DER FARBEN

von E. GUICHARD ✲

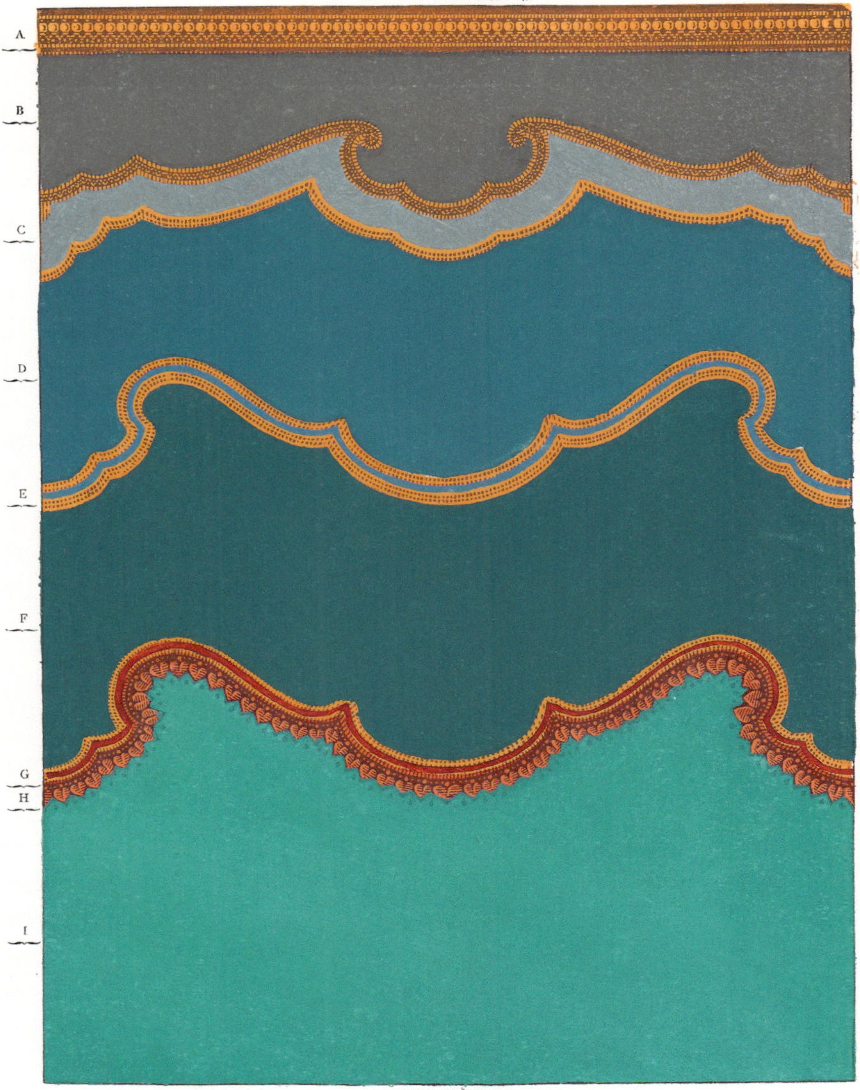

A

B

C

D

E

F

G

H

I

## TAPETEN

Wenn die Gruncfarbe einer Tapete wie I ist, so kann der Fries wie F und die Borde wie A, O und H sein.

## VORHÄNGE und PORTIÈREN

Ist die Farbe der Tapete wie I, so kann die Grundfarbe der Vorhänge wie F sein, mit Bordüren wie I und Franzen oder Gimpen wie A, G und H. — Wählt man die Vorhänge von derselben Farbe wie die Tapete, so wird man gut thun, um Eintönigkeit zu vermeiden, die Farbe F für die Gallerieüberhänge (lambrequins) der Fenster zu nehmen.

## THÜREN, LAMBRIS und KARNIESSE (GESIMSE, franz. CORNICHES)

Zu den Thüren und Lambris nimmt man die Farben B, C, D und E. — Der Theil des Karniesses, welcher den Plafond berührt, muss in etwas lichteren Farbentönen gehalten sein als die Thüren und Lambris; — man nehme dazu daher nur die Töne C, D, E, nämlich die Farbe C als Grundfarbe des Karniesses, die Farbe D für die Wölbung desselben und die Farbe E für das an den Plafond angrenzende Gesims. — Die Farbe A kann in bescheidenem Mass zu feinen Zwischenlinien benutzt werden; statt dessen kann man übrigens auch Gold nehmen oder diese Verzierung ganz weglassen.

## FRAUENKLEIDUNG

Die soeben angeführten Farbenzusammentellungen werden auch bei der feinen Damentoilette ihre Wirkung nicht verfehlen.

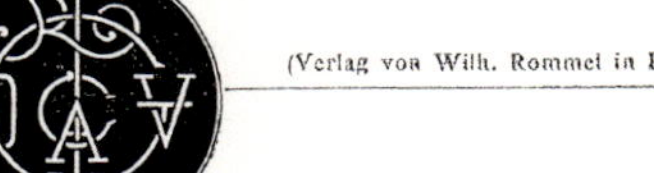

Alle Rechte vorbehalten.

(Verlag von Wilh. Rommel in Frankfurt a. M.)

# HARMONIE DER FARBEN

von E. GUICHARD ✻

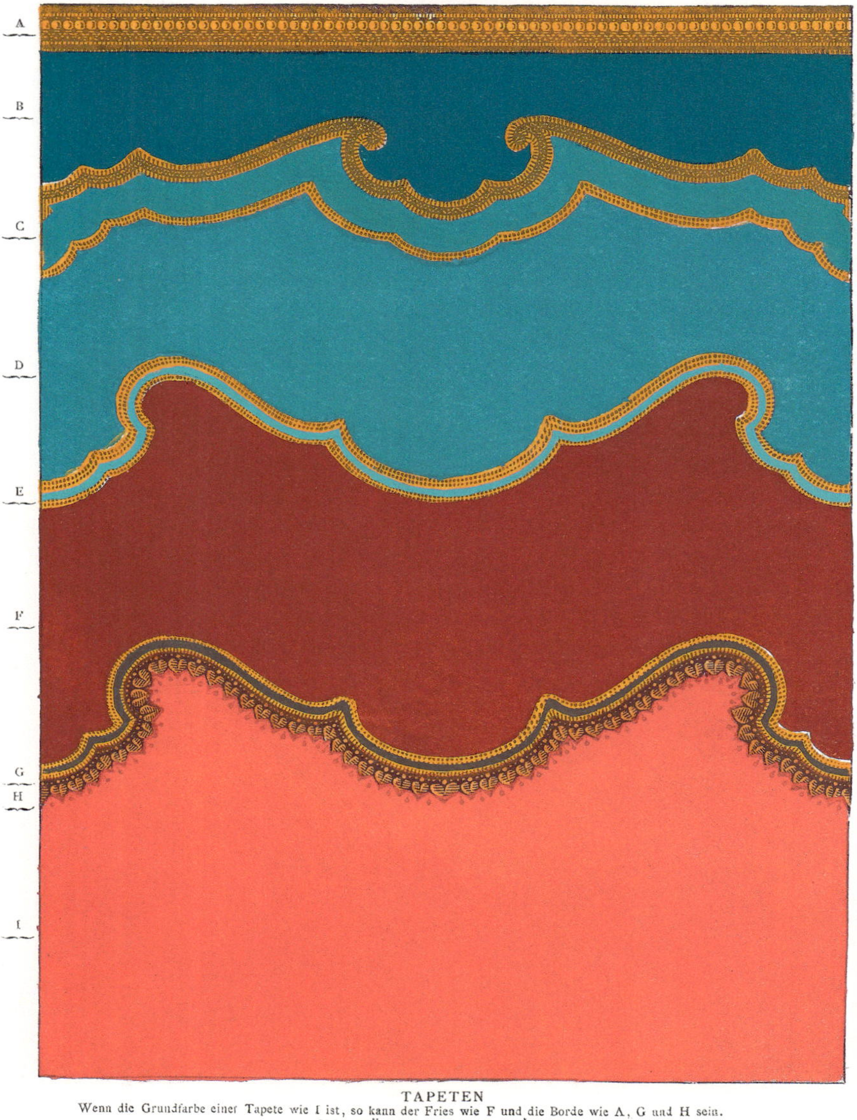

A

B

C

D

E

F

G

H

I

## TAPETEN

Wenn die Grundfarbe einer Tapete wie I ist, so kann der Fries wie F und die Borde wie A, G und H sein.

## VORHÄNGE und PORTIÈREN

Ist die Farbe der Tapete wie I, so kann die Grundfarbe der Vorhänge wie F sein, mit Bordüren wie I und Franzen oder Gimpen wie A, G und H. — Wählt man die Vorhänge von derselben Farbe wie die Tapete, so wird man gut thun, um Eintönigkeit zu vermeiden, die Farbe F für die Gallerieüberhänge (lambrequins) der Fenster zu nehmen.

## THÜREN, LAMBRIS und KARNIESSE (GESIMSE, franz. CORNICHES)

Zu den Thüren und Lambris nimmt man die Farben B, C, D und E. — Der Theil des Karniesses, welcher den Plafond berührt, muss in etwas lichteren Farbentönen gehalten sein als die Thüren und Lambris; — man nehme dazu daher nur die Töne C, D, E, nämlich die Farbe C als Grundfarbe des Karniesses, die Farbe D für die Wölbung desselben und die Farbe E für das an den Plafond angrenzende Gesims. — Die Farbe A kann in bescheidenem Mass zu feinen Zwischenlinien benutzt werden; statt dessen kann man übrigens auch Gold nehmen oder diese Verzierung ganz weglassen.

## FRAUENKLEIDUNG

Die soeben angeführten Farbenzusammenstellungen werden auch bei der feinen Damentoilette ihre Wirkung nicht verfehlen.

Alle Rechte vorbehalten.

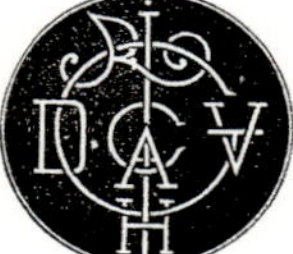

(Verlag von Wilh. Rommel in Frankfurt a. M.)

# HARMONIE DER FARBEN

von E. GUICHARD ✻

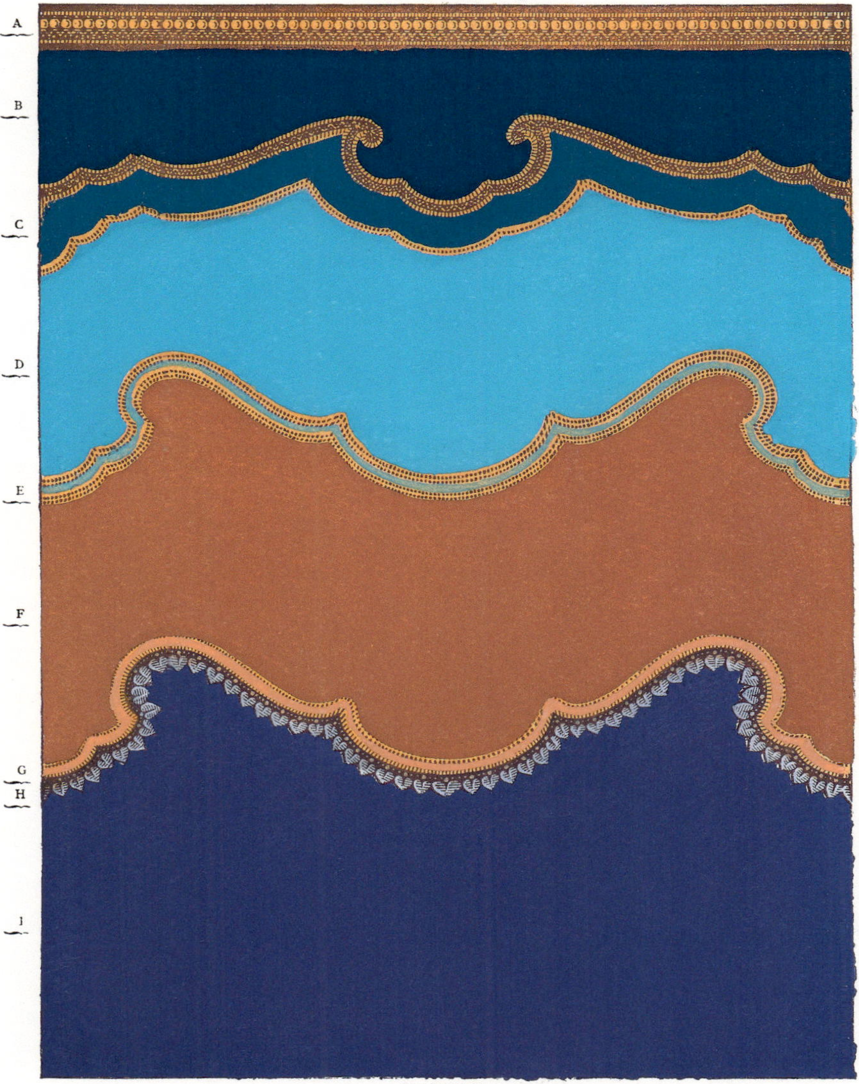


## TAPETEN

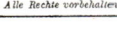

Wenn die Grundfarbe einer Tapete wie I ist, so kann der Fries wie F und die Borde wie A, G und H sein.

## VORHÄNGE und PORTIÈREN

Ist die Farbe der Tapete wie I, so kann die Grundfarbe der Vorhänge wie F sein, mit Bordüren wie I und Franzen oder Gimpen wie A, G und H. — Wählt man die Vorhänge von derselben Farbe wie die Tapete, so wird man gut thun, um Eintönigkeit zu vermeiden, die Farbe F für die Gallerieüberhänge (lambrequins) der Fenster zu nehmen.

## THÜREN, LAMBRIS und KARNIESSE (GESIMSE, franz. CORNICHES)

Zu den Thüren und Lambris nimmt man die Farben B, C, D und E. — Der Theil des Karniesses, welcher den Plafond berührt, muss in etwas lichteren Farbentönen gehalten sein als die Thüren und Lambris; — man nehme dazu daher nur die Töne C, D, E, nämlich die Farbe C als Grundfarbe des Karniesses, die Farbe D für die Wölbung desselben und die Farbe E für das an den Plafond angrenzende Gesims. — Die Farbe A kann in bescheidenem Mass zu feinen Zwischenlinien benuzt werden; statt dessen kann man übrigens auch Gold nehmen oder diese Verzierung ganz weglassen.

## FRAUENKLEIDUNG

Die soeben angeführten Farbenzusammenstellungen werden auch bei der feinen Damentoilette ihre Wirkung nicht verfehlen.

*Alle Rechte vorbehalten.*

(Verlag von Wilh. Rommel in Frankfurt a. M.)

DCAVH

## Charles Lacouture (1832–1908)

# RÉPERTOIRE CHROMATIQUE

## solution raisonnée et pratique des problèmes les plus usuels dans l'étude et l'emploi des couleurs

### A Chromatic Repertory

*16 plates, 31.6 x 25.7 cm | 12 ½ x 10 ⅛ in., Paris, 1890*
*London, Royal College of Art, Colour Reference Library*

This work, conceived and written by the French botanist and university professor of natural history Charles Lacouture, was intended as a homage to his fellow Frenchman Chevreul's work on colour earlier in the 19th century (pp. 216–237). While Lacouture greatly admired his predecessor, he also recognised some of the shortcomings of Chevreul's colour classification system, notably in relation to its usefulness to practising artists, designers and craftsmen. With his *Répertoire chromatique* he aimed to simplify and extend the system to which he and so many others were indebted, by composing an easy-to-read and updated textbook and guidebook for the use of colour. Its title (perhaps surprisingly, the book was never published in other languages) translates as 'A chromatic repertory, a logical and practical solution to the most frequent problems encountered in the study and use of colours', and in his text Lacouture concentrated on materials and objects, alongside the quality of pigments and paints, and how and why they deteriorate. By the end of the 19th century the fugitive nature of many colours and the damaging effect of light exposure had become a popular topic of discussion among manufacturers and colour researchers, partly caused by the advent of more intense, artificial lighting combined with the mass production of painting materials.

*Répertoire chromatique* is illustrated with 29 high-quality aquatinted colour plates and further uncoloured diagrams, with the coloured, full-page plates being particularly sophisticated in design and production. The leading image, which appears on the frontispiece (p. 279), has the title "Rose Synoptique" and introduces Lacouture's six principal colours and their six mixtures (or "second-order colours"), visualised as a 12-petal flower-head. The purest manifestation is shown at the root of each flower petal, with the hues lightening towards the outer tips. This is a variation on the classic colour wheel as proposed in the 18th century by Harris (pp. 118–123) and adapted by several other colour theorists since. A key to the diagram is printed on its transparent tissue guard.

Lacouture's most complex and aesthetically pleasing plate is entitled "Trilobe Synoptique", and is another synoptic diagram but this time divided into three 'lobes'. Here, the trichromatic system is presented as sections of overlapping

# ROSE SYNOPTIQUE

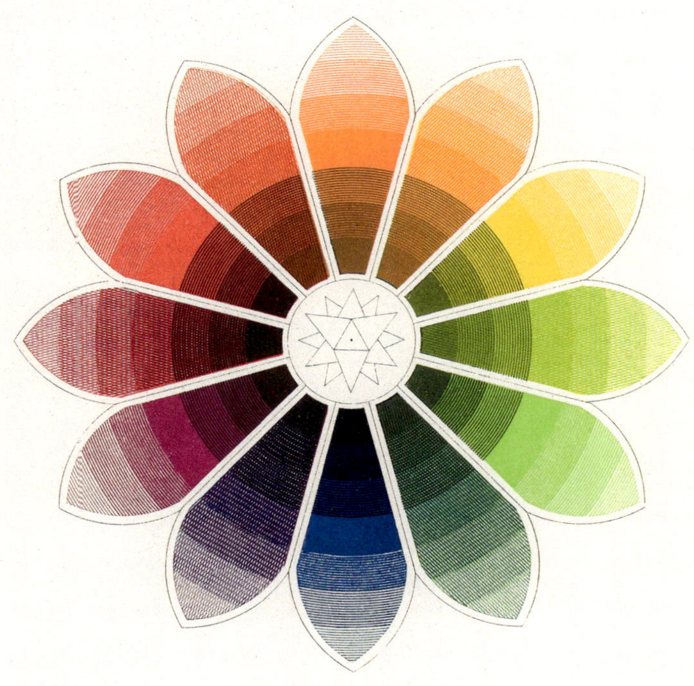

**N. B.** Fermer l'atlas pour soustraire ces planches à la lumière aussitôt qu'on n'a plus besoin d'en faire usage.

Chromolith. G. Severeyns.

# TRILOBE SYNOPTIQUE

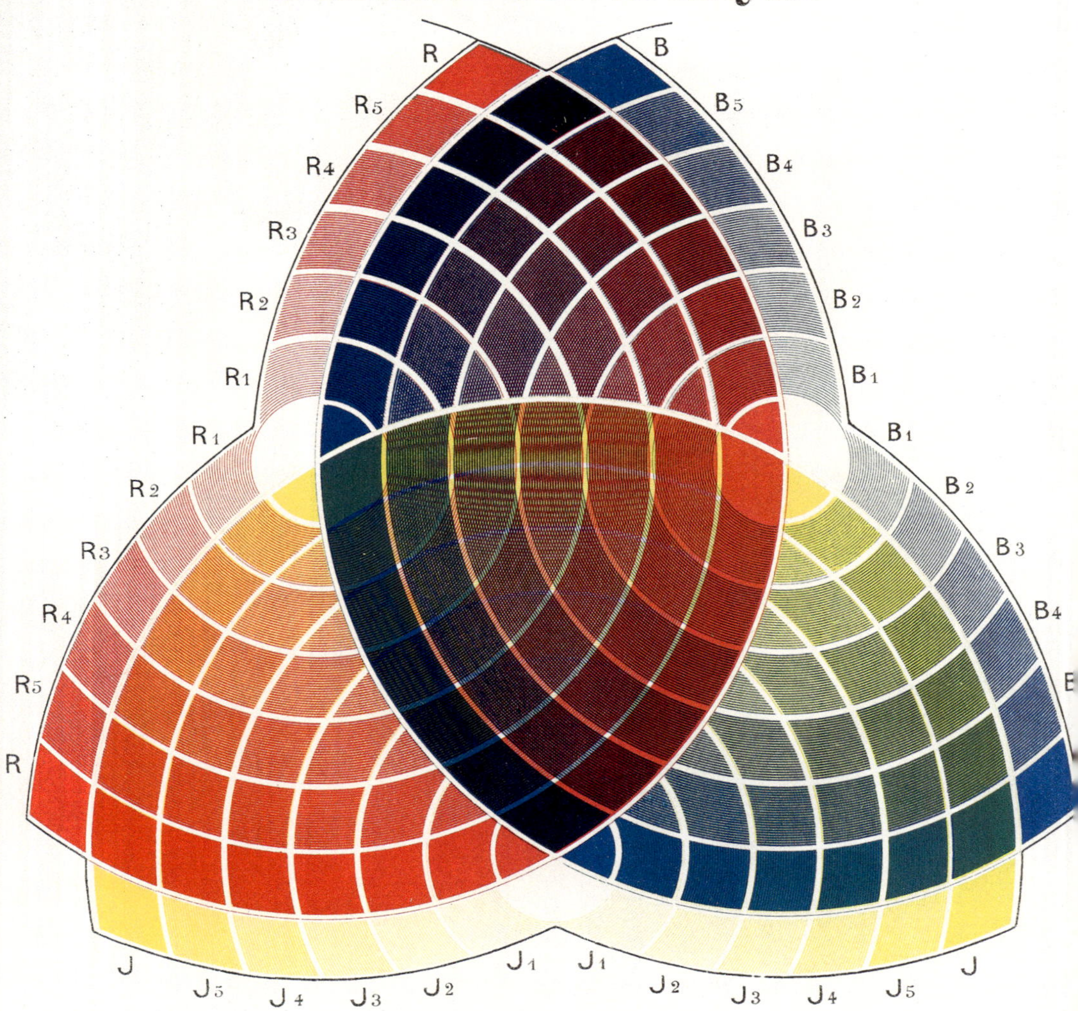


**N. B.** Fermer l'atlas pour soustraire ces planches à la lumière aussitôt qu'on n'a plus besoin d'en faire usage.

Chromolith. G. Severeyns.

RÉPERTOIRE CHROMATIQUE 2me section PLANCHE II

# LE ROUGE

ses gammes lavées, rabattues et grisées

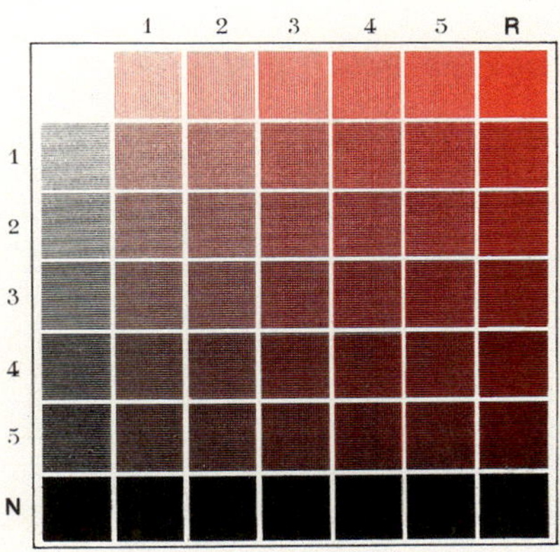


N. B. Fermer l'atlas pour soustraire ces planches à la lumière aussitôt qu'on n'a plus besoin d'en faire usage.

Chromolith. G. Severeyns.

circles of the primaries red, yellow and blue, which in the process form wing-like shapes that display the many different areas of mixtures of the 12 main colours in their gradations from light through grey to dark (*claires, grisées, assombries*). The primaries are marked and numbered along the outer edge of each wing, allowing for the exact identification of each tint. The remaining plates in Lacouture's book depict individual colours and their mixtures in the form of square grids similar to those designed by Robert Ridgway (pp. 288–297) and Maerz and Paul (pp. 316–325), and a variation of a colour triangle that appears always in six gradations. In all Lacouture's coloured plates white is represented by the colour of the printing paper, while the intensity of the hues and their darker gradations is created by increasing the density of graphic lines, thus avoiding the mixing of printing inks altogether.

## Chromatisches Repertoire

Diese Abhandlung, konzipiert und verfasst von Charles Lacouture, einem französischen Botaniker und Universitätsprofessor für Naturgeschichte, war als Hommage an das Werk von Michel-Eugène Chevreul aus dem frühen 19. Jahrhundert gedacht (S. 216–237). Lacouture bewunderte seinen Landsmann und Vorgänger sehr, erkannte in dessen System der Farbklassifizierung jedoch auch einige Schwächen, insbesondere im Hinblick auf die Anwendbarkeit für praktizierende Künstler, Gestalter und Handwerker. Mit *Répertoire chromatique* wollte er das System vereinfachen und erweitern, dem er und so viele andere verpflichtet waren, indem er ein leicht lesbares und aktualisiertes Lehr- und Handbuch für den Farbgebrauch zusammenstellte. Der Titel des Werks, das (vielleicht überraschend) niemals in anderen Sprachen erschien, lautet übersetzt „Chromatisches Repertoire, eine logische und praktische Lösung für die häufigsten Probleme bei der Erforschung und Anwendung von Farben". Im Text konzentrierte sich Lacouture auf farbige Materialien und Objekte, auf die Qualität von Pigmenten und Farben und auf die Frage, wie und warum sie an Substanz einbüßten. Im ausgehenden 19. Jahrhundert waren die flüchtige Natur vieler Farben und die schädliche Wirkung des Lichts unter Farbenherstellern und Farbforschern zum verbreiteten Diskussionsthema geworden, unter anderem ausgelöst durch die Einführung stärkerer künstlicher Lichtquellen in Kombination mit der Massenproduktion von Malmaterialien.

*Répertoire chromatique* ist mit 29 hochwertigen Aquatinta-Farbtafeln und weiteren nicht kolorierten Diagrammen bebildert, wobei die ganzseitigen Farbtafeln besonders aufwendig gestaltet und produziert wurden. Das tonangebende Bild auf dem Frontispiz trägt den Titel „Rose synoptique" (S. 279) und stellt die sechs Hauptfarben Lacoutures und ihre sechs Mischfarben (oder „Farben zweiter Ordnung") in Gestalt einer zwölfblättrigen Blüte vor. Die reinste Manifestation zeigt sich im Zentrum der Blüte, während die einzelnen Blütenblätter zu den Spitzen hin immer heller werden. Im Kern haben wir es mit einer Variation des klassischen Farbkreises zu tun, wie er in den 1760er-Jahren von Moses Harris (S. 118–123) vorgeschlagen und seither von mehreren anderen Farbtheoretikern übernommen und angepasst wurde.

Lacoutures komplexeste und ästhetisch ansprechendste Tafel, ein weiteres synoptisches Diagramm, ist mit „Trilobe synoptique" betitelt und diesmal in drei „Lappen" unterteilt. Das trichromatische System wird hier von sich überschneidenden Kreisstücken in den drei Grundfarben Rot, Gelb und Blau dargestellt. Sie bilden flügelartige Formen, auf denen die zahlreichen Mischungen der zwölf Hauptfarben in ihren Abstufungen von Hell über Grau bis Dunkel (*claires*, *grisées*, *assombries*) abzulesen sind. Die Grundfarben wurden an den Außenkanten der Flügel gekennzeichnet und nummeriert, um jeden Farbton genau bestimmen zu können. Die übrigen Tafeln in Lacoutures Buch zeigen einzelne Farben und ihre Mischungen in Form von quadratischen Rastern ähnlich denen von Robert Ridgway (S. 288–297) und Maerz und Paul (S. 316–325) sowie eine Variation eines Farbdreiecks, das immer in sechs Abstufungen erscheint. In allen farbigen Tafeln Lacoutures steht die Farbe des Druckpapiers für Weiß, während die Intensität der Farbtöne und ihrer dunkleren Schattierungen durch die jeweilige Stärke der Farblinien erzeugt wird. Das Anmischen von Druckfarben wurde so vollständig vermieden.

# Le VERT

ses gammes lavées, rabattues et grisées

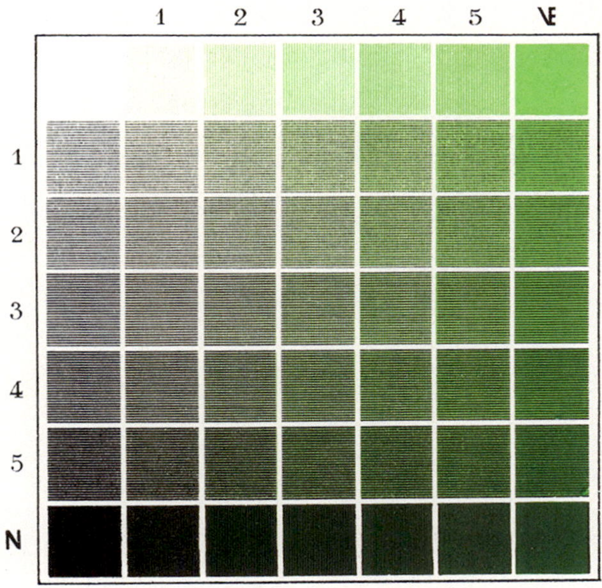


N. B. Fermer l'atlas pour soustraire ces planches à la lumière aussitôt qu'on n'a plus besoin d'en faire usage.

Chromolith. G. Severeyns.

# L'ORANGÉ-JAUNE

ses gammes de nuances

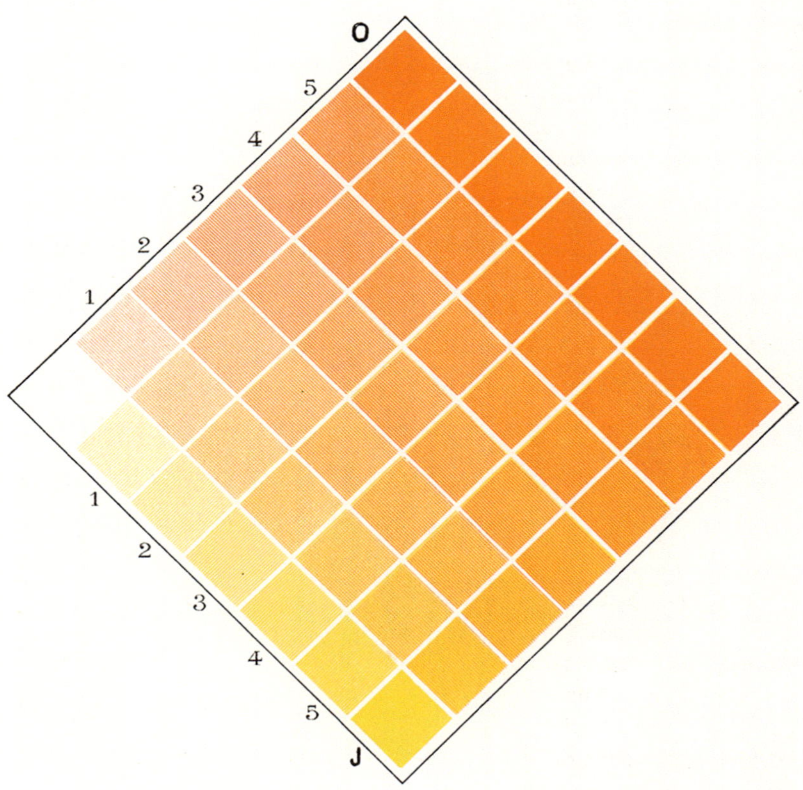


**N. B.** Fermer l'atlas pour soustraire ces planches à la lumière aussitôt qu'on n'a plus besoin d'en faire usage.

Chromolith. G Severeyns.

## Répertoire chromatique

Conçu et rédigé par Charles Lacouture, botaniste et professeur d'histoire naturelle français, cet ouvrage est pensé comme un hommage à l'œuvre réalisée par Michel-Eugène Chevreul au début du XIXe siècle (p. 216–237). Grand admirateur de son prédécesseur, Lacouture met néanmoins en évidence les défauts de la classification chromatique de Chevreul, notamment quant à son utilité pour les peintres, dessinateurs et artisans. Avec son *Répertoire chromatique*, il veut simplifier et augmenter un système auquel, comme tant d'autres, il doit beaucoup, en réalisant un manuel facile à lire et mis à jour, qui soit aussi un guide pratique pour l'emploi des couleurs. Dans cet ouvrage qui, étonnamment peut-être, n'a été traduit en aucune langue, Lacouture s'intéresse aux matériaux et aux objets, ainsi qu'à la qualité des pigments et des peintures, et explique comment et pourquoi ceux-ci se détériorent. À la fin du XIXe siècle, la nature éphémère de nombreuses couleurs et les dommages causés par l'exposition à la lumière font partie des débats courants parmi les fabricants et les coloristes, notamment en raison de l'avènement de l'éclairage artificiel plus intense, associé à la production industrielle des matériaux de peinture.

Le *Répertoire chromatique* est illustré de graphiques sans couleurs et de 29 planches pleine page, à l'aquatinte en couleurs de grande qualité, dont la conception et la réalisation sont particulièrement raffinées. Intitulée « Rose synoptique », l'image qui orne le frontispice (p. 279) présente les six couleurs principales et les six mélanges (« couleurs dérivées de son ordre ») de Lacouture, sous la forme d'une fleur à 12 pétales. L'état d'intensité maximale des couleurs est visible au centre de la fleur, les tonalités s'éclaircissant de plus en plus vers l'extrémité des pétales. Il s'agit avant tout d'une variante du cercle chromatique classique proposé par Moses Harris dans les années 1760 (p. 118–123) et remanié par plusieurs théoriciens à sa suite. La légende de ce graphique est imprimée sur une page de protection transparente en papier de soie.

La planche la plus complexe et la plus réussie sur le plan esthétique s'intitule « Trilobe synoptique », graphique divisé, comme son nom l'indique, en trois lobes. Ce système trichromatique est formé de sections de cercles entrecroisés figurant les couleurs primaires rouge, jaune et bleu. Celles-ci créent à leur tour des « ailes » réunissant les nombreux segments composés de mélanges des 12 couleurs principales, dans leurs gradations « claires, grisées, assombries ». Le long des contours extérieurs, les couleurs primaires sont désignées par une lettre et un chiffre, chaque teinte étant ainsi identifiable avec précision. Les autres planches de l'ouvrage de Lacouture représentent les teintes et leurs mélanges sous la forme de grilles composées de carrés, semblables à celles de Robert Ridgway (p. 288–297) et de Maerz et Paul (p. 316–325), ainsi que des variations d'un triangle aux bords arrondis, toujours présenté en six gradations. Dans toutes les planches, le blanc est figuré par la couleur du papier, tandis que l'intensité des tons et de leurs gradations sombres est produite par la densité des traits, ce qui évite le mélange des encres d'impression.

# L'ORANGÉ

ses gammes de nuances

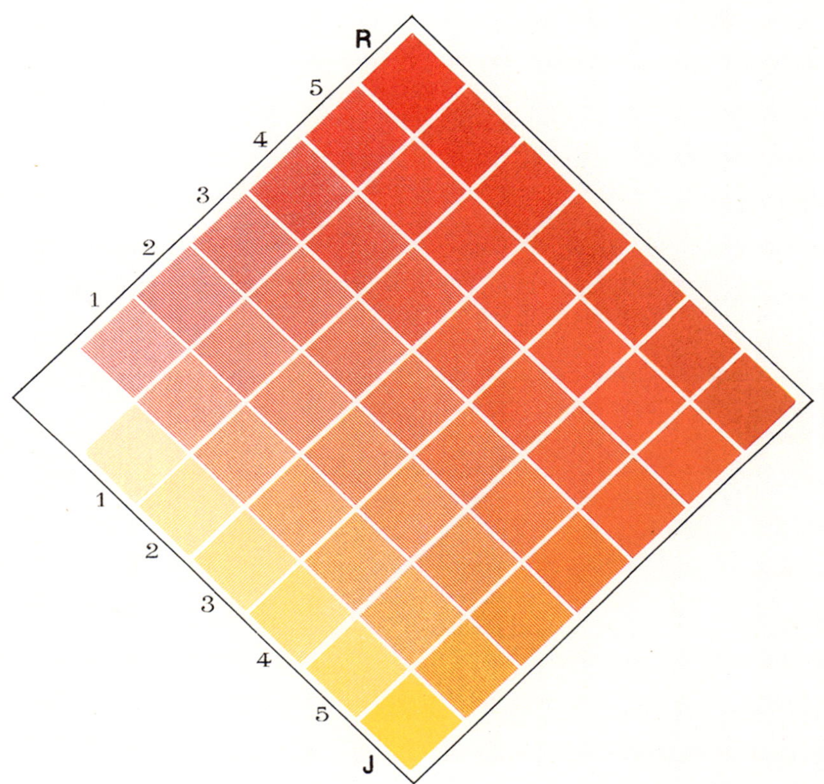


**N. B.** Fermer l'atlas pour soustraire ces planches à la lumière aussitôt qu'on n'a plus besoin d'en faire usage.

Chromolith. G. Severeyns.

# Le VERT

ses gammes de nuances

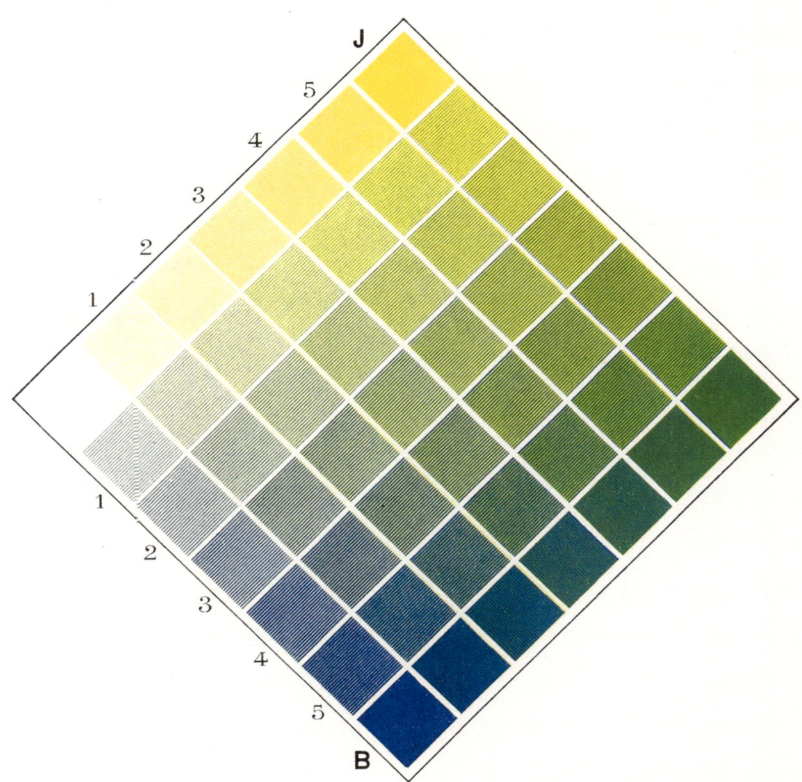


**N. B.** Fermer l'atlas pour soustraire ces planches à la lumière aussitôt qu'on n'a plus besoin d'en faire usage.

Chromolith. G. Severeyns.

## Robert Ridgway (1850–1929)

# COLOR STANDARDS AND COLOR NOMENCLATURE

*17 plates, 23 x 14 cm | 9 x 5½ in., Washington, D.C., 1912*
*New Haven, Yale University, Robert B. Haas Family Arts Library Special Collections, Faber Birren Collection of Books on Color*

The American ornithologist Robert Ridgway was strongly influenced by the work of Werner and Syme and their attempts at colour standardisation (pp. 240–249), both in visual terms and with regard to the naming and description of colours. In turn, Ridgway was later referred to as a major historical source for Maerz and Paul's *Dictionary of Color* (pp. 316–325), while he also included references to his own work in *Color Standards and Color Nomenclature* since he had first published an illustrated collection of colour names 26 years earlier, namely *A Nomenclature of Colors for Naturalists, and Compendium of Useful Knowledge for Ornithologists*, illustrated with hand-coloured charts and diagrams. His lifelong interest in colour standardisation and his desire to improve his own system resulted in this second, elegant and meticulously researched book which also reflects the advances in colour science that had taken place between the 1880s and 1910s.

Ridgway set his standards high, providing clear definitions of colour terminology and compiling a list of 1,115 individual colours together with their proportional composition, as well as a concise list of recent colour literature. His title-page image illustrates the 'Maxwell disks' method for calculating the proportional composition of colours in the book, based on a colour wheel of 36 segments and interlocking coloured cardboard discs. In the 1850s, the Scottish physicist James Clerk Maxwell had

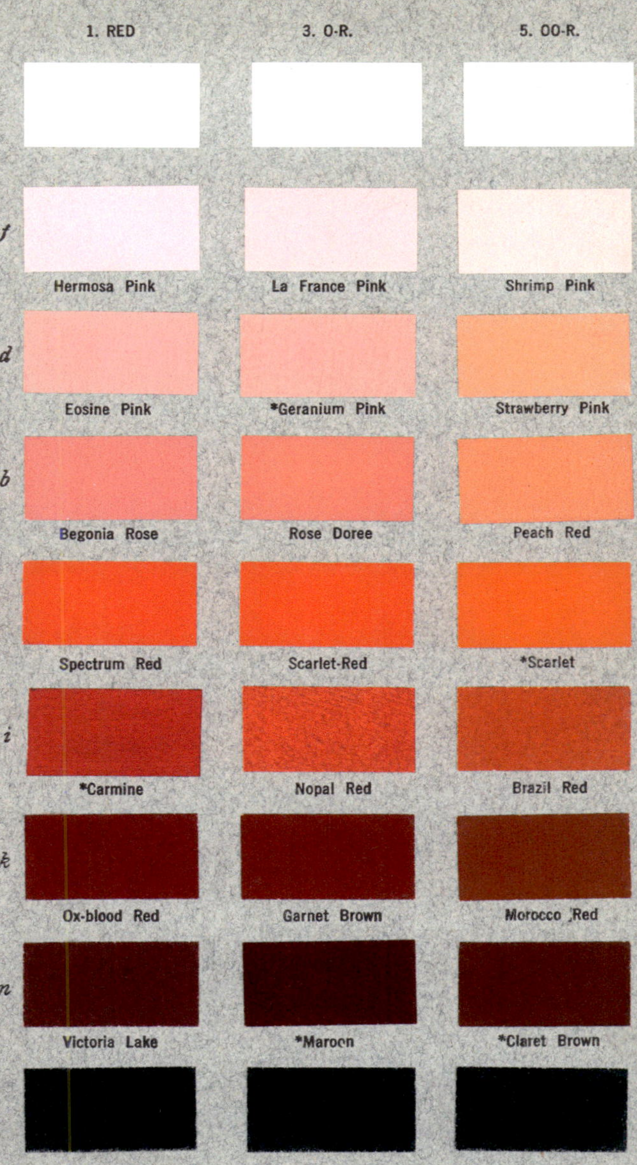
Plate I
1. RED
3. O-R.
5. OO-R.
f
Hermosa Pink
La France Pink
Shrimp Pink
d
Eosine Pink
*Geranium Pink
Strawberry Pink
b
Begonia Rose
Rose Doree
Peach Red
Spectrum Red
Scarlet-Red
*Scarlet
i
*Carmine
Nopal Red
Brazil Red
k
Ox-blood Red
Garnet Brown
Morocco Red
m
Victoria Lake
*Maroon
*Claret Brown

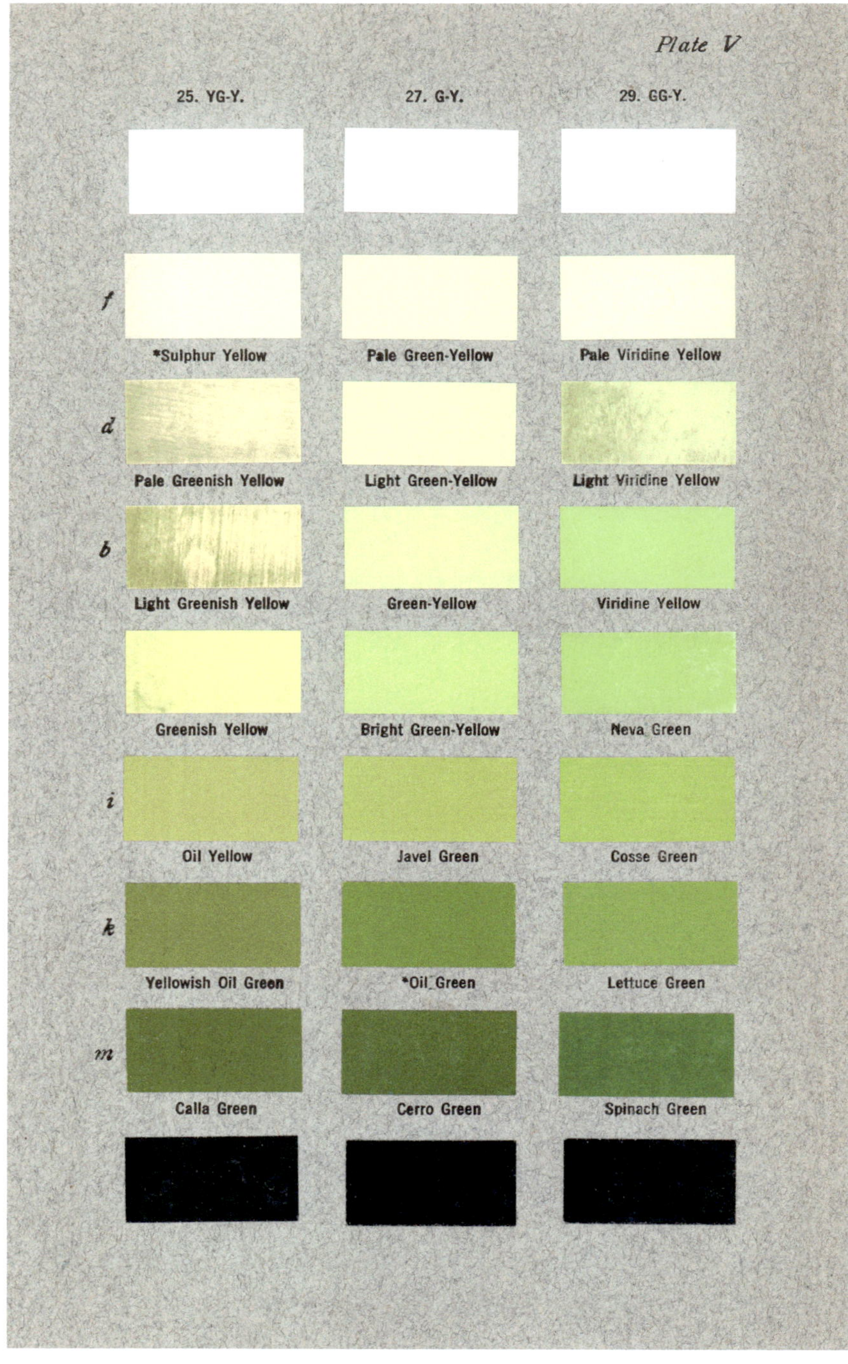
Plate V
25. YG-Y.
27. G-Y.
29. GG-Y.
f
*Sulphur Yellow
Pale Green-Yellow
Pale Viridine Yellow
d
Pale Greenish Yellow
Light Green-Yellow
Light Viridine Yellow
b
Light Greenish Yellow
Green-Yellow
Viridine Yellow
Greenish Yellow
Bright Green-Yellow
Neva Green
i
Oil Yellow
Javel Green
Cosse Green
k
Yellowish Oil Green
*Oil Green
Lettuce Green
m
Calla Green
Cerro Green
Spinach Green

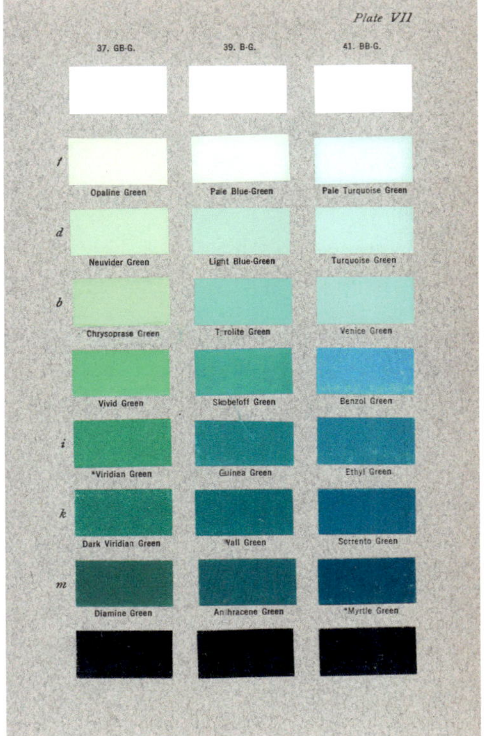


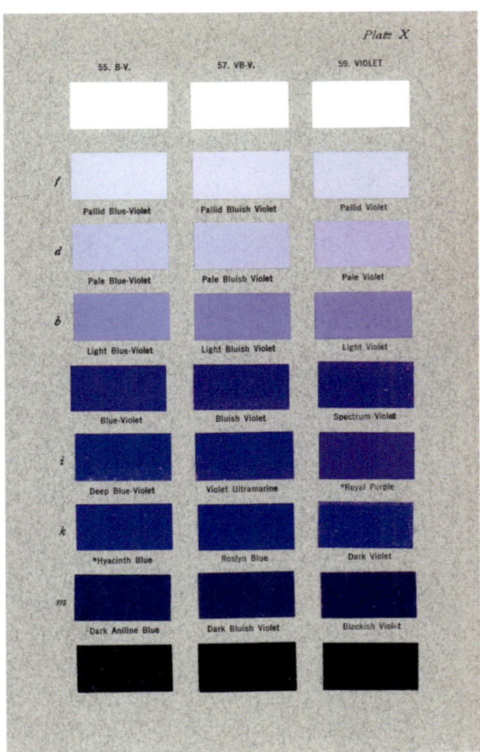


devised a range of spinning tops and discs with which he could demonstrate certain aspects of colour vision and optical colour mixture.

The most important feature, announced on the title-page, is the set of 53 coloured plates, which together provide a physical representation of the 1,115 named colours. Each plate is mounted with 27 colour chips, showing a gradual change in hue, using the spectrum colours and their intermediates in their purest manifestation in the first 12 plates; these are followed by sets in which the admixture of neutral greys is increased steadily, dulling the colours gradually. The final plate consists entirely of shades of grey between white in the top left corner and slate black in the bottom right.

Ridgway was particularly concerned about reliable representation of the colours listed in the book, and sought to avoid variations between different copies by painting uniform sheets of paper for each colour for the entire print run of 5,000, then cutting these sheets into small strips. He also warned readers not to expose the plates to light for prolonged periods, which indicates how advanced his understanding was of the fugitive nature of printed colour. Ridgway's choice of pigments for the illustrations, which omitted almost all organic colours, also reflects this: "The pigments used in the preparation of these Plates are the most durable known, those which have been proven unstable having been, as far as possible, discarded."

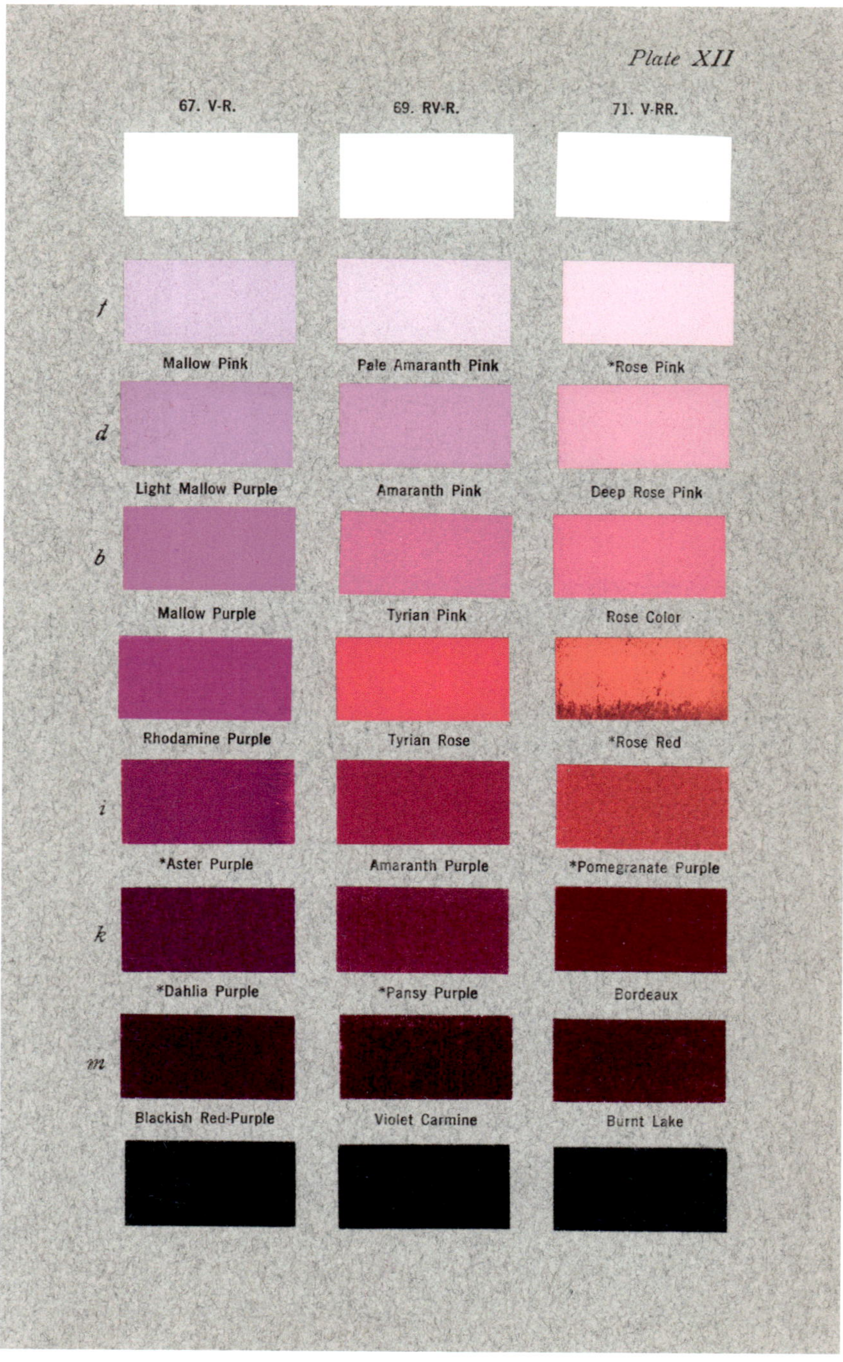
Plate XII
67. V-R.
69. RV-R.
71. V-RR.
f
Mallow Pink
Pale Amaranth Pink
*Rose Pink
d
Light Mallow Purple
Amaranth Pink
Deep Rose Pink
b
Mallow Purple
Tyrian Pink
Rose Color
Rhodamine Purple
Tyrian Rose
*Rose Red
i
*Aster Purple
Amaranth Purple
*Pomegranate Purple
k
*Dahlia Purple
*Pansy Purple
Bordeaux
m
Blackish Red-Purple
Violet Carmine
Burnt Lake

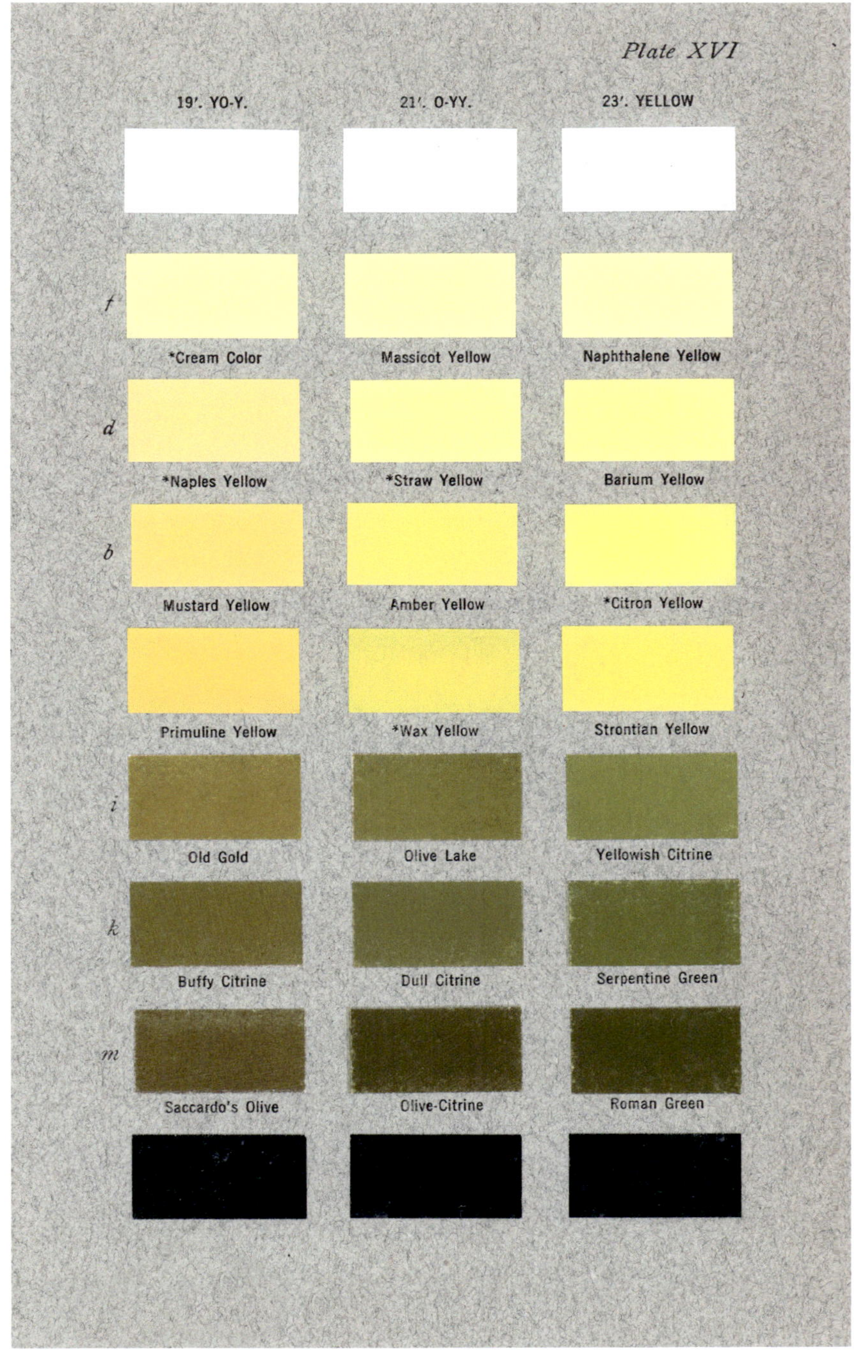
Plate XVI
19'. YO-Y.
21'. O-YY.
23'. YELLOW
f
*Cream Color
Massicot Yellow
Naphthalene Yellow
d
*Naples Yellow
*Straw Yellow
Barium Yellow
b
Mustard Yellow
Amber Yellow
*Citron Yellow
Primuline Yellow
*Wax Yellow
Strontian Yellow
i
Old Gold
Olive Lake
Yellowish Citrine
k
Buffy Citrine
Dull Citrine
Serpentine Green
m
Saccardo's Olive
Olive-Citrine
Roman Green

## Farbstandards und Farbnomenklatur

Der amerikanische Ornithologe Robert Ridgway war stark beeinflusst von Werner und Syme und deren Versuchen, sowohl in optischer Hinsicht als auch bei der Benennung und Beschreibung von Farben einen Farbstandard zu entwickeln (S. 240–249). Er selbst wurde später als wichtige historische Quelle für das *Dictionary of Color* von Maerz und Paul (S. 316–325) bezeichnet. In *Color Standards and Color Nomenclature* wiederum bezog er sich auch auf sein eigenes Werk, hatte er doch 26 Jahre zuvor mit *A Nomenclature of Colors for Naturalists, and Compendium of Useful Knowledge for Ornithologists* eine erste Sammlung von Farbbezeichnungen veröffentlicht, die mit handkolorierten Tabellen und Diagrammen illustriert war. Sein lebenslanges Interesse an der Normierung von Farben und sein Bestreben, das eigene System zu verbessern, führten zu diesem zweiten, eleganten und akribisch recherchierten Buch, das auch die Fortschritte der Farbwissenschaft in den 1880er- bis 1910er-Jahren widerspiegelte.

Ridgway legte die Messlatte hoch. Er formulierte eindeutige Definitionen für die Farbterminologie und erstellte eine Liste von 1.115 Einzelfarben mit ihrer jeweiligen Zusammensetzung sowie eine kurze Bibliografie der jüngeren Farbliteratur. Die Abbildung auf seiner Titelseite veranschaulicht die Berechnung der Farbzusammensetzungen im Buch nach der Methode der „Maxwell'schen Farbscheiben", die auf einem Farbkreis mit 36 Segmenten und ineinandergreifenden Scheiben aus farbigem Karton basierte. Der schottische Physiker James Clerk Maxwell hatte in den 1850er-Jahren Farbscheibenkreisel entwickelt, mit denen er bestimmte Aspekte des Farbensehens und der additiven Farbmischung demonstrieren konnte.

Der wichtigste Bestandteil des Buches waren, wie auf der Titelseite angekündigt, die 53 Farbtafeln mit den Darstellungen der insgesamt 1.115 benannten Farben. Jede Tafel zeigt anhand von 27 aufgeklebten farbigen Rechtecken, wie der Farbton der Spektralfarben und ihrer Zwischenfarben auf den ersten zwölf Tafeln in ihrer reinsten Form verwendet werden. Die letzte Tafel besteht ausschließlich aus Grautönen, aufgefächert zwischen Weiß oben links und Schieferschwarz unten rechts.

Ridgways besonderes Anliegen war die zuverlässige Wiedergabe der im Buch aufgelisteten Farben. Weil er Abweichungen zwischen den einzelnen Buchexemplaren vermeiden wollte, trug er jede Farbe einheitlich für die gesamte Auflage von fünftausend Büchern auf Papierbögen auf, die er anschließend in kleine Streifen zerschnitt. Seiner Leserschaft riet er, die Tafeln nicht für längere Zeit dem Licht auszusetzen, womit deutlich wurde, dass er hinsichtlich der flüchtigen Natur gedruckter Farben auf dem neuesten Stand war. Auch seine Pigmentauswahl, bei der er fast vollständig auf organische Farben verzichtete, spiegelt dies wider: „Die bei der Erstellung dieser Tafeln verwendeten Pigmente sind die beständigsten, die wir kennen, während jene, die sich als instabil erwiesen haben, so weit wie möglich aussortiert wurden."

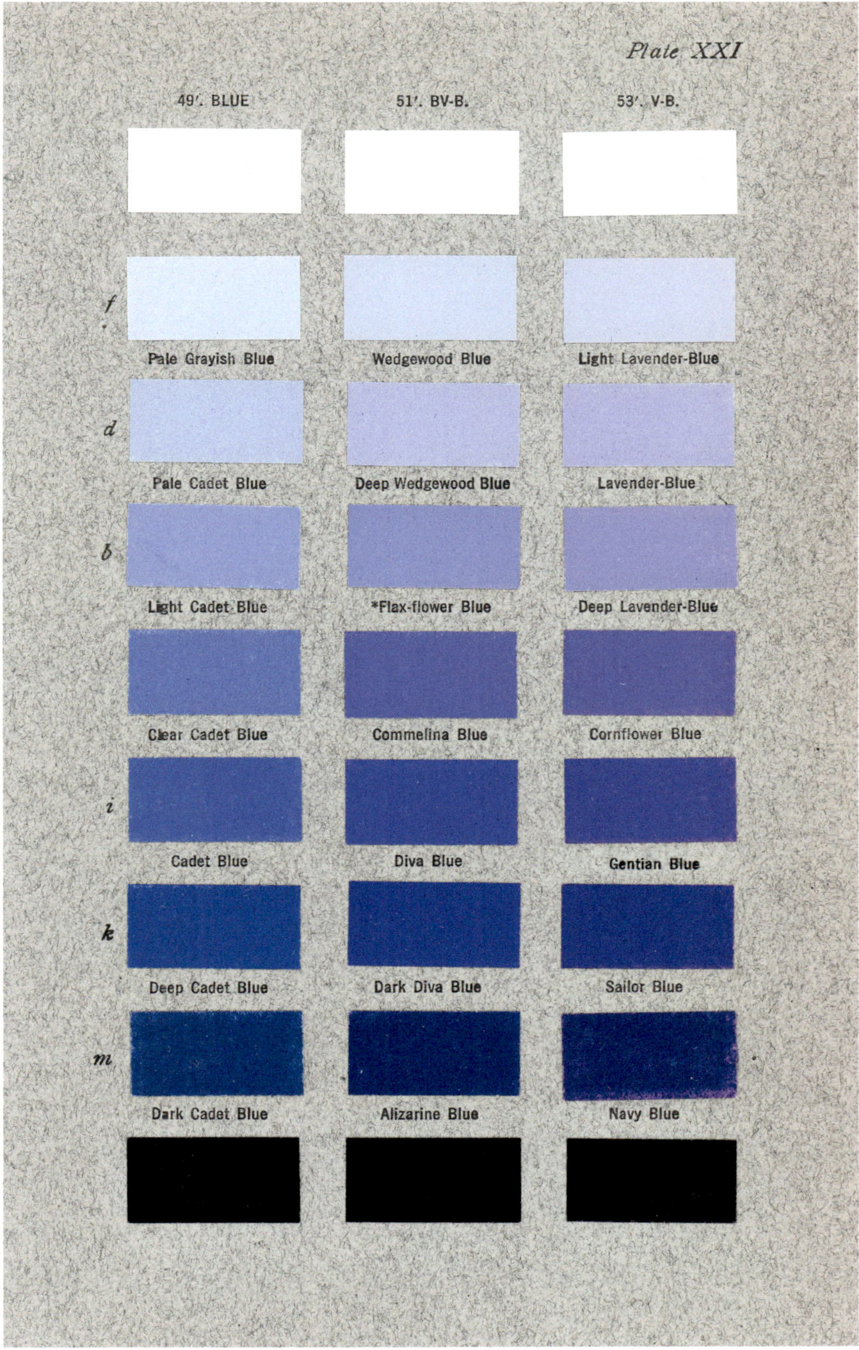
Plate XXI
49'. BLUE
51'. BV-B.
53'. V-B.
f
Pale Grayish Blue
Wedgewood Blue
Light Lavender-Blue
d
Pale Cadet Blue
Deep Wedgewood Blue
Lavender-Blue
b
Light Cadet Blue
*Flax-flower Blue
Deep Lavender-Blue
Clear Cadet Blue
Commelina Blue
Cornflower Blue
i
Cadet Blue
Diva Blue
Gentian Blue
k
Deep Cadet Blue
Dark Diva Blue
Sailor Blue
m
Dark Cadet Blue
Alizarine Blue
Navy Blue

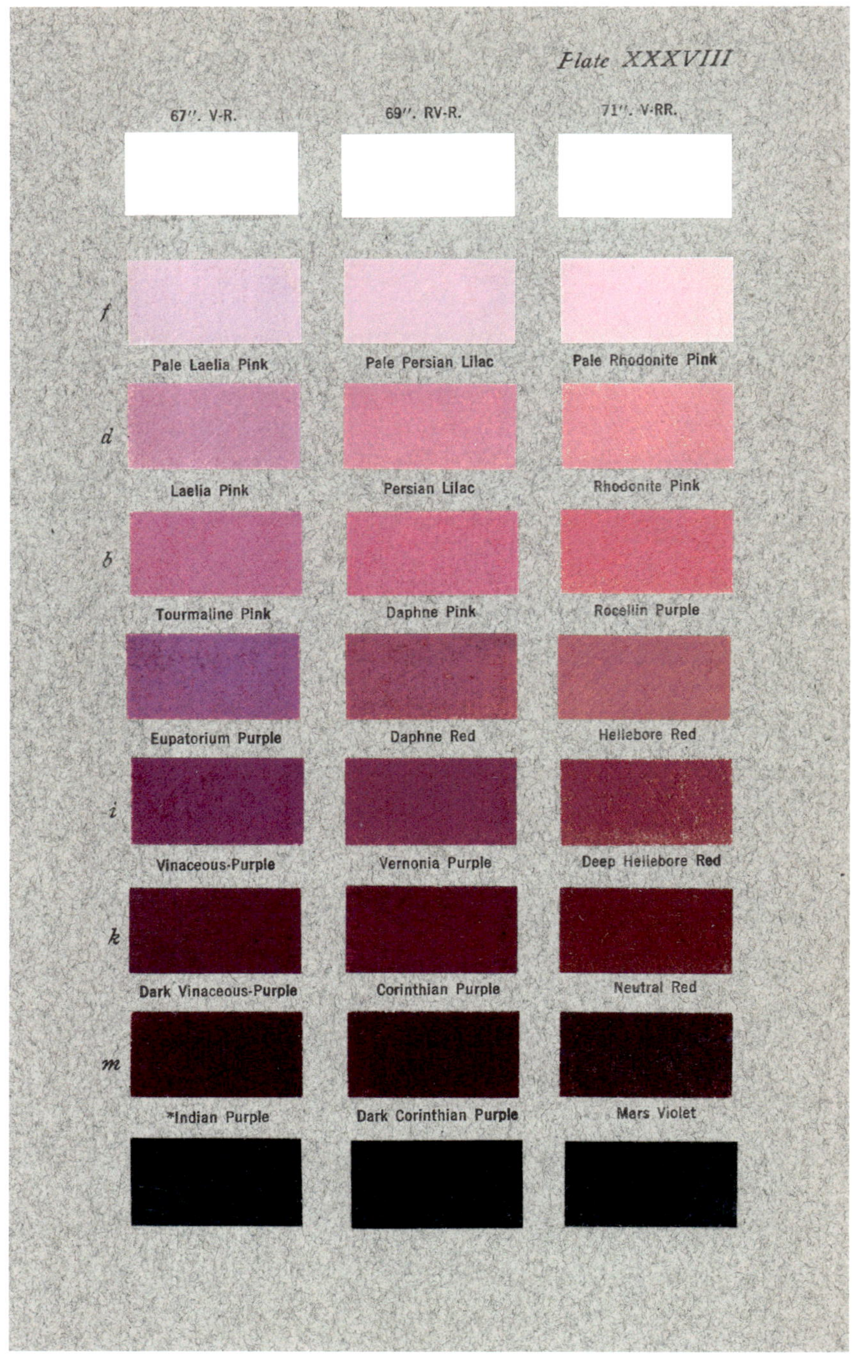
Plate XXXVIII
67''. V-R.
69''. RV-R.
71''. V-RR.
f
d
b
i
k
m
Pale Laelia Pink
Pale Persian Lilac
Pale Rhodonite Pink
Laelia Pink
Persian Lilac
Rhodonite Pink
Tourmaline Pink
Daphne Pink
Rocellin Purple
Eupatorium Purple
Daphne Red
Hellebore Red
Vinaceous-Purple
Vernonia Purple
Deep Hellebore Red
Dark Vinaceous-Purple
Corinthian Purple
Neutral Red
*Indian Purple
Dark Corinthian Purple
Mars Violet

## Normes et nomenclatures des couleurs

Ornithologue américain, Robert Ridgway est très influencé par les tentatives de standardisation des couleurs entreprises par Werner et Syme (p. 240–249), tant visuellement que dans la manière de nommer et de décrire les couleurs. Ridgway, qui sera à son tour cité comme l'une des sources historiques majeures du *Dictionary of Color* de Maerz et Paul (p. 316–325), mentionne aussi ses travaux antérieurs dans ces *Color Standards and Color Nomenclature*. En effet, vingt-six ans auparavant, il a publié un recueil de noms de couleurs, *A Nomenclature of Colors for Naturalists, and Compendium of Useful Knowledge for Ornithologists*, illustré de tableaux et de graphiques coloriés à la main. L'intérêt qu'il a porté tout au long de sa vie à la standardisation des couleurs et son souhait de perfectionner son système l'amènent à faire paraître ce deuxième ouvrage, élégant fruit de recherches approfondies, qui témoigne en outre des progrès effectués dans la science des couleurs des années 1880 aux années 1910.

Avec une grande exigence, Ridgway offre une terminologie claire des couleurs et répertorie 1 115 teintes et les proportions qui les composent, ainsi qu'une liste concise d'ouvrages de son temps sur le sujet. L'image de la page de titre illustre la méthode des « disques de Maxwell » – employée dans l'ouvrage pour le calcul des proportions des couleurs – à l'aide d'un cercle chromatique formé de 36 segments et de disques colorés en carton qui s'emboîtent. Dans les années 1850, James Clerk Maxwell, physicien écossais, avait conçu des dispositifs de toupies et de disques, grâce auxquels il démontrait certains aspects de la vision en couleurs et des mélanges de couleurs optiques.

La pièce maîtresse du livre de Ridgway est, comme l'annonce la page de titre, l'ensemble de 53 planches en couleurs, représentant les 1115 teintes inventoriées. Sur chaque planche, sont montés 27 échantillons colorés présentant des changements progressifs de tonalité. Les 12 premières planches montrent les couleurs du spectre et les teintes intermédiaires dans leur intensité maximale sur la ligne horizontale médiane. Viennent ensuite des groupes de couleurs auxquelles des gris neutres sont ajoutés graduellement, afin de ternir les teintes. La dernière planche est entièrement composée de nuances de gris, depuis le blanc de l'angle supérieur gauche jusqu'à la teinte ardoise de l'angle inférieur droit.

Soucieux de fournir une représentation fiable des couleurs répertoriées dans son livre, Ridgway veut éviter les variations d'un exemplaire à l'autre et a l'idée de peindre uniformément des feuilles de papier pour chaque couleur des 5000 exemplaires du tirage, puis de découper chaque feuille en petites bandes. En outre, il avertit les lecteurs de ne pas exposer trop longtemps les planches à la lumière, montrant ainsi qu'il est très conscient de la nature fragile de la couleur imprimée. Le choix des pigments employés dans les illustrations, qui laisse de côté presque toutes les teintes organiques, en est aussi la preuve : « Les pigments utilisés pour la préparation de ces planches sont les plus pérennes que nous connaissions actuellement, ceux qui se sont montrés instables ayant été, dans la mesure du possible, écartés. »

## Elizabeth Burris-Meyer (1899–1969)

# HISTORICAL COLOR GUIDE

*30 plates, 23 x 17.5 cm | 9 x 6 ⅞ in., New York, 1938*
*Montreal, Canadian Centre for Architecture*

Elizabeth Burris-Meyer is still an under-researched and underappreciated writer, educator and commentator on 20th-century colour. She has hardly been discussed in colour literature, and little is known about her life, despite the fact that her publishing output was extensive. When this first *Historical Color Guide* by her was issued she was working as Dean of the Tobé-Coburn School for Fashion Careers in New York, a newly founded training institution for the fashion and beauty industries. She was previously educated at the University of Michigan, and subsequently taught design at the Paris and New York branches of the New York School of Fine and Applied Art (later known as Parsons New School of Design). Her first published work was the substantial *Color and Design in the Decorative Arts* (1935), in which she demonstrated a thorough understanding of art history and colour science, together with an ability to write and educate in a clear and accessible manner about colour and its applications. Amongst other topics she discussed Albert Henry Munsell's colour concepts and systems, and reproduced one of his colour wheels and some of his other diagrams. Her book also included a colour card with 66 pasted-in and named swatches of "representative colors in common use in merchandising, advertising, and dress", together with a perforated paper screen designed to isolate colours or colour groups on the card and thereby assist the user in finding harmonious arrangements. Burris-Meyer applied this practical, informed and concise style in all her publications.

# PRIMITIVES

Bali GY 8/6

Blcssom Y 9/10

Fungus RP-R 5/8

Calabash R-YR 6/10

Shadow RP 4/4

# ITALIAN PRIMITIVE

| | |
|---|---|
| Sky | PB 6/10 |
| Coral | R 5/10 |
| Hibiscus | YR 8/4 |
| Lime | Y 9/12 |
| Olive | Y-GY 6/4 |

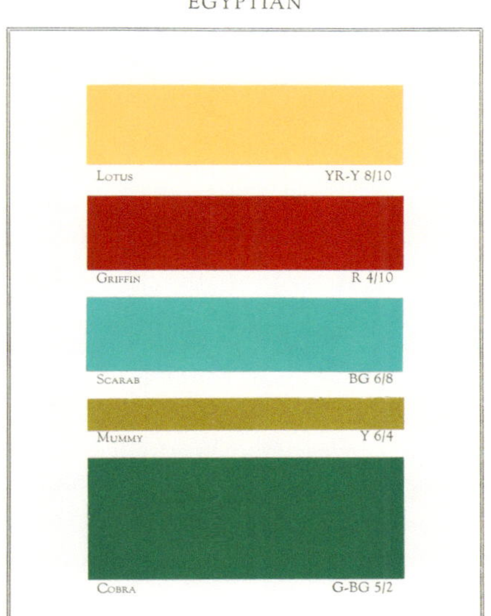


2

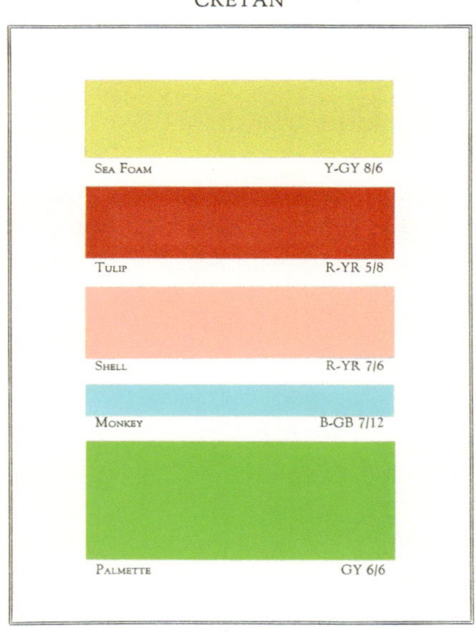


3

With the *Historical Color Guide* her purpose was to provide "a book of representative traditional color schemes derived from examples of the decorative arts from all fields", predominantly intended for designers, merchants, decorators and architects. Across 30 plates, each provided with five printed colour strips and an accompanying page of commentary, Burris-Meyer presented a historical, global and cultural overview of colour schemes throughout the centuries. She arranged these plates by theme, from the so-called "Primitives" found on tribal carvings and textiles, on by way of Ancient Egypt, the Classical world, Chinese examples and Persian Miniatures, through specific periods and phases such as the Italian Renaissance and the English "mauve decade", to individual artists' palettes for Van Gogh and Gauguin. Each colour sample is numerically marked according to Munsell's notation system, and the book was rounded off with a numbered colour index. The concept and style of Burris-Meyer's *Historical Color Guide* bear a close resemblance to Thomas Parsons's *A Tint Book of Historical Colours*, published in London four years earlier, and there is no doubt that Burris-Meyer took inspiration from it. However, where Parsons's book concentrated specifically on architectural colour, Burris-Meyer was aiming for a far wider range of application. She wrote several other books on design, interior decoration and fashion, always including colour charts, and in 1947 published a companion volume to this book, her *Contemporary Color Guide*.

## Historischer Farbführer

Als Autorin und Pädagogin, die sich mit den Farben des 20. Jahrhunderts beschäftigte, wird Elizabeth Burris-Meyer bis heute von der Forschung vernachlässigt und zu wenig geschätzt. In der Farbliteratur wird sie so gut wie nicht erwähnt, und obwohl sie viel veröffentlicht hat, ist über ihr Leben wenig bekannt. Als ihr *Historical Color Guide* erschien, war sie Direktorin der Tobé-Coburn School for Fashion Careers in New York, einer neu gegründeten Ausbildungseinrichtung für die Mode- und Kosmetikindustrie. Sie hatte die University of Michigan besucht und anschließend in Paris und New York an der New York School of Fine and Applied Art (der späteren Parsons New School of Design) Gestaltung unterrichtet. Ihre erste Veröffentlichung war der umfangreiche Band *Color and Design in the Decorative Arts* (1935), in dem sie nicht nur ein umfassendes Verständnis von Kunstgeschichte und Farbwissenschaft, sondern auch die Fähigkeit unter Beweis stellte, auf klare und verständliche Weise über Farbe und ihre Anwendungen zu schreiben. So behandelte sie unter anderem die Farbtheorien und -systeme von Albert Henry Munsell und reproduzierte neben einem Farbkreis noch weitere seiner Diagramme. Ihr Buch enthielt auch eine Farbkarte mit 66 eingeklebten und namentlich benannten Mustern von „repräsentativen Farben, die in Handel, Werbung und Mode allgemein in Gebrauch sind", ergänzt um eine perforierte Papierschablone, mit der sich Farben oder Farbgruppen auf der Karte abgrenzen ließen, um das Auffinden harmonischer Kombinationen zu vereinfachen. Diesen praxisorientierten, sachkundigen und prägnanten Stil verwendete Burris-Meyer in allen ihren Veröffentlichungen.

Der *Historical Color Guide* sollte „ein Buch der repräsentativen traditionellen Farbkonzepte, abgeleitet von Beispielen aus allen Bereichen der dekorativen Kunst" sein, das sich vorrangig an Designer, Händler, Dekorateure und Architekten richtete. Auf dreißig Tafeln mit jeweils fünf gedruckten Farbstreifen und einer Seite Begleittext präsentierte Burris-Meyer einen globalen historischen und kulturellen Überblick über Farbzusammenstellungen quer durch die Jahrhunderte. Sie ordnete die Tafeln thematisch an, von den „Urfarben" auf Schnitzereien und Textilien alter Stammeskulturen über Altägypten, die Antike, Beispiele aus China, persische Miniaturen, bestimmte Perioden und Phasen wie die italienische Renaissance oder die „mauve decade" in England (1890er-Jahre) hin zu den Künstlerpaletten van Goghs und Gauguins. Jedes Farbmuster ist mit einer Nummer nach Munsells Notationssystem versehen, die sich im abschließenden Farbregister wiederfindet. In Konzeption und Stil erinnert der *Historical Color Guide* stark an *A Tint Book of Historical Colours* von Thomas Parsons, das vier Jahre zuvor in London erschienen war und Burris-Meyer zweifellos beeinflusst hatte. Doch wo sich Parsons Buch speziell auf Architekturfarben konzentrierte, zielte Burris-Meyer auf ein weit größeres Anwendungsspektrum ab. Sie schrieb mehrere andere Bücher über Design, Innenausstattung und Mode, die stets Farbtabellen enthielten, und veröffentlichte 1947 mit dem *Contemporary Color Guide* einen Begleitband zu ihrem *Historical Color Guide*.

# ITALIAN RENAISSANCE

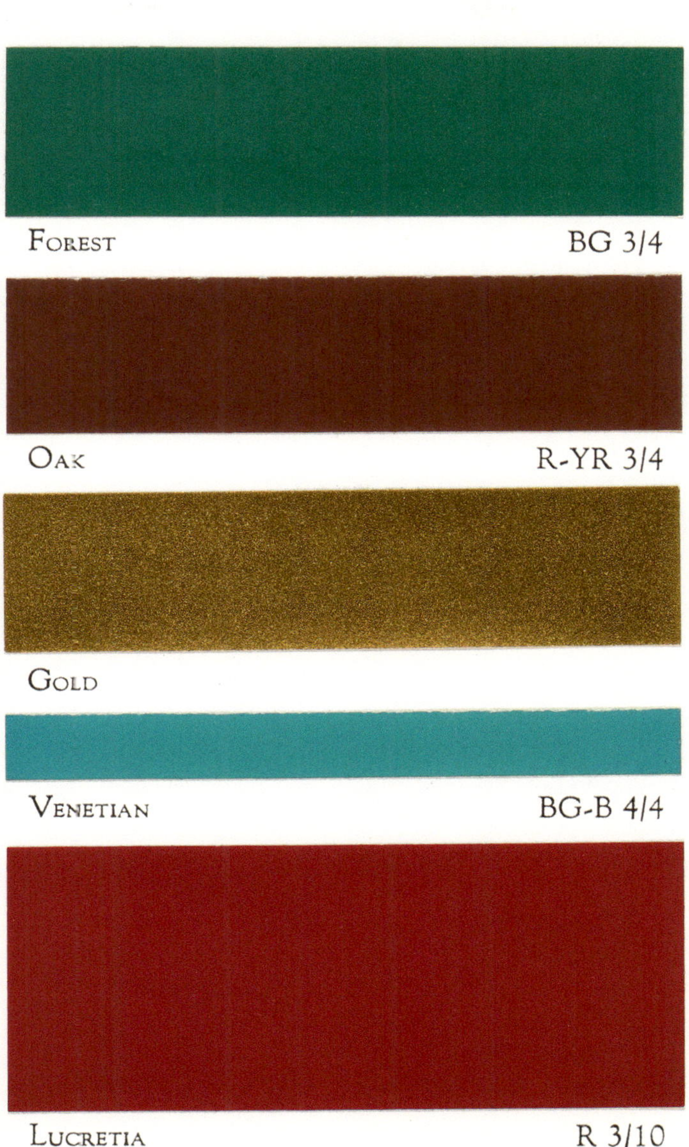

# FLEMISH PRIMITIVE

| | |
|---|---|
| Bruges | Y-RY 3/8 |
| L'arbre | GY 6/4 |
| La Jeunesse | PB 8/2 |
| La Joie | R-YR 8/8 |
| La Morte | Y-GY 3/2 |

## Guide historique de la couleur

Pédagogue et exégète de la couleur au XXe siècle, Elizabeth Burris-Meyer est une autrice sous-estimée et trop peu étudiée. On ignore presque tout de la vie de cette femme qui, alors qu'elle a énormément publié, est quasiment absente des écrits sur le sujet. Quand paraît son premier « Guide historique de la couleur », Burris-Meyer est doyenne de l'École Tobé-Coburn des carrières de la mode, à New York, institution alors récemment fondée pour former aux métiers de la mode et de la beauté. Après des études à l'Université du Michigan, elle enseigne le dessin dans les antennes parisienne et new-yorkaise de l'École des beaux-arts et arts appliqués de New York (connue depuis sous le nom de Parsons New School of Design). En 1935, elle publie son premier ouvrage, *Color and Design in the Decorative Arts*, où elle fait montre d'une très grande connaissance de l'histoire de l'art et de la science des couleurs, ainsi que d'une capacité à écrire sur la couleur et ses applications et à dispenser un enseignement clair et accessible. Elle s'intéresse notamment aux conceptions et systèmes chromatiques d'Albert Henry Munsell et reproduit un cercle chromatique et d'autres graphiques de cet auteur. Son ouvrage comprend également une carte en couleurs sur laquelle sont collés 56 échantillons, chacun doté d'une appellation, figurant les « couleurs représentatives couramment employées dans le commerce, la publicité et l'habillement », ainsi qu'une feuille de papier perforée destinée à isoler les teintes ou groupes de teintes de cette carte, afin de permettre à l'utilisateur de trouver des combinaisons harmonieuses. Dans tous ses ouvrages, Burris-Meyer a recours à cette méthode pratique, documentée et concise.

L'objectif de ce guide est de proposer « un ouvrage représentatif des coloris traditionnels inspirés d'exemples des arts décoratifs de tous les domaines », principalement à destination des dessinateurs, marchands, décorateurs et architectes. Grâce à 30 planches, chacune comportant cinq bandes de couleurs imprimées et accompagnée d'une page de commentaires, Burris-Meyer présente un panorama historique et culturel des couleurs du monde entier au fil des siècles. Elle organise ces planches de manière thématique, en commençant par ce qu'elle appelle les « primitives », visibles dans les gravures et textiles tribaux, puis passe à l'Égypte ancienne, au monde classique, à des exemples chinois et aux miniatures persanes, et s'intéresse à des périodes spécifiques comme la Renaissance italienne et la « décennie mauve » anglaise des années 1890, ainsi qu'à la palette de peintres comme Van Gogh ou Gauguin. Chaque échantillon de couleur est numéroté selon le système de notation de Munsell et l'ouvrage s'achève par un index chromatique numéroté. La conception et le style de l'*Historical Color Guide* de Burris-Meyer ressemblent beaucoup à ceux d'un ouvrage de Thomas Parsons intitulé *A Tint Book of Historical Colours*, paru quatre ans plus tôt à Londres et dont l'autrice s'est à coup sûr inspirée. Mais, tandis que Parsons s'intéresse avant tout à la couleur en architecture, Burris-Meyer vise des applications beaucoup plus nombreuses. Elle a signé d'autres livres consacrés aux arts graphiques, à la décoration d'intérieur et à la mode qui comprennent tous des tableaux de couleurs et, en 1947, publie un complément à cet ouvrage, intitulé *Contemporary Color Guide*.

# FRENCH, STAINED GLASS

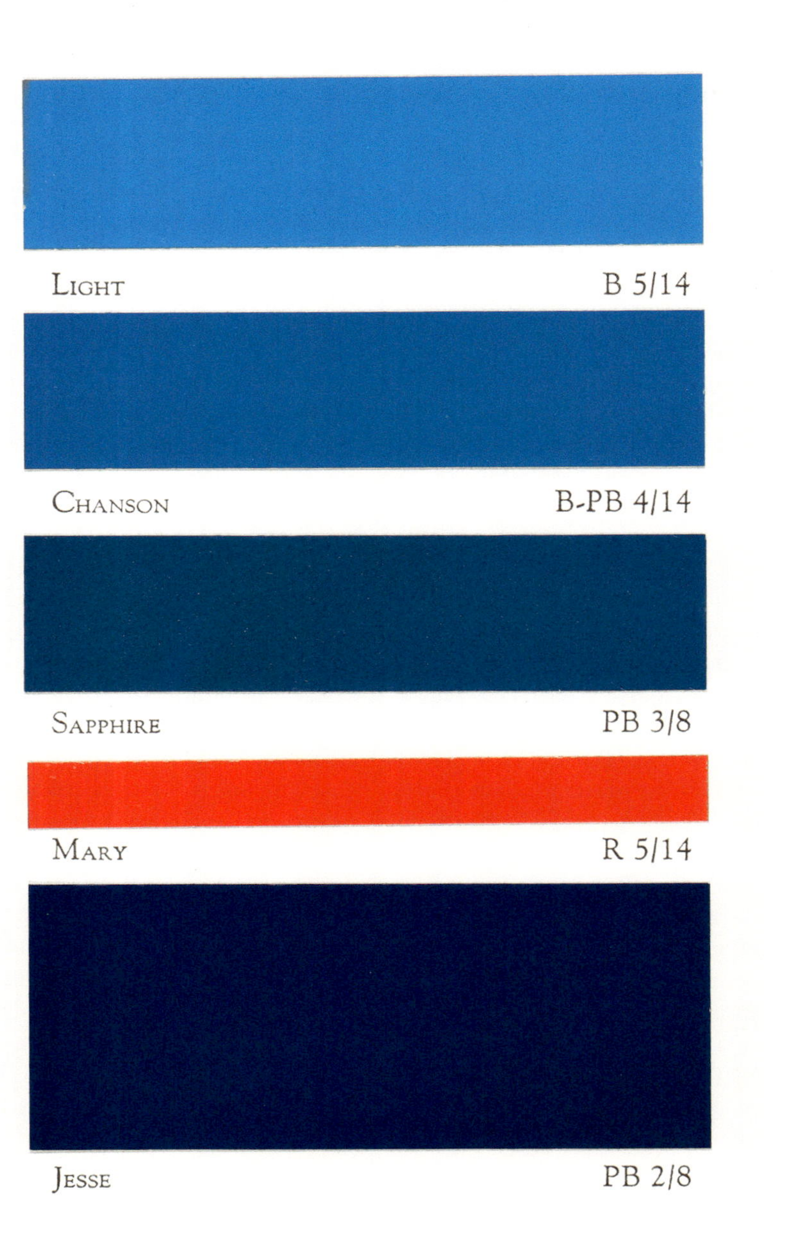

# ENGLISH, VICTORIAN

| | |
|---|---|
| LAVENDER | R-PR 5/6 |
| HELIOTROPE | R-PR 7/6 |
| WAISTCOAT | G-YG 4/6 |
| BLACK WALNUT | YR 3/2 |
| PLUSH | P 3/6 |

# FRENCH, LOUIS XV

| | |
|---|---|
| Mignonette | PB-P 6/8 |
| Watteau | B-PB 7/6 |
| Avril | GY 8/6 |
| L'amour | R 8/10 |
| Pouf du Vent | P-RP 8/4 |

# FRENCH, LOUIS XVI

Le Grec — R-YR 5/10

L'argent

Faun — Y-RY 8/2

Violette — P 5/6

Allure — B-PB 9/2

# CHINESE, BUDDHIST

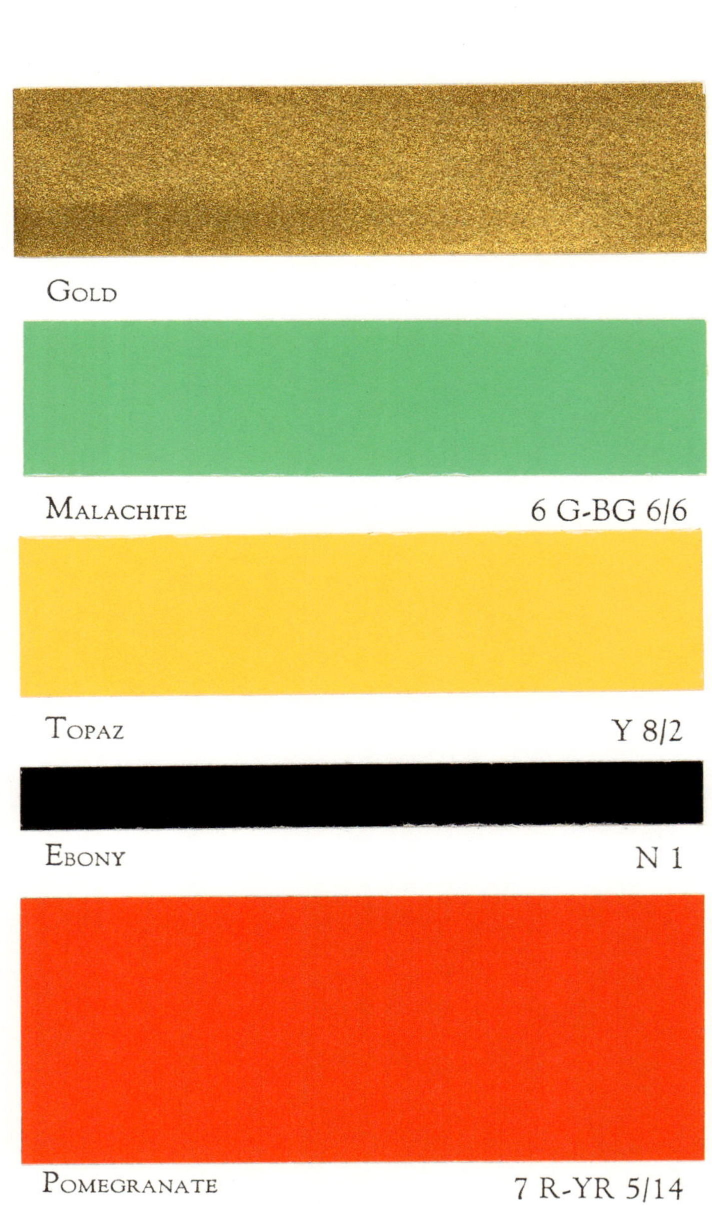

# INDIAN

Krishna PB-P 2/6

Elephant RP-R 8/8

Dhāk Y 8/12

Flame R 5/14

Jade G 6/10

# SPANISH, VELASQUEZ

| | |
|---|---|
| Imperial | RP-R 3/8 |
| Ethiopian | Y-RY 3/2 |
| Infanta | 8 R-YR 5/10 |
| Gold | Y-RY 6/10 |
| Pearl | YR-Y 9/2 |

# SPANISH, EL GRECO

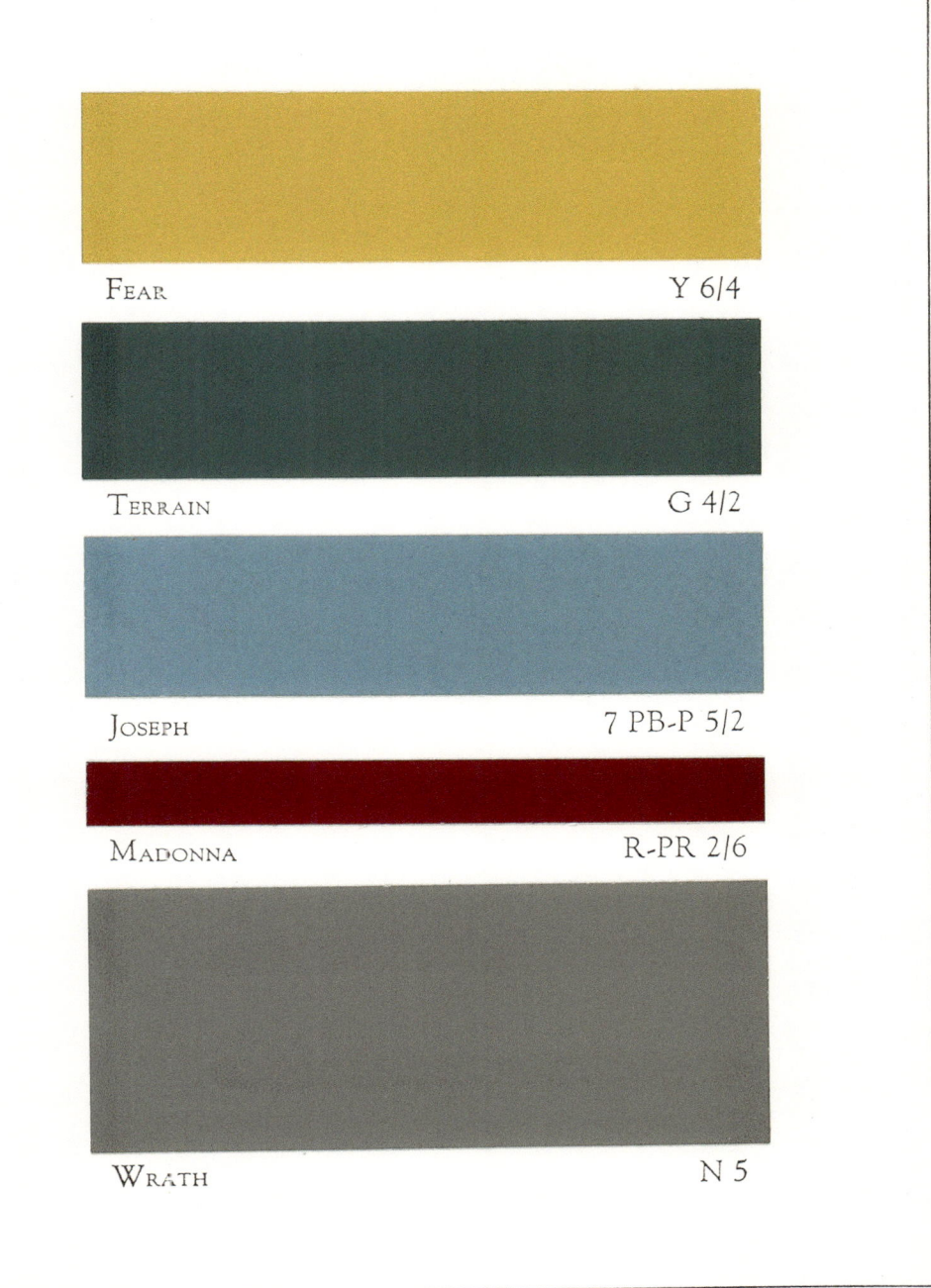

Fear Y 6/4

Terrain G 4/2

Joseph 7 PB-P 5/2

Madonna R-PR 2/6

Wrath N 5

# VAN GOGH

| | |
|---|---|
| Electric | BG-B 6/12 |
| Sunflower | Y 8/6 |
| Ciel | PB 6/10 |
| Marigold | R-YR 6/10 |
| Cobalt | PB 3/12 |

# GAUGUIN

| | |
|---|---|
| Amethyst | P 4/2 |
| Mid-night | P 3/2 |
| Leaf | GY 7/10 |
| Breadfruit | Y 5/4 |
| Carnation | RP 7/12 |

## Aloys John Maerz (1885–1972), Morris Rea Paul (1895–1970)

# A DICTIONARY OF COLOR

*19 plates, 29.5 x 21.5 cm | 11⅝ x 8½ in., New York, 1950*
*Sussex, collection of the author*

The *Dictionary of Color* was an unprecedented effort to gather, codify and visually represent colour names in the English language. It was perhaps the most ambitious book on colour to be published in the interwar years, when the first edition appeared in 1930, and it was followed 20 years later by a second edition, which is the one presented here. The book is hugely impressive in the scope of its research, its graphic design and the quality of its colour plates, and it is fast becoming one of the most desirable and collectable of all 20th-century books on the subject. The compilers of the colour names were two American scientists with strong international connections, Maerz being the Director of the American Color Research Laboratory while Paul worked as a colour consultant for several institutions. Their intention was to collate the most extensive list of colour names in the English language, ignoring numerical systems and instead looking to turn their research findings into a useful system of classification. Their sources included major U.S. and English paint and varnish manufacturers, the Textile Color Card Association of the United States, various French colour names used in English and names for certain natural and synthetic dyestuffs, all accompanied by a select choice of colour literature. As historical and current references, Robert Ridgway (pp. 288–297) and Albert Henry Munsell (pp. 380–389) were singled out for their importance.

Maerz and Paul structured their system by dividing colour into seven groups, following the prismatic spectrum: "red to orange, orange to yellow, yellow to green, green to blue-green, blue-green to blue, blue to red, and purple to red". Each group is represented by eight high-quality plates, successively showing gradations of colour from full strength towards white and black. The 56 tables depict 12 x 12 and 12 x 6 colour grids, adding up to a total of over 7,000 individual colours. The coloured grids each have an uncoloured opposite, marked with colour names as identified by Maerz and Paul printed in the small squares.

*A Dictionary of Color* is part of a long tradition of attempts to compile the myriad ways in which designers, manufacturers, artists and industries talk about colour and describe it. Conceptually, the book has an early ancestor in Richard Waller's "catalogue" of colours in four languages, from 1686, but ultimately the shimmering double-plates of the *Dictionary* reveal as much as anything how limited language is compared to the actual range of colours, for there are many empty white squares, where no name was found or given for a subtle variation of the tints or shades illustrated opposite.

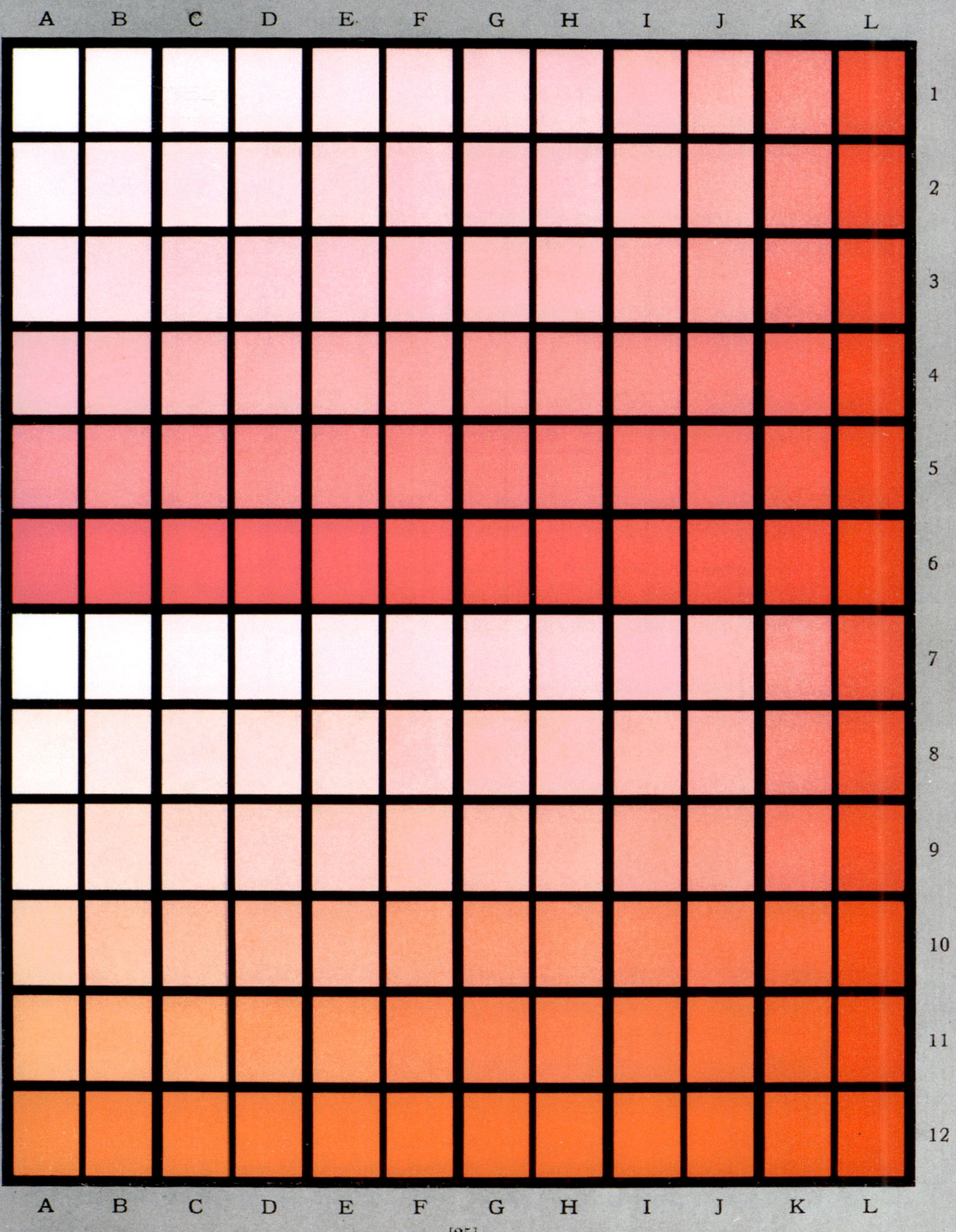

A B C D E F G H I J K L

1

2

3

4

5

6

7

8

9

10

11

12

A B C D E F G H I J K L

PLATE 12

| | A | B | C | D | E | F | G | H | I | J | K | L | |
|---|---|---|---|---|---|---|---|---|---|---|---|---|---|
| 1 | | | | | | | | | | | | Oil Y. | 1 |
| 2 | Moonmist | **FLAX** Pebble– Peanut+ | | | Sallow | | | | Hay | Absinthe Y. | | Chartreuse Gr. Olive Y | 2 |
| 3 | **ATMOS-PHERE** Mauve Blush | Lark **PARCH-MENT**+ | **OLD IVORY** | **CRASH** | | | | | | | Cloudy Amber | Pyrite Y | 3 |
| 4 | | Long Beach+ | Malacca | Tanaura | | | | | | | | Sulphine Y | 4 |
| 5 | **PEARL-BLUSH** Rosetan– | **FALLOW** | Manila | | India Buff | | | | | **LIGHT STONE** | | | 5 |
| 6 | **ALESAN FRENCH NUDE**– Café-au-lait+ | Tansan+ | Lariat | Honey-suckle | Walnut Taffy | | | Roe | Powdered Gold | **HONEY MIDDLE STONE**+ | Burnt+ Yellow-stone | Tennis | 6 |
| 7 | **BLUSH** Josephine Rose Blush 2 | **CORK** | Papyrus | **BRAN** | **CINNA-MON** | | **PABLO** | Macaroon | Desert | | Samovar | Burnished Gold | 7 |
| 8 | Formosa | | | | | | | | **TOPAZ** | | Spruce Y | Antique Gold | 8 |
| 9 | Paloma | Rose Am-ber | | | | | | Harvest | | | | Yucatan Cathay– Mexican+ French Y | 9 |
| 10 | Maya | | | | | Caramel | | Amber-glow | | Burma | Chinese Gold | Mast Colour | 10 |
| 11 | | | | | | | | | | | | **TAN** Leather Oriole | 11 |
| 12 | Talavera | Eldorado | Indian | Spa-Tan | | Sunstone | | | | | | Punjab | 12 |
| | A | B | C | D | E | F | G | H | I | J | K | L | |

[46]

## Wörterbuch der Farben

*A Dictionary of Color* war der nie dagewesene Versuch, englischsprachige Farbnamen zu sammeln, mit einem Code zu versehen und bildlich darzustellen. Vielleicht war es sogar das ehrgeizigste Farbenbuch der Zwischenkriegszeit, als es 1930 in erster Auflage erschien. Die zweite, hier vorgestellte Auflage, folgte zwanzig Jahre später. Außerordentlich beeindruckend sind der Rechercheumfang des Buches, seine grafische Gestaltung und die Qualität seiner Farbtafeln, die es schnell zu einem der begehrtesten und sammelwürdigsten aller sich mit dem Thema Farbe befassenden Bücher des 20. Jahrhunderts werden ließen. Die Sammler der Farbnamen waren zwei amerikanische Wissenschaftler mit sehr guten internationalen Be-

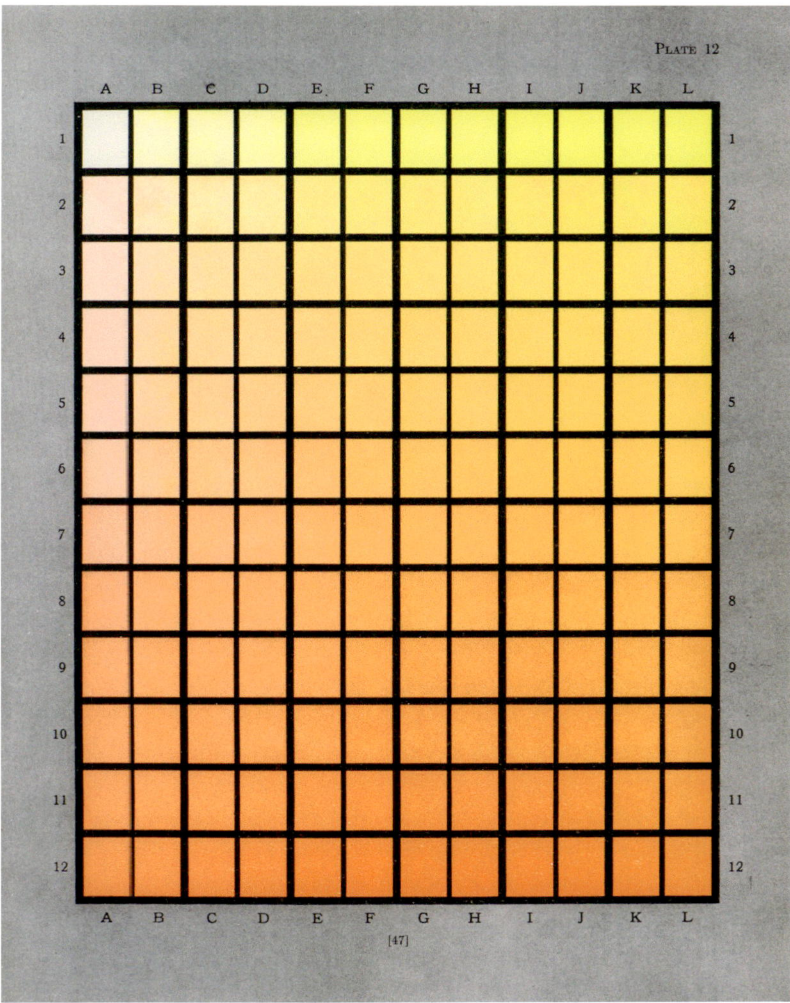


ziehungen. Maerz leitete das American Color Research Laboratory, Paul war als Farbberater für verschiedene Institutionen tätig. Gemeinsam wollten sie die umfangreichste Liste von Farbbezeichnungen in der englischen Sprache zusammenstellen, wobei sie numerische Systeme außer Acht ließen, um ihre Forschungsergebnisse stattdessen in ein hilfreiches Klassifikationssystem zu überführen. Zu ihren Quellen zählten große Farben- und Lackhersteller in England und den USA, die amerikanische Textile Color Card Association, verschiedene französische, auch im Englischen gebräuchliche Farbnamen, die Bezeichnungen für bestimmte natürliche und synthetische Farbstoffe sowie eine ausgewählte Reihe von Büchern aus der Farbliteratur. Als bedeutende historische und aktuelle Quellen wurden Robert Ridgway

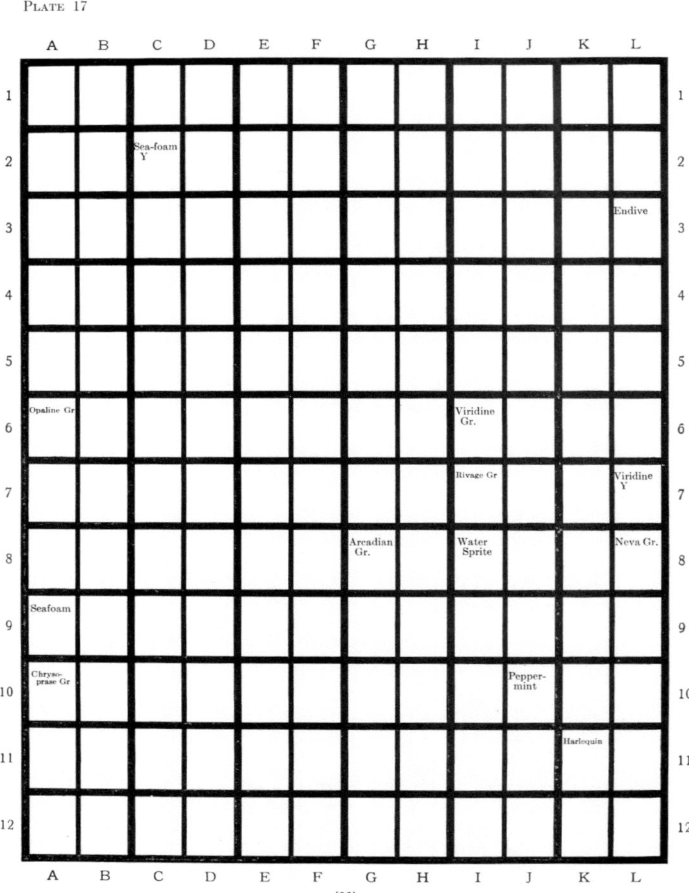


(S. 288–297) und Albert Henry Munsell (S. 380–389) hervorgehoben.

Maerz und Paul strukturierten ihr System, indem sie die Farben in Anlehnung an das prismatische Spektrum in sieben Gruppen einteilten: „Rot bis Orange, Orange bis Gelb, Gelb bis Grün, Grün bis Blaugrün, Blaugrün bis Blau, Blau bis Rot und Violett bis Rot“. Auf jeweils acht fortlaufenden Tafeln von höchster Qualität sind die Farbabstufungen zu sehen, die für jede Gruppe von Farbtönen in voller Leuchtkraft bis zu Weiß und Schwarz reichen. Aus den zwölf mal zwölf oder sechs mal zwölf Felder umfassenden Rastern der insgesamt 56 Tafeln ergeben sich mehr als siebentausend Einzelfarben. Jedem farbigen Raster wurde ein nicht koloriertes Raster gegenübergestellt, in dessen kleine Felder die von

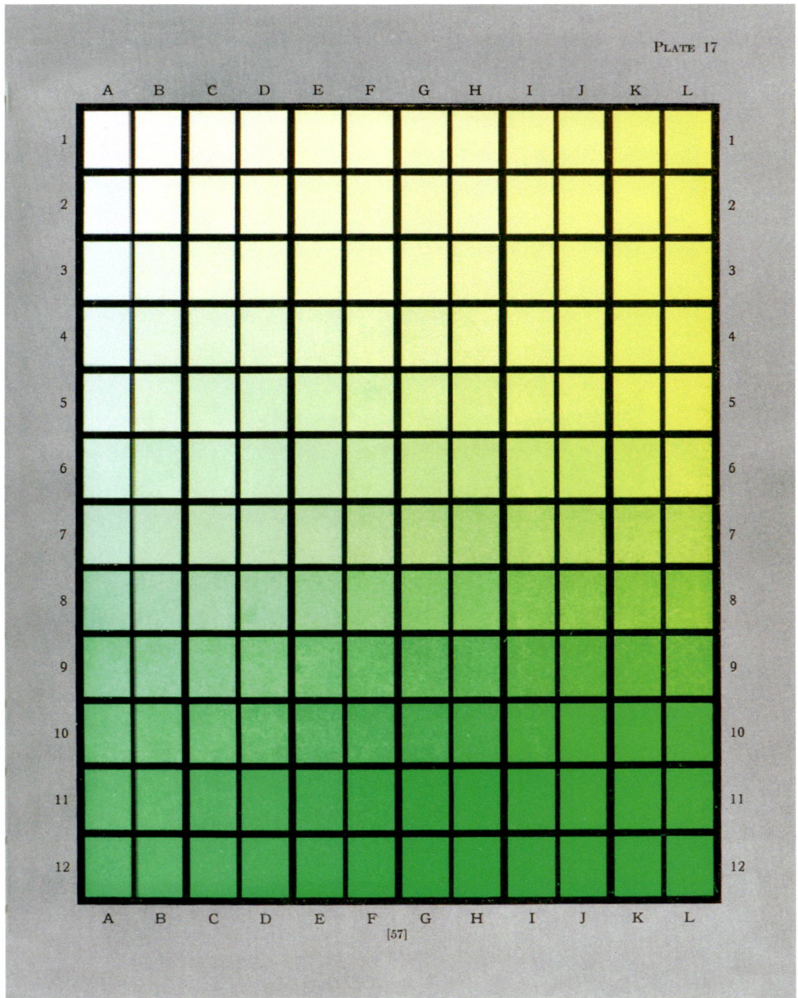


Maerz und Paul identifizierten Farbnamen eingetragen sind.

*A Dictionary of Color* ist Teil einer langen Tradition, die unzähligen Methoden zusammenzutragen, nach denen Gestalter, Produzenten, Künstler und Industrien über Farbe sprechen und sie beschreiben. Konzeptuell hat das Buch einen frühen Vorgänger in Richard Wallers „Katalog" der Farben in vier Sprachen aus dem Jahr 1686, doch letzten Endes offenbaren die schimmernden Doppeltafeln des *Dictionary* nur einmal mehr, wie begrenzt die Sprache im Vergleich zur tatsächlichen Bandbreite der Farben ist. So blieben viele weiße Felder leer, weil für die subtilen Variationen der daneben abgebildeten Farbtöne oder Schattierungen keine Namen gefunden oder vergeben werden konnten.

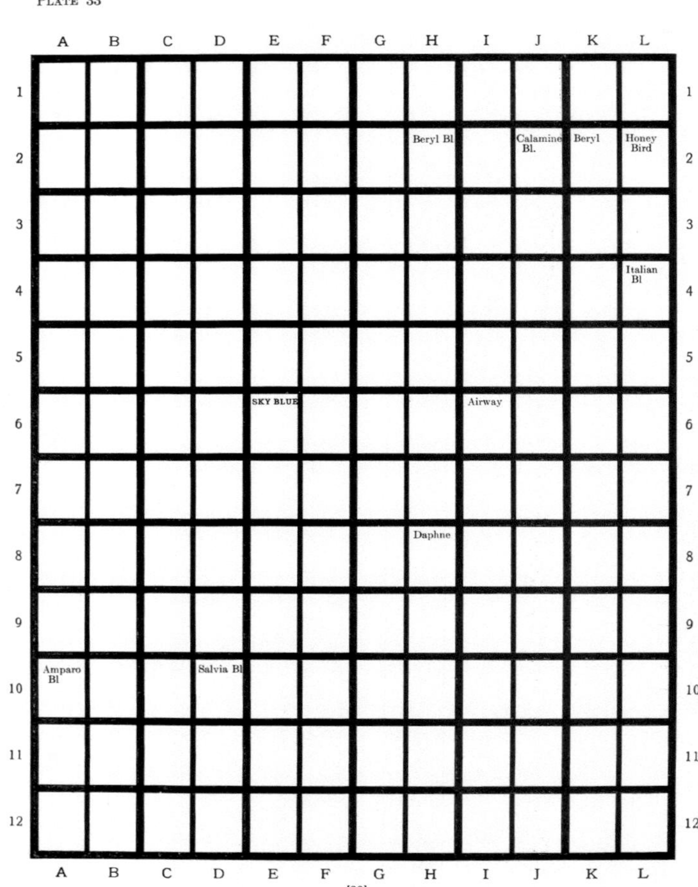


## Dictionnaire de la couleur

Ce «Dictionnaire de la couleur» tente pour la toute première fois de réunir, codifier et représenter visuellement les noms de couleur de la langue anglaise. C'est peut-être l'ouvrage de l'entre-deux-guerres le plus ambitieux sur le sujet lorsque paraît sa première édition en 1930, suivie, vingt ans plus tard, d'une seconde édition, présentée ici. Très impressionnant par l'envergure de ses études, sa conception graphique et la qualité de ses planches en couleurs, ce dictionnaire est en passe de devenir l'un des ouvrages les plus recherchés des collectionneurs parmi les livres du XXe siècle consacrés au sujet. Les compilateurs de ces noms de couleurs sont deux Américains entretenant de solides relations avec d'autres chercheurs du monde entier : Maerz est directeur de l'Ameri-

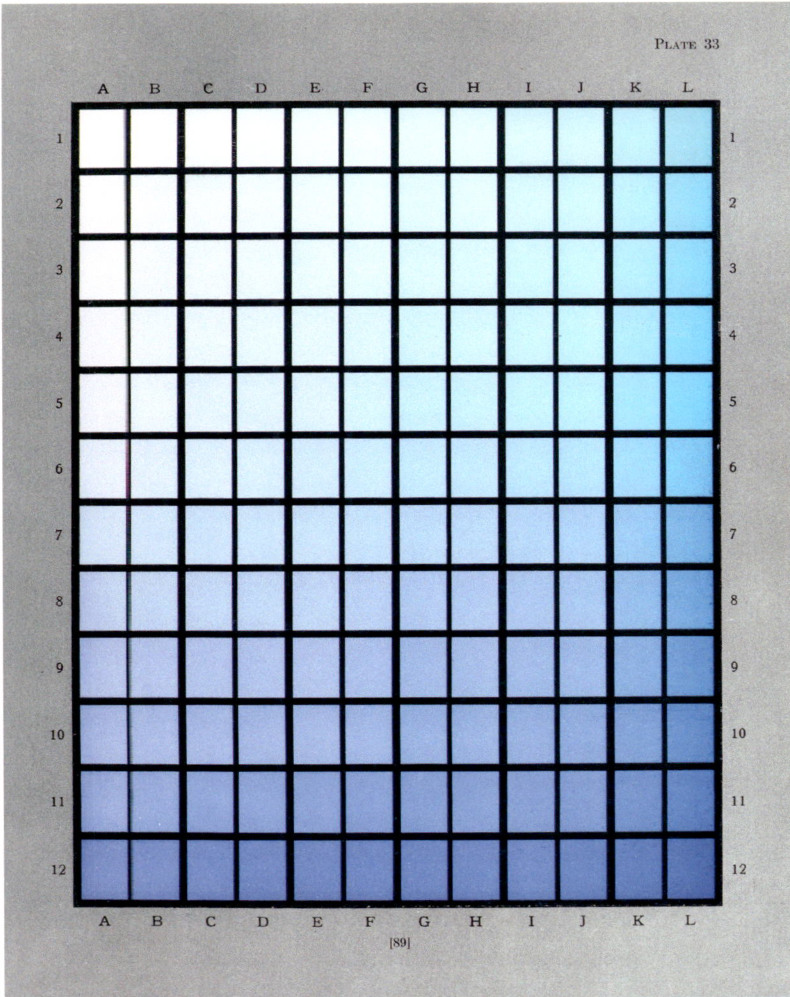


can Color Research Laboratory, Paul est coloriste, conseiller de plusieurs institutions. Leur projet consiste à établir la liste la plus exhaustive possible des noms de couleurs en anglais, sans tenir compte des systèmes numériques, et à organiser leurs résultats grâce à une méthode pratique de classification. Leurs sources sont les grands fabricants américains et anglais de peintures et de vernis et la Textile Color Card Association des États-Unis, et les auteurs adoptent les noms de couleurs français employés en anglais, ainsi que les dénominations de certains colorants naturels et synthétiques, le tout s'accompagnant d'une sélection d'ouvrages sur le sujet. Les auteurs soulignent l'importance historique et contemporaine des œuvres de Robert Ridgway (p. 288–297) et d'Albert Henry Munsell (p. 380–389).

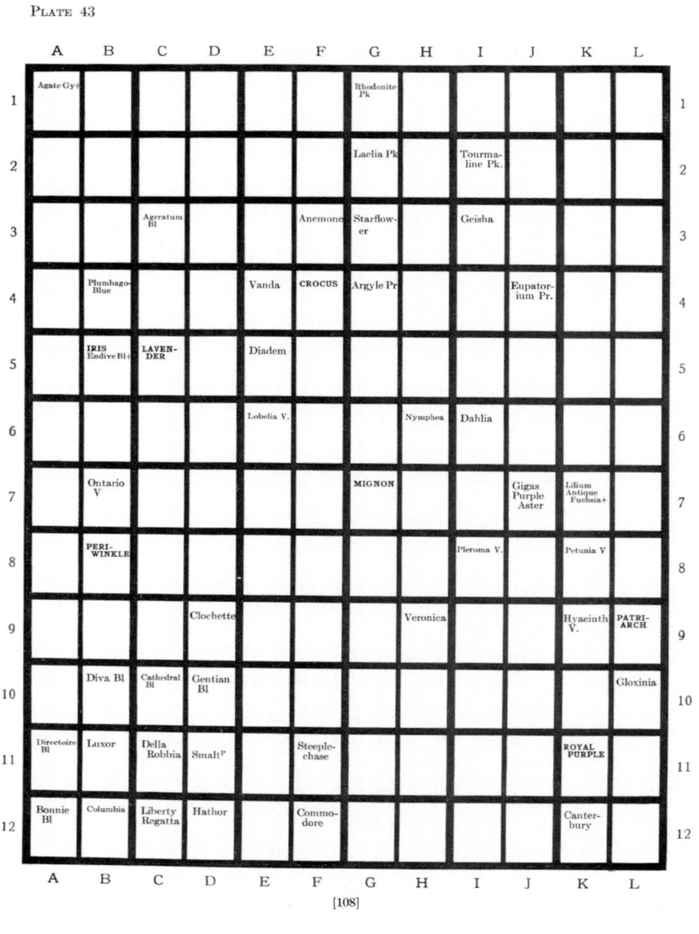

PLATE 43

| | A | B | C | D | E | F | G | H | I | J | K | L | |
|---|---|---|---|---|---|---|---|---|---|---|---|---|---|
| 1 | Agate Gy+ | | | | | | Rhodonite Pk | | | | | | 1 |
| 2 | | | | | | | Laelia Pk | | Tourmaline Pk. | | | | 2 |
| 3 | | | Ageratum Bl | | | Anemone | Starflower | | Geisha | | | | 3 |
| 4 | | Plumbago-Blue | | | Vanda | **CROCUS** | Argyle Pr | | | Eupatorium Pr. | | | 4 |
| 5 | | **IRIS** Endive Bl+ | **LAVENDER** | | Diadem | | | | | | | | 5 |
| 6 | | | | | Lobelia V. | | | Nymphea | Dahlia | | | | 6 |
| 7 | | Ontario V | | | | | **MIGNON** | | | Gigas Purple Aster | Lilium Antique Fuchsia+ | | 7 |
| 8 | | **PERIWINKLE** | | | | | | | Pleroma V. | | Petunia V | | 8 |
| 9 | | | | Clochette | | | | Veronica | | | Hyacinth V. | **PATRIARCH** | 9 |
| 10 | | Diva Bl | Cathedral Bl | Gentian Bl | | | | | | | | Gloxinia | 10 |
| 11 | Directoire Bl | Luxor | Della Robbia | Smalt$^{P}$ | | Steeplechase | | | | | **ROYAL PURPLE** | | 11 |
| 12 | Bonnie Bl | Columbia | Liberty Regatta | Hathor | | Commodore | | | | | Canterbury | | 12 |
| | A | B | C | D | E | F | G | H | I | J | K | L | |

[108]

Maerz et Paul construisent leur système en divisant les couleurs en sept groupes, suivant l'ordre des couleurs du spectre: «du rouge à l'orange, de l'orange au jaune, du jaune au vert, du vert au bleu-vert, du bleu-vert au bleu, du bleu au rouge et du violet au rouge». Chaque groupe est représenté par huit planches de grande qualité, montrant les gradations successives d'une couleur saturée, déclinée vers le blanc et vers le noir. Les 56 tableaux réunissent des grilles de 12 x 12 et 12 x 6 couleurs, pour un total de plus 7000 teintes. Chaque grille chromatique possède son équivalent sans couleurs, les noms des teintes identifiées par Maerz et Paul figurant dans les rectangles.

Le *Dictionary of Color* s'inscrit dans la lignée des tentatives de compilation des innombrables méthodes avec lesquelles dessinateurs,

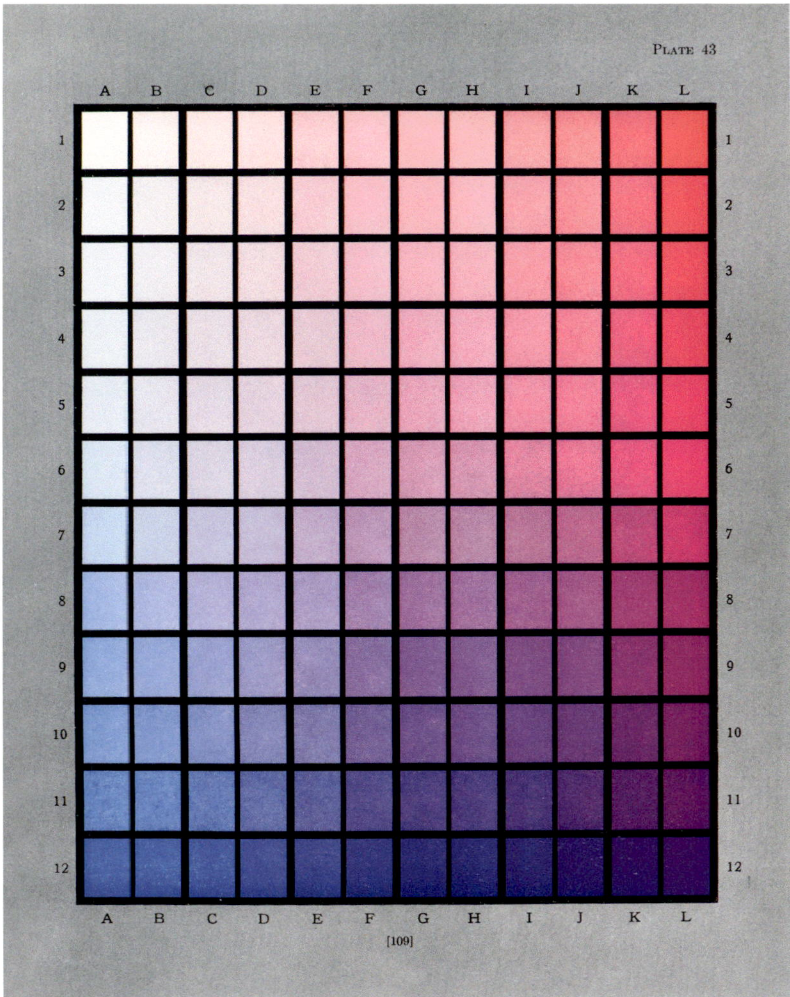


fabricants, peintres et autres corps de métiers qualifient et décrivent la couleur. Sur le plan conceptuel, cet ouvrage a pour précurseur le « catalogue » des couleurs de Richard Waller, publié en 1686 en quatre langues. En définitive, les doubles pages chatoyantes de ce dictionnaire démontrent à quel point les langues sont limitées pour décrire toute la gamme des couleurs, car de nombreux rectangles sont dépourvus de toute appellation susceptible de désigner la variation subtile d'une teinte ou d'une nuance présente dans la grille correspondant.

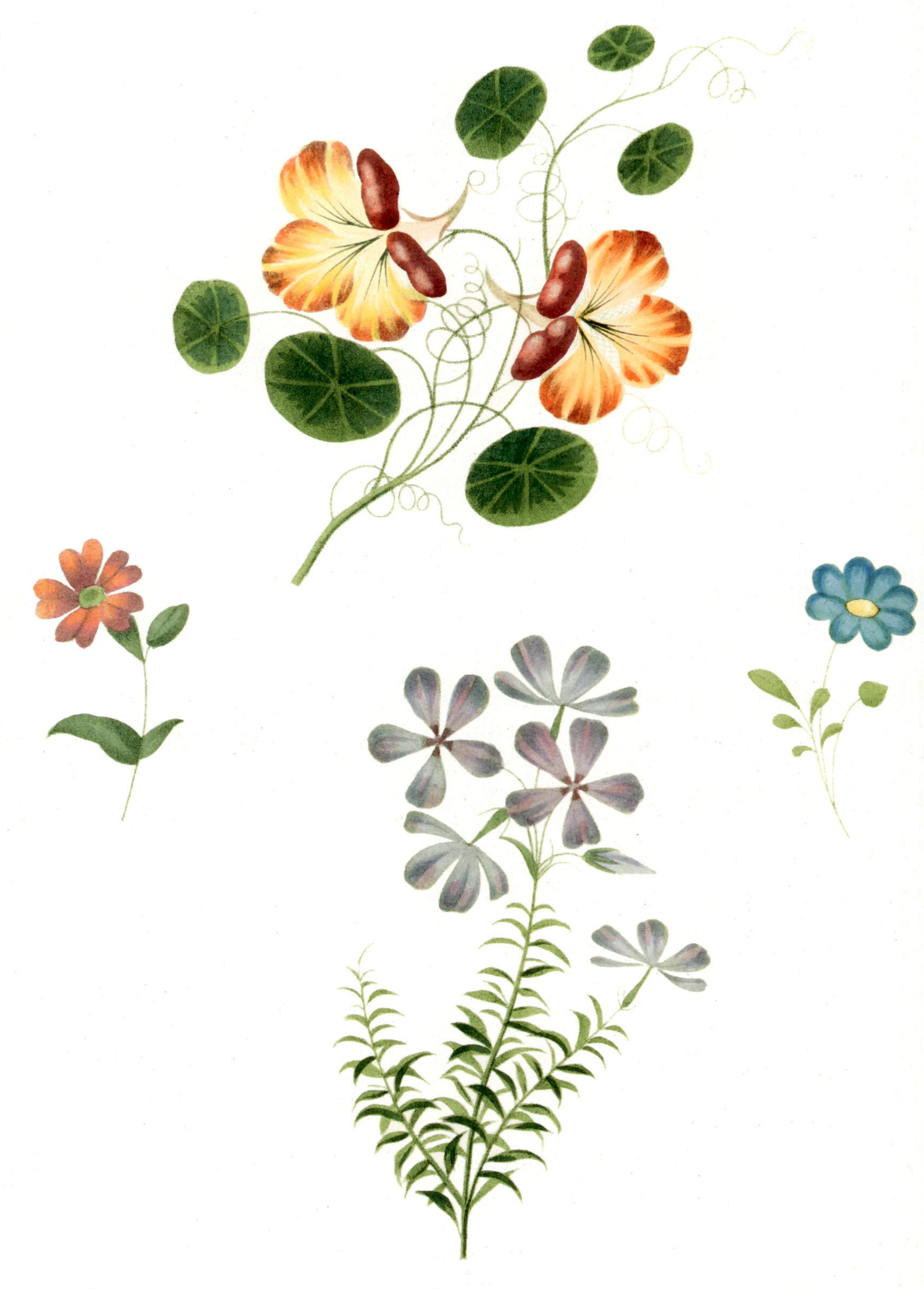

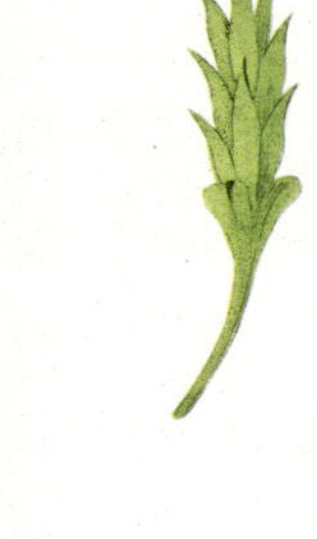

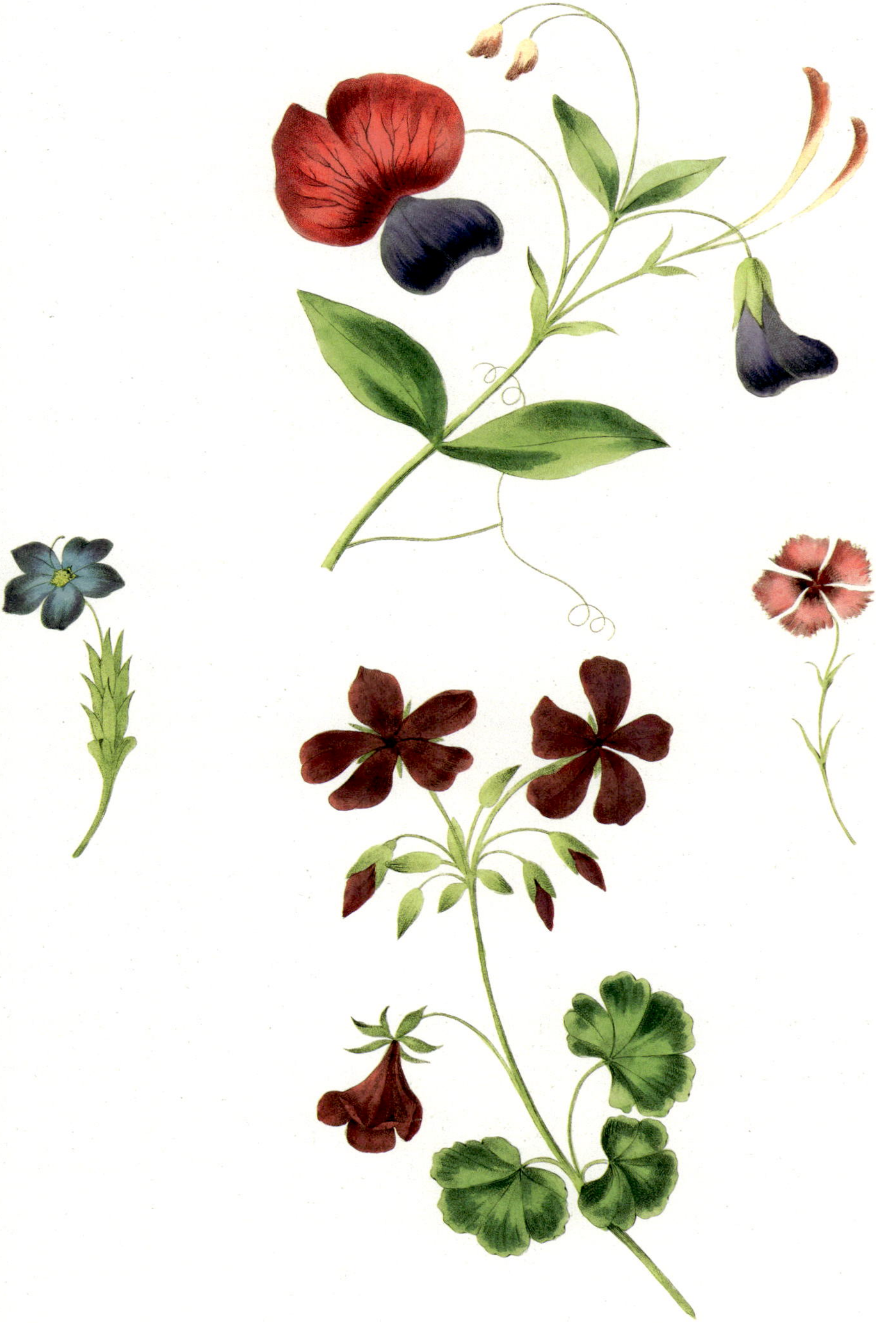

Painted by G. Brookshaw

Published by Longman Hurst, Rees, Orme & Brown & J. Lepard 108 Strand

A NEW TREATISE

ON

# FLOWER PAINTING,

OR

EVERY LADY HER OWN DRAWING MASTER:

CONTAINING

FAMILIAR AND EASY INSTRUCTIONS

FOR ACQUIRING

*A perfect Knowledge of Drawing Flowers with Accuracy and Taste:*

ALSO

COMPLETE DIRECTIONS FOR PRODUCING THE VARIOUS TINTS.

BY GEORGE BROOKSHAW, ESQ.

AUTHOR OF THE POMONA BRITANNICA.

LONDON:

PRINTED FOR LONGMAN, HURST, REES, ORME, AND BROWN, PATERNOSTER-ROW;
J. BOOTH, DUKE-STREET, PORTLAND-PLACE;
AND
J. LEPARD, 108, STRAND.

AUG. APPLEGATH AND HENRY MITTON, PRINTERS, 24, NELSON-SQUARE, SURREY-ROAD.
1816.

have looked like at the time when the book was published. Brookshaw's *New Treatise* contains a further 12 engraved and partly coloured plates showing plants and flowers in various stages of depiction.

The publishing history of this book and its author's career is somewhat complicated. Brookshaw originally worked as a cabinet-maker in the latter part of the 18th century, specialising in items with painted floral designs, before becoming a botanical illustrator and painting instructor. He published several further editions of this work soon after it first appeared, together with supplements showing more flower groups as well as illustrations of birds and groups of fruit. Brookshaw may have published earlier versions of it too, between 1797 and 1803, under the pseudonym "G. Brown", or else perhaps plagiarised from those works. His *Pomona Britannica*, published in 1817, is a masterpiece amongst 19th-century British illustrated books, featuring 90 superb aquatints of different fruits.

|  |  |  |
|---|---|---|
| *Apple Green.* | No. 1. | This tint is made by mixing gamboge and a very little Prussian blue. |
| *Pea Green.* | No. 2. | This tint is made with gamboge, and still more blue than in the last. |
| *Grass Green.* | No. 3. | This tint is made by mixing gamboge, and blue worked thicker. |
| *Dark Green.* | No. 4. | This tint is made by mixing gamboge, blue, and a little yellow oker. |
| *Darker Green.* | No. 5. | This tint is gamboge, more blue, and more yellow oker. |
| | No. 6. | This tint is the same as the last, with a little sap green in it. |
| *Sap Green.* | No. 7. | This tint is sap green alone. |
| | No. 8. | This tint is made with sap green and dark blue. |

| | | |
|---|---|---|
| *Blue.* | No. 1. | This tint is Prussian blue worked very thin with water. |
| | No. 2. | This tint is Prussian blue worked not so thin with water. |
| | No. 3. | This tint is Prussian blue worked thicker with more colour. |
| | No. 4. | This tint is Prussian blue its full colour. |
| *Pink.* | No. 1. | This tint is lake worked thin with water. |
| | No. 2. | This tint is lake worked thicker in colour. |
| | No. 3. | This tint is lake worked thicker than the last. |
| | No. 4. | This tint is clear lake worked its full colour. |

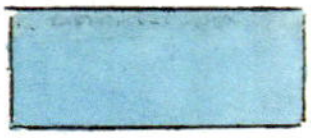

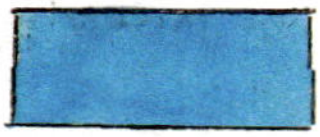

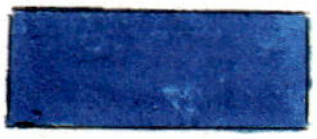

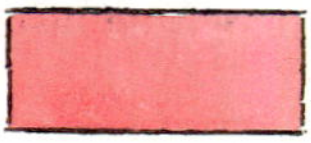

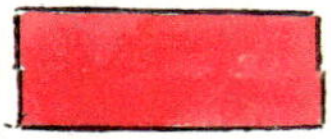

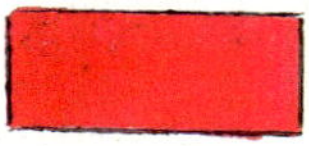

No. 1.

*Purples.*  This tint is lake and blue worked thin.

No. 2.

 This tint is the same as the above, only with more lake.

No. 3.

 This tint is lake and blue worked thicker than No. 1.

No. 4.

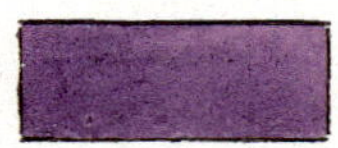 This tint is lake and blue, but more lake than No. 3.

No. 5.

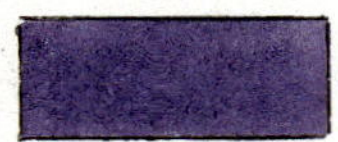 This tint is lake and blue worked stronger than No. 3.

No. 6.

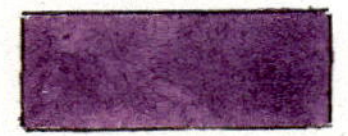 This tint is lake and blue, but more lake than No. 5.

No. 7.

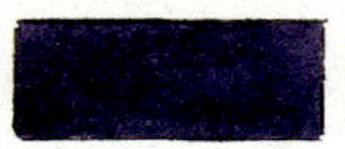 This tint is lake and blue worked dark.

No. 8.

 This tint is lake and blue, with more lake than No. 7.

No. 9.

 This tint is dark blue, glazed with lake twice over

No. 1.

*Red.*

This tint is vermillion worked thin.

No. 2.

This tint is vermillion worked stronger.

No. 3.

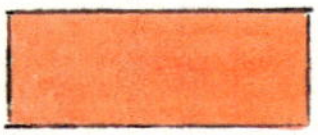

This tint is vermillion worked its full colour.

No. 4.

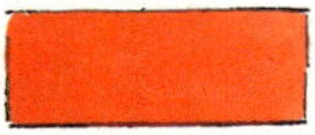

This tint is vermillion glazed over with lake.

No. 1.

*Crimson.*

This tint is vermillion and lake worked thin.

No. 2.

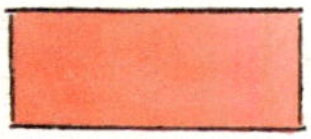

This tint is vermillion and lake worked stronger.

No. 3.

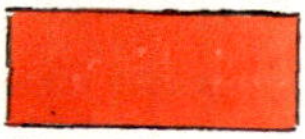

This tint is vermillion and lake worked still stronger.

No. 4.

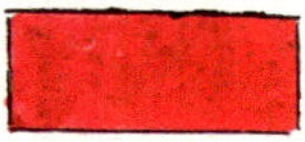

This tint is lake worked its full colour.

## Neue Abhandlung über Blumenmalerei; oder Jede Dame ihre eigene Zeichenlehrerin

Mit Beginn des 19. Jahrhunderts hatte die Aquarellmalerei unter Amateurkünstlern eine solche Beliebtheit erreicht, dass sie oft zur informellen Ausbildung junger Frauen gehörte. Mit Motiven aus der Natur konnte sie zahlreiche Formen annehmen – von malerischen Landschaften unweit des eigenen Zuhauses über die Dokumentation von Reisen in andere Länder (sofern man die Gelegenheit dazu hatte) bis hin zum Kopieren der Natur in kleinerem Maßstab, etwa in der Abbildung von Pflanzen. Wenngleich die Grenzen zwischen Blumenmalerei und formaler botanischer Illustration durchlässig sein konnten, war das Blumenmalen im Allgemeinen oft weiblich konnotiert und wurde zum Teil auch genutzt, um den Handlungs- und Bewegungsfreiraum von Frauen einzuschränken. Während Mary Gartside (um 1755–1819) ihre Handbücher für Blumenmalerei auf eine auch abstrakte und theoretische Ebene hob, verharrte Brookshaws *New Treatise on Flower Painting* fest im Genre der instruktiven Malhandbücher für Frauen und konzentrierte sich hauptsächlich auf die Technik. Das Buch bot „vertraute und einfache Anweisungen, um vollkommene Kenntnisse des genauen und geschmackvollen Blumenzeichnens zu erwerben". Jede „Dame" (wie es auf der Titelseite hieß) war sehr wahrscheinlich stolze Besitzerin eines Malkastens, der mit einer Auswahl vorgefertigter Farbblöcke bestückt war. Ihnen lieferte Brookshaws Handbuch „vollständige Anleitungen für die Herstellung der verschiedenen Farbtöne", die zusammen mit diesen praktischen und neuerdings verfügbaren Künstlermaterialien zu verwenden waren. In einer mehrseitigen Liste wurde neben jedem der über fünfzig handgemalten Farbmuster in wenigen Worten erklärt, wie diese Farbe mit Wasser anzurühren oder aus mehreren Farben anzumischen war. Zusammen führen die Muster in einer lebhaften Momentaufnahme vor Augen, wie diese speziellen Wasserfarbtöne wohl aussahen, als das Buch erschien. Brookshaws *New Treatise* enthält in jeweils doppelter Ausführung zwölf weitere, zum Teil kolorierte Kupfertafeln von Blättern, Blumen und Blütenzweigen in verschiedenen Stadien ihrer Darstellung.

Die Publikationsgeschichte dieses Buches und die Karriere seines Autors sind etwas verschlungen, da Brookshaw im ausgehenden 18. Jahrhundert zunächst als Möbeltischler tätig war, der sich auf Objekte mit Blumendekor spezialisiert hatte, bevor er Pflanzenillustrator und Mallehrer wurde. Kurz nach der Erstauflage veröffentlichte er weitere Ausgaben des Buches jeweils mit Nachträgen, die zusätzliche Blumengruppen und Illustrationen von Vögeln und Früchten umfassten. Möglicherweise brachte er zwischen 1797 und 1803 unter dem Pseudonym „G. Brown" auch frühere Ausgaben auf den Markt oder bediente sich als Plagiator aus diesen Werken. Sein 1817 erschienenes *Pomona Britannica* ist mit neunzig herausragenden Früchtetafeln in Aquatintatechnik ein Meisterwerk unter den britischen Bildbänden des 19. Jahrhunderts.

No. 1.

*Yellow.*

This tint is gamboge worked thin with water.

No. 2.

This tint is gamboge worked strong.

No. 1.

*Orange Tint.*

This tint is gamboge with very little vermillion to it.

No. 2.

This tint is gamboge and more vermillion.

No. 3.

This tint is the next degree of darker shade to the last; and is gamboge, vermillion, and burnt terra de siena.

No. 4.

This is the next tint darker: this is burnt terra de siena.

No. 1.

*Browns.*

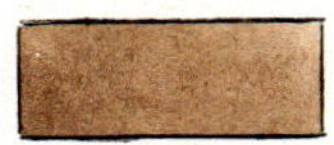

This tint is burnt umber worked thin with water.

No. 2.

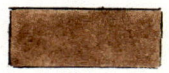

This tint is burnt umber, worked thicker than No. 1.

No. 3.

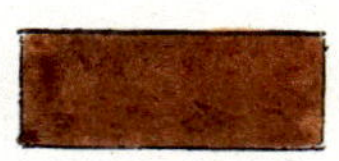

This is burnt umber worked strong.

No. 4.

This is burnt umber, glazed over with burnt terra de siena, and is sometimes required to strengthen the darkest orange tints.

No. 1.

*Shadow for White.*

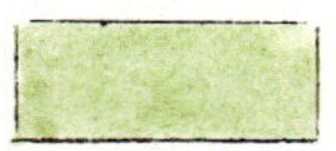

This tint is blue and yellow oker very faint.

No. 2.

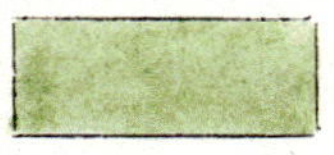

This tint is blue and yellow oker a degree stronger.

No. 3.

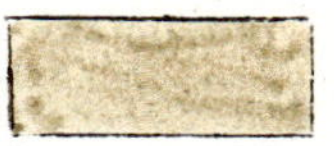

This tint is blue and yellow oker, with a faint tinge of burnt umber.

No. 4.

This tint is blue, burnt umber, and raw terra de siena.

## Nouveau traité de peinture florale, que toute dame doit pouvoir maîtriser

Au début du XIXe siècle, la peinture à l'aquarelle est devenue extrêmement populaire parmi les artistes amateurs et fait généralement partie de l'éducation informelle reçue par les jeunes femmes. Avec la nature pour sujet, cette activité prend de multiples formes, qu'il s'agisse de saisir des paysages près de chez soi, de rendre compte de voyages dans d'autres contrées (pour qui a l'occasion de voyager), ou encore de copier ce qu'offre la nature à plus petite échelle, comme avec la peinture de végétaux. Même si la frontière entre la peinture florale et l'illustration botanique à proprement parler peut être poreuse, peindre des fleurs est bien souvent considéré comme l'apanage des femmes, voire un moyen de restreindre leur sphère d'action et de mouvement. Alors que Mary Gartside (vers 1755–1819) avait poussé plus loin l'abstraction et la théorie, le « Nouveau traité de peinture florale » de Brookshaw ne déroge pas au genre codifié du manuel pédagogique pour femmes et fait la part belle à la technique. Le livre offre des « instructions courantes et faciles pour l'acquisition d'un parfait savoir-faire afin de dessiner des fleurs avec goût et précision ». Toute « dame », comme l'indique le titre, se doit de posséder à l'époque une boîte de couleurs garnie d'un choix de tablettes d'aquarelle industrielle. L'ouvrage donne « toutes les indications pour produire différentes teintes », destinées à être mises en application à l'aide de ce matériel de beaux-arts nouveau et commode. Les indications sont assorties de listes d'échantillons de plus de 50 teintes, toutes peintes à la main, avec des instructions simples pour les créer en mélangeant les couleurs. Les échantillons choisis nous renseignent de façon frappante sur l'aspect de ces teintes d'aquarelle à l'époque de la publication de ce « Nouveau traité ». L'ouvrage de Brookshaw contient en outre 12 gravures partiellement colorées figurant des plantes et des fleurs à plusieurs étapes de leur représentation.

Retracer l'historique de l'ouvrage et la carrière de son auteur s'avère compliqué. À la fin du XVIIIe siècle, Brookshaw travaille comme ébéniste spécialisé dans les motifs floraux, avant de devenir illustrateur botanique et professeur de peinture. Plusieurs éditions de cet ouvrage verront le jour peu après la première publication, ainsi que des fascicules présentant des illustrations d'oiseaux et de groupes de fleurs et de fruits. Brookshaw a peut-être publié des versions préalables entre 1797 et 1803, sous le pseudonyme de G. Brown, ou encore plagié ces travaux antérieurs. Quoi qu'il en soit, son *Pomona Britannica*, recueil de 90 splendides aquatintes de différents fruits publié en 1817, figure parmi les chefs-d'œuvre de l'illustration britannique du XIXe siècle.

No. 1.

*Yellow Oker.* This tint is yellow oker worked thin.

No. 2.

This tint is yellow oker worked strong.

No. 1.

*Raw terra de Siena.* This tint is raw terra de siena worked thin.

No. 2.

This tint is raw terra de siena worked strong.

No. 1.

*Burnt terra de Siena.* This tint is burnt terra de siena worked thin.

No. 2.

This tint is burnt terra de siena worked strong.

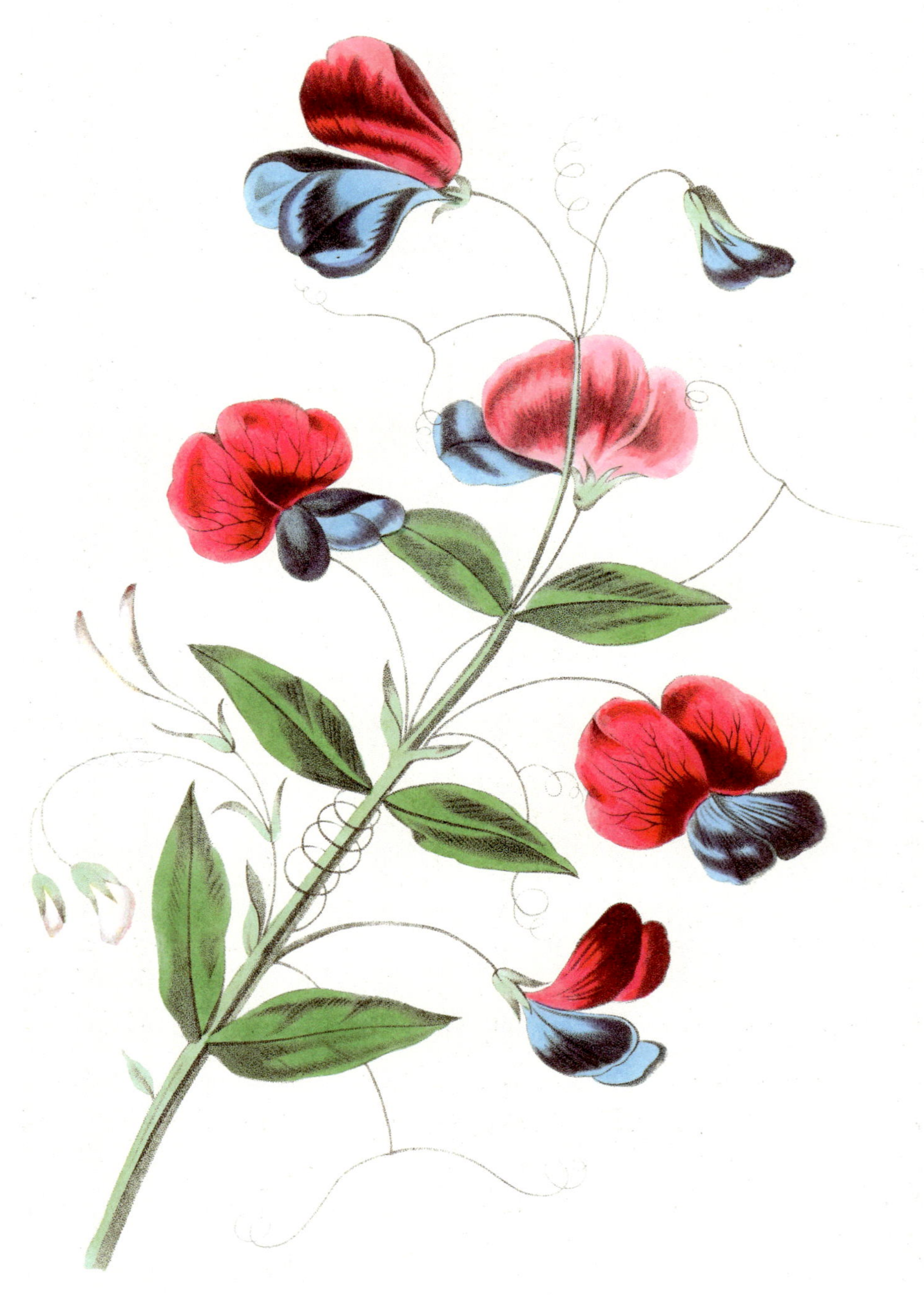

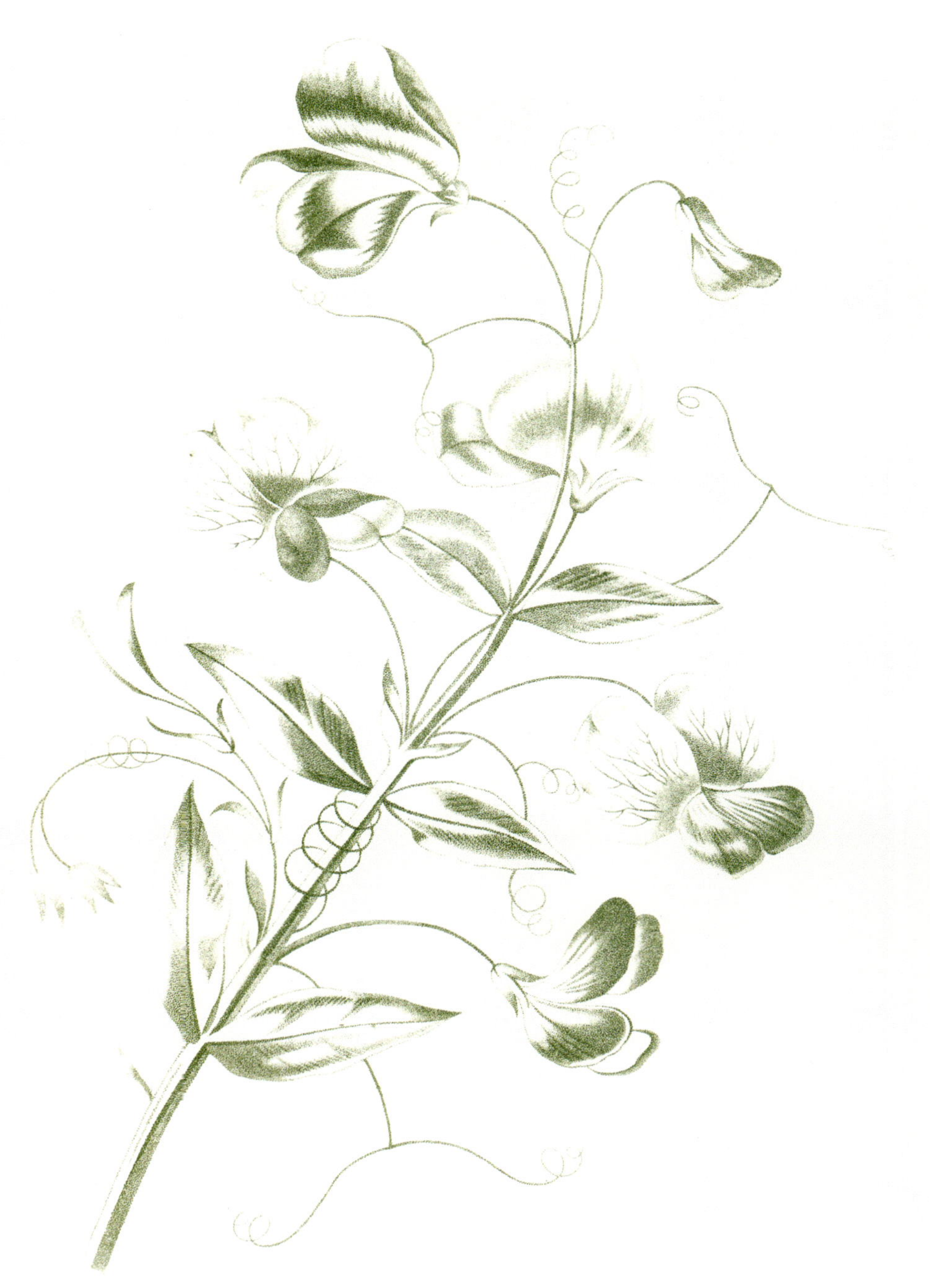

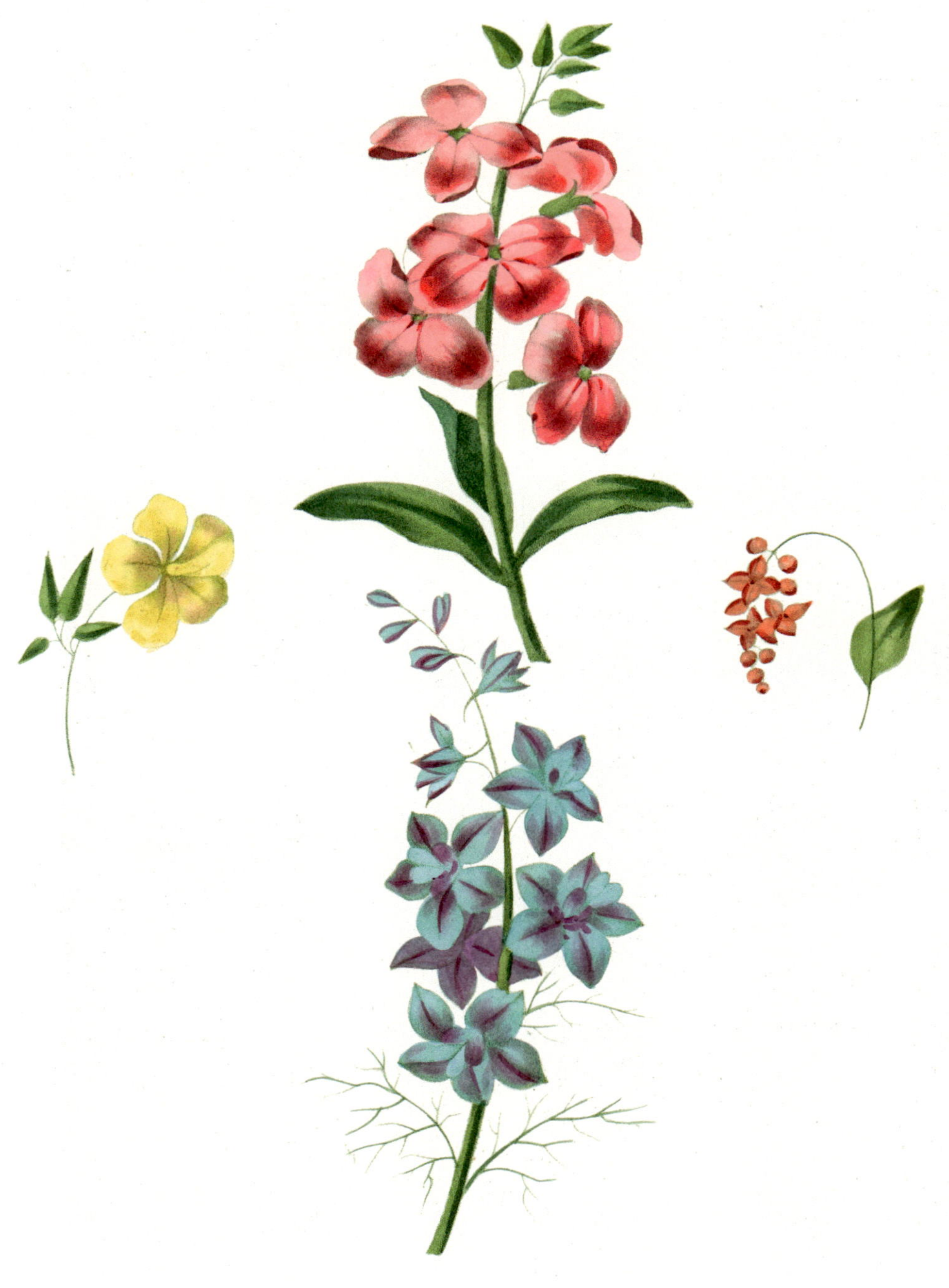

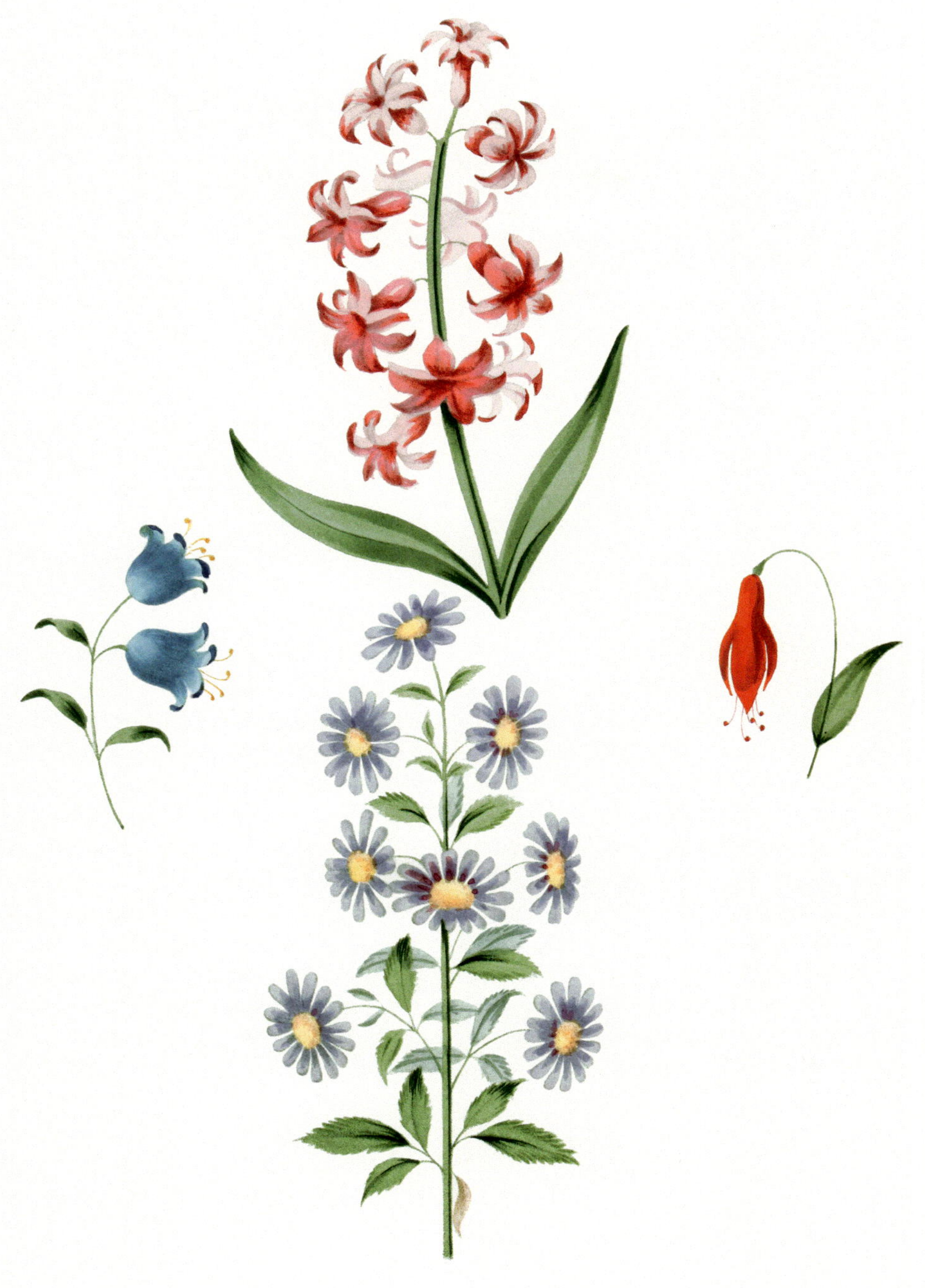

## George Barnard (*c.* 1807–*c.* 1890)

# THE THEORY AND PRACTICE OF LANDSCAPE PAINTING IN WATER-COLOURS

*9 plates, 27 x 18.1 cm | 10 ⅝ x 7 ⅛ in., London, 1885*
*Los Angeles, Getty Research Institute*

The British landscape artist and drawing teacher George Barnard was active at a time when great technical innovations were under way, which variously helped to make day-to-day life more colourful than before, from the goods that could now be brought in and quickly produced by means of steam power to the discovery and large-scale manufacture of aniline dyes. Barnard had a great interest in science and was strongly influenced by the work of George Field, whose pigments he used, as well as that of others working with colour such as David Brewster, Goethe and Chevreul.

*The Theory and Practice of Landscape Painting in Water-Colours* was first published in parts and then in book form, with a first edition in 1855 (the 1885 edition is reproduced here). It was intended as a comprehensive guidebook for amateur artists as well as students of art and is a substantial work, including 26 chromolithographs printed using the "Leighton Brothers' Chromatic Process" in addition to dozens of small engravings intercut within the text. As with David Cox's *Series of Progressive Lessons*, some of the plates and engravings illustrate the different stages of picture composition and are based on Barnard's own artwork.

The most interesting plates though are those which illustrate basic colour theory and Barnard's own colour concepts as applied to painting and material colour. His designs are simple and effective, and make good use of the possibilities provided by lithographic printing and the book's large format. His main colour order diagram is a vertically stretched rhombus or diamond shape, in which are arranged "twenty-five of the most useful pigments", each shown in a lighter and darker version. Barnard also included a number of plates that illustrate his interpretation of simultaneous colour contrast, among them a pair that allows readers

THE PRISMATIC SPECTRUM.

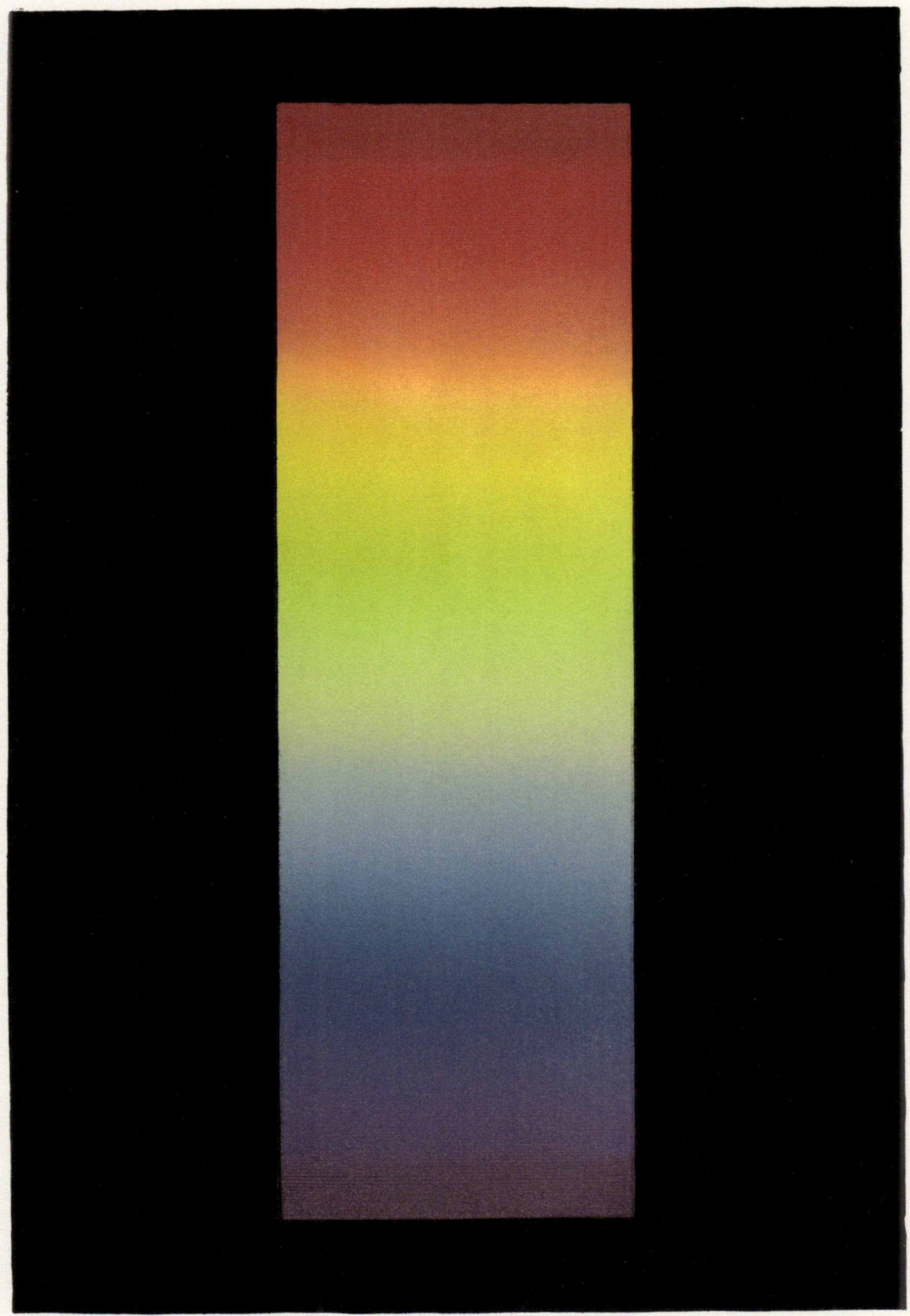

LEIGHTON. BROS.

PLATE 2.

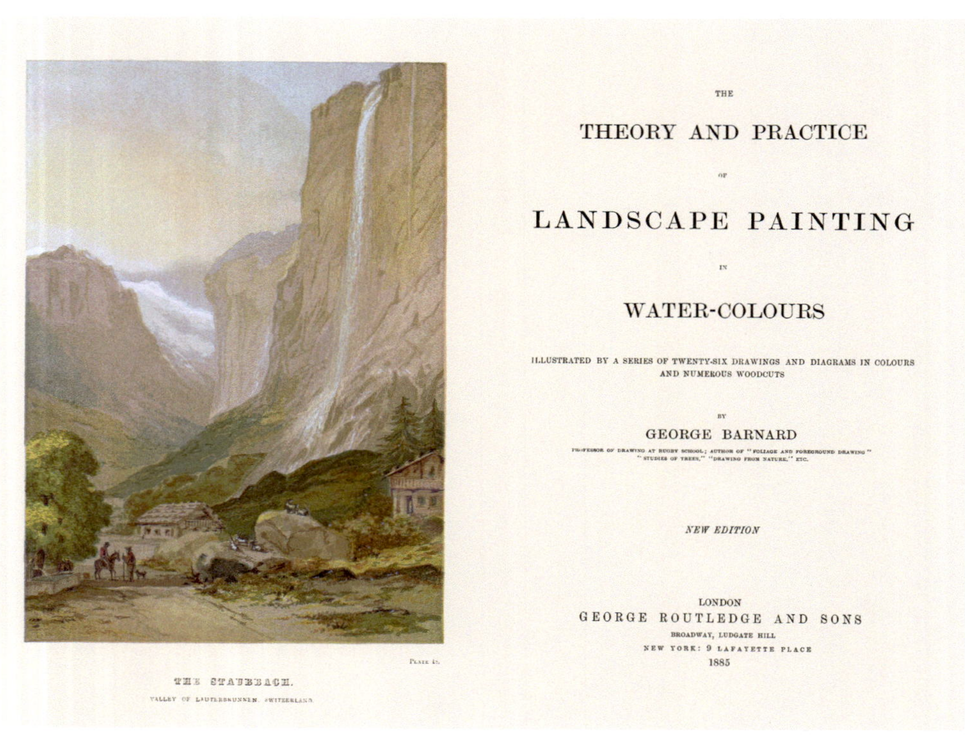

THE STAUBBACH.

VALLEY OF LAUTERBRUNNEN, SWITZERLAND.

THE

THEORY AND PRACTICE

OF

LANDSCAPE PAINTING

IN

WATER-COLOURS

ILLUSTRATED BY A SERIES OF TWENTY-SIX DRAWINGS AND DIAGRAMS IN COLOURS
AND NUMEROUS WOODCUTS

BY

GEORGE BARNARD

PROFESSOR OF DRAWING AT RUGBY SCHOOL; AUTHOR OF "FOLIAGE AND FOREGROUND DRAWING"
"STUDIES OF TREES," "DRAWING FROM NATURE," ETC.

*NEW EDITION*

LONDON
GEORGE ROUTLEDGE AND SONS
BROADWAY, LUDGATE HILL
NEW YORK: 9 LAFAYETTE PLACE
1885

to carry out simple optical experiments themselves. A recently discovered sketchbook that has been attributed to Barnard (pp. 47–49) confirms his systematic working methods, such as the meticulous manner in which he recorded colours and pigments in relation to compositions. The sketchbook also includes a draft version for plate 26, entitled "Contrasts of Colour", which features rough blot shapes to illustrate colour contrasts and harmonies. Conceptually, these bear a resemblance to Mary Gartside's blots from 1805, and there is certainly a chance that Barnard knew her *Essay on Light and Shade* (pp. 164–175). His book went into several new and enlarged editions up until 1885.

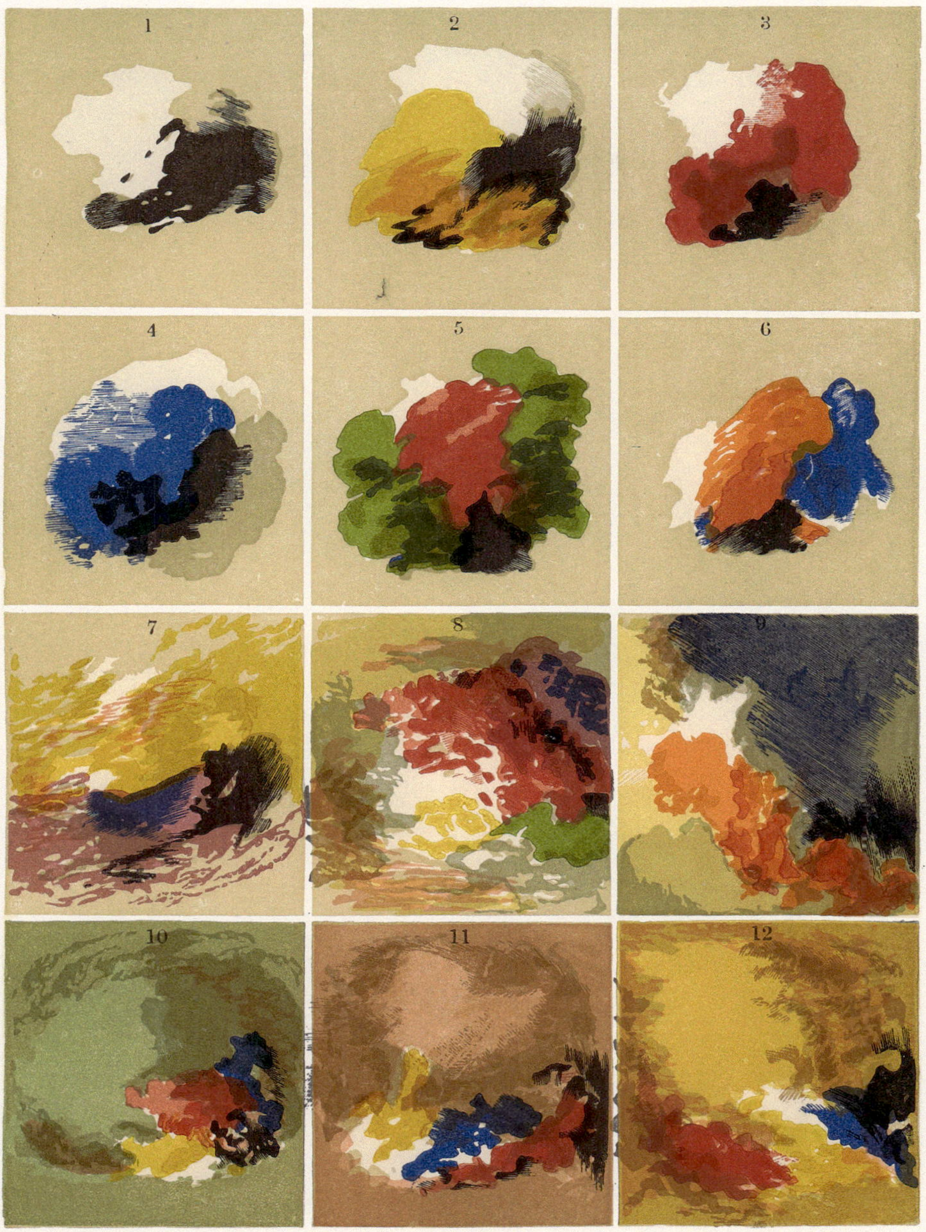


LEIGHTON, BROS.

PLATE 23.

CONTRASTS OF COLOUR.

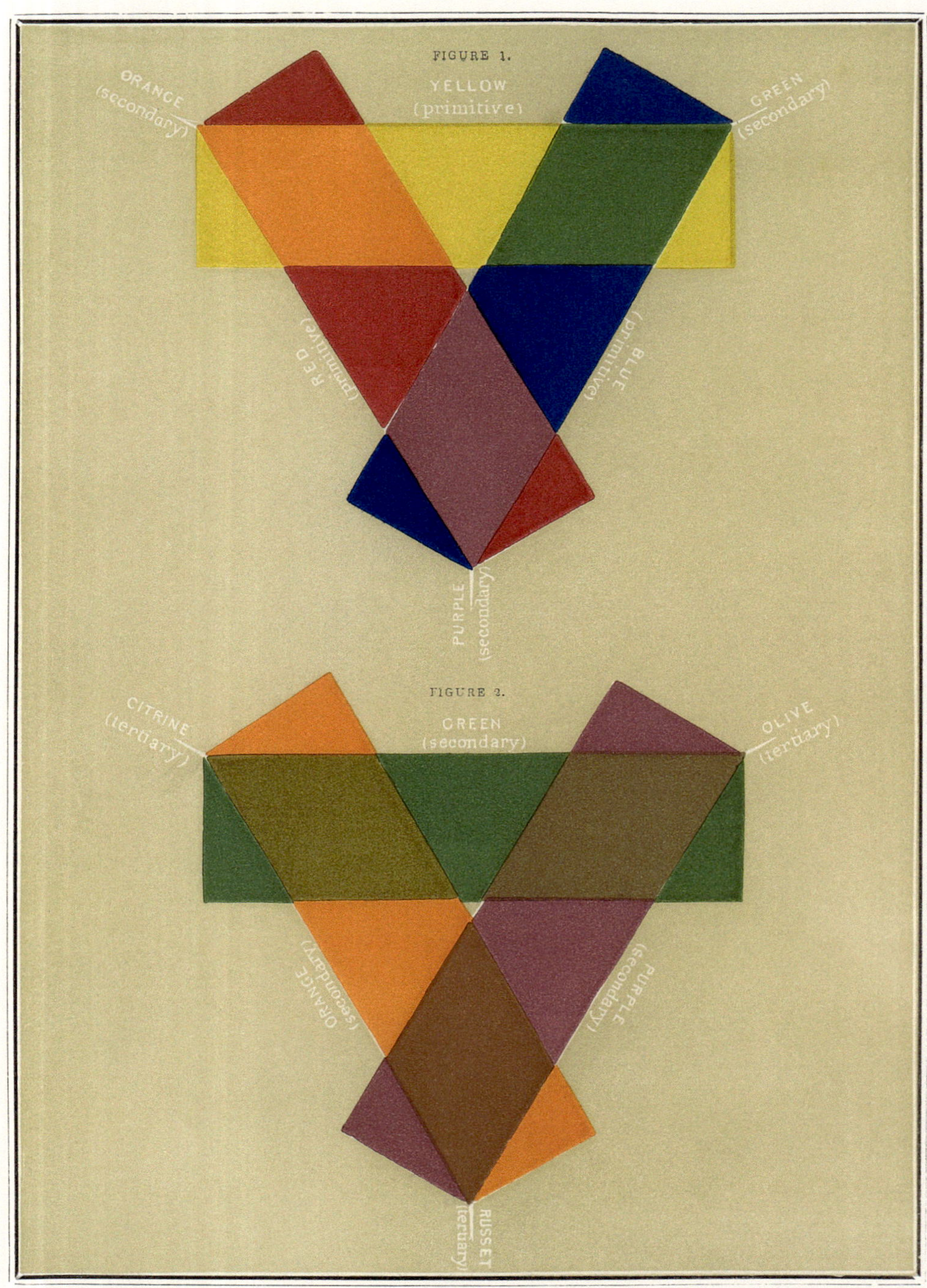
FIGURE 1.
ORANGE (secondary)
YELLOW (primitive)
GREEN (secondary)
RED (primitive)
BLUE (primitive)
PURPLE (secondary)
FIGURE 2.
CITRINE (tertiary)
GREEN (secondary)
OLIVE (tertiary)
ORANGE (secondary)
PURPLE (secondary)
RUSSET (tertiary)

## Theorie und Praxis der Landschaftsmalerei mit Wasserfarben

Der britische Landschaftsmaler und Zeichenlehrer George Barnard war zu einer Zeit tätig, in der große technische Neuerungen den Alltag auf unterschiedliche Weise bunter machten als zuvor – von den Waren, die jetzt importiert oder mithilfe der Dampfkraft schnell produziert werden konnten, bis hin zur Entdeckung und großflächigen Herstellung von Anilinfarben. Barnard war wissenschaftlich interessiert und beeinflusst von George Field, dessen Pigmente er verwendete, aber auch von anderen Farbtheoretikern wie David Brewster, Goethe und Chevreul.

*The Theory and Practice of Landscape Painting in Water-Colours* wurde zunächst fortlaufend in Einzelbeiträgen und dann 1855 erstmals in Buchform veröffentlicht (hier wird die Ausgabe von 1885 gezeigt) und als ausführliches Handbuch für Amateurkünstler und Kunststudenten gedacht. Das Werk enthält 26 Farblithografien, die nach dem „Chromatischen Verfahren der Brüder Leighton" gedruckt wurden, sowie Dutzende kleinerer Kupferstiche im laufenden Text. Wie bei *A Series of Progressive Lessons* von David Cox illustrieren einige Tafeln und Stiche anhand von Barnards eigenen Kunstwerken die verschiedenen Stadien der Bildkomposition.

Die interessantesten Tafeln sind jedoch jene, die sich mit den Grundlagen der Farbtheorie und Barnards eigenen Farbvorstellungen im Hinblick auf Malerei und stoffliche Farben befassen. Seine Zeichnungen sind einfach und wirkungsvoll und nutzen die Möglichkeiten der Lithografie und das große Buchformat gewinnbringend aus. Sein wichtigstes Farbordnungsdiagramm ist eine lang gezogene Raute, in der „fünfundzwanzig der brauchbarsten Pigmente" angeordnet sind, jeweils dargestellt in einer helleren und einer dunkleren Variante. Mehrere Tafeln veranschaulichen zudem Barnards Interpretation des simultanen Farbkontrasts, darunter ein Tafelpaar, das die Leserschaft selbst zur Durchführung einfacher optischer Experimente einlädt. Ein vor Kurzem entdecktes und Barnard zugeschriebenes Skizzenbuch (S. 47–49) bestätigt seine systematischen Arbeitsmethoden, etwa die akribische Art, Farben und Pigmente in Bezug auf Bildkompositionen zu dokumentieren. Es enthält auch die Entwurfsversion für eine Tafel 26 mit dem Titel „Farbkontraste", die in groben Flecken Farbkontraste und Farbharmonien verbildlicht. In ihrer Anlage erinnern die Formationen an Mary Gartsides Farbflecken von 1805, und es könnte gut sein, dass Barnard ihre Abhandlung *An Essay on Light and Shade* (S. 164–175) kannte. Sein eigenes Buch erschien bis 1885 in mehreren neuen und erweiterten Auflagen.

## La théorie et la pratique de la peinture de paysage à l'aquarelle

La période d'activité du George Barnard, peintre de paysage et professeur de dessin, correspond à une époque de grandes innovations techniques où la couleur est largement introduite dans la vie courante: quantité d'articles sont désormais produits rapidement grâce à la machine à vapeur et on a mis au point et lancé une production à grande échelle de teintures à l'aniline. Passionné de science, Barnard est fortement influencé par l'œuvre de George Field dont il utilise les pigments, ainsi que ceux d'autres spécialistes de la couleur tels que David Brewster, Goethe et Chevreul.

*The Theory and Practice of Landscape Painting in Water-Colours*, a d'abord été publié sous forme de fascicules avant de faire l'objet d'un livre paru en 1855 (l'édition de 1885 est reproduite ici). Ce guide complet pour les peintres amateurs et les étudiants des beaux-arts est un volumineux ouvrage contenant 26 chromolithographies imprimées grâce au « procédé chromatique des Frères Leighton », ainsi que des dizaines de petites gravures insérées dans le texte. Comme dans *A Series of Progressive Lessons* de David Cox, on trouve ici des planches et des gravures illustrant différentes étapes de la composition d'une image et inspirées des propres tableaux de Barnard. Les planches les plus intéressantes restent cependant celles qui illustrent les fondements de la théorie chromatique et les conceptions que Barnard applique à la peinture et aux couleurs matérielles. Son graphisme simple et efficace tire le meilleur parti des possibilités offertes par la lithographie et par le grand format du livre. Sa principale représentation de l'ordre chromatique est un losange disposé verticalement, dans lequel sont agencés « vingt-cinq des pigments les plus utiles », chacun montré en deux tonalités, claire et foncée.Barnard intègre également plusieurs planches illustrant son interprétation du contraste simultané des couleurs, dont deux qui permettent au lecteur de mener quelques expériences optiques simples. Un carnet de croquis récemment découvert et attribué à Barnard (p. 47–49) confirme ses méthodes systématiques de travail, comme sa manière méticuleuse de référencer les couleurs et les pigments correspondant à chaque composition. Le carnet en question comprend aussi une ébauche d'une planche 26, intitulée « Contrastes de couleur », où figurent des taches grossières de couleurs illustrant les contrastes et harmonies chromatiques. Cette conception rappelle fortement les taches proposées par Mary Gartside en 1805 dans son *Essay on Light and Shade* (p. 164–175), référence probable de Barnard. L'ouvrage de Barnard est plusieurs fois réédité et augmenté jusqu'en 1885.

# HARMONIOUS ARRANGEMENT

OF TWENTY-FIVE OF THE MOST USEFUL PIGMENTS.

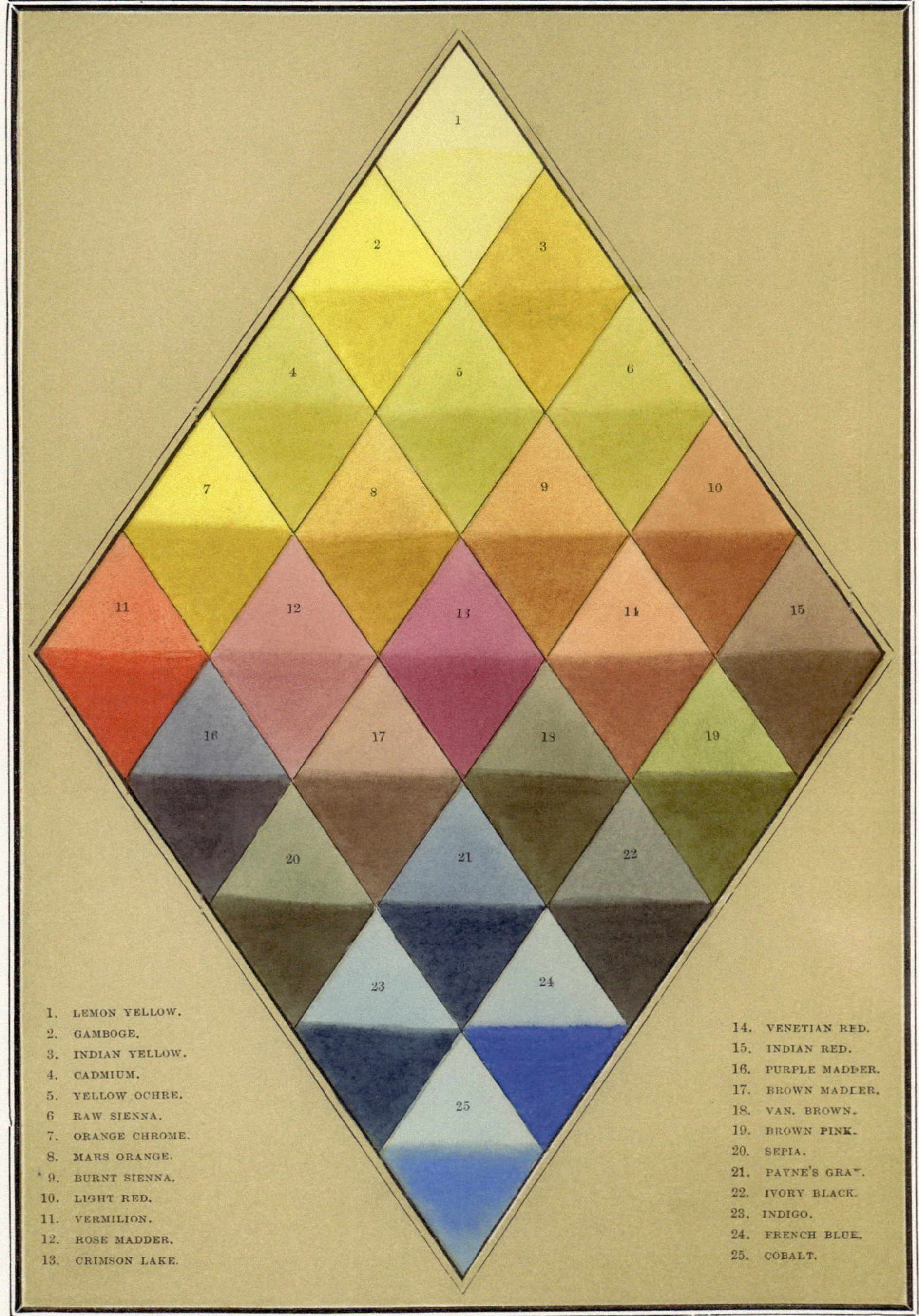


LEIGHTON, BROS.

PLATE 4.

## Bonnie E. Snow (1865–1925), Hugo B. Froehlich (1862–1925)

# THE THEORY AND PRACTICE OF COLOR

*10 plates, 26 x 20 cm | 10 ¼ x 7 ⅞ in., New York & Chicago, 1918*
*New Haven, Yale University, Robert B. Haas Family Arts Library Special Collections, Faber Birren Collection of Books on Color*

While little today is known about the two American authors of this concise overview of colour theory presented in a practical context, Bonnie Snow and Hugo Froehlich's book was intended to provide the "ordinary" reader with the basic rules and principles of colour, so that it could be enjoyed more fully and used more efficiently in art, advertising and elsewhere. It was written in an engagingly narrative and slightly didactic style, which the pair had developed in the course of their previous work. In around 1904 Snow and Froehlich had begun publishing a series of textbooks and educational course-books for children and young readers (pp. 22–23, 27), published with the same Prang Educational Company that issued the book presented here. These small-format booklets were designed to train children in drawing, painting, paper collage and other creative occupations, but in a refreshing departure colour use was given greater prominence than drawing technique, and the illustrations relating to colour theory and composition are charming, inventive and effective. They include colour wheels shaped like flower-heads, sunsets in winter and goldfish swimming in a jar. The authors' ability to simplify complex content is also evident in *The Theory and Practice of Color*, their only known work for older readers. The book was part of Prang's series of "Quarto Art Books", which covered various aspects of art, crafts, design and art history, and although it is a slim volume it was the highest-priced book in the series on account of its colour illustrations. A printed image of a prismatic scale forms the frontispiece and indicates that optical colour theory will be explained in the text. This image is followed by nine plates of colour charts which together present hundreds of hand-painted samples in circular and rectangular shapes, pasted on to the pages. A "value scale" using two colours demonstrates a neutral grey-scale, while a sequence of further charts shows primaries, binaries, colours in lighter tints and darker shades, complementaries and mixtures of these colours in several combinations and proportions. The book is an overlooked gem in colour history and an important example of educational literature from the early 20th century. There are few physical depictions of colour order, grading and mixture that are so neatly presented and executed.

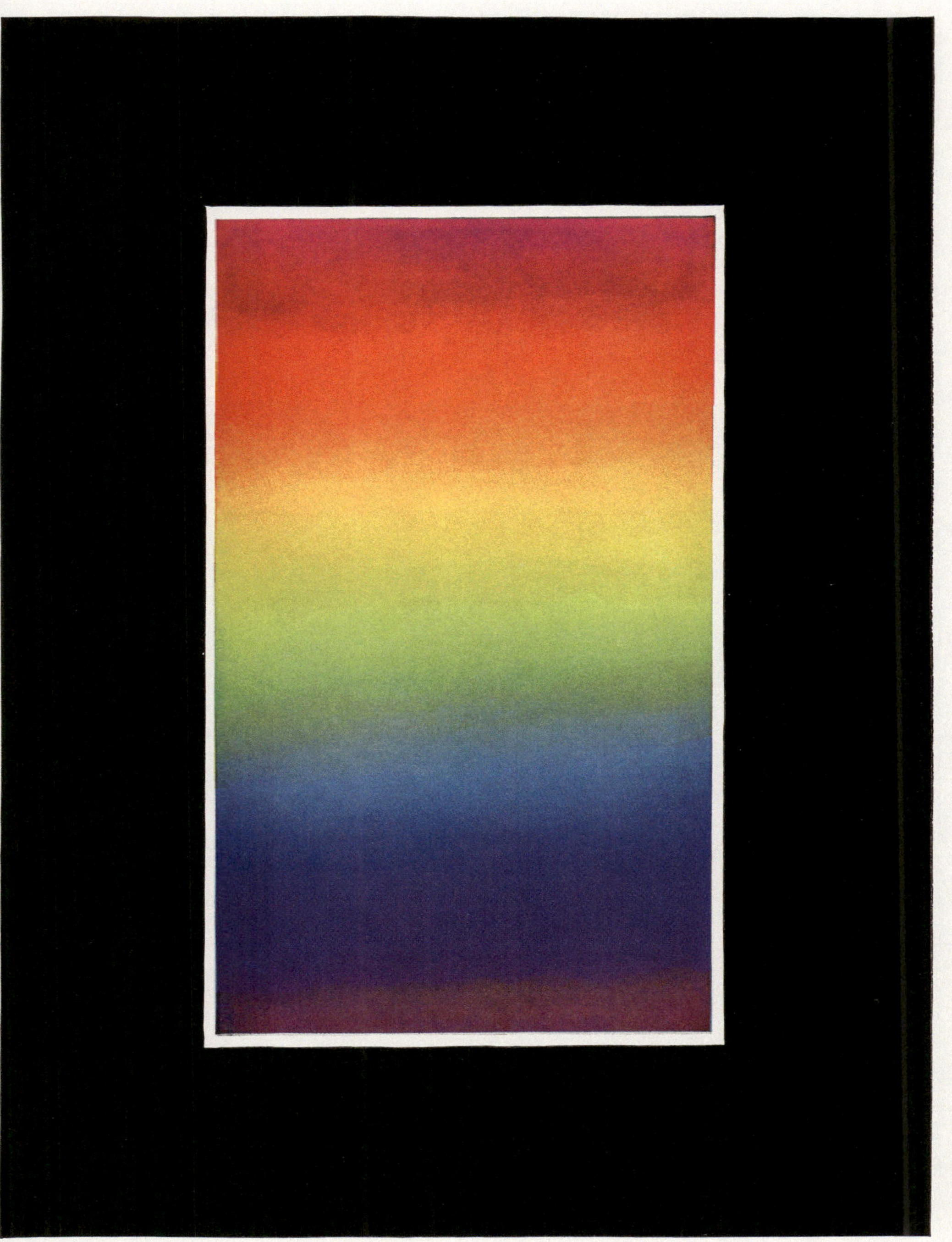

A Symbol of the Rainbow

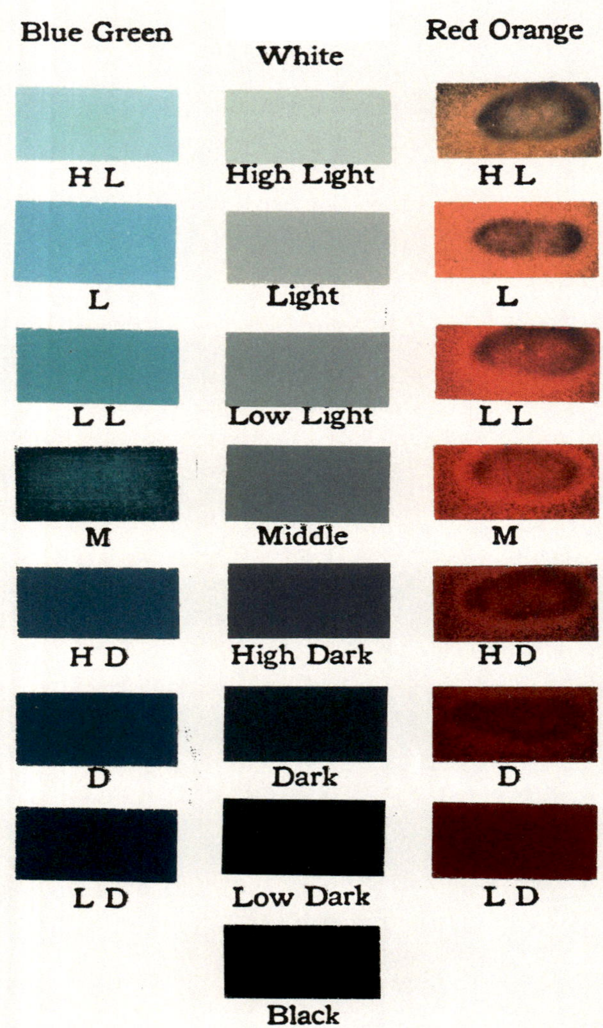


VALUE SCALE IN TWO COLORS
AND NEUTRAL TONES

## Theorie und Praxis der Farbe

Über die beiden amerikanischen Autoren dieses kurzen Überblicks über die Farbtheorie in einem praktischen Kontext ist heute wenig bekannt. Man weiß jedoch, dass Bonnie Snow und Hugo Froehlich den „gewöhnlichen" Leser mit den Grundregeln und -prinzipien von Farbe vertraut machen wollten, damit man sich daran erfreuen und sie in Kunst, Werbung und anderen Bereichen effizienter einsetzen konnte. Das Buch wurde in einem einnehmend erzählerischen und wenig didaktischen Stil verfasst, den das Autorenpaar im Verlauf seiner bisherigen Arbeit entwickelt hatte. Um 1904 hatten Snow und Froehlich begonnen, eine Serie von Schulbüchern und lehrreichen Fachbüchern für Kinder und Jugendliche zu veröffentlichen (S. 22–23, 27), die wie der hier vorgestellte Band von der Prang Educational Company verlegt wurden. Mithilfe der kleinformatigen Büchlein sollten Kinder das Zeichnen, Malen, Collagieren und andere kreative Betätigungen erlernen. Im Vergleich zu anderen Lehrbüchern wirkt es hier erfrischend, dass den Farben mehr Platz eingeräumt wird als der Zeichentechnik und dass die Illustrationen zu Farbtheorie und Bildaufbau charmant, ideenreich und wirkungsvoll daherkommen. Sie beinhalten Farbkreise mit Blütenköpfen als Muster, Sonnenuntergänge im Winter und Goldfische im Glas.

Die Fähigkeit der Autoren, komplexe Inhalte zu vereinfachen, zeigt sich auch in *The Theory and Practice of Color*, ihrem einzigen bekannten Buch für eine ältere Leserschaft. Das Werk war Teil der von Prang herausgegebenen Serie „Quarto Art Books", die verschiedene Aspekte aus Kunst, Kunsthandwerk, Gestaltung und Kunstgeschichte abdeckte. Trotz des geringen Umfangs war es aufgrund seiner Farbillustrationen das teuerste Buch der Reihe. Das gedruckte Bild einer prismatischen Farbskala bildet das Frontispiz und deutet an, dass die Theorie der immateriellen Farben im Text erläutert wird. Auf dieses Bild folgen über das Buch verteilt neun Tafeln mit Farbtabellen, die zusammen Hunderte von handgemalten und aufgeklebten Farbmustern in Form von Kreisen und Rechtecken präsentieren. Eine am Beispiel von zwei Farben aufgestellte „Werteskala" weist in der Mitte eine neutrale Grauskala auf. Alle weiteren Tafeln zeigen Primär- und Sekundärfarben, Farben in helleren Tönen und dunkleren Schattierungen, Komplementärfarben und Mischungen dieser Farben in verschiedenen Kombinationen und Zusammensetzungen. Das Buch ist ein vergessenes Juwel der Farbgeschichte und ein bedeutendes Beispiel für die Bildungsliteratur des frühen 20. Jahrhunderts. Es gibt nur wenige Darstellungen der Ordnung, Abstufung und Mischung von Farben, die so feinsäuberlich aufbereitet und ausgeführt sind.

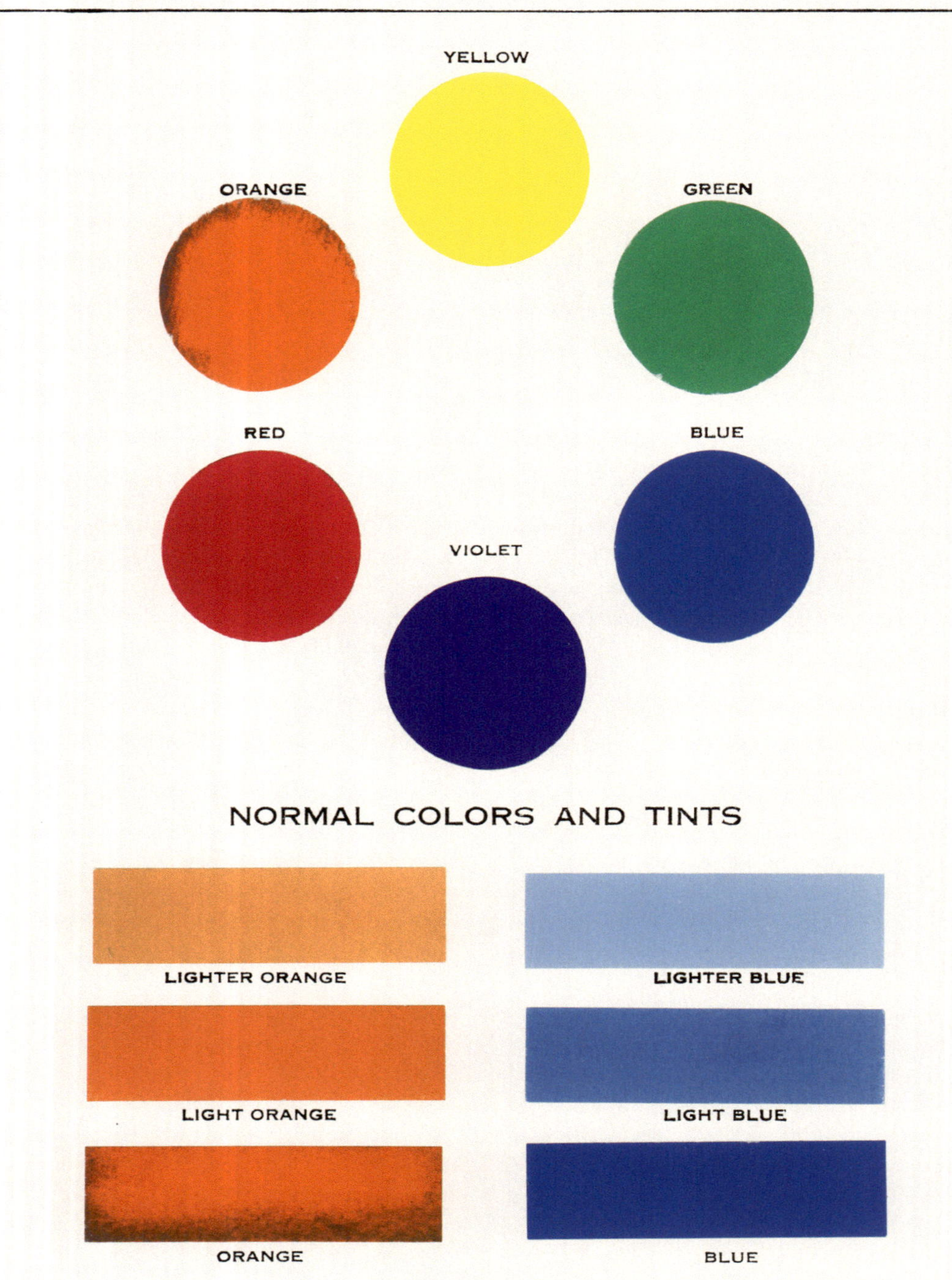
YELLOW
ORANGE
GREEN
RED
BLUE
VIOLET
NORMAL COLORS AND TINTS
LIGHTER ORANGE
LIGHTER BLUE
LIGHT ORANGE
LIGHT BLUE
ORANGE
BLUE

CHART THREE

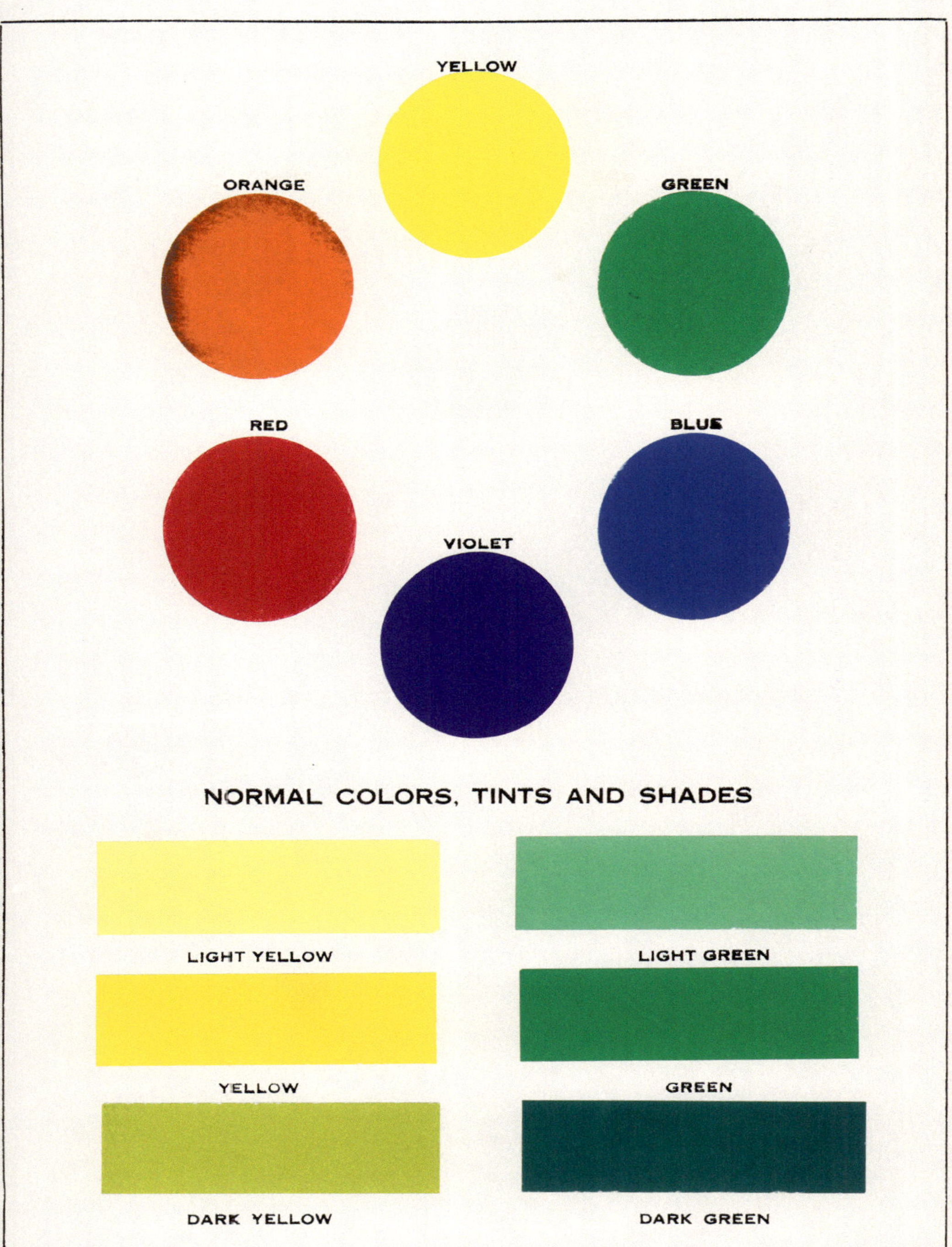
YELLOW
ORANGE
GREEN
RED
BLUE
VIOLET
NORMAL COLORS, TINTS AND SHADES
LIGHT YELLOW
LIGHT GREEN
YELLOW
GREEN
DARK YELLOW
DARK GREEN

CHART FOUR

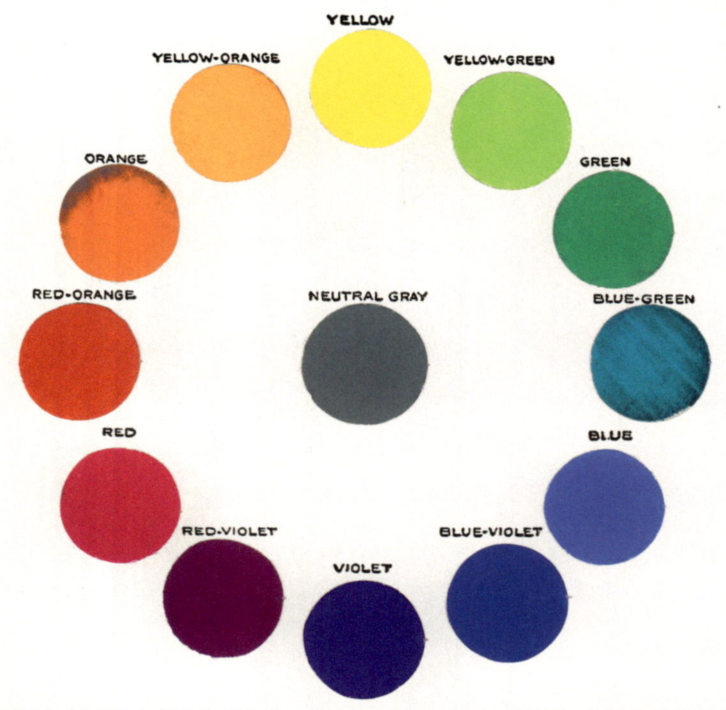


## PRIMARY COLORS BINARY COLORS AND HUES

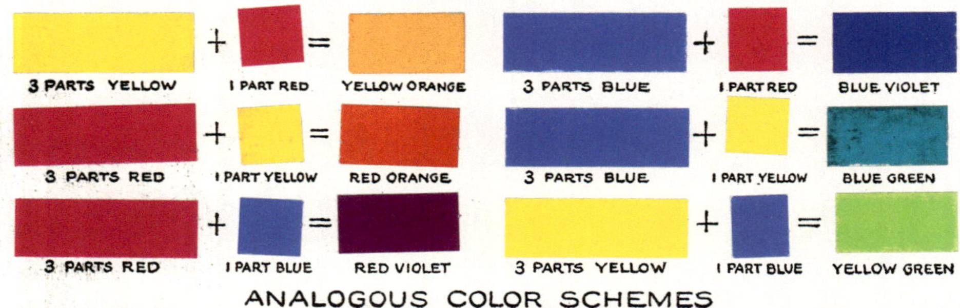


## ANALOGOUS COLOR SCHEMES

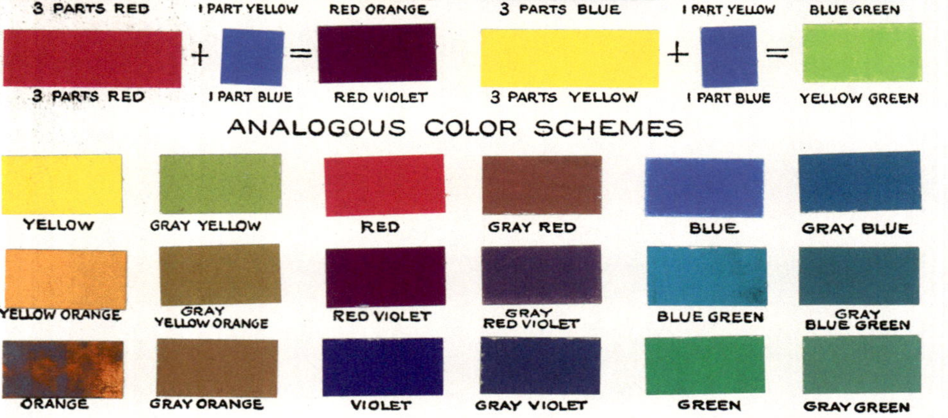

## Théorie et pratique de la couleur

On sait peu de choses des deux auteurs américains de ce panorama concis des théories de la couleur, proposé dans un but pratique. Bonnie Snow et Hugo Froehlich entendent fournir au lecteur « ordinaire » les règles de base et les principes de la couleur, pour un usage plus efficace dans les domaines artistique et publicitaire, entre autres. Le duo écrit dans un style narratif plaisant et discrètement didactique qu'ils ont mis au point au fil de leurs ouvrages précédents. Vers 1904, Snow et Froehlich commencent en effet à publier des manuels scolaires et ouvrages pédagogiques pour enfants et jeunes lecteurs (p. 22–23, 27), édités, comme l'ouvrage présenté ici, par Prang Educational Company. Ces publications de petit format sont conçues pour que les enfants s'adonnent au dessin, à la peinture et au collage, entre autres occupations manuelles, mais proposent une alternative bienvenue : l'usage de la couleur y est plus important que la technique du dessin, et les illustrations au service de la théorie de la couleur et de la composition sont charmantes, inventives et efficaces. Ainsi, les cercles chromatiques adoptent des formes de corolles de fleurs, de couchers de soleil en hiver ou de poissons nageant dans un bocal. Cette capacité à simplifier des contenus complexes est aussi à l'œuvre dans *The Theory and Practice of Color*, seul titre connu que les auteurs destinent à un public plus âgé. L'ouvrage fait partie de la collection Quarto Art Books que publie Prang, consacrée à plusieurs aspects de la peinture, de l'artisanat, des arts graphiques et de l'histoire de l'art. Malgré son nombre de pages modeste, c'est le livre le plus onéreux de la collection de par ses illustrations en couleurs. La gamme prismatique du frontispice annonce que la théorie de la couleur optique sera expliquée. Viennent ensuite neuf planches de tableaux chromatiques présentant des centaines de pastilles circulaires ou rectangulaires, coloriées manuellement et collées sur les pages. L'échelle des gris est mise en évidence par apposition avec une « échelle de valeur » de deux autres couleurs. Toute une série de tableaux traitent ensuite des couleurs primaires et binaires, des tons clairs et des nuances sombres, des complémentaires et des mélanges selon différentes combinaisons et proportions. L'ouvrage constitue un trésor oublié de l'histoire de la couleur et un exemple remarquable de la littérature pédagogique du début du XXe siècle. Les représentations physiques de l'ordre chromatique, des dégradés et des mélanges sont rarement exécutées avec un tel soin.

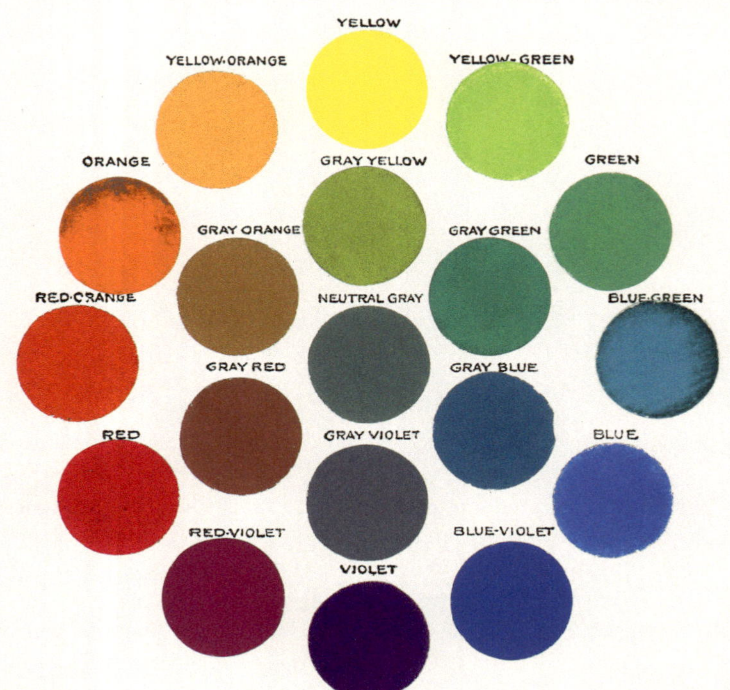
YELLOW
YELLOW-ORANGE
YELLOW-GREEN
ORANGE
GRAY YELLOW
GREEN
GRAY ORANGE
GRAY GREEN
RED-ORANGE
NEUTRAL GRAY
BLUE-GREEN
GRAY RED
GRAY BLUE
RED
GRAY VIOLET
BLUE
RED-VIOLET
BLUE-VIOLET
VIOLET

COLORS IN FULL INTENSITY AND GRAYED COLORS

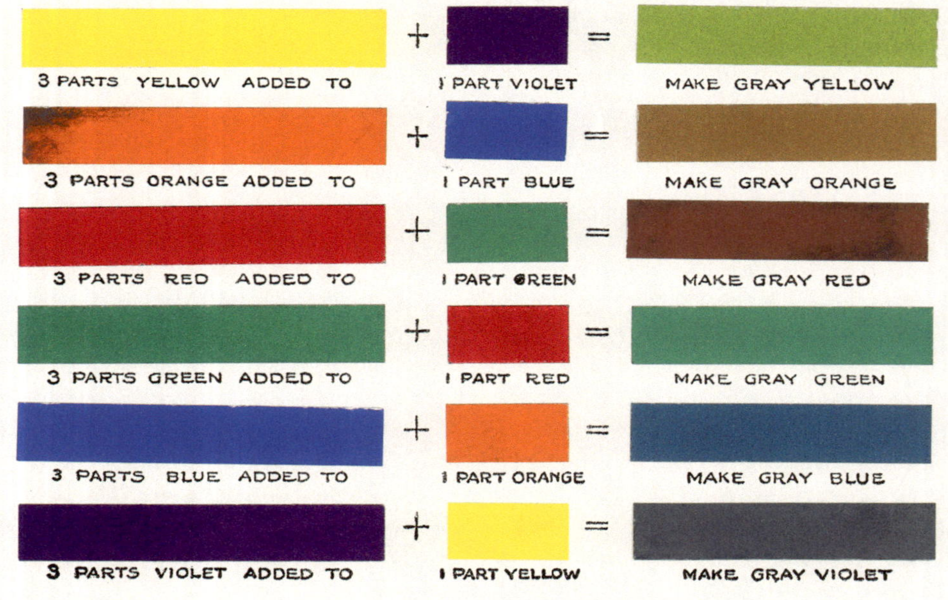
3 PARTS YELLOW ADDED TO + 1 PART VIOLET = MAKE GRAY YELLOW
3 PARTS ORANGE ADDED TO + 1 PART BLUE = MAKE GRAY ORANGE
3 PARTS RED ADDED TO + 1 PART GREEN = MAKE GRAY RED
3 PARTS GREEN ADDED TO + 1 PART RED = MAKE GRAY GREEN
3 PARTS BLUE ADDED TO + 1 PART ORANGE = MAKE GRAY BLUE
3 PARTS VIOLET ADDED TO + 1 PART YELLOW = MAKE GRAY VIOLET

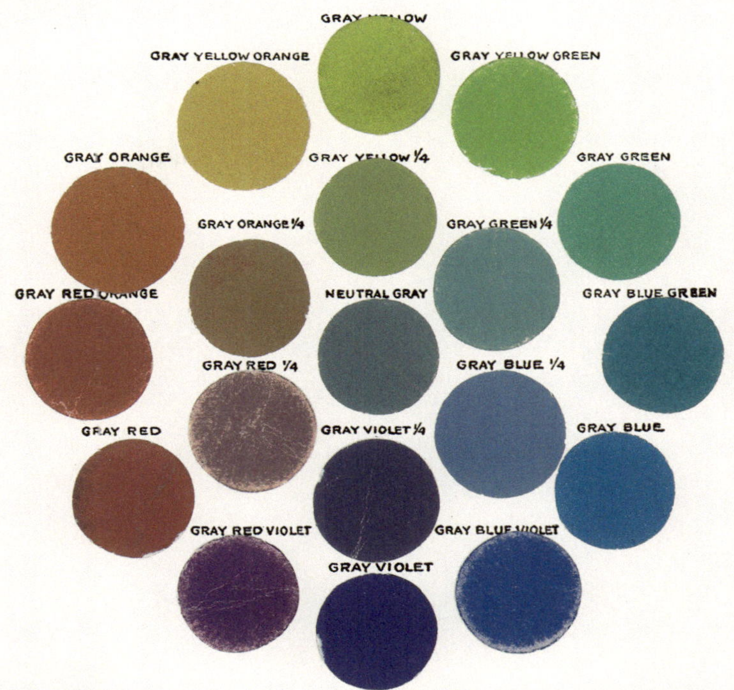


## COLORS IN ONE-HALF AND IN ONE-FOURTH INTENSITIES

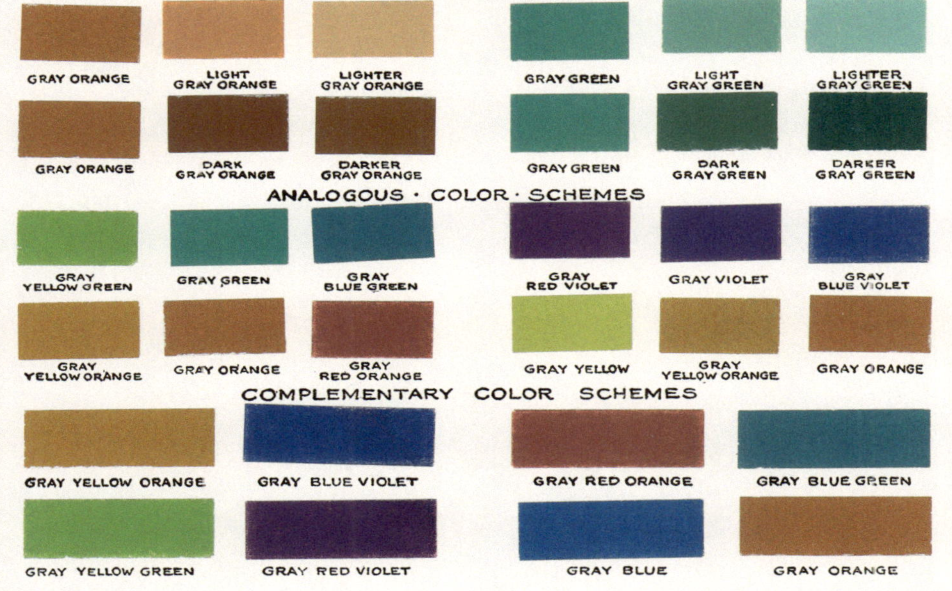

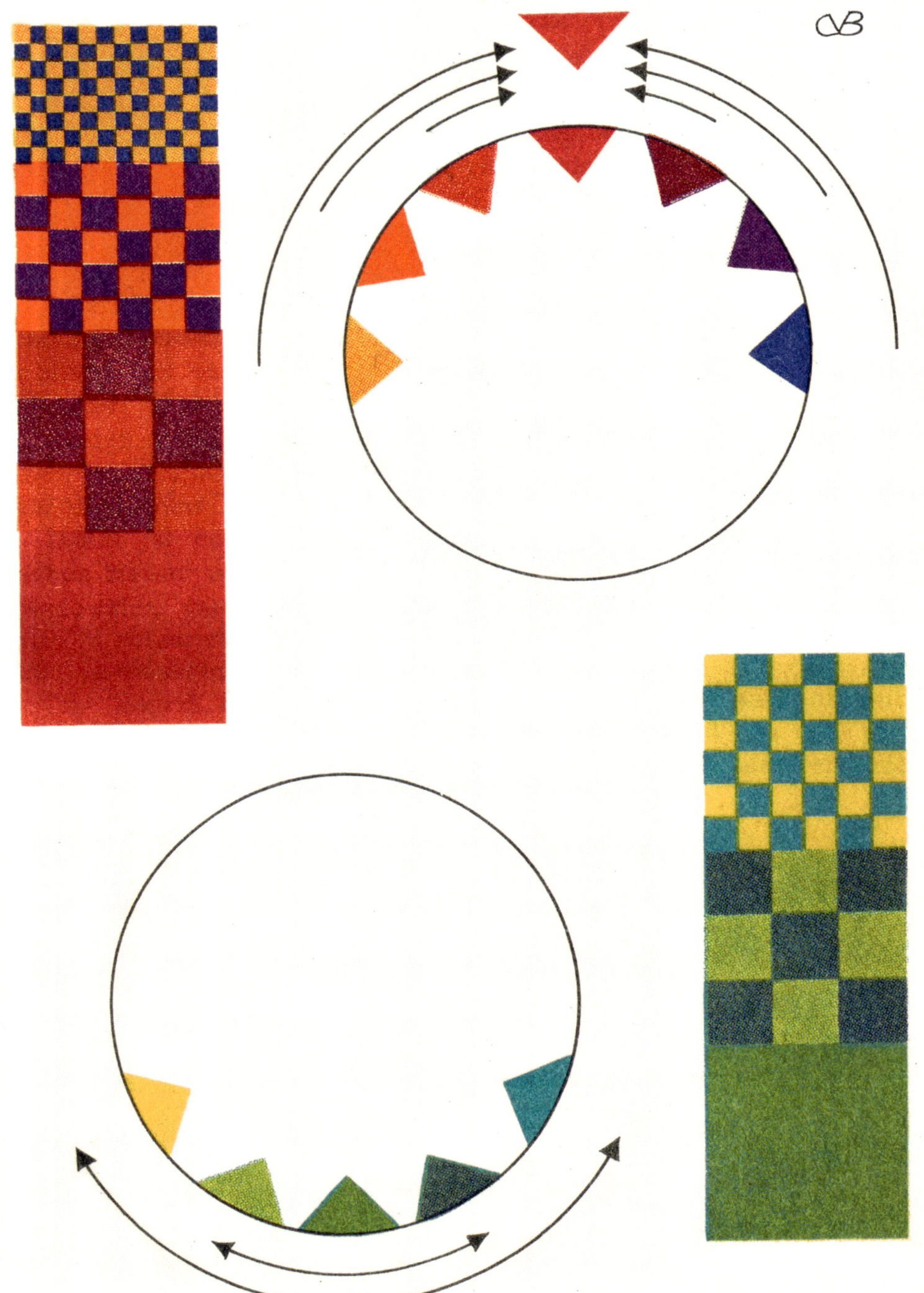

## Chapter 6

# *Colour Breaking Free:* THE EARLY 20th CENTURY

## 1902–1930

## Emily Noyes Vanderpoel (1842–1939)

# COLOR PROBLEMS

## A Practical Manual for the Lay Student of Color

*46 plates, 21 x 16 cm | 8 ¼ x 6 ¼ in., New York, London, Bombay, 1902*
*New Haven, Yale University, Robert B. Haas Family Arts Library Special Collections, Faber Birren Collection of Books on Color*

Emily Noyes Vanderpoel was a New York-born artist, teacher and advocate of the right of women to a full education. In 1902 her book *Color Problems* was published, which she described as a "practical manual" although it was very much concerned as well with pushing the boundaries of the genre. Vanderpoel was widely read on the subject of colour and was especially indebted to Goethe's work, but in the same way as Chevreul and others before her she cast the net of application for her studies beyond the realm of mere painting, noting that, "a better understanding of color would also be of great value to decorators, designers, lithographers, florists, dressmakers, and milliners; women in their dress and home decoration, and many others". Keeping her text as brief as possible she instead put a great deal of effort into the book's 117 full-page lithographed plates, which were printed on thick, textured paper.

Vanderpoel's plates include some standard images of optical range, colour gradation, a colour wheel and tables of complementary colours, but others are much more experimental and give a sense of a highly analytical mind with a deep understanding of compositional harmony. Most of the plates show a high degree of abstraction, including several with colour "notes" and "harmonies" that are presented by means of impressionistic brushstrokes. Meanwhile, other diagrams are marked by a fine geometrical sharpness, including a group of images of colour contrast that resemble Josef Albers's much later colour squares. Five plates feature circles of complementary colour mixtures inspired by Milton Bradley's (1836–1911) "color machine", a mechanical "color-disk rotating mechanism" that had been patented in 1893. Beyond all these, however, Vanderpoel's most notable diagrams are her 54 "color analyses" in which she sought to break down artefacts or ornamental patterns into their chromatic components and use these as the colour key for a 10 x 10 grid of squares. She also included celluloid colour transparencies in the book, to be used as overlays with some of the plates. *Color Problems* was a commercial success and was reprinted just 12 months after its first publication. It marked a significant new milestone in publishing on colour by women, and in her concluding comments in the text Vanderpoel confidently noted that "No woman has a right to say she has no influence, conscious or unconscious, on the world around her".

PLATE I

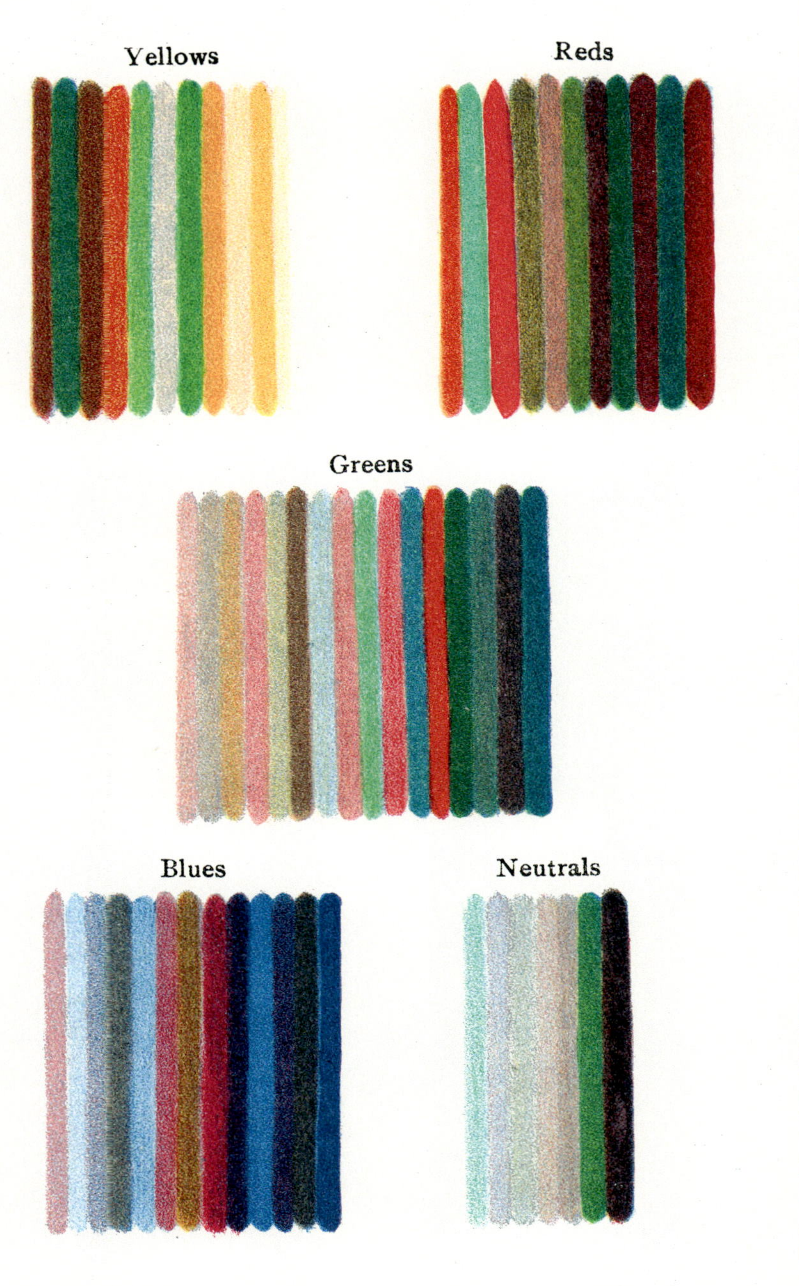


WOOLS AS SORTED BY A COLOR-BLIND MAN

PLATE II

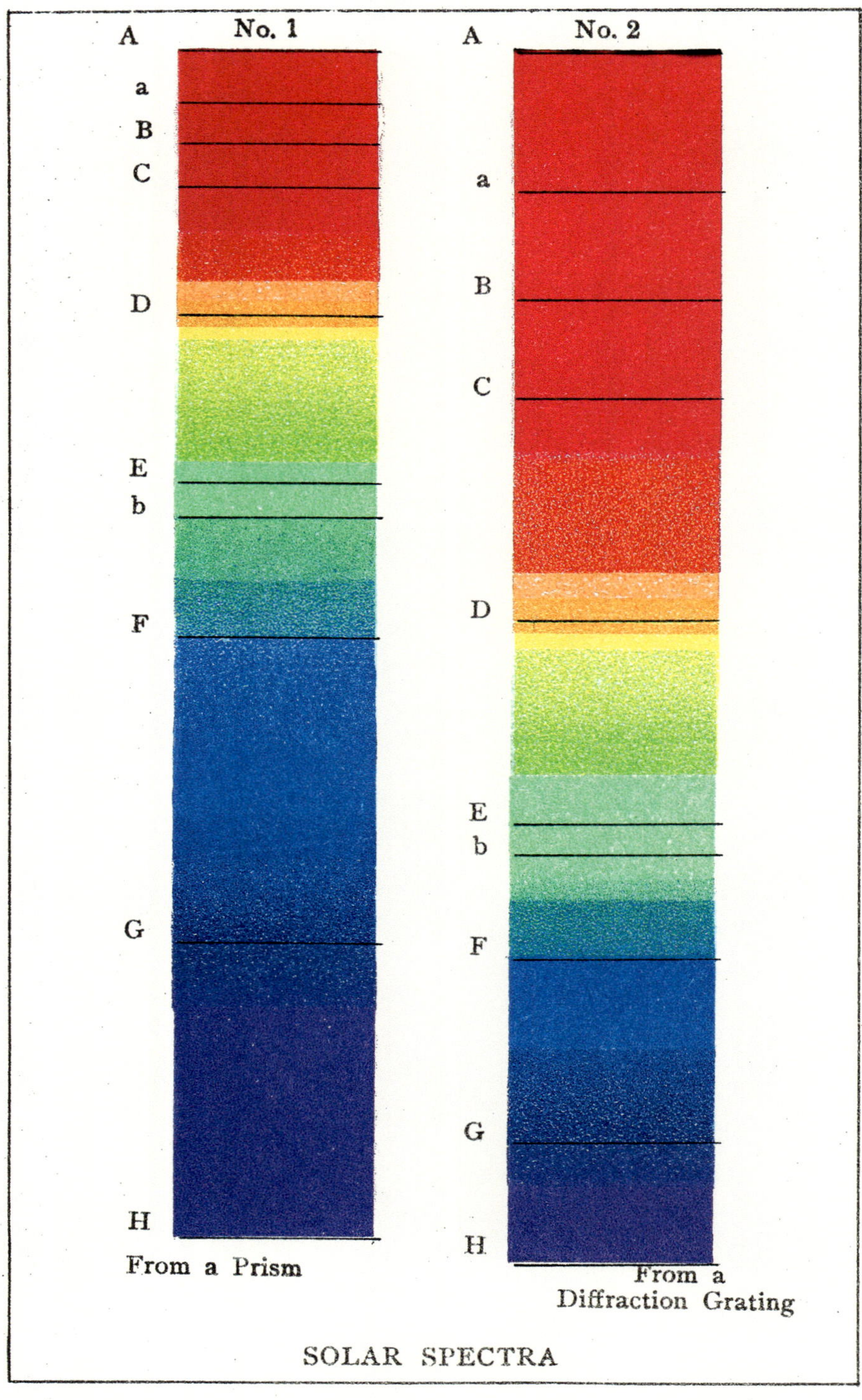


SOLAR SPECTRA

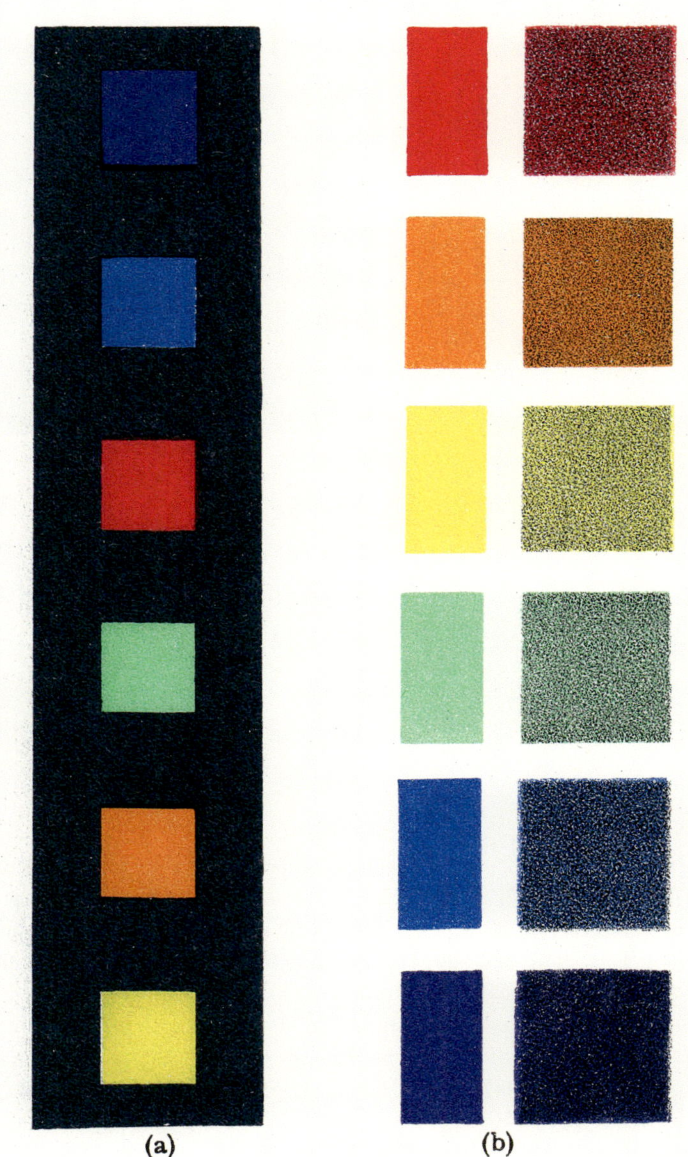


THE SPECTRAL COLORS

(a) In their order of Luminosity
(b) Pure and Grayed

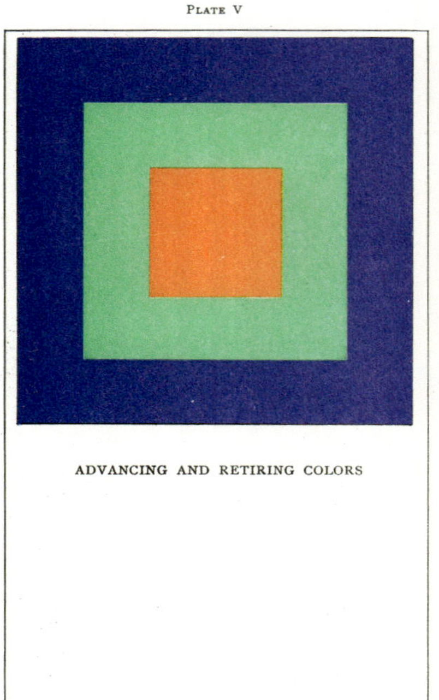


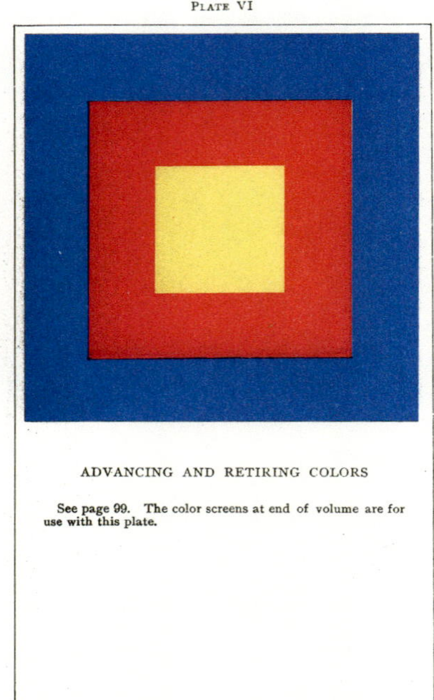

PLATE VI
ADVANCING AND RETIRING COLORS
See page 99. The color screens at end of volume are for use with this plate.


## Farbprobleme. Ein praktisches Laienhandbuch für Farbenschüler

Die in New York geborene Künstlerin und Lehrerin Emily Noyes Vanderpoel setzte sich unter anderem für das Recht von Frauen auf eine vollwertige Ausbildung ein. 1902 erschien ihr Farbenbuch *Color Problems*, das sie als „praktisches Handbuch" bezeichnete, obwohl es vor allem auch die Grenzen des Genres sprengen sollte. Vanderpoel war in Farbfragen sehr belesen und besonders dem Werk Goethes verpflichtet, doch wie Chevreul und andere vor ihr bezog sie die Anwendbarkeit ihrer Studien nicht nur auf die Malerei – denn, so Vanderpoel in ihrem Vorwort, „ein besseres Farbverständnis wäre auch für Dekorateure, Designer, Lithografen, Floristen, Schneider und Hutmacher, für Frauen beim Dekorieren ihrer Wohnräume und Kleider und für viele andere von großem Wert". Ihren Text hielt sie so knapp wie möglich und investierte stattdessen viel Mühe in die 117 ganzseitigen lithografierten Bildtafeln, die sie auf dickes, strukturiertes Papier drucken ließ.

Einige ihrer Tafeln zeigen übliche Abbildungen des optischen Bereichs, Farbabstufungen, einen Farbkreis und Tabellen von Komplementärfarben, andere geben sich weitaus experimenteller und vermitteln den Eindruck eines äußerst analytischen Geistes mit einem tiefen Verständnis für harmonische Kompositionen. Die meisten Tafeln sind in hohem Maße

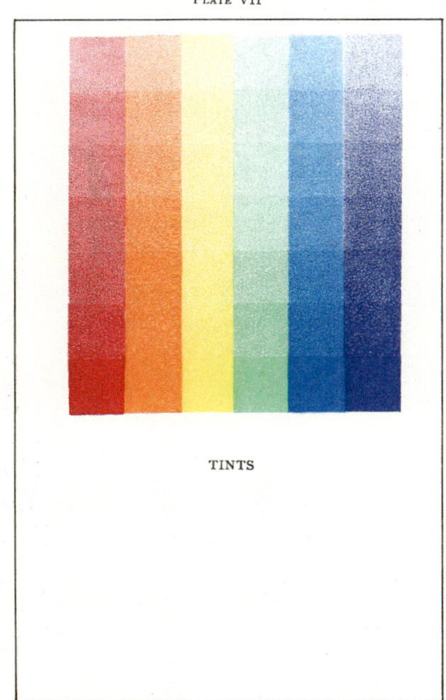


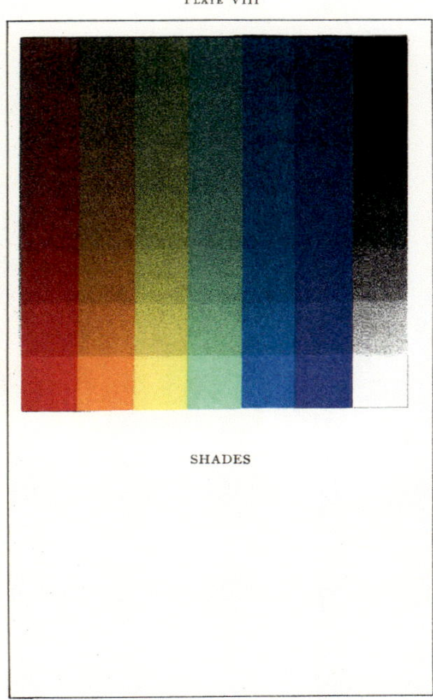


abstrakt, so auch mehrere, die mithilfe impressionistischer Pinselstriche „Farbnotizen“ und „Farbharmonien“ präsentieren. Andere Diagramme, wie eine Gruppe von Farbkontraststudien, die an die späteren Farbquadrate von Josef Albers erinnern, zeichnen sich durch eine feine geometrische Strenge aus. Fünf Tafeln zeigen Kreise mit Komplementärfarbmischungen, die von einer ebenfalls abgebildeten „Farbmaschine“ angeregt waren, einer mechanischen „Rotationsvorrichtung für Farbscheiben“, auf die Milton Bradley (1836–1911) seit 1893 ein Patent hielt. Die über all das hinaus bemerkenswertesten Diagramme Vanderpoels sind jedoch ihre 54 „Farbanalysen“, in denen sie Artefakte oder ornamentale Muster in ihre farblichen Komponenten zerlegte und diese als Farbschlüssel in ein Raster aus zehn mal zehn Feldern übertrug. Darüber hinaus fügte sie dem Buch Farbfolien aus Zelluloid bei, die man über einzelne Tafeln legen sollte. Der Erfolg von *Color Problems* war so groß, dass das Buch bereits zwölf Monate nach seinem Erscheinen nachgedruckt werden musste. Für die Veröffentlichung von Farbenbüchern durch Frauen stellte es einen wichtigen Meilenstein dar. In den Schlussbemerkungen ihres Textes merkte Vanderpoel selbstbewusst an: „Keine Frau hat das Recht zu behaupten, sie habe, bewusst oder unbewusst, keinen Einfluss auf ihre Umgebung.“

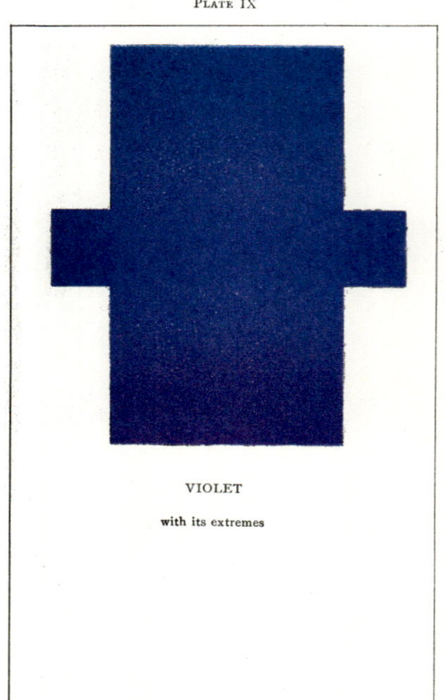


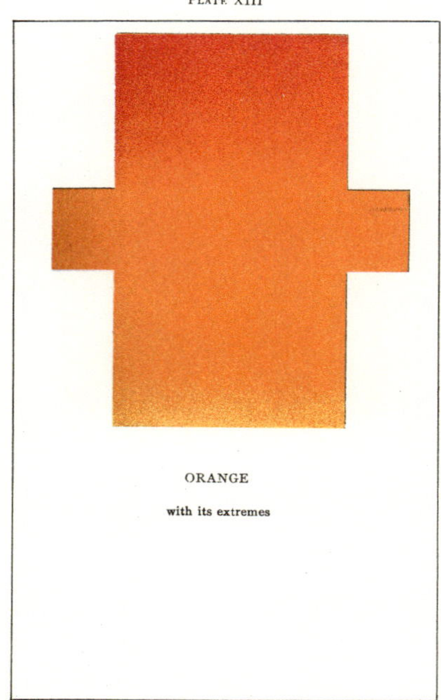


## Problèmes de la couleur, manuel pratique pour s'initier à la couleur

Née à New York, Emily Noyes Vanderpoel est une artiste, enseignante et militante pour le droit des femmes à l'éducation.En 1902, elle publie *Color Problems*, qu'elle décrit comme un « manuel pratique » bien qu'elle y repousse véritablement les limites du genre. Vanderpoel est une grande connaisseuse des recherches antérieures sur la couleur et reconnaît devoir beaucoup notamment à Goethe, mais, à l'instar de Chevreul et d'autres avant elle, elle énonce que son champ d'études s'applique bien au-delà de la peinture. Elle souligne ainsi « qu'une meilleure compréhension de la couleur est fort profitable aux décorateurs, dessinateurs, lithographes, fleuristes, couturiers, modistes, aux femmes pour leur garde-robe et la décoration intérieure, et à bien d'autres ». Pour accompagner un texte aussi concis que possible, elle propose 117 planches lithographiées, imprimées en pleine page sur du papier épais et texturé.

Les planches de Vanderpoel proposent des représentations classiques du spectre lumineux et des gradations des couleurs, un cercle chromatique et des tableaux des couleurs complémentaires. D'autres, plus expérimentales, témoignent d'un esprit hautement analytique et d'un sens profond de la composition harmonieuse. Abstraites pour la plupart, elles sont faites de touches impressionnistes qui sont

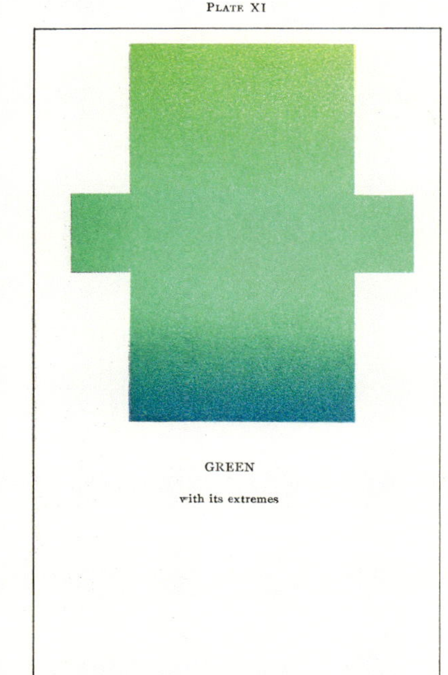


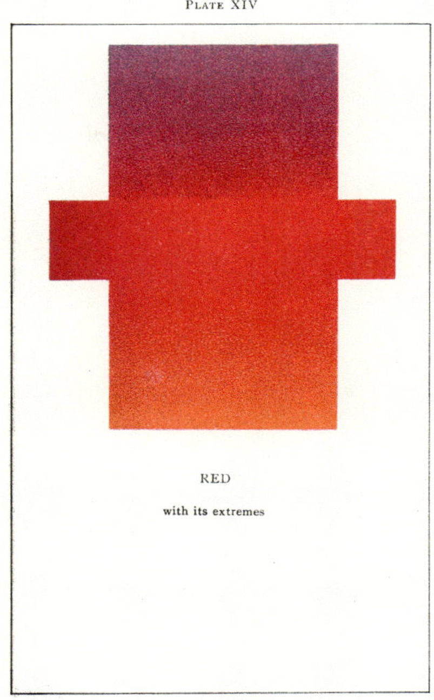


autant de « notes » et d'« harmonies » de couleurs. Par ailleurs, d'autres graphiques se caractérisent par une netteté toute géométrique, tel le groupe de contrastes de couleurs qui semble annoncer les carrés de Josef Albers, bien plus tardifs. Cinq planches présentent des cercles de mélanges de couleurs complémentaires inspirés par la « machine à couleur » de Milton Bradley (1836–1911), un « dispositif circulaire et rotatif des couleurs » breveté en 1893. Mais les propositions les plus remarquables de Vanderpoel sont ses 54 graphiques baptisés « analyses de couleurs ». Elle y cherche à séparer les composants chromatiques d'objets et de motifs ornementaux et à en coder les teintes dans des grilles carrées de 10 cases de côté. Elle glisse aussi dans le livre des feuilles de celluloïde transparent à appliquer sur certaines planches. Fort de son succès commercial, *Color Problems* est réimprimé douze mois à peine avec sa première publication. Il constitue une étape importante dans la littérature sur la couleur écrite par les femmes. Vanderpoel conclut l'ouvrage sur une prise de position : « Aucune femme n'est en droit de dire qu'elle n'a pas d'influence, consciemment ou inconsciemment, sur le monde qui l'entoure. »

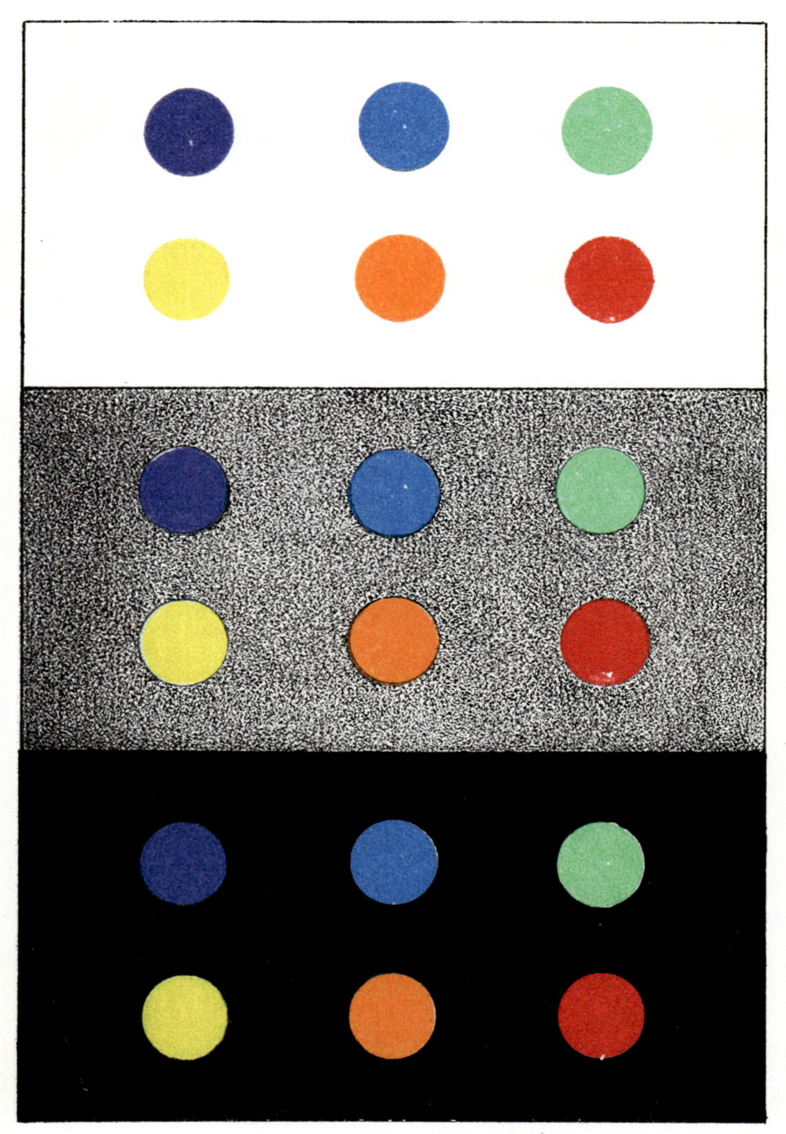

SPECTRAL COLORS
ON BLACK, WHITE AND GRAY

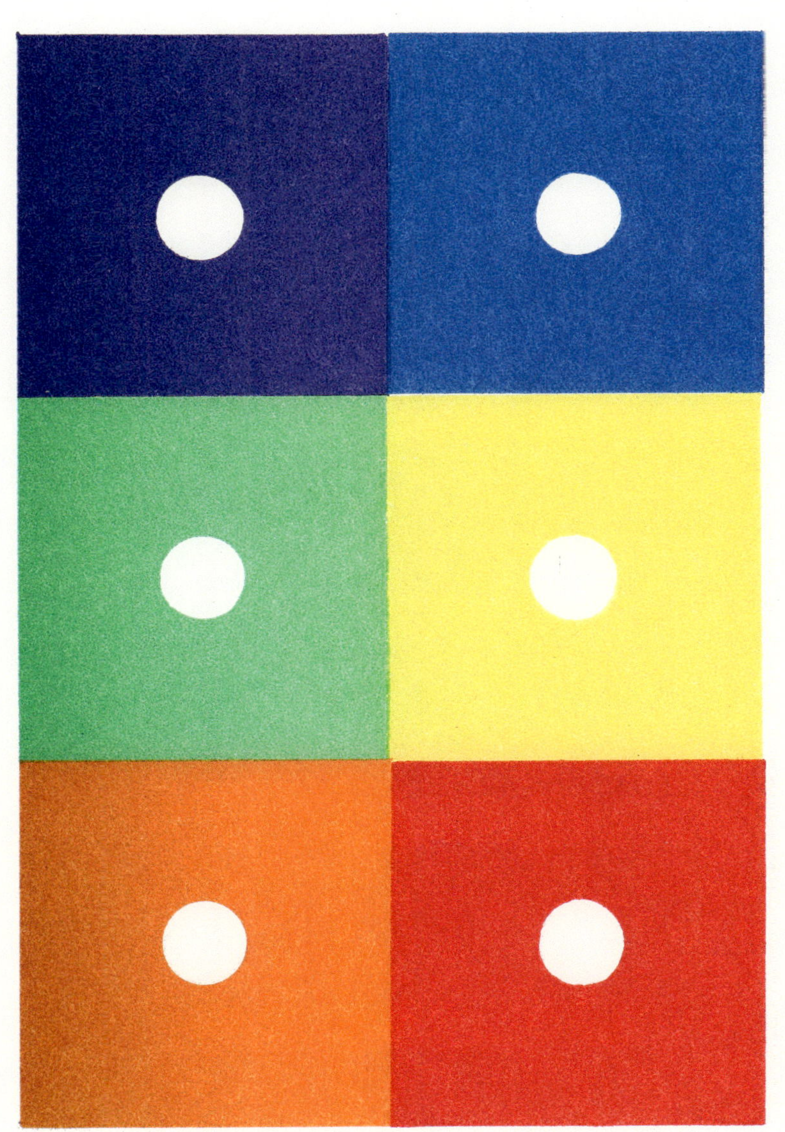

WHITE
ON SPECTRAL COLORS

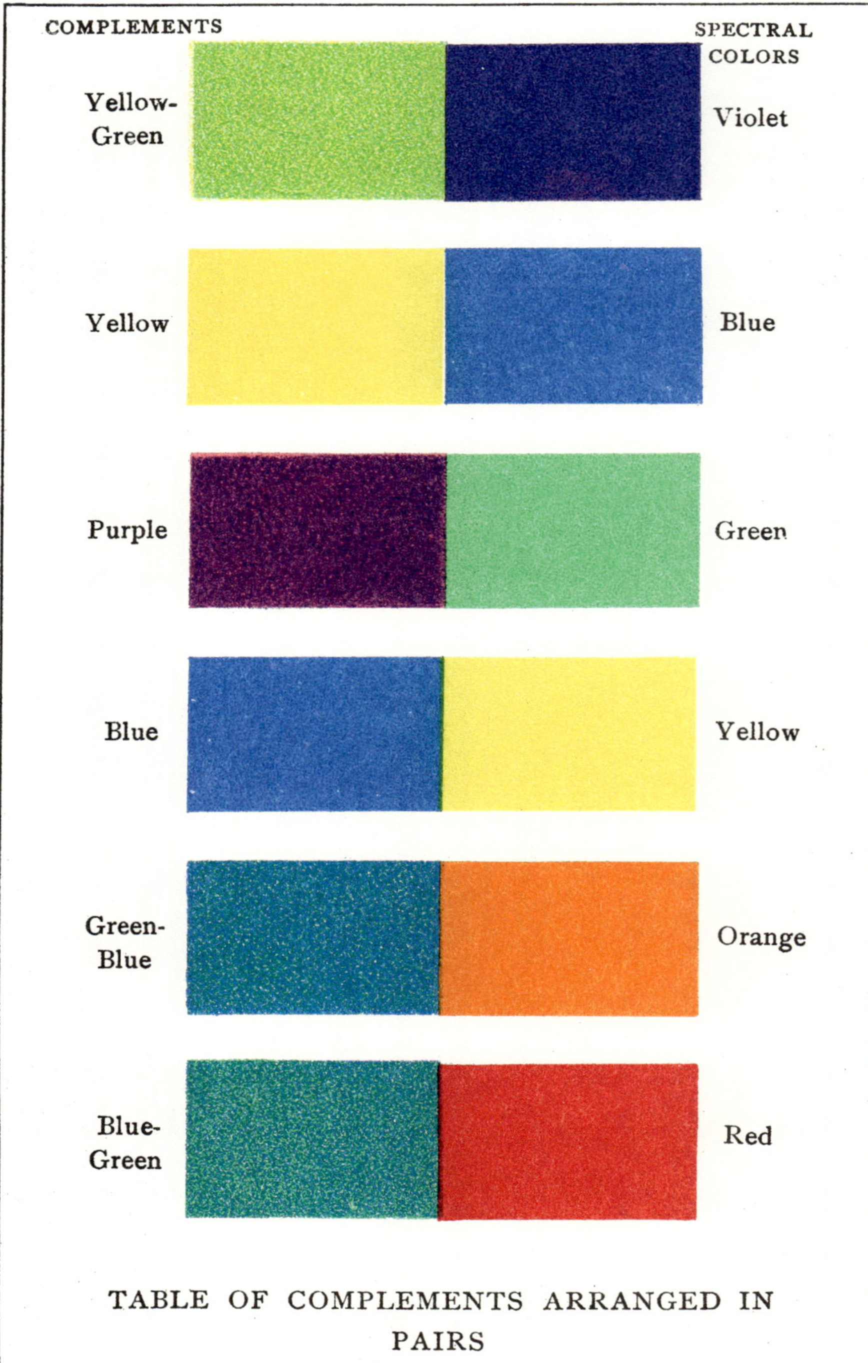


TABLE OF COMPLEMENTS ARRANGED IN PAIRS

Plate XXIX

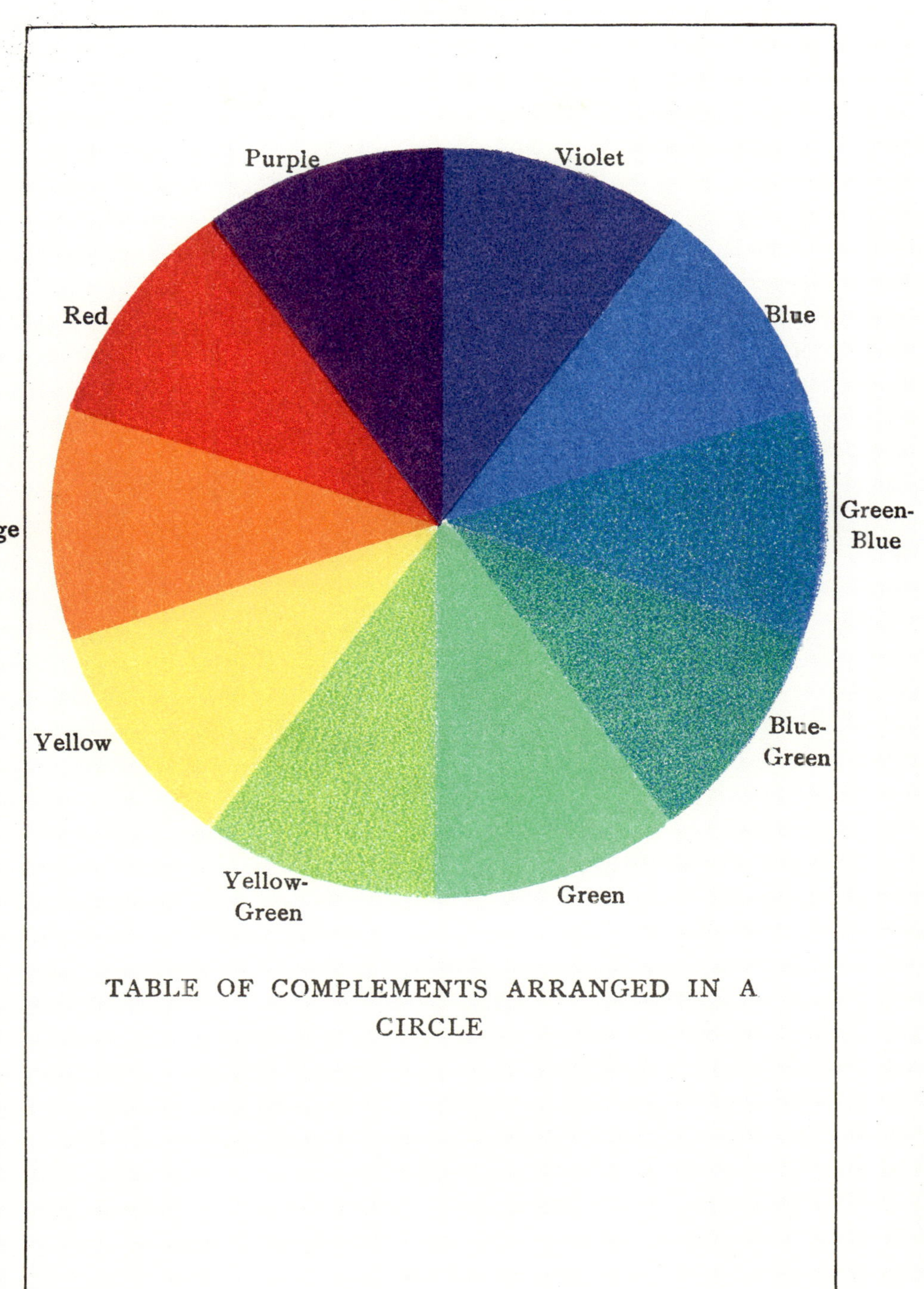


TABLE OF COMPLEMENTS ARRANGED IN A CIRCLE

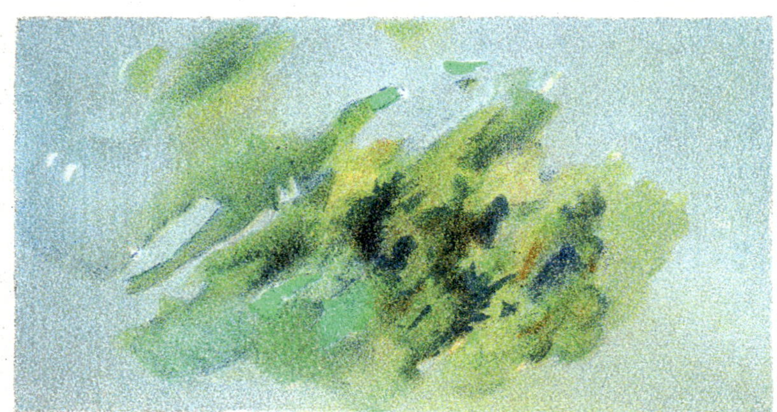

A HARMONY OF ONE COLOR

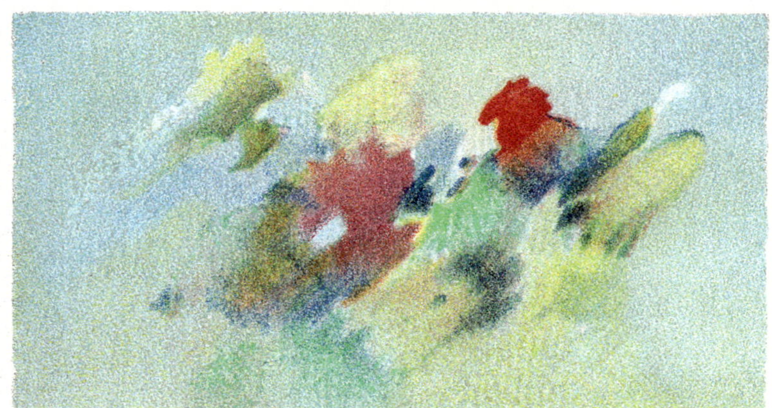

A HARMONY OF CONTRAST

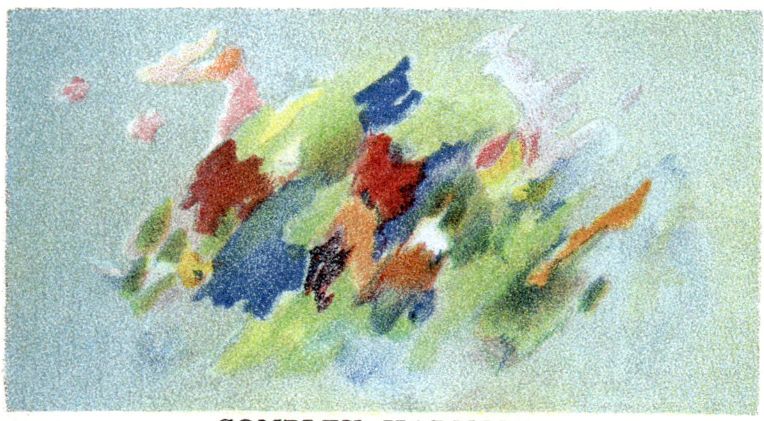

COMPLEX HARMONY

HARMONY BY GRADATION

From Orange to Cream-White

From Yellow to Yellow-White

From Green to Green-White

From Blue to Blue-White

THE TRUE CHARACTER OF SOME OF THE SO-CALLED "WHITES"

(which are really pale tints)

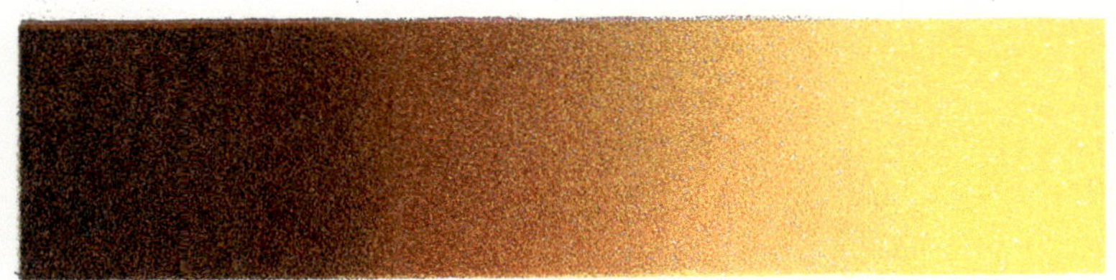

From Brown to Yellow

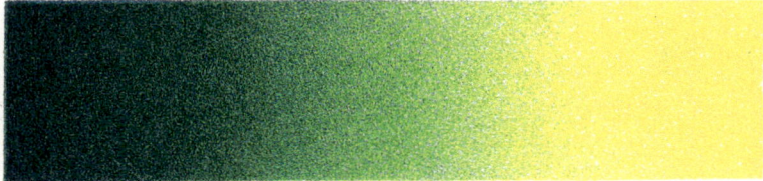

From Green to Yellow

From Pink to Yellow

From Red to Yellow

SOME CHANGES BY GRADATION FROM ONE COLOR TO ANOTHER

## Albert Henry Munsell (1858–1918)

# ATLAS OF THE MUNSELL COLOR SYSTEM

*15 plates, 28 x 35.5 cm | 11 x 14 in., Malden, Massachusetts, 1915*
*University of Vermont, Silver Special Collections Library*

The American Albert Henry Munsell was one of several educators in the early 20th century who worked to bring order to what was perceived by some as the chromatic chaos of the 19th century. His aim was to develop a system that would be easy to understand, would identify colours accurately and could be used in all forms of art education. The basis of Munsell's concept was that colour is three-dimensional and may be anchored in relation to three qualities: *hue* (the colour itself, such as red, yellow, blue etc.), *value* (that is brightness, or the amount of white or black within a colour) and *chroma* (the saturation or brilliance of a colour). He visualised his concept in the form of an irregular three-dimensional model resembling a tree, in which the colours were represented as branches of different lengths and at different heights, protruding from a central stem of neutral greys with black at the bottom and white at the top. Each colour could be identified by its location on this spatial model and referred to using precise alphanumerical coordinates instead of unreliable colour names.

Munsell first published his general concept in 1905 in *A Color Notation*, a small, practical handbook intended to help standardise how colour was taught in schools. It contained woodcut illustrations that were somewhat limited in size, while later editions were published with a "Munsell Student Chart" and a set of 26 coloured "Munsell chips". When his *Atlas* was published 10 years later this was now a sophisticated and large-format visualisation of his concept. It contained 15 plates with colour charts produced with hand-painted colour samples, not dissimilar to those seen in the work of his predecessor Patrick Syme (pp. 240–249), and indeed Munsell's work in turn inspired that of his contemporary Wilhelm Ostwald. Some of Munsell's plates also have overlays that can be lifted, as, for example, on the chart depicting the "Axis of the Color Tree" (pp. 384/385). His system proved to be hugely successful and was soon adopted internationally and used in all manner of different disciplines and industries. Munsell continued to issue further books visualising his system, including *A Grammar of Color* which was eventually published posthumously by the Strathmore Paper Company in 1921, but none matched the sophistication and elegance of the *Atlas* of 1915.

MUNSELL COLOR SYSTEM

# ATLAS

—OF—

## COLOR CHARTS

COPYRIGHT BY A. H. MUNSELL, 1907-1915.
PATENTED JUNE 26, 1906.

CHART
H

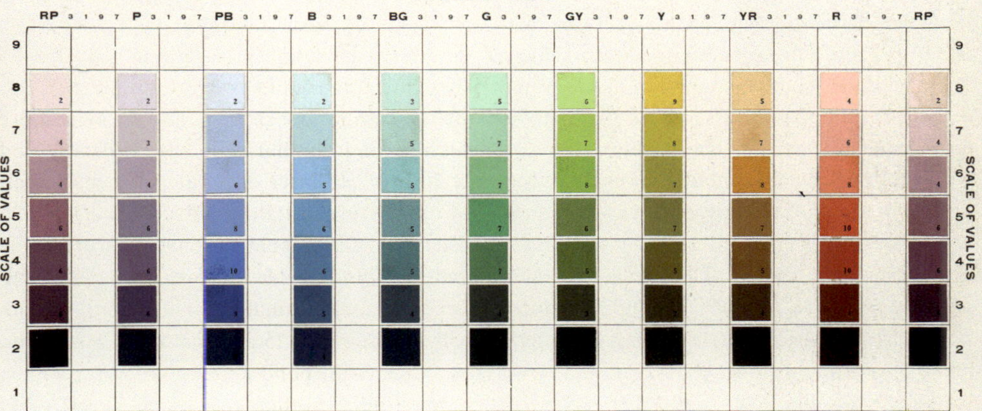

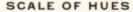

## CHART H

### INDEX FOR COLOR NOTATION

This chart suggests all color paths and records each step by a simple NOTATION. The ten steps of hue are written RP (red-purple), P (purple), PB (purple-blue), B (blue), BG (blue-green), G (green), GY (green-yellow), Y (yellow), YR (yellow-red or orange), and R (red).

Initials at the top of the chart trace the Sequence of Hues; numerals at the side trace the Sequence of Values and the small numeral printed on each color step is an index of its Chroma, *i. e.* strength or saturation. The color step made of vermilion bears the chroma numeral 10—it is at the value level 4—and in the red column R. This step is written $5R\frac{4}{10}$, as explained in a previous introduction and in chapter VI of "A Color Notation."

If this chart were bent around the equator of the color sphere forming a cylindrical envelope, it would imitate a Mercator chart of the globe, each hue taking the place of a meridian and each value level representing a parallel of latitude, while the chroma numerals would correspond to altitudes.

Were this cylinder cut open on the red-purple meridian (RP) it would spread out to form this Hue Chart—green being at its center with yellow and red (warm hues) to the right, and blue and purple (cool hues) to the left.

Colors shown on this chart form the *irregular outside* of the color tree, between which and the neutral gray trunk are the intermediate degrees of weaker chroma, which appear on the succeeding charts R. Y. G. B. P. and 20. 30. 40. 50. 60. 70. 80. of the system.

AVOID DUST, HANDLING AND EXPOSURE TO STRONG LIGHT.

## Atlas des Munsell-Farbsystems

Der Amerikaner Albert Henry Munsell war einer von mehreren Pädagogen des frühen 20. Jahrhunderts, die Ordnung in die von einigen als chromatisches Chaos des 19. Jahrhunderts wahrgenommene Farbenlehre bringen wollten. Ihm schwebte ein leicht verständliches Farbsystem vor, das Farben exakt bestimmen würde und für jede Form der Kunsterziehung einsetzbar wäre. Seiner Theorie lag die Vorstellung zugrunde, dass Farbe dreidimensional ist und sich an drei Eigenschaften festmachen lässt: dem *Farbton* (der Farbe an sich, etwa Rot, Gelb oder Blau usw.), der *Wertigkeit* (also dem Helligkeitsgrad, der in einer Farbe enthaltenen Menge von Weiß oder Schwarz) und der *chroma* (also der Intensität oder Leuchtkraft einer Farbe). Als Bild für sein System wählte Munsell ein unregelmäßiges dreidimensionales Modell, das einem Baum ähnelte. Die Farben wurden von unterschiedlich langen Ästen dargestellt, die in verschiedenen Höhen einem zentralen Stamm aus neutralen Grautönen mit Schwarz am unteren und Weiß am oberen Ende entwuchsen. Anhand ihrer Lage in diesem räumlichen Modell konnte jede beliebige Farbe identifiziert und mit präzisen alphanumerischen Koordinaten anstelle von unzuverlässigen Farbnamen bezeichnet werden.

Munsell veröffentlichte seine Ideen zuerst 1905 in *A Color Notation*, einem kleinen, praktischen Handbuch, das helfen sollte, den Farbunterricht an Schulen zu vereinheitlichen. Es enthielt Holzschnittillustrationen, die in der Größe etwas begrenzt waren, bevor spätere Auflagen mit einer „Munsell-Schülerkarte“ und 26 farbigen „Munsell-Plättchen“ herausgegeben wurden. Mit dem zehn Jahre später erschienenen *Atlas* gelang Munsell eine anspruchsvolle und großformatige Visualisierung seines Systems, die unter anderem 15 Tafeln mit Farbtabellen enthielt. Die handbemalten Farbmuster, die Munsell hierfür verwendete, waren denen seines Vorgängers Patrick Syme (S. 240–249) nicht unähnlich; im Gegenzug inspirierte sein eigenes Werk *Die Farbenfibel* seines Zeitgenossen Wilhelm Ostwald. Einige Tafeln, wie das Schaubild „Achse des Farbbaums“ (S. 384/385), sind zudem mit abhebbaren Schablonen ausgestattet. Munsells System erwies sich als Riesenerfolg und wurde bald von etlichen Fachdisziplinen und Branchen weltweit übernommen und angewandt. Der Autor selbst ließ weitere Bücher folgen, um sein System zu veranschaulichen, darunter *A Grammar of Color*, das jedoch erst 1921 postum von der Strathmore Paper Company herausgegeben wurde. Die Vollkommenheit und Eleganz des 1915 erschienenen *Atlas* erreichte keines von ihnen.

## Atlas du système chromatique de Munsell

Albert Henry Munsell fait partie d'une poignée de pédagogues du début du XXe siècle qui, aux États-Unis, cherchent à ordonner ce qui est alors perçu par certains comme le chaos chromatique du siècle précédent. Il se donne pour objectif de mettre au point un système qui identifie les couleurs avec précision, soit facile à comprendre et exploitable dans toutes les formes d'apprentissage artistique. Munsell fonde sa conception sur le fait qu'une couleur possède trois dimensions et peut être rapportée à trois qualités : la *teinte* (la couleur elle-même : rouge, jaune, bleu, etc.), la *valeur* (sa luminosité, selon la quantité de blanc ou de noir qu'elle contient) et le *chroma* (sa saturation ou intensité). Il envisage un modèle de forme irrégulière en trois dimensions ressemblant à un arbre, où les couleurs sont représentées comme des branches de différentes longueurs, qui émergent à différentes hauteurs d'un tronc central de gris neutres, où le noir figure en bas et le blanc, en haut. Chaque couleur peut ainsi être identifiée par son emplacement dans cet espace et désignée par des coordonnées alphanumériques précises, plutôt que par des noms de couleurs hasardeux.

Munsell a déjà fait connaître les grandes lignes de sa conception en 1905 dans *A Color Notation*, petit manuel pratique destiné à standardiser la façon dont la couleur est enseignée à l'école. Il contient des illustrations gravées sur bois relativement limitées en taille. Des éditions ultérieures intègrent le « Tableau de Munsell pour les élèves » et une série de 26 échantillons coloriés, les « Éclats de Munsell ». Dix ans plus tard, dans l'*Atlas* présenté ici, la visualisation de sa conception est bien plus élaborée et bénéficie d'un format plus grand. Quinze planches offrent des tableaux chromatiques d'échantillons peints à la main, qui rappellent ceux de son prédécesseur Patrick Syme (p. 240–249) et, à leur tour, inspireront les recherches d'un contemporain de Munsell, Wilhelm Ostwald. Certaines planches sont pourvues d'un cache transparent que l'on peut soulever, comme par exemple celle décrivant l'« Axe de l'arbre chromatique » (p. 384/385). Le système de Munsell, qui rencontre un énorme succès international, est adopté dans de nombreuses disciplines et secteurs. L'auteur fera paraître d'autres ouvrages proposant sa conception visuelle, dont *A Grammar of Color* que publie The Strathmore Paper Company en 1921 à titre posthume, mais aucun n'égale la sophistication et l'élégance de cet *Atlas* de 1915.

**MUNSELL COLOR SYSTEM**

# ATLAS

—OF—

**COLOR CHARTS.**

COPYRIGHT BY A. H. MUNSELL. 1907-1915.
PATENTED JUNE 26, 1906.

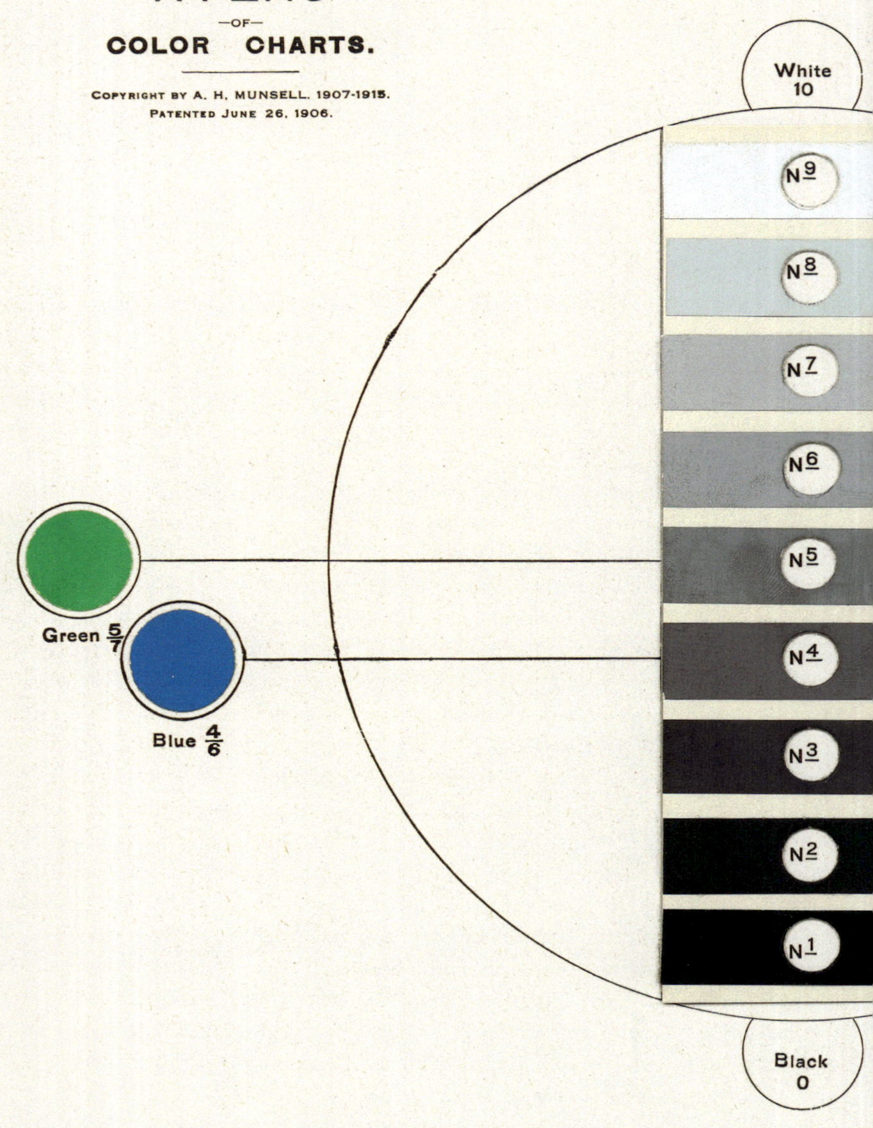

Yellow $\frac{8}{9}$

Red $\frac{4}{10}$

Purple $\frac{3}{6}$

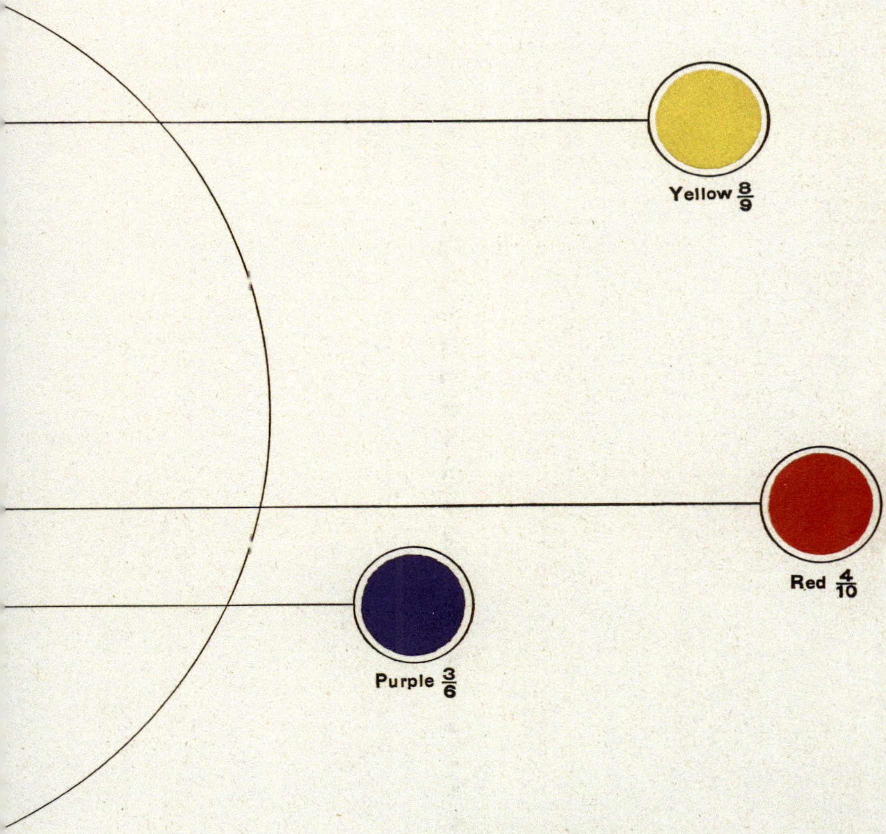

## CHART V. AXIS of the color tree.

(A scale of neutral values 0—10.)

VALUE, i.e. the amount of light reflected from pigments, is the second dimension or quality of color, — the other two being HUE and CHROMA.

A scale of neutral or gray values extends from the extreme of whiteness (10) to the extreme of blackness (0), and is represented on this chart by the hinged and perforated card. The value of any color is readily found by sliding it behind these perforations until a point is reached where the luminosity of the color matches that of a step in the gray scale. Should the value fall between two of these steps, the interval may be given decimally.

Thus the yellow has a value of eight (8), green is five (5), red and blue four (4), purple three (3). Personal bias plays no part in this measured scale of value. It is established by a special instrument adopted in the course of optical measurements, at the Mass. Institute of Technology, and known as the Munsell Photometer.

These pigment colors vary not only in their VALUE, but also in their CHROMA,—as fully shown on Chart C, which explains why the color branches extending outward from the neutral axis are of uneven length. See chapters II and III of the teacher's handbook, "A COLOR NOTATION."

PROTECT THE CHART FROM DUST AND HANDLING.

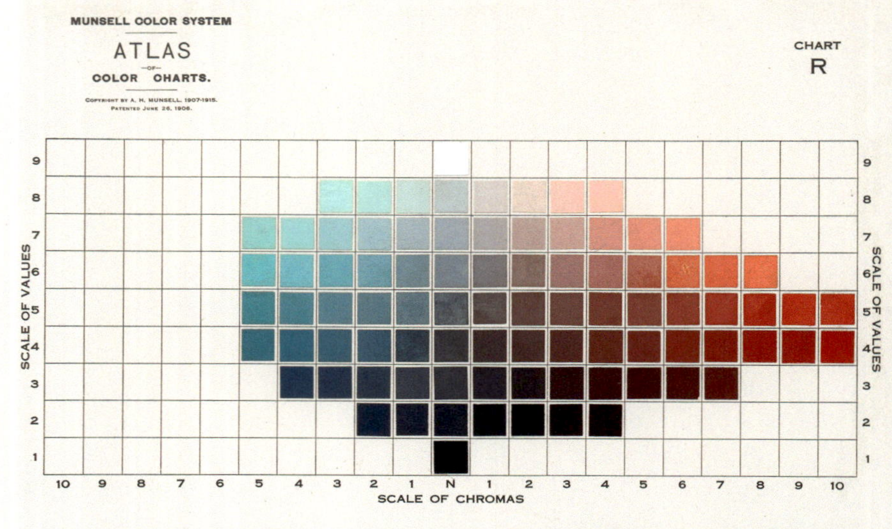


## RED AND BLUE-GREEN CHART

This chart presents a vertical plane passed through the axis of the color solid and bearing the complementary hues, red and blue-green. This pair of opposite hues is shown in regular measured scales from black to white and from grayness to the strongest color made in stable pigment.

VALUES of red and blue-green range vertically from black (0) to white (10). CHROMAS or strengths of color range horizontally from neutral gray to the maximum (10).

Each step in these color scales bears an appropriate symbol describing its light and its strength. Thus $R\frac{4}{10}$ is vermilion, the standard red of the system, which exhibits 100% of chromatic strength and reflects the same amount of light as $N^{4}/$ of the value scale. Its opposite $BG\frac{4}{5}$ reflects the same amount of light but only 50% of chroma. To balance this pair the areas must be inversely as the chroma, i. e., since blue-green is but half as strong as vermilion red, twice as much is required for a balance Attention to these measures leads to pleasing combinations.

Any chosen steps of red and blue-green upon this chart may be balanced by noting their symbols:– thus light blue-green ($BG\frac{6}{4}$) balances dark red ($R\frac{3}{2}$), when the areas are inversely as the product of the symbols viz:–six parts of light blue green and twenty-four parts of dark red.

Chapters III and IV of the handbook, "A Color Notation," describe these balances and their combinations with other hues. The symbol on each color step is its NAME, a measure of its light and strength by which it is to be memorized, written and reproduced.

AVOID DUST, HANDLING AND EXPOSURE TO STRONG LIGHT.

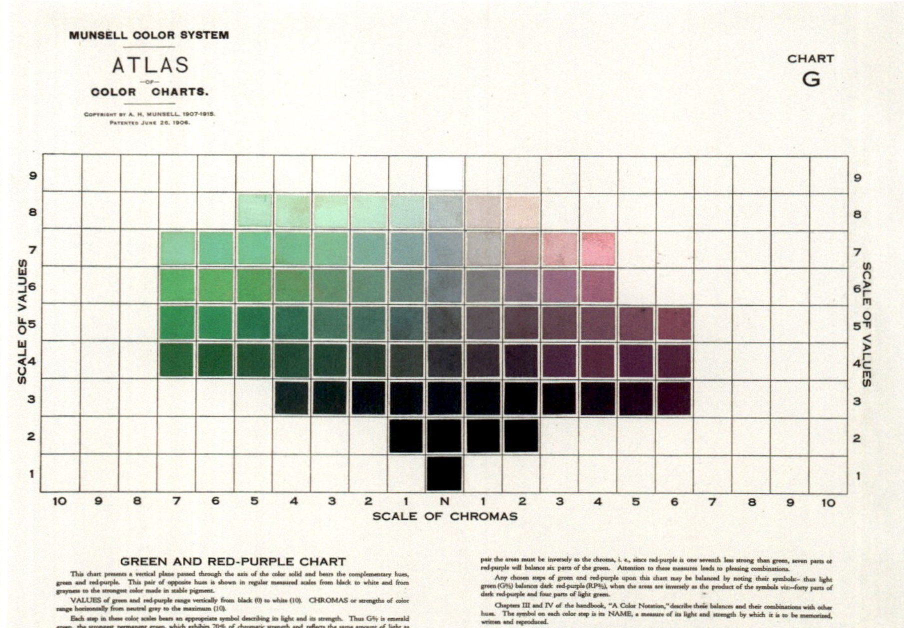


## GREEN AND RED-PURPLE CHART

This chart presents a vertical plane passed through the axis of the color solid and bears the complementary hues, green and red-purple. This pair of opposite hues is shown in regular measured scales from black to white and from grayness to the strongest color made in stable pigment.

VALUES of green and red-purple range vertically from black (0) to white (10). CHROMAS or strengths of color range horizontally from neutral gray to the maximum (10).

Each step in these color scales bears an appropriate symbol describing its light and its strength. Thus $G\frac{5}{7}$ is emerald green, the strongest permanent green, which exhibits 70% of chromatic strength and reflects the same amount of light as $N^{5}/$ of the value scale. Its opposite $RP\frac{5}{6}$ reflects the same amount of light but only 60% of chroma. To balance this pair the areas must be inversely as the chroma, i. e., since red-purple is one seventh less strong than green, seven parts of red-purple will balance six parts of the green. Attention to these measures leads to pleasing combinations.

Any chosen steps of green and red-purple upon this chart may be balanced by noting their symbols:– thus light green ($G\frac{8}{5}$) balances dark red-purple ($RP\frac{2}{2}$), when the areas are inversely as the product of the symbols viz:–forty parts of dark red-purple and four parts of light green.

Chapters III and IV of the handbook, "A Color Notation," describe these balances and their combinations with other hues. The symbol on each color step is its NAME, a measure of its light and strength by which it is to be memorized, written and reproduced.

AVOID DUST, HANDLING AND EXPOSURE TO STRONG LIGHT.

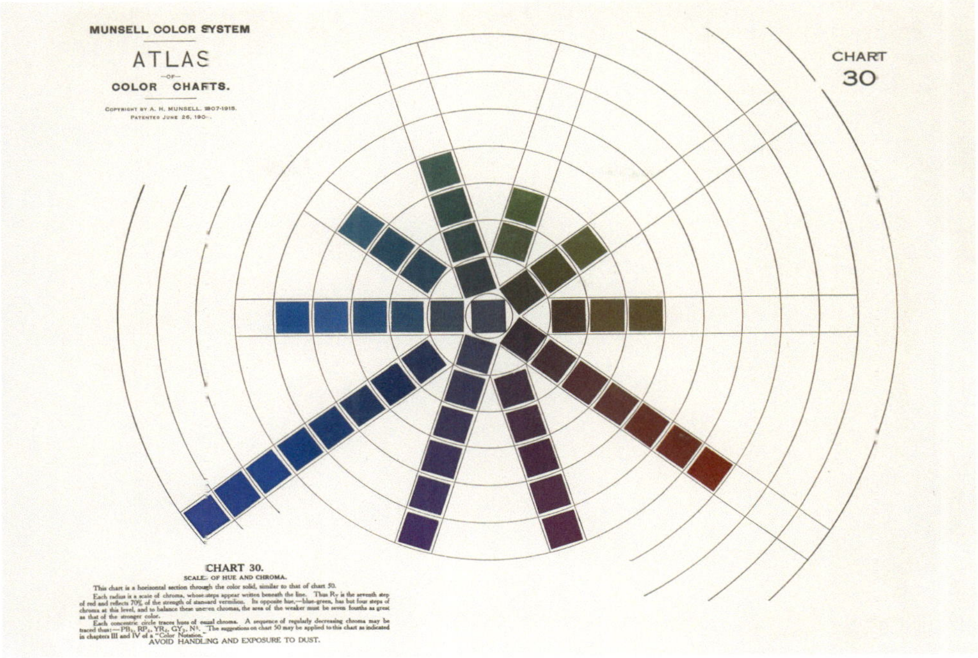

MUNSELL COLOR SYSTEM

ATLAS

—OF—

COLOR CHARTS.

COPYRIGHT BY A. H. MUNSELL. 1907-1915.
PATENTED JUNE 26, 190-.

CHART
30

CHART 30.

SCALE OF HUE AND CHROMA.

This chart is a horizontal section through the color solid, similar to that of chart 50.

Each radius is a scale of chroma, whose steps appear written beneath the line. Thus $R_7$ is the seventh step of red and reflects 70% of the strength of standard vermilion. Its opposite hue,—blue-green, has but four steps of chroma at this level, and to balance these uneven chromas, the area of the weaker must be seven fourths as great as that of the stronger color.

Each concentric circle traces hues of equal chroma. A sequence of regularly decreasing chroma may be traced thus:—$PB_1$, $RP_4$, $YR_4$, $GY_3$, $N^3$. The suggestions on chart 50 may be applied to this chart as indicated in chapters III and IV of a "Color Notation."

AVOID HANDLING AND EXPOSURE TO DUST.

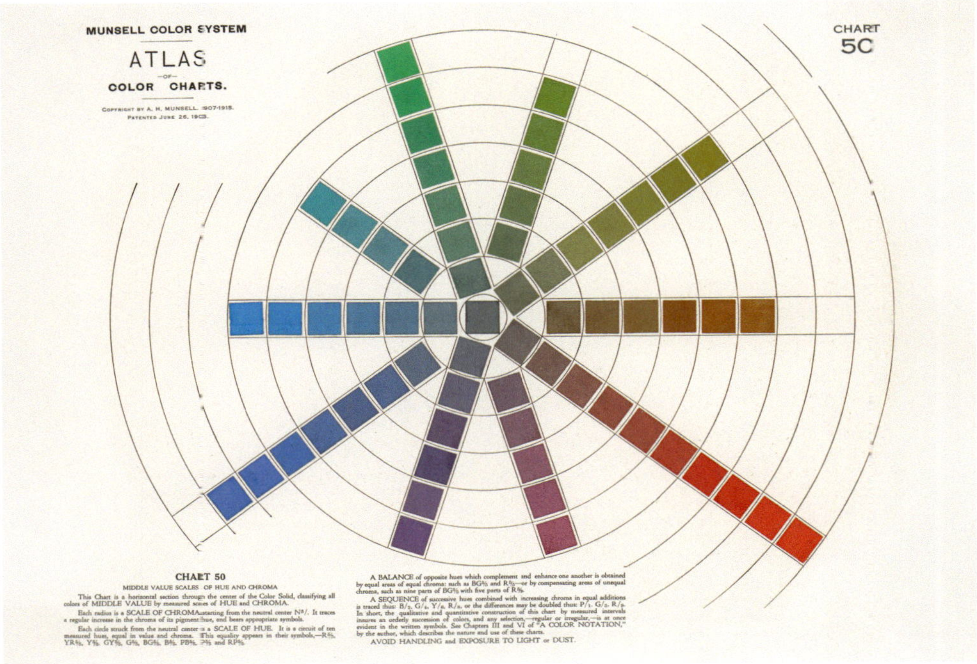

MUNSELL COLOR SYSTEM

ATLAS

—OF—

COLOR CHARTS.

COPYRIGHT BY A. H. MUNSELL. 1907-1915.
PATENTED JUNE 26, 1903.

CHART
5C

CHART 50

MIDDLE VALUE SCALES OF HUE AND CHROMA

This Chart is a horizontal section through the center of the Color Solid, classifying all colors of MIDDLE VALUE by measured scales of HUE and CHROMA.

Each radius is a SCALE OF CHROMA starting from the neutral center N5/. It traces a regular increase in the chroma of its pigment hue, and bears appropriate symbols.

Each circle struck from the neutral center is a SCALE OF HUE. It is a circuit of ten measured hues, equal in value and chroma. This equality appears in their symbols,—R5/5, YR5/5, Y5/5, GY5/5, G5/5, BG5/5, B5/5, PB5/5, P5/5 and RP5/5.

A BALANCE of opposite hues which complement and enhance one another is obtained by equal areas of equal chroma: such as BG5/5 and R5/5—or by compensating areas of unequal chroma, such as nine parts of BG5/5 with five parts of R5/9.

A SEQUENCE of successive hues combined with increasing chroma in equal additions is traced thus: B/2, G/4, Y/6, R/8, or the differences may be doubled thus: P/1, G/5, R/9. In short, the qualitative and quantitative construction of this chart by measured intervals insures an orderly succession of colors, and any selection,—regular or irregular,—is at once evident in the written symbols. *See* Chapters III and VI of "A COLOR NOTATION," by the author, which describes the nature and use of these charts.

AVOID HANDLING and EXPOSURE TO LIGHT or DUST.

**MUNSELL COLOR SYSTEM**

# ATLAS

—OF—

## COLOR CHARTS.

COPYRIGHT BY A. H. MUNSELL. 1907-1915.
PATENTED JUNE 26, 1906.

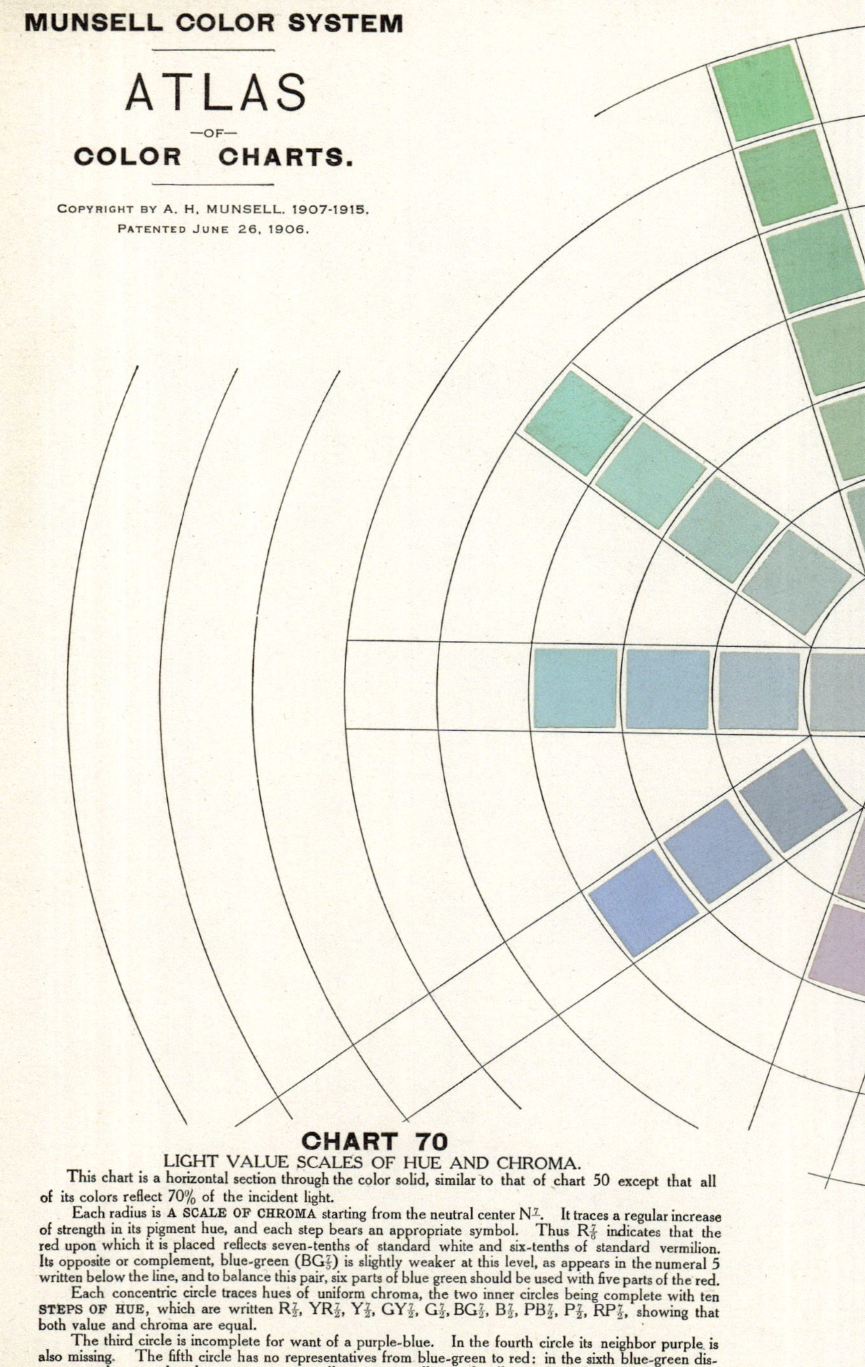

## CHART 70

LIGHT VALUE SCALES OF HUE AND CHROMA.

This chart is a horizontal section through the color solid, similar to that of chart 50 except that all of its colors reflect 70% of the incident light.

Each radius is **A SCALE OF CHROMA** starting from the neutral center $N\frac{7}{}$. It traces a regular increase of strength in its pigment hue, and each step bears an appropriate symbol. Thus $R\frac{7}{6}$ indicates that the red upon which it is placed reflects seven-tenths of standard white and six-tenths of standard vermilion. Its opposite or complement, blue-green ($BG\frac{7}{5}$) is slightly weaker at this level, as appears in the numeral 5 written below the line, and to balance this pair, six parts of blue green should be used with five parts of the red.

Each concentric circle traces hues of uniform chroma, the two inner circles being complete with ten **STEPS OF HUE**, which are written $R\frac{7}{2}$, $YR\frac{7}{2}$, $Y\frac{7}{2}$, $GY\frac{7}{2}$, $G\frac{7}{2}$, $BG\frac{7}{2}$, $B\frac{7}{2}$, $PB\frac{7}{2}$, $P\frac{7}{2}$, $RP\frac{7}{2}$, showing that both value and chroma are equal.

The third circle is incomplete for want of a purple-blue. In the fourth circle its neighbor purple is also missing. The fifth circle has no representatives from blue-green to red: in the sixth blue-green disappears: the seventh only presents green, yellow-green, yellow and yellow-red, while the eighth circle is represented by yellow alone.

These radii describe the unequal strength of pigments at this level of the color solid and should be contrasted with chart 30 where the relations of strength and weakness are reversed.

For a study of balances and sequences on this chart see Chapters III and IV of "A Color Notation" by the author.

AVOID HANDLING AND EXPOSURE TO DUST.

CHART

70

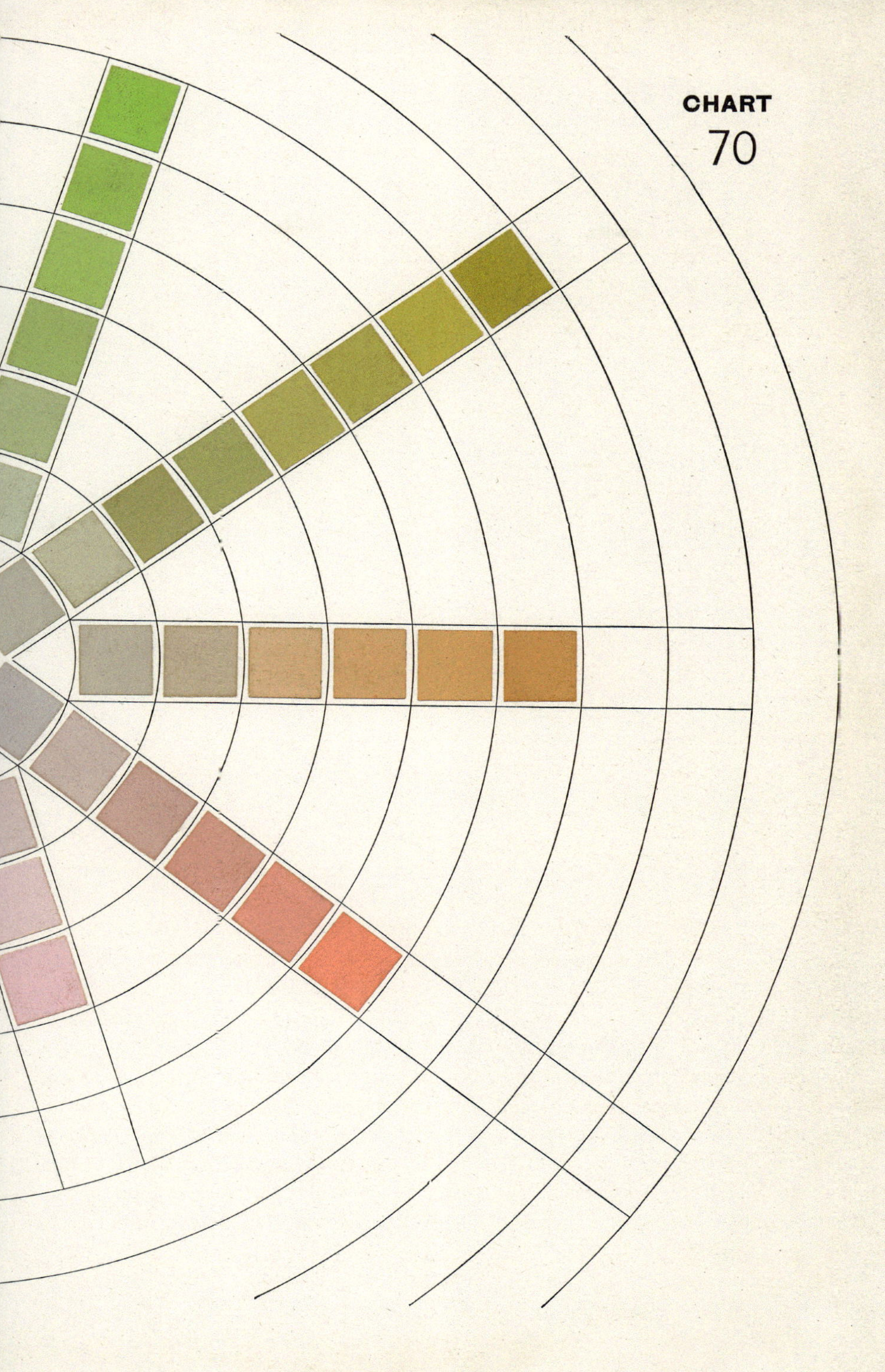

## Christine Ladd-Franklin (1847–1930)

# COLOUR AND COLOUR THEORIES

*9 plates, 22 x 13.5 cm / 8 ⅝ x 5 ¼ in., London & New York, 1929*
*Sussex, collection of the author*

Although it was published in 1929, *Colour and Colour Theories* was first conceived in the 19th century and is therefore an important indicator of developments in colour research over that period, as well as the restrictions women still faced at the time in higher education. Connecticut-born Christine Ladd-Franklin succeeded in entering colleges and attending university courses despite the rules that were then in place, sometimes by hiding the fact that she was a woman. With the assistance of the English mathematician James Sylvester she was admitted to John Hopkins University, where she studied mathematics under Sylvester and logic with Charles Sanders Peirce. Although she completed all the requirements for a Ph.D. – and in the process became the first woman in the United States to do so – the university did not allow her to graduate, and she had to wait until 1926 for this to be rectified, 44 years after she had earned her doctorate.

Ladd-Franklin was concerned with how individual colour "sensation" could be explained in relation to the anatomy of the human eye. She had a profound knowledge of the prevailing theories of colour vision in the 19th century and had worked in Germany for several years with the pioneering researchers in this field, Hermann von Helmholtz, Ewald Hering, and their fellow scientists. As early as 1892 Ladd-Franklin had proposed her own theory of colour vision in a series of essays written

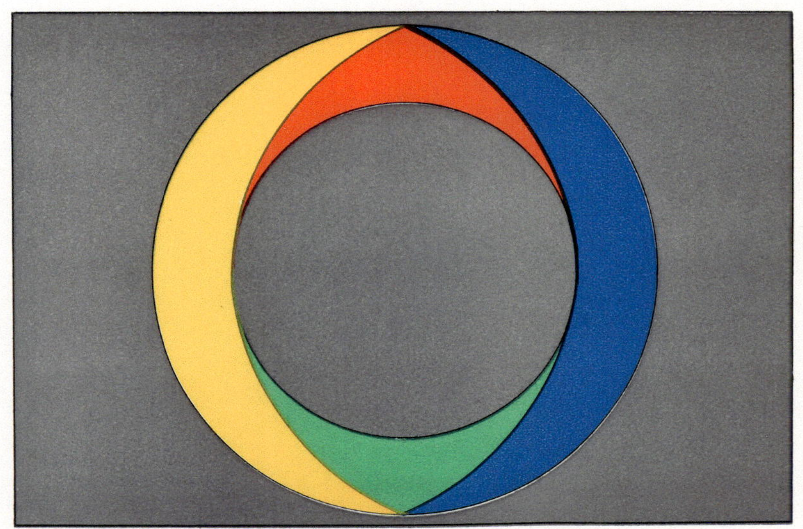

I. FIRST CRUDE ANALYSIS OF THE COLOUR SENSE

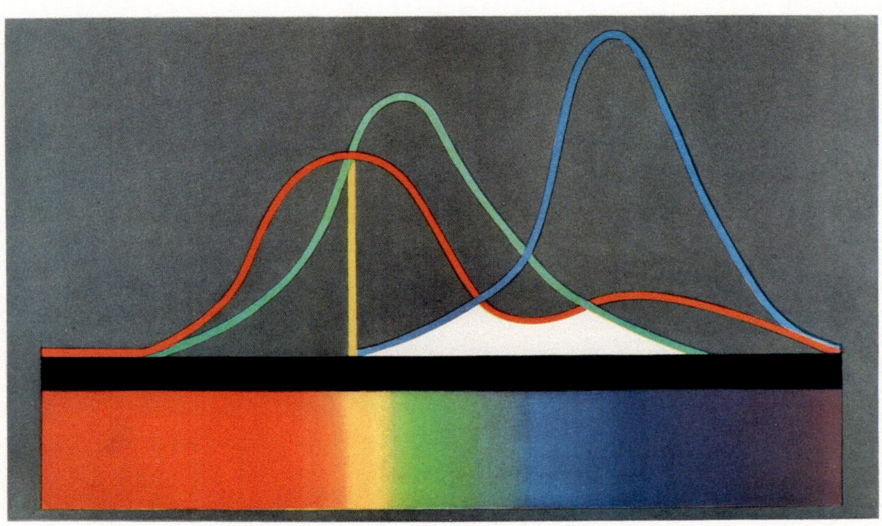

II. SCIENTIFIC ANALYSIS OF THE SPECTRUM: HELMHOLTZ-KONIG

## DEVELOPMENT OF THE COLOUR SENSE

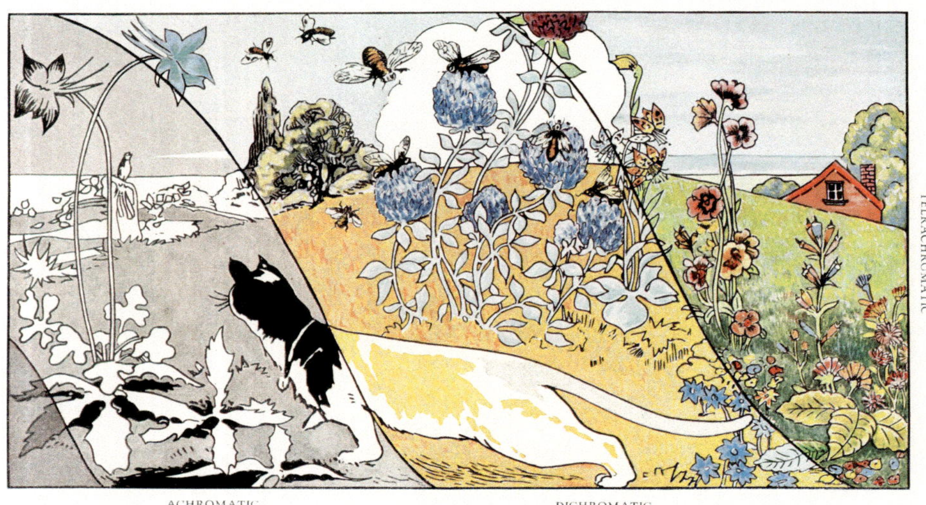


in German and English, which took a critical view of the two rival theories proposed by Helmholtz and Hering. She argued for an evolutionary, or developmental theory of colour vision, beginning with a single light-sensitive chemical in prehistoric times that gave animals an achromatic black-and-white vision. Over time this molecular activity became differentiated into two processes, with one part recognising "warm" tones (yellow) and the other "cold" (blue), thus leading to dichromatic vision, as is found still in certain insects. Human trichromatic vision would represent a further evolutionary split when yellow differentiated into red and green, which Ladd-Franklin then extended to a theory of tetrachromatic human vision. One instance she put forward in support of her argument referred to colour blindness which was known to occur only in certain colour pairs.

The full extent of Ladd-Franklin's studies and research was not published until 1929 when this book was issued. She commissioned the colour plates specially, which she considered a "kintergarten [*sic*] method of enabling one to hold in mind all at once the curiously complicated [...] phenomena of colour", and while her theories are now mostly discredited or have been superseded, there can be no question that she contributed significantly to an understanding of colour psychology in relation to colour vision.

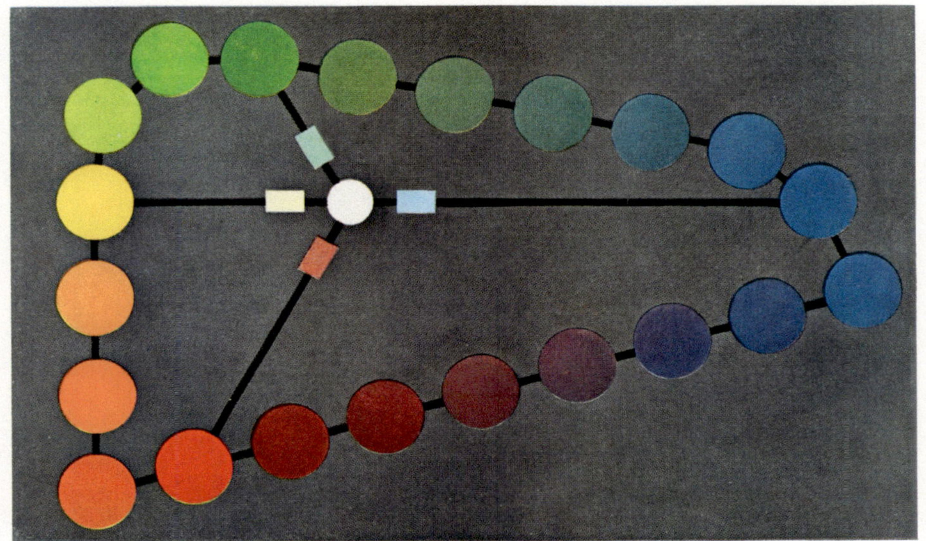

III. THE COLOUR TRIANGLE

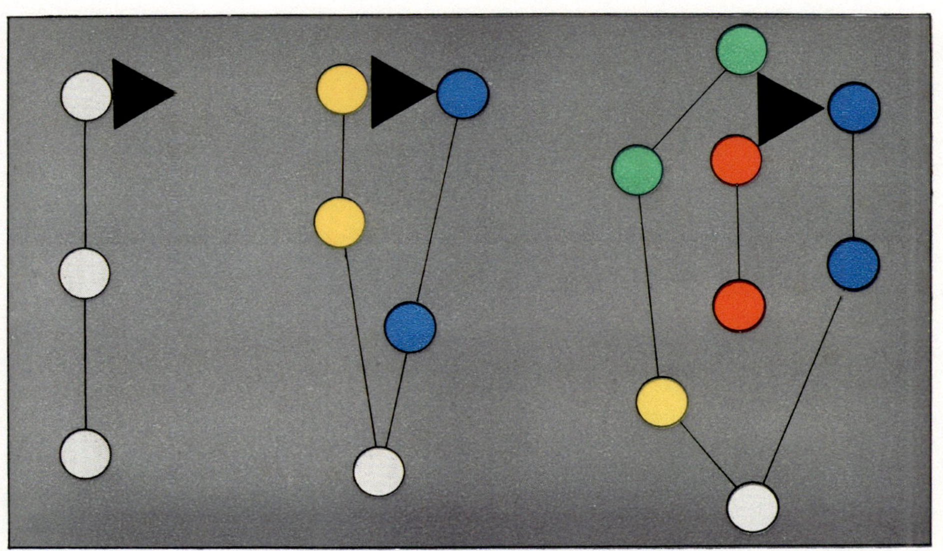

IV. THE STAGES OF DEVELOPMENT—THEORETICAL

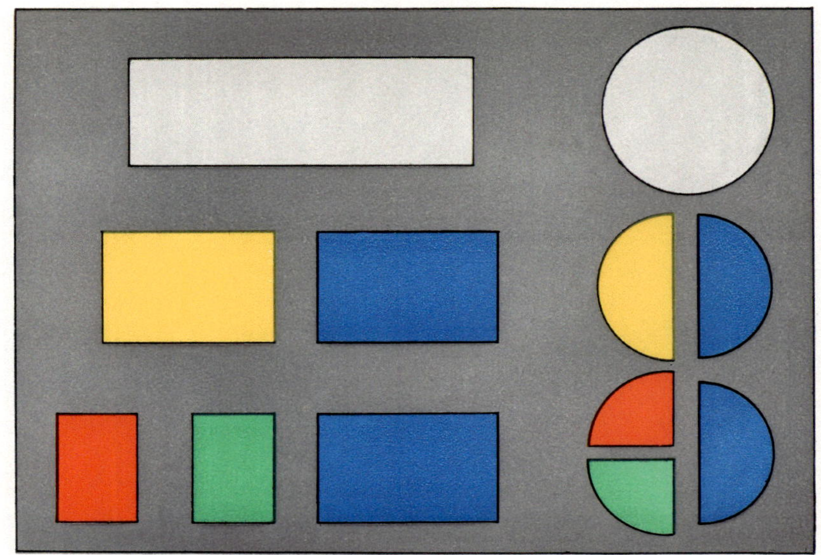

V. THE STAGES OF DEVELOPMENT—*Left*, ACTUAL *Right*, THEORETICAL

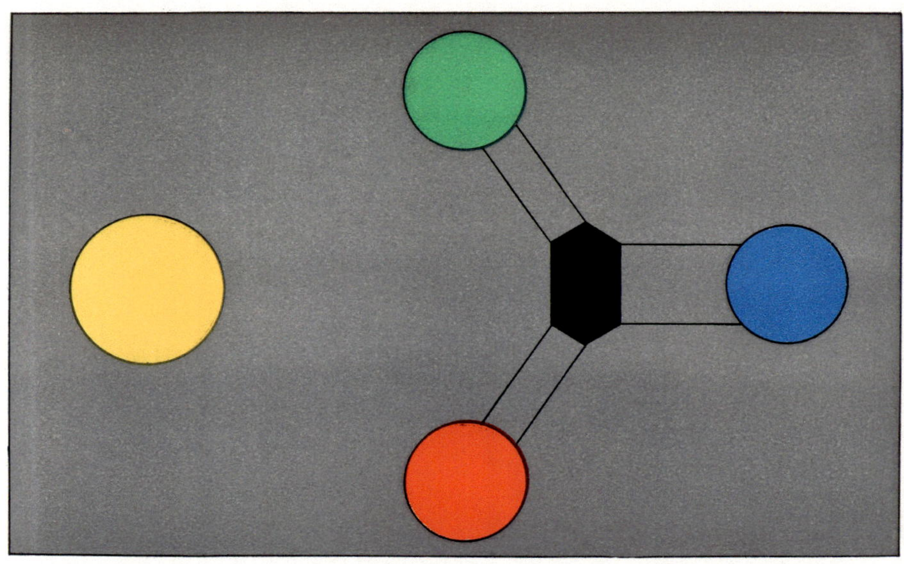

VI. THE ASSUMED COLOUR-MOLECULE—TOGETHER WITH SECONDARY YELLOW

## Farbe und Farbtheorien

Obwohl es 1929 veröffentlicht wurde, reichen die Wurzeln von *Colour and Colour Theories* bis ins 19. Jahrhundert zurück. Das Buch ist daher ein wichtiger Indikator für die Entwicklung der Farbforschung in dieser Zeit und für die Einschränkungen, denen Frauen im damaligen Hochschulwesen unterworfen waren. Die im US-Bundesstaat Connecticut geborene Christine Ladd-Franklin setzte sich klug über die geltenden Vorschriften zum Collegezugang und Hochschulstudium hinweg und hatte Erfolg, indem sie mitunter sogar ihre weibliche Identität verbarg. Mit Unterstützung des englischen Mathematikers James Sylvester wurde sie an der Johns Hopkins University zugelassen, wo sie bei Sylvester Mathematik und bei Charles Sanders Peirce Logik studierte. Obwohl sie – als erste Frau in den USA überhaupt – alle für eine Promotion erforderlichen Leistungen erbrachte, verweigerte ihr die Universität den Abschluss. Sie musste bis 1926 warten, ehe diese Entscheidung korrigiert wurde – ganze 44 Jahre, nachdem sie den Doktorgrad eigentlich erworben hatte.

Ladd-Franklin beschäftigte die Frage, wie die individuelle „Empfindung" von Farbe in Bezug auf die Anatomie des menschlichen Auges zu erklären war. Sie kannte die im 19. Jahrhundert vorherrschenden Theorien des Farbensehens und hatte in Deutschland mehrere Jahre lang mit Hermann von Helmholtz, Ewald Hering und deren Kollegen, den wegweisenden Forschern auf diesem Gebiet, zusammengearbeitet. Schon 1892 hatte sie in einer Reihe von Aufsätzen auf Deutsch und Englisch ihre eigene Theorie des Farbensehens vorgelegt, die sich kritisch mit den beiden konkurrierenden Theorien von Helmholtz und Hering auseinandersetzte. Sie selbst plädierte für eine Evolutions- oder Entwicklungstheorie des Farbensehens, das in prähistorischer Zeit mit einer einzigen lichtempfindlichen Chemikalie begann und Tieren ein unbuntes Schwarz-Weiß-Sehen ermöglichte. Mit der Zeit spaltete sich diese Molekulartätigkeit in zwei Prozesse auf. Ein Teil erkannte „warme" Töne (Gelb), der andere „kalte" (Blau), was zum Zweifarbensehen führte, wie es heute noch bei manchen Insekten zu finden ist. Das Dreifarbensehen des Menschen steht für eine weitere evolutionäre Aufspaltung von Gelb in Rot und Grün, die Ladd-Franklin dann zu einer Theorie des menschlichen Vierfarbensehens erweiterte. Ein Beleg, den sie zur Unterstützung ihrer Argumentation vorbrachte, bezog sich auf die Farbenfehlsichtigkeit, von der man wusste, dass sie nur bestimmte Farbpaare betraf.

Der ganze Umfang der Studien und Forschungsarbeiten Ladd-Franklins wurde erst 1929 mit dem hier vorgestellten Farbenbuch sichtbar. Die Farbtafeln dafür gab sie speziell in Auftrag. Dabei hielt sie Farbdiagramme eigentlich für eine „Kintergartenmethod [sic], die uns befähigt, die merkwürdig komplizierten [...] Farbphänomene auf einmal im Kopf zu behalten". Während ihre Theorien heute größtenteils in Misskredit geraten oder überholt sind, kann es keinen Zweifel geben, dass Ladd-Franklin maßgeblich zu einem besseren Verständnis des Zusammenhangs zwischen Farbensehen und Farbpsychologie beigetragen hat.

## Couleur et théories chromatiques

Publié en 1929, *Colour and Colour Theories* a pourtant été conçu à la fin du siècle précédent. À ce titre, il est un témoignage important de l'évolution de la recherche sur la couleur, ainsi que des limitations que subissent encore alors les femmes dans l'accès aux études supérieures. Née dans le Connecticut, Christine Ladd-Franklin a habilement transgressé les règles d'accès aux cours délivrés dans les universités, allant parfois jusqu'à cacher qu'elle était une femme. Elle étudie les mathématiques auprès de l'Anglais James Sylvester, qui l'a fait admettre à la Johns Hopkins University, ainsi que la logique auprès de Charles Sanders Peirce. Elle remplit toutes les conditions pour rédiger sa thèse et devient la première femme aux États-Unis à parvenir à ce niveau. Cependant, l'université ne lui permet pas d'obtenir son doctorat, ce qui ne sera réparé qu'en 1926, soit quarante-quatre ans après la fin de son cursus.

Ladd-Franklin cherche particulièrement à expliquer comment l'anatomie de l'œil humain produit la « sensation » d'une couleur. Elle est très au fait des théories sur la vision de la couleur qui prévalent au XIXe siècle et a travaillé plusieurs années en Allemagne avec les pionniers de la recherche dans ce domaine, Hermann von Helmholtz, Ewald Hering et leurs collègues scientifiques. Dès 1892, Ladd-Franklin a proposé sa propre théorie de la vision des couleurs et critique les deux théories rivales de Helmholtz et Hering dans une série d'essais écrits en allemand et en anglais. Elle y soutient une théorie évolutionniste : un élément chimique photosensible unique aurait donné aux animaux, depuis la préhistoire, une vision achromatique en noir et blanc. Au fil du temps, cette activité moléculaire se serait différenciée en deux processus, l'un permettant de reconnaître les teintes « chaudes » (jaune), l'autre les « froides » (bleu), et aurait donné lieu à la vision dichromatique que l'on trouve chez certains insectes. La vision trichromatique humaine aurait correspondu à une séparation ultérieure dans cette évolution, soit la division du jaune en rouge et vert, et abouti plus tard encore, selon Ladd-Franklin, au tétrachromatisme chez l'humain. Le daltonisme, réputé n'affecter que la vision de certaines paires chromatiques, est un argument de plus pour étayer sa thèse.

La sortie de cet ouvrage en 1929 représente la première publication de la totalité des recherches de Ladd-Franklin. Elle fait faire tout spécialement les planches en couleurs, les considérant comme « une méthode de *kintergarten* [*sic*] pour permettre à chacun d'envisager dans sa totalité le phénomène [...] curieusement compliqué de la couleur ». Si ses théories ont été largement battues en brèche depuis, sa contribution a de toute évidence été significative dans la compréhension de la psychologie de la couleur par rapport à la vision des couleurs.

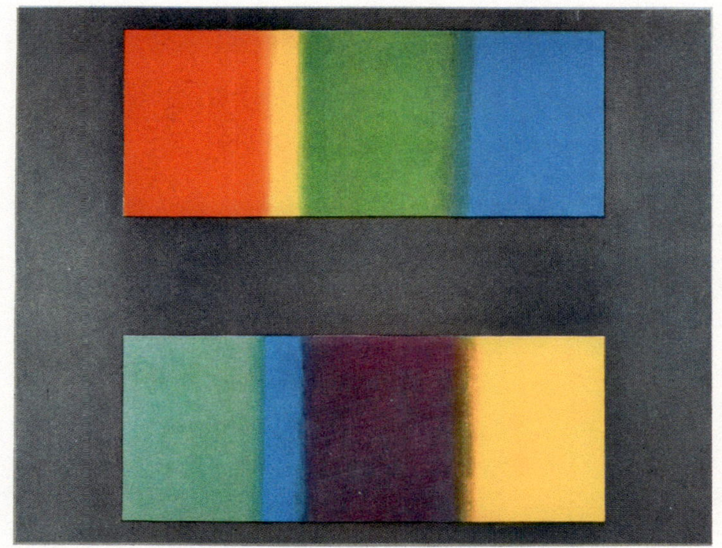

VII. *Above*, THE SPECTRUM. *Below*, ITS RESIDUAL IMAGE

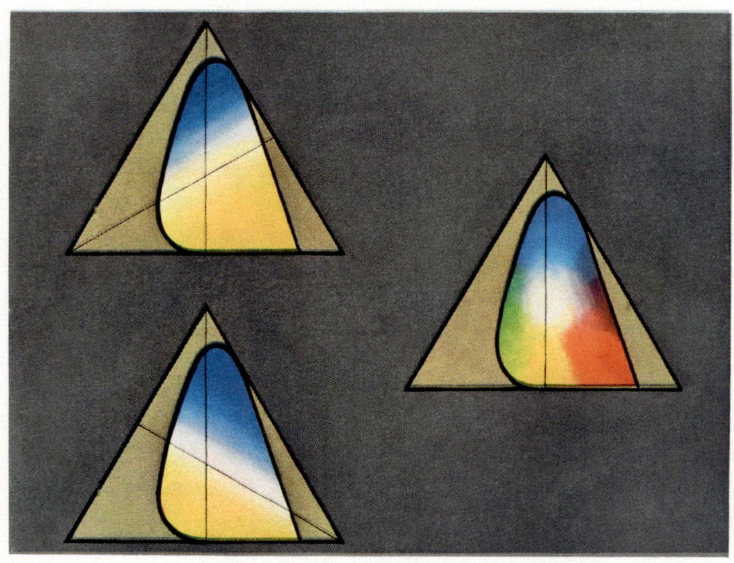

VIII. *Left*, ATAVISTIC DICHROMATIC VISION OF THE TWO TYPES
*Right*, NORMAL TETRACHROMATIC VISION

## Carry van Biema (1881–1942)

# FARBEN UND FORMEN ALS LEBENDIGE KRÄFTE

**Colours and Forms as Living Forces**
*19 plates, 21.8 x 15.4 cm | 8 ⅝ x 6 in., Jena, 1930*
*Berlin, Universität der Künste*

A deeply personal and intellectual work, *Farben und Formen als lebendige Kräfte* was intended to combine scholarship with practical advice. In this it fully reflected its author's upbringing and vocation since Carry van Biema had decided when she was still young that she would be an artist, which she then managed to combine with teaching art and art history. She moved between her birthplace Germany and the Netherlands, where her family came from, for work and exhibiting her own art. Van Biema mixed with members of German avant-garde groups while studying old masters and foundational texts, including Goethe's writings on colour. The person who most influenced her approach to colour was Adolf Hölzel (1853–1934), a German abstract painter and teacher at the Königliche Akademie der bildenden Künste in Stuttgart (Stuttgart Academy of Arts) where Van Biema attended classes from 1914 to 1919, overlapping as a student there with Johannes Itten. In the absence of any published work by Hölzel, Van Biema intended to bring his theories to wider public attention, and this she eventually did with *Farben und Formen*, which was divided into three parts: an introduction to the basics of painting and composition, an overview of Goethe's *Zur Farbenlehre* and an introduction to Hölzel's colour theory.

The bold modernist cover of *Farben und Formen* was designed by the German Expressionist Max Thalmann (1890–1944), and the book itself contains 21 chromolithographic plates depicting colour diagrams and artworks, together with 81 black and white photographic images. Van Biema's plates are particularly innovative in having an interactive element, since each one is overlaid with a transparent tissue guard printed with graphic shapes and text labels that relate to the image underneath. It was an extremely simple and effective idea that made it easier for the reader to understand concepts such as the golden ratio or the structure of various colour diagrams.

Although the book was not positively received by Hölzel, it was widely discussed in Germany and during the early 1930s Van Biema appears to have enjoyed both intellectual fulfilment and professional success. It was not to last, however, for since she was Jewish she faced persecution under the Nazi regime. Van Biema temporarily found shelter in the Netherlands but was eventually deported and murdered in Auschwitz concentration camp. Most copies of her book are thought to have been destroyed by the Nazis.

TAFEL I

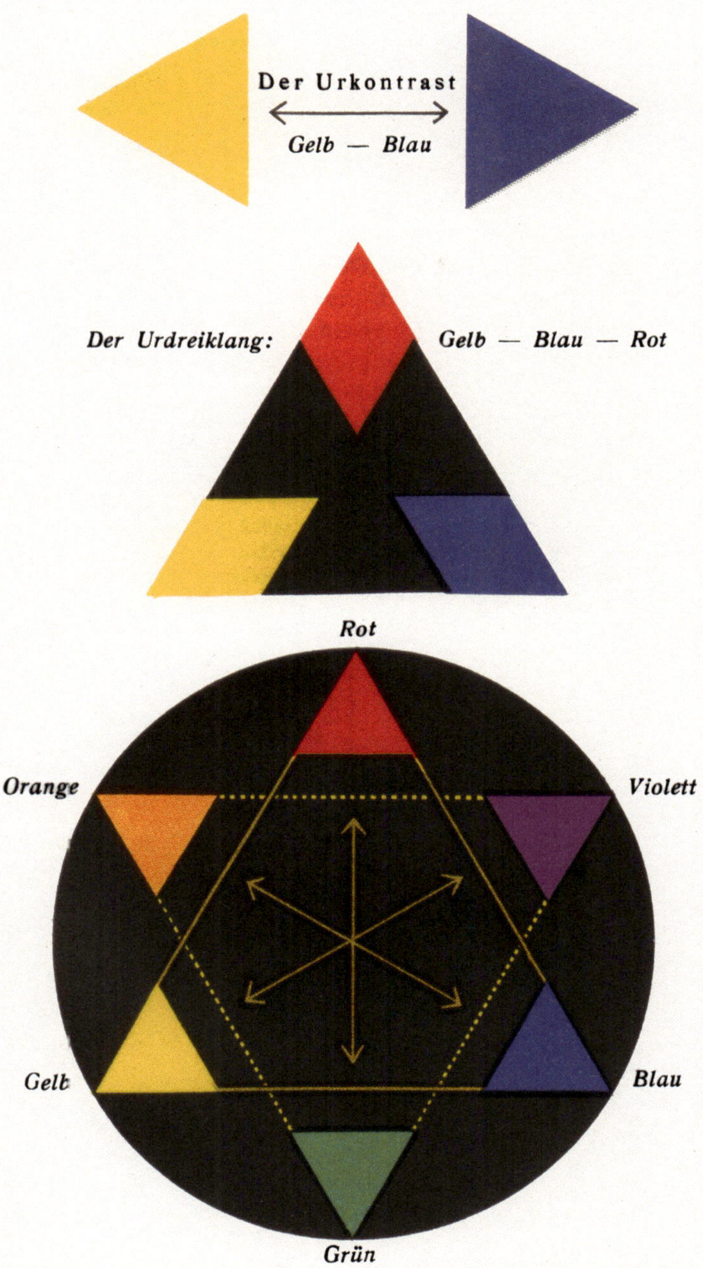


DER GOETHESCHE FARBKREIS
(Die Pfeile bezeichnen die komplementären Paare)

## DER ÄQUIVALENTE FARBKREIS NACH SCHOPENHAUER

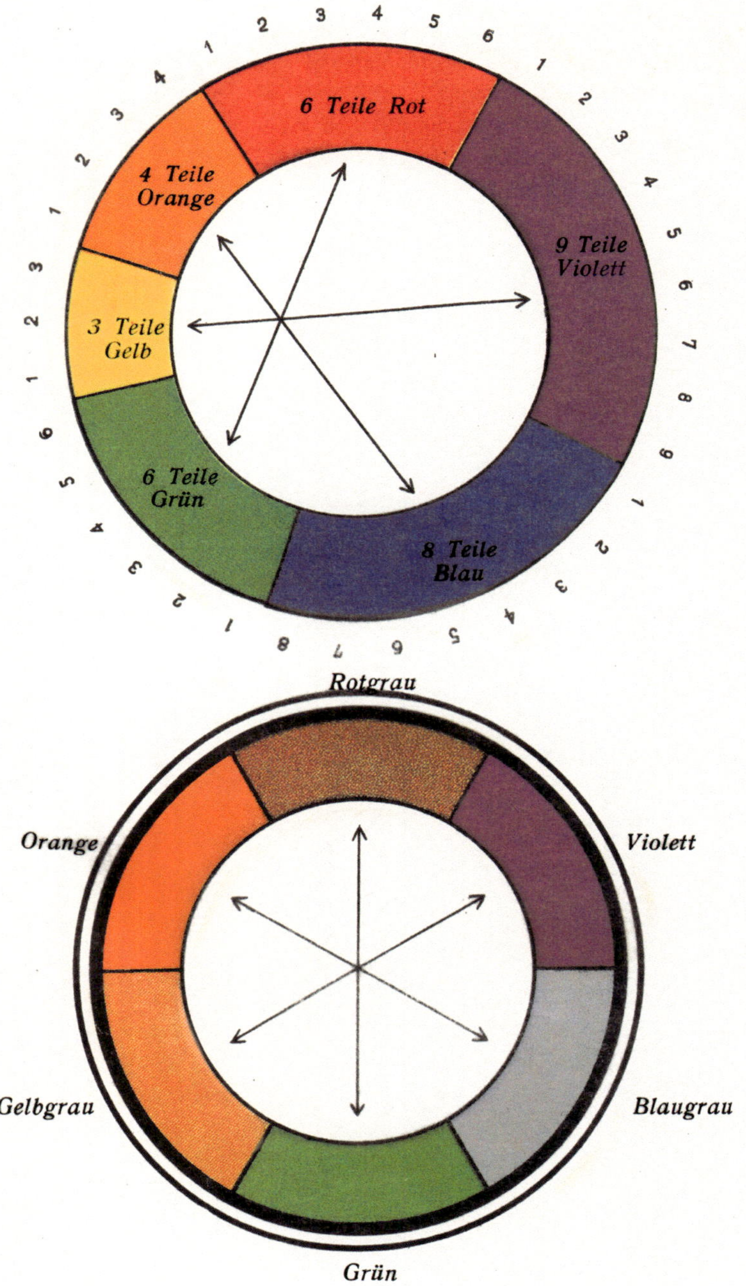


## DER MISCHFARBENKREIS

Die tertiären Farben haben die Plätze der Urfarben eingenommen

## Farben und Formen als lebendige Kräfte

*Farben und Formen als lebendige Kräfte* war ein zutiefst persönliches und intellektuelles Buch, das Wissenschaft und praktische Ratschläge miteinander verbinden sollte. Darin spiegelte es vollumfänglich die Erziehung und Berufung seiner Autorin wider. Schon als Jugendliche hatte Carry van Biema beschlossen, Künstlerin zu werden. Später dann gelang es ihr, neben der Malerei Kunst und Kunstgeschichte zu unterrichten. Um zu arbeiten und ihre eigene Kunst auszustellen, pendelte sie zwischen ihrem Geburtsland Deutschland und den Niederlanden, dem Herkunftsland ihrer Familie. Sie verkehrte mit Mitgliedern avantgardistischer Künstlergruppen in Deutschland und beschäftigte sich gleichzeitig mit Alten Meistern und Grundlagentexten wie Goethes Schriften über Farbe. Den größten Einfluss auf ihren Zugang zur Farbe hatte der deutsche Abstraktionist Adolf Hölzel (1853–1934), der an der Königlichen Akademie der bildenden Künste in Stuttgart lehrte, wo van Biema von 1914 bis 1919 teils zeitgleich mit Johannes Itten studierte. Weil es von Hölzel wenig Schriftliches gab, wollte van Biema seine Theorien einer breiteren Öffentlichkeit bekannt machen und setzte ihr Vorhaben mit *Farben und Formen als lebendige Kräfte* in die Tat um. Das Buch war in drei Teile untergliedert: eine Einführung in die Grundlagen der Malerei und Komposition, einen Überblick über Goethes Farbenlehre und eine Einführung in Hölzels Farbtheorie.

Den modernen Einband von *Farben und Formen* entwarf der deutsche Expressionist Max Thalmann (1890–1944). Das Buch selbst enthält 21 farblithografische Tafeln mit Abbildungen von Farbdiagrammen und Kunstwerken, ergänzt um 81 Schwarz-Weiß-Reproduktionen. Als besondere Neuerung fügte van Biema jeder ihrer Bildtafeln ein interaktives Element hinzu, ein Deckblatt aus transparentem Seidenpapier, das mit grafischen Formen und Beschriftungen bedruckt war, die sich auf das darunterliegende Bild bezogen. Dieser überaus simple und wirkungsvolle Einfall erleichterte es der Leserschaft, Ideen wie den Goldenen Schnitt oder den Aufbau verschiedener Farbdiagramme nachzuvollziehen.

Obwohl Hölzel selbst das Buch nicht gut aufnahm, wurde es in Deutschland in weiten Kreisen diskutiert. Entsprechend scheint seine Autorin in den frühen 1930er-Jahren sowohl geistige Erfüllung als auch beruflichen Erfolg genossen zu haben. Beides sollte nicht von Dauer sein, denn als Jüdin wurde van Biema vom NS-Regime verfolgt. Vorübergehend fand sie Schutz in den Niederlanden, wurde jedoch schließlich deportiert und im Konzentrationslager Auschwitz ermordet. Die meisten Exemplare ihres Buches fielen vermutlich dem Zerstörungswahn der Nationalsozialisten zum Opfer.

## FARBENSTIMMUNGEN AUS DEM NEUNTEILIGEN DREIECK

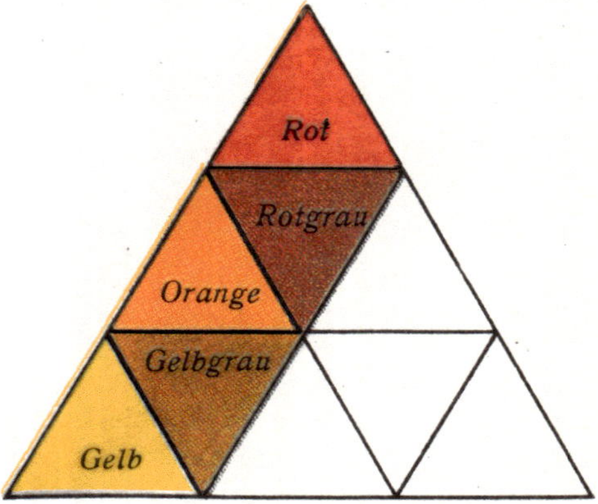

Rot
Rotgrau
Orange
Gelbgrau
Gelb

*leuchtend*

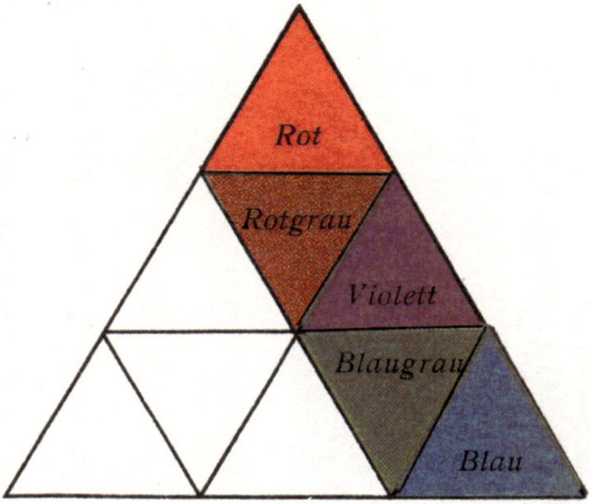

Rot
Rotgrau
Violett
Blaugrau
Blau

*ernst*

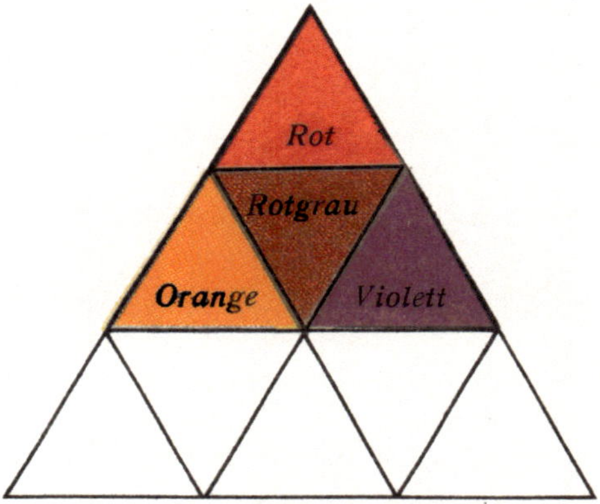

Rot
Rotgrau
Orange
Violett

*mächtig*

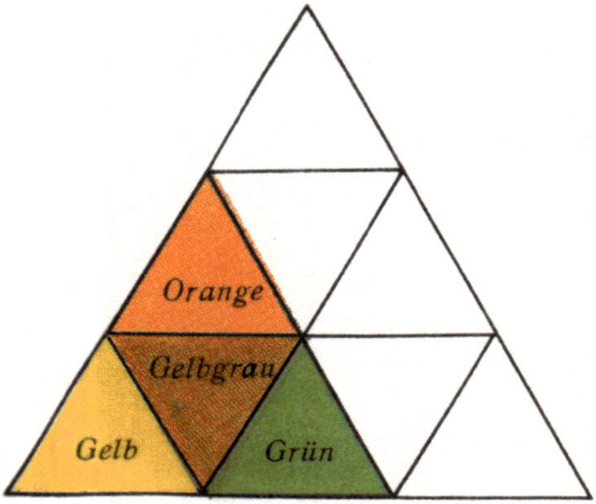

Orange
Gelbgrau
Gelb
Grün

*heiter*

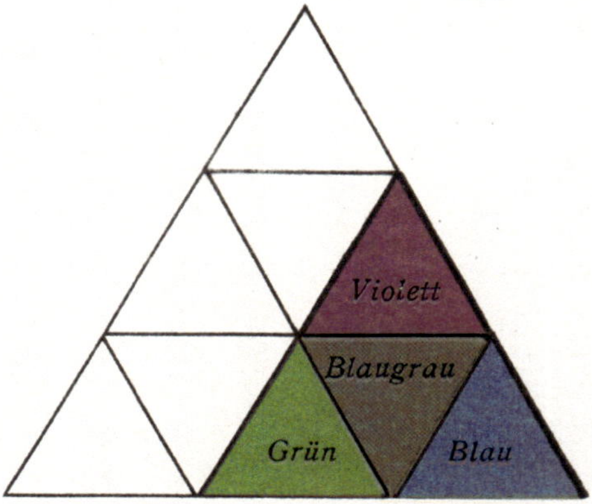

Violett
Blaugrau
Grün
Blau

*melancholisch*

Die Seiten und Ecken ergeben ausgesprochene Farbenstimmungen. (Seite 107 und 113)

## DAS BEKANNTE NEUNTEILIGE FARBENDREIECK

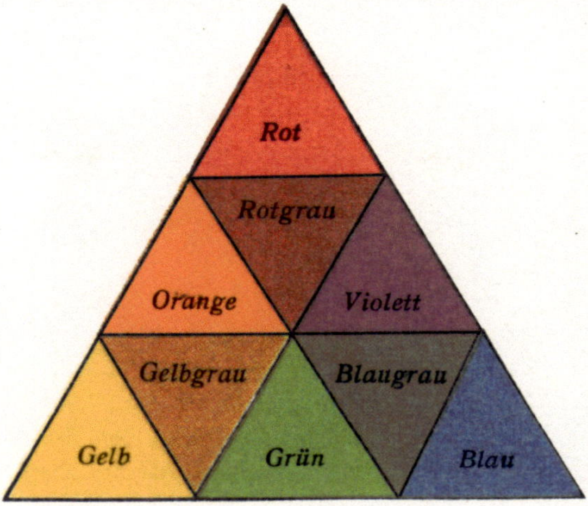

Rot
Rotgrau
Orange
Violett
Gelbgrau
Blaugrau
Gelb
Grün
Blau

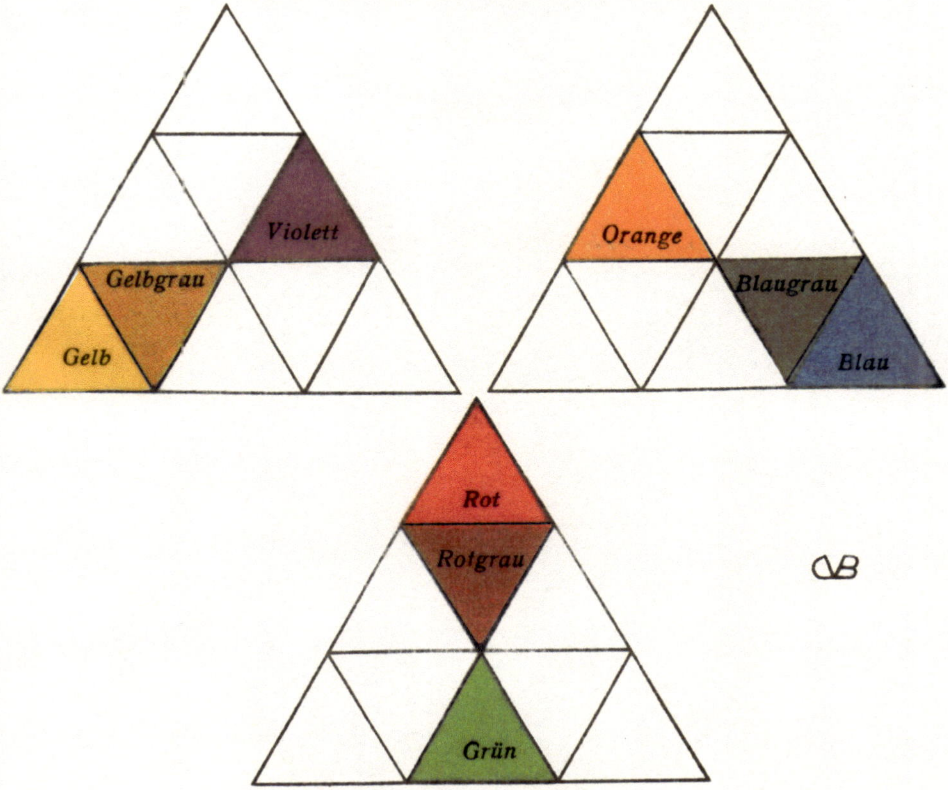

Violett
Gelbgrau
Gelb

Orange
Blaugrau
Blau

Rot
Rotgrau
Grün

**Unten drei schöne komplementäre Akkorde, bei denen die tertiären Farben die Übergänge bilden. (Seite 107) Hier sieht man zugleich eine günstige Anordnung und Strichlage der Farben im Bildganzen. (Seite 189)**

DER ACHTTEILIGE ODER DIATONISCHE FARBKREIS

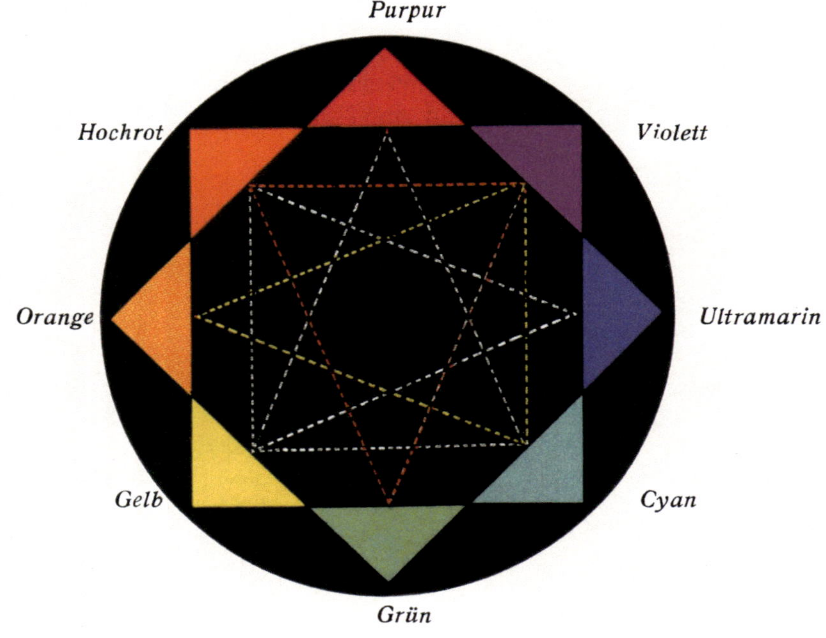


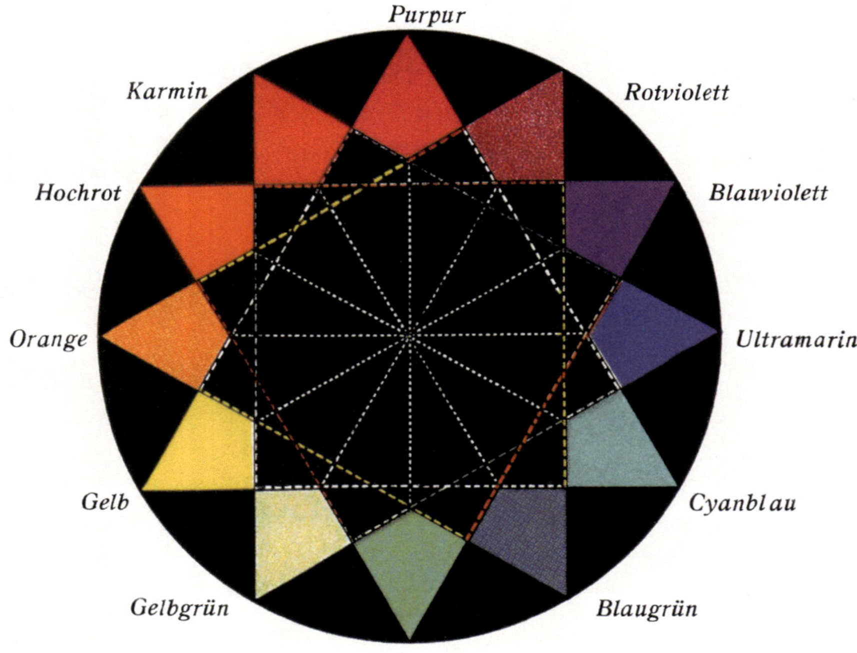


DER ZWÖLFTEILIGE FARBKREIS

DER ALTBEKANNTE ZWÖLFTEILIGE FARBKREIS
(Die Pfeile bezeichnen die komplementären Paare)

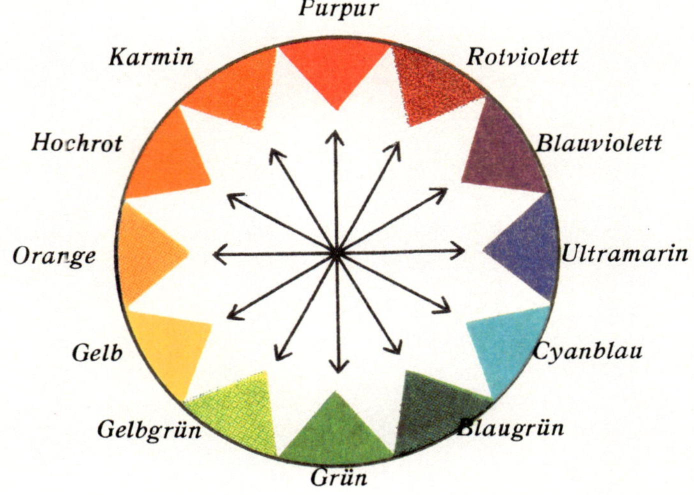


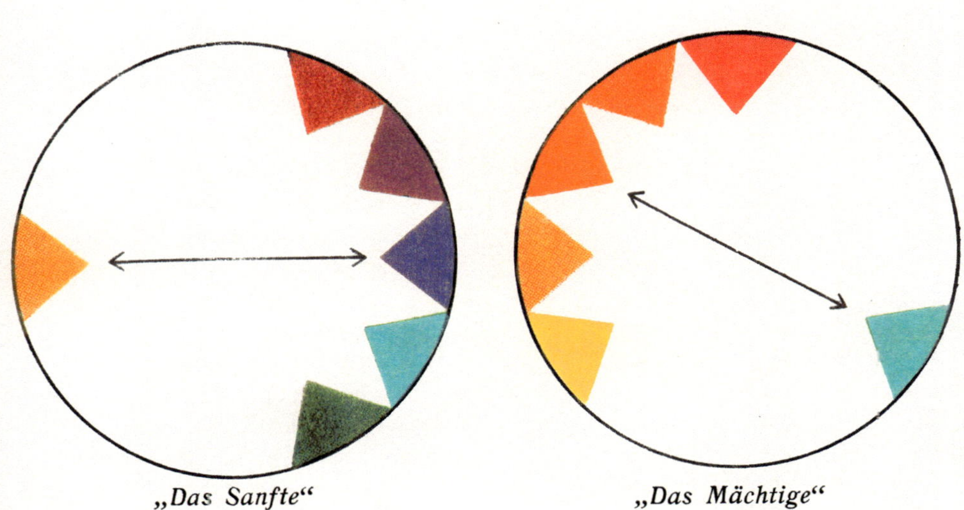

*„Das Sanfte“* *„Das Mächtige“*

DUR- UND MOLLKLANG NACH GOETHE

## Les couleurs et les formes, forces vitales

Ouvrage profondément intellectuel et personnel, *Farben und Formen als lebendige Kräfte* vise à marier pédagogie et conseils pratiques. En cela, il reflète pleinement l'éducation et la vocation de son autrice. Carry van Biema a en effet décidé très jeune qu'elle serait artiste, ce qu'elle a ensuite réussi à mener de front avec l'enseignement de l'art et de l'histoire de l'art. Elle voyage régulièrement entre son Allemagne natale et les Pays-Bas, d'où est originaire sa famille, pour son travail et pour exposer ses œuvres. Elle fréquente les groupes de l'avant-garde allemande tout en étudiant les maîtres de la peinture classique et les textes fondateurs, dont les écrits de Goethe sur la couleur. Mais dans son approche du sujet, elle est surtout influencée par Adolf Hölzel (1853–1934), peintre abstrait allemand qui enseigne à la Königliche Akademie der bildenden Künste (Académie royale des beaux-arts) à Stuttgart, où van Biema suit des cours de 1914 à 1919, en partie au même moment que Johannes Itten. Hölzel n'ayant jamais publié d'ouvrage, van Biema se propose de faire connaître ses théories au public. C'est là l'objet de *Farben und Formen*, qui est divisé en trois parties : une présentation des bases de la peinture et de la composition, une vue d'ensemble du *Zur Farbenlehre* de Goethe et une introduction à la théorie de la couleur de Hölzel.

La couverture, audacieusement moderniste, est signée par l'expressionniste allemand Max Thalmann (1890–1944). L'ouvrage contient 21 œuvres d'art et tableaux chromatiques chromolithographiés, ainsi que 81 photographies en noir et blanc. Les planches de van Biema sont particulièrement novatrices par leur élément interactif : chacune est recouverte d'un papier de soie transparent imprimé de formes graphiques et de brefs textes en lien avec les images. Une idée extrêmement simple et efficace pour faciliter la compréhension de concepts tels que le nombre d'or ou la structure des différents graphiques chromatiques.

Bien que l'ouvrage soit assez mal accueilli par Hölzel lui-même, il est largement commenté en Allemagne et, au début des années 1930, van Biema semble avoir connu à la fois l'épanouissement intellectuel et la réussite professionnelle. Cela ne dure pas : juive, elle subit la persécution du régime nazi. Après avoir provisoirement trouvé refuge aux Pays-Bas, van Biema est finalement déportée et assassinée au camp de concentration d'Auschwitz. La plupart des exemplaires de son livre ont probablement été détruits par les nazis.

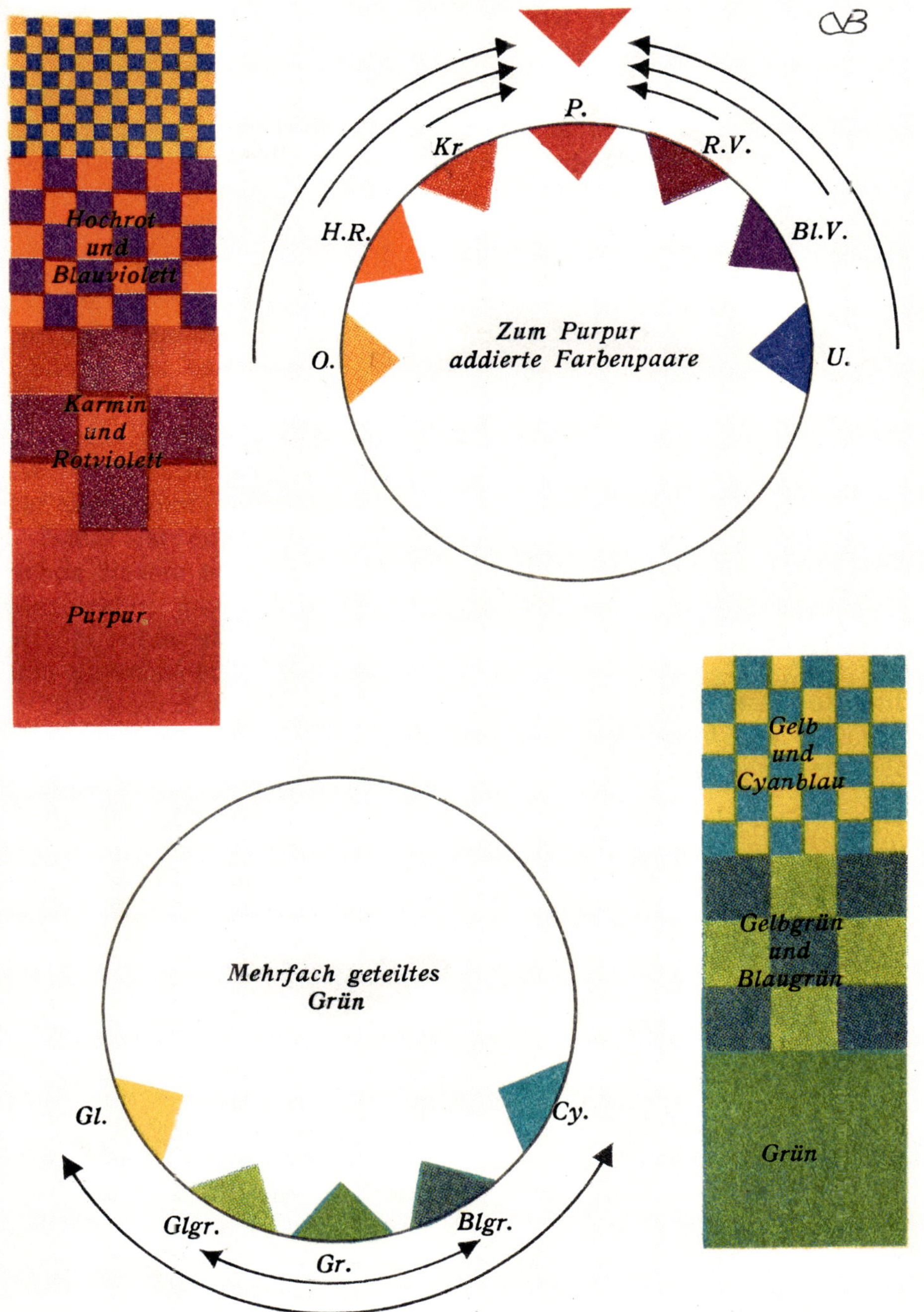


DIVIDIEREN UND ADDIEREN DER FARBEN

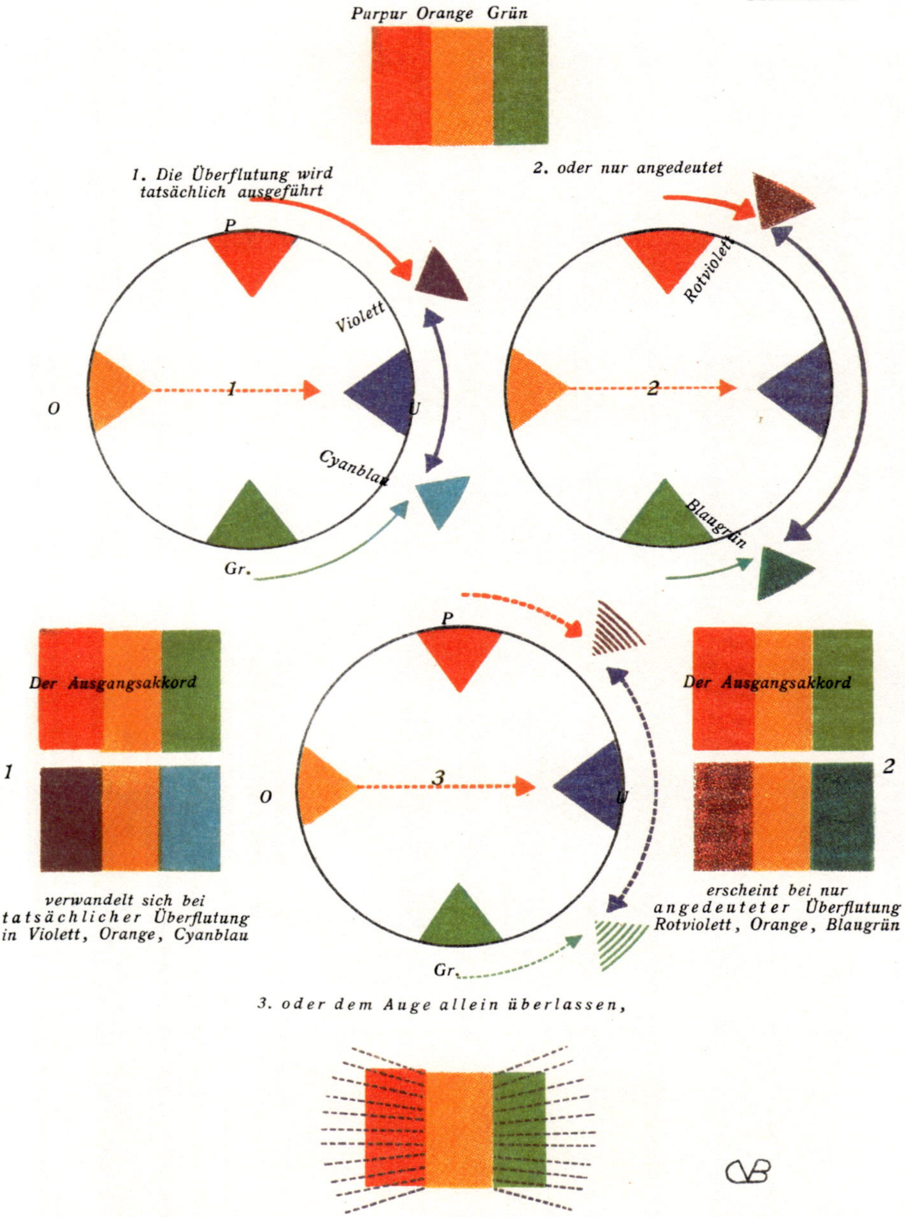

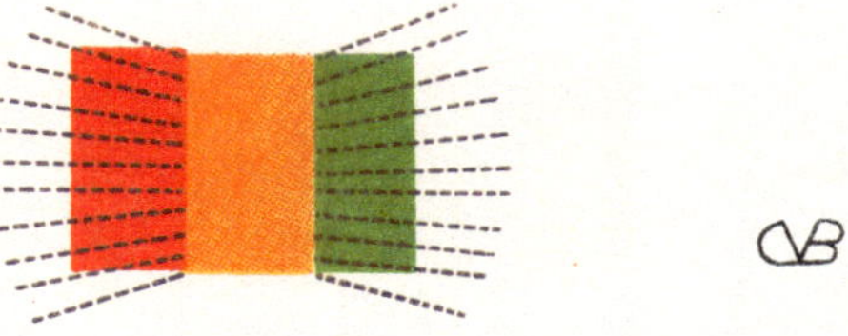

denn es sieht über der roten und grünen Fläche das Blau vibrieren

# VERSCHIEDENARTIGE AUSNÜTZUNG EINER KOMPLEMENTÄRÜBERFLUTUNG

„Wir blicken von einem Gegenstand auf den andern . . . und werden nicht gewahr, daß sich von dem vorhergehenden etwas in den nachfolgenden hinüberschleicht.“ Goethe

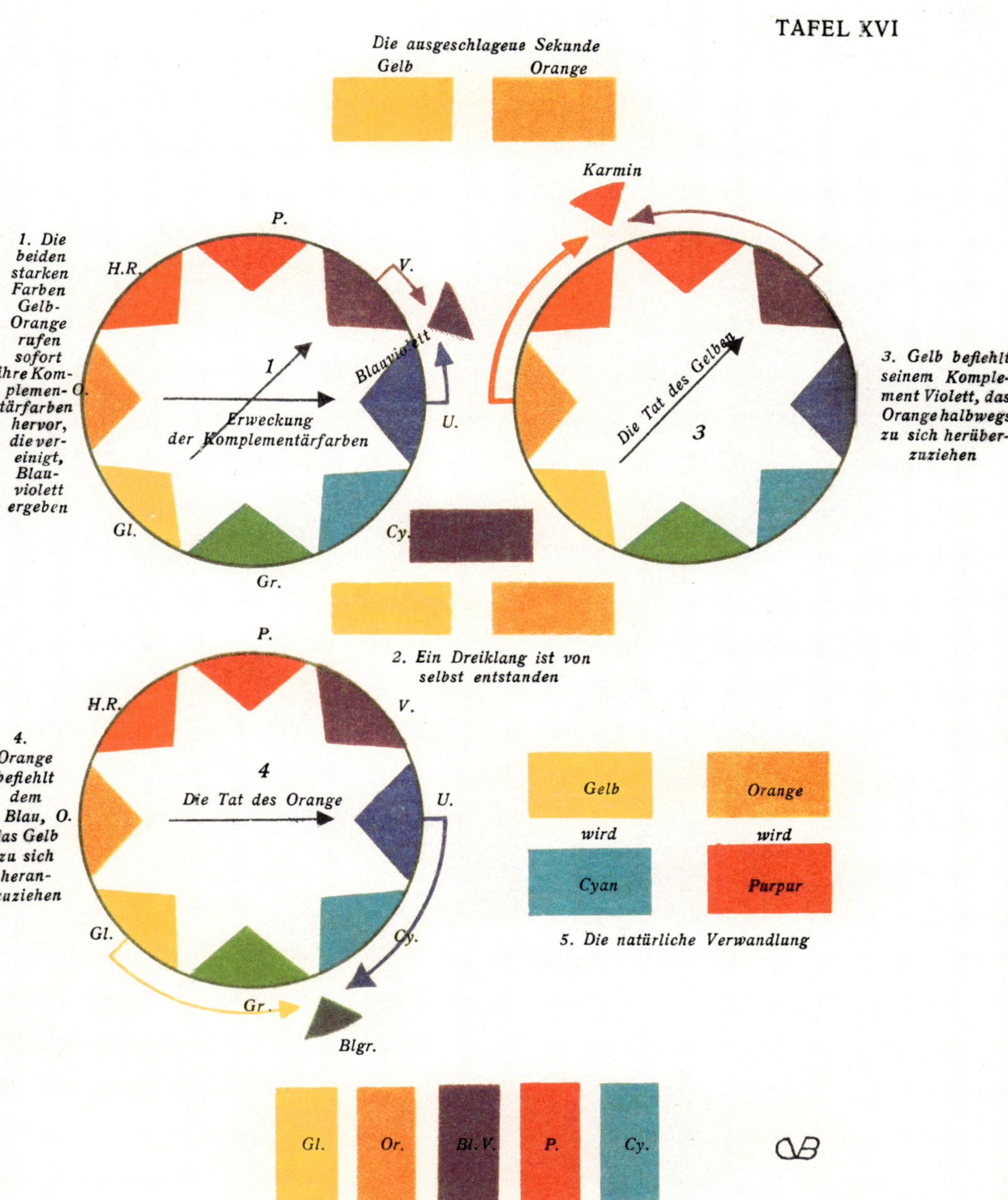
Die ausgeschlageue Sekunde
Gelb
Orange
Karmin
P.
1. Die beiden starken Farben Gelb-Orange rufen sofort ihre Komplementärfarben hervor, die vereinigt, Blauviolett ergeben
H.R.
V.
Blauviolett
1
O.
Erweckung der Komplementärfarben
U.
Gl.
Cy.
Gr.
Die Tat des Gelben
3
3. Gelb befiehlt seinem Komplement Violett, das Orange halbwegs zu sich herüberzuziehen
2. Ein Dreiklang ist von selbst entstanden
P.
H.R.
V.
4. Orange befiehlt dem Blau, O. das Gelb zu sich heranzuziehen
4
Die Tat des Orange
U.
Gl.
Cy.
Gr.
Blgr.
Gelb
Orange
wird
wird
Cyan
Purpur
5. Die natürliche Verwandlung
Gl.
Or.
Bl. V.
P.
Cy.
6. Die neu entstandene Farbenreihe

## DER KAMPF ZWEIER GLEICHSTARKER FARBEN UM DIE VORHERRSCHAFT

„(Zwei Farben) können aufgehoben, neutralisiert, indifferenziert werden, so daß beide zu verschwinden scheinen, aber sie lassen sich auch umkehren, und diese Umkehrung ist im allgemeinen die zarteste Sache von der Welt.“ Goethe

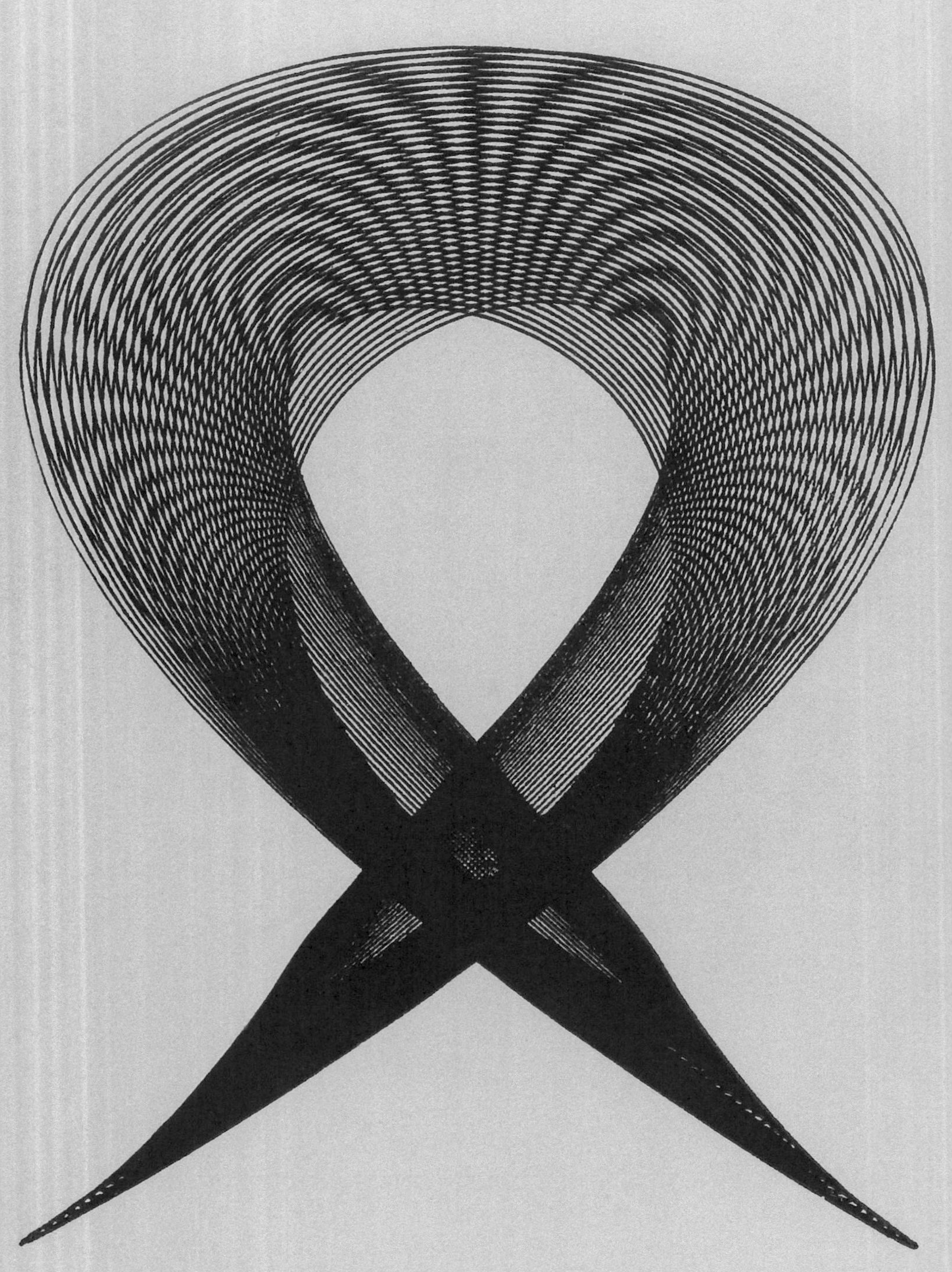

Chapter 7

# *The Sound of Colour:* SPIRITUALISM, OCCULTISM AND MUSIC

1902–1946

## Charles Webster Leadbeater (1854–1934)

# MAN VISIBLE AND INVISIBLE

### Examples of Different Types of Men as Seen by Means of Trained Clairvoyance

*25 plates, 23 x 14 cm / 9 x 5 ½ in., London, New York, 1902*
*Copenhagen, Det Kongelige Bibliotek (The Royal Danish Library)*

While this is not explicitly a book about colour, its content relies heavily on colour concepts and in particular on colour symbolism. The book's frontispiece (p. 413) shows a table of 25 colours, each symbolising a human emotion or disposition. These relate to the human auras that are described and illustrated later in the book, and the values assigned to each unnamed colour in the table provide a direct insight into the theosophical concepts of spiritual colour that were championed by the book's author. A light yellow square thus signifies "Highest Intellect", brown with red streaks indicates "Jealousy" and a saturated blue in the top row corresponds to "Pure Religious Feeling". In the text Charles Leadbeater explained that, "Before we can intelligently study the detail of these various [astral] bodies, we must familiarize ourselves with the general meaning of the various shades of colour in them, as indicated in our frontispiece. It will be realised that almost infinite variety is possible in their combination."

Three subsequent plates illustrate the theosophical concept of the "Planes of Nature", which relate to different states of consciousness, or being, and some of which are denoted with terms derived from Sanskrit and Buddhism. The book's most striking illustrations, however, are the 22 plates showing astral bodies surrounded by colourful auras. They were illustrated by the theosophist Count Maurice Prozor and copied for reproduction by another initiate, Gertrude Spink. The body is always represented by the outline of a man, possibly based on classical sculptures or Leonardo da Vinci's *Vitruvian Man* (*c.* 1490), and like that image it is trapped within a rounded perimeter. This is the aura, which is delineated as an ovoid form filled with varying shades of colour and often overlaid with geometric shapes, which indicate disruption, chaos or negative emotions. While these mostly abstract compositions with their pronounced colour symbolism are visually fascinating, they are also socially problematic, since three of the images illustrate a figure referred to as "The Savage", meaning a lower stage of evolution, or a "poor and undeveloped mind-body". A modern perspective would acknowledge the racist overtones in such terminology, in the depictions of Black bodies with certain exaggerated features, and in the language used to describe them.

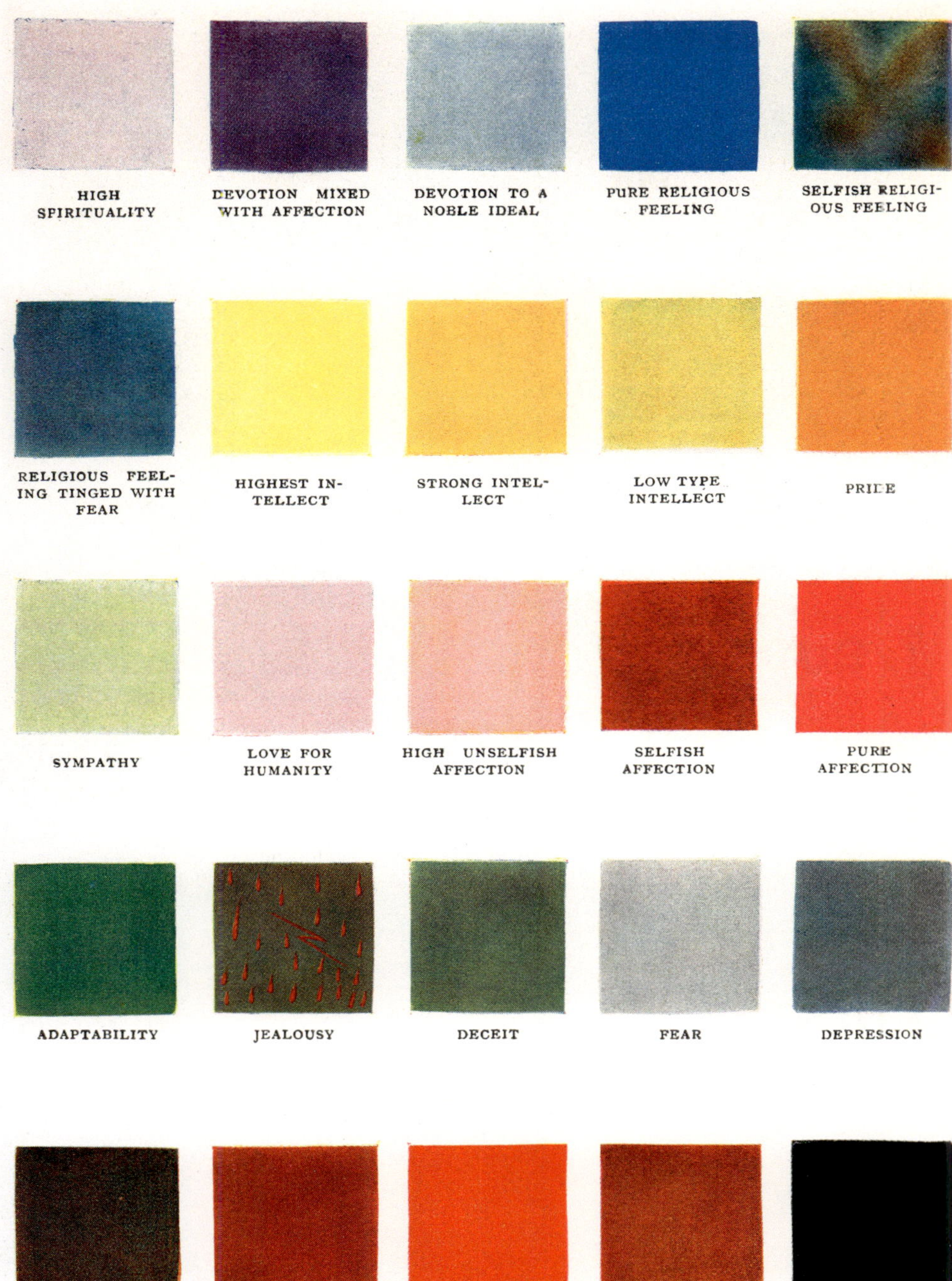
HIGH SPIRITUALITY
DEVOTION MIXED WITH AFFECTION
DEVOTION TO A NOBLE IDEAL
PURE RELIGIOUS FEELING
SELFISH RELIGIOUS FEELING
RELIGIOUS FEELING TINGED WITH FEAR
HIGHEST INTELLECT
STRONG INTELLECT
LOW TYPE INTELLECT
PRIDE
SYMPATHY
LOVE FOR HUMANITY
HIGH UNSELFISH AFFECTION
SELFISH AFFECTION
PURE AFFECTION
ADAPTABILITY
JEALOUSY
DECEIT
FEAR
DEPRESSION
SELFISHNESS
AVARICE
ANGER
SENSUALITY
MALICE

# PLANES OF NATURE

| | Plane | | Sub-planes | |
|---|---|---|---|---|
| 7 | MAHÂPARANIRVÂNIC | | FIRST | TRIPLE MANIFESTATION |
| 6 | PARANIRVÂNIC | | SECOND | |
| 5 | NIRVÂNIC | | ATOMIC<br>SPIRIT | THIRD<br>THREEFOLD SPIRIT in MAN |
| 4 | BUDDHIC | | ATOMIC<br>The Reincarnating Ego or Soul in Man | INTUITION |
| 3 | MENTAL | ARUPA | ATOMIC | INTELLIGENCE<br>CAUSAL BODY |
| | | RUPA | | MENTAL BODY |
| 2 | ASTRAL | | ATOMIC | ASTRAL BODY |
| 1 | PHYSICAL | | ATOMIC<br>SUB-ATOMIC<br>SUPER-ETHERIC<br>ETHERIC | ETHERIC DOUBLE |
| | | | GASEOUS<br>LIQUID<br>SOLID | DENSE BODY |

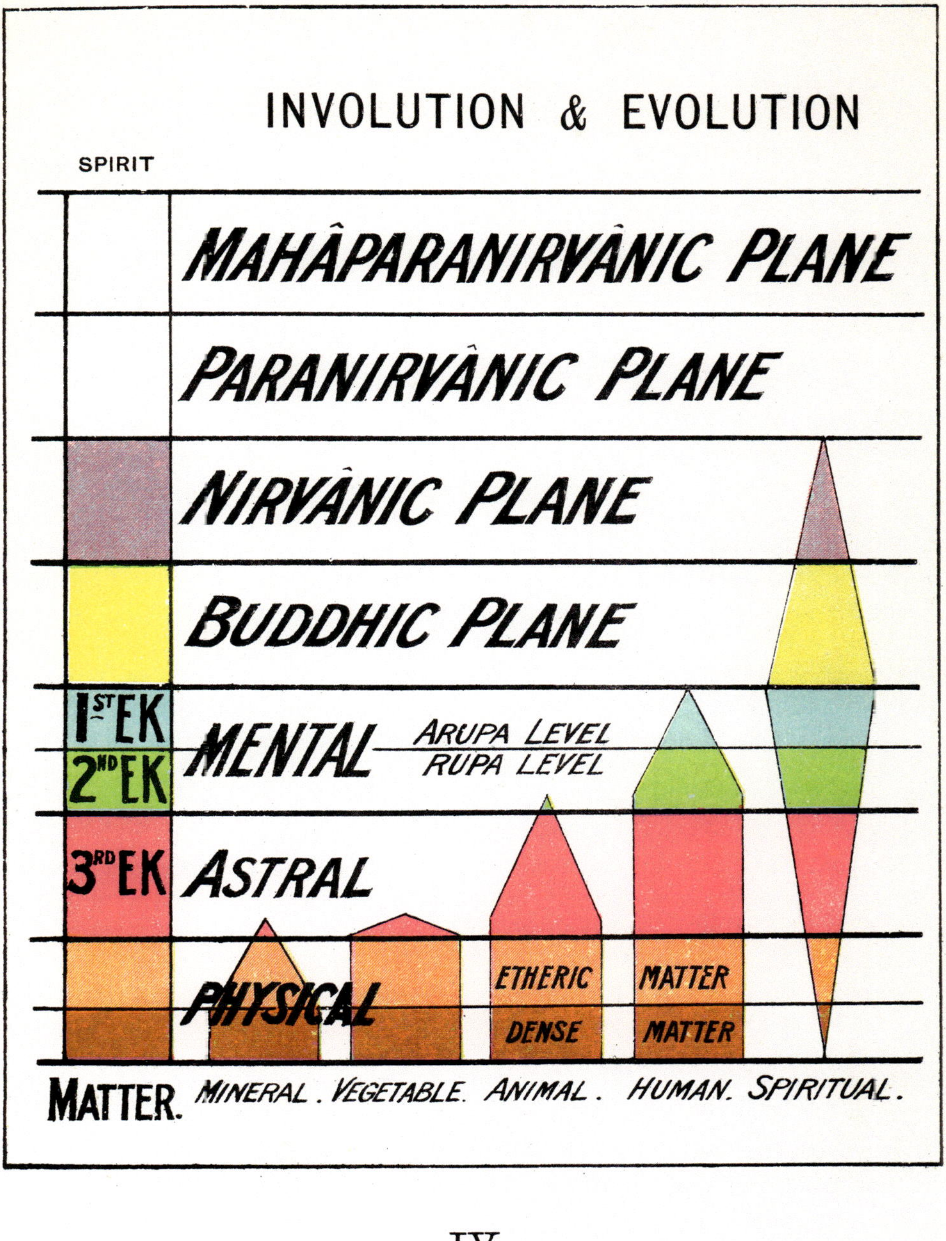

# INVOLUTION & EVOLUTION

SPIRIT

MAHÂPARANIRVÂNIC PLANE

PARANIRVÂNIC PLANE

NIRVÂNIC PLANE

BUDDHIC PLANE

1ST EK
2ND EK
MENTAL — ARUPA LEVEL / RUPA LEVEL

3RD EK
ASTRAL

PHYSICAL
ETHERIC MATTER
DENSE MATTER

MATTER. MINERAL. VEGETABLE. ANIMAL. HUMAN. SPIRITUAL.

IV.

## Der sichtbare und der unsichtbare Mensch

Handelt dieses Buch auch nicht ausdrücklich von Farbe, so stützt sich sein Inhalt doch maßgeblich auf Farbtheorien und speziell auf die Symbolik von Farben. Das Frontispiz (S. 413) zeigt 25 Farben, die jeweils eine menschliche Emotion oder Veranlagung symbolisieren. Diese beziehen sich auf die Auren des Menschen, die im Buch später beschrieben und veranschaulicht werden. Die den unbenannten Farben in der Tabelle zugeordneten Werte verschaffen einen direkten Einblick in die theosophischen Vorstellungen von spiritueller Farbe, die der Buchautor selbst vertrat. Ein hellgelbes Quadrat zum Beispiel steht für „sehr hohe Verstandeskraft", Braun mit roten Streifen signalisiert „Eifersucht", und ein gesättigtes Blau in der oberen Reihe kennzeichnet ein „reines religiöses Empfinden". Im Text erläuterte Charles Leadbeater: „Ehe wir die Einzelheiten in den verschiedenen Körpern mit Verständnis betrachten können, müssen wir uns mit der allgemeinen Bedeutung der Farbenschattierungen bekannt machen, die die Farbentafel uns gibt. Außer den vorliegenden gibt es natürlich eine undarstellbare Menge von Variationen, die durch Mischung und Verbindung der Farben entstehen."

Die drei folgenden Tafeln illustrieren das theosophische Konzept der „Naturebenen", die mit verschiedenen Bewusstseins- oder Seinszuständen in Zusammenhang stehen und zum Teil aus dem Sanskrit oder dem Buddhismus abgeleitete Namen tragen. Die erstaunlichsten Illustrationen des Buches sind jedoch die 22 Tafeln, die von farbenprächtigen Auren umgebene Astralkörper zeigen. Sie wurden von dem Theosophen Maurice Graf Prozor gestaltet und von Gertrude Spink, einer weiteren Eingeweihten, für die Reproduktion kopiert. Der stets als Umriss einer männlichen Gestalt in ein Oval gestellter Körper geht möglicherweise auf antike Skulpturen oder Leonardo da Vincis vitruvianischen Menschen (um 1490) zurück. Dieses mit wechselnden Farbtönen gefüllte Oval ist die Aura, es wird oft von geometrischen Formen überlagert, die auf Zerrissenheit, Chaos oder negative Gefühle hindeuten. Während diese meist abstrakten Kompositionen mit ihrer ausgeprägten Farbsymbolik optisch faszinieren, müssen sie heute gesellschaftlich als problematisch gelten, denn drei Bilder zeigen eine Gestalt, die „der Wilde" genannt wird. Dahinter verbirgt sich eine tiefer stehende Entwicklungsstufe oder, wie es wörtlich heißt, „ein verhältnismäßig unentwickelter Gedankenkörper". Einer modernen Sichtweise würden die rassistischen Untertöne dieser Terminologie nicht verborgen bleiben, die wir auch aus der Darstellung von schwarzen Körpern mit bestimmten übertriebenen Merkmalen und aus der Sprache kennen, mit der sie beschrieben werden.

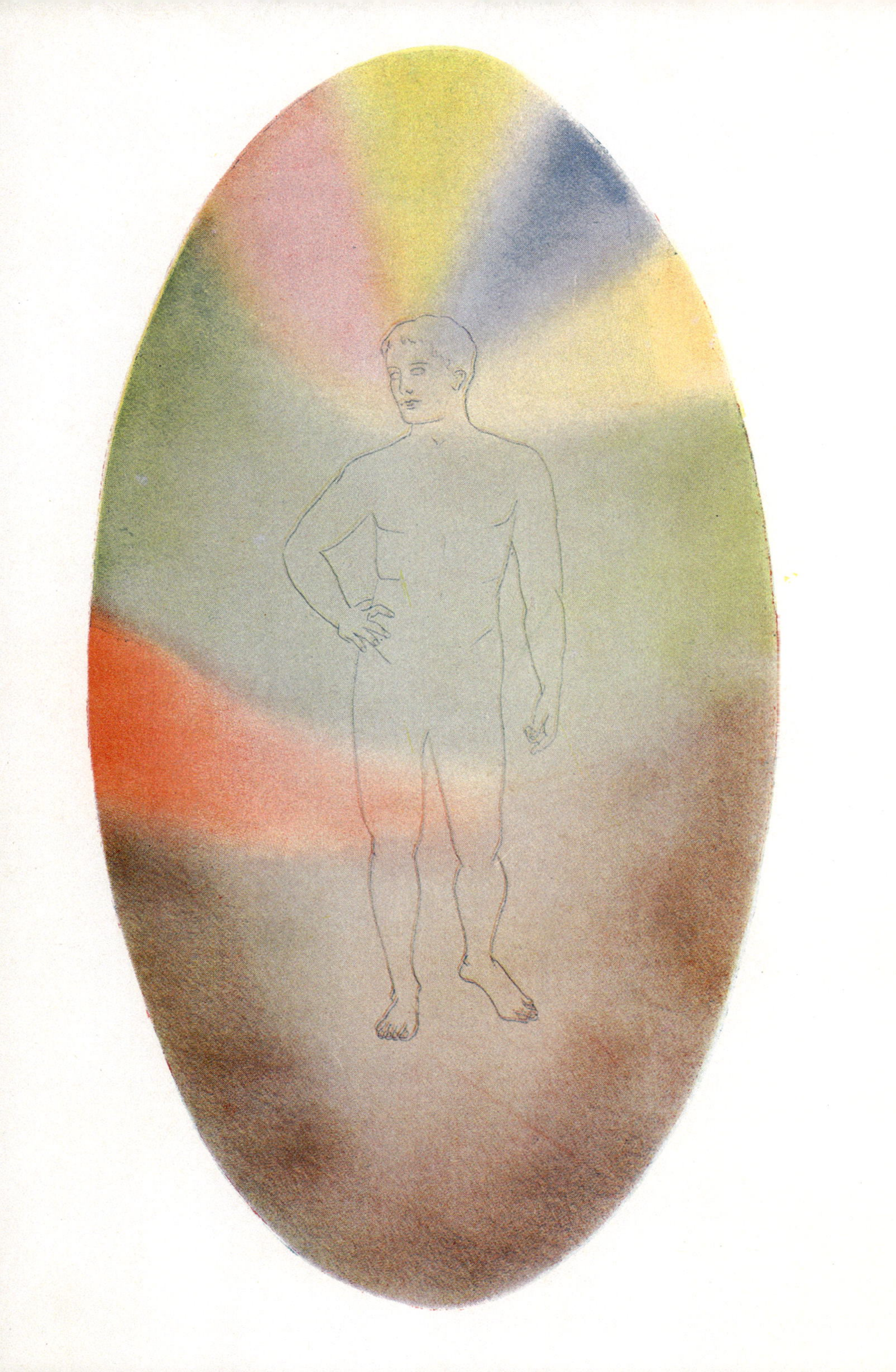

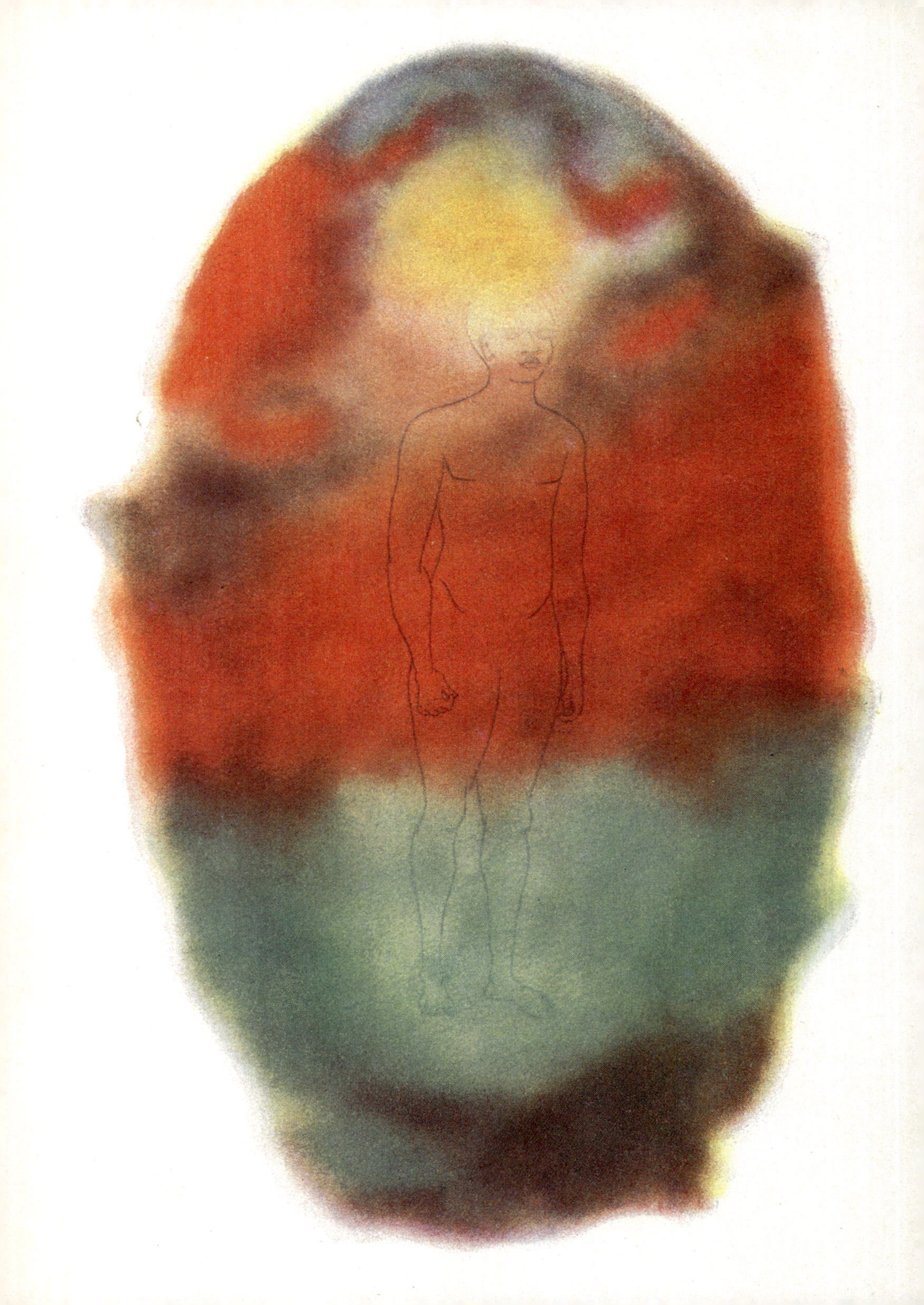

## L'Homme visible et invisible

*L'Homme visible et invisible* ne porte certes pas explicitement sur la couleur mais s'appuie fortement sur les conceptions chromatiques, et notamment le symbolisme, pour illustrer ses « Exemples de différents types d'hommes tels qu'ils peuvent être observés par un clairvoyant exercé ». Le frontispice (p. 413) présente un tableau de 25 couleurs, qui symbolisent chacune une émotion ou une disposition humaine et se retrouvent dans les auras humaines décrites et illustrées plus loin dans l'ouvrage. Les couleurs ne sont pas nommées, et les valeurs qui leur sont assignées dans le tableau témoignent des concepts théosophiques de la couleur spirituelle défendus par l'auteur. Ainsi, un carré jaune pâle y signifie un « intellect supérieur », le brun ponctué de rouge indique la « jalousie » et le bleu profond de la rangée du haut correspond à un « pur sentiment religieux ». Charles Leadbeater explique : « Pour être à même d'entreprendre une étude intelligente de ces divers corps dans leur détail, nous devrons au préalable nous familiariser avec la signification générale des teintes variées qu'ils présentent (on en trouvera l'indication dans notre frontispice). La combinaison de ces couleurs principales rend possible une variété presque infinie de teintes secondaires. »

Les trois planches suivantes illustrent le concept théosophique des « plans de la Nature », liés aux différents états de conscience ou d'existence, et dont certains sont désignés par des mots dérivés du sanskrit et de la tradition bouddhiste. Les illustrations les plus marquantes de l'ouvrage sont cependant les 22 planches montrant les corps astraux entourés d'auras colorées. Elles ont été réalisées par le comte Maurice Prozor, théosophe, et reproduites par une autre initiée, Gertrude Spink. Le corps est toujours figuré par la silhouette d'un homme, peut-être inspirée de sculptures classiques ou bien de par *L'Homme de Vitruve* de Léonard de Vinci (vers 1490) et entourée de la même manière d'une forme arrondie. L'aura est représentée par un périmètre ovale empli de couleurs variées, parfois agrémentées de formes géométriques indiquant une perturbation, le chaos ou des émotions négatives. Ces compositions principalement abstraites, renforcées par leur symbolisme chromatique, restent visuellement fascinantes. Cependant, elles sont aussi problématiques : trois d'entre elles sont légendées « Le sauvage », autrement dit un stade inférieur d'évolution ou un « corps mental fort pauvre et sous-développé ». Un point de vue moderne repère forcément ici un sous-entendu raciste, ainsi que dans certaines représentations caricaturales de corps noirs et dans les termes qui les décrivent.

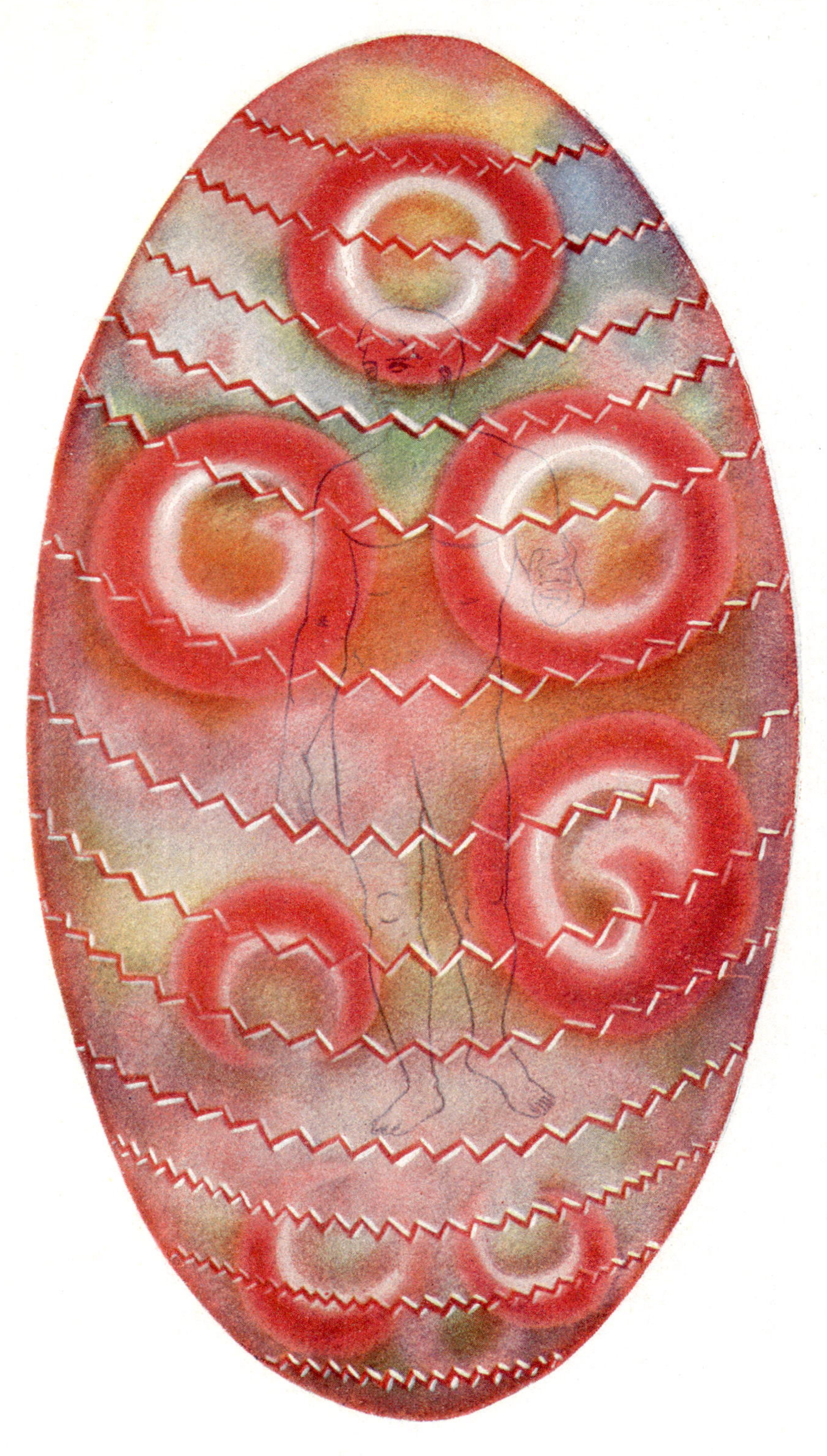

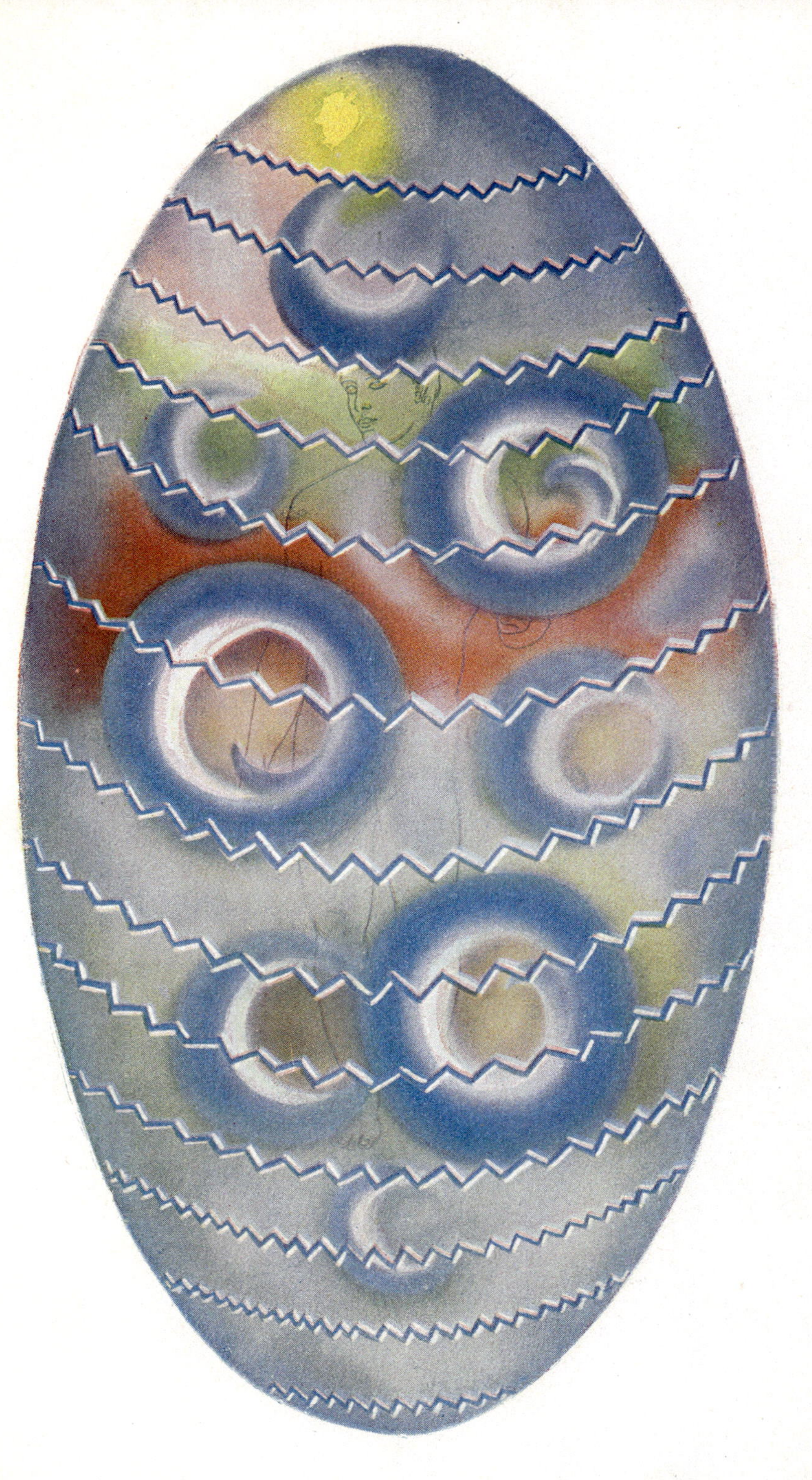

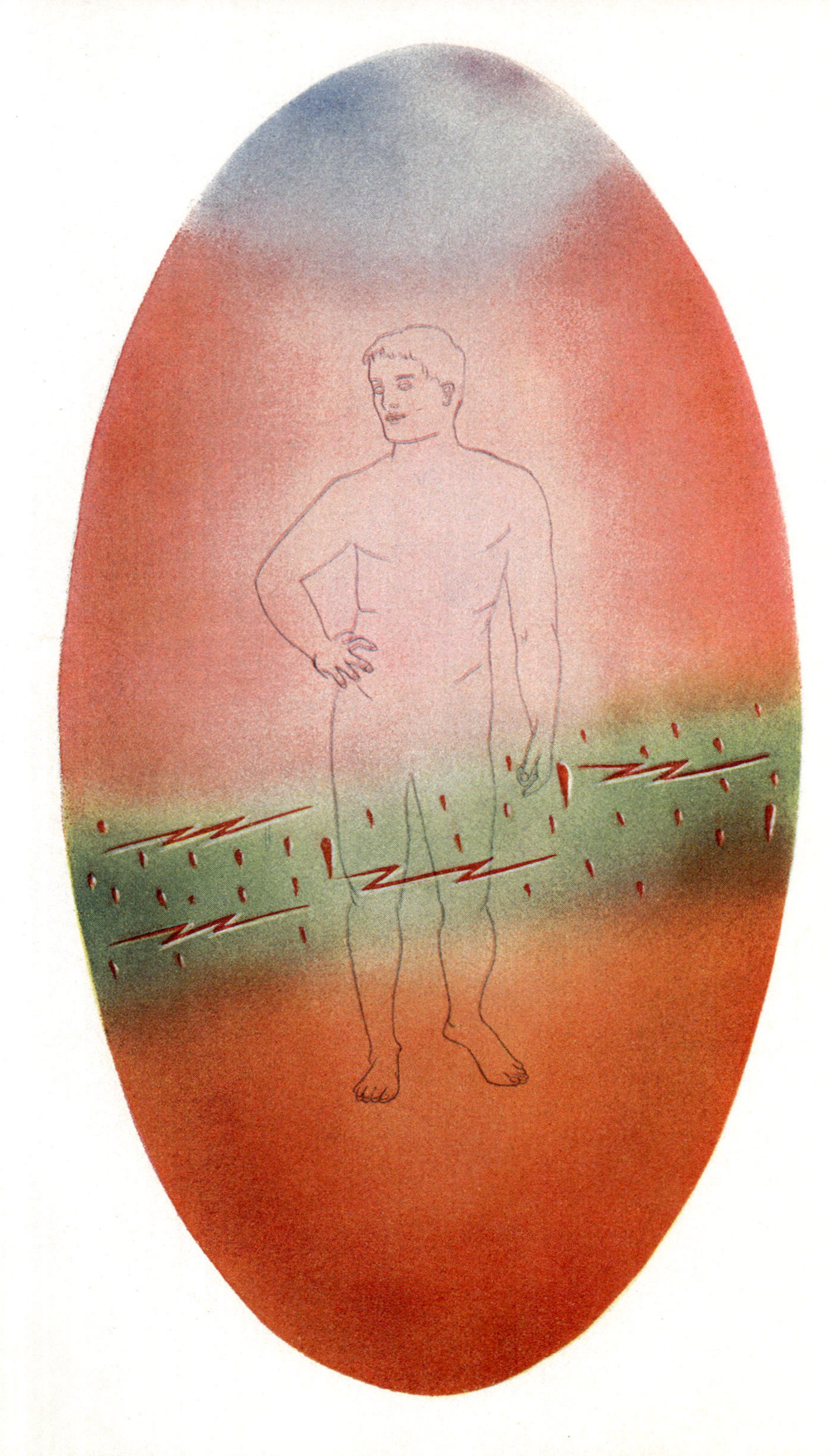

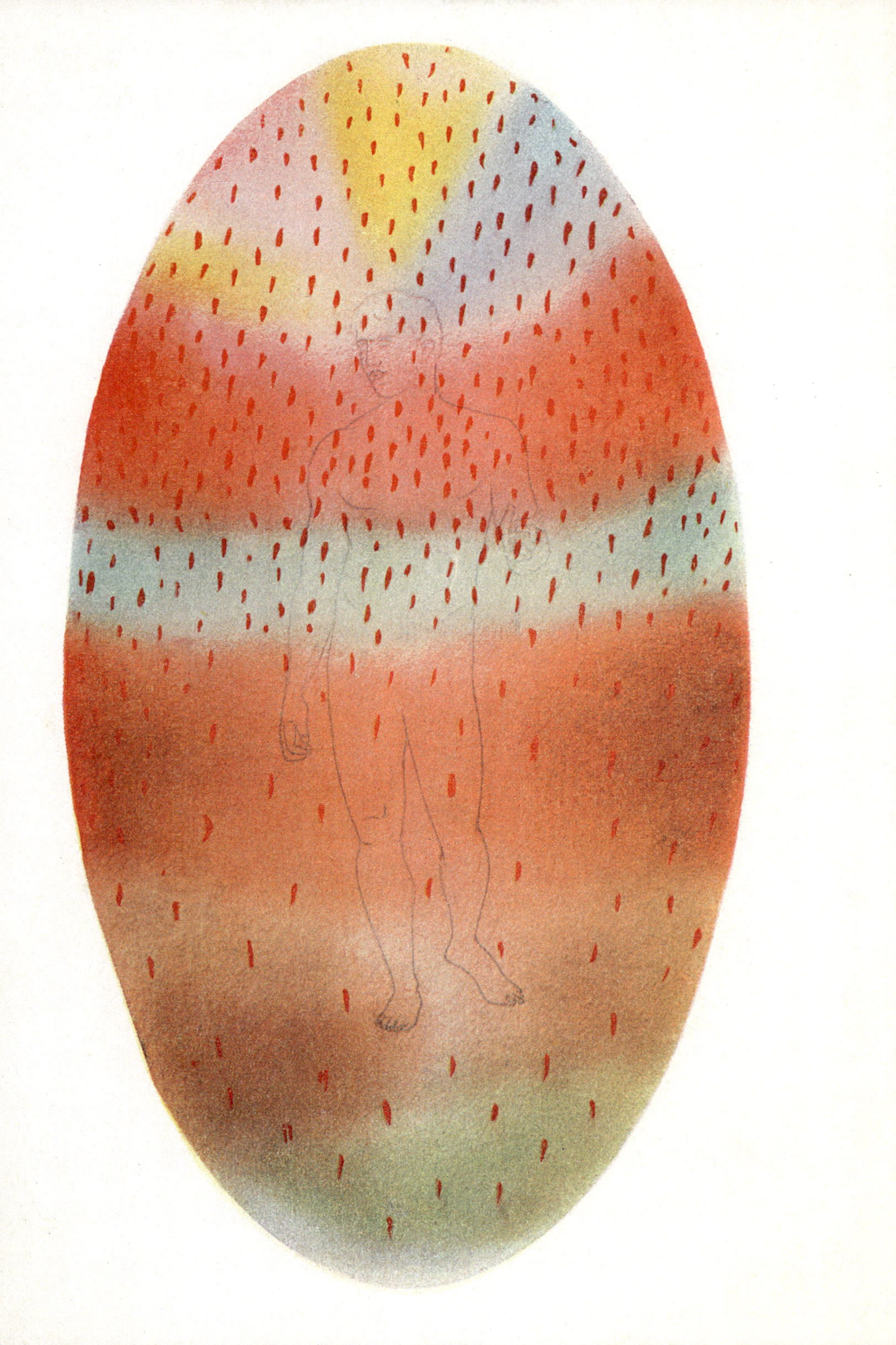

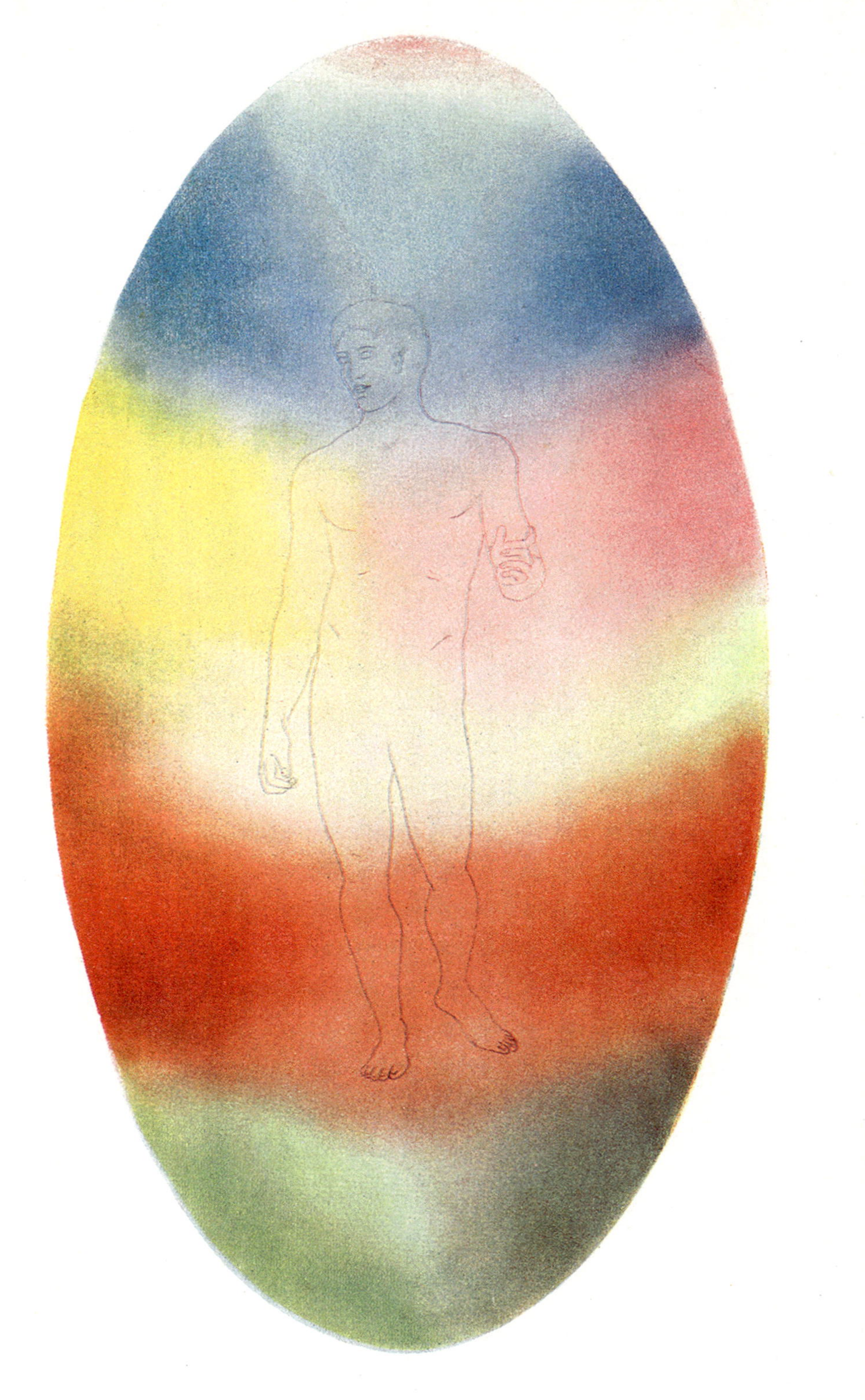

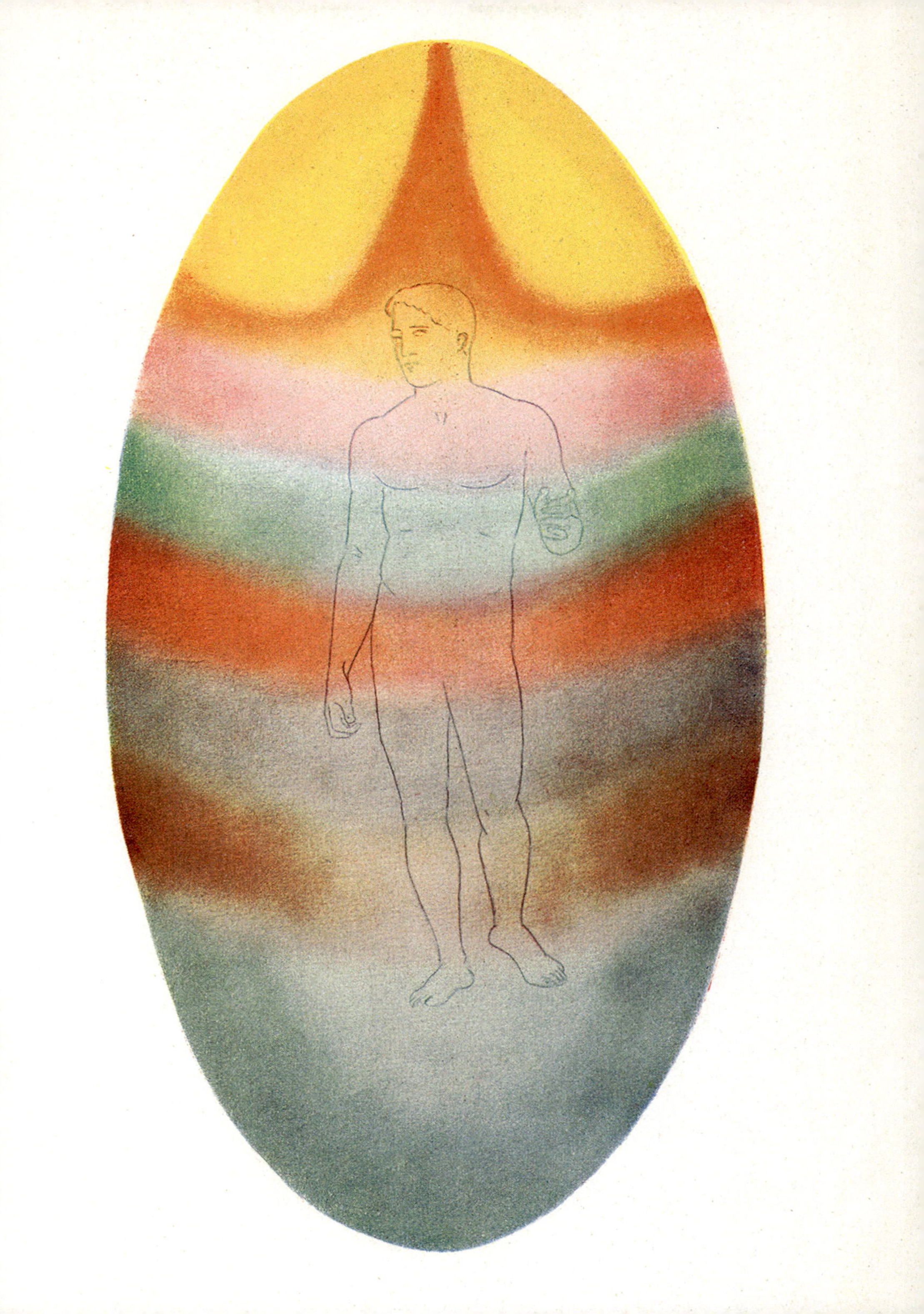

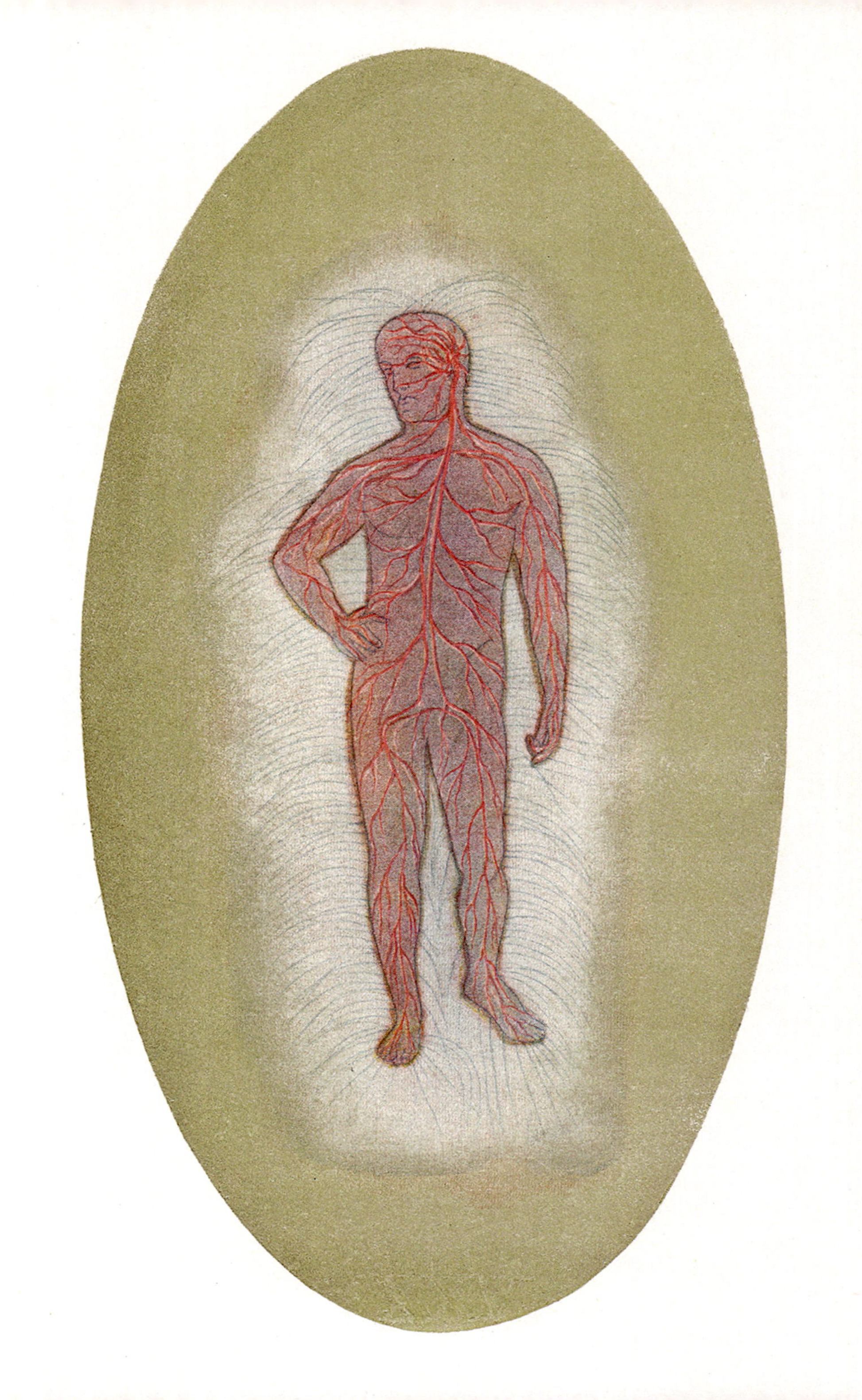

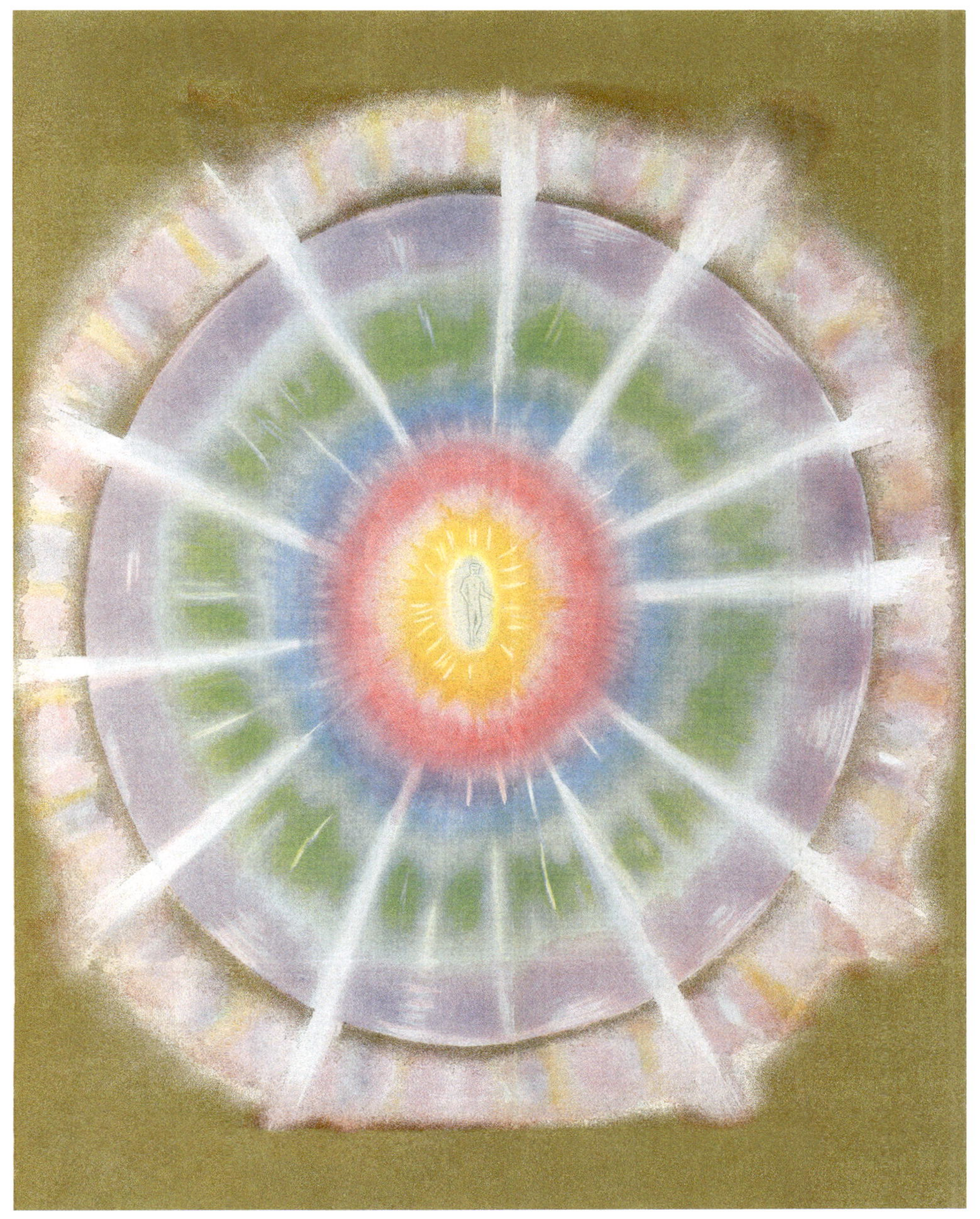

## Annie Besant (1847–1933), Charles Webster Leadbeater

# THOUGHT-FORMS: A RECORD OF CLAIRVOYANT INVESTIGATION

*51 illustrations across 26 plates, 21 x 13.2 cm | 8 ¼ x 5 ¼ in., London, 1905*
*Heidelberg, Universitätsbibliothek*

Annie Besant was a formidable educator, socialist, political activist and campaigner for women's rights, who rose quickly through the ranks of the Theosophical Society. She first met Charles Leadbeater in 1894, and they became lifelong friends. This book on how ideas and thoughts present themselves physically and visually was their greatest collaboration.

The first plate, "Key to the Meanings of Colours", was recycled from Leadbeater's *Man Visible and Invisible* (1902) with the same colour symbolism in place. With *Thought-forms* the authors intended to carry the "general subject of the aura" further and to do so they based the illustration of their images on three general principles, of which colour formed the first: "1. Quality of thought determines colour. 2. Nature of thought determines form. 3. Definiteness of thought determines clearness of outline." This was then conceptualised further by identifying three classes of thought-forms, namely thinkers or human figures, material objects, and those which represented a state of mind, corresponding to the "astral and mental" planes. Besant and Leadbeater only regarded this third group as being worthy of transforming into images, and the 58 illustrations that appear in the book are based on artwork by various friends of theirs who are thanked in the foreword for the hard task of painting "in earth's dull colours the forms clothed in the living light of other worlds".

The last three thought-forms are markedly different from the others in that they represent music instead of an individual's thoughts, and depict a Mendelssohn piano piece, a choral work by Gounod and an orchestral excerpt by Wagner (p. 434). In contrast to all the other images these three each feature a representational picture of a church with a tall tower, from which the musical forms emerge like colourful clouds. Mendelssohn's music produces irregular and broken lines of crimson, yellow and blue emanating from and engulfing the church, while Gounod's rising chorus floats several hundred feet above the church tower, in a mushroom-cloud of polychrome vapour. The most spectacular image relates to Wagner's music, which takes the form of a billowing mountain-range of colour hovering high above the church which is dwarfed beneath. It is a bombastic finish to this extraordinary book and a great example of the theosophists' interest in synaesthetic experiences.

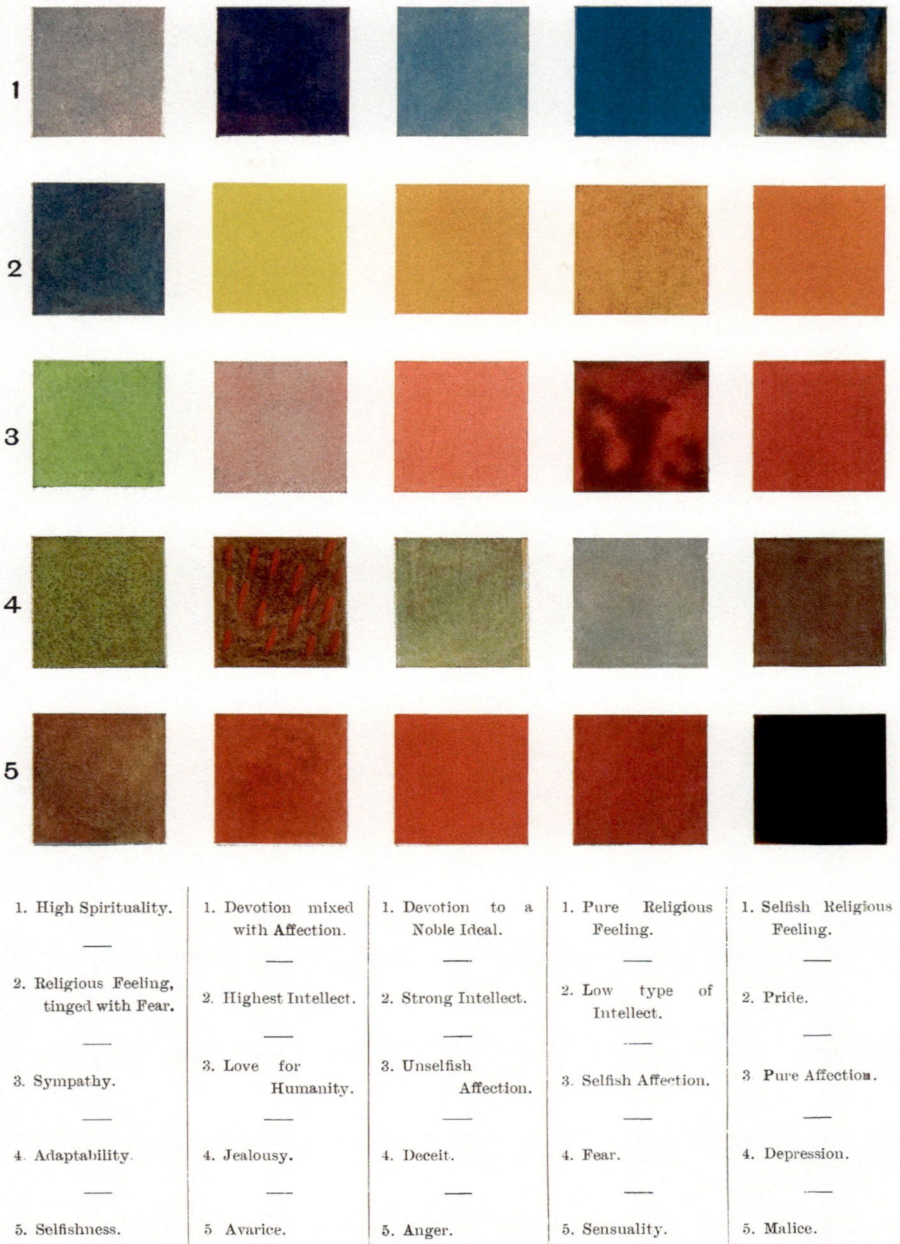


KEY TO THE MEANINGS OF COLOURS.

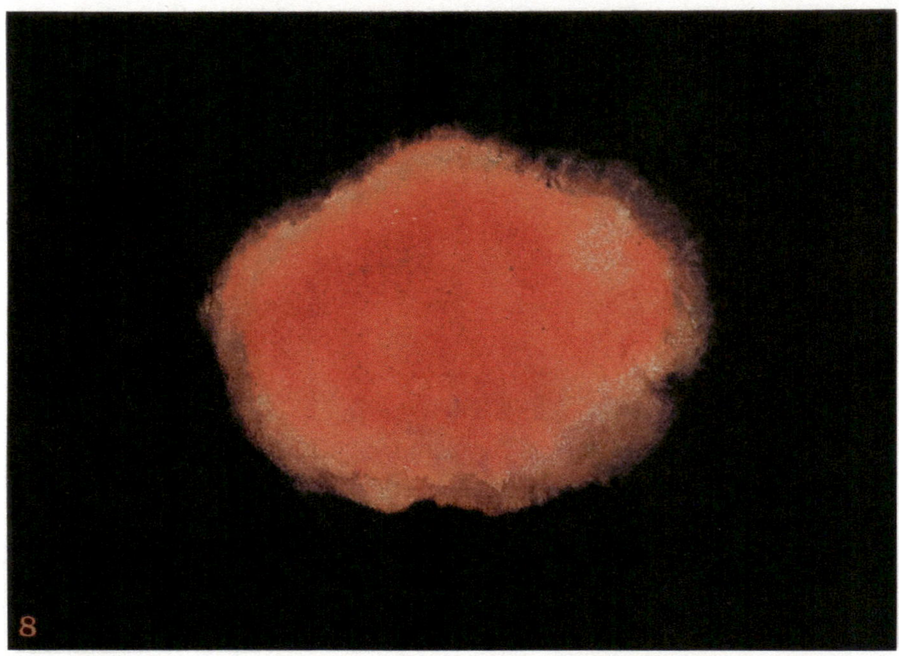
8

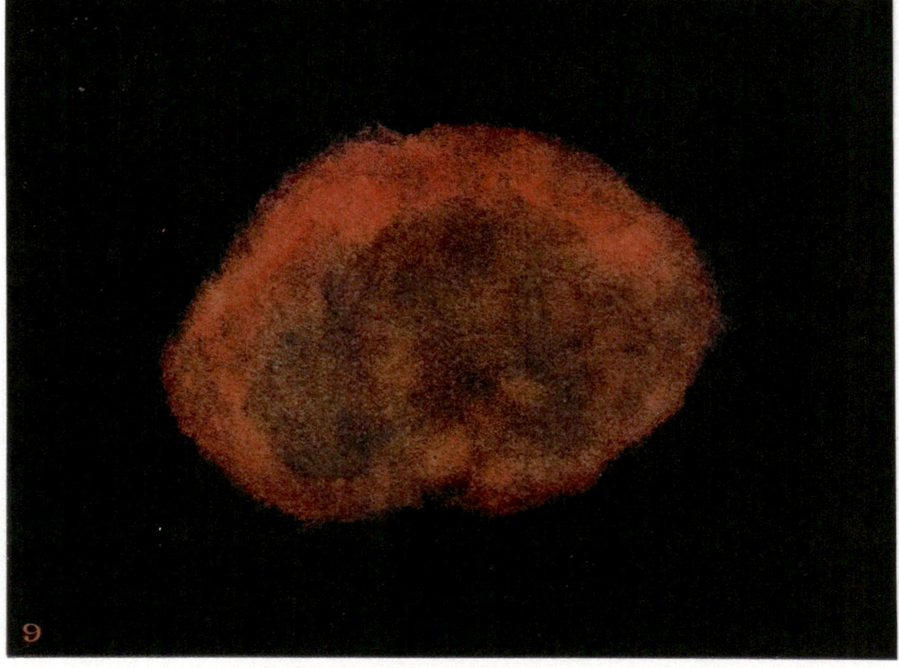
9

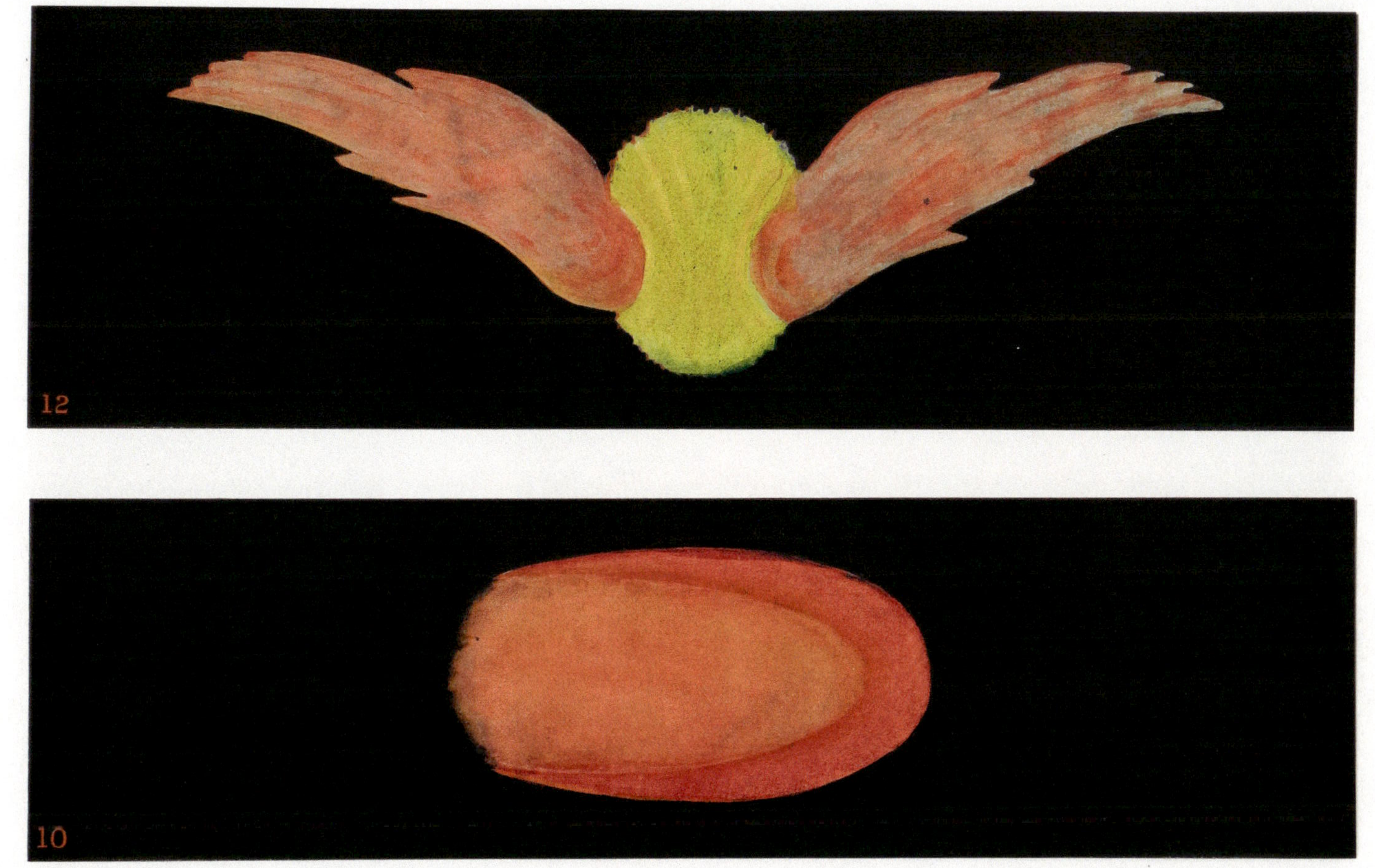
12
10

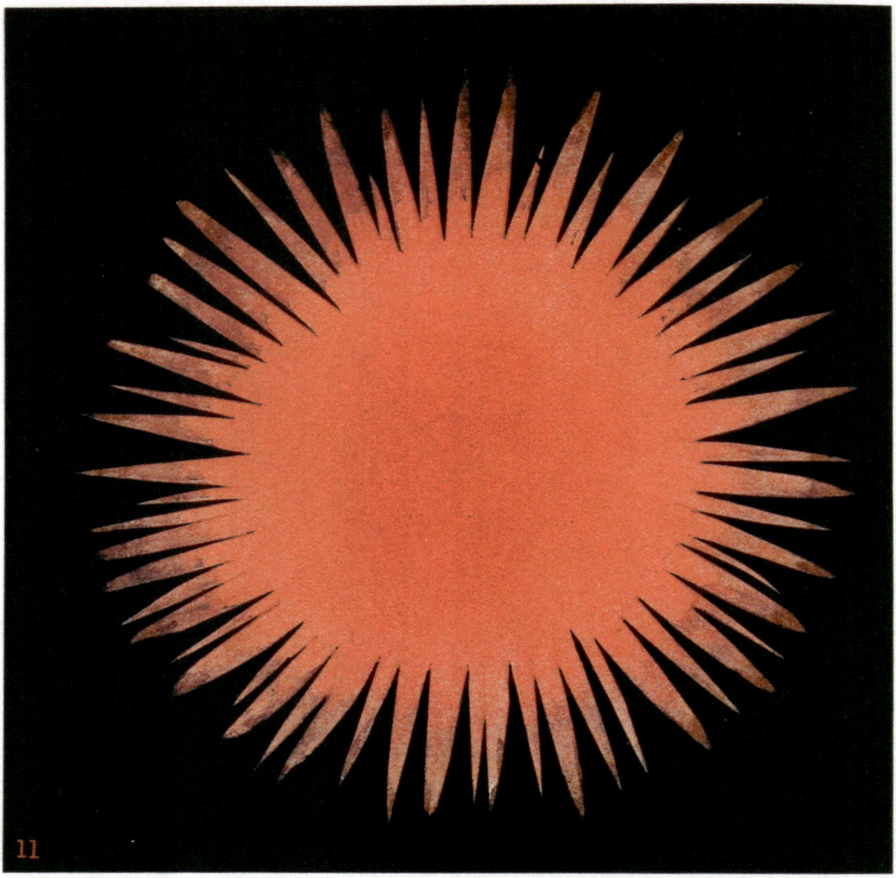

11

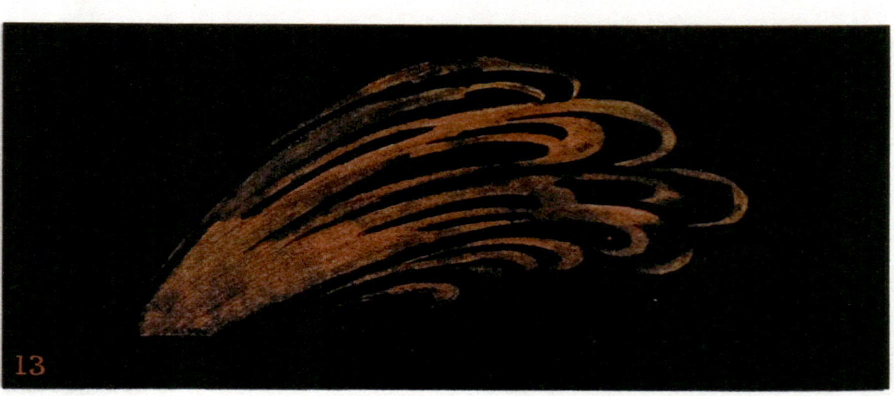

13

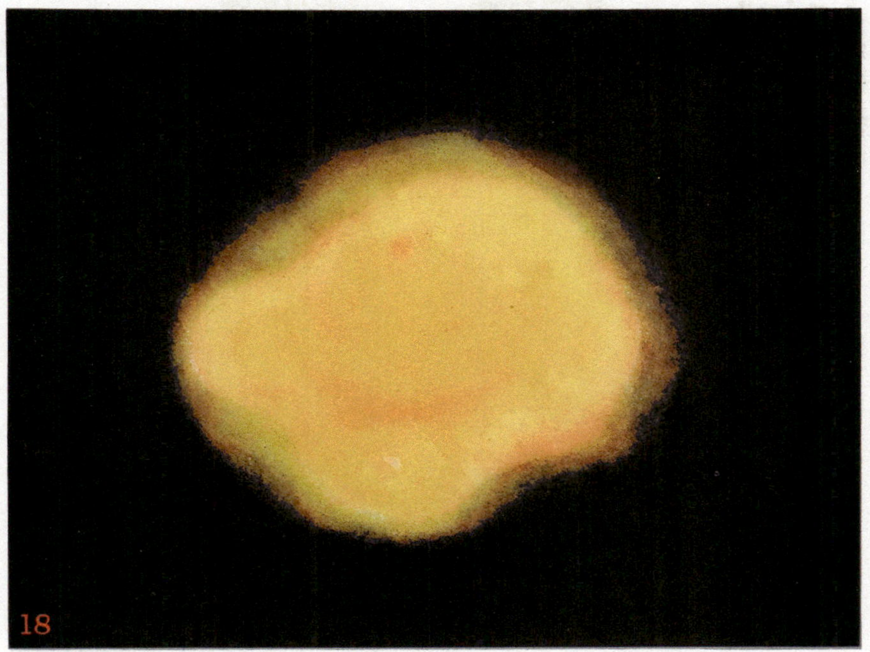
18

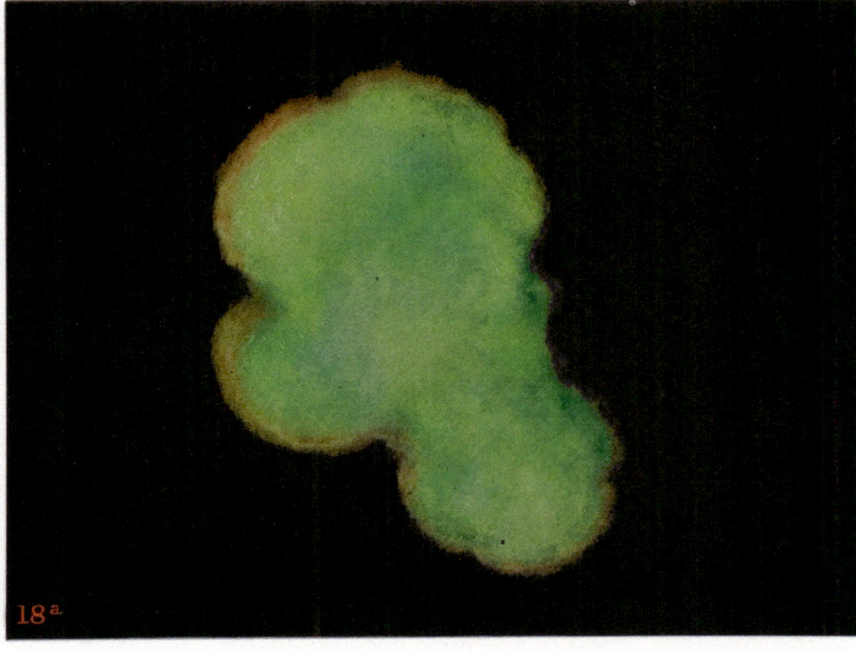
18a

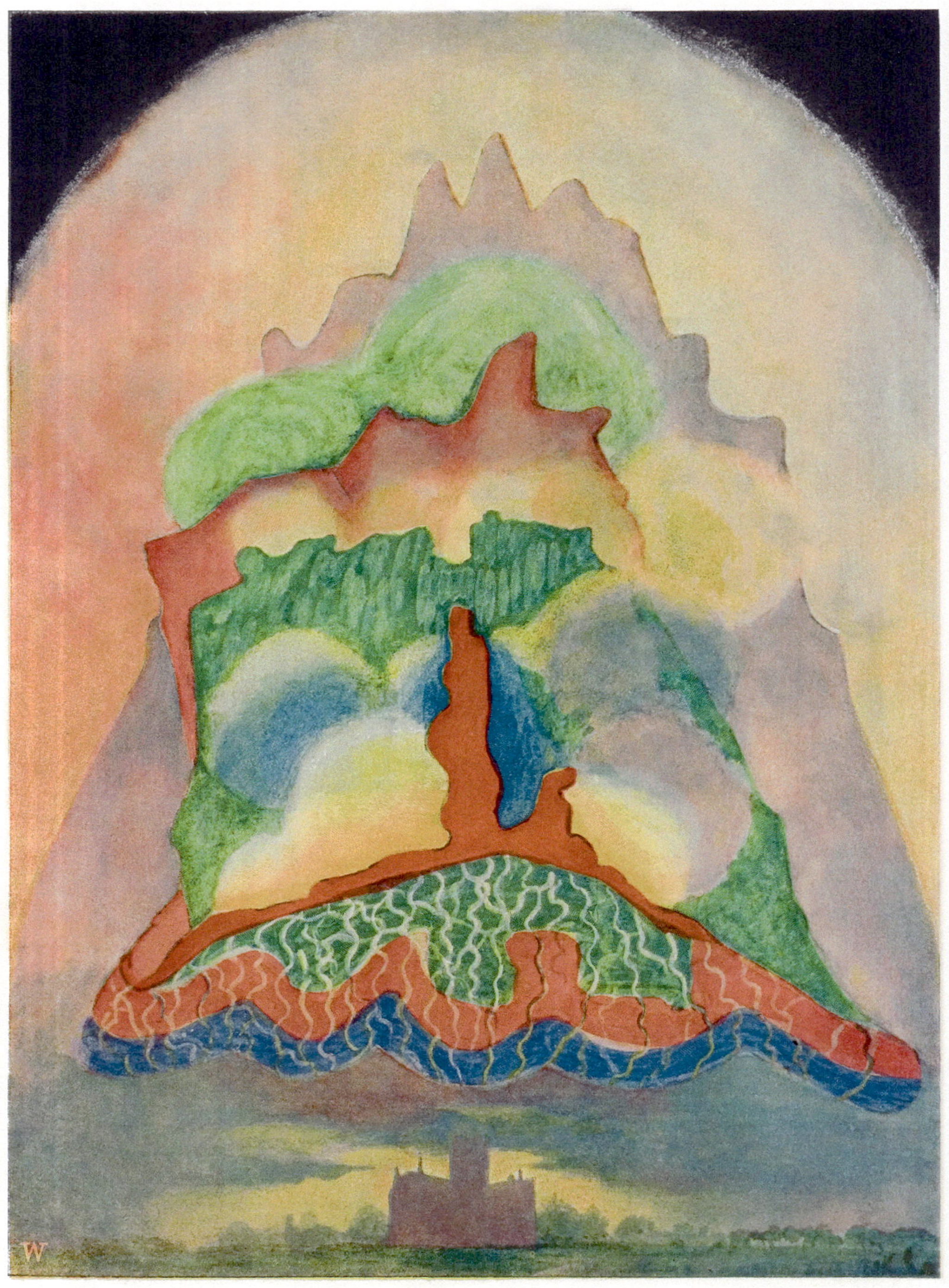

## Gedankenformen: Ein Protokoll hellseherischer Erkundung

Die beeindruckende Pädagogin, Sozialistin, politische Aktivistin und Frauenrechtlerin Annie Besant arbeitete sich in der Theosophischen Gesellschaft schnell nach oben. 1894 lernte sie Charles Leadbeater kennen, mit dem sie ein Leben lang befreundet blieb. Dieses Buch über die physischen und visuellen Erscheinungsformen von Ideen und Gedanken war ihre wichtigste gemeinsame Arbeit.

Die erste Farbtafel, „Schlüssel zum Verständnisse der Farbenbedeutung", übernahmen sie mitsamt der Farbsymbolik aus Leadbeaters *Man Visible and Invisible* (1902). Mit *Thought-forms* („Gedankenformen") wollten die Autoren das zuvor „nur ganz allgemein" behandelte Thema der Aura weiterentwickeln und richteten ihre Abbildungen entsprechend nach drei allgemeinen Grundsätzen aus, deren erster die Farbe betraf: „1. Die *Beschaffenheit* des Gedankens bestimmt seine Farbe. 2. Die *Natur* des Gedankens bestimmt seine Form. 3 Die *Bestimmtheit* des Gedankens ist die Ursache der Schärfe seiner Umrisse." Im nächsten Schritt legten sie drei Klassen von Gedankenformen fest: Bilder des Denkers oder anderer menschlicher Gestalten, Bilder von materiellen Gegenständen und schließlich Gedanken, die einen Gemütszustand verkörpern und damit der astralen und mentalen Naturebene zuzuordnen sind. Nur diese dritte Gruppe hielten Besant und Leadbeater für würdig, nutzbringend in Bilder umgewandelt zu werden. Die 58 Illustrationen ihres Buches beruhen auf den Kunstwerken dreier Freundinnen und Freunde, denen im Vorwort für den mühevollen Versuch gedankt wird, „die in das lebendige Licht höherer Welten gehüllten Formen mit den trüben irdischen Farben zu malen".

Die letzten drei Gedankenformen unterscheiden sich deutlich von allen übrigen, indem sie anstelle der Gedanken einer Person Musik repräsentieren: ein Klavierstück von Mendelssohn, ein Chorwerk von Gounod und einen Orchesterauszug von Wagner (S. 434). Anders als alle übrigen Illustrationen zeigen diese drei das gegenständliche Bild einer Kirche mit Vierungsturm, aus der wie farbige Wolken die musikalischen Formen empordringen. Die Musik Mendelssohns erzeugt unregelmäßige, durchbrochene Linien in Karminrot, Gelb und Blau, die vom Turm ausgehend die Kirche einhüllen, während Gounods aufstrebender Chor als polychromer Rauchpilz einige Hundert Meter über dem Kirchturm steht. Die spektakulärste Abbildung bezieht sich auf Wagners Werk, das in Gestalt einer wogenden Bergkette hoch über der Kirche schwebt und sie zwergenhaft erscheinen lässt. Dieses bombastische Finale eines außergewöhnlichen Buches steht beispielhaft für das Interesse der Theosophen an synästhetischen Erfahrungen.

## Formes-pensées, registre de la recherche clairvoyante

Remarquable pédagogue, socialiste, militante des droits des femmes, Annie Besant est vite devenue une figure de proue de la Société théosophique. Quand elle rencontre Charles Leadbeater en 1894, c'est le début d'une longue amitié. Cet ouvrage consacré à la façon dont les idées et les pensées se présentent physiquement et visuellement est leur plus belle collaboration.

La première planche, «Note pour la signification des couleurs», reprise de l'ouvrage de Leadbeater, *Man Visible and Invisible* (1902), utilise le même symbolisme chromatique. Avec ces *Formes-pensées*, les auteurs tentent d'approfondir le «sujet général de l'aura» en fondant leurs illustrations sur trois principes généraux, à commencer par la couleur: «1. La qualité des pensées détermine la couleur. 2. La nature des pensées détermine la forme. 3. La précision des pensées détermine la netteté des contours.» La conceptualisation va plus loin et identifie trois catégories de formes-pensées, à savoir les penseurs ou figures humaines, les objets matériels et ceux représentant un état d'esprit, qui correspondent aux plans «astral ou mental». Aux yeux de Besant et Leadbeater, seul ce troisième groupe mérite d'être rendu par des images. Les 58 illustrations qui figurent dans le livre s'inspirent d'œuvres de plusieurs amis, remerciés dans l'introduction pour la «tâche difficile» de «rendre au moyen des sombres couleurs terrestres les formes revêtues par la lumière vivante des mondes de l'au-delà.»

Les trois dernières formes-pensées diffèrent clairement des autres puisqu'elles représentent non plus des pensées isolées mais de la musique, soit une pièce pour piano de Mendelssohn, une œuvre chorale de Gounod et une œuvre pour orchestre de Wagner (p. 434). On y reconnaît la même église avec son haut clocher, d'où émergent les formes visuelles correspondant à la musique. La musique de Mendelssohn produit des lignes brisées et irrégulières de rouge cramoisi, jaune et bleu qui émanent de l'église et l'enveloppent; le chœur de Gounod, en s'élevant, forme un nuage-champignon de vapeur polychrome qui flotte à plusieurs dizaines de mètres au-dessus du clocher. L'image la plus spectaculaire est celle générée par la musique de Wagner: une sorte de chaîne montagneuse multicolore semble s'envoler et planer au-dessus de l'église, rendue minuscule. Un finale grandiose pour ce livre extraordinaire et un splendide exemple de l'intérêt des théosophes pour les expériences synesthésiques.

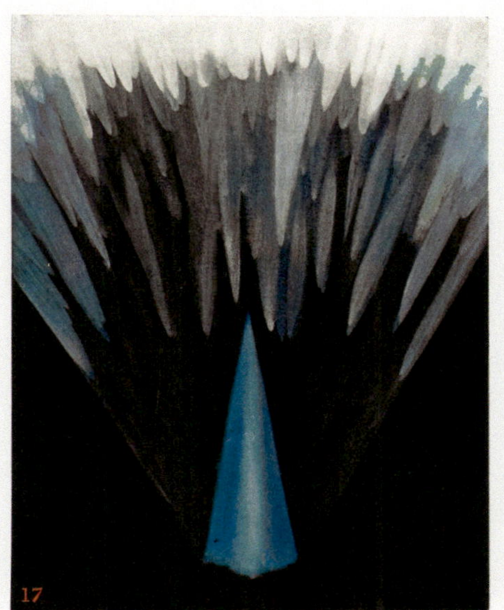
17

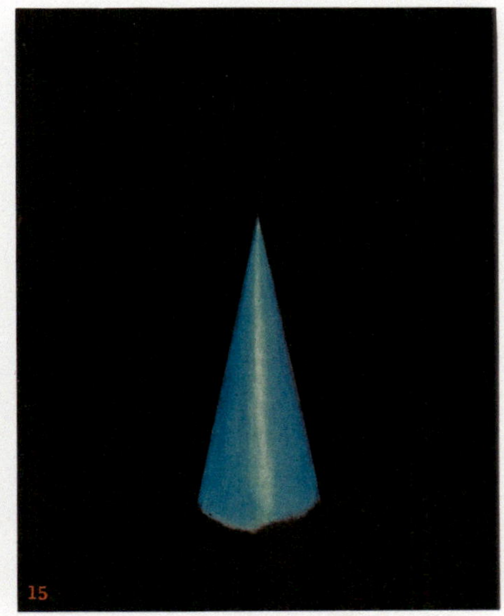
15

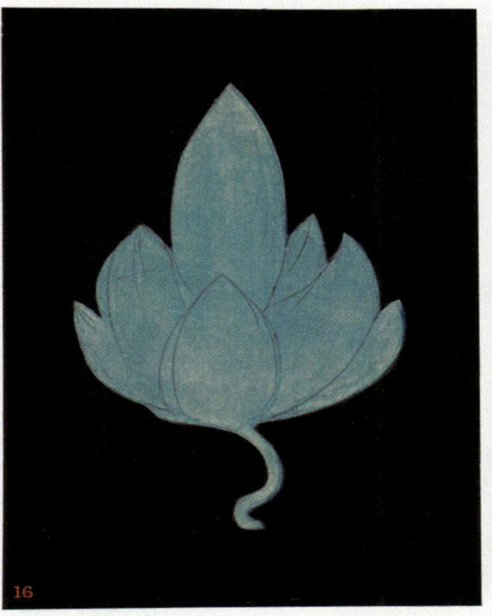
16

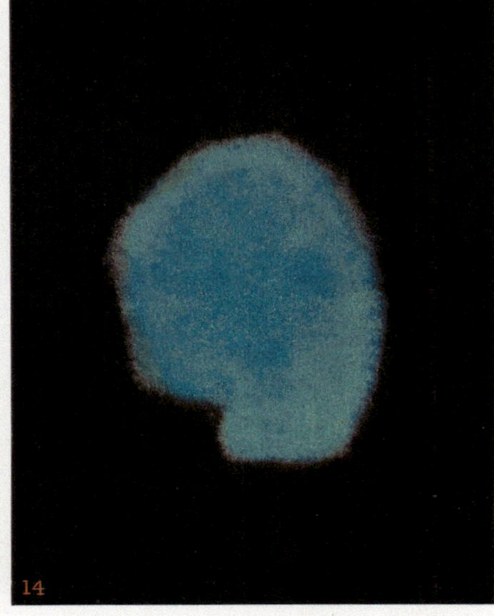
14

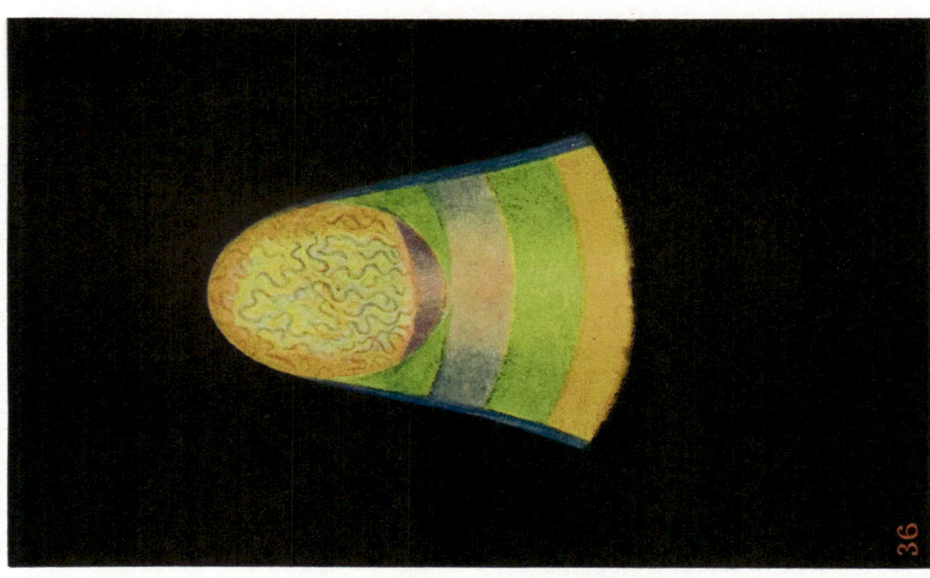

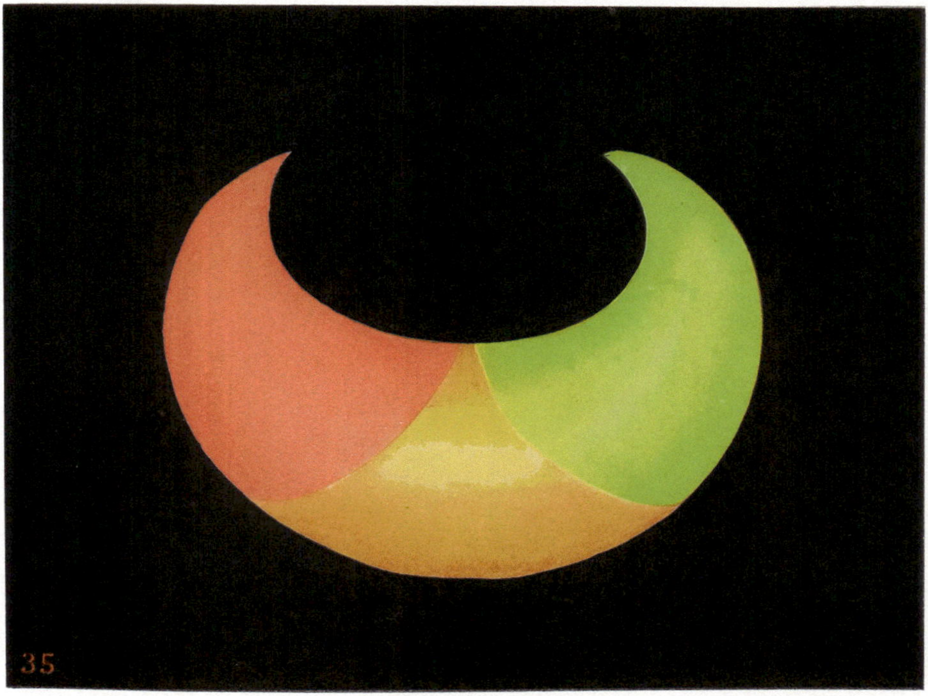

35

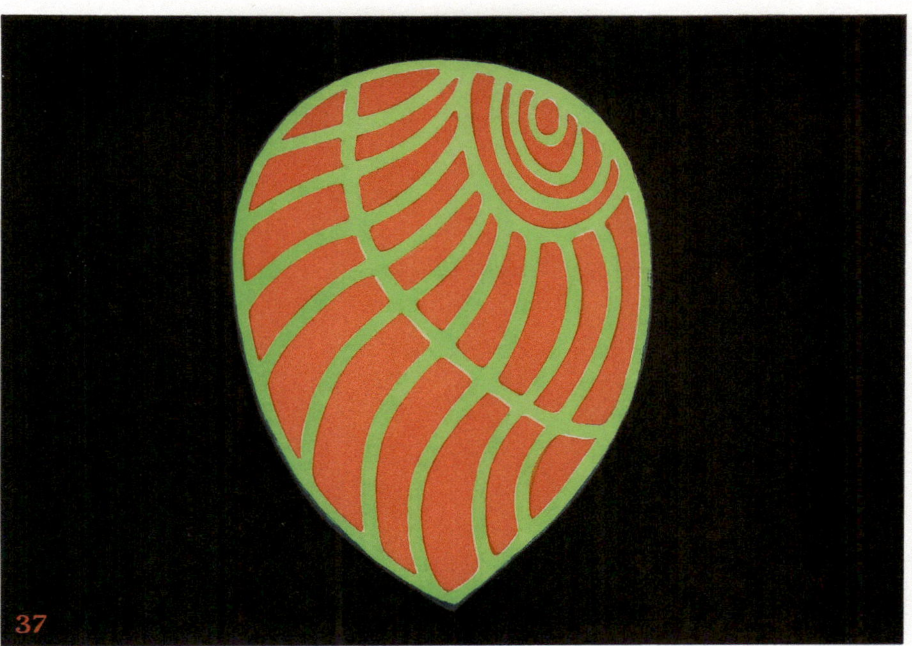
37

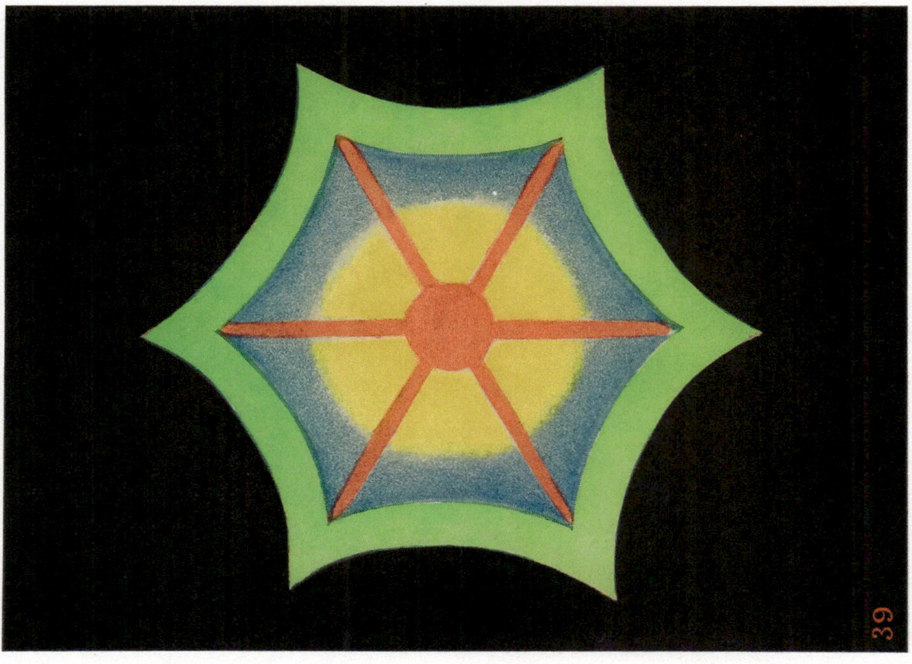
39

## Alexander Wallace Rimington (1854–1918)

# COLOUR-MUSIC: THE ART OF MOBILE COLOUR

*10 plates, 20 x 14 cm | 7 ⅞ x 5 ½ in., London, 1912*
*Sussex, collection of the author*

In June 1895 the painter Alexander Wallace Rimington gave a talk at St. James's Hall in Piccadilly, central London, in which he proposed a new form of art: colour music. So far, he claimed, there had been no pure art that dealt with colour alone, and he was convinced that he had found a way to unlock colour's expressive potential. Rimington announced to the audience that he had recently taken out a patent on a "colour organ", a device that functioned so that when any note was played on the keyboard it would project corresponding coloured rays of light. He likened the keyboard of an organ to a painter's palette and talked of bold visions involving synaesthetic colour-music compositions before giving a practical demonstration of his colour organ, using music by Wagner and Chopin.

Rimington was not the first person to have built an instrument that could play colour as in the early 18th century the French Jesuit and mathematician Louis-Bertrand Castel designed and built an ocular harpsichord that could play light through pieces of coloured glass. He followed this later by designing an organ that would play sounds and make coloured strips of paper appear at the same time.

Of course, Rimington had the advantage of living in the age of electrification, and while he was aware that the mechanism of his device was complicated and sensitive, by means of electricity he was able to shine a powerful ray of light through two large prisms contained inside it. The prisms split the light into the colours of the spectrum with the help of a series of diaphragms, which could be isolated, combined and controlled using the keyboard and pedals, and then projected on to a large screen.

He spent many years perfecting his invention and poured all his research work and excitement into this book. The cover illustration shows a mountainous landscape across which float colourful lines of musical notation, while the frontispiece, entitled "Nature's Colour Scale", depicts the natural visible spectrum in the form of a rainbow. Both images were based on Rimington's own artwork. The book also includes several black-and-white photographs showing the design and mechanism of his colour organ, as well as many elegant coloured diagrams that illustrate the analogy between musical and chromatic scales, chords, melodies and harmonies.

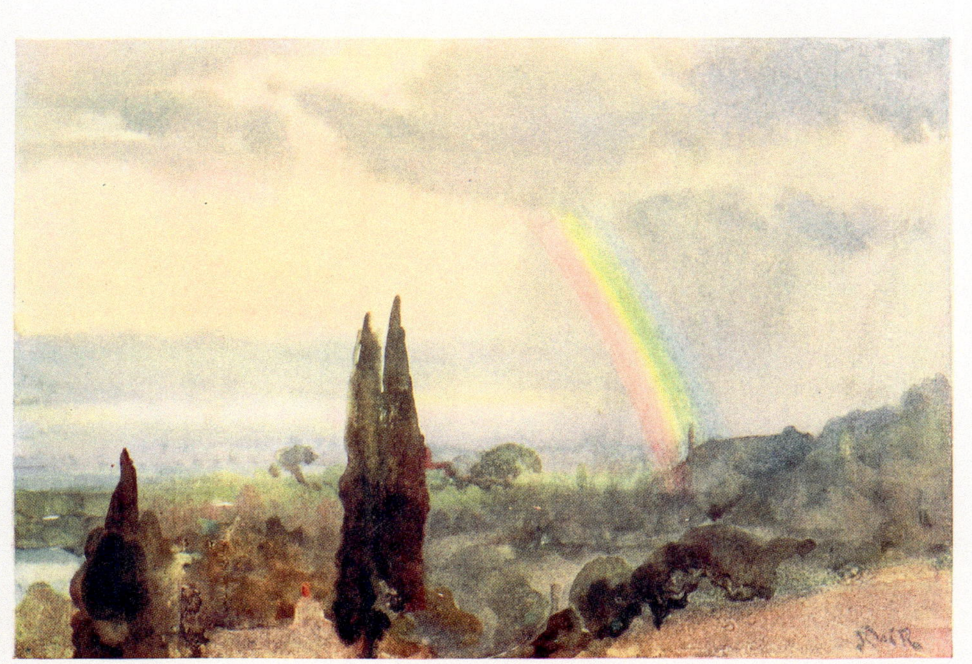

NATURE'S COLOUR SCALE.

*Frontispiece.*

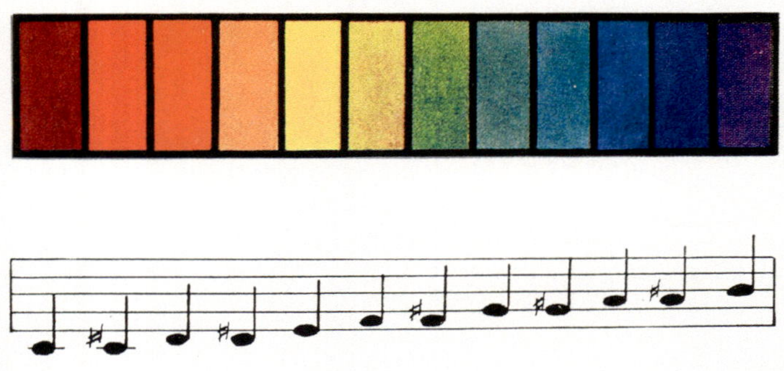

Chromatic scale in Music and Colour.
Shewing correspondence of intervals when C = lowest spectrum red.

## Farbenmusik: Die Kunst der beweglichen Farbe

Im Juni 1895 hielt der Maler Alexander Wallace Rimington in der St. James's Hall an der Piccadilly im Zentrum Londons einen Vortrag, in dem er für eine neue Kunstform warb: die Farbenmusik. Bis dahin, so Rimington, habe es keine reine Kunst gegeben, die sich allein mit Farbe beschäftigte. Nun aber war er überzeugt, eine Methode gefunden zu haben, um das Ausdruckspotenzial von Farben zu erschließen. Rimington verkündete dem Publikum, er habe er sich kürzlich eine „Farbenorgel" patentieren lassen, einen Apparat, der beim Anschlag einer Note auf der Tastatur entsprechende farbige Lichtstrahlen auswarf. Er verglich das Manual einer Orgel mit einer Malpalette und sprach in kühnen Visionen von synästhetischen Farbenmusikstücken, bevor er mit Kompositionen von Wagner und Chopin eine praktische Vorführung seiner Farbenorgel gab.

Rimington war nicht der erste Erbauer eines Instruments, das Farbsequenzen spielen konnte. Im frühen 18. Jahrhundert entwarf und konstruierte der französische Jesuitenpater und Mathematiker Louis-Bertrand Castel ein „Augencembalo", das Licht durch farbiges Glas werfen konnte. Später ließ er eine Orgel folgen, bei der zu jedem gespielten Ton ein farbiger Papierstreifen zum Vorschein kam.

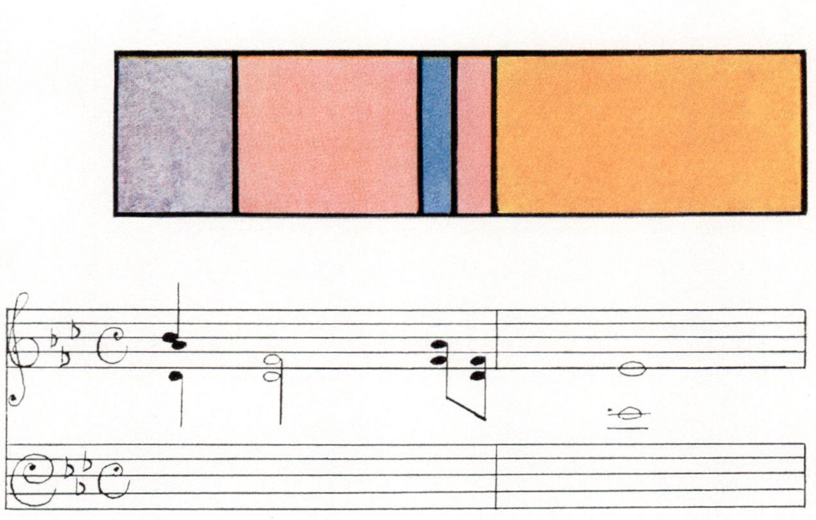

Diagram to illustrate introduction of the element of time into colour effects—the duration of the colour chords upon the screen corresponding to the musical notation.

Natürlich hatte Rimington den Vorteil, im Zeitalter der Elektrifizierung zu leben. In dem Bewusstsein, dass der Mechanismus seines Instruments kompliziert und empfindlich war, lenkte er mit elektrischem Strom einen starken Lichtstrahl durch zwei große Prismen in dessen Inneres. Die Prismen spalteten das Licht mithilfe einer Reihe von Blenden in die Spektralfarben auf, die sich unter Einsatz von Tastatur und Pedalen isolieren, kombinieren und steuern und sodann auf eine große Leinwand projizieren ließen.

Über viele Jahre war der Künstler damit beschäftigt, seine Erfindung zu perfektionieren, und ließ seine gesamte Forschungsarbeit und Begeisterung in dieses Buch einfließen. Die Einbandillustration zeigt eine Gebirgslandschaft, über die bunte Notenbänder hinwegschweben, während im Frontispiz mit dem Titel „Die Farbskala der Natur“ das natürliche sichtbare Spektrum in Form eines Regenbogens aufscheint. Beide Bilder basierten auf Rimingtons eigenen Werken. Neben mehreren Schwarz-Weiß-Fotografien von der Farbenorgel des Künstlers und ihren Mechanismen enthält das Buch zudem zahlreiche elegante Farbdiagramme, in denen die Analogie zwischen Ton- und Farbenleitern sowie musikalischen und chromatischen Akkorden, Melodien und Harmonien veranschaulicht wird.

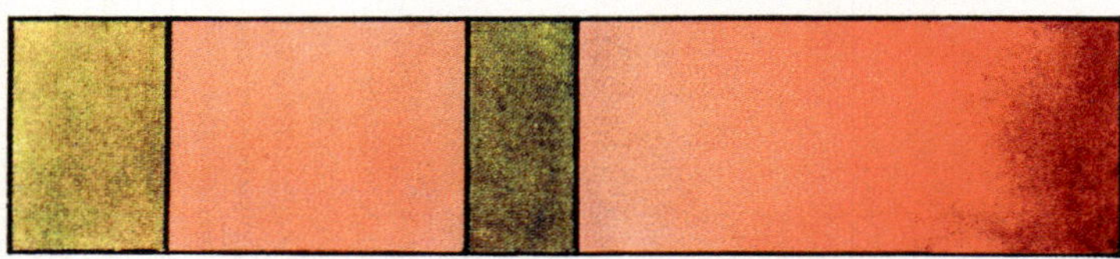

Illustrating a colour phrase, in which the fourth note is gradually increased in strength by the swell pedal of the colour organ.

## Couleur-musique : l'art de la couleur mobile

En juin 1895, le peintre Alexander Wallace Rimington donne une causerie au St. James's Hall à Piccadilly, au centre de Londres, où il propose une nouvelle forme d'art : la musique en couleurs. De son point de vue, aucun art véritable n'a jusqu'à présent traité de la couleur seule, et il est persuadé d'avoir trouvé une façon de libérer le plein potentiel expressif de celle-ci. Rimington annonce au public qu'il a fait breveter un « orgue de couleurs » : à chaque note jouée sur le clavier, des rais de lumière de la teinte correspondante sont projetés. Il compare l'orgue à la palette du peintre, relate des visions remarquables de compositions synesthésiques mélangeant couleurs et musique, puis fait la démonstration de son dispositif en jouant des partitions de Wagner et de Chopin.

Rimington n'est pas le premier à construire un instrument qui joue des couleurs : au début du XVIIIe siècle, le mathématicien jésuite français Louis-Bertrand Castel a conçu et construit un clavecin oculaire, capable de faire passer la lumière à travers des morceaux de verre coloré. Plus tard, il conçoit un orgue qui produit des sons et fait apparaître des bandes de papier coloré en même temps.

Rimington a bien sûr l'avantage de vivre à l'époque de l'électrification. Il sait que le mécanisme de son appareil est fragile et compli-

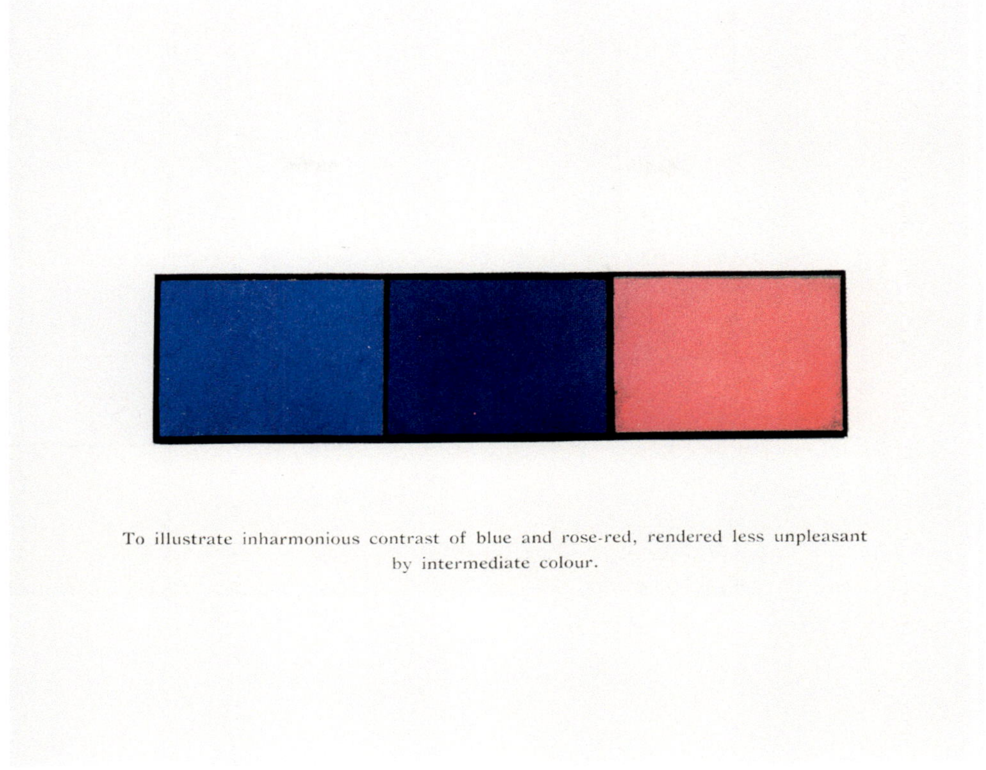

To illustrate inharmonious contrast of blue and rose-red, rendered less unpleasant by intermediate colour.

qué, mais l'électricité lui permet de produire un puissant rayon lumineux qui passe à travers deux prismes placés à l'intérieur. Les prismes font jaillir les couleurs du spectre à l'aide d'une série de diaphragmes, qui peuvent être isolés, combinés et contrôlés au moyen du clavier et des pédales de l'orgue, et projetés sur un grand écran.

L'artiste travaille d'arrache-pied pendant des années pour perfectionner son invention, et son ouvrage « Couleur-musique : l'art de la couleur mobile » est le fruit de toutes ces recherches passionnées. L'illustration de couverture montre un paysage montagneux sous lequel figure une portée musicale multicolore. Sur celle du frontispice, intitulée « Gamme de couleurs de la nature », un arc-en-ciel déploie le spectre visible naturel. Les deux images sont tirées d'œuvres de Rimington. L'ouvrage compte aussi quelques photographies en noir et blanc présentant le fonctionnement de l'orgue de couleurs, ainsi que d'élégants graphiques en couleurs illustrant l'analogie entre les gammes musicale et chromatique, les accords, les mélodies et les harmonies.

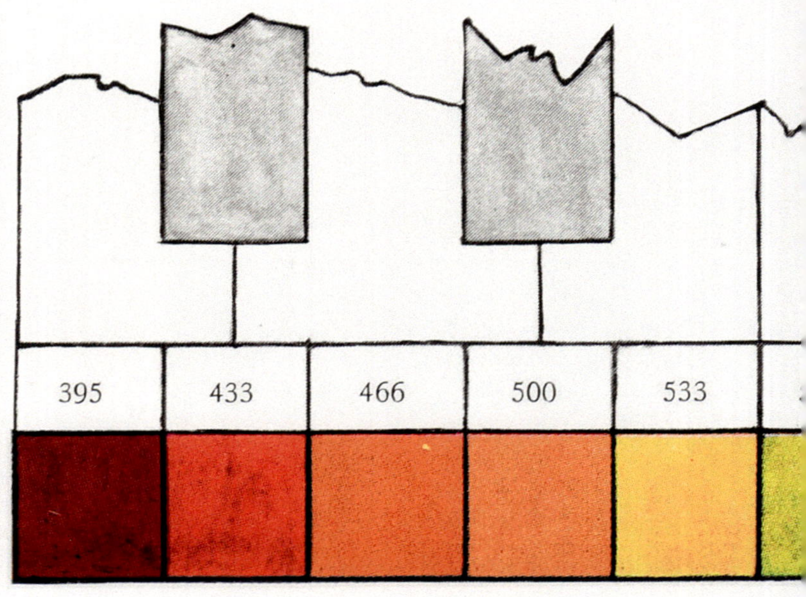


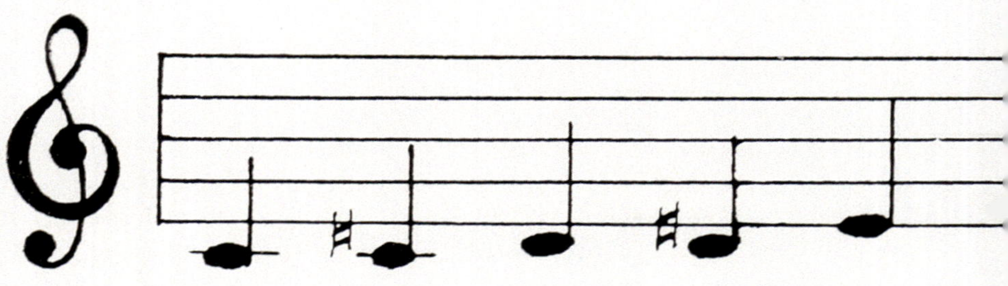

To shew normal division of colour scale upo
of execution are employed. The figures in
frequencies of aether vibration in millions of
given in pigments, and of course do not corr
ir

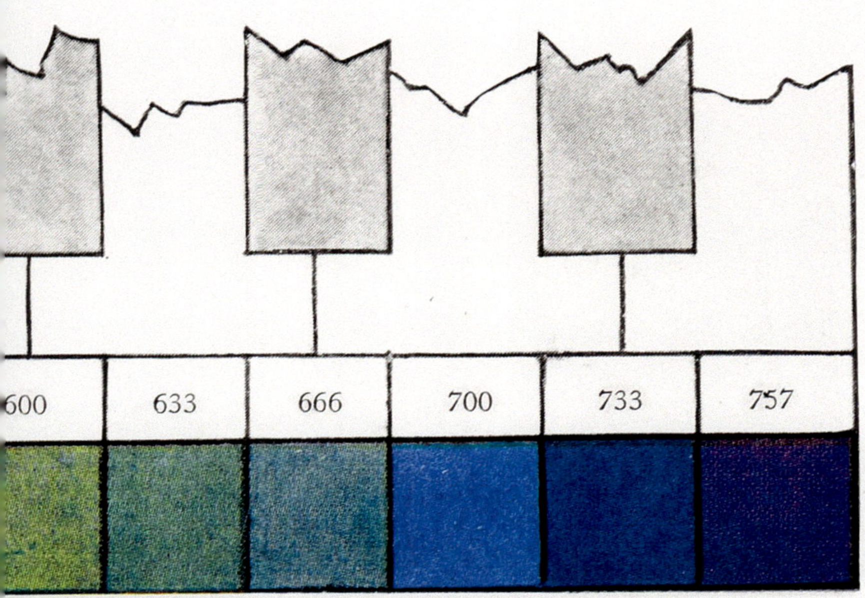


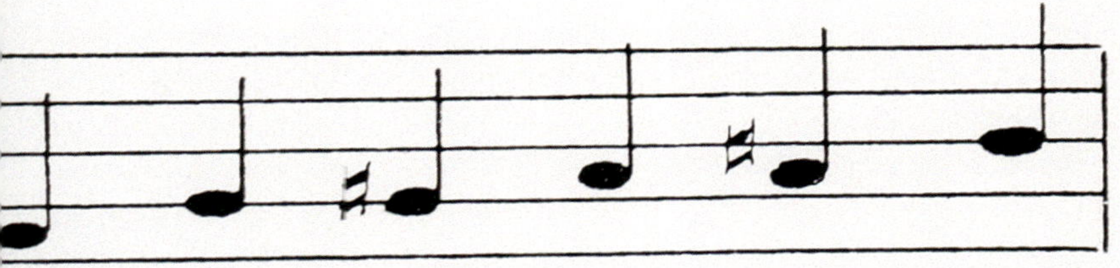

oard of colour organ, colour musical methods
aces above the colours give the approximate
per second. The colours cannot be accurately
more than roughly to those produced by the
nt.

## Maria Schindler (unknown), Eleanor C. Merry (1873–1956)

# PURE COLOUR

*23 plates, 22 x 13.5 cm | 8 ⅝ x 5 ¼ in., London, 1946*
*Sussex, collection of the author*

This book is a remarkable collaboration between two women in London immediately after the Second World War, both of whom were students of Rudolf Steiner's spiritual science and had a keen interest in European folklore, mythology, art and colour in particular. The English-born Eleanor Merry had studied in Vienna in the 1920s, where she met Steiner. Together with Maria Schindler, whose biographical data have so far not come to light, she directed the New School of Painting in North London in the 1940s. Both women were prolific authors who wrote a number of books on spiritual science and European folklore, and *Pure Colour* was their first known publication.

The book comprises three parts which examine the nature, power and impact of colour, using Goethe's colour theory as a principal theme. Part I, by Schindler, is an illustrated essay on how this theory can be applied to painting, which guides the reader through the basics of Goethe's *Zur Farbenlehre*, reinterpreting his colour circles and suggesting a series of painting exercises. Merry wrote Part II, "Painting and Imagination", which discusses intellectual and emotional approaches to colour painting, again using Goethe as a guideline. Part III consists of three extracts from Goethe's writings on colour in English, translated by Merry, which include the first published English translation of "Contributions to Optics" (*Beyträge zur Optik*, 1791/92).

*Pure Colour* includes a selection of black-and-white plates that were intended to be looked at through a three-sided prism, recreating some of Goethe's own colour experiments. Some copies of the book also included instructions on how to make a water prism, as a further experiment that could be easily conducted by readers. The colour plates, based on pastel drawings by Schindler and watercolours by Merry, provide visual examples of the painting exercises suggested in the text. They have a strong spiritual feel and are surprisingly vivid and luminous, not least when the poor printing materials and paper available in the aftermath of the war are taken into consideration. A revised edition of Schindler's part of the book was reprinted in 1964, on better paper and with even more luminous colour plates.

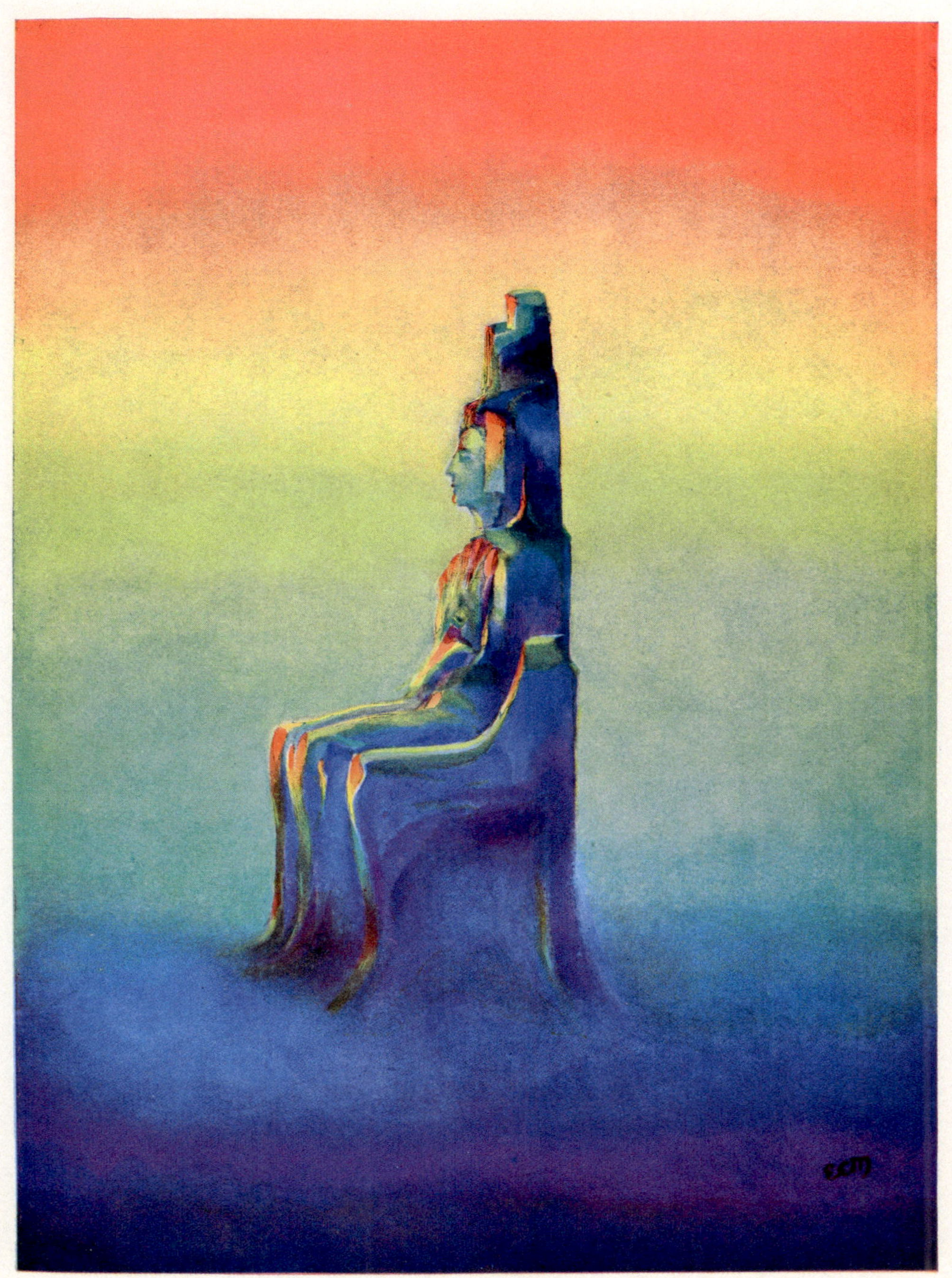

FRONTISPIECE

Exercise in prismatic colours

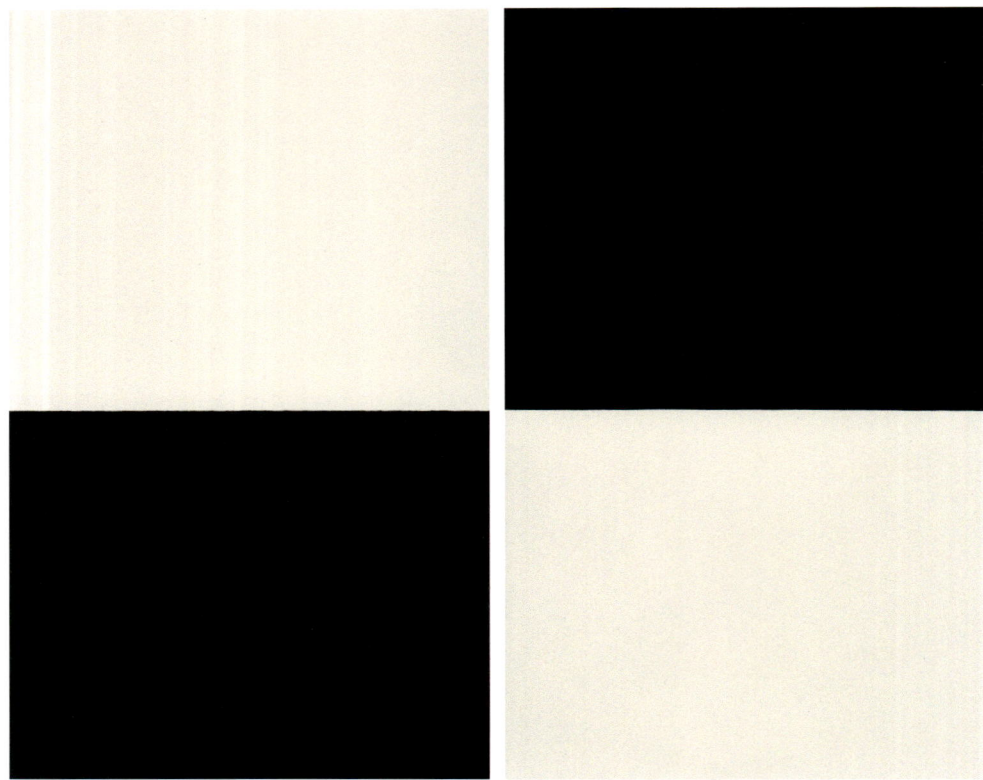

## Reine Farbe

Dieses Buch, das unmittelbar nach dem Zweiten Weltkrieg in London entstand, ist das bemerkenswerte Gemeinschaftsprojekt zweier Frauen, die beide Studentinnen Rudolf Steiners anthroposophischer Lehren waren und sich brennend für die Gebiete der europäischen Folklore, der Mythologie, der Kunst und besonders für das der Farben interessierten. Die gebürtige Engländerin Eleanor Merry studierte in den 1920er-Jahren in Wien, wo sie Steiner kennenlernte. Gemeinsam mit Maria Schindler, deren biografische Daten bis heute im Verborgenen liegen, leitete sie in den 1940er-Jahren die New School of Painting im Norden Londons. Beide Frauen waren äußerst produktive Autorinnen und schrieben zahlreiche Bücher über die Geisteswissenschaft und europäisches Volkstum. Das Werk *Pure Colour* war ihre erste bekannt gewordene Publikation.

Das aus drei Teilen bestehende Buch untersucht das Wesen, die Kraft und die Wirkung von Farbe und stützt sich dabei als Hauptthema auf die Farbtheorie Goethes. Der von Schindler verfasste Teil I ist ein illustrierter Aufsatz über die Anwendbarkeit dieser Theorie auf die Malerei. Er führt die Leserschaft durch die Grundlagen von Goethes *Zur Farbenlehre*, interpretiert seine Farbkreise neu und macht Vorschläge für eine Reihe von Malübungen. Merry schrieb den zweiten Teil, der unter der

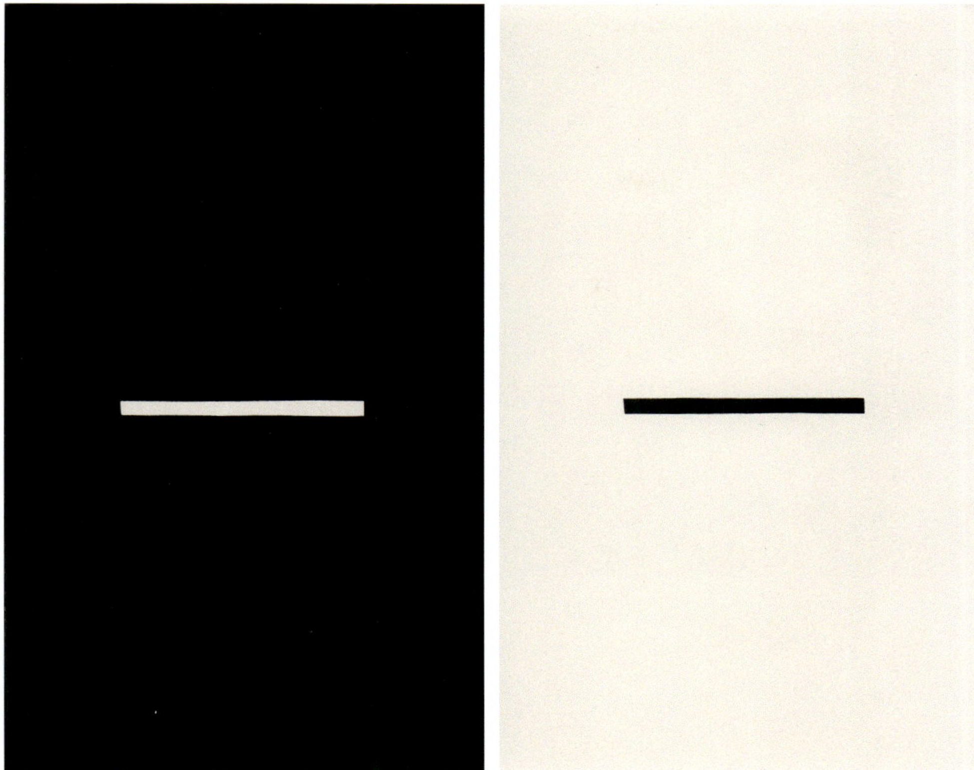

Überschrift „Malerei und Vorstellungskraft“ intellektuelle und gefühlsbetonte Zugänge zur Farbmalerei behandelt, abermals mit Goethe als Richtschnur. Teil III versammelt drei von Merry ins Englische übersetzte Auszüge aus Goethes Schriften über Farbe, darunter die erste jemals erschienene englische Übersetzung von *Beyträge zur Optik* (1791/92).

*Pure Colour* enthält eine Auswahl schwarzweißer Bildtafeln, die durch ein dreiseitiges Prisma zu betrachten waren, um einige der Farbexperimente Goethes nachzuvollziehen. Einigen Buchexemplaren war überdies eine Anleitung zum Bau eines Wasserprismas beigelegt, um den Lesern die Durchführung dieser und anderer Experimente zu ermöglichen. Die Farbtafeln, die auf Pastellzeichnungen von Schindler und Aquarellen von Merry basieren, zeigen Bildbeispiele für die im Text vorgeschlagenen Malübungen. Sie vermitteln eine überzeugende spirituelle Stimmung und wirken überraschend lebendig und strahlend – erst recht, wenn man die minderwertigen Druckmaterialien und verfügbaren Papiere nach dem Krieg berücksichtigt. Eine durchgesehene Auflage des von Schindler verantworteten Buchabschnitts erschien 1964 auf besserem Papier und mit noch leuchtenderen Farbtafeln.

Plate VIII

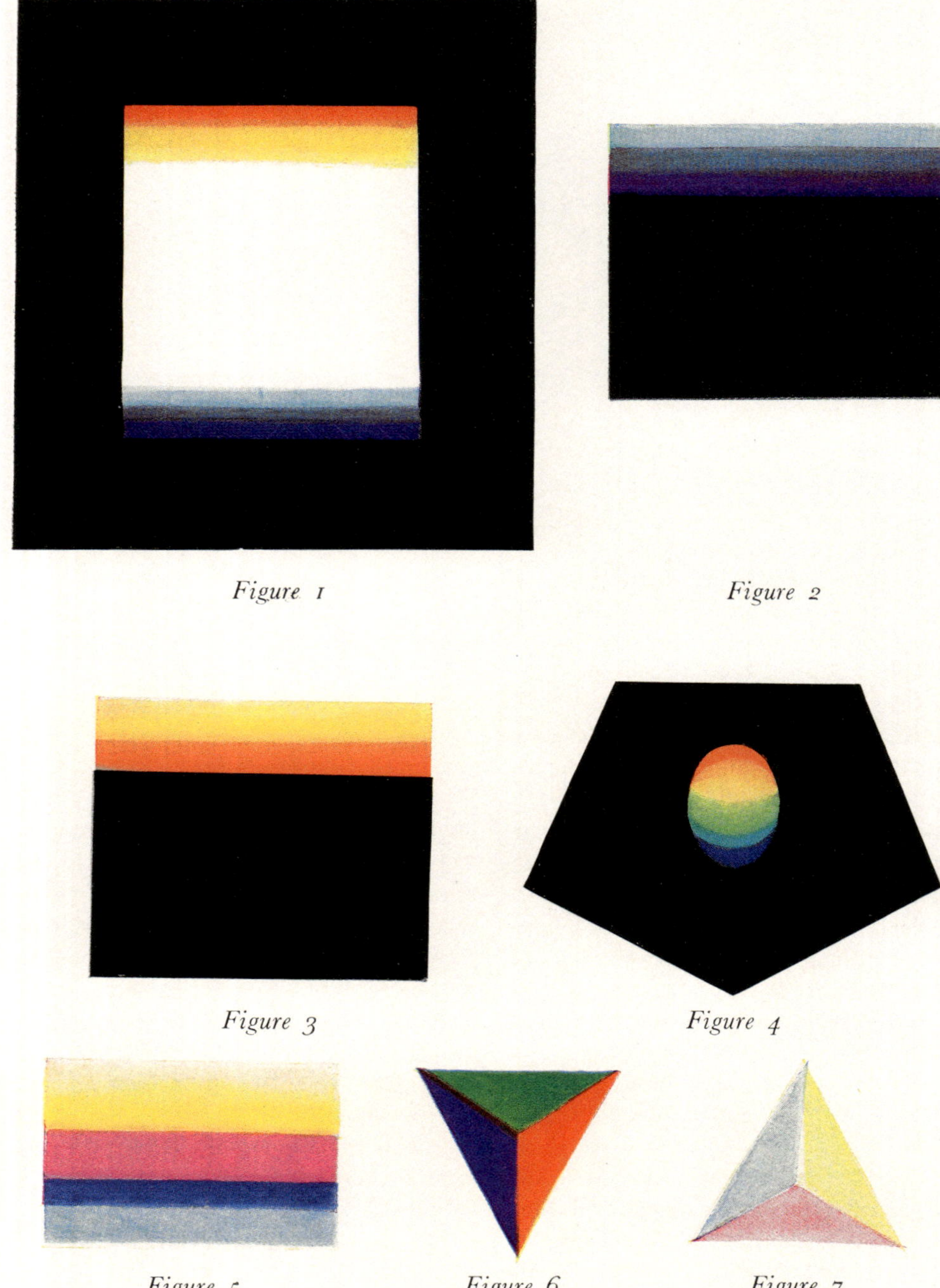

*Figure 1*

*Figure 2*

*Figure 3*

*Figure 4*

*Figure 5*

*Figure 6*

*Figure 7*

## Couleur pure

Cet ouvrage est le fruit d'une remarquable collaboration entre deux femmes, dans le Londres de l'immédiat après-guerre. Toutes deux étudient la science spirituelle de Rudolf Steiner et se passionnent pour les traditions populaires, la mythologie et la peinture, notamment la couleur, dans la culture européenne. Dans les années 1920, Eleanor Merry, née en Angleterre, a étudié à Vienne, où elle a rencontré Steiner. Dans les années 1940, avec Maria Schindler, dont la vie reste à ce jour un mystère, Merry dirige la New School of Painting dans le nord de Londres. Les deux femmes, autrices prolifiques, font paraître plusieurs ouvrages sur le spiritualisme et le folklore européen. *Pure Colour* est leur première publication connue.

L'ouvrage contient trois parties qui étudient la nature, la puissance et l'impact de la couleur en se fondant sur la théorie de la couleur de Goethe. La première partie, signée Schindler, est un essai illustré sur la façon dont cette théorie peut s'appliquer à la peinture : le lecteur y découvre les principes du *Zur Farbenlehre* de Goethe, avec une réinterprétation des cercles chromatiques, et peut s'adonner à une série d'exercices picturaux. Dans la deuxième partie, « Peinture et imagination », Merry analyse les approches intellectuelle et émotionnelle des couleurs en peinture, toujours avec Goethe comme fil d'Ariane. La troisième partie propose trois extraits des écrits de Goethe sur la couleur, traduits en anglais par Merry, dont la toute première traduction dans cette langue des « Contributions *à l'optique* » (*Beyträge zur Optik*, 1791/92).

*Pure Colour* contient également une sélection de planches en noir et blanc à observer à travers un prisme à trois facettes afin de recréer certaines expériences de Goethe. Certains exemplaires du livre contiennent des instructions pour fabriquer un prisme à eau permettant d'effectuer d'autres expériences. Les planches en couleurs, reproductions de dessins au pastel de Schindler et des aquarelles de Merry, sont autant d'exemples des exercices picturaux suggérés dans le texte. Elles dégagent une profonde spiritualité et sont étonnamment vives et lumineuses au regard de la piètre qualité du matériel d'impression et des pénuries de papier de l'après-guerre. Une édition révisée de la partie de Schindler verra le jour en 1964, sur un meilleur papier et avec des planches encore plus éclatantes.

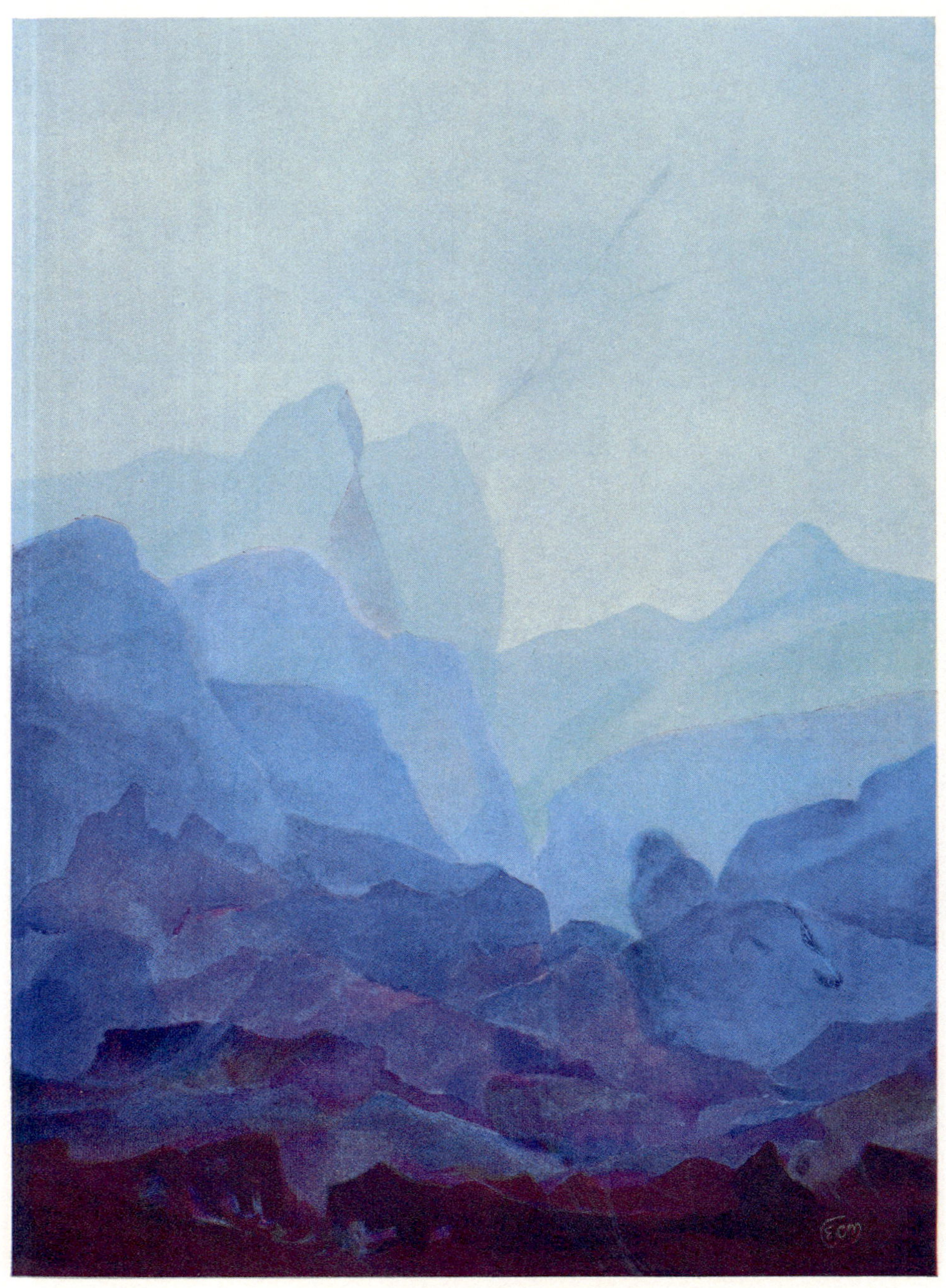

Exercise in blue and violet
(Water-colour)

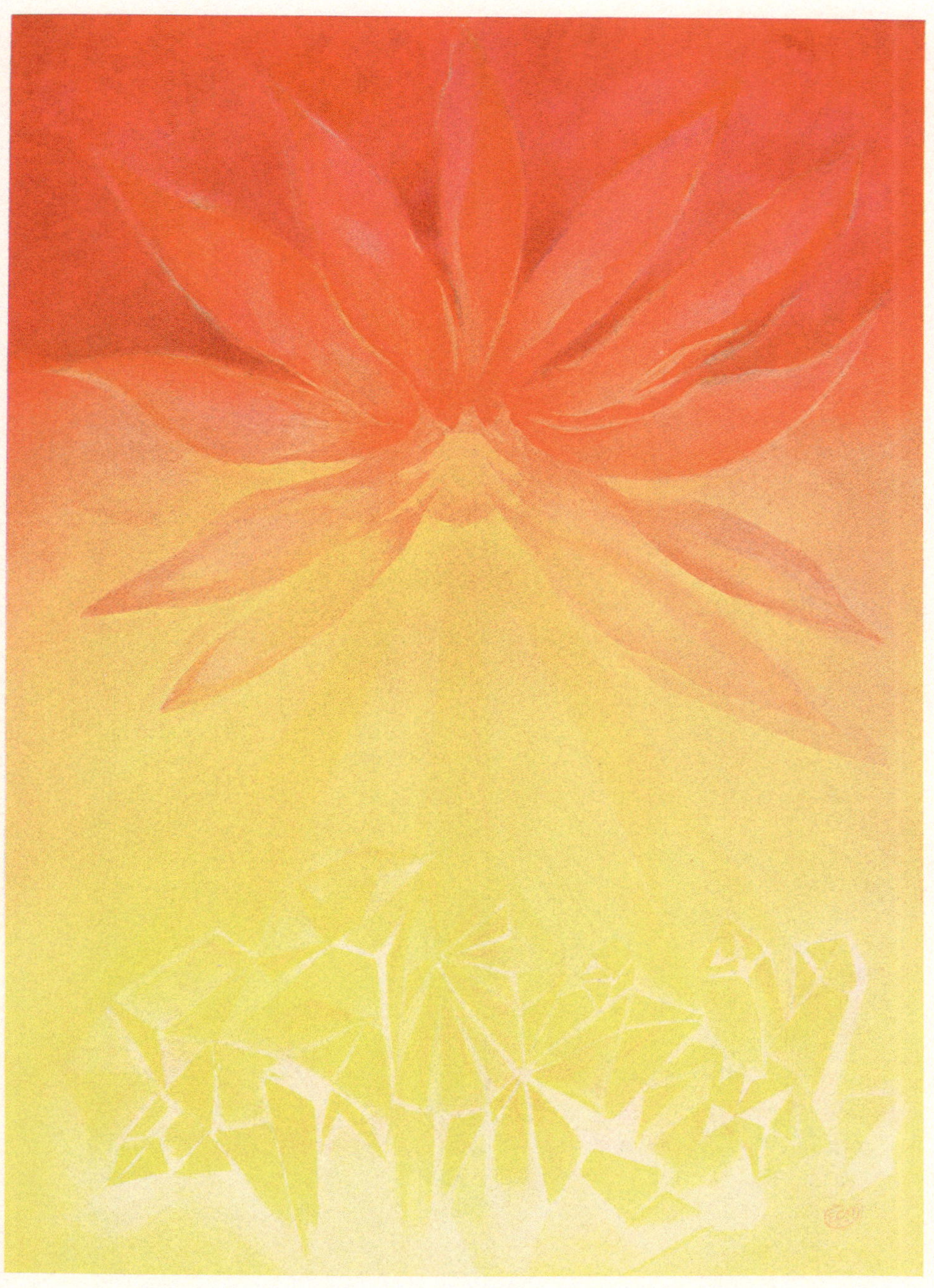

Exercise in red and yellow
(Water-colour)

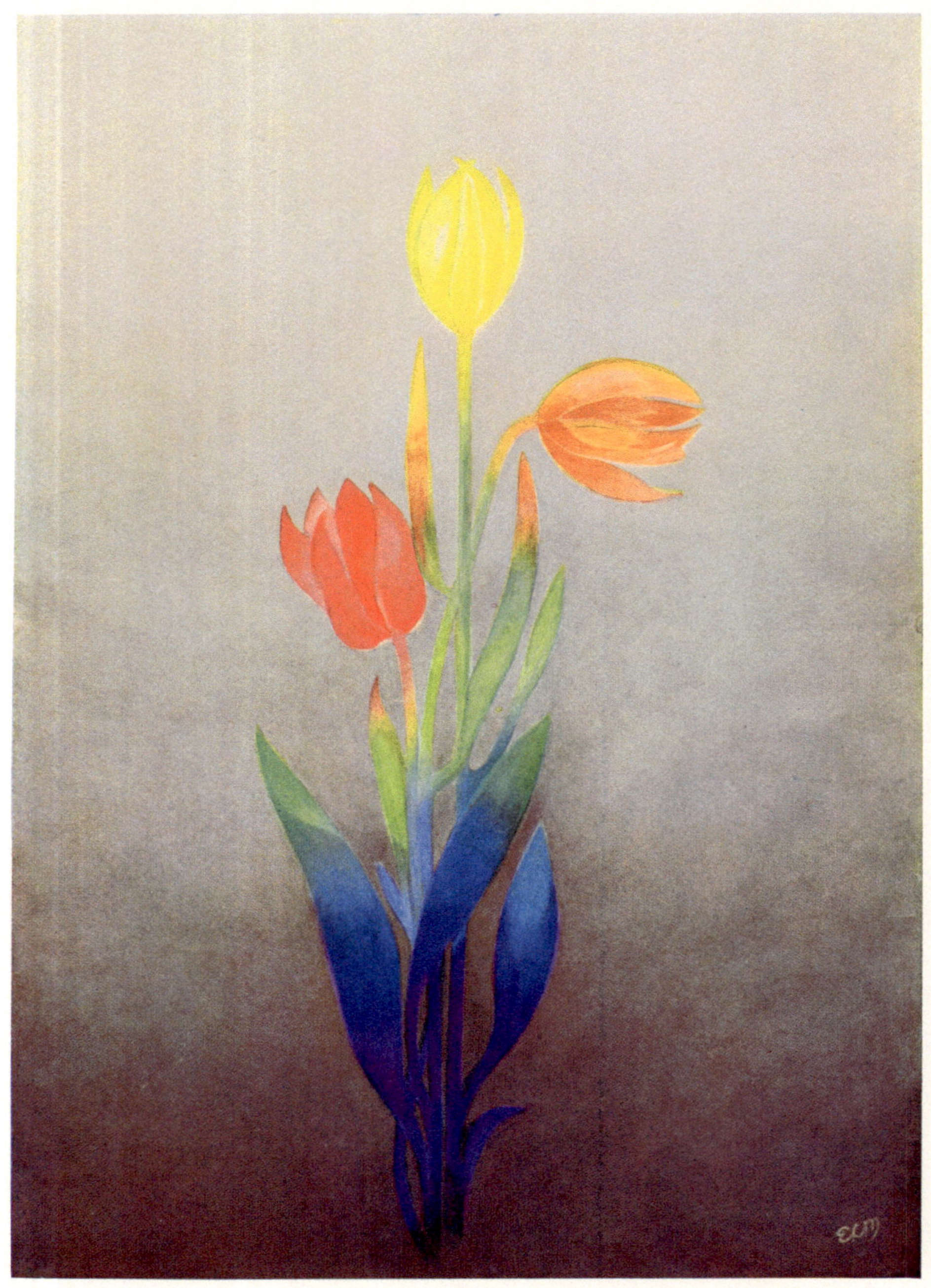

Exercise on the relation of colours to grey (Water-colour)

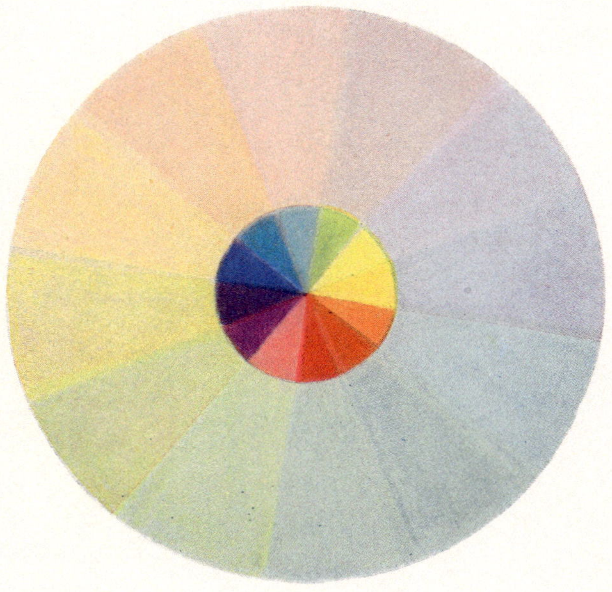

Physiological colour circle. In the centre prismatic colours and adjoining each one, the after-image

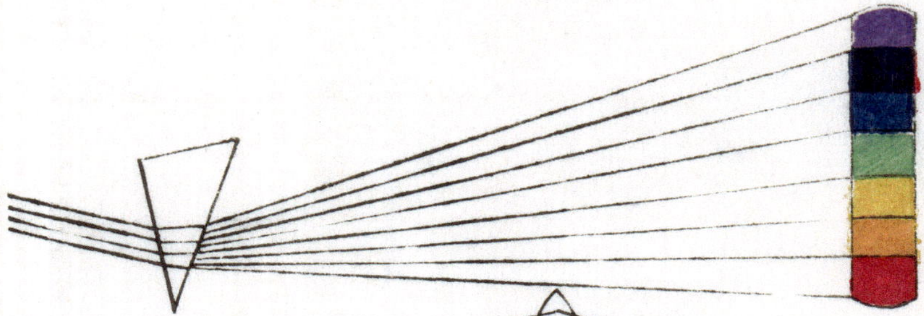

第一圖

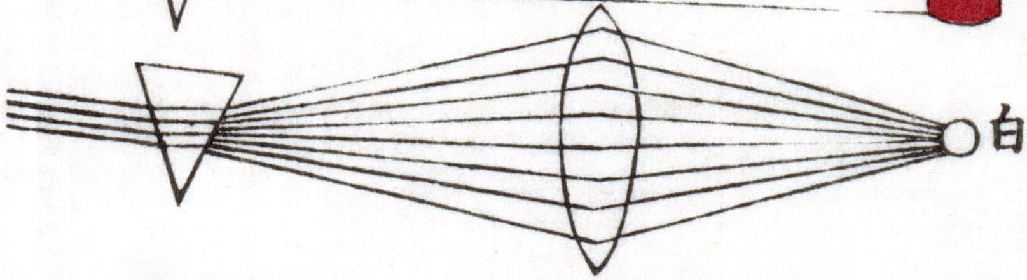

七色

第二圖

白

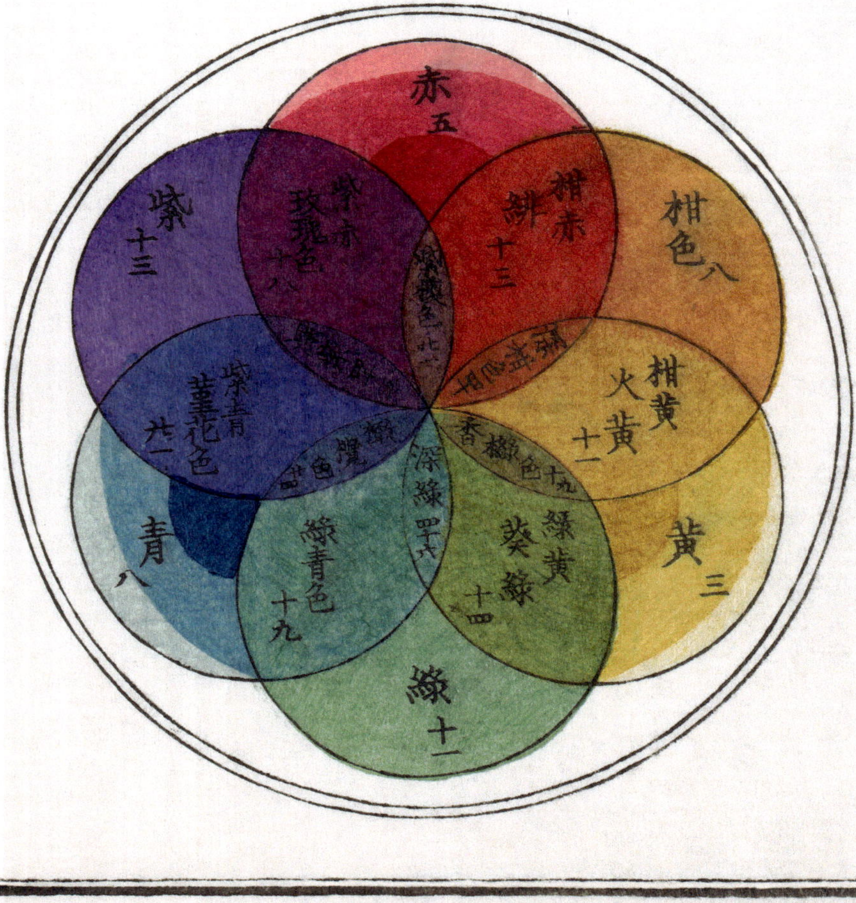

赤 五

紫 十三

紫赤 玫瑰色 十八

柑赤 緋 十三

柑色 八

柑黄 火黄 十一

香櫞色 十九

黄 三

綠黄 葵綠 十四

深綠 四十六

綠 十一

綠青色 十九

青 八

紫青 菫花色 十六

Chapter 8

# *Looking Beyond:* EASTERN COLOUR CONCEPTS

1876–1934

## Masanori Iehara, Kan'ichiro Shiozu (dates unknown)

# GAKKO HITSUYO IROZU MONDO

## A Book of Questions and Answers about Colour for Use in Schools

*2 plates, 21 x 12.5 cm | 8 ¼ x 4 ⅞ in., Tokyo, 1876*
*Berkeley, University of California, C.V. Starr East Asian Library*

The influence of Japanese aesthetics on Western culture in the latter part of the 19th century cannot be overestimated. Soon after Japan opened up to trade with the rest of the world in the 1850s, Japanese motifs became ubiquitous in painting and design, as well as literature and fashion, while *Japonisme* and Aestheticism developed as exciting new artistic styles and movements that reflect the fascination in Europe and the United States with this previously inaccessible culture. Concurrently, a growing interest about Western culture developed among the Japanese, and this filtered down into ideas about colour theory and colour teaching.

*Gakko hitsuyo irozu mondo* is a small textbook on colour for schools, and seems to have been the first such that was inspired by Western models. The 22 folded sheets of printed text are illustrated with two hand-coloured plates of colour diagrams, and additional small colour squares within the running text. Conceptually the graphic design of the plate with the colour chart is based on a system that corresponds to the seven Newtonian colours, with the three primaries yellow, red and blue being given special status (p. 461, top right). The flower-shaped colour wheel in the second plate is clearly an adaptation of George Field's "Scale of Chromatic Equivalents", a colour compass that described colour mixture and contrasts and which had been designed by Field in England in the 1810s. It was first published in an uncoloured version in 1835 as the frontispiece to *Chromatography*, and a coloured version subsequently appeared in other books by Field from 1841. Above the much-simplified version of Field's diagram in this textbook are small images of Newton's prismatic experiments relating to the splitting of white light into the visible spectrum of colours. The presence of these ghosts of diagrams by Field and Newton in a Japanese school primer from the 1870s raises intriguing questions. How did they make their journey around the globe? Which versions did the authors see, and were they able to read the accompanying English text? And how did they fit existing Japanese colour concepts and linguistic terms into an earlier European colour system? It is, in any case, a wonderful example of global cross-cultural exchange in the 19th century.

BERKELEY LIBRARY UNIVERSITY OF CALIFORNIA

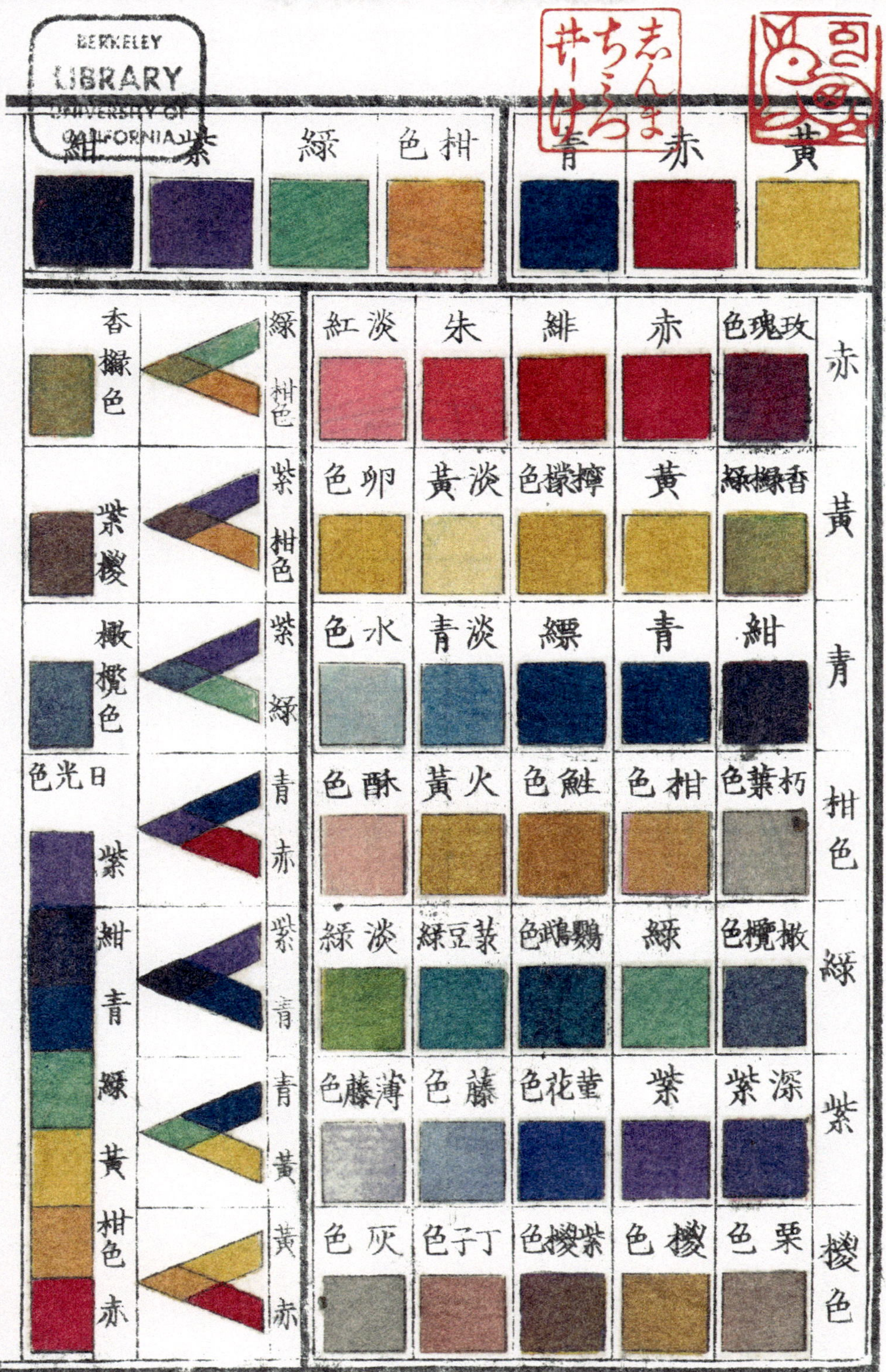


501341

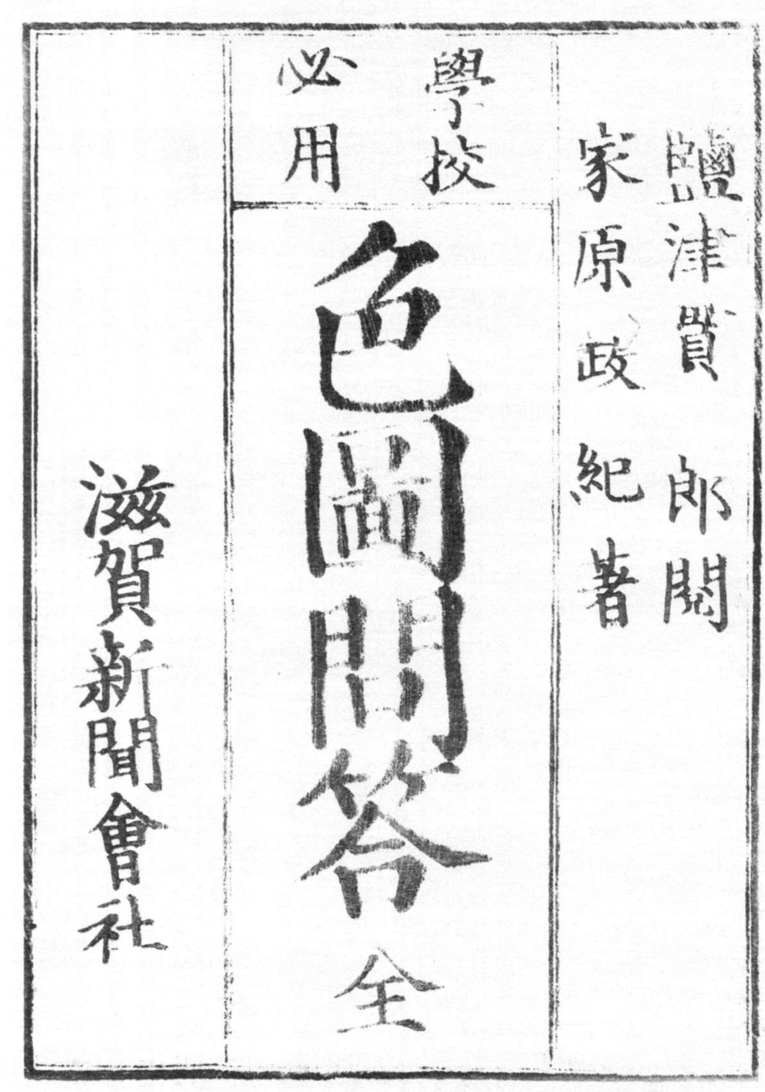

鹽津貫一郎閲
家原政紀著

學校必用

色圖問答　全

滋賀新聞會社

## Ein Buch der Fragen und Antworten über Farbe für den Schulgebrauch

Der Einfluss der japanischen Ästhetik auf die westliche Kultur im späten 19. Jahrhundert ist nicht zu unterschätzen. Kurz nachdem sich Japan in den 1850er-Jahren dem Welthandel geöffnet hatte, waren japanische Motive in Malerei und Gestaltung, aber auch in Literatur und Mode allgegenwärtig. Mit dem Japonismus und dem Ästhetizismus entwickelten sich aufregende neue Kunststile und -strömungen, in denen sich die Begeisterung Europas und Amerikas für diese zuvor unzugängliche Kultur widerspiegelte. Gleichzeitig wuchs in Japan das Interesse an der westlichen Kultur, was sich unter anderem in Gedanken zur Farbtheorie und zum Farbunterricht niederschlug.

*Gakko hitsuyo irozu mondo* ist ein kleines Farblehrbuch für Schulen und scheint das erste seiner Art gewesen zu sein, das von westlichen Vorbildern angeregt war. Die 22 gefalteten und bedruckten Doppelbögen sind mit Farbdiagrammen auf zwei handkolorierten Tafeln und kleinen Farbquadraten im laufenden Text bebildert. Die grafische Gestaltung der Farbtabelle beruht auf einem System, das den sieben Newton'schen Farben entspricht, wobei den drei Grundfarben Gelb, Rot und Blau eine Sonderstellung eingeräumt wird (S. 461, oben rechts). Bei dem blütenförmigen Farbkreis auf der zweiten Bildtafel handelt es sich eindeutig um eine Bearbeitung der „Chromatischen Äquivalente“ von George Field. Field hatte seinen Farbkompass mit Beschreibungen von Farbmischungen und Farbkontrasten in den 1810er-Jahren in England entworfen. 1835 wurde er als nicht koloriertes Schaubild im Frontispiz zu *Chromatography* zum ersten Mal abgedruckt, ab 1841 erschien er in anderen Büchern Fields auch in einer kolorierten Fassung. Oberhalb der stark vereinfachten Version des Field'schen Diagramms in diesem Lehrwerk finden sich kleinere Abbildungen der prismatischen Experimente Newtons zur Aufspaltung des weißen Lichts in die Farben des sichtbaren Spektrums. Die Darstellung dieser rudimentären Diagramme nach Field und Newton in einer japanischen Schulfibel aus den 1870er-Jahren wirft interessante Fragen auf. Wie gelangten sie auf die andere Seite der Welt? Welche Fassungen haben die Autoren gesehen, und konnten sie den englischen Begleittext lesen? Wie ordneten sie bestehende japanische Farbenlehren und sprachliche Begriffe in ein älteres europäisches Farbsystem ein? In jedem Fall ist ihr Buch ein wunderbares Beispiel für den weltweiten kulturübergreifenden Austausch im 19. Jahrhundert.

## Livre de questions et réponses sur la couleur à l'usage des écoles

L'influence de l'esthétique japonaise sur la culture occidentale dans la dernière partie du XIXe siècle est énorme. Le Japon se rouvre au commerce avec le reste du monde dans les années 1850 et, très vite, les motifs japonais deviennent omniprésents dans la peinture et les arts graphiques, dans la littérature et la mode. L'essor du japonisme et de l'esthétisme, nouveaux styles et mouvements artistiques, témoigne alors de la fascination en Europe et aux États-Unis pour cette culture si longtemps inaccessible. Parallèlement, l'intérêt croissant que suscite la culture occidentale auprès des Japonais se diffuse dans les théories chromatiques et les enseignements qu'ils élaborent.

Ce petit « Livre de questions et réponses sur la couleur à l'usage des écoles » semble être le premier manuel à s'inspirer des modèles occidentaux. Imprimé sur 22 feuillets pliés, le texte s'accompagne de deux planches de tableaux chromatiques coloriés à la main et de petits carrés de couleur dans le corps du texte. En termes conceptuels, le graphisme du tableau chromatique se fonde sur un système correspondant aux sept couleurs newtoniennes : les trois primaires jaune, rouge et bleu ont une position à part (p. 461, en haut à droite). Le cercle chromatique en forme de fleur de la deuxième planche est une adaptation évidente des « Équivalents chromatiques » de George Field, boussole qui décrit les mélanges et les contrastes de couleurs, conçue en Angleterre dans les années 1810. D'abord publiée dans sa version achromatique en 1835 sur le frontispice de *Chromatography*, elle paraît en couleurs dans d'autres ouvrages de Field à partir de 1841. Dans le manuel japonais, au-dessus de cette version très simplifiée du tableau de Field, des petites illustrations figurent les expériences du prisme de Newton montrant que les couleurs du spectre visible proviennent de la dispersion de la lumière blanche. La présence de tels échos aux systèmes de Field et Newton dans un livre d'écolier japonais des années 1870 est assez intrigante. Comment ces représentations ont-elles fait le tour du globe ? Quelles versions les auteurs en ont-ils vues, et étaient-ils en mesure de lire les textes d'accompagnement en anglais ? Comment ont-ils allié les conceptions chromatiques et termes japonais existants avec un système chromatique européen plus ancien ? Quoi qu'il en soit, c'est un merveilleux exemple d'échange interculturel mondial au XIXe siècle.

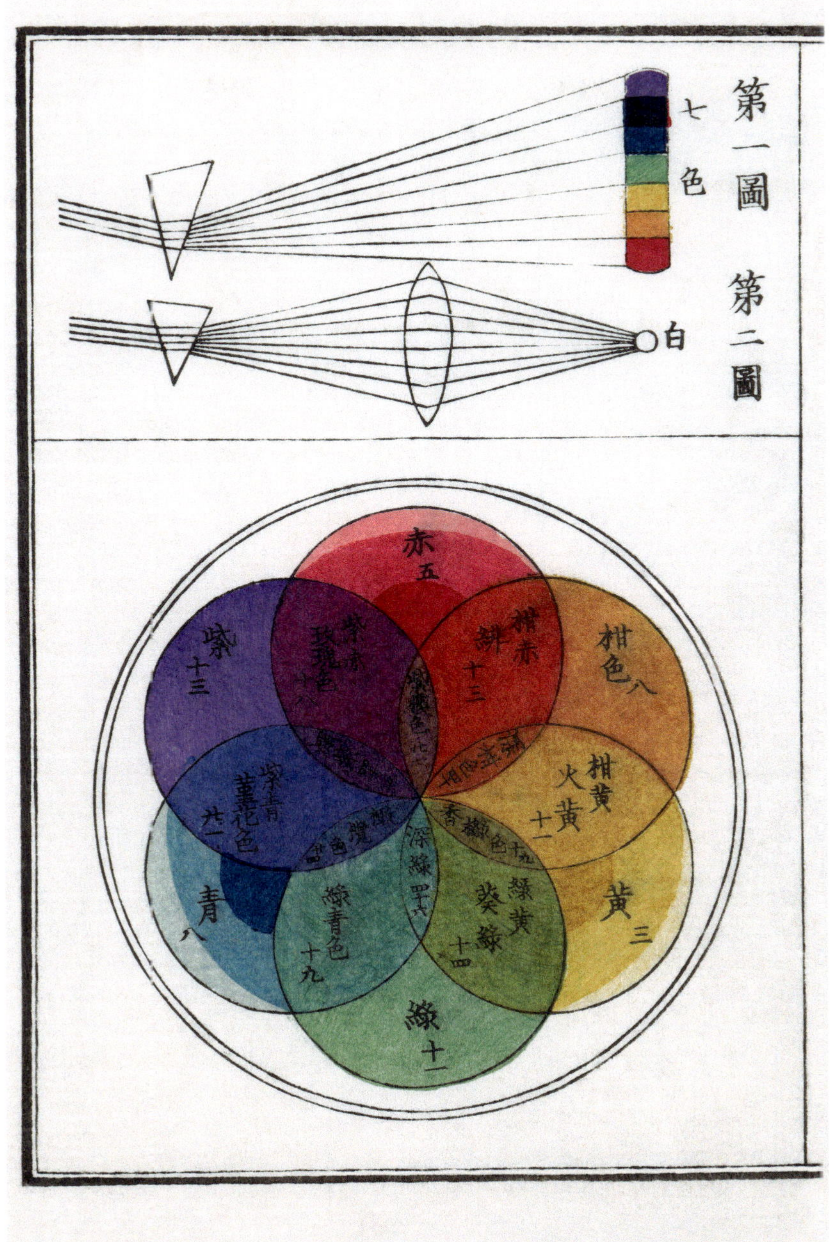
第一圖
七色
第二圖
白
赤 五
紫 十三
柑色 八
黄 三
綠 十一
青 八

**Sanzō Wada (1883–1967)**

# HAISHOKU SŌKAN

## Colour Schemes

*34 plates, 19.5 x 13 cm | 7 ⅝ x 5 ⅛ in., Tokyo, 1933/34*
*San Marino, California, The Huntington Library, Art Museum, and Botanical Gardens*

Sanzō Wada collected colours in the same way as a lepidopterist seeks out butterflies. He became an artist and illustrator when still in his teenage years, and later studied Western painting at the Tokyo School of Fine Arts, with the patronage of the painter Kuroda Seiki (1866–1924). Sanzō travelled to France in 1909, sponsored by the Ministry of Education, and stayed in Europe for more than five years before returning to Japan in 1915 by way of an extended detour through India, Java and Burma. By the early 1920s he had become a highly respected figure in the Japanese art world.

Wada developed a passion for colour early in his career and collected tens of thousands of colour samples in many different materials. While he was in Europe, he familiarised himself with the canon of Western colour literature, including the works of Munsell, Ostwald, Ridgway and most likely Chevreul. Being acutely aware of the lack of colour standardisation in his home country he began working on a system of nomenclature, and quickly became Japan's leading colour theorist. In 1927 he founded the Japan Standard Color Association, which is still in operation today and now known as the Japan Color Research Institute.

Wada's first published colour nomenclature appeared in 1931, as *Shikimei sōkan*, which took the form of a booklet accompanied by 160 colour samples mounted on accordion-folded cards. He continued to expand this system over the years, and between 1933 and 1934 he assembled *Haishoku sōkan*, which was intended as a comprehensive listing and a dictionary of colours. The 40-page booklet was issued with a set of cards in six volumes, showing 348 colour combinations based on 159 colours, each being numbered and named in Japanese and English. The 176 printed accordion-cards presented mounted samples of two-, three- and four-colour combinations. This collection was followed by *Haishoku sōkan B*, issued in 12 monthly instalments between 1934 and 1935, which included combinations of up to seven different colours. As with his previous works of nomenclature, readers had the option to cut out the printed colour samples so as to create or recreate their own combinations. Wada published many more books of colour standards, nomenclature and other works on Japanese and Western design and colour theory, including *The Story of Color* in 1952 and the *Munsell Renotation Color Book* in 1963, both of which were directly informed by Munsell's colour system.

多色配合の例（一）

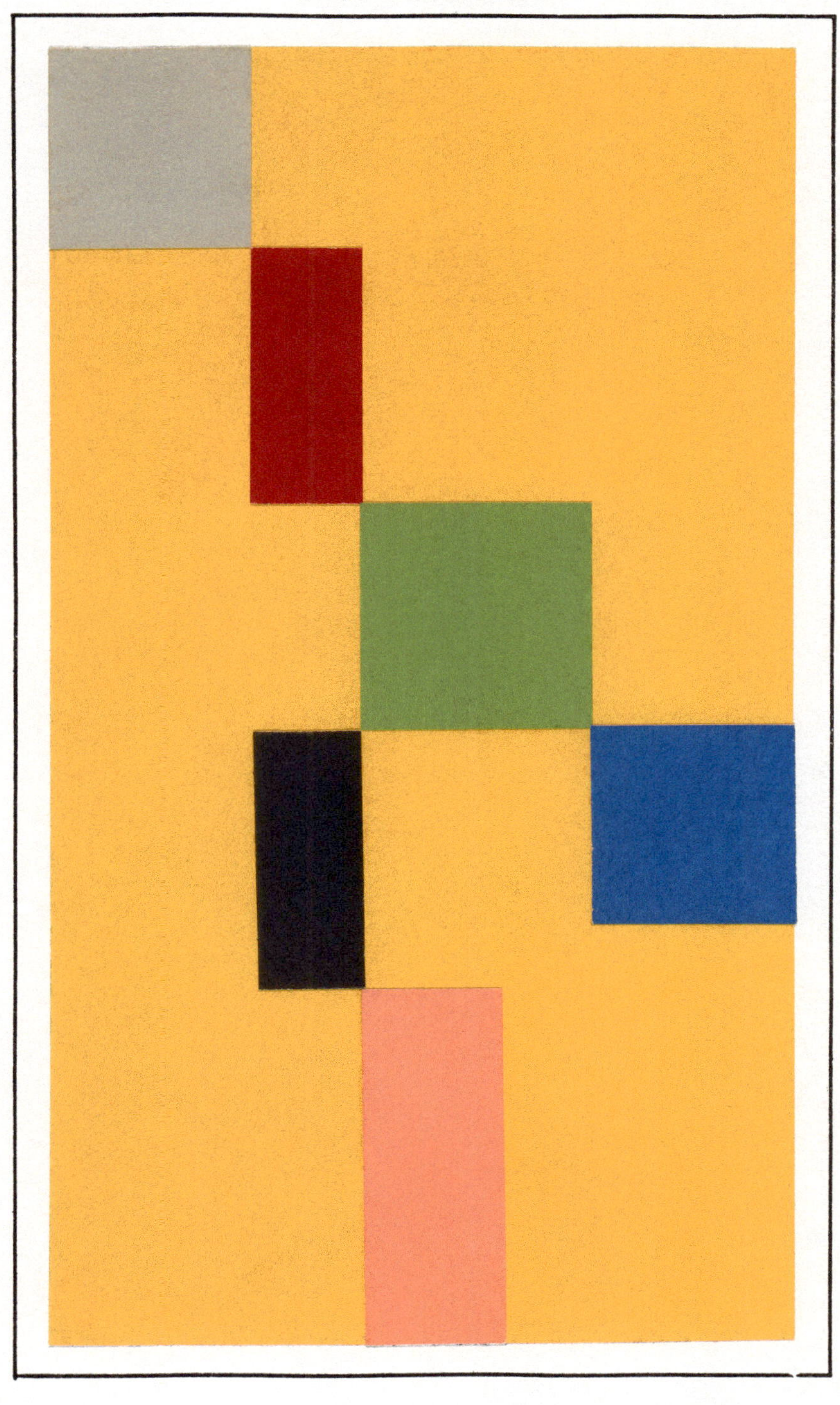

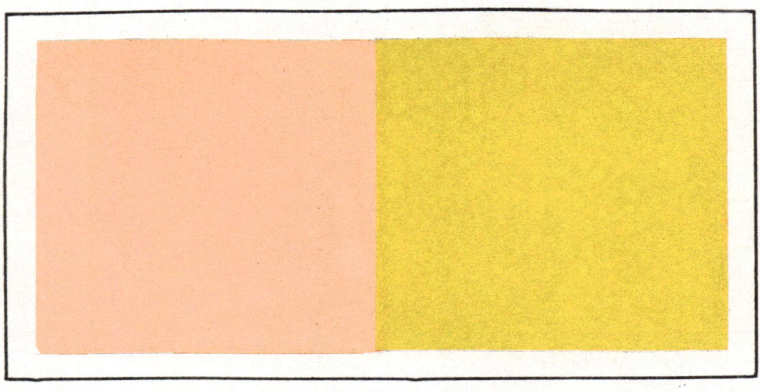

はだいろ
肌　色
Seashell Pink

かなりやいろ
金絲雀色
Lemon Yellow

たうしよく
橙　色
Orange

くろいろ
黒　色
Black

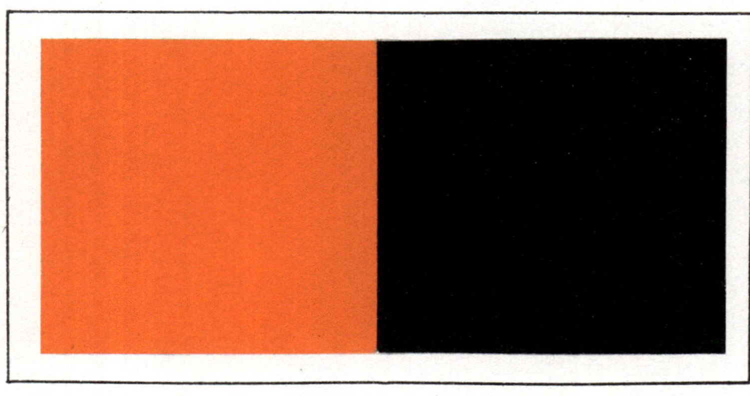

## Farbzusammenstellungen

Sanzō Wada sammelte Farben wie ein Lepidopterologe Schmetterlinge. Bereits im Jugendalter wurde er Künstler und Illustrator und studierte später mit Unterstützung des Malers Kuroda Seiki (1866–1924) Malerei an der Kunstakademie Tokio. Vom japanischen Bildungsministerium gefördert, reiste Wada 1909 nach Frankreich und kehrte nach mehr als fünf Jahren in Europa und einem ausgedehnten Umweg über Indien, Java und Burma erst 1915 nach Japan zurück. Anfang der 1920er-Jahre war er in der japanischen Kunstwelt zu einer hoch angesehenen Persönlichkeit aufgestiegen.

Schon in den Anfangstagen seiner Karriere entwickelte Wada eine Leidenschaft für Farbe und sammelte Zehntausende von Farbmustern in vielen verschiedenen Materialien. Während seiner Zeit in Europa machte er sich mit dem Kanon der westlichen Farbliteratur vertraut, las Werke von Munsell, Ostwald, Ridgway und höchstwahrscheinlich auch von Chevreul. Weil er sich der fehlenden Farbstandards in seinem Heimatland nur allzu bewusst war, begann er an einem Nomenklatursystem zu arbeiten und wurde schnell zum führenden Farbtheoretiker Japans. 1927 gründete er die japanische Gesellschaft für Standardfarben, die heute als japanisches Farbforschungsinstitut bekannt und noch immer aktiv ist.

Wadas erste Farbnomenklatur, *Shikimei sōkan*, erschien 1931 als Büchlein mit 160 Farbmustern, die auf Karten in Leporellofalz montiert waren. Über die Jahre entwickelte er sein System weiter und stellte zwischen 1933 und 1934 *Haishoku sōkan* zusammen, das als umfassende Auflistung und Farbenzyklopädie gedacht war. Das vierzigseitige Büchlein wurde mit einem Kartensatz in sechs Bänden herausgegeben, der anhand von 159 Farben insgesamt 348 nummerierte und auf Englisch und Japanisch bezeichnete Farbkombinationen präsentierte. Die 176 zu einem Leporello gefalteten und bedruckten Karten zeigten Kombinationen aus jeweils zwei, drei oder vier aufgeklebten Farbmustern. Auf diese Sammlung folgte *Haishoku sōkan B*. Das zwischen 1934 und 1935 in zwölf Lieferungen publizierte Werk enthielt Kombinationen von bis zu sieben verschiedenen Farben. Wie bei Wadas früheren Nomenklaturen konnten die Leserinnen und Leser diese gedruckten Farbmuster ausschneiden, um ihre eigenen Farbkombinationen zu erstellen oder wiederherzustellen. Von Wada erschienen viele weitere Bücher mit Farbstandards und Nomenklaturen, aber auch andere Schriften über Design und Farbtheorie nach japanischer und westlicher Prägung, darunter 1952 *The Story of Color* und 1963 das *Munsell Renotation Color Book*. Beide waren unmittelbar von Munsells Farbsystem inspiriert.

( 25 )

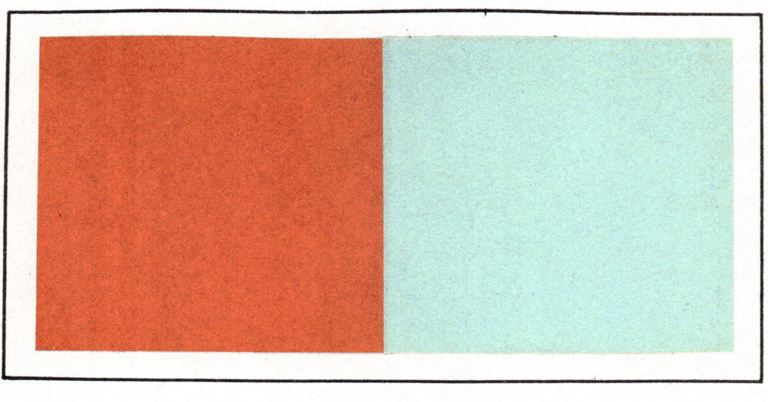

すゞめちや
雀　　茶
Etruscan Red

みづいろ
水　　色
Nile Blue

こびちやいろ
媚　茶　色
Pale Raw Umber

きんちや
金　　茶
Golden Yellow

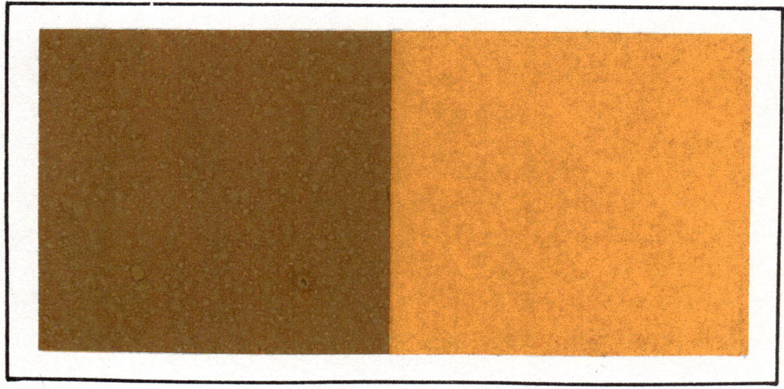

( 26 )

## Combinaisons des couleurs

Sanzō Wada rassemble les couleurs comme un lépidoptériste collectionne les papillons. Devenu peintre et illustrateur dès l'adolescence, il étudie ensuite la peinture occidentale à l'École des beaux-arts de Tokyo auprès de son mentor, le peintre Kuroda Seiki (1866–1924). Avec le soutien du ministère japonais de l'Éducation, Wada part pour la France en 1909 et passera plus de cinq ans en Europe. Il rentre au Japon en 1915 en faisant de larges détours par l'Inde, Java et la Birmanie. Au début des années 1920, il est une figure très respectée dans les arts japonais.

Passionné dès sa jeunesse par la couleur, Wada collecte des dizaines de milliers d'échantillons de couleurs de différents matériaux. En Europe, il se familiarise avec les canons établis par la littérature occidentale sur le sujet, notamment à travers Munsell, Ostwald, Ridgway et très probablement Chevreul. Cherchant à pallier le manque de normes chromatiques dans son pays natal, il s'attelle à la création d'une nomenclature et devient rapidement le principal théoricien de la couleur de son pays. En 1927, il fonde la Japan Standard Color Association, toujours active désormais sous le nom de Japan Color Research Institute.

La première nomenclature proposée par Wada, *Shikimei sōkan*, paraît en 1931. C'est un opuscule illustré de 160 échantillons de couleurs collés sur des pages cartonnées pliées en accordéon. De 1933 à 1934, l'auteur complète ce système jusqu'à réunir ses *Haishoku sōkan* («Combinaisons des couleurs»), qu'il conçoit comme un catalogue exhaustif et un dictionnaire des couleurs. Le livre de 40 pages est édité en six volumes de pages cartonnées, présentant au total 348 combinaisons chromatiques à partir de 159 teintes, chacune étant numérotée et nommée en japonais et en anglais. Les échantillons collés sur 176 pages en accordéon sont constitués de combinaisons de deux, trois ou quatre couleurs. Ce recueil est suivi de «Combinaisons des couleurs B» (*Haishoku sōkan B*), qui présente des combinaisons de deux à sept couleurs et paraît par livraisons mensuelles de 1934 à 1935. Comme dans les précédentes nomenclatures, les lecteurs ont la possibilité de découper les échantillons de couleurs imprimés afin de créer ou recréer leurs propres combinaisons. Wada publiera de nombreux autres ouvrages de standardisation chromatique. Parmi ses autres travaux sur la théorie de la couleur et le graphisme au Japon et en Occident, on retiendra *The Story of Color* en 1951 et *Munsell Renotation Color Book* en 1963, tous deux établis directement à la lumière du système chromatique de Munsell.

( 29 )

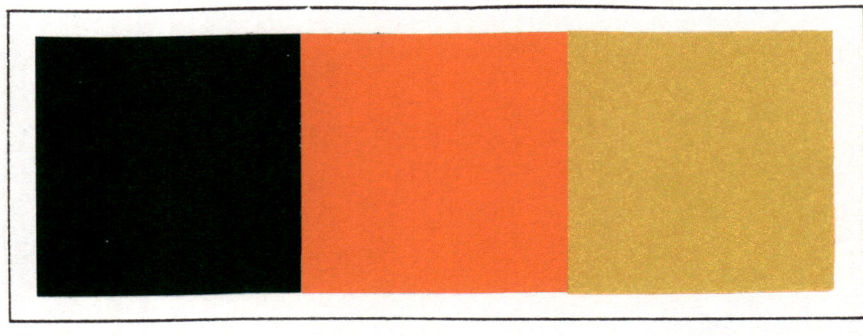

| てついろ | たうしよく | あぶらいろ |
| --- | --- | --- |
| 鐵 色 | 橙 色 | 油 色 |
| Deep Slate Green | Orange | Olive Ocher |

| はだいろ | なたねいろ | うらはいろ |
| --- | --- | --- |
| 肌 色 | 菜 種 油 色 | 裏 葉 色 |
| Seashell Pink | Citron Yellow | Glaucous Green |

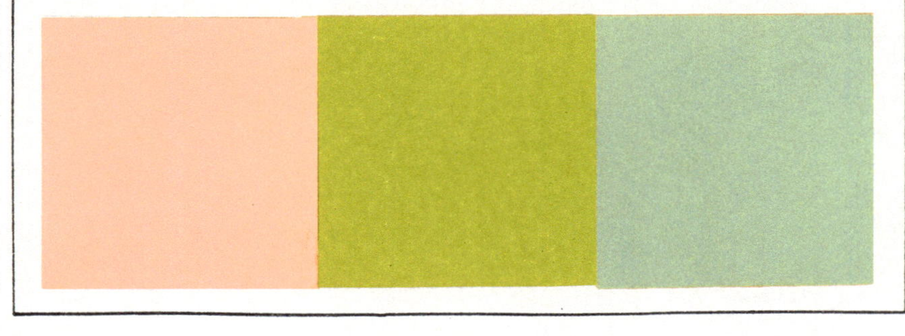

( 30 )

( 27 )

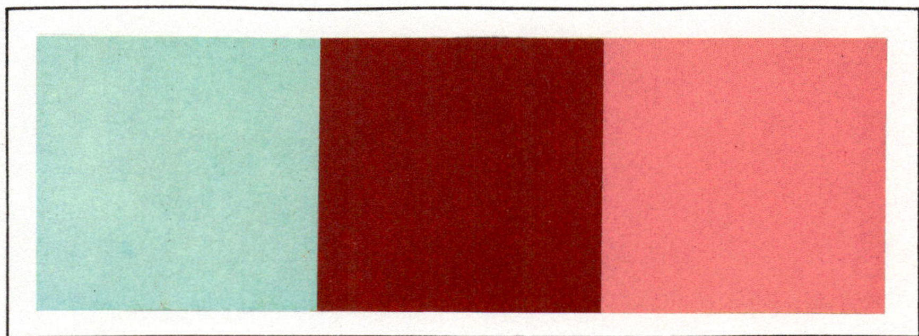

| びやくろく<br>白緑<br>Turquoise Green | べにゑびちや<br>紅海老茶<br>Vandyke Red | こうばいいろ<br>紅梅色<br>Spinel Red |
|---|---|---|
| やまぶきいろ<br>山吹色<br>Orange Yellow | はなあさぎ<br>花浅葱<br>Cerulian Blue | あぶらいろ<br>油色<br>Olive Ocher |

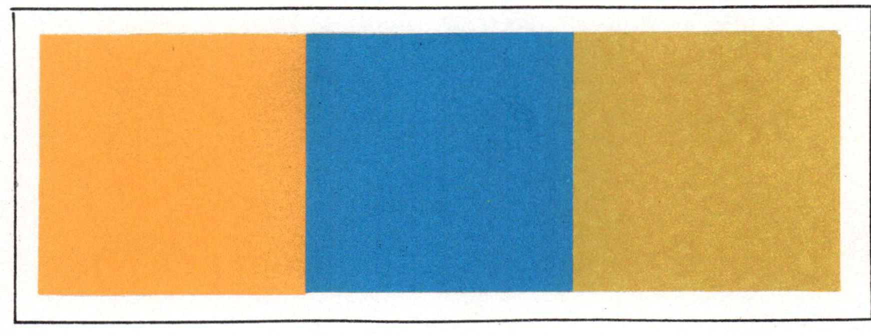

( 28 )

( 93 )

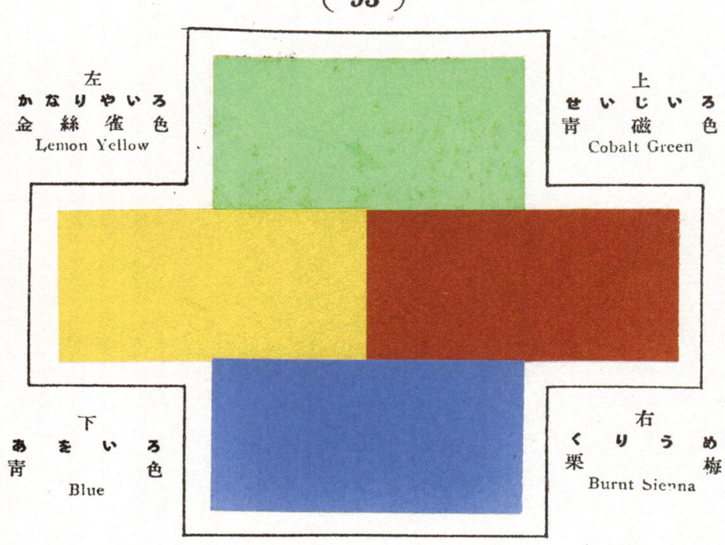
左
かなりやいろ
金絲雀色
Lemon Yellow
上
せいじいろ
青磁色
Cobalt Green
下
あをいろ
青色
Blue
右
くりうめ
栗梅
Burnt Sienna

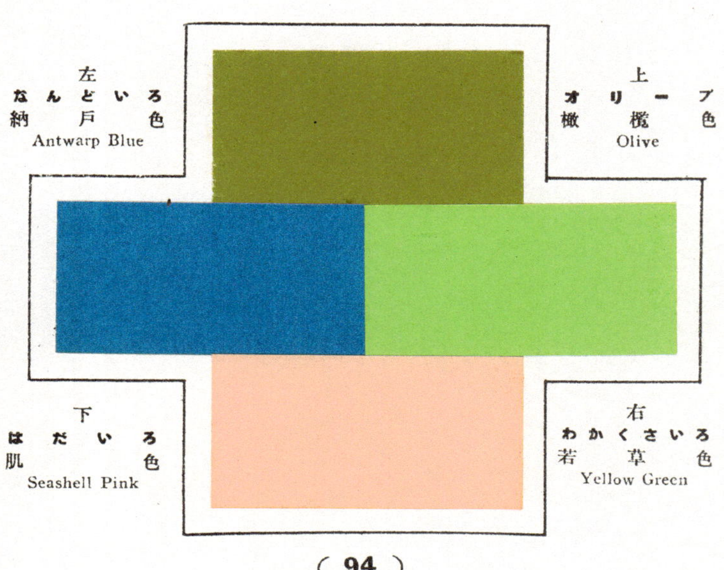
左
なんどいろ
納戸色
Antwarp Blue
上
オリーブ
橄欖色
Olive
下
はだいろ
肌色
Seashell Pink
右
わかくさいろ
若草色
Yellow Green

( 94 )

（ 67 ）

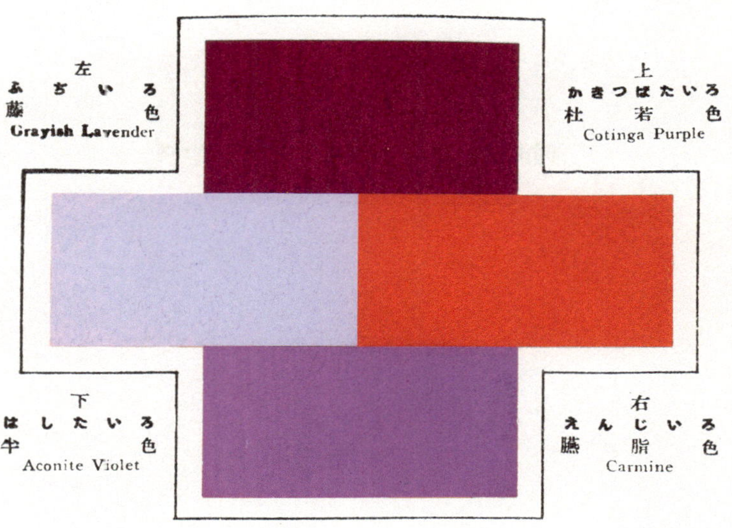

左
ふぢいろ
藤色
Grayish Lavender
上
かきつばたいろ
杜若色
Cotinga Purple
下
はしたいろ
半色
Aconite Violet
右
えんじいろ
臙脂色
Carmine


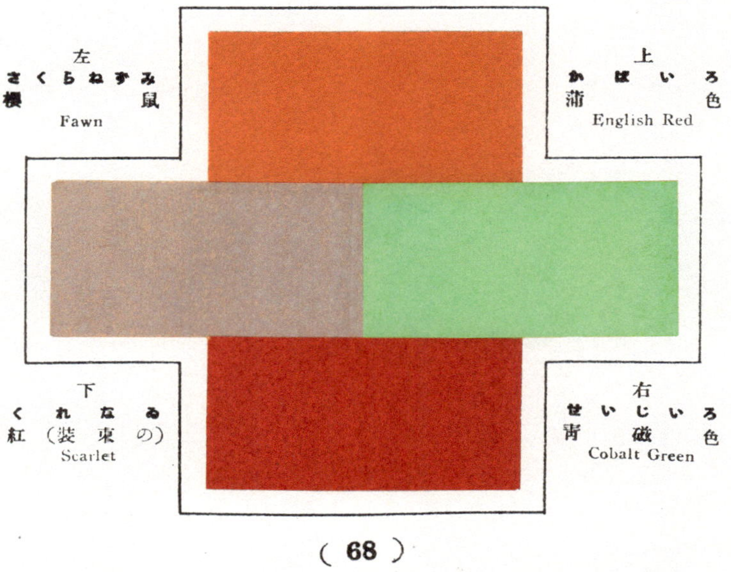

左
さくらねずみ
櫻鼠
Fawn
上
かばいろ
蒲色
English Red
下
くれなゐ
紅（裝束の）
Scarlet
右
せいじいろ
青磁色
Cobalt Green


（ 68 ）

( 73 )

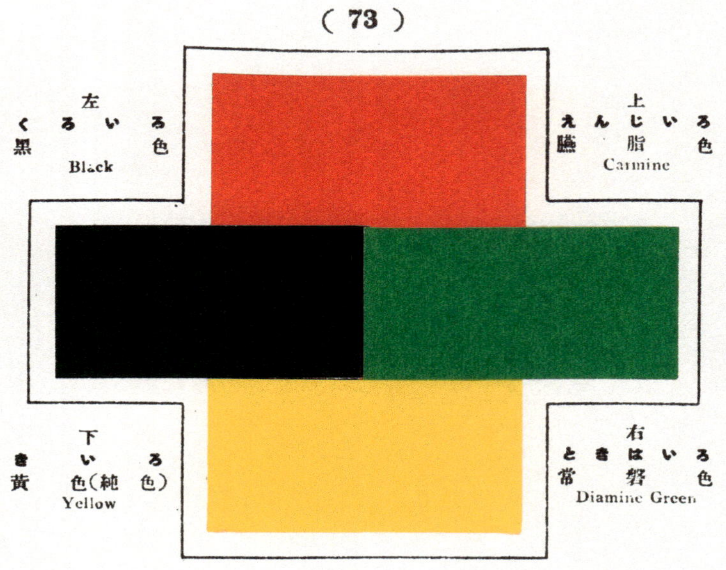
左
くろいろ
黒色
Black
上
えんじいろ
臙脂色
Carmine
下
きいろ
黄色（純色）
Yellow
右
ときはいろ
常磐色
Diamine Green

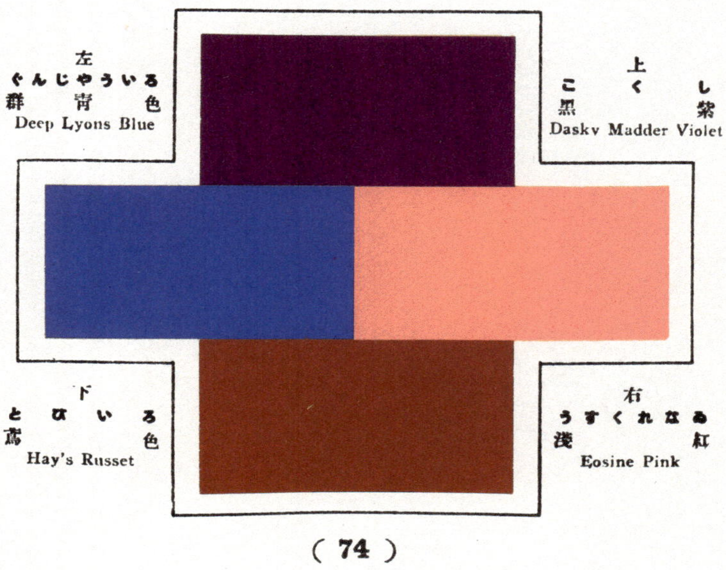
左
ぐんじやういろ
群青色
Deep Lyons Blue
上
こくし
黒紫
Dasky Madder Violet
下
とびいろ
鳶色
Hay's Russet
右
うすくれなゐ
淺紅
Eosine Pink

( 74 )

多色配合の例（二）

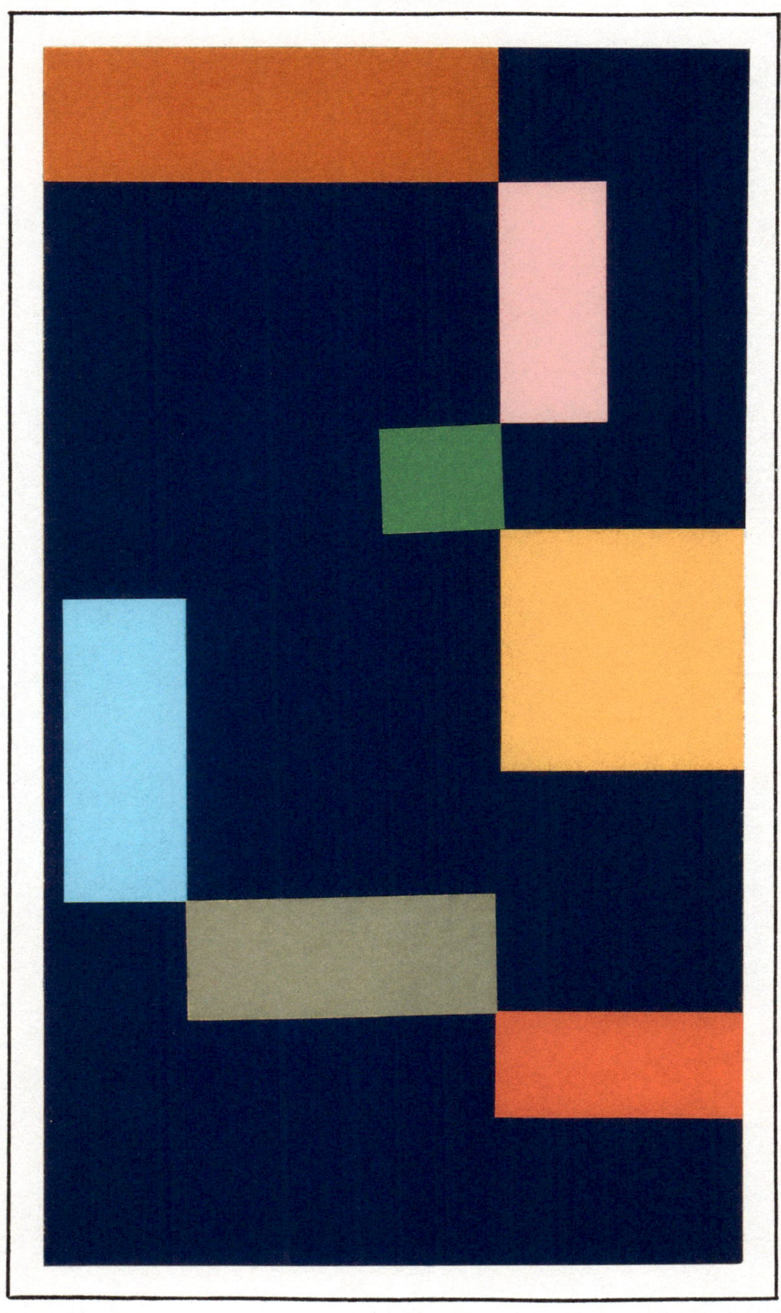

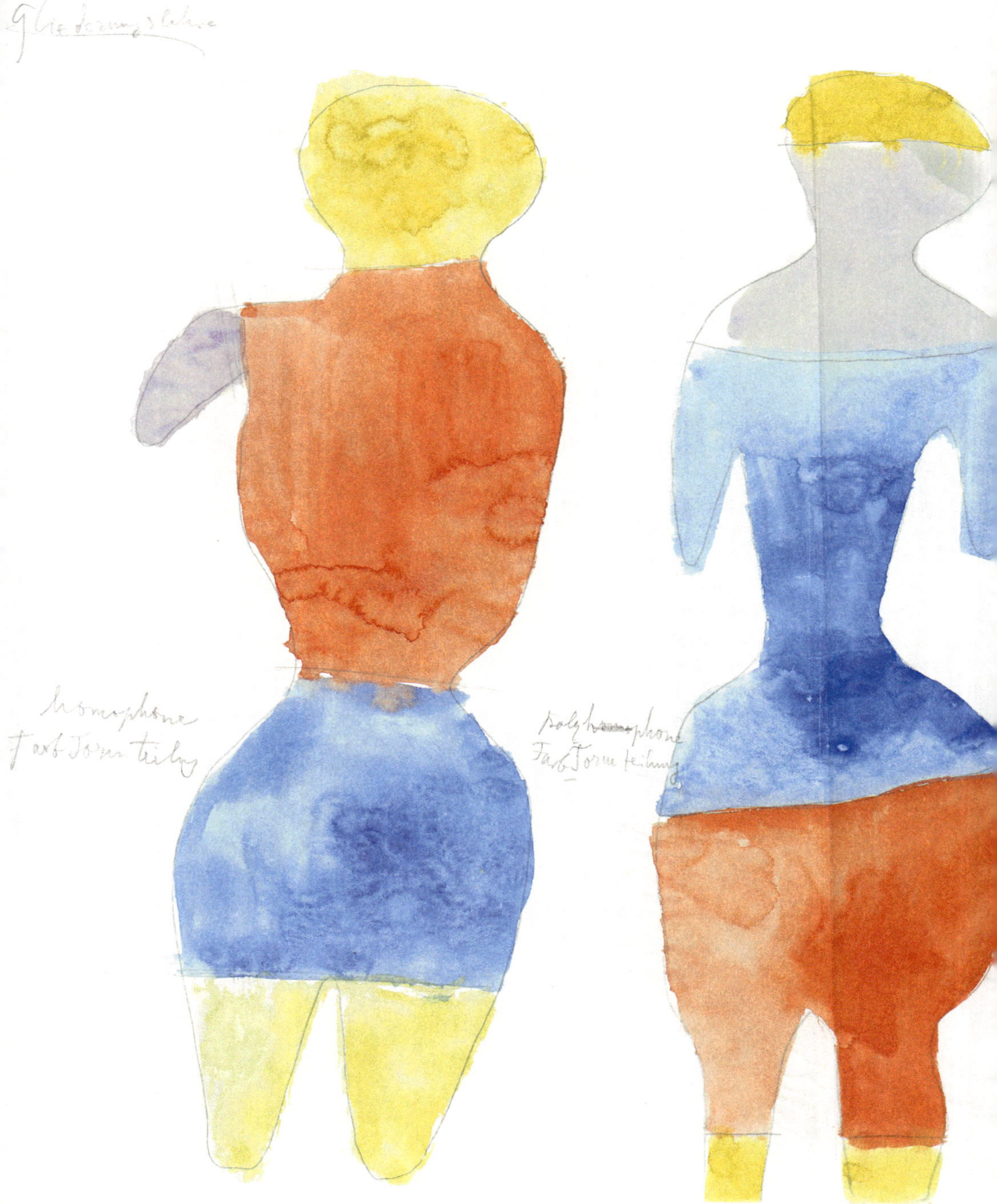

Gliederungslehre

homophone
Farbformteilung

poly~~homo~~phone
Farbformteilung

## Chapter 9

# *Interaction and Abstraction:* BAUHAUS AND BEYOND

## 1919–1963

## Josef Matthias Hauer (1883–1959)

# 12-TEILIGER FARB-KLANG-KREIS

### 12-part Colour-Sound Circle

*Ink and pencil drawing on paper, 34 x 21 cm | 13 ⅜ x 8 ¼ in., 1919*
*Vienna, Museum Moderner Kunst Stiftung Ludwig*

The Viennese composer Josef Matthias Hauer was a pioneer in the development of 12-tone music in the early 20th century. After overcoming serious illness in his twenties he began experimenting with atonal, rhythmic music, thereby celebrating his "spiritual rebirth". As discussed previously in the chapter on the "Sound of Colour", some degree of belief in spiritualism was widely held amongst writers, artists and performers from the time of the later 19th century onwards, and there was a long history of relating music to colour. In Hauer's view, music should not be a process of self-expression but rather an exercise in selfless contemplation, thus reflecting the universal order of the cosmos. This was in some respects an interpretation of the Romantic notion of placing the individual into a universal context, but it resulted in thoroughly modern, non-traditional musical compositions and collaborations.

Hauer had a brief friendship with Johannes Itten, who was running a private art school in Vienna between 1916 and 1919. Both men were intrigued by the correlations between colour, sound and form. Hauer was deeply impressed by Itten's art, and engaged in an extended correspondence with him beginning in 1919 when Itten left Vienna to go and teach at the Bauhaus in Weimar. Their discussions inspired Hauer to rewrite his essay of 1918, *Über die Klangfarbe* (On tone colour), and republish it in 1920 as *Vom Wesen des Musikalischen* (On the essence of music).

A further consequence of this creatively charged encounter was the colour-tone circle shown here that Hauer drew, divided into 12 equal parts and in which the warm colours were to represent musical fifths (*Quinten*) and the cold colours fourths (*Quarten*). The coloured segments were cut from coloured paper and pasted on to the sheet, with the outer tonal circle being drawn in pencil. Hauer sent his diagram to Itten, perhaps with the idea that he might be able to run a teaching module on colour and music at the Bauhaus, but nothing came of it and their friendship soon faltered. Itten presented his own colour circle shortly afterwards, also based on 12 parts and musical analogies.

Die Intervalle der zwölfstufigen Temperatur

andräuml. · chromatisch angeordnet:

physisch

reine Oktav g

kleine Sekund

große Sekund

kleine Terz

große Terz

reine Quart

übermäß. Quart

reine Quint

kleine Sext

große Sext

kleine Septime

große Septime

12. 7. 2. 9. 4. 11. 6. 1. 8. 3. 10. 5.

## 12-teiliger Farb-Klang-Kreis

Der Wiener Komponist Josef Matthias Hauer gehörte im frühen 20. Jahrhundert zu den Pionieren der Zwölftonmusik. Nachdem er in seinen Zwanzigerjahren eine ernsthafte Erkrankung überlebt hatte, begann er mit atonaler, rhythmischer Musik zu experimentieren, um seine „geistige Wiedergeburt“ zu feiern. Wie bereits im Kapitel „Der Klang der Farbe“ erwähnt, war der Glaube an das Spirituelle unter Schriftstellern, Künstlern, Schauspielern und Musikern seit dem späteren 19. Jahrhundert weit verbreitet. Hinzu kam eine lange Geschichte der Verbindung zwischen Musik und Farbe. Aus Hauers Sicht sollte Musik nicht die eigene Persönlichkeit ausdrücken, sondern eine Übung in selbstloser Betrachtung sein und so die universelle Ordnung des Kosmos widerspiegeln. In mancherlei Hinsicht war dies eine Interpretation der romantischen Vorstellung vom Individuum, das in einen weltumfassenden Kontext gestellt wird. Bei Hauer entstanden daraus durch und durch moderne, nichttraditionelle musikalische Kompositionen und Kooperationen.

Für kurze Zeit war Hauer mit Johannes Itten befreundet, der von 1916 bis 1919 in Wien eine private Kunstschule betrieb. Beide waren fasziniert von den Entsprechungen zwischen Farbe, Klang und Form. Hauer war zudem tief beeindruckt von Ittens Kunstschaffen und pflegte einen regen Briefwechsel mit ihm, nachdem dieser Wien 1919 verlassen hatte, um am Bauhaus in Weimar zu unterrichten. Ihre Diskussionen inspirierten Hauer, seinen 1918 verfassten Aufsatz *Über die Klangfarbe* umzuschreiben und 1920 unter dem Titel *Vom Wesen des Musikalischen* neu zu veröffentlichen.

Eine weitere Folge ihrer kreativ aufgeladenen Begegnung war der von Hauer entworfene, in zwölf gleich große Segmente unterteilte Farb-Klang-Kreis, der hier zu sehen ist. Darin standen die warmen Farben für Quinten und die kalten Farben für Quarten. Die farbigen Segmente wurden aus Buntpapier ausgeschnitten und auf das Blatt geklebt, der darumgelegte Notenkreis mit Bleistift zu Papier gebracht. Hauer schickte sein Diagramm womöglich mit der Idee an Itten, dass er am Bauhaus einen Kurs über Farbe und Musik abhalten könnte, doch daraus wurde nichts, und schon bald verlief ihre Freundschaft im Sand. Itten stellte kurze Zeit später seinen eigenen Farbkreis vor, der ebenfalls auf zwölf Teilen und musikalischen Analogien beruhte.

## Cercle chromatique tonal en douze segments

Le compositeur viennois Josef Matthias Hauer est un pionnier du développement de la musique dodécaphonique au début du XXe siècle. Guéri d'une grave maladie vers l'âge de 20 ans, il fait des expériences de musique rythmique atonale, célébrant par là sa « renaissance spirituelle ». Comme évoqué dans le chapitre consacré au « Son de la couleur », les croyances dans le spiritisme sont largement répandues depuis la fin du siècle précédent chez les écrivains, les peintres et les artistes de la scène, et les liens entre musique et couleur sont déjà amplement étudiés. Du point de vue d'Hauer, la musique n'a pas vocation à être une expression de soi, mais plutôt un exercice de contemplation altruiste et un reflet de l'ordre universel du cosmos. À certains égards, c'est une interprétation de la notion romantique qui considère l'individu dans un contexte universel, mais qui donne lieu à des compositions et des collaborations musicales en profonde rupture avec la tradition.

Hauer vit une brève amitié avec Johannes Itten, qui dirige une école d'art privée à Vienne entre 1916 et 1919. Tous deux sont fascinés par les corrélations entre couleur, son et forme. Hauer, profondément impressionné par la peinture d'Itten, entame une longue correspondance avec celui-ci en 1919, lorsque Itten quitte Vienne pour aller enseigner au Bauhaus, à Weimar. Leurs échanges mèneront Hauer à réécrire son essai de 1918, *Über die Klangfarbe* (« Sur le timbre »), et à le republier en 1920 sous le titre *Vom Wesen des Musikalischen* (« De l'essence du fait musical »).

Autre production découlant de cette rencontre féconde : le cercle chromatique tonal d'Hauer, divisé en 12 parties égales, qui est présenté ici. Les couleurs chaudes y représentent les quintes musicales (*Quinten*), les couleurs froides, les quartes (*Quarten*). Les segments sont découpés dans du papier de couleur et collés sur la feuille, et le cercle tonal extérieur est dessiné au crayon. Hauer a fait parvenir son tableau à Itten, peut-être dans la perspective que celui-ci mette au point un module pédagogique sur la couleur et la musique au Bauhaus, mais en vain, et leur amitié s'est étiolée. Peu de temps après, Itten présentera son propre cercle chromatique, également en 12 sections avec des analogies musicales.

## Paul Klee (1879–1940)

# BILDNERISCHE FORM- UND GESTALTUNGSLEHRE

### Pictorial Doctrine on Form and Creation

*21 illustrated pages, cover: 21 x 17.6 cm | 8 ¼ x 6 ⅞ in., single sheets of varying sizes, Weimar, 1921–1931*
*Bern, Zentrum Paul Klee*

In the autumn of 1920, Paul Klee was invited by telegram to join the recently founded Bauhaus in Weimar as a teaching "Master". By the following spring Klee had moved to Weimar where he taught at the Bauhaus for the next 10 years, at first giving classes on bookbinding and glass painting but eventually moving on to *Gestaltungslehre* (design doctrine), which also covered colour. Klee was passionate about colour and its potential as an expressive and formal tool, and had been greatly influenced by the work of Cézanne, Van Gogh and Robert and Sonia Delaunay. He was also briefly associated with the avant-garde group Der Blaue Reiter, which had been formed in 1911 by a number of artists including Kandinsky, while a trip he made to North Africa in 1914 further heightened his sense of colour. During Klee's time at the Bauhaus he created some of his best-known abstract works, and most of these are thought to have benefited by the opportunity he had there to develop his didactic colour theory.

Klee was not a trained teacher and as such prepared for each of his lessons in great detail, over the years producing thousands of pages of notes and sketches. His collected notes and lectures from the Bauhaus, the *Paul Klee Notebooks*, reveal a methodical yet playful mind, focused yet intuitive, and provide a fascinating insight into his creative and didactic processes and his love of colour. Klee may have planned to publish them in their entirety, but during his lifetime they only appeared in condensed form as a 50-page booklet in 1925 in the *Bauhausbücher* series, with the title *Pädagogisches Skizzenbuch* (Pedagogical sketchbook). Klee emigrated to Switzerland in 1933, fleeing the Nazi regime, and had to leave his papers behind. Miraculously, they survived. They were sent to him in a large trunk and are now kept in the Zentrum Paul Klee in Bern where they are referred to as his *Bildnerische Form- und Gestaltungslehre*. After Klee's death some of his papers were published in book form, first in the 1950s in a heavily criticised edition by Jürg Spiller, and later as a facsimile and transcription edited by Jürgen Glaesemer. In 2012 the Zentrum Paul Klee digitised all 3,900 pages of the notebooks and made them available online, together with transcriptions and annotations, making this vital body of 20th-century art and colour theory freely available.

In derselben Weise (könnte) kann ich nun die blaue und die gelbe rbreichweite betrachten

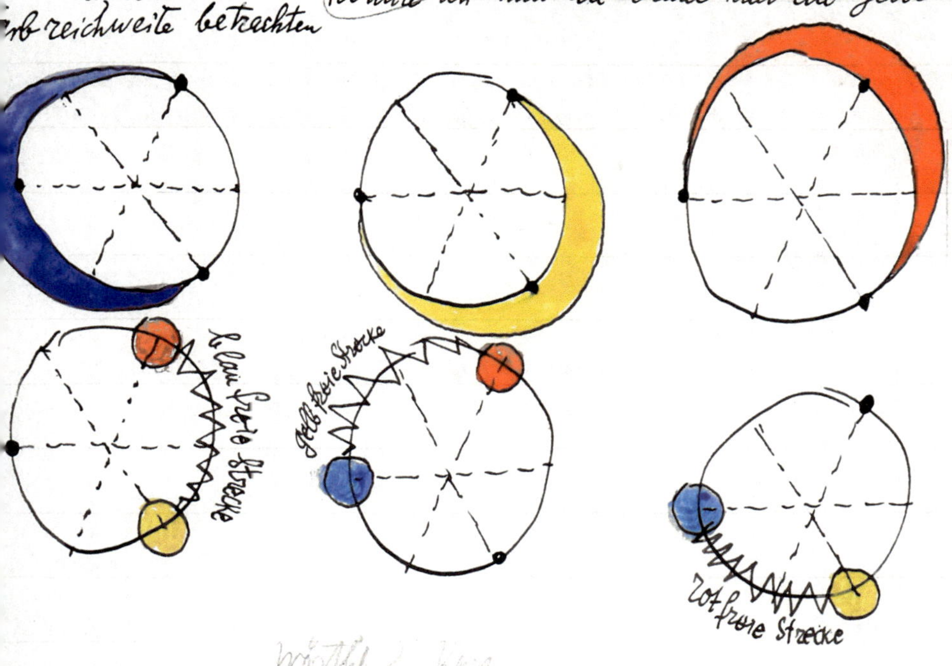


fig. 5

Ich will mich aber etwas (kürzer) fassen und aus der Anschauung der Skizzen einfach herauslesen:

Sowohl Blau, als Gelb und Rot haben auf dem Kreisumfang eine Reichweite von zwei Dritteln. Das letzte Drittel aber bleibt jeweils frei, blaufrei, gelbfrei oder rotfrei. Und zwar liegt das blaufreie Drittel zwischen den beiden Gipfelpunkten Gelb und Rot, das gelbfreie Drittel zwischen den beiden Gipfelpunkten Blau und Rot und das rotfreie Drittel zwischen dem blauen und dem gelben Gipfel.

Es bleibt also ~~aber~~ jeder Gipfel, jeder Culminationspunkt auf einen Moment hin frei von den Farbeinfluss der beiden Nachbargipfel.

Und so kann ich also jetzt (nicht nur) sagen (Rot ist nicht Grün, sondern auch) Rot ist nicht Blau und nicht Gelb, wenn es auch

~~Rot=grünen~~ schwarz-weissen Beziehungen erinnern, nur dass es sich für diesmal erstens um ~~Blau~~ Gelb handelt. Dann werde ich Gelb Rot darstellen und dann Rot-Blau, um ~~also~~ (in dieser Weise) wieder zum Ausgangspunkt zu gelang[…]
Und zwar diesmal nur fünfgliedrig. (~~Arithmetisch~~)

fig. 10

| | | |
|---|---|---|
| 4 Blau + 0 Gelb | Blau | |
| 3 " + 1 " | blaugrün | od. grün[…] |
| 2 " + 2 " | grün | |
| 1 " + 3 " | grüngelb | od. gelbg[…] |
| 0 " + 4 " | Gelb | |
| 4 Gelb + 0 Rot | Gelb | |
| 3 " + 1 " | gelborange | od. orange |
| 2 " + 2 " | orange | |
| 1 " + 3 " | orangerot | od. roto[…] |
| 0 " + 4 " | Rot | |
| 4 Rot + 0 Blau | Rot | |
| 3 " + 1 " | rotviolett | od. viol. r[…] |
| 2 " + 2 " | violett | |
| 1 " + 3 " | violettblau | od. blauv[…] |
| 0 " + 4 " | Blau | |

fig. 10

Dieser arithmetischen Tabelle entspricht der einzig befriedigende praktische Weg, die peripherale Farbbewegung darzustellen. Denn wenn die Tatsache des Anwachsens, Kulminierens und Abnehmens unberücksichtigt bleibt, erreicht man, ~~zumal beim Aquarell wo der weisse Untergrund stark mitspricht~~ (im Vergleich zu den Hauptfarben zu dunkle […]) zu helle Hauptfarben und zu dunkle Mischungen.

~~Also~~ Links der Plan für die Operation, in der Mitte die Berechnung des ~~direkten~~ unmittelbaren Gehaltes, rechts die Charakterisierung der Mischungen, die Effekte der Operation, der indirekte Gehalt.

Demnach ist grün der indirekte (od. mittelbare) Gehalt von Blau und Gelb zu

[g]leichen Teilen, und analog verhalten sich orange und violett wie [W]irkungen: zu ihren Ursachen Gelb Rot bezw. Rot Blau. Wir [s]ind also wohl berechtigt, den rechts erscheinenden Farben verschiedenen [R]ang beizumessen. [Prima Secundaria]

Die Geometrische ~~Anschauung~~ Darstellung des ganzen Geschehens wird [u]ns dies mit noch knapperer Deutlichkeit zeigen.

| | | | Rang |
|---|---|---|---|
| 4 Blau + 0 Gelb | = | Blau | I |
| 3 " + 1 " | = | blaugrün | III |
| 2 " + 2 " | = | grün | II |
| 1 " + 3 " | = | grüngelb | III |
| 0 " + 4 " | = | Gelb | I |
| 1 Rot + 3 " | = | gelborange | |
| 2 " + 2 " | = | Orange | II |
| 3 " + 1 " | = | orangerot | |
| 4 " + 0 " | = | Rot | I |
| 3 " + 1 Blau | = | rotviolett | |
| 2 " + 2 " | = | violett | II |
| 1 " + 3 " | = | violettblau | |
| 0 " + 4 " | = | Blau | I |

fig. 11

Jetzt springt der secundäre Charakter der drei Mischungen direct ins [Au]ge. Ihre Einordnung in die primäre Blau- Gelb- und Rot bewegung [k]ann klarer nicht zum Ausdruck kommen. Die Ursächlichkeit der drei Primären

180.

ist deutlich veranschaulicht, ebenso wirkt die Abhängigkeit der drei Secundä[ren] entsprechend dem Verhältnis von Ursache und Wirkung.
Und jetzt beginnt jener Kanon über seine Notierung hinaus zu erklingen

fig 12

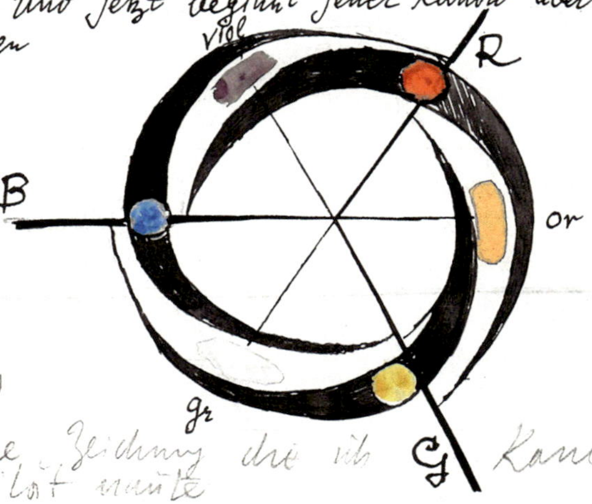

viol
R
B
or
gr
G

Dies ist) Ich jene Zeichnung die ich ~~Kanons~~ Kanon der farbigen Totalität nannte

Er kreist dreiteilig, wobei die Gliederung bestimmt wird durch die drei Gipfelpunkte der Primären. An diesen Gipfelpunkten ereig[net] sich ausserdem noch das Einsetzen und Verklingen der beiden andern hier nicht kulminierenden Primaeren. ~~Dazwischen er-sche~~ Zwischen den drei Kulminationen aber erscheinen da, wo sich die beiden Stimmen, die eben kulminierende und die neu einsetzende sich zunehmend und noch abnehmend begegnen, (wo sie gleichwertig sind) die Secundären, ~~eine nach dem andern~~ in jedem Abschnitt wieder eine andere Secundäre.

/ Die drei Kulminationspunkte der Primaeren kann ich nun um die Inferiorität der Secundären in der allereinfachsten Weise darzustellen ohne ~~auf~~ dem Kreis festhalten und ~~zu~~ zu einer andern Form verbinden.

Wenn das reine Rot auf seinem Gipfel weder Blau noch Gelb enthalten soll, weder bläulich kühl noch gelblich warm sein soll, so kann das im Sinne der natürlich kreisenden Bewegung, welche von einer zu- und abnehmenden Übergänglichkeit genährt w[ird] nur an einer einzigen kurzen Stelle wahr sein. Ebenso verhält

## Bildnerische Form- und Gestaltungslehre

Im Herbst 1920 wurde Paul Klee telegrafisch eingeladen, sich dem kürzlich gegründeten Bauhaus in Weimar als „Meister" anzuschließen. Bevor das nächste Frühjahr anbrach, war Klee nach Weimar umgezogen, wo er für die nächsten zehn Jahre am Bauhaus unterrichtete. Nach anfänglichen Kursen in Buchbinderei und Glasmalerei wechselte er schließlich zur Gestaltungslehre, die auch den Bereich der Farbe abdeckte. Maßgeblich beeinflusst von Cézanne und van Gogh, aber auch von den Werken Robert und Sonia Delaunays, interessierte sich Klee brennend für Farbe und ihr Potenzial als Mittel von Ausdruck und Form. Für kurze Zeit war er zudem eng mit der avantgardistischen Künstlergruppe Der Blaue Reiter verbunden, die Wassily Kandinsky und weitere Gleichgesinnte 1911 gegründet hatten. Auch eine 1914 unternommene Reise nach Nordafrika verstärkte seinen Sinn für Farbe. Während seiner Zeit in Weimar und Dessau schuf Klee einige seiner berühmtesten abstrakten Gemälde. Ein Großteil dieser Werke soll davon profitiert haben, dass ihm am Bauhaus die Gelegenheit geboten wurde, seine didaktische Farbtheorie zu entwickeln.

Klee war kein gelernter Pädagoge und bereitete daher jede seiner Unterrichtsstunden akribisch vor. Über die Jahre fertigte er Tausende von Seiten mit Notizen und Skizzen an. Seine gesammelten Aufzeichnungen und Vorträge aus der Bauhauszeit offenbaren einen methodischen, aber spielerischen Geist, fokussiert und doch intuitiv, und gewähren faszinierende Einblicke in die kreative und didaktische Arbeitsweise des Künstlers und seine Liebe zur Farbe. Womöglich hatte Klee geplant, die Notizen in ihrer Gesamtheit zu veröffentlichen, doch zu seinen Lebzeiten erschien 1925 in der Reihe der Bauhausbücher lediglich ein fünfzigseitiges Büchlein mit dem Titel *Pädagogisches Skizzenbuch*, das seine Lehren in komprimierter Form zusammenfasste. Auf der Flucht vor dem NS-Regime emigrierte Klee 1933 in die Schweiz und musste seine Papiere zurücklassen. Wie durch ein Wunder blieben sie erhalten und erreichten ihn in einer großen Kiste. Heute werden sie im Zentrum Paul Klee in Bern verwahrt, wo sie unter der Bezeichnung *Bildnerische Form- und Gestaltungslehre* archiviert sind. Nach Klees Tod wurden einige seiner Papiere in Buchform publiziert, zunächst in den 1950er-Jahren in einer stark kritisierten Ausgabe von Jürg Spiller und später als faksimilierte Ausgabe mit Transkription, herausgegeben von Jürgen Glaesemer. 2012 digitalisierte das Zentrum Paul Klee alle 3.900 Seiten der Notizbücher, stellte sie mitsamt Transkriptionen und Anmerkungen online und machte so dieses wesentliche Konvolut der Kunst- und Farbtheorie des 20. Jahrhunderts frei zugänglich.

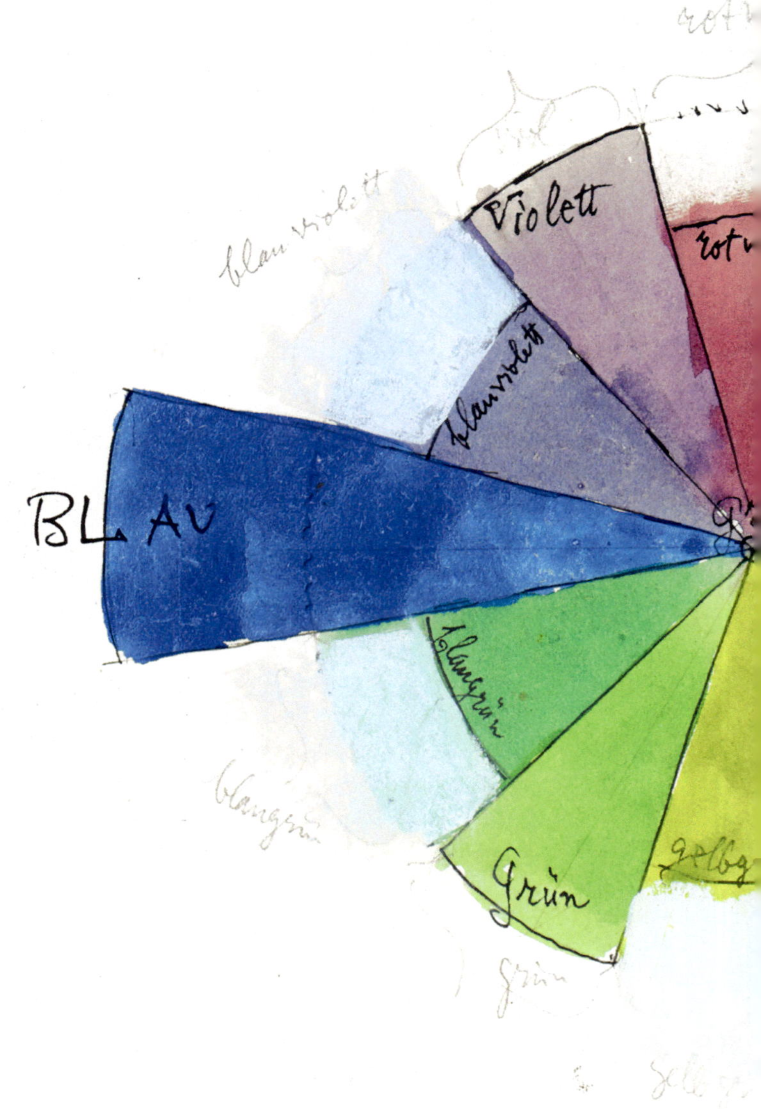


1)

Der wissenschaftliche Teil bezieht sich nach landläufigem Ge
Dabei wird der psychologische Teil vernachlässigt, z. B.
verlangt die Dreiteilung bzw Sechsteilung des Kreises. (

2)

Die Bestimmung von Reinrot ist schwerer als die Bestimmung der beiden andern farbigen Elemente. Nachdem also Reinblau und reingelb fester stehn als reinrot, so richte man reinrot so ein, dass es einerseits mit reinblau ein gutes Violett gibt und andersseits mit reingelb zusammen ein gutes grün. Dann ist schon viel gewonnen.

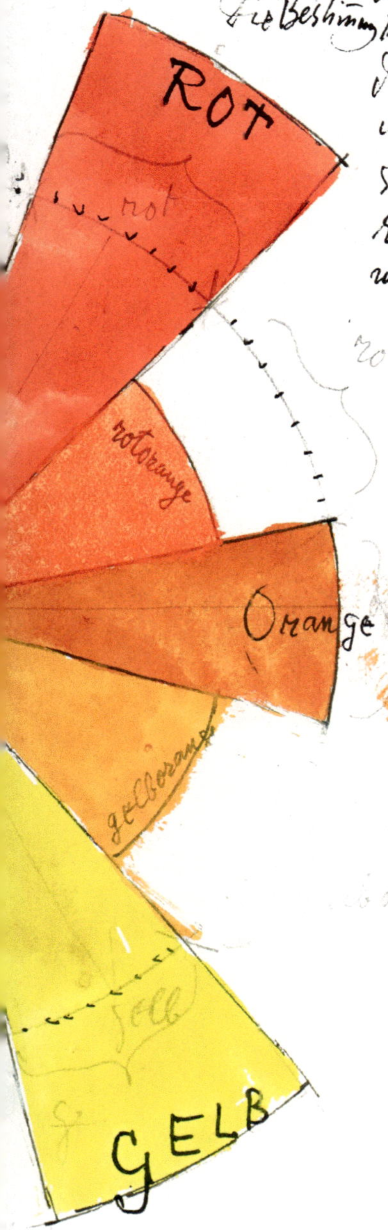

Die diametral Kontraste sind auf dem Erfahrungsweg, der Einwirkung und Beeinflussung in Bezug auf d. Gegenfarbe auf das Auge festzusetzen. Wenn dann zB. zu Rot ein grün festgestellt werden sollte das nicht ganz das grün zwischen Gelb und Blau ist so ist das ein geringeres Unglück, als die Vier- bezw 8 teilung des Kreises. Die tut wirklich weh!

uf den mathematisch logischen Nachweis der Richtigkeiten-
o. Die Psychologie des farbenkünstlerischen Menschen
dem Kreis verwandtere Zahl als 1/8 !)

ROT
rotorange
Orange
gelborange
GELB

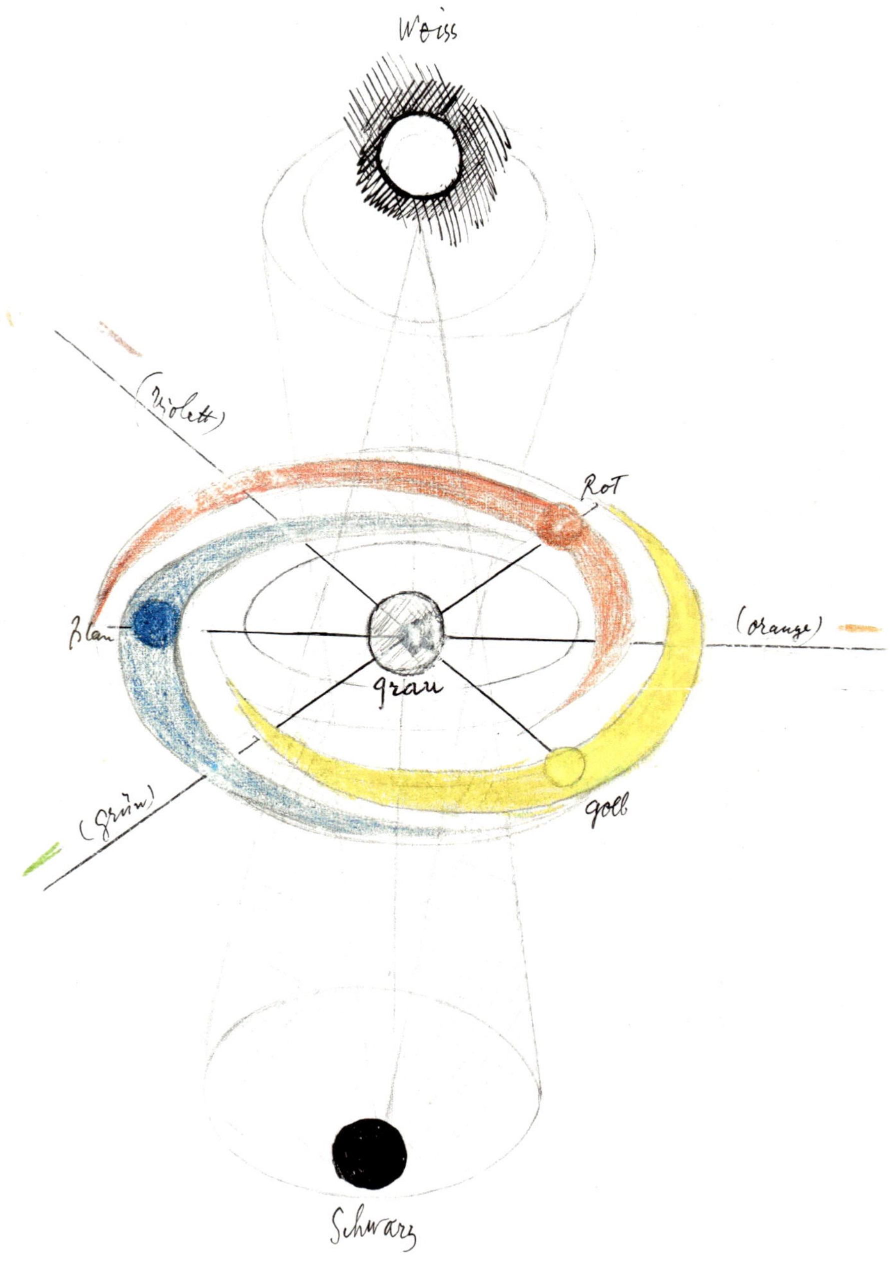

Weiss
(Violett)
Rot
Blau
(orange)
grau
(grün)
gelb
Schwarz

## Théorie de la mise en forme picturale

À l'automne 1920, Paul Klee reçoit un télégramme l'invitant à rejoindre le Bauhaus, tout récemment fondé à Weimar, comme « maître professeur ». Dès le printemps suivant, Klee y entame une décennie d'enseignement, d'abord avec des cours de reliure et de peinture sur verre, puis il s'oriente peu à peu vers la *Gestaltungslehre* (théorie des formes picturales), qui comprend aussi la couleur. Très influencé par les œuvres de Cézanne, de Van Gogh et de Robert et Sonia Delaunay, il se passionne pour la couleur et le potentiel formel et expressif qu'elle recèle. Klee participe brièvement au groupe d'avant-garde Der Blaue Reiter (Le Cavalier bleu), formé en 1911 par plusieurs artistes dont Kandinsky. Par ailleurs, un voyage en Afrique du Nord, en 1914, a beaucoup influé sur sa perception de la couleur. Pendant qu'il enseigne au Bauhaus, Klee crée certaines de ses plus célèbres toiles abstraites, pour la plupart considérées comme le fruit de l'élaboration de sa théorie chromatique dans ce cadre didactique.

Klee, qui débute dans l'enseignement, prépare ses cours dans les moindres détails et produit ainsi, au fil des années, des milliers de pages de notes et de croquis. Le recueil de ses notes et cours du Bauhaus, publié en français sous le titre *Paul Klee, cours du Bauhaus*, révèle un esprit méthodique et précis, mais néanmoins espiègle et intuitif, et constitue une découverte fascinante de sa démarche créative et pédagogique et de son amour de la couleur. Si Klee prévoyait peut-être de publier l'intégralité de ces notes, elles n'ont paru de son vivant que dans un opuscule de 50 pages, en 1925, dans la collection Bauhausbücher, sous le titre *Pädagogisches Skizzenbuch* (« Carnet de croquis pédagogiques »). En 1933, Klee émigre en Suisse pour fuir le régime nazi. Il doit abandonner ses textes et notes qui, miraculeusement, survivront et lui seront envoyés plus tard dans une grande malle. Ils sont désormais conservés au Centre Paul-Klee à Berne sous le nom donné par l'artiste : *Bildnerische Form- und Gestaltungslehre* (Théorie de la mise en forme picturale). Après la mort de Klee, certains de ses documents sont publiés pour la première fois dans les années 1950 à l'occasion d'une édition très controversée de Jürg Spiller, puis en fac-similé et dans une transcription établie par Jürgen Glaesemer. En 2012, le Centre Paul-Klee numérise les 3 900 pages des carnets qu'il publie en ligne, ainsi que des transcriptions et annotations, mettant ainsi gratuitement à disposition ce corpus exceptionnel de la peinture et de la théorie de la couleur du XXe siècle.

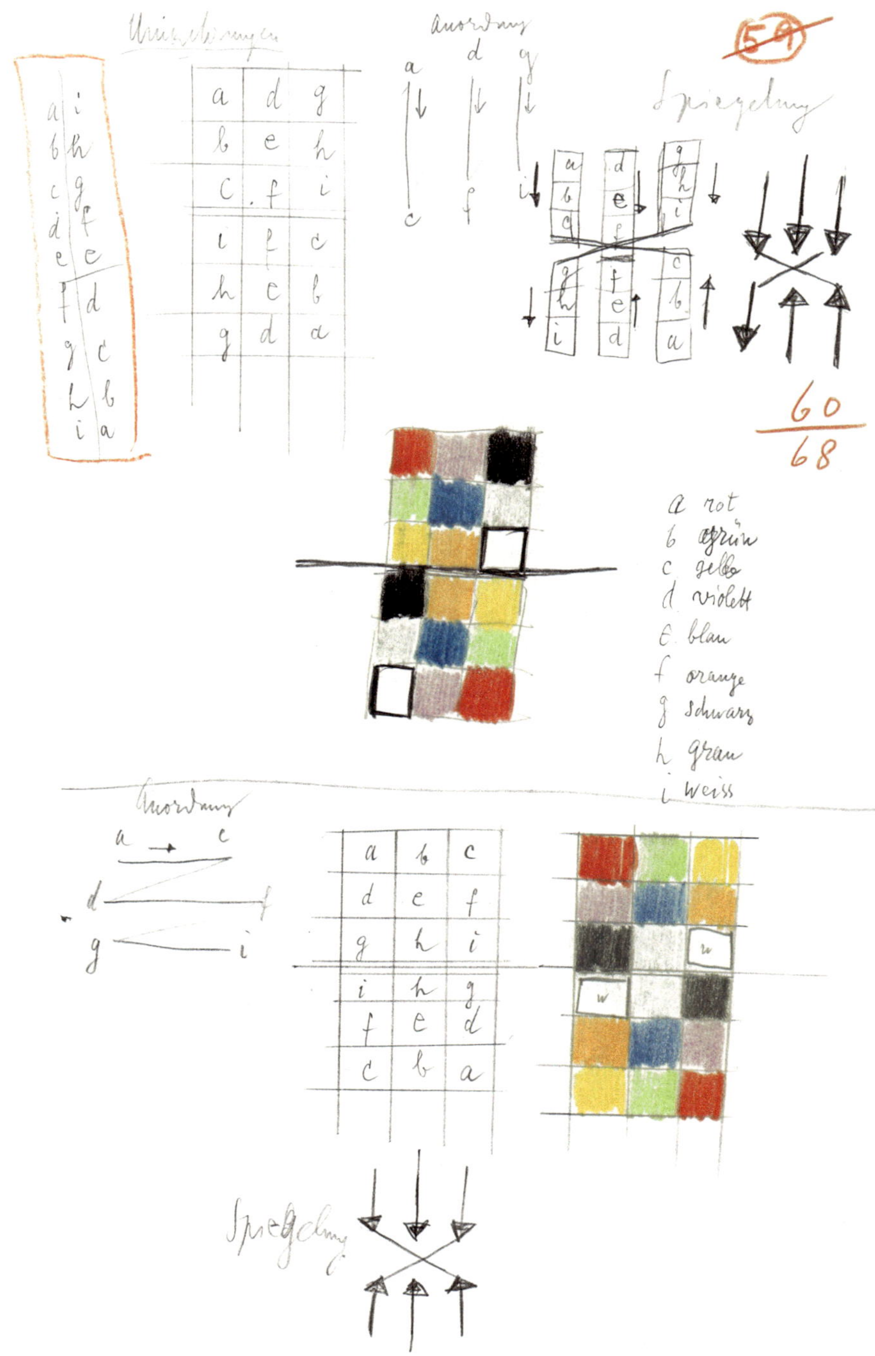
Umkehrungen
Anordnung
Spiegelung
60
68
a rot
b grün
c gelb
d violett
e blau
f orange
g schwarz
h grau
i weiss
Anordnung
Spiegelung

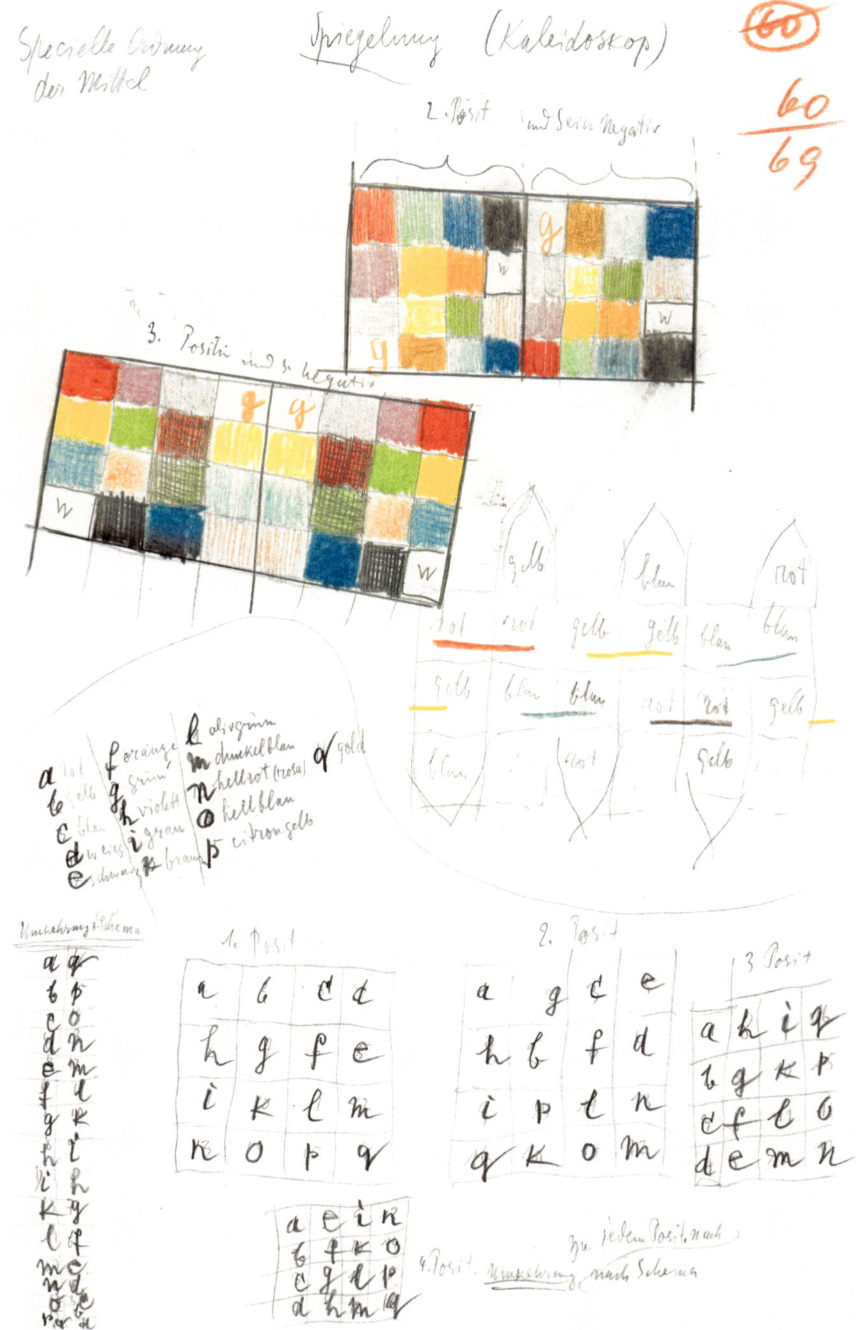
Specielle Ordnung der Mittel
Spiegelung (Kaleidoskop)
60
60
69
2. Posit und sein Negativ
3. Positiv und sein Negativ
gelb
blau
rot
a rot
b gelb
c blau
d weiss
e schwarz
f orange
g grün
h violett
i grau
k braun
l olivgrün
m dunkelblau
n hellrot (rosa)
o hellblau
p citrongelb
q gold
Umkehrung & Schema
1. Posit
2. Posit
3 Posit
4. Posit
zu jedem Posit. nach Umkehrung nach Schema

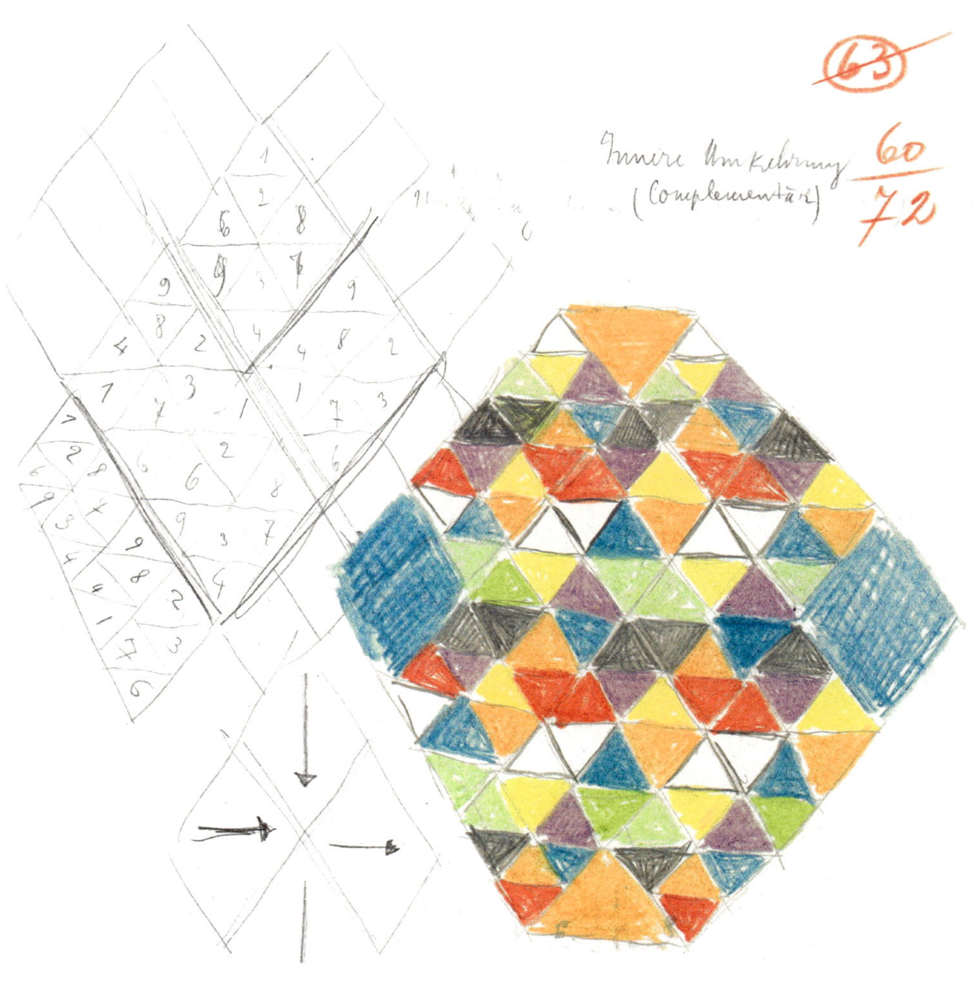
63
Innere Umkehrung
(Complementär)
60
72

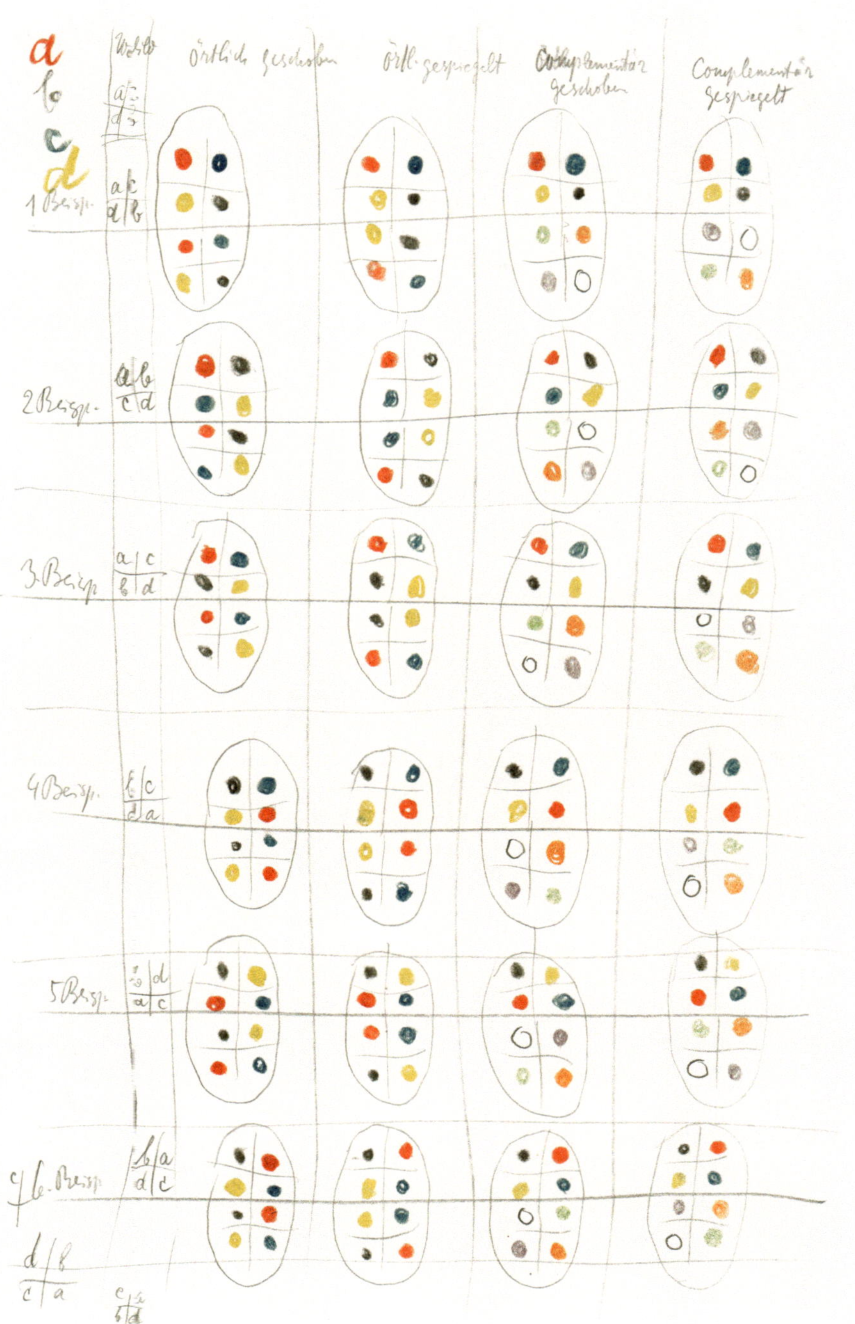
a
b
c
d
örtlich geschoben
örtl. gespiegelt
Complementär geschoben
Complementär gespiegelt
1 Beisp.
2 Beisp.
3. Beisp.
4 Beisp.
5 Beisp.
6. Beisp.

**Josef Albers (1888–1976)**

# INTERACTION OF COLOR

*16 loose plates, 33 x 25.3 cm / 13 x 10 in., New Haven, Connecticut, 1963*
*Göttingen, Niedersächsische Staats- und Universitätsbibliothek*

Josef Albers's engagement with colour can be divided into three phases, which demonstrate a clear development from one to the next: firstly, his involvement with the Bauhaus in the 1920s and 1930s, then his *Homage to the Square* series of paintings from 1950 onwards and lastly the publication of *Interaction of Color* in 1963. Albers was originally a student at the Bauhaus under Johannes Itten in the early 1920s, and later became a teacher there, delivering the preliminary course in conjunction with László Moholy-Nagy (1895–1946) before eventually teaching on his own. He completely restructured the course, although colour played a surprisingly small part in it. However, his own art from this period, much of it involving geometric glass designs, foreshadows his interest in precise outlines and the phenomenology of overlaid transparent colour.

After the Bauhaus closed down in 1933, Albers and his wife Anni emigrated to America, where he taught at the progressive Black Mountain College in Asheville, North Carolina, before joining Yale University where he taught design. Travels to Mexico further sharpened Albers's concepts of colour and abstract art, and in 1950 he embarked on his long series of 'hard-edge paintings', *Homage to the Square*, in which he experimented with a strict geometric pattern of three or four overlapping squares, positioned towards the bottom of the composition. He created these in hundreds of different colour combinations, first by using a palette knife and then with oil paints on board. Albers later began exploring the possibilities of silkscreen printing and soon became an advocate of the technique as an art form, choosing it for *Interaction of Color*, a mainly visual textbook in which he wanted to "place practice before theory" and show "what happens between colors". It was first published by Yale University Press in a limited edition with 150 silkscreen-printed plates of superior quality, showing Albers's distinctive geometric shapes and diagrams that were reminiscent of the paper cut-outs he used in teaching. It was republished as a more affordable pocket-format paperback in 1971 and has never been out of print since. In 2009 Yale reproduced the original silkscreen edition in a lavish new edition of this popular and elegant book on 20th-century colour.

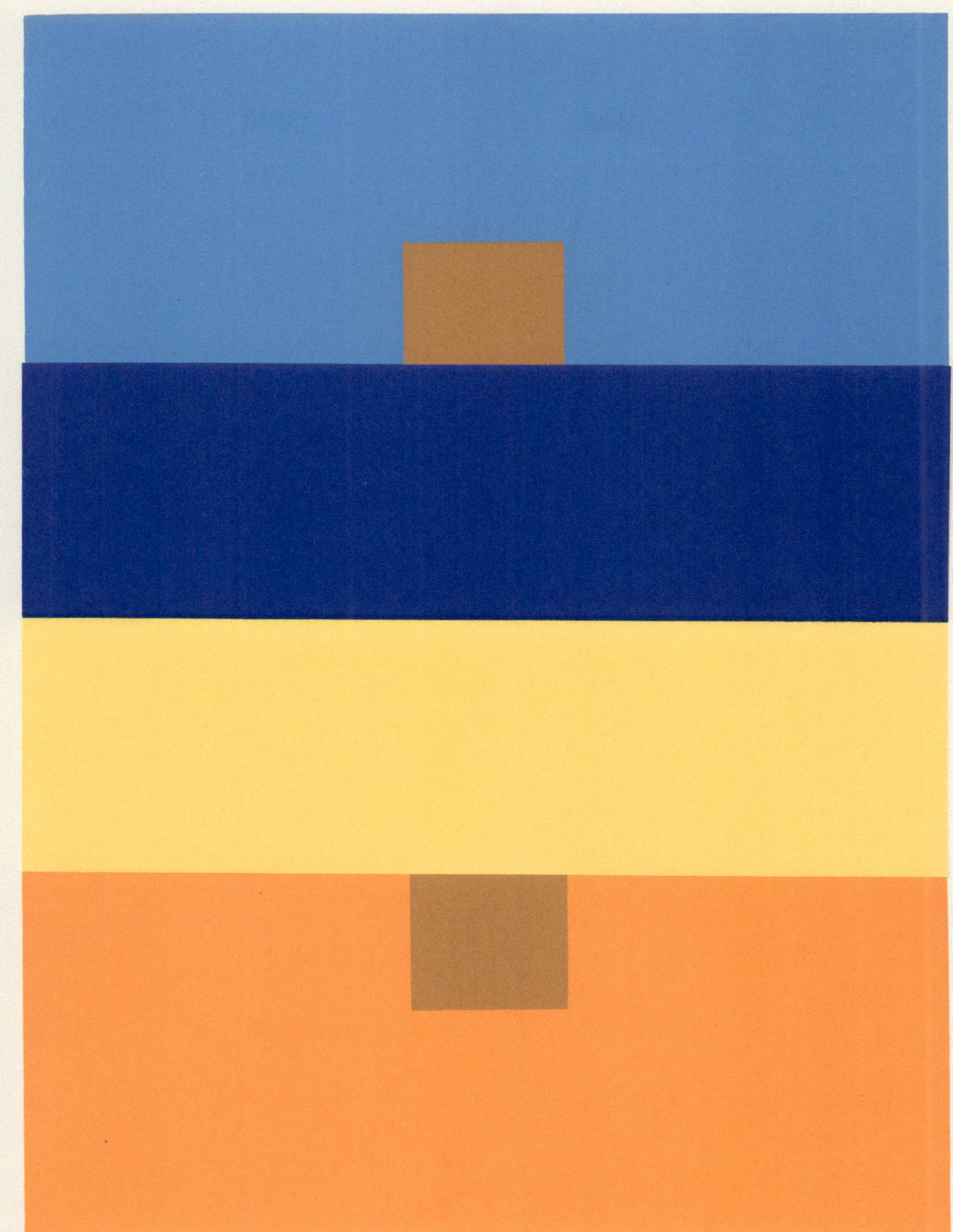

## Wechselwirkung der Farbe

Josef Albers' Beschäftigung mit Farbe lässt sich in drei Phasen unterteilen, die eine eindeutige Entwicklung aufweisen: Auf seine Zeit am Bauhaus in den 1920er- und 1930er-Jahren folgte ab 1950 die Gemäldeserie *Homage to the Square* und zuletzt *Interaction of Color*. In den 1920er-Jahren war Albers ursprünglich als Schüler von Johannes Itten ans Bauhaus gekommen, wurde dort anschließend Lehrer und unterrichtete gemeinsam mit László Moholy-Nagy (1895–1946) den Vorkurs, bevor er schließlich in Eigenregie Klassen übernahm. Obwohl er den Kurs vollkommen umstrukturierte, spielte Farbe darin eine erstaunlich geringe Rolle. Doch Albers' eigene Kunst aus dieser Periode, darunter zahlreiche geometrische Glasarbeiten, nimmt bereits sein Interesse an präzisen Konturen und der Phänomenologie übereinandergelegter transparenter Farben vorweg.

Nach der Schließung des Bauhauses 1933 emigrierten Albers und seine Frau Anni in die USA, wo Albers unweit von Asheville, North Carolina, am progressiven Black Mountain College unterrichtete, bevor er als Dozent für Gestaltung an die Yale University wechselte. Auf Reisen nach Mexiko konnte er seine Vorstellungen von Farbe und abstrakter Kunst weiter schärfen. 1950 schließlich nahm er die Arbeit an seiner nahezu unendlichen Serie von Hard-Edge-Gemälden auf: In *Homage to the Square* experimentierte er mit einem streng geometrischen Muster aus drei oder vier ineinandergeschachtelten Quadraten, die er am unteren Rand der Komposition ausrichtete. Albers schuf diese Bilder in Hunderten von unterschiedlichen Farbkombinationen, zunächst mit einem Palettenmesser, dann mit Ölfarben auf Holz. Später begann, er die Möglichkeiten des Siebdrucks auszuloten, wurde bald zum Verfechter dieses Verfahrens als Kunstform und wählte es auch für *Interaction of Color*. Sein überwiegend aus Abbildungen aufgebautes Lehrbuch sollte „die Praxis vor die Theorie" stellen und zeigen, „was zwischen den Farben geschieht". Es erschien zuerst 1963 bei der Yale University Press in einer limitierten Auflage mit 150 Siebdrucktafeln von überragender Qualität. Die unverwechselbaren geometrischen Formen und Diagramme darin erinnerten an die Scherenschnitte aus Papier, die Albers im Unterricht verwendete. 1971 erschien *Interaction of Color* im erschwinglicheren Taschenbuchformat und wird seither immer wieder neu aufgelegt. 2009 brachte der Verlag die ursprüngliche Siebdruckausgabe in einer aufwendigen Neuauflage dieses populären und eleganten Buches über Farbe im 20. Jahrhundert heraus.

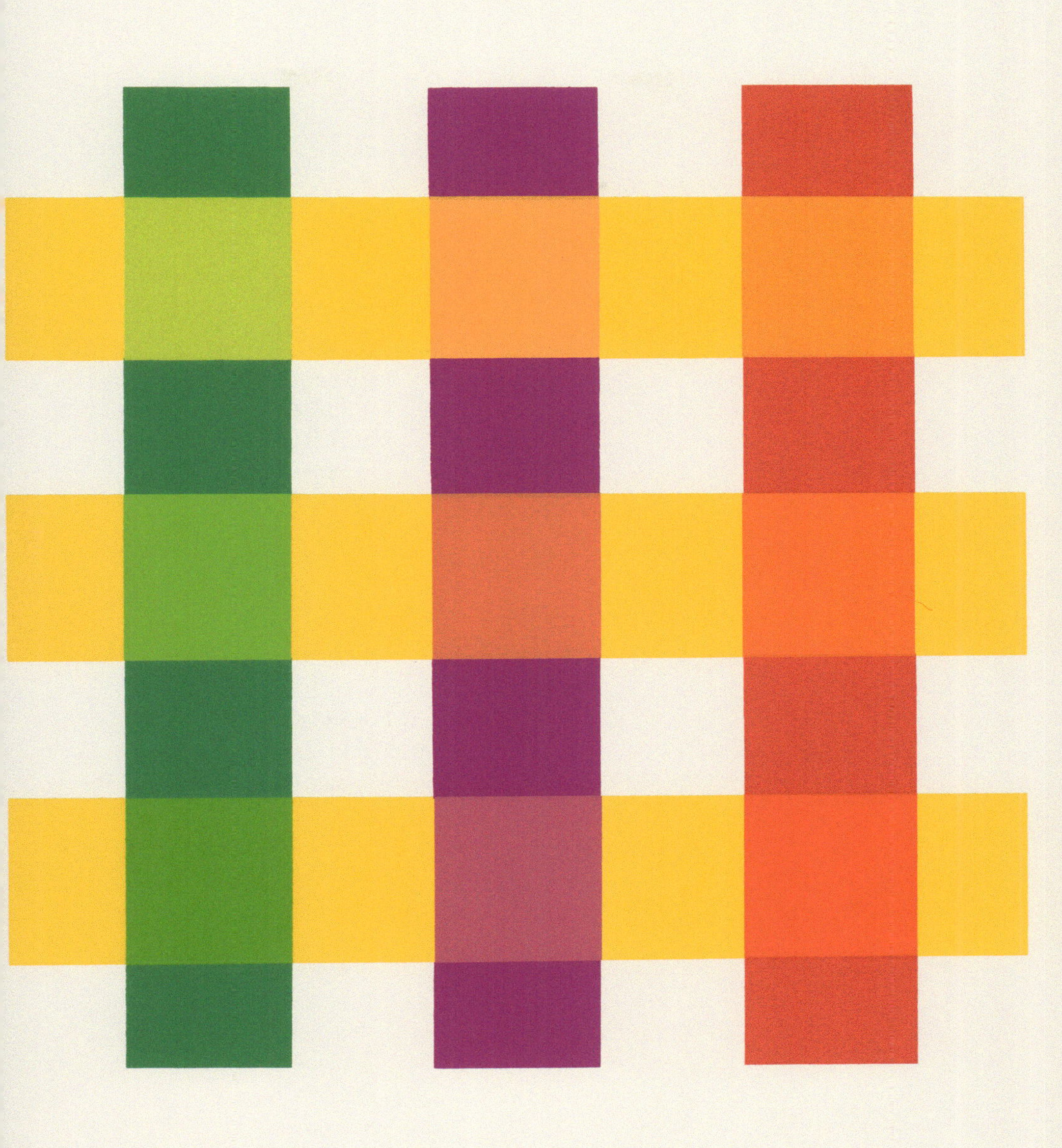

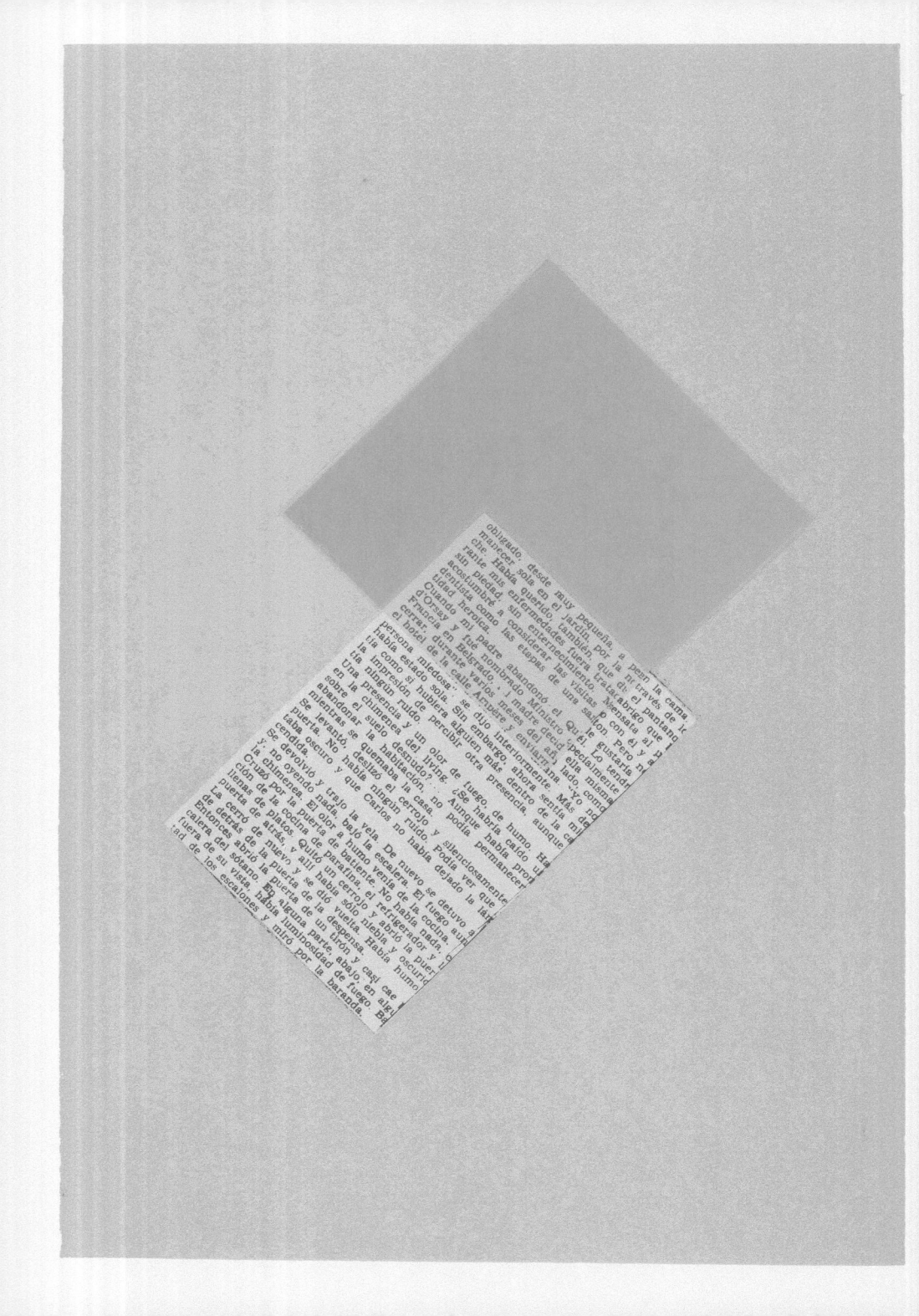

obligado, desde muy pequeña, a
manecer sola en el jardín, por
che. Había querido, también, que
rante mis enfermedades fuera tratada
sin piedad, sin enternecimiento.
acostumbré a considerar las visitas
dentista como las etapas de una
tidad heroica.
Cuando mi padre abandonó el
d'Orsay y fué nombrado Ministro
Francia en Belgrado,
cerrar, durante varios meses del añ
el hotel de la calle
persona miedosa", se dijo interiormente. Más
había estado sola. Sin embargo, ahora sentía
tía como si hubiera alguien más dentro de la ca
la impresión de percibir otra presencia, aunque
tía ningún ruido. ¿Se habría caído
Una presencia y un olor de fuego, de humo.
en la chimenea del living. Aunque había
sobre el suelo desnudo?... no podía permanecer
abandonar la habitación,
mientras se quemaba la casa.
Se levantó, deslizó el cerrojo y silenciosamente
puerta. No había ningún ruido. Podía ver que
taba oscuro y que Carlos no había dejado la
cendida.
Se devolvió y trajo la vela. De nuevo se detuvo
y, no oyendo nada, bajó la escalera. El fuego
la chimenea. El olor a humo venía de la cocina.
Cruzó por la puerta de batiente. No había nada,
ción de la cocina de parafina, el refrigerador y
llenas de platos. Quitó un cerrojo y abrió la
puerta de atrás, y allí había sólo niebla y
La cerró de nuevo y se dió vuelta. Había humo
de detrás de la puerta de la despensa.
Entonces abrió la puerta de un tirón y casi cae
calera del sótano. En alguna parte, abajo, en
fuera de su vista, había luminosidad de fuego.
tad de los escalones y miró por la baranda.

## L'Interaction des couleurs

Les travaux de Josef Albers sur la couleur suivent trois phases qui témoignent clairement de son évolution : tout d'abord, son implication au Bauhaus dans les années 1920 et 1930, puis sa série de tableaux *Homage to the Square* à partir de 1950 et, pour finir, la publication de *Interaction of Color* en 1963. Albers commence au Bauhaus comme élève de Johannes Itten, au début des années 1920, et y devient plus tard enseignant chargé du cours préparatoire en tandem avec László Moholy-Nagy (1895–1946). Une fois responsable de son propre cours, il restructure entièrement celui-ci et, étonnamment, la couleur n'y joue qu'un rôle limité. Cependant, les œuvres qu'il réalise alors, notamment des motifs géométriques sur verre, annoncent son intérêt pour les contours précis et la phénoménologie de la superposition des couleurs par transparence.

Après la fermeture du Bauhaus en 1933, Albers émigre aux États-Unis avec son épouse Anni. Il enseigne à l'université libre expérimentale du Black Mountain College à Asheville (Caroline du Nord) avant de rejoindre l'Université Yale pour y enseigner le *design*. Plusieurs voyages au Mexique aiguisent les conceptions d'Albers sur la couleur et l'art abstrait et, en 1950, il se lance dans sa longue série de peinture *hard edge* (« à bords durs »), *Homage to the Square*. Dans cette expérience strictement géométrique, il trace trois ou quatre carrés enchâssés les uns dans les autres, positionnés vers le bas de la composition. Il décline le même motif en des centaines de combinaisons chromatiques, d'abord au couteau à palette puis à la peinture à l'huile sur Isorel. Albers s'essaye plus tard à la sérigraphie et devient vite un ardent défenseur de cette technique comme forme artistique à part entière. C'est elle qu'il choisit pour *Interaction of Color*, un manuel principalement visuel dans lequel il veut « placer la pratique avant la théorie » et montrer « ce qui se produit entre les couleurs ». L'ouvrage, paru d'abord chez Yale University Press dans une édition limitée contenant 150 planches sérigraphiées de qualité supérieure, montre les formes et tableaux géométriques caractéristiques d'Albers, rappelant les papiers découpés qu'il utilisait dans ses cours. Republié en poche en 1971, il n'a cessé d'être réédité depuis. En 2009, Yale propose un nouveau tirage somptueux de l'édition sérigraphiée originale de ce célèbre et élégant ouvrage sur la couleur du XXe siècle.

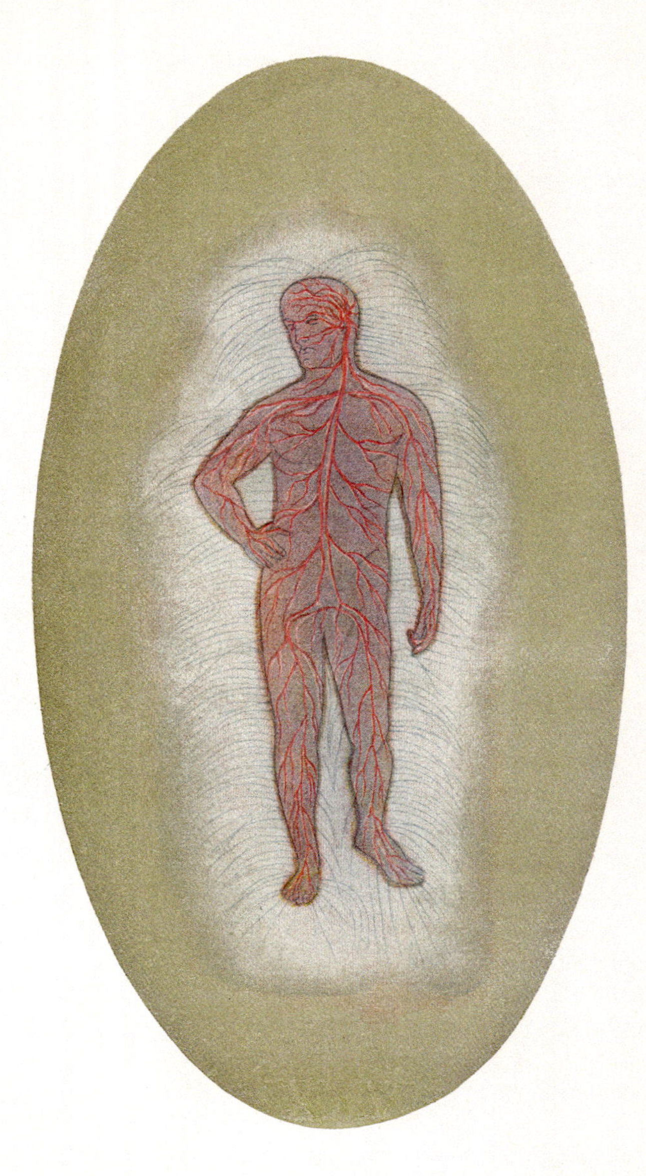

# APPENDIX

# Editorial Notes

### Remarks on the Editions and Plates

As a general rule, these volumes have sourced and reproduced first editions of the chosen works. Where a later edition of the book is more lavishly illustrated or rendered in a superior quality, however, this has then been shown at the expense of a first edition. These individual exceptions to the rule are discussed in further detail in the accompanying chapter texts. The specifications indicating the number of pages or plates featured refer to the quantity reproduced in this edition, rather than the total included in the original work.

### Technical Terms

**Achromatic colour:** Achromatic colours have no hue and can be described as colourless. They consist of the so-called neutral greys, whites and blacks, and they are effectively mixtures of just white and black. They are different from monochromatic colours or colour schemes, which consist of a single hue, mixed only with white, grey or black.

**Additive (immaterial) colour mixture:** Mixtures of light of different wavelengths (or colours) that create secondary, lighter tones. The three primaries of coloured light are red, blue and green. Combining all additive colours results in white light.

**Subtractive (material) colour mixture:** Mixtures of physical colours, such as raw pigments or paints, that result in an absorption or subtraction of light, and a darkening of the colours. The three primaries of subtractive colour are usually taken to be cyan (blue), magenta (red) and yellow.

**Trichromatic colour vision:** A theory of colour vision based on three types of colour receptors in the retina of humans and certain animals, making visible the colours red, green and blue, and their mixtures.

**Visible spectrum:** The range of colour visible to the human eye, from red to violet, via orange, yellow, green, blue and indigo.

# Acknowledgements

### The Publisher

For her insightful expertise and thoughtful contributions, and for lending her steadfast support to this publication in every stage of its realisation, we would like to thank the author of this book, Alexandra Loske. We would also like to extend our gratitude to Graham Fudger for the photography of books and objects from Alexandra Loske's private collection, as well as to the photographer Justin Lubliner.
While we appreciate the support of all libraries, museums and collections involved in the licensing and provision of image material, we would like to extend our particular thanks to Andres Betschart (Werner Spillmann Collection, Winterthur), Kathy Bohlman and Maria Zapata (Faber Birren Collection of Books on Color, Yale University, New Haven), Jennifer Cohlman Bracchi (Cooper Hewitt, Smithsonian Design Museum Library, New York), Mario Einaudi and Dan Lewis (The Huntington Library, Art Museum, and Botanical Gardens, San Marino, California), Neil Parkinson (Colour Reference Library, Royal College of Art, London) and Sean Rippington (The University of St Andrews Library, Fife).

### The Author

This was a collaborative project, from conception to finish, and would not have been possible without the excellent team at TASCHEN, several colleagues in the field of colour, and the photographer Graham Fudger. Special thanks are due to Neil Parkinson at the Royal College of Art, London, for his expertise and friendship over the years, and to Stephen Pavey and Jochen Menge, for giving me books, advice and support over many years.

Alexandra Loske is a British-German art historian, writer and museum curator, with a particular interest in the role of women in the history of colour. She received her Ph.D. from the University of Sussex and is currently Curator of the Royal Pavilion and Historic Properties in Brighton, England. She has lectured and been published widely on colour and other topics, and her recent publications include *Colour: A Visual History* (2019), *A Cultural History of Color in the Age of Industry* (2021) and *The Artist's Palette* (2024). She has curated and contributed to many exhibitions on colour, including "Turner et la Couleur" / "J. M. W. Turner: Adventures in Colour" at the Hotel de Caumont, Aix-en-Provence and Turner Contemporary, Margate (2016/17). Her most recent curated exhibition was "Colour: A Chromatic Promenade through the Royal Pavilion" at Brighton & Hove Museums (2025).

# Index

# Photo Credits

The publisher wishes to thank the museums, libraries, archives and all other institutions mentioned in the captions and in the credits for their kind assistance.
The credit "Sussex, collection of the author" in the image captions refers to books and objects held in the private collection of Alexandra Loske.

© akg-images: pp. 30, 33.
Alamy: p. 15.
Allen Phillips / Wadsworth Atheneum: p. 42.
Bayerische Staatsbibliothek, Munich: Math.a. 23 m: pp. 129–133, 193–199; Lithogr. 206: front cover.
Bayerische Staatsgemäldesammlungen – Sammlung Moderne Kunst in der Pinakothek der Moderne, Munich: p. 67.
Bibliothèque Méjanes, Aix-en-Provence (1692, Ms. 1389): pp. 84, 87–101.
Birmingham Museums: p. 21.
bpk | Hamburger Kunsthalle | Christoph Irrgang: spine, p. 26; bpk | Hamburger Kunsthalle | Elke Walford: p. 29; bpk | Klassik Stiftung Weimar | Mokansky, Olaf: pp. 36, 37.
Bridgeman Images: pp. 6, 16; © British Library Board. All Rights Reserved / Bridgeman Images: pp. 114–115.
By courtesy of the Hilma af Klint Foundation. Photo: Moderna Museet, Stockholm: pp. 56, 68, 69.
Canadian Centre for Architecture: pp. 299–315.
© Centre Pompidou, MNAM-CCI, Dist. RMN-Grand Palais/image Centre Pompidou, MNAM-CCI: p. 75.
The Cleveland Museum of Art, Ohio, Gift of the John Huntington Art and Polytechnic Trust, 1914.680: p. 9.
Collection from Winsor & Newton Archive: p. 50.
Collection of the author, Sussex; photography © Graham Fudger: pp. 22, 23, 24, 27, 47–49, 51, 73 top right, 73 bottom, 108, 120, 165–175, 201–207, 317–325, 391–397, 441–447, 449–457.
Colour Reference Library, Royal College of Art (photo: Sarah Mercer): back cover, pp. 1, 2, 5, 134–141, 152, 217–227, 278–287.
Courtesy of the Library of The University of California, Berkeley: pp. 458, 460–465.
Courtesy of Princeton University Library: pp. 125–128.
Courtesy of the Smithsonian Libraries and Archives, Washington, D.C.: endpapers, pp. 103–108, 238, 271–277.
Courtesy of the University of St Andrews Libraries and Museums: For ND1285.W4: pp. 240–249; ND1285.H2N7E46: pp. 261–269.
© Estate of Roy de Maistre (© Caroline de M. Walker; © Joanna Green); Image © Art Gallery of New South Wales, WA2.1969.a-b: p. 76.
© The Estate of Yves Klein / VG Bild-Kunst, Bonn 2025 (Foto: © Rheinisches Bildarchiv Köln, rba_d038911): p. 79.
Faber Birren Collection of Books on Color, Robert B. Haas Family Arts Library Special Collections, Yale University: pp. 229–237, 289–297, 365–379.
© The Fitzwilliam Museum, Cambridge: p. 34 bottom left
Folger Shakespeare Library, Washington, D.C.: pp. 13, 14.
Getty Research Institute, Los Angeles: pp. 126, 143–151, 209, 345–351.
配色總鑑 / 編纂者和田三造 (Haishoku sōkan / hensansha Wada Sanzō), RB 721911, The Huntington Library, Art Museum, and Botanical Gardens, San Marino, California: pp. 467–477.
Isabella Stewart Gardner Museum, Boston: p. 60.
Photo: Jens Ziehe, 2014 / © 2014 Olafur Eliasson: p. 81; Vanhaerents Art Collection, Brussels (no. 57): p. 81 top left; Bob and René Drake, Amsterdam (no. 58): p. 81 top right
© The Josef and Anni Albers Foundation / VG Bild-Kunst, Bonn 2025: pp. 499–502.
Det Kongelige Bibliotek (The Royal Danish Library), Copenhagen: pp. 413–427, 504.
Library of Congress, Rare Book and Special Collections Division: pp. 154–163.
Foto © mumok – Museum moderne Kunst Stiftung Ludwig Wien, Sammlung Dieter und Gertraud Bogner im mumok: p. 481.
Digital image, The Museum of Modern Art, New York / Scala, Florence: p. 70.
Mylands | mylands.com: pp. 82/83.
Niedersächsischse Staats- und Stadtsbibliothek, Göttingen: pp. 501, 502.
Rare Book Collection. The Louis Round Wilson Special Collections Library. University of North Carolina at Chapel Hill: pp. 251–259.
© Royal Academy of Arts, London; photographer: John Hammond: p. 20.
sammlung angela thomas schmid, haus bill: p. 479.
Städtische Galerie im Lenbachhaus und Kunstbau München, Gabriele Münter Stiftung, 1957: p. 66.

© Photo: Tate: pp. 38, 39, 41, 45, 55, 58, 65, 74.
© Trustees of Winifred Nicholson: p. 34 top right
© Tullie, Carlisle: p. 34 top right
Universität der Künste Berlin, Universitätsbibliothek: 8 G 395: pp. 362, 399–409.
Universitätsbibliothek Heidelberg: pp. 412, 428–439.
© Universitätsbibliothek der Humboldt-Universität zu Berlin, Historische Sammlungen: 2942:tafe:F8: pp. 185–191.
University of Glasgow, Department of Special Collections: pp. 328–343.
University of Vermont, Silver Special Collections Library: pp. 381–389.
Van Gogh Museum, Amsterdam (Vincent van Gogh Foundation): p. 52.
Wellcome Collection, London: pp. 18, 177–183, 210–215.
Winterthurer Bibliotheken, Sammlung Winterthur, Farb-Sammlung Werner Spillmann: pp. 62, 113–116, 119–123.
Zentrum Paul Klee, Bern, Bildarchiv: pp. 478, 485–497.

*Front and back cover*
Matthias Klotz
**Gründliche Farbenlehre**
(*A Comprehensive Doctrine on Colour*), 1816
(see page 192)

*Spine*
Philipp Otto Runge
**Farben-Kugel**
(*Colour Globe*), 1810
(see page 124)

*Endpapers*
Édouard Guichard
**L'Harmonie des couleurs / Die Harmonie der Farben**
(*The Harmony of Colours*), 1880–1882
(see page 270)

*Pages 1, 2, and 5*
Michel-Eugène Chevreul
**De la loi du contraste simultané des couleurs**
(*On the Principles of Simultaneous Contrast in Colours*), 1839
(see page 216)

*Page 504*
Charles Webster Leadbeater
**Man Visible and Invisible**, 1902
(see page 412)

*Page 511*
Maria Schindler, Eleanor C. Merry
**Pure Colour**, 1946
(see page 448)

*Page 512*
Édouard Guichard
**L'Harmonie des couleurs / Die Harmonie der Farben**
(*The Harmony of Colours*), 1880–1882
(see page 270)

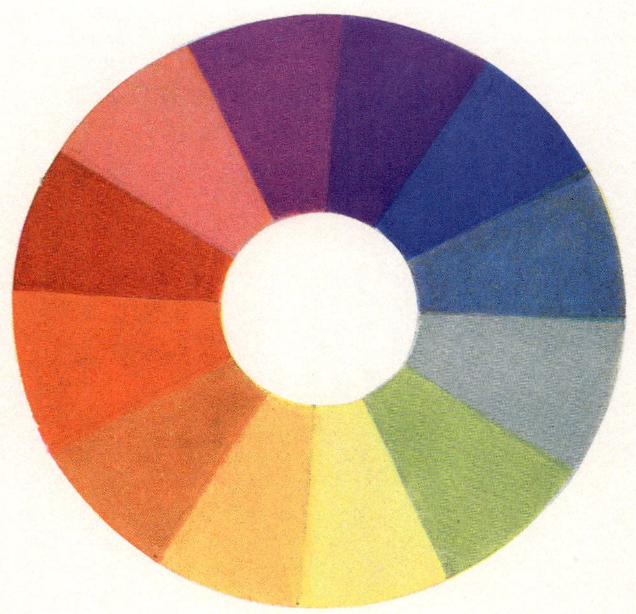

Naturalistic colour circle

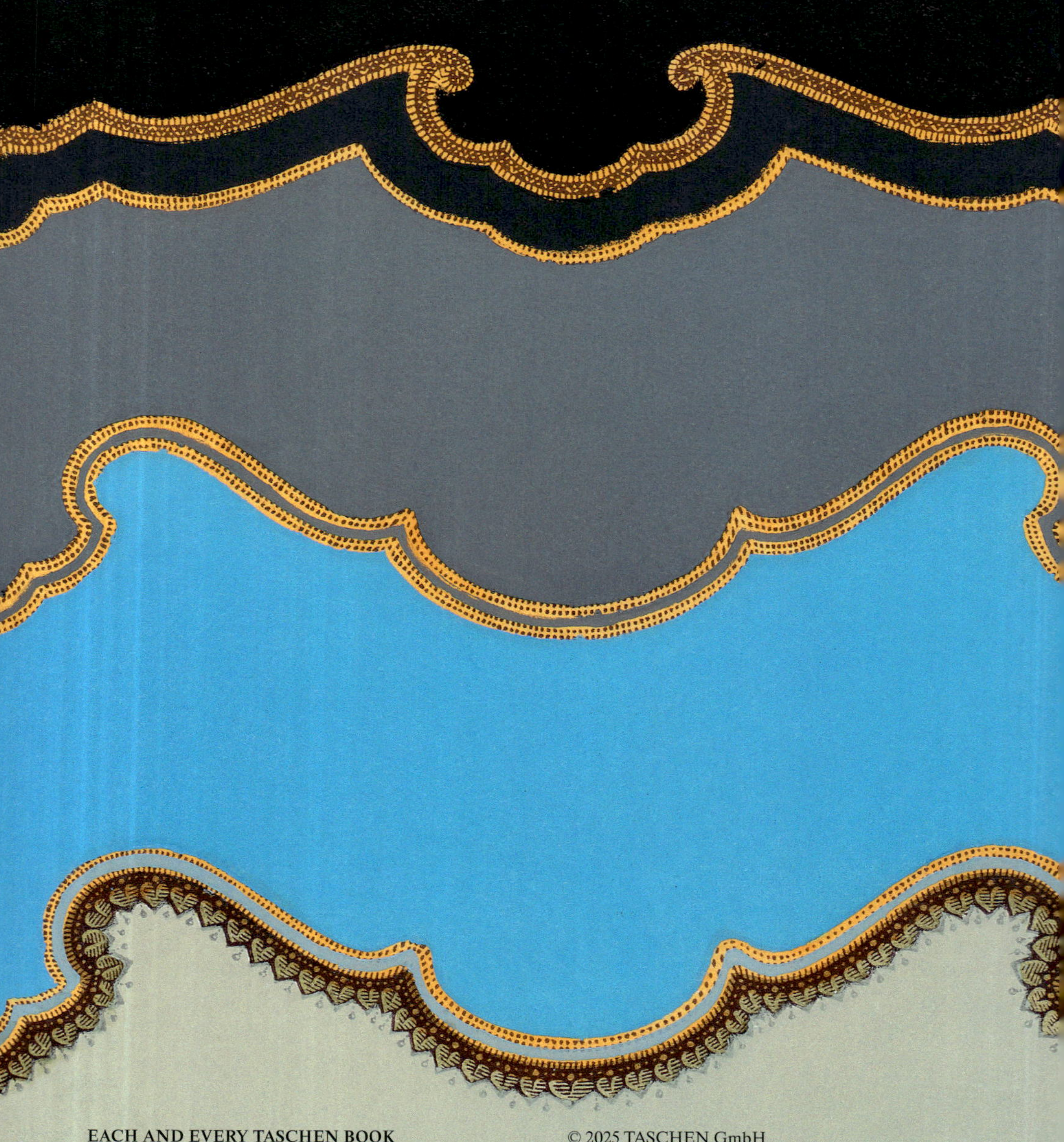

**EACH AND EVERY TASCHEN BOOK PLANTS A SEED!**
Each year, we offset our annual carbon emissions with carbon credits at the Instituto Terra, a reforestation program in Minas Gerais, Brazil, founded by Lélia and Sebastião Salgado. To find out more about this ecological partnership, please check: www.taschen.com/institutoterra.
**Inspiration: unlimited. Carbon footprint: (almost) zero.**

Want to see more? Visit taschen.com to view our current publications, browse our latest magazine, and subscribe to our newsletter.

© 2025 TASCHEN GmbH
Hohenzollernring 53, D–50672 Köln
**www.taschen.com**

*Project management:* Mahros Allamezade, Tom Pitt-Brooke, Cologne
*Design:* Andy Disl, Los Angeles
*German translation:* Kurt Rehkopf, Hamburg
*French translation:* Jean-François Cornu, Hélène Geniez, France

Printed in Bosnia-Herzegovina
ISBN 978-3-7544-0124-8